D1460567

HOTEL SVATY JAN
VYSEHRADRASKA 28

The AA KEYGuide
Prague

By Michael Ivory
and Heather Maher

Contents

KEY TO SYMBOLS

- ✚ Map reference
- ✉ Address
- ☎ Telephone number
- 🕐 Opening times
- 💷 Admission prices
- Ⓜ Metro station
- 🚍 Tram or bus number
- 🚆 Train station
- ⛴ Ferry/boat
- 🚗 Driving directions
- ℹ Tourist office
- 🎫 Tours
- 📖 Guidebook
- 🍴 Restaurant
- ☕ Café
- 🛍 Shop
- 🍸 Bar
- 🚻 Toilets
- 🛏 Number of rooms
- 🅿 Parking
- 🚭 No smoking
- ❄ Air conditioning
- 🏊 Swimming pool
- 🏋 Gym
- ❓ Other useful information
- ▷ Cross reference
- ★ Walk start point

HOW TO USE THIS BOOK

Understanding Prague is an introduction to the city, its geography, economy and people. **Living Prague** gives an insight into the city today, while **The Story of Prague** takes you through its past.

For detailed advice on getting to Prague—and getting around once you are there—turn to **On the Move**. For useful practical information, from weather forecasts to emergency services, turn to **Planning**.

Prague's key attractions are listed alphabetically in **The Sights** and are located on the maps on pages 56–59. The key sightseeing areas are described on pages 60–63 and are circled in blue on the map on the inside front cover.

Turn to **What to Do** for information on shops, entertainment, nightlife, sport, health and beauty, children's activities and festivals and events. Entries are listed by theme, then alphabetically. Shops are located on the maps on pages 158–161 and entertainment venues on the maps on pages 170–173. The top shopping areas are described on pages 155–157 and circled in green on the map on the inside front cover.

Out and About offers walks around Prague, a river trip and excursions that encourage you to explore further afield.

Eating and Staying gives you selected restaurants and hotels, listed alphabetically. Restaurants are located on the maps on pages 226–229 and hotels on the maps on pages 246–249.

Map references refer to the locator maps within the book or the street atlas at the end. For example, the Národní muzeum (National Museum) has the grid reference ✚ 59 G7, indicating the page on which the map is found (59) and the grid square in which the museum sits (G7). The grid on the locator maps within the book is the same as the grid on the atlas at the back of the book.

UNDERSTANDING PRAGUE

Utterly enchanting at first acquaintance, Prague reveals the complexities of its character only to those who take the time to savour it more fully. To appreciate today's Prague, you need to experience its lively nightlife and state-of-the-art shopping complexes, just as much as its incomparable artistic and architectural heritage. Since the fall of Communism, Prague has become one of the most popular city-break destinations in Europe. Millions flock here every year, drawn by the city's justified reputation as the continent's most perfectly preserved historic capital city. Every layer of a long history is here to be explored, but there's an urgency about the place as well; with entry into the web of Western institutions and alliances, the people of Prague and the Czech Republic are now facing the challenges of globalization and the temptations of lifestyle options and consumer choice.

FINDING YOUR WAY AROUND

Part of the allure of Prague is its complex, sometimes labyrinthine character. Much of Staré Město (Old Town) and Malá Strana consist of a maze of crooked streets and narrow alleyways. Doorways and other openings tempt the passer-by to penetrate one of the 'three Ps', *průchod*, *pavlač* or *pasáž*. A *průchod* or through-passageway will often lead to a secret courtyard or a *pavlač*, closely packed, old-style dwellings reached by galleries running round a central light-well. The *pasáž* is a late 19th- or early 20th-century invention, a shopping arcade leading deep into the interior of a building complex, perhaps with cinemas, cafés, nightclubs and other places of entertainment. Together the three Ps can make it possible to navigate your way around town without ever emerging onto the street.

Other parts of the city are less of a warren. Rational town planning got off to an early start in Prague. The straight streets of the market area around Havelská street were clearly designed on an early surveyor's drawing board, while Nové Město (New Town), with its logically laid out streets and squares—like the broad boulevard of Václavské náměstí (Wenceslas Square)—is the supreme example of medieval urban planning. Here it is easier to find your way around, but getting lost in Prague is part of the experience of the place; however great your confusion, sooner or later you will find a recognizable landmark, or emerge onto the riverbank.

The Vltava is an essential element in the cityscape; rather than separating the different parts of the city, it brings them together with a glorious set of bridges, each with its individual character. Nature plays a role too; many city views have as their background, not just the Castle on its rock spur above the river, but the greenery of Petřín Hill or Letná Plain. And as well as these extensive open spaces, there are other leafy parks and lovely gardens offering respite from excessive sightseeing.

POLITICS AND ECONOMICS

Under the long presidency (1989–2003) of Václav Havel, Prague sometimes seemed to be the capital of a country poised between East and West, offering an alternative to both discredited Communism and unbridled capitalism. But however inspiring, Havel was often more admired abroad than at home. His successor, the one-time prime minister and present president, Václav Klaus, is a committed free-marketeer and a determined Eurosceptic, who pointedly took a holiday the day his country joined the European Union in 2004. On the whole, his fellow country-men have accepted integration into Western alliances, including NATO, though often with a lack of enthusiasm; the Czech Republic is the only former Soviet satellite in which an unreconstructed Communist party commands a substantial measure of support.

Prague, like most capital cities, is not represen-tative of the country as a whole. While parts of the Czech Republic still struggle to overcome the economic legacy of Communism, the capital has thrived, enjoying very low rates of unemploy-ment. This success, however, is potentially precarious, based as it is on the service sector, above all on tourism.

PEOPLE AND LANGUAGE

Not so long ago a city populated almost exclu-sively by Czechs, Prague has been touched by global trends in recent years. Influences have included not just the constant streams of foreign

PRAGUE'S DISTRICTS AT A GLANCE

THE HISTORIC FOUR TOWNS
Originally independent towns in their own right, they now make up the historic core of the city.

Hradčany The Castle quarter is built on a rock spur commanding the bend in the River Vltava and the rest of the city.
Malá Strana Sometimes called the Lesser Town or Quarter, between the riverbank and the Castle hill, this is the most perfectly preserved district, with a wealth of aristocratic palaces and gardens, including the greenery of Petřín Hill.

A decorative street lamp casts a shadow on a house on Karlova street in Staré Město (below)

Detail of an art nouveau relief panel (left). Strolling across Karlův most (Charles Bridge; below)

Staré Město The Old Town, on the east bank of the Vltava, is contained within the river bend, bounded by boulevards running along the line of its long-demolished medieval walls, and focused on Staroměstské náměstí (Old Town Square) with its town hall and astronomical clock. The Old Town includes Josefov, the former Jewish ghetto.
Nové Město The New Town, a planned development of the 14th century, extends south and east of the Old Town, and is focused on a series of former marketplaces, including Václavské náměstí (Wenceslas Square). It is the city's commercial heart.

INNER DISTRICTS
These densely built-up 19th- and early 20th-century suburbs surround the historic core of Prague.

Vyšehrad Centred on the clifftop citadel overlooking the Vltava to the south of Nové Město (New Town).
Vinohrady A middle-class, late 19th- to early 20th-century suburb southeast of Nové Město.
Žižkov A working-class equivalent of Vinohrady, to the east of Nové Město.
Karlín A mixed, partly industrial riverside district northeast of Nové Město.
Holešovice A mixed district, tucked into a loop of the Vltava, with some visitor attractions, including the parkland of Letná Plain.
Smíchov A developing, former working-class district south of Malá Strana.

OUTER DISTRICTS
Dejvice and Střešovice Attractive villa and university quarters north and northwest of Hradčany.
Troja A downstream, semi-rural riverside district with a zoo, botanical gardens and a palace.
Zbraslav A once independent town, now part of Greater Prague, on the west bank of the Vltava, 12km (7.5 miles) south of the city's core.

tourists, but immigrant workers from less well-off countries further east and a variety of expatriate communities. Many of the latter are Americans, though the heady post-Velvet Revolution era, when Prague was thought of as the 1990s equivalent of Left Bank Paris of the 1920s and '30s, has passed its heyday. German, once the city's second—if not its first—language, has been displaced by English. Few of the city's visitors from abroad try to master Czech, deterred by its formidable grammar, multitude of accents, seemingly vowelless sentences, and that almost unpronounceable ř. It's a Slavonic tongue, related to Russian and more closely to Polish. It is even

closer to Slovak, and until the Velvet Divorce which split Czechoslovakia, the two languages were indiscriminately mixed on radio and TV. Nowadays younger members of both nationalities are finding it harder to understand each other.

Frequently misunderstood are the Czech Republic's Roma community. Most of them are descendants of Slovak gypsies, transported westwards following World War II to help revive the depopulated German Sudetenland. They were once cared for in a coercive way by the Communist regime, but many are now adrift in a rapidly changing society. In Prague, they have tended to settle in inner districts like Smíchov and Žižkov.

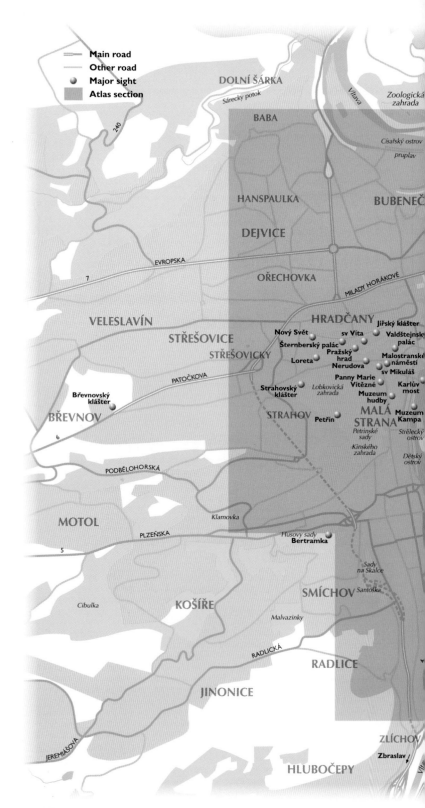

Main road
Other road
Major sight
Atlas section

DOLNÍ ŠÁRKA

Sárecky potok

Vltava

Zoologická
zahrada

240

BABA

Císařský ostrov

pruplav

HANSPAULKA

BUBENEČ

DEJVICE

EVROPSKA

7

OŘECHOVKA

MILADY HORÁKOVÉ

VELESLAVÍN

HRADČANY

Jiřský klášter

STŘEŠOVICE

Nový Svět

sv Víta

Valdštejnský
palác

STŘEŠOVICKY

Šternberský palác

Pražský
hrad

PATOČKOVA

Loreta

Nerudova

Malostranské
náměstí

sv Mikuláš

Břevnovský
klášter

Strahovský
klášter

Lobkovická
zahrada

Panny Marie
Vítězné

Karlův
most

BŘEVNOV

Muzeum
hudby

Muzeum
Kampa

6

STRAHOV

Petřin

MALÁ
STRANA

Petřinské
sady

Střelecký
ostrov

Kinského
zahrada

Dětský
ostrov

PODBĚLOHORSKÁ

MOTOL

Klamovka

PLZEŇSKÁ

Husovy sady
Bertramka

5

Sady
na Skalce

Cibulka

KOŠÍŘE

Malvazinky

SMÍCHOV

Santoška

RADLICKÁ

RADLICE

JINONICE

JEREMIÁŠOVA

ZLÍCHOV

Zbraslav

Vlt

HLUBOČEPY

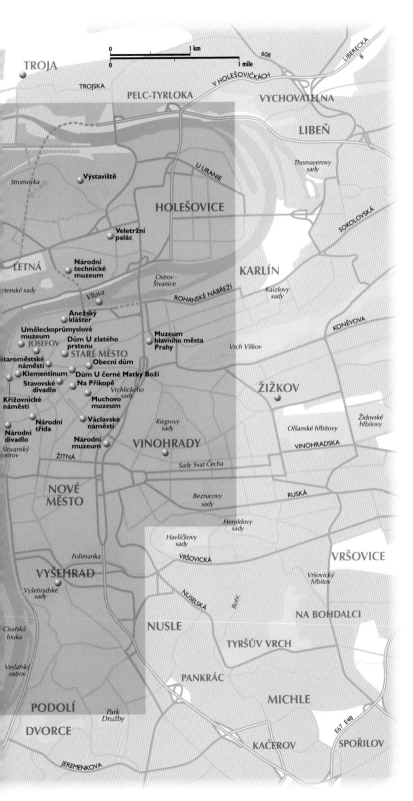

TROJA

TROJSKA

PELC-TYRLOKA

V HOLEŠOVIČKÁCH

VYCHOVATELNA

608

LIBEŇ

LIBERECKÁ
8

Stromovka

Výstaviště

U URANIE

Thomayerovy
sady

HOLEŠOVICE

Veletržní
palác

SOKOLOVSKÁ

LETNÁ

Národní
technické
muzeum

etenské sady

Vltava

Ostrov
Štvanice

KARLÍN

ROHANSKÉ NÁBŘEŽÍ

Kaizlovy
sady

KONĚVOVA

Anežský
klášter

Uměleckoprůmyslové
muzeum
JOSEFOV

Dům U zlatého
prstenu

STARÉ MĚSTO

Muzeum
hlavního města
Prahy

Vrch Vítkov

taroměstské
náměstí

Obecní dům

Klementinum

Dům U černé Matky Boží

Stavovské
divadlo

Na Příkopě

Vrchlického
sady

ŽIŽKOV

Křižovnické
náměstí

Muchovo
muzeum

Národní
třída

Václavské
náměstí

Riegrovy
sady

Olšanské hřbitovy

Židovské
hřbitovy

Národní
divadlo

Slovanský
ostrov

Národní
muzeum

VINOHRADY

VINOHRADSKÁ

ŽITNÁ

Sady Svat Čecha

NOVÉ
MĚSTO

Bezrucovy
sady

RUSKÁ

Heroldovy
sady

Havlíčkovy
sady

Folimanka

VRŠOVICKÁ

VRŠOVICE

VYŠEHRAD

Vršovický
hřbitov

Vyšehradské
sady

NUSELSKÁ

Botič

NA BOHDALCI

Císařská
louka

NUSLE

TYRŠŮV VRCH

Veslařský
ostrov

PANKRÁC

MICHLE

PODOLÍ

Park
Družby

E67 E48

DVORCE

KAČEROV

SPOŘILOV

JEREMENKOVA

0   1 km
0   1 mile

BEST CHURCHES AND MONASTERIES

Bazilika svatého Jiří (▷ 110): Behind the baroque façade of St. George's Basilica is an austere Romanesque interior, the finest in the country.

Chrám Matky Boží před Týnem (▷ 114): The Church of Our Lady before Týn's twin towers dominate the Old Town Square.

Loreta (▷ 86–87): Crowds still flock to the Loreto shrine, with its gorgeous baroque façade, carillon, courtyard and *santa casa.*

Strahovský klášter (▷ 118–119): Strahov Monastery is a sprawling complex of churches, courtyards, libraries and an art gallery.

Svatého Mikuláš (▷ 122–123): The city's greatest baroque church, the Church of St. Nicholas, has an interior of the utmost flamboyance and a superb dome visible from all over Prague.

Svatého Víta (▷ 126–129): A thousand years of the Czech lands' Christian heritage are encapsulated in St. Vitus Cathedral.

Detail of the ceiling frescoes (above) in St. George's Basilica

BEST LANDMARKS

Karlův most (▷ 80–83): Lined with baroque statuary and thronged by entertainers and trinket sellers, the great stone Charles Bridge, built by Emperor Charles IV in the 14th century, spans the Vltava and is one of Prague's great gathering places.

Obecní dům (▷ 100–101): The Municipal House, a triumph of art nouveau architecture, is a fine example of this exuberant style.

Pomník Jana Husa (▷ 112, 114): The extraordinary art nouveau statue of Jan Hus in Staroměstské náměstí (Old Town Square) is a popular meeting place.

A view of Old Town Square (above)

Pražský hrad (▷ 106–111): Presiding over the city, 1,000-year-old Prague Castle is virtually a town in its own right, as well as the treasure house of the Czech nation's history and culture.

Staroměstská radnice (▷ 112): An eccentric assemblage of ancient buildings, the Old Town Hall draws the crowds to the hourly spectacle offered by its world-famous Orloj (Astronomical Clock).

The Astronomical clock

Staronová synagóga (▷ 75–76): The Old-New Synagogue, at the heart of what used to be the ghetto, is a poignant reminder of the history of Prague's Jewish community.

Wenceslas monument (▷ 135): The patron saint of the Czechs, Václav, sits astride his steed at the top of the square named after him.

Prague at dusk (above). A fine altarpiece (below) in St. Agnes's Convent

BEST MUSEUMS AND GALLERIES

Anežský klášter (▷ 64–66): St. Agnes's Convent houses some of the finest works of medieval painting and sculpture in Europe.

Dům U zlatého prstenu (▷ 71): The House at the Golden Ring is home to the city's extensive collection of modern Czech art.

Jiřský klášter (▷ 72–73): Some of the most glorious works of art from Prague's Renaissance and baroque eras can be seen in the restored Convent of St. George in the Castle precincts.

Národní muzeum (▷ 95): The National Museum, at the upper end of Václavské náměstí (Wenceslas Square), displays rambling collections of stuffed birds, mineral specimens and much more.

Národní technické muzeum (▷ 96): The National Technical Museum is worth a visit for its superb exhibits of old-timers of road and rail.

Šternberský palác (▷ 116–117): The Sternberg Palace is a dignified setting for the nation's fine collection of European art.

THE BEST OF PRAGUE

Uměleckoprůmyslové muzeum (UPM, ▷ 132–133): The Decorative Arts Museum has outstanding collections of glass, ceramics, furniture and more.

Veletržní palác (▷ 139–141) One of the great pioneering buildings of Modernist architecture, the Trade Fair Palace makes a wonderful home for 19th-, 20th- and 21st-century Czech art.

A Škoda convertible in the Trade Fair Palace

BEST PALACES

Černínský palác (▷ 70): The vast Černín Palace was such an over-ambitious project that it bankrupted its aristocratic builder.

Dům pánů z Kunštátu a Poděbrad (▷ 70–71): The medieval House of the Lords of Kunštát and Poděbrady offers a glimpse into Prague's past.

Palác Kinských (▷ 115): The Palác Kinských is Prague's loveliest rococo palace, once lived in by Franz Kafka's family.

Schwarzenberský palác (▷ 120–121): Destined to become a home of the National Gallery, the Schwarzenberg is the most splendidly sgraffitoed of all Prague's palaces.

Trojský zámek (▷ 130–131): Count Sternberg's palatial country seat has some over-the-top baroque sculpture and decoration.

BEST PARKS AND GARDENS

Jižní zahrady (▷ 111): The Castle's exquisitely landscaped South Gardens offer a wonderful summer promenade, with romantic views over the rooftops of Malá Strana.

Kampa Park (▷ 194): A restful riverside park on Kampa Island.

Královská zahrada (▷ 84): The Royal Garden is a tranquil and leafy retreat.

Sgraffito decoration (above) on the Schwarzenberg Palace. Stained-glass detail (top) in the Decorative Arts Museum

Vrtbovská zahrada (▷ 146): Hidden away at the foot of Petřín Hill, the Vrtba Garden is the loveliest of all the city's baroque landscapes.

Zahrady pod pražským hradem (▷ 146): The restored, terraced baroque Palace Gardens step down gracefully from the Castle to the aristocratic palaces of Malá Strana.

BEST VIEWPOINTS

Staroměstská mostecká věž (▷ 82): The great length and graceful curving alignment of Karlův most (Charles Bridge) are best appreciated from the top of the Old Town Bridge Tower.

Staroměstská radnice (▷ 112): The reward for toiling up the tower of the Old Town Hall is a view over ancient red-tiled rooftops and down to the cobblestones of the square.

Svatého Mikuláš (▷ 122–123): It's a long climb to the top of the bell-tower of the Church of St. Nicholas, but once there you can look out over Malá Strana in the company of stone baroque saints atop the parapet.

Svatého Víta (▷ 126–129): The viewing gallery of St. Vitus Cathedral's central tower offers a superb panorama over Prague, as well as a close-up view of the building's Gothic structure.

BEST PLACES TO SHOP

Botanicus (▷ 166): A huge selection of beautifully-packaged natural, organic products from soaps to spices.

Český Granát Turnov (▷ 167): The Czech-designed and crafted jewellery sold here is made using authentic Bohemian garnets.

Ivana Follová Art & Fashion Gallery (▷ 164): A combined artisans gallery and fashion store, selling unique designs.

Moser (▷ 163): This Czech crystal company has been producing crystal stemware for royal tables across the world since 1857.

Exquisite Moser glassware (right)

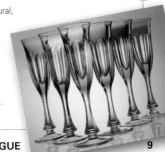

THE BEST OF PRAGUE

BEST NIGHTLIFE

Café Imperial (▷ 183): This huge café, dating from 1918, has an ornate mosaic ceramic-tile interior and festive café-society vibe.

Duplex (▷ 181): A glamorous rooftop club/lounge/restaurant with a massive balcony overlooking Wenceslas Square.

Radost FX (▷ 185): This cult-status club has a global disco, a vegetarian café, and a cool Moroccan-themed lounge and bar.

U Vejvodu (▷ 185): A lively, authentic Czech beer hall on three levels with hearty food and several excellent beers on tap.

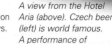

BEST PLACES TO EAT

Alcron (▷ 230): You can enjoy excellent fish dishes in this small restaurant, just off the lobby of the Radisson SAS Hotel.

The Café Imperial (above)

David (▷ 234): This restaurant, in a quiet lane in Malá Strana, offers reinvented versions of traditonal Bohemian dishes.

Kampa Park (▷ 235): In a great location, close to Karlův most (Charles Bridge), this stylish restaurant serves fine food.

Pálffy Palác (▷ 239): Dine in baroque splendour in the second-floor dining room of this palace in Malá Strana.

BEST PLACES TO STAY

Aria (▷ 251): This unique hotel, with a musical theme, has rooms named after musicians and a music salon.

Carlo IV (▷ 252): Relax in one of Prague's most opulent hotels and enjoy the stylish surroundings.

Four Seasons (▷ 254): Close to Karlův most (Charles Bridge), this elegant hotel is a conversion of three historic buildings.

U zlaté studně (▷ 261): This charming hotel, in a superb location near the castle, has luxurious bedrooms and great city views.

A view from the Hotel Aria (above). Czech beer (left) is world famous. A performance of Cinderella at the Státní opera Praha (below)

TOP EXPERIENCES

Enjoy an evening at the opera in the Národní divadlo (National Theatre, ▷ 94), Státní opera Praha (State Opera, ▷ 121) or the Stavovské divadlo (Estates Theatre, ▷ 120).

Feast on traditional Bohemian food at a super-pub like Kolkovna (▷ 236).

Get lost in the labyrinth of lanes and courtyards between Staroměstské náměstí (Old Town Square, ▷ 112–115) and Betlémské náměstí.

Listen to a chamber concert in an historic interior such as the Mirror Hall of the Klementinum (▷ 84) or the hall of the Music Museum (▷ 91).

Sail slowly down the Vltava aboard a pleasure steamer as dusk gathers and watch as floodlights begin to illuminate the buildings (▷ 218).

Sip a coffee or cocktail in sumptuous surroundings such as the café in the Obecní dům (Municipal House, ▷ 100–101).

Stroll across Karlův most (Charles Bridge) to Staré Město (Old Town) and watch the hourly show of the Orloj (Astronomical Clock, ▷ 112) in Staroměstské náměstí (Old Town Square).

Tap your foot to the marches and polkas played by the military band in the Castle's Jižní zahrady (South Gardens, ▷ 111).

Taste a well-kept and expertly drawn Pilsner or Staropramen in a cellar pub or, in summer, a beer garden.

Treat yourself to a gourmet meal in a terrace restaurant with a panoramic view, such as U zlaté studně (▷ 244) just below the Castle.

Try the unique dark beer brewed on the premises at the ancient U Fleků pub (▷ 185).

Visit the Castle (Pražský hrad, ▷ 106–111) to marvel at Svatého Víta (St. Vitus Cathedral) and wander down charming Zlata ulička (Golden lane).

Art nouveau detail in the Obecní dům

Living Prague

Christmas traditions in Prague: delicious cakes (left), a festive market in the Old Town Square (right) and carp sellers (below right).
The Parnas restaurant (below) in the Old Town has a superb art deco interior

Food and Drink

The dining scene in Prague is getting more sophisticated and varied all the time, but blink and some restaurants will have come and gone. Although Czechs still love their cabbage, *knedlíky* (dumplings) and pork, that hasn't stopped organic vegetarian cafés, Thai curry houses, Greek tavernas, French bistros, Japanese sushi bars and Pakistani grills from finding success. Prague is still some way off being a gastronomic capital, but the number of local chefs taking culinary chances with innovative dishes using locally produced ingredients is on the rise. Some of the top restaurants may be in international hotels—the dining rooms in the Four Seasons and Radisson are widely acclaimed—but their kitchens are run by Czech chefs, and as many Praguers as guests are requesting reservations. The Kampa Group, which owns Brasserie Provence, Kampa Island, Bazaar and Square, consistently wows diners with its restaurant kitchens and interior design.

In contrast to Czech cooking, Czech beer has been winning awards for years. Centuries spent refining brewing techniques and strict purity laws that date from medieval times are two

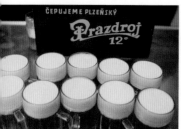

reasons why *pivo* is so revered. Czechs enjoy a reputation for producing the best-tasting beer in the world, with no greater fans than themselves. No one even raises an eyebrow at the sight of someone in a café enjoying a freshly pulled beer at 10 in the morning.

A fishy, festive tradition

At the height of the advent season, when almost every square has a Christmas tree and a wooden hut selling mulled wine, a fishy tradition also takes place. The customary Christmas Eve meal of *kapr* (carp) supports a cottage industry of fish farms in the country, where ponds hold thousands of the fish. Every December they're hauled to Prague in tanks, and carp sellers set up a sturdy table and a splashing tub full of fish. Customers point to the one they want and minutes later are handed the fillets. Those who want an even fresher fish will take a live carp home and keep it in their bathtub until the appointed hour. There are lots of recipes—from carp soup to carp balls—but it isn't the taste that makes the fish so popular. If you put one of the scales in your purse or wallet it is said that money will come your way in the New Year.

Czech beer is world famous (above). If the bowl of doughnuts (below) disappears from the bar in the Café Imperial—look out!

Prague pub U Tygra (above). A traditional Czech dish (left)

Waiter, there's a doughnut in my soup!

The majestic art deco Café Imperial (▷ 232), with its high ceilings, giant picture windows and ceramic secessionist-era wall tiles, has reigned on the corner of Na poříčí and Zlatnická since 1914. But it's only since the 1990s that the patrons came up with an unusual gimmick whereby you can slap 1,943Kč on the bar and in exchange receive a bowl of yesterday's doughnuts, with the manager's permission to throw them at other customers. The notice on the menu advertising this bizarre, but legitimate, offer warns that it is only for 'sober people more than 21 years of age', and advises customers that 'the bowl is visibly stationed on our bar' so 'if you don't see it there, leave quickly', as someone has bought it and you stay at your own risk. Photos near the door attest to the number of times stale doughnuts have gone flying here.

Battle of the breweries

Who owns the right to call its beer 'Budweiser'? That's the crux of an ongoing battle between the Czech brewery Budějovický Budvar and the American brewery giant Anheuser-Busch. This David and Goliath struggle has been playing out in European courts since the early 1990s, and as of 2005 more than 40 trademark and patent cases were still pending. Anheuser-Busch, which has made 'Budweiser' since the late 19th century, wants the Budějovický brewery to stop selling its beer under the 'Budweiser' name in about 60 countries. But several national courts have ruled in favour of the Czech brewer, citing its more than 700 years of beer-making and historic use of the 'Budweiser Budvar' brand—a derivative of 'Budweis', the German name for České Budějovice where the beer is brewed.

Fast-food, Czech-style

Prague has its share of KFCs and McDonald's, but many people still prefer the Czech version of fast food, which is served throughout the city at stand-up buffets called *bufet* or *jídelna*. Lunch remains the most important meal for Czechs, and although salads and sandwiches are catching on, anything other than a hot, hearty meal is unthinkable for many people, even if the modern workday means it must be eaten quickly. For about 60Kč, customers can get a traditional meal such as pork, dumplings and sauerkraut, or with a glass of beer for around 18Kč more. There are no chairs, just high tables where diners stand and eat, but the prices are inexpensive and the portions are big, so no one usually complains.

Oenophile

There's no danger of wine surpassing beer as Prague's drink of choice, but *vino* has been increasing in popularity for two big reasons: imports are cheaper and the country's winemakers are improving. As a result, the number of wine bars and stores has skyrocketed. Petr Pipek, the executive chef at two of the city's gourmet restaurants, Flambée and Rybí trh (▷ 240), owns Wine Shop Ungelt (▷ 166) in Staré Město. A stone spiral stairway leads to a 14th-century cellar that's cooled to a constant 14°C (57°F). This is where he keeps his individually selected collection of some of the finest varieties in the world, including bottles from the best Moravian vineyards. Sceptics who doubt that a Czech sauvignon can compete with its French counterpart should simply ask for a taste; the staff are always proud to pour one.

Performing at the Bertramka (below)

The Prague Spring music festival in the National Museum (above).
A performance of *Cinderella* at the Státní opera Praha (right).
Modern art (below right)

The Arts

Mission Impossible

Prague has been the setting for dozens of films, but the one that awakened modern audiences to its splendour was *Mission Impossible* (1996). The spy movie featured scenes along the Vltava, on Karlův most (Charles Bridge) and in the cobblestone streets of Malá Strana. More than 10 years on, fans are still seeking out its locations. The scene with Tom Cruise and a CIA official at the restaurant on Staroměstské náměstí, however, poses a problem. Sensing a trap, Cruise sticks a piece of gum to the window and an explosion blows out the glass and shatters a wall-sized fish tank. Cruise dives through the air and escapes through the square. Few people realise that there is no such restaurant. The scene was filmed inside a studio—only the shots of the square are real.

Bronze babies climb the TV Tower (right)

Ever since Wolfgang Amadeus Mozart premièred his opera *Don Giovanni* at the Stavovské divadlo (Estates Theatre) in 1787, Prague has occupied a special place in the hearts of classical music lovers. Celebrated 19th-century composers Antonín Dvořák (1841–1904) and Bedřich Smetana (1824–84) solidified the city's lyrical reputation—the annual Prague Spring music festival opens with a performance of Smetana's *Má vlast (My Country)*—and on any given day you can hear strains of classical music pouring out of churches, buildings and schools. The concert scene has an egalitarian nature—at all but the most regal venues the dress code is smart but not formal, and students mingle with wealthy patrons.

Classical music is just one of the many creative expressions celebrated in this city, which takes pride in its history of artistic achievement—Franz Kafka's likeness is everywhere, from bookstores to T-shirts—yet has a growing appetite for the modern. Prague's abundance of fascinating architecture includes baroque, art nouveau, and early 20th-century Czech Cubist buildings. A more recent addition to the city's landscape is the Tančící dům (Dancing Building) on the river bank—its shape resembling two dancers. The Gothic cathedrals that pierce the sky gave Prague the nickname 'City of a hundred spires' but at street level, there's a vibrant and forward-looking sensibility: just look at the sculptures of giant bronze babies on Žižkov's TV tower.

A graceful performer at the Státní opera Praha (left). The striking Tančící dům (Dancing Building; right)

Mimers on Celetná street (above). A beautiful display of Moser glassware (right)

Prague hosted CowParade in 2004 (right)

Popular puppetry

In Prague, puppets and puppet shows aren't just for children. Collectors pay good money for hand-carved marionettes, and the city has several playhouses that bring these dolls to life in popular performances. At the oldest such theatre, the adventures of a father and son puppet duo have been captivating both children and adults for more than 50 years. The Spejbl and Hurvínek Theatre (▷ 178) was founded in 1945 by Josef Skupa, a former German prisoner of war. The theatre's longevity is probably due to its unique combination of make-believe and message: every play contains a life lesson of some sort and several are even aimed exclusively at adult audiences. In the most popular such play, the father, Spejbl, and son, Hurvínek, contemplate no less than the meaning of human existence.

CowParade

The 'CowParade' originated in Zurich in 1998 and since then has taken place in many other cities, including New York, Chicago, Washington, Dublin, Stockholm, Manchester and Brussels. In the summer of 2004, 204 brightly painted, life-size fibreglass cows were displayed in Prague. Celebrities, artists and schools participated in the design and painting, and each cow was sponsored by a company or a business. Eurotel Praha was the co-organizer of the project, along with the city of Prague. The event was simply a public exhibition that local artists and organizations took part in to entertain the public. The benefit for the sponsors was that their name was on the plaque accompanying the cow they paid for.

Švandovo's subtitles

Prague's strong playhouse tradition was born in the 1940s, with comedies that subtly mocked the German occupiers, and peaked in the 1960s, when 'absurdism' gave voice to opponents of the Communist government. Today dozens of theatres stage contemporary plays and reinterpret the classics, but the performances have always been in Czech. All that changed in 2005, when the ultra-modern Švandovo divadlo (▷ 174) became the first playhouse to install 'subtitle' technology. More common in opera houses, the system allows audience members to see a simultaneous English translation of the dialogue being spoken on a screen below the stage. Švandovo's subtitled performances have been a hit with non-Czech audiences.

The glass of kings

Czechs take a great pride in their international reputation for producing delicate and exciting designs in crystal and glassware. Their world-famous wares have found their way into dozens of royal house-holds, from Saudi Arabia to Buckingham Palace. In 2004, two of Europe's royal weddings toasted with stemware produced by Moser: Crown Prince Felip of Spain and his wife Letizia Ortiz drank from 'Copenhagen' crystal, and Crown Prince Frederik of Denmark and his wife, Mary Donaldson, from the company's 'Splendid' crystal. Moser glass is the gold standard for Czech crystal. Founded in 1857 by Ludwig Moser, it still uses the lead-free technique it perfected 150 years ago. Moser was appointed Court Purveyor for Austro-Hungarian Emperor Franz Joseph I in 1873 and since then the company has been called 'the glass of kings'.

Exhibits from the Museum of Communism (above and below). Dior in Prague (below left)

Yoko Ono visits the John Lennon Wall—its graffiti was a source of conflict between the city's youth and the secret police in the 1980s (above). Former Gestapo headquarters (left) on Politických vězňů street

The Communist
Legacy

Reminders of the more than 40 years that the Czechs spent under Communist rule are everywhere in Prague: on busy Milady Horákové Street, named for a woman who was executed for resisting the regime; in the hulking building on Politických vězňů (Political Prisoners) street, where citizens disappeared into secret police headquarters; and in the names of the fallen on a plaque on the Český rozhlas (Czech Radio) building, which broadcast SOS messages during the Warsaw Pact invasion in August 1968 as Praguers battled Soviet troops outside on Vinohradská street. On bustling Václavské náměstí (Wenceslas Square) even a sunny day can feel sombre when passing the plaque that marks where student Jan Palach set fire to himself in 1969 to protest against Soviet-imposed normalization.

In the years since the regime was pulled down by the Velvet Revolution of 1989, Czechs have struggled with how to correct the wrongs of the past without disrupting the present. Lustration laws have prevented some members of the former regime from holding public office, and the files of the secret police have been opened to the public. The years following the revolution have been difficult but healing ones, and Czechs have made great strides. In May 2004, on Staroměstské náměstí—the site of countless Communist rallies and popular protests—the Czech flag took its place alongside all the other flags of the European Union. There is a feeling now that the future is bright.

Museum of Communism

Sandwiched rather incongruously between a McDonald's and a Benetton on Na příkopě is a door that leads into Prague's past. The Museum of Communism (▷ 93) is full of objects from the Communist years, and gives visitors the chance to see the grim reality of life from 1948 to 1989. Among the exhibits are a barren shop with just two kinds of canned goods on its shelf, and a 1950s-era classroom with Russian-language textbooks on the desks. Busts of Lenin, propaganda posters urging citizens to harvest more grain, and photographs of the Warsaw Pact invasion bring the oppressiveness of the regime to life. Perhaps the most chilling re-creation is that of a police interrogation room, complete with a trench coat hanging behind a metal desk and a typewriter for taking 'confessions'. Every few minutes, the black rotary phone rings ominously.

Sprawling *Paneláky* on the southwest outskirts of Prague (left)

The Plastic People of the Universe (below left) are still popular today

The basement of the Pension Unitas (below) was once used by the Czech Communist secret police

Many Praguers go to their *Chatas* for the weekend (below)

P6-P21

Chata culture

To Praguers 'I'm going to my country house' doesn't have the same ring of snobbery it might elsewhere. As one newspaper put it, 'Here, having a second home is not just the domain of the upper crust, but truly a movement of the masses.' *Chatas* are the small wooden cottages that many city residents dash off to every Friday afternoon. This country-house culture sprang up after World War II, when land and homes that had been occupied by ethnic Germans—controversially driven off when Germany was defeated —became available. It even flourished under the Communist regime, as city-dwellers sought relief from the oppression of the state. The government looked the other way as small country plots changed hands, believing, according to some historians, that if people were out weeding their gardens, they would be too busy to plan a government coup.

Plastic People of the Universe

Modern audiences who hear the Plastic People of the Universe (PPU) play are getting more than a concert for their money, they're getting a piece of Iron Curtain history. The PPU was once synonymous with 'dissident rock', and today their fans include the sons and daughters of Czechs who risked arrest more than three decades ago to attend their banned performances. The Prague band played music inspired by New York's Velvet Underground and attracted legions of followers, but were banned by the Communist regime. After 1989, the PPU re-emerged onto the music scene and were invited to play all over the world. In 2005, the musicians gave a performance at Švandovo divadlo in honour of a joint appearance by the legendary singer Lou Reed and Václav Havel, Czechoslovakia's first 'dissident president'.

The modern *paneláky*

Just a few metro stops from the baroque, Gothic and Renaissance buildings in central Prague there are vast stretches of concrete tower blocks called *paneláky*. An estimated 2 million *panelák* apartments were built by the Communist regime, all with the same cheap, pre-fabricated materials. Today the suburban spaces these tower blocks occupy is in big demand, and real estate companies have started buying up multiple apartments and tearing down the walls to create trendy lofts. Some developers are building a new generation of blocks, with quality materials and views of the country-side. More than 200,000 Praguers still live in *panelák* flats and housing cooperatives spent 220 million crowns in 2004 on improvements. The most popular trend is to paint the exterior the same yellow, blue and green shades used on the beautiful old buildings in central Prague.

Paying for prison

Guests at the Pension Unitas have an unusual choice when they check in: they can opt for a traditional room with the usual amenities, or pay around 1,000Kč to sleep in one of the prison cells in the basement, where the Czech Communist secret police used to interrogate, torture and jail opponents of the regime. One of the most famous prisoners was Czechoslovakia's first post-Communist president, Václav Havel, who spent time in the cell known as 'P6' for various dissident crimes. All of the tiny cell-rooms have iron bunk beds, curtains on the barred windows and carpeted floors, and some even have a sink, but they still have the heavy iron door that sealed prisoners inside. The Unitas's low prices and central location (Bartolomějská 9, Nové Město) make it popular with backpackers, however even the sounds of a cheery hostel can't banish the ghosts of the past completely.

Relaxing with a good book on Karlův most (Charles Bridge; right)

Children looking at the mushrooms on display at an exhibition on Žofín Island (above). Footballer Martin Zbončák of Slavia Praha (right)

Culture and
Leisure

The Slavic culture is not usually associated with the word 'carefree' but in Prague this perception is contradicted every time you see the crowds of rollerbladers in the parks, groups toasting each other with *na zdraví!* in pubs, and couples strolling along the riverbank. The city itself seems to encourage delight: How can anyone brood when Prague Castle lights up like something out of a Hans Christian Andersen fairy tale every evening? Or when a metro carriage opens and a crowd of giggling students in formal dress pours out, on the way to their first ball?

Leisure activities are easy to find: there's live music everywhere, from the corner pub to the downtown club. At Christmas, the local squares are full of craft markets and even on cold days people take their time as they sip hot wine. At Easter, still-bare trees are festooned with pastel-hued ribbons and plastic eggs. When the first warm days of spring coax up the crocuses, it's a mad dash to the greenhouse to load up on seedlings for the garden. Outdoor cafés are packed and the jazz boats on the Vltava start chugging along on their nightly cruises. The city settles into a lazy routine, and everyone goes a little more slowly. After all, no one can really hurry on cobblestones.

An eye-catching hairstyle adds the finishing touch to this smart outfit (right)

Houby hunting

A strange sight appears on the Prague metro in late summer and early autumn: grown men carrying wicker baskets. At the last stop on the line, they exit the station along with their wives and children, and stride purposefully into the nearest woods. They are in search of wild mushrooms. *Houby* hunting is immensely popular with Czechs; one study claims 80 per cent of the population has gone foraging at least once in their lives. Throughout the three-month season, Praguers armed with baskets or mesh bags ride the metro out to the forest, collect their bounty and then pickle, dry or use it straight away in traditional recipes like *houbová polévka* (mushroom soup). The pastime is popular because it embodies traditional Czech values such as family togetherness, appreciation of nature and frugality.

The Aristocratic Gala Ball (left)

The high-speed 'Red Bull Crashed Ice' race in Prague (below)

New Year's Eve in the Old Town Square (above). A scene from the *Nagano* opera (below)

Lenka Šmídová shows off her silver medal at the 2004 Summer Olympics in Athens (right)

A ball of a time

From November to the end of March, Praguers of every age put on their dancing shoes and head out into the cold winter night to attend the many cultural and social balls that are held across the city. Every *ples* (ball) has a theme: there's a Hunters' Ball, Municipal House Ball, Africa Ball, Moravian Ball and even an Erotic Ball. Most are open to the public, but some, like the political party balls, require a connection. Inside, the fashion runs the gamut from short and sparkly to long and conservative, but the point isn't to have the best dress or nicest suit, it's to dance to as many songs as your feet will allow you. Waiters push carts tinkling with bottles of Bohemia Sekt, strangers invite each other onto the dance floor, and no one even thinks of going home until the orchestra starts packing up.

Lifting a glass

As the bistro is to Paris, and the pub is to Dublin, the *hospoda* is to Prague. For many, the local *hospoda* is a second living room, a place to gather with friends around a wooden table after work and leave the day's worries behind. With waiters who automatically bring another beer when they see an empty glass, the point of these places has always been drinking, not dining. But modern lifestyles have taken a toll on the traditional *hospoda*, and the Czech brewery Pilsner Urquell has capitalized on consumer demand by opening its own versions: Kolkovna (▷ 236) and Olympia (▷ 238). Both brew-pubs are bright, clean and have large menus of Czech and even vegetarian dishes. Reservations are a must, since locals fill the tables every night, but some tourists who visit either place might be dismayed to find that the concept of a nonsmoking section still hasn't caught on.

The landlocked sailor

Czechs are avid outdoor sports enthusiasts. In summer the countryside is packed with cyclists, hikers and canoeists, and in winter the mountains teem with skiers, snowboarders and climbers. The idea of someone from this landlocked country taking home an Olympic medal in ocean sailing sounds implausible, yet that's exactly what Lenka Šmídová did in the 2004 Summer Olympics in Athens. She won the silver medal—the first sailing medal ever for a Czech—in the 'Europe' category, and received a hero's welcome when she arrived back in Prague. For a time, the smiling Šmídová was seen and heard everywhere: in newspapers and magazines, on radio and television. Ironically, this modest champion—she once shrugged 'Whoever makes the least mistakes wins'—spends nine months a year outside the Czech Republic, practicing on the ocean.

Singing goalies

To the casual observer, ice hockey and opera have nothing in common. To Martin Smolka and Jaroslav Dušek, the composer and librettist of the Czech opera *Nagano: Start of the Legend*, the similarities are endless. Both involve highly trained 'performers' and pre-performance rituals. and, as Dušek explained 'opera singers, similarly to the players, are forced to give their physical best'. And Czechs are crazy about both. Given all that, the idea of an opera based on the Czech Republic's famous 1998 Olympic victory in Nagano, Japan—where they beat their arch-rival Russia 1–0—doesn't seem so strange. *Nagano* had its première at the Stavovské divadlo (Estates Theatre) in April 2004, on the same stage where Mozart debuted *Don Giovanni* in 1787, and its singing goalies were a big hit with fans of hockey and classical music alike. It has now become one of the most popular operas in Prague.

A crowd watching the changing of the guard at the Castle (right)

Painting portraits on Charles Bridge (above). Sightseeing in a vintage Czech car (below)

Karlův most (Charles Bridge) is a magnet for tourists (above). Garnet jewellery for sale (below)

Tourism in Prague

With a population of just 1.2 million, Prague's annual tourism numbers would give anyone a moment's pause: 3.7 million people visited the city in 2004, making the ratio of visitors to residents 3:1. The fact that Prague was hidden behind the Iron Curtain until 1990 still makes it something of a tourist novelty, and that, combined with the fact that its ancient heart has escaped wartime destruction, has made it a prime destination. The largest tourist contingents are from Germany, Britain and the US, followed closely by Italy. Prague Castle on any given day—be it dreary, snowy or sunny—is a happy sea of camera-toting visitors speaking a cacophony of foreign languages.

Tourism is a serious source of revenue for the city, and brings in billions of crowns each year, which helps fund municipal services like the metro and historic building renovations. Gradually, Prague has evolved to accommodate the many people who come here to spend money and see the sights. In most restaurants and shops, credit cards are now accepted, and opening hours have been extended. Ruzyně Airport is building a new wing and metro lines have been lengthened. The negatives are the same as for any popular tourist destination: shops selling souvenirs and inflated prices in restaurants near the centre. Although it's hard to get a seat on the popular No. 22 or 23 trams during the summer, the constant flow of international visitors gives Prague an undeniable energy. Without them, the city might feel empty.

No stags please!

Don't be surprised if you see a sign on the door of a bar that says 'No stags'. Ever since low-cost airlines began flying the UK–Prague route in 2001, the Prague stag party phenomenon has been causing headaches for the city. Every weekend planeloads of 'lads' arrive for 48 to 72 hours of partying. The groups are easy to spot, not least because their shirts usually advertise their role as 'usher' or 'best man' at the forthcoming wedding. Some pub owners have had enough of the raucous behaviour and banned stags from their establishments. The City Council is even considering changing the public drinking laws. It's still legal to weave down a Prague street clutching an open bottle of beer, but perhaps not for much longer.

A stylish souvenir: beautiful Bohemian glass (right)

Prague is a popular destination for stag parties (above). The so-called green fairy (right)

Maintenance work being carried out on the moving figures of the Astronomical clock on Old Town Square (above)

Taken for a ride

In late 2004, the newspaper *Mladá fronta Dnes* published the results of an investigation into the city's taxi ranks and reported that many drivers were overcharging their non-Czech speaking passengers. When he read this, Mayor Pavel Bém decided to conduct his own experiment. He put on a false moustache and dark sunglasses, and in an Italian accent hailed two taxis, separately, near Staroměstské náměstí. The results were as the newspaper had said: one driver overcharged the mayor by 200 percent, the other by 500 percent. Bém was convinced of the corruption and ordered the authorities to increase fines dramatically for drivers who overcharge. He also announced that more inspectors would be conducting secret checks. Now Prague cabbies never know if the person in their back seat has a city map, or a citation book, in their pocket.

What's a Staroměstské náměstí?

Throughout the three central districts in Prague—Nové Město, Staré Město and Malá Strana—there's plenty of evidence that tourists are a major part of city life. Shiny metal squares embedded in pavements (sidewalks) mark the former royal path, now known as 'The Silver Route', and restaurants advertise their 'tourist menu' of Czech specials. But few people would consider the brown arrowed signs on street corners tourist aids. In the 1990s, tourism officials decided to help foreign visitors find the most popular sights in the city, so they spent millions manufacturing directional signs to point the way to each one. But they made a mistake: all the signs were written in Czech. The cost of the project meant the signs had to go up anyway, and the sight of tourists squinting at them in confusion is common all over the city.

Return of the green fairy

It is said to have driven Dégas, Van Gogh and Toulouse-Lautrec, among others, insane. Though it has been banned for almost 100 years in the US and many other countries, it's legal in the Czech Republic. Absinthe, also called 'the green fairy' for its emerald tint and legendary effect, contains wormwood oil and the chemical thujone. In high enough doses, thujone can trigger hallucinations, and artists of the late 19th and early 20th centuries claimed this gave them creative inspiration. The liqueur's outlaw status elsewhere has given rise to a small but growing number of 'absinthe tourists' who come to Prague determined to experience it first hand. But modern absinthe contains a fraction of the wormwood oil of yesteryear, so while the drinker will almost surely end up with a hangover, a green fairy sighting is far less likely.

Back in time

Ascending the spiral staircase to the Grand Café Orient, in the Czech Cubist Museum, it's easy to feel that each step is bringing you closer to another era. The café is in the Dům U černé Matky Boží (Black Madonna House), which was built in 1911–12 by Josef Gočár, and is considered a perfect example of Czech Cubism. The original café was open for just 10 years before it closed in the 1920s when Cubism went out of fashion. When the café reopened in spring 2005, it looked like time had stood still for more than 80 years, even though the space had at one time been taken over by offices. Using the architect's original sketches, the owners have re-created the original café, using excellent reproductions of the brass chandeliers, dark panelled booths and original buffet bar. A visit to this Cubist café—even for a simple espresso—is truly memorable.

Floating cranes on the river, near Charles Bridge, repairing the damage caused by the floods (left)

Ducks swimming over a flooded area of the historic Malá Strana district in August 2002 (below)

Prague Zoo's official mascot is the daughter (above) of Gaston the sea lion

After the
Floods

Of all the trials Prague has endured throughout its history, the floods of August 2002 rank fairly high: thousands of people were evacuated and the costs reached around 70 billion crowns in structural damage and lost tourism. The city, however, has made a remarkably swift recovery. Many of the businesses on Kampa Island were ruined but took the opportunity to make improvements as they rebuilt. Scores of old flooded apartment buildings that were crumbling before the floods hit have been restored to their original splendour. Most importantly, perhaps, the city is building a new flood wall and has developed an early warning system in case the waters start to rise again. The floating cranes working busily near Karlův most (Charles Bridge) are a reminder that nature once got the better of Prague; the people strolling across the bridge demonstrate that life goes on here, as it always has.

Gaston's legacy

Long after the flood waters had receded, Prague received an unexpected gift from Gaston, the brave sea lion who escaped from his pen at the city zoo during the flood. Gaston swam 120km (75 miles) downstream along the Vltava and then the Elbe before being recaptured near Dresden in Germany. A few days later, he died of exhaustion and the people around the world who had followed his journey mourned. However, 10 months later, in June 2003, Gaston's mate Bára delivered a female pup that zookeepers said could only be a daughter of Gaston. The whiskered pup was publicly christened Abeba—which means 'flower' in an African language—and a crowd of onlookers drank a toast in her honour. Abeba is now Prague Zoo's official mascot and a reminder to everyone who sees her of Gaston's brave odyssey.

Soggy statistics

During the floods, more than 20,000 residents were evacuated from the city's riverside Karlín district. Today the area shows the results of a rapid recovery effort with dozens of new and reconstructed buildings. But one casualty wasn't as easily repaired. The library containing the historical archives of the Czech Statistical Office lost a considerable amount of irreplaceable socio-economic data going as far back as the Austro-Hungarian Empire. The office has now moved to a location far from the river, the soggy record books that were saved are in a freezer—the first step in the restoration process—and the remaining archives are stored in the vault of the Czech National Bank.

A helping hand

Roman Halama's boat rental on Žofín Island has been in his family for over 50 years. The flood waters carried some of his boats out to sea, others were sunk. For two weeks Roman, his wife Lida, and their friends dragged up boats from the muddy bottom and made repairs—incredibly by the end of August they were back in business.

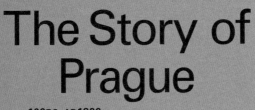

The Story of Prague

The Beginnings of Prague

A combination of forests, fertile soil, fordable river and easily defended rock outcrops made the site that became Prague an attractive place to settle, even in the earliest times. In the last centuries BC, the area supported the Celtic people called the 'Boii' by the Romans, a name which has survived in the form of Bohemia. In the final century BC, the Celts, with their relatively advanced culture, were driven out by the Marcomans, a Germanic tribe, who held sway over the area for several hundred years until, in the 6th century AD, they were overcome by Slavs moving in from the north and east.

Initially divided into at least a dozen quarrelsome clans, the Slavs of central Bohemia were eventually united under the Přemyslid family, who ruled first as dukes, then as kings, until the beginning of the 14th century. Among their number was perhaps the most famous Czech of all, the so-called 'Good King' Václav or Wenceslas (later patron saint of the country). The original Přemyslid stronghold was at Levý Hradec, just to the north of today's city, where Duke Bořivoj erected the country's first Christian church in the mid-9th century. A few years later, Bořivoj moved the ducal seat to the rock spur overlooking the Vltava at Hradčany, thereby becoming the founder of the city subsequently known as Praha (Prague). In the beginning, the duke and his retinue seem to have lived in a kind of oversized log cabin, but the Church of Our Lady he built here (the foundations of which were only discovered in the 1950s), was a substantial structure of stone.

100 BC

A vaulted 13th-century basement in Prague's Old Town (right)

Legendary Libussa

The central figure in the legend of the founding of Prague is the beautiful and wise Princess Libuše (Libussa), who ruled the Czechs from the Vyšehrad rock, where she dispensed justice beneath a lime tree, sacred to the Slavs. Uneasy at being ruled by a woman, her male subjects encouraged her to find a husband. She chose a humble ploughman called Přemysl, who gave his name to the royal house. Looking out from Vyšehrad towards the wooded heights of Hradčany one evening, Libussa fell into a trance, in which the vision of a great city was revealed to her 'whose glory shall reach unto the stars'. Her nobles were ordered to search the forest for a man fashioning the stone sill (*práh*) of a house, for this would be the site of her new stronghold, Praha.

The Jewish badge in the form of a hat (top) was introduced in 1215. The doorway of St. Martin's Rotunda at Vyšehrad (below), Prague's oldest surviving Romanesque building

The war of the maidens

The role played by women in the court of the early Czech rulers was much resented by its male members, and their intrigues led to the withdrawal of the privileges of the court maidens. Led by the spirited Vlasta, the angry women began to study the art of war, learning to ride and use the sword and bow. When the male mockery continued, they left Praha to build their own stronghold, Děvín ('Maiden's Castle'), from where they sallied forth to trap and kill their adversaries. The young and handsome Ctirad was offered a drink of mead by the lovely Šárka but as he drank, he was seized by other female warriors, tortured and put to death. Male revenge followed; despite the girls' resistance, Děvín fell, and those maidens not killed were forced into marriage.

The good and saintly king

Prince Václav (Wenceslas) was the grandson of Bořivoj and his consort Ludmila. In the early 10th century, the Přemyslid court was riven with factional strife, not least because of quarrels between Christians and those who had reverted to pagan practices. Ludmila, a Christian, was killed by her heathen daughter, Drahomíra, the mother of Wenceslas. In 929 or 935, Wenceslas was assassinated by his brother Boleslav, though in this case it seems that politics was the motive. Wenceslas may have been thought too conciliatory to his German neighbours in Saxony and Bavaria. Whatever the reason for his murder, he was soon canonized, and ever since has been invested with every ideal quality by the inhabitants of Bohemia.

A visitor's tale

The old east–west trade route along the Danube was blocked by the advance of the much-feared and still pagan Hungarians, and Prague, which by the middle of the 10th century still consisted only of Hradčany and Malá Strana, lay conveniently astride the alternative northern route. In 965, it was described for the first time by an observant visitor from Spain. Sent to report on central Europe by the Caliph of Tortosa, and writing in Arabic, the Jewish merchant Ibrahim ibn Ya'qub described a solid-seeming city built of limestone. According to him it teemed with merchants from distant parts and of different origins—Turkey and Russia, Jews and Muslims—all engaged in buying goods such as slaves, tin and furs. It was a 'place made richer by commerce than all others'.

Statue of St. Wenceslas (left). Slavs arrive at Vyšehrad (below right)

A king of gold and iron

The kingdom of Bohemia reached its greatest size under Otakar II (c1233–78), who extended its borders into Austria and almost to the Adriatic. Foreign rivals respected the military strength of this 'Ruler of Iron', who won his epithet by exploiting the kingdom's abundant resources of precious metals. Half-German himself, with a Hohenstaufen mother, Otakar further developed his realm by inviting German farmers, traders and technicians into the country, to clear forests, found new towns and promote commercial and industrial activity. German burghers dominated the civic life of Prague, which had spread across the river to the Old Town, its districts linked by one of the wonders of the age, the Romanesque Judith Bridge. Otakar met his death on the field of battle, defeated by a Habsburg, an ominous name for the further course of Czech history.

AD1300

A carving of St. Agnes (above left), founder of St. Agnes's Convent in Prague in the 1230s

Princess Libuše depicted in a 19th-century drawing (left)

A 2nd–1st century BC Celtic head in the La Tene style (above left), found within a sacred enclosure in Bohemia

THE BEGINNINGS OF PRAGUE 25

At the Heart of Europe

Czechs still look back on the middle of the 14th century as a Golden Age in their country's history. Under the wise and vigorous rule of Charles IV, who was Holy Roman Emperor as well as King of Bohemia, Prague became an imperial capital, one of the largest and most beautiful cities in Europe. Charles founded the first university in central Europe, spanned the Vltava with the splendid bridge now named after him and began the construction of the Gothic cathedral on Hradčany. His most ambitious project was the Nové Město (New Town), the planned extension of Prague which was so far-sighted that it coped with the city's growth for 500 years. But when Charles was succeeded by his son, Wenceslas IV, in 1378, the kingdom began to fall apart, undermined by religious strife.

Church corruption had reached such a pitch that radical clergymen like Jan Hus (c1372–1415), a Protestant before his time, found a ready hearing, not least among the Czech-speaking urban poor, resentful of their richer German fellow citizens. Banned from preaching his fiery sermons in Prague's Bethlehem Chapel, Hus eventually met a grisly fate at the stake, but his followers—the Hussites—fired by the conviction that they were 'Warriors of God', spread their subversive beliefs throughout the country and beyond. For a while, their fanaticism and their revolutionary military tactics gave them victory over the superior forces sent against them by Pope and Emperor, but by the mid-15th century, the movement had split, and calm of a kind returned to the country under the rule of a provincial nobleman, George of Poděbrady, the only native Czech ever to be elected king.

The Powder Tower (left) in the Old Town was built in 1475

Charles the collector

King-Emperor Charles IV had a many-sided personality, and some aspects of his character were decidedly odd. Among them was an obsessive interest in religious relics, which he housed in the great purpose-built castle at Karlštejn. His collection had got off to a good start, with inherited artefacts that included fragments of Christ's Cross and the lance that pierced his side. Friends and allies were leaned on to provide further choice objects. The French Dauphin was persuaded to part with some very precious relics—two thorns from Christ's crown. From Hungary came the tablecloth used at the Last Supper and from Constantinople the authenticated bones of Abraham.

Karlštejn Castle (below)

1300

The first defenestration (above)

Charles and the Czech crown

Charles IV was a determined inventor of traditions, among them the cult of St. Wenceslas. The Good King's crown jewels were brought out and refashioned into the crown which was used for Charles' coronation in 1346. One of the holy thorns donated by the French Dauphin was inserted into the sapphire cross forming part of the crown, which could not be removed from its place of safe keeping until the day of the coronation. The belief that only a future king might place the crown on his head was scorned by Nazi Reichsprotektor Heydrich in 1942, who had himself photographed doing just that. Six weeks later he was dead, assassinated by Czechoslovak parachutists sent from England.

Burn him!

Exasperated by Jan Hus's heretical views and his contempt for their corrupt ways, the Church hierarchy summoned him to appear before a grand council in the Swiss city of Constance in 1414. Hus hoped to win over his adversaries by argument, and although he was given assurances of safe conduct, he was later sentenced to be burned at the stake. But first he had to be humiliated. He was stripped of his clerical robes and made to wear a ridiculous paper hat, then he was dragged off past a blazing bonfire fed by his confiscated books and taken to a malodorous dump on the edge of town. Bound to a pole, he was offered a last chance to recant. He refused, the fire was lit, and the great preacher died with a prayer on his lips. His ashes were cast into the Rhine.

The first defenestration

The tradition in Prague of hurling your opponents from a window to settle political arguments seems to have been established in July 1419. This was when a Hussite priest named Jan Želivský led an angry crowd to the Town Hall of Nové Město (New Town), where the councillors had imprisoned a number of citizens who had taken part in a forbidden demonstration. Anger turned to fury when stones were thrown from an upper window; the locked doors were beaten down, the mob stormed upstairs, released the prisoners, and threw the councillors out of the window onto the pikes and lances of the waiting crowd. Those who survived had their heads smashed in on the cobblestones. Želivský himself continued to stir up trouble, until he too met a violent end, beheaded in the courtyard of the Town Hall of Staré Město (Old Town).

Victory on Vítkov Hill

The Hussites owed much of their success in battle to their one-eyed general Jan Žižka (1360–1424), a squire from southern Bohemia. Žižka made a virtue of his peasant followers' lack of sophisticated weaponry, teaching them to use their flails and scythes to deadly effect. His most spectacular victory was achieved in 1420 against Emperor Sigismund's well-equipped and numerically superior Crusader army, drawn up on Letná Plain. On the summit of Vítkov Hill on the far side of the Vltava, Žižka built barricades from whatever materials could be found, including pews ransacked from a nearby church. When Sigismund's mounted knights attacked, they were halted by Hussites (women among them) fighting with fanatic ferocity. Milling around in confusion, the horsemen fell victim to Žižka's counter-attack, many of them plunging to their death down the hill's cliff-like slopes.

A statue of Charles IV (above)

Religious reformer Jan Hus (above) was burned at the stake in 1415 (below)

1500

A bronze relief (below) on the base of the statue of St. John of Nepomuk (▷ 30) on Charles Bridge

The 14th-century Charles Bridge (left)

AT THE HEART OF EUROPE **27**

Darkness Falls

When Emperor Rudolf II decided in 1583 to make Prague his capital city, his Habsburg dynasty had already been ruling the Czech lands for half a century. In total, the reign of this Roman Catholic, Germano-Spanish family lasted for four centuries, ending only in the abdication of Emperor Karl in 1918. Rudolf's rule was relatively benign; compromises were made with the country's Protestant majority, and the court became a European focus of culture, attracting painters, sculptors, architects and craftsmen, as well as astronomers, astrologers and alchemists. But the bachelor Emperor became increasingly eccentric and his politics more unfathomable, until in 1611 he was deposed by his brother Matthias, who moved the court back to Vienna. All over central Europe, Catholic-Protestant relations were deteriorating; in 1618, the signal for the outbreak of the Thirty Years War was given when a group of Protestant noblemen threw the Emperor's representatives from the windows of Prague Castle. In 1620, the Protestant army was routed in the Battle of the White Mountain, and what many Czechs call the *Temno*, the time of darkness, began; homegrown forms of religious worship were forbidden, a foreign-born aristocracy was imported, thousands of Protestants were forced to emigrate, and the Czech language lost out to German.

Tin-nosed Tycho

One of the eminent scientists drawn to Rudolf's court was the Danish astronomer and mathematician Tycho Brahe (1546–1601). Tycho arrived in Prague in 1599 with his astrolabes, hourglasses and sextants, as well as his famous tin nose, a replacement for the real one which had been sliced off in the course of a duel. While alchemists Edward Kelley (1555–95) and John Dee (1527–1608) worked in the castle laboratories vainly trying to turn base metal into gold for the Emperor, Tycho and his assistant Johannes Kepler (1571–1630) plotted the course of the planets for their imperial master with rather more success. Poor Tycho had to endure a horrible end; not wanting to leave his host's table to relieve himself, his bladder burst and he spent five days in agony before dying.

Tycho Brahe (above) and his astronomical sextant (left)

1500

A statue of Rabbi Loew (above). Engraving of the Battle of White Mountain (right)

The Rabbi and the Golem

Emperor Rudolf was interested in the occult. One of those who advised him on its mysteries was the Rabbi Loew (c1520–1609), who on occasion was summoned in secret to the Castle, where the emperor listened to him hidden behind a screen. The Rabbi is credited with the creation of the Golem, Prague's own version of the Frankenstein monster. Fashioned at midnight out of mud from the banks of the Vltava, the robotic Golem becomes the Rabbi's faithful servant and protector of the ghetto. But one night the ritual which sends him to sleep is neglected and the Golem runs wild, terrifying the populace. Eventually the Rabbi pacifies him; the monster crumbles into clay and his remains are placed in the loft of the Old-New Synagogue.

Another defenestration

Provoked by constant Catholic pressure, a band of Protestant noblemen stormed into the Castle on the morning of 23 May 1618, intent on confronting Emperor Matthias's representatives. Two imperial councillors were released, but two others, Vilem Slavata and Jaroslav Martinic, were forced out through a window of the Old Royal Palace (▷ below left). Slavata clung to the sill for a while until someone broke his knuckles with the hilt of a dagger. For good measure, secretary Filip Fabricius was thrown out too. Astonishingly, all survived the 15m (50ft) fall, their landing softened by a huge heap of manure. The unfortunate secretary was subsequently rewarded for his trouble by being raised to the ranks of the aristocracy, with the title of 'Von Hohenfall' (Sir Philip of High Fall).

The White Mountain

The White Mountain— Bílá Hora—is the name given to the bleak limestone plateau west of Prague. Here, on 8 November 1620, the most fateful battle in Czech history was fought, between the Bohemian Protestant army and the Catholic forces of the Emperor. The Protestants had the advantage of occupying the top of the hill and, with so much at stake, their morale should have been better than that of their adversaries. But their commander-in-chief, King Frederick, chose to stay in the Castle rather than appear on the field of battle, and many of his soldiers seemed to prefer the fleshpots of Prague to the perils of soldiering. Within an hour, the battle had become a rout, with the Protestant troops streaming back to the city in disorder. The next day the Catholic army entered Prague without a shot being fired.

21 June 1621

On this date, a gruesome spectacle was enacted in Prague to make it quite clear who were now the rulers of Bohemia. The master of ceremonies was Prince Karl von Liechtenstein, a former Protestant who had prudently converted to Catholicism. To the deafening sound of drums, and in the presence of countless armed men, a group of Protestant 'rebels', including some of the defenestrators of 1618, were brought to Staroměstské náměstí (Old Town Square) for execution. On a scaffold draped in black, the aristocrats among them were beheaded, the commoners hanged. Special torments were reserved for some. Bits of corpses were exposed on Žižkov Hill, while a dozen severed heads were carried off to decorate the Staroměstská mostecká věž (Old Town Bridge Tower).

White crosses on Old Town Square (right) show where Protestant 'rebels' were executed in 1621

1700

Italian-inspired sgraffito decoration on the façade of the Dům U Minuty (left) on Old Town Square. Rudolf II and courtiers at the Belvedér (below)

From Darkness to Light

Despite its name, there was a lot of light during the dark days of the *Temno*. This was the age of the baroque, when aristocrats competed to build the most ostentatious palaces, and when the triumphant Catholic Church wooed congregations with ever more opulent settings for worship. Though no longer the capital (Emperor Matthias had moved the court back to Vienna in 1612), and with its population halved, Prague became one of the most beautiful cities in Europe. By the middle of the 18th century, it had become thoroughly Germanized, with Czech relegated to the status of a dialect spoken by peasants, coachmen, and washerwomen. Emperor Joseph's advocacy of German as the sole official language of the Empire might have killed it off altogether, but by this time interest was growing in the Czech nation's history and heritage.

In a great upsurge of activity, which came to be known as the National Awakening, intellectuals such as Josef Jungmann (1773–1847) revived and codified the language, while historian František Palacký (1798–1876) explored the nation's forgotten past. During the 19th century, Prague was transformed from a seemingly German city into a thoroughly Czech one. One of the causes of this change was industrialization. Bohemia and Moravia had become the industrial powerhouse of the Austro-Hungarian Empire; Prague expanded rapidly, drawing in Czech workers from the countryside. The city decked itself out with great institutional buildings like the Národní Muzeum (National Museum), proud symbols of the revival of Czech confidence.

Nepomuk

One problem facing the hierarchy of the 17th-century Catholic Church was the popularity among the populace of Jan Hus, a condemned heretic. To provide people with a more appropriate martyr, they successfully built up the cult of another 14th-century figure, the Vicar General of St. Vitus Cathedral, Jan Nepomuk. In addition to his normal duties, Nepomuk was the queen's confessor. Ordered by her jealous husband, King Václav IV, to reveal the secrets of the confessional, the cleric refused. Furious, the king gave the order for Nepomuk to be dealt with. In 1393 thuggish underlings tortured him, trussed him up in a sack, then took him to Karlův most (Charles Bridge) and threw him over the parapet to his death. A statue of Nepomuk now stands at the spot where he was thrown in.

Statue of St. John of Nepomuk on Charles Bridge (above)

1700

The impressive interior of Prague's main railway station, Hlavní nádraží (below)

Detail of a gilded sunburst decorating a lamp-post (top)

Prague's coat of arms features on the 19th-century calendar of the Astronomical clock (above)

Enlightened emperor

Emperor Joseph II was a true son of the 18th century Enlightenment, who hoped to turn his largely feudal realm into a modern, centralized state run on rational lines. Many of his ideas seemed eminently reasonable, among them universal education, abolition of serfdom, freedom of religion and emancipation of the Jews. Unfortunately, Joseph was not the most sensitive of men. His appreciation of music was summed up in the film *Amadeus* (1984) by his remark 'Too many notes, Mozart!' He genuinely thought that making German the sole official language would 'create a sense of fraternity', and was surprised when mourners objected to their loved ones being buried in sacks rather than coffins in order to save timber. In Prague, his 'rationalization' of religion led to the loss of half the city's churches and two-thirds of its monasteries, many of them converted into barracks, depots and warehouses.

Patriotic Palacký

František Palacký (1798–1876) is chiefly remembered for his monumental *History of the Czech Nation in Bohemia and Moravia*, written over a period of more than 40 years between 1830 and his death. Brought up in a Germanicized world, Palacký initially found it easier to think and write in German, and only later was his history translated into Czech. To begin with, he was no foe of the Habsburg Empire, maintaining that 'If Austria did not exist, she would have to be invented.' But when the Empire proved incapable of responding to the growing Czech demand for national recognition, Palacký changed his mind, declaring 'We were here before Austria, and we will be here when she is gone.'

František Palacký (1798–1876)

Street battles

The growing control of Prague by its Czech population was reflected in the way streets were named by the city government. Traditional street names were bilingual, written in a flowery Gothic script, with German first, Czech second. Very few remain, among them Georgi Gasse/Jiřská ulice (St. George's Lane) in the Castle. When Czechs began to dominate the city council from the 1860s onwards, this was felt to be intolerable. First the order came to reverse the sequence, with the Czech name put before the German. Then in 1892, after the last German representatives had resigned from the council, it was decided to eliminate the German. Henceforth street names would only be in Czech, with white lettering on a background of red—the national colour (▷ below).

Café society

In the last years of the Habsburg monarchy, Prague became a vibrant focus of literary life, much of it taking place in cafés, of which there were more than a hundred. They served less as places of refreshment than as forums for discussion, as reading rooms, even as work stations. Each was presided over by the imperious figure of a head waiter, who might with luck provide an impoverished scribbler with the occasional loan. The German, mostly Jewish writers like Franz Kafka (1883–1924) frequented the Café Arco, and bore with pride their title of 'Arconauts'. The Czechs preferred the Union, referred to as the 'Unionka', while the famous Slavia, with its view of the Vltava, attracted both nationalities.

An equestrian portrait of Emperor Joseph II (left)

Many of the cafés in Prague had a literary focus in the early 20th century (below)

Czechoslovakia: Rise and Fall

In World War I the Czechs, as Austrian citizens, had to fight alongside Kaiser Wilhelm's Germany against their Russian fellow Slavs. Many deserted, with whole units leaving their trenches and crossing over to the Russian lines. In the mean time, émigrés such as Tomáš Masaryk (1850–1937), Edvard Beneš (1884–1948) and the Slovak Milan Štefánik (1880–1919) persuaded the Western Allies to support the creation of an independent Czech and Slovak state out of the ruins of the Habsburg Empire. On 28 October 1918, in Prague's Obecní dům (Municipal House), the new Republic of Czechoslovakia was proclaimed, with Masaryk as its president.

A model democracy in many ways, the new state was fatally flawed from the start. The 7 million Czechs barely formed a majority, and the largest minority—3.1 million—was made up of their old adversaries, the Germans. Rule from an assertively Czech Prague was deeply resented by the Germans living in what came to be called the Sudetenland, especially when the Great Depression of the early 1930s affected them disproportionately. Hitler exploited their grievances, threatening war if they were not allowed to return '*heim ins Reich*' (home to the Reich). In September 1938, Britain and France signed the Munich Agreement which rendered Czechoslovakia defenceless by giving Hitler the Sudetenland. A few months later, in March 1939, Germany forced Slovakia to secede, and what was left of the country was incorporated into the Third Reich as the 'Protectorate of Bohemia-Moravia'. The German occupation continued until the end of World War II. In 1945 President Beneš hoped Czechoslovakia could act as a bridge in an increasingly divided Europe. This was not to be.

A woman weeps as she salutes the German troops in 1938 (left)

The Legions

Tens of thousands of Czechs and Slovaks were fighting as legionnaires on the Allied side by 1918. Recruited from deserters, POWs and émigrés, substantial numbers served on the Western Front and in Italy, but by far the largest contingent was in Russia. When the Bolsheviks made peace with Germany, the Czechoslovak Legion there found itself in an extremely awkward situation. The decision to extricate it via Vladivostok and the US led it on a legendary 'long march' which took two years to complete, from 1918 to 1920. At one point the Legion found itself in control of the whole length of the Trans-Siberian railway, fighting off attacks by Trotsky's Red Army. The legionnaires' exploits are commemorated in the sculpture adorning the Bank of the Legions in Prague's Na poříčí street.

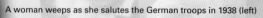

1914

A 1927 poster (above) advertising the Grand Restaurant in Prague

First philosopher president

The philosophy professor Tomáš Garrigue Masaryk (1850–1937), fondly referred to as T.G.M, was the son of a Slovak coachman and a German-speaking Moravian mother. An enemy of prejudice and everything irrational, he entered public life as an exposer of nationalistic forgeries and an opponent of anti-Semitism. He was already elderly as he travelled the world pleading the Czechoslovak cause during World War I, and served three terms as president of the new state, reviewing his troops on horseback for the last time at the age of 83. Such sprightliness was legendary; in the 1920s, rather than go around to the front door of the Thunovský palác (Thun Palace) for a tête-à-tête with the British Ambassador, Masaryk would nip down a private ladder from the Castle into the Embassy garden.

Adolf Hitler entered the Sudetenland with his army, stopping along the route to join his officers at a field dinner (below left)

17 November 1939

Hitler's promise that Czechs would be able to live 'a full national life' within the German Reich was soon revealed as empty. A student celebration of Independence Day on 28 October 1939 was broken up brutally and a medical student named Jan Opletal shot dead. Further demonstrations and confrontations followed his funeral, then, in the small hours of 17 November, university dormitories were raided; nine students were shot and 1,200 others arrested at random and sent off to concentration camps in Germany. The Governor of Bohemia-Moravia, Reichsprotekor Konstantin von Neurath, ordered the closure of all Czech universities and institutions of higher education. Their buildings were given to the Wehrmacht and the SS, and their libraries dispersed. Lecturers subsequently found they risked execution for teaching in private.

Hangman Heydrich

The appointment in 1941 of SS Obergruppenführer Reinhard Heydrich as acting Reichsprotektor heralded a devastating reign of terror which destroyed the underground resistance movement. At the same time, the Czech workforce, whose collaboration was vital to the Nazi war effort, was seduced with extra rations and good working conditions. Dismayed by these developments, the Czechoslovak government in exile in Britain sent a group of parachutists to assassinate Heydrich. On 27 May 1942, two of them—one Czech, one Slovak—waylaid 'The Hangman' as he drove into Prague from his country residence. A tommy-gun jammed, but a hand-grenade dealt Heydrich a fatal wound. The parachutists fled the scene, but were later betrayed; they met their deaths in the crypt of the Svatého Cyrila a Metoděje (Church of St. Cyril and St. Methodius).

Lidice

Lidice, a mining village just outside Prague, was the victim of one of the worst atrocities in World War II. Outraged at Heydrich's assassination, the Germans, on the flimsiest of pretexts, sealed off the village on the night of 9 June 1942; its male inhabitants were shot on the spot, the women and children carted off to concentration camps. Miners coming off the night shift were arrested and killed too. Army engineers set about destroying all traces of Lidice, and Nazi propaganda boasted that corn would grow where the village once stood. But the action backfired, and instead Lidice became a symbol worldwide of Nazi brutality and Czech victimhood. After the war, the site became a national monument, and a new Lidice was built alongside it.

A collage composed of pictures of the men murdered by the Nazis at Lidice in 1942 (below)

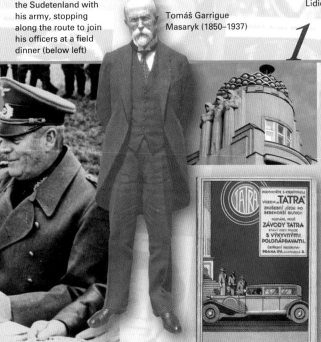

1945

Tomáš Garrigue Masaryk (1850–1937)

Detail of three cloaked figures at the top of the art nouveau Koruna Palace on the corner of Wenceslas Square (above left).
A 1930s advert for the Czech Tatra tourer car (left)

Communism to
Revolution

At the end of World War II most of the Czech Republic was liberated from the Nazis by the Red Army, giving Soviet-style Communism a huge boost. Free elections made the Communists the largest party, and their leader, Klement Gottwald, became prime minister. In February 1948 the Communists staged a *coup d'état*—Communist militiamen filled the streets and took over public buildings and counter-demonstrations were broken up. Gottwald proclaimed his triumph to the masses in Old Town Square and President Beneš gave in to the threat of force. Tens of thousands of Czechs fled abroad. Thousands more were arrested, all private industry was nationalized, and Czechoslovakia became a satellite of Stalin's Soviet Union.

In 1968 Communist Party leader Alexander Dubček (1921–92), led an attempt, known as the 'Prague Spring', to revive Czechoslovak Communism by making it responsive to the wishes of the people. Its brutal crushing by Soviet tanks in August of that year ushered in two decades of political and cultural repression. The vast majority of Czechs and Slovaks kept their heads down, focusing on family life. Some brave spirits kept the flag of freedom flying, among them playwright Václav Havel and his fellow signatories of 'Charter 77', which called on the government to respect its own laws. By the end of the 1980s, the whole Communist pack of cards in Eastern Europe had begun to collapse. In Prague, the bloodless 'Velvet Revolution' of November 1989 was coordinated by Havel and his colleagues, encouraged by mass demonstrations in the city. The cry went up Havel na hrad (Havel to the Castle), and he became President.

Liberation

In early May 1945, with the Red Army approaching from the east and the Americans from the west, Prague rose up against its Nazi occupiers. Most German soldiers wanted to escape Russian wrath by surrendering to the Americans but the Gestapo and SS fought on savagely. Hundreds of Czech fighters and civilians perished as the conflict continued and German shell-fire destroyed the north wing of the Staroměstské radnice (Old Town Hall). Desperate appeals for help went out on Prague Radio to General Patton's forces in liberated Plzeň. The crowds in Prague went wild as a pair of American jeeps entered the city, but it was only a reconnaissance mission; the Allies had agreed that Prague was to be liberated by the Russians. Red Army tanks rolled into town on 9 May, handing the Soviet Union and local Communists a huge propaganda victory.

1945

Czechs dressed as US soldiers celebrate the anniversary of VE Day (right)

Soviet troops entering Prague in May 1945 (above)

Show trial, Stalin style

One of the most fanatical members of the Communist government was Rudolf Slánský (1901–52), untiring in his persecution of 'traitors, class enemies and bourgeois nationalists'. People like Jiří Mucha, the son of the painter Alfons, were sent to the uranium mines, while political opponents like the former female MP Milada Horáková were executed. But the tyrannical machinery of repression Slánský had set up ended by devouring its maker. With help from specialists sent from Moscow by Stalin, trumped-up charges were fabricated against him and other old Communists. Arrested, he and the others were tortured and brainwashed into admitting to a host of improbable crimes, including acting as 'agents of Imperialism' and 'Zionist conspirators'. Of the 13 high-ranking Party men subsequently executed, 10, including Slánský, were of Jewish origin.

Alexander Dubček speaks to a crowd of 500,000 Czechs during the Velvet Revolution (below left)

2–0

The Soviet invasion of August 1968 left Czechs and Slovaks stunned. For a while, with Alexander Dubček still at least nominally in charge, it seemed as if something of the spirit of the Prague Spring might be saved. But in March 1969, the Czechoslovak ice-hockey team beat their Russian opponents two-nil. Within minutes of the game ending, tens of thousands had torn themselves away from their TV sets and converged ecstatically on Václavské náměstí (Wenceslas Square), singing, shouting and writing the score on every available surface. Matters got out of hand when part of the crowd attacked the offices of Aeroflot, the Soviet airline, comprehensively trashing it. This was too much for the Russians; Dubček was eased out of office, replaced by *apparatchiks* (servants of the government) ready to do their masters' bidding.

Jan Palach

On 16 January 1969, in a gesture resonant with the memory of martyred Jan Hus, the 21-year-old philosophy student Jan Palach poured petrol over himself at the top of Václavské náměstí (Wenceslas Square) and set himself alight. Three days later he was dead. The note he left behind simply demanded freedom of the press and the closure of a Soviet-inspired propaganda bulletin, but he inevitably became a symbol of protest against the invasion, and his funeral procession through Prague was followed by half a million mourners. Palach was buried in Olšany cemetery (▷ 99), but when his grave attracted too many pilgrims, his body was dug up by the secret police, cremated, and the ashes reburied in his home village. Only after 1989 were they returned to Olšany.

A memorial to Jan Palach (above), who set himself on fire in political protest in 1969

17 November 1989

On the evening of 17 November 1989, to mark the 50th anniversary of the murder by the Nazis of medical student Jan Opletal (▷ 33), an officially sanctioned demonstration of some 50 000 young people wound its way from Vyšehrad to the Národní divadlo (National Theatre). As the column made its way along Národní třída towards Václavské náměstí (Wenceslas Square), it found its route blocked by riot police. Some of the marchers sat down, sang the national anthem and chanted slogans. Suddenly, the police attacked, causing panic among those unable to escape. Many were beaten and badly hurt, and it seemed that one demonstrator had been killed. The event was quickly dubbed the 'Massacre', and became one of the sparks that ignited the Velvet Revolution. But the death of the demonstrator turned out to be a rumour put out by the secret police, for reasons that remain inscrutable to this day.

The small shrine (above) set up to commemorate student Jan Palach

Czechs stage a sit-down protest in Wenceslas Square during the uprising of 1968 (left)

Modern Prague

By the turn of the 21st century, Havel's hopes of a 'Third Way' between capitalism and Communism had been dashed. Prague was now the capital of a more or less 'normal' Western country, with a democratically elected government and a privatized economy. Longstanding problems between Czechs and Slovaks had been solved in the 'Velvet Divorce', though the split of Czechoslovakia into separate republics had never been put to the two peoples in the form of a referendum. The Czech Republic became a member of NATO in 1999 and the European Union in 2004. The most obvious effect of change in Prague was in the condition of buildings; the pervasive greyness and decay of the Communist era vanished as new owners repaired and repainted their property. Western tourists who had avoided the city in Cold War days now made up for lost time.

Foreigners

Prosperous, with almost no unemployment, and now part of the European Union, Prague is a magnet for people from countries farther to the east. Most of them are Ukrainians, officially some 60,000 in total—unofficially far more. They are easily outnumbered by a flood of people coming from the opposite direction; the Czech Republic attracts over a hundred million visitors a year, though not all of them come to Prague. In the early post-1989 days the majority were Germans or Austrians, but today the British are the biggest contingent, carried here in a couple of hours aboard a budget jet.

The great flood

The flood of August 2002 (▷ 22) was all the worse for being unexpected, and even as the water rose around them, Praguers could hardly believe it was happening. Billions of crowns worth of damage was done to the city, but recovery was remarkably swift, and few visible signs of the inundation remain, apart from the tide-marks on certain buildings.

Václav v. Václav

Both post-1989 presidents—Havel, in office until 2003, and Klaus who succeeded him—are called Václav (Wenceslas), but the men themselves could not be more different. Havel's view of politics as a branch of moral philosophy contrasts with his opponent's concentration on practical matters, particularly economics. Outward-looking Havel relishes appearing on the world stage, unlike Euro-sceptic Klaus, who stayed away from celebrations marking the Czech Republic's entry to the European Union. Two images seem to sum up these contrasting characters: for Havel, the huge red neon heart his friends placed atop the Castle; for Klaus, the monster election poster sited prominently in the city.

Václav Havel's giant neon heart (below)

1989–Today

A T-shirt illustrates the split of Czechoslovakia into the Czech and Slovak Republics in 1993 (above)

Young Czechs celebrate the Czech Republic joining the European Union in 2004 (right)

On the Move

want.
nects
metro, but
route.
airport with
minus of
western
may be more
some destina-
No. 225 joins the
Nové Butovice.
y night-time bus
No. 510) is provided
e airport to the Divoká

On the
Move

and
want.
nects
metro, but
route.
airport with
minus of
western
may be more
some destina-
No. 225 joins the
Nové Butovice.
y night-time bus
No. 510) is provided
e airport to the Divoká

<table>
</table>

On the
Move

and
want.
nects
metro, but
route.
airport with
minus of
western
may be more
some destina-
No. 225 joins the
Nové Butovice.
y night-time bus
No. 510) is provided
e airport to the Divoká

ARRIVING

Arriving by Air

ON THE MOVE

Prague, in the heart of central Europe, is very accessible by air, only an hour or two from many of the continent's major cities. The redevelopment and expansion of the city's only airport at Ruzyně has greatly improved conditions, while the entry of the Czech Republic into the European Union in 2004 has reduced entry formalities to a minimum.

The advent of short-haul, budget airlines has simplified travel and brought down costs, making a short break in Prague an easy and economical possibility for many people. As well as being linked directly to many European destinations, the city can also be reached direct from the US and Canada (New York, Montreal, Toronto), and with just one connecting flight from many destinations world-wide.

Ruzyně Airport (PRG) is 19km (12 miles) northwest of central Prague. Its buildings and facilities are modern and well maintained and well capable of handling the volume of traffic. Routes to and from the plane through passport control and customs are much quicker than they used to be and are signposted in English as well as Czech. At present there is only one terminal for use by travellers, but a second is due to be completed by 2006.

Facilities and amenities in the arrival hall and elsewhere in the terminal include bars, cafés, restaurants and cafeterias, left luggage, a broad range of shops, and money-changing facilities. There is an airport information desk (tel 220 111 111), while tourist information is provided by private hotel and travel agencies. Automated reservation of accommodation is available in the baggage hall and the Prague Transport Authority (Dopravní podnik hl.m.Prahy—DPP)

USEFUL TELEPHONE NUMBERS	
Arrival/departure information	220 113 314 or 220 113 321
First aid	220 113 301-2
Pharmacy	220 116 662
Post office	222 241 180
VIP lounges	220 562 525

has an information office in the arrival hall (tel 220 115 404, open daily 7am–10pm).

GETTING TO PRAGUE FROM THE AIRPORT

Though the airport has no rail link, transfer to central Prague is quite straightforward and there is a choice of options (▷ 38–39).

By public transport

This is a very economical and reliable way of getting to most parts of Prague. Departing from the bus station immediately in front of the terminal, city bus No. 119 connects the airport with Dejvická metro station, from where it is only a few stops to stations serving central Prague. The bus sets down and picks up at a small number of

intermediate stops and takes around 25 minutes from airport to station. Buses run between 4am and midnight, at intervals of 7 to 8 minutes during peak times, or around 30 minutes in early morning/late evening. The metro runs every few minutes between 5am and midnight. You will need an ordinary public transport ticket (20Kč), which can be obtained from the DPP office in the terminal, from a ticket machine at the bus stop, or from the driver (in which case it will cost 25Kč). It must be validated (▷ 44) and allows travel throughout the city for up to 1 hour, or 1.5 hours outside peak times. You can change between bus, metro tram as many times as you City bus No. 254 also co the airport to Dejvická has a more roundabo Bus No. 100 links th Zličín station, the t metro Line B in th suburbs, which convenient fo tions, while same line a

An hou service from th

A ČSA Czech Airlines plane taxies along a runway (above)

Šárka tram terminus. From here, night tram No. 51 runs every half hour to Nádraží Strašnice via Náměstí Republiky (Republic Square) and Václavské náměstí (Wenceslas Square) and other stops in central Prague, including Lazarská, where it connects with all the other night trams.

By minibus
The CEDAZ company has a desk in a prominent position in the arrival hall, and runs a minibus service to Dejvická metro station and to Náměstí Republiky (Republic Square) close to the Obecní dům (Municipal House) and the Prašná brána (Powder Tower) in central Prague. The trip to the metro takes about 15 minutes and costs 60Kč, to Náměstí Republiky about 30 minutes and costs 90Kč. Minibuses leave from the front of the terminal every half hour between 5.30am and 9.30pm. The minibuses will also take you directly to your hotel or to a private address for a set fee.

By taxi
FIX has the monopoly on taxi services from the airport and operates from a desk in the arrivals hall. Prague taxi drivers are notorious for overcharging (▷ 21) but this firm seems to have reined in the worst excesses. Variable but defined rates are charged according to the distance you travel, and you should make sure that the fare is

MAJOR AIRLINES	
AIRLINE	**WEBSITE**
American Airlines	www.aa.com
Air Canada	www.aircanada.ca
Air France	www.airfrance.com
Alitalia	www.italiatour.com
Austrian Airlines	www.aua.com
British Airways	www.britishairways.com
Czech Airlines	www.czechairlines.com
Easyjet	www.easyjet.com
EUjet	www.eujet.com
Jet2	www.jet2.com
KLM Royal Dutch Airlines	www.klm.nl
Lufthansa	www.lufthansa.com

CAR RENTAL COMPANIES		
COMPANY	**TELEPHONE**	**WEBSITE**
Alimex ČR Rent a car	220 114 860	www.alimexcr.cz
Avis	220 114 270	www.avis.cz
Budget	220 113 253	www.budget.cz
CS-Czechocar	220 113 116	www.czechocar.cz
Dvořák Rent a Car	220 113 676	www.dvorak-rentacar.cz
Europcar	220 113 207	www.europcar.cz
Hertz	220 114 340	www.hertz.cz
Sixt	220 114 554	www.e-sixt.cz

agreed in advance. The journey to central Prague should not cost more than 500Kč.

By car
You are likely to find a car more of a hindrance than a help in Prague. Traffic is heavy, parking is difficult and virtually everywhere in the city can be reached using the integrated public transport system. However, a car can be very useful if you wish to visit locations beyond the city, including some of the excursions described on pages 204–217.

Several of the major car rental companies are represented at the airport, but it is usually less expensive to arrange car rental in advance. It may be cheaper still to rent a vehicle from one of the local companies (▷ above). You will need to produce your driving licence, be more than 21 years of age, and guarantee payment with a credit card.

A 1.5km (1-mile) spur road leads from the airport to Route No. 7 running northwest from Prague. For central Prague follow signs to Centrum or Praha.

Arriving By Train

As well as operating services throughout the Czech Republic, the national rail company České Drahy (ČD) liaises with the railways of neighbouring countries to provide international links. Direct services connect Prague with cities in Austria, Germany and several countries in Eastern Europe, and a single change of train brings many other cities within reach.

ON THE MOVE

INTERNATIONAL TRAINS

● It is possible to travel by train from London to Prague via the Channel Tunnel but this will normally involve at least two changes of train and use of night services. Given the speed and relatively low cost of flights, the rail option between the UK and Prague is really only relevant for those planning to combine a visit to the Czech Republic with other travel on the Continent. Eurostar trains link London and Ashford International with Paris-Nord and Bruxelles-(Brussels)- Midi. Journey times from London are 2 hours 35 minutes to Paris and

2 hours 30 minutes to Brussels. Running smoothly at a maximum speed of 300kph (186mph), the trains have been upgraded and feature first-class restaurant cars and buffet facilities.

● Thalys trains run between Brussels and Cologne and are similar to Eurostar trains.

● Long-distance rail travel within Germany and on to the Czech Republic is normally by ICE (InterCityExpress) or EC (EuroCity) trains, which are of an equivalent or superior standard. Between Cologne and Frankfurt trains use a new section of rail line, allowing ultra-high speeds.

● The modern overnight trains run by German Railways between Brussels-Berlin and Frankfurt-Prague provide comfortable accommodation in sleeping cars (one, two or three berths) and couchettes (four or six berths), as well as in ordinary coaches. Snacks and drinks are usually available.

STATIONS IN PRAGUE

Most, but not all, international trains serving Prague arrive at Praha hlavní nádraží, the city's main railway station. This is an old station with splendid but decaying art nouveau buildings and a more modern concourse where the main facilities (ticket offices, left luggage, information, shops, etc.) are located. The station is on the edge of the historic heart of the city, less than a 10-minute walk from Václavské náměstí (Wenceslas Square), and has its own metro station.

Two other stations are served by international trains: Praha-Smíchov in the southwestern suburbs and Praha-Holešovice in the north. Both are modern constructions and are served by the metro, but are in a rather run-down condition.

Praha hlavní nádraží is not necessarily the most convenient station at which to arrive, and certain international trains not terminating in Prague only call at Praha-Holešovice. Depending on your final destination in the city you should check which of the city's three principal stations best serves your needs, bearing in mind that they are all connected directly to the efficient metro and public transport system. There is an international rail information office at Praha hlavní nádraží (on the south side of the building, upstairs from the main hall).

USEFUL CONTACTS

COMPANY	TELEPHONE	WEBSITE
Eurostar (in Britain)	08705 186 186/0870 160 6600	www.eurostar.com
(from outside Britain)	0044 1233 617 575	
Deutsche Bahn (German Railways)	0870 243 5363	www.bahn.de
České Drahy (Czech Railways)	221 111 122	www.cd.cz

INTERNATIONAL RAIL SERVICES TO PRAGUE

COUNTRY	CITY	JOURNEY TIME	TRAINS DAILY
Austria	Vienna	4.5 hours	5
Germany	Berlin	5 hours	7
	Dresden	3 hours	7
	Frankfurt	8 hours	1
	Hamburg	7 hours	2
	Munich	6 hours	3
	Nuremberg	5 hours	2
Hungary	Budapest	7 hours	2
Poland	Warsaw	12 hours	1
Slovakia	Bratislava	5–5.5 hours	2

INDIRECT SERVICES (CHANGE NECESSARY)

London–Prague
From London-Waterloo: Change at Bruxelles-(Brussels)-Midi, Köln (Cologne) and Frankfurt Hbf (night train Frankfurt–Prague). Journey time: 17 hours
From London-Waterloo: Change at Bruxelles-(Brussels)-Midi and Berlin (night train Brussels–Berlin, luxury sleeping accommodation available). Journey time: 20 hours

Paris–Prague
From Paris-Est: Change at Karlsruhe, Frankfurt Hbf, Dresden. Journey time: 13.5 hours
From Paris-Nord: Change at Köln (Cologne), Frankfurt-Flughafen, Frankfurt Hbf, Dresden. Journey time: 13.5 hours

Arriving by Long-distance Bus

Long-distance bus services linking Prague with other European cities, including London, are run by a number of companies. Fares are cheaper than by rail, and in some cases journey times are shorter.

Coaches are generally modern vehicles, in good condition, with on-board toilets, air-conditioning and reclining seats. On longer trips, stops for food and refreshment are made at service areas, and basic refreshments may be available on board. The trip from London involves spending a night on the bus. Services usually terminate at Prague's Florenc bus station, a seemingly rather chaotic, but in fact quite efficient establishment with basic facilities. It is on the edge of the historic centre, less than a 10-minute walk from the Prašná

LONG-DISTANCE BUS SERVICES FROM THE UK

Anglia International (Part of Eurobus Group), tel 0870 608 8806;
www.anglia-lines. co.uk
London Victoria–Prague Florenc, 3 times weekly. Journey time: 21.5 hours
Capital Express, tel 220 870 368 (London: 020 7243 0488); www.capitalexpress.cz
London Victoria–Prague Florenc, up to 10 times weekly. Journey time: 17.5 hours
Kingscourt Express (Long-established Czech-based company), tel 0800 496 0001;
www.kce.cz
London Victoria–Prague Florenc, 6 times weekly in summer. Journey time: 19.5 hours
National Express (Associated with Eurolines Group), tel 0870 514 3219;
www.eurolines.co.uk
London Victoria–Prague Florenc, 5 times weekly. Journey time: 21.5 hours

brána (Powder Tower) and Obecní dům (Municipal House). There are good connections to all parts of the city by underground railway from Florenc metro station and by tram from nearby stops.

ČSAD

The Czech Republic's former national bus company has been divided into a number of operators, who between them run services to European destinations as various as Amsterdam and Warsaw. Timetable and fare information is most easily obtained from: www.jizdnirady.cz

The chart on the left shows the distances in kilometres between major European cities

	Amsterdam	Belgrade	Berlin	Bern	Bratislava	Brussels	Bucharest	Budapest	Copenhagen	Ljubljana	London	Luxembourg	Madrid	Moscow	Paris	Prague	Rome	Sarajevo	Warsaw	Vienna	Zagreb
Belgrade	1718																				
Berlin	655	1247																			
Bern	838	1363	922																		
Bratislava	1225	577	671	938																	
Brussels	206	1673	763	637	1181																
Bucharest	2181	619	1646	1893	977	2136															
Budapest	1398	388	864	1111	194	1353	788														
Copenhagen	920	1832	564	1378	1255	1048	2231	1449													
Ljubljana	1241	530	999	836	435	1153	1146	443	1656												
London	533	2039	1090	947	1546	370	2502	1719	1375	1537											
Luxembourg	386	1469	762	431	1010	213	1965	1183	1066	956	582										
Madrid	1800	2573	2343	1535	2458	1599	3189	2489	2642	2046	1750	1662									
Moscow	2449	2084	1830	2644	1885	2556	1758	1831	2385	2300	2888	2523	4138								
Paris	525	1800	1068	592	1340	324	2295	1513	1367	1287	475	407	1300	2861							
Prague	891	904	341	769	328	902	1304	522	927	664	1272	731	2300	1855	1031						
Rome	1658	1282	1493	932	1175	1457	1898	1198	2126	755	1772	1275	1945	3040	1417	1281					
Sarajevo	1727	303	1389	1372	707	1682	824	539	2143	539	2052	1478	2581	2370	1779	1046	1291				
Warsaw	1202	1056	584	1402	643	1309	1240	668	1138	1057	1641	1281	2891	1247	1596	612	1797	1207			
Vienna	1148	622	629	861	66	1103	1022	240	1214	378	1473	933	2380	1923	1233	285	1117	758	681		
Zagreb	1326	394	988	968	417	1281	1009	347	1741	135	1647	1074	2177	2178	1406	645	887	400	1039	359	

Arriving by Car

ON THE MOVE

Due to the distance involved and the excellence of the city's public transportation system, which makes using a car unnecessary, there is little point in driving from Britain to Prague (a journey of about 1250km/777 miles from London via Dover–Calais). However, if you intend to visit other destinations en route and explore more of the Czech Republic once you arrive, bringing your own car may well be justified.

Prague is the hub of the Czech Republic's main road and motorway system. Principal routes are identified by a one or two figure number, motorways by a D (*dalnice*—motorway) and a single number. Designated European through routes (E) are identified by a white one- or two-figure number on a green background. Two main routes link the capital with Germany and on to other countries in western Europe. The D8/E55 runs north from Prague to Dresden, and (as E55) continues to Berlin and to Rostock on the Baltic. The D5/E50 runs west past Plzeň to connect with the autobahn network of Bavaria and western Germany.

Frontier crossings have been or are being modernized and, with the entry of the Czech Republic into the European Union, border formalities are now simpler and delays for private cars are minimal. Be aware that a charge is levied for the use of motorways and other divided highways in the Czech Republic. Proof of payment is in the form of a *vignette* or sticker which can be bought at the frontier, at most filling stations and at post offices, and must be displayed on the car's windscreen. A sticker valid for 10 days costs 150Kč, for a month 250Kč.

For more details on driving in Prague and the Czech Republic, ▷ 52.

DRIVING ROUTES

Most people driving from Britain to the Czech Republic will use the short sea route from Dover to Calais or the rail shuttle through the Channel Tunnel. Other car ferry services run between Dover and Dunkerque (Dunkirk), Harwich and Hoek van Holland (Hook of Holland), between Hull and Zeebrugge or Rotterdam.

A longer crossing, between Harwich and Cuxhaven in Germany, shortens the road distance considerably, but involves an overnight trip aboard the ferry.

and Nürnberg (Nuremberg) to E50, crossing the Czech frontier at Waidhaus (Rozvadov), and continuing on E50/D5 to Prague. Only a short section east of Nuremberg is not of motorway standard.

A slightly longer, but easy to follow, alternative is to remain on E40 right across Germany, joining E55 near Dresden, crossing the border at Zinnwald (Cínovec). The existing 75km (46-mile) single-carriageway main road section between Dresden and Lovosice in the Czech Republic is due to be replaced by a motorway in 2008.

A motorway sign directs drivers towards Prague

From Calais, the most direct route—almost wholly on motorways—is via E40 through Belgium to Köln (Cologne) in Germany, then via E35, E41 and E45 past Frankfurt, Würzburg

From Cuxhaven, the most direct route is via E234, E45, E30, and E49, passing Bremen, Hanover, Magdeburg, and Leipzig, then via E55 as above (total distance 730km/454 miles).

CROSS-CHANNEL AND NORTH SEA FERRIES

COMPANY	ROUTE	TELEPHONE	WEBSITE
DFDS Seaways	Harwich–Cuxhaven	0870 533 3000	www.dfdsseaways.co.uk
Hoverspeed	Dover–Calais	0870 240 8070	www.hoverspeed.com
Norfolk Line	Dover–Dunkirk	0870 870 1020	www.travel.norfolkline.com
P&O	Dover–Calais, Hull–Zeebrugge/Rotterdam	0870 520 2020	www.poferries.com
SeaFrance	Dover–Calais	0870 571 1711	www.seafrance.com
Stena Line	Harwich–Hook of Holland/Rotterdam	0870 570 7070	www.stenaline.com

GETTING AROUND

Prague is proud of its integrated public transport system, based on trams, buses, the metro and even a funicular. The system gives reliable access to virtually any destination in the city, though journeys using more than one mode of transport may take some time, and conditions can get very crowded during peak times. Fares are inexpensive and ticketing is straightforward, with a number of special bargains for short-term visitors.

The system is run by Dopravní podnik hl.m.Prahy (DPP—Capital City of Prague Transport Authority), which ensures coordination between the various methods of transport. Many, if not most, journeys involve a change from one form to another, not least because metro stations are relatively far apart and function largely as hubs for onward travel by tram and bus. The map on page 47 shows these interrelationships, while for a complete overview of the network it is worth buying the DPP plan města 1:23 000, a beautifully produced and regularly revised large-scale city plan showing all transport routes in detail (39Kč). An alternative is the booklet and map *Guide to Prague by the Metro*, one of a series of public transport guides to world cities published in the USA by Michael Brein.

Services are generally frequent during the day, more so during the rush hours, and there is a useful skeleton service of trams and buses at night.

DPP

The DPP information office in the arrivals hall at Ruzyně Airport is open daily 7am–10pm, tel 220 115 404. As well as tickets, maps and other publications, DPP information offices provide advice on routes, fares, times and temporary alterations to services. Travel information can also be obtained by phone (tel 296 19 18 17, lines open daily 7am–9pm) or online at www.dpp.cz.

DPP has information offices, usually with English-speaking staff, at the airport and at the following Metro stations:
Anděl In the station hall (open Mon–Fri 7am–6pm, tel 222 646 055).

Prague's modern metro system is reliable and easy to use

Černý Most At the northern end of the station next to bus stops (open Mon–Fri 7am–6pm, tel 222 647 450).
Můstek In the underground concourse beneath Jungmannovo náměstí (open Mon–Fri 7am–6pm, tel 222 646 350).
Muzeum In the underground concourse (open daily 7am–9pm, tel 222 623 777).
Nádraží Holešovice By the exit to Plynární street (open Mon–Fri 7am–6pm, tel 220 806 790).

PLANNING AHEAD

It is worth considering how you are going to set about exploring Prague and the way in which the public transport system can help you. While the city's historic centre can be explored on foot—some of it only on foot—it covers an extensive area, parts of which are hilly. It can be quite exhausting to walk from Staré Město (Old Town), across Karlův most (Charles Bridge), then climb the alleyways and steps of Malá Strana up to the Castle and back again. Familiarize yourself with a map of the city and be prepared to spend a little time planning your trips around town, particularly those which involve a change from metro to tram and vice-versa. The route followed by trams Nos. 22 and 23 is particularly useful for visitors, taking a scenic trip from Nové Město (New Town) across the Vltava, through the heart of Malá Strana, then effortlessly up the steep slope to the gates of the Castle (▷ 106–111). It can be joined at various points, including the key metro stations of Národní třída and Malostranská.

Trams (left) form an essential part of the transportation system in Prague

Taking a bus tour of the city (below) is a good way to see the sights, ▷ 218

ON THE MOVE

TIPS
● Smoking is not permitted on any form of public transport, including metro stations. ● Children under 6 travel free. ● A possible alternative to a 3-day or similar public transport pass is the 'Prague Card', which, for 1,120Kč gives access (for a whole year) either free or at a reduced rate to numerous Prague attractions, as well as unlimited use of public transport for 3 days (or 7 days for an additional 60Kč, and 14 days for an additional 120Kč). It is available at a number of outlets, including the Euroagentur Praha desk at the airport and First Prague Information Centre, Václavské náměstí 37; www.praguecard.info ● The young and fit are expected to give up their seats to the elderly and infirm on the metro and on all forms of public transport. Locals do this without being asked.

TICKETS AND PASSES

Single tickets are available from information offices, hotel desks, some newsagents/ tobacconists and department stores, travel agents, windows at some metro stations, P.I.S. offices (▷ 271), and from ticket machines at all metro stations and some tram and bus stops. With the exception of 24-hour tickets, which can be obtained from the machines, travel passes and season tickets are only available from information offices and windows at metro stations.

● **Single tickets** These are of two types, costing 14Kč and 20Kč (half-price for children between 6 and 15). The 14Kč ticket is called a *nepřestupní jízdenka* or no-transfer ticket; it permits single journeys lasting up to 20 minutes by bus or tram without changing, or metro trips between no more than five stations (which may include a change from one line to another). The 20Kč ticket is a *přestupní jízdenka* or transfer ticket. It allows travel over the whole system with any number of changes, as

long as the journey is completed within 75 minutes. (1.5 hours in the evening). You may find that the no-transfer ticket will be the right one for shorter trips.

● **Travel passes** These save lots of fiddling with single tickets, but are worthwhile only if you intend to use public transport several times a day. They are available for 24-hours (adult 80Kč, child 40Kč for trips within the central area; adult 120Kč, child 60Kč for travel throughout the city), for 3 days/72 hours (220Kč), 7 days/168 hours (280Kč), and 15 days/360 hours (320Kč). Your name and date of birth must be written on the ticket.

● **Season tickets** These are worth considering if you are staying for some time in Prague. A monthly/30-day ticket costs 460Kč (adult), 115Kč (child); a quarterly ticket 1260Kč (adult), 315Kč (child) and a yearly ticket 4150Kč (adult), 1040Kč (child). When purchasing one you will need to present ID and a passport-sized photograph.

● **Luggage tickets** Substantial items of luggage require a 10Kč ticket.

● **Validating tickets** Tickets are only valid for travel once they have been inserted into a validating machine. These are located close to the doors on trams and buses and on the approach to the platforms at metro stations (usually at the top of the escalators). Insert the ticket face up into the machine in the direction of the printed arrow. You MUST validate the ticket in this way; inspectors in civilian clothes (but with a numbered ID) roam the network on the lookout for naive foreigners who are unaware of local ways or imagine that mere purchase of a ticket is sufficient. Ignorance of the rules is no excuse and if you are caught with a blank ticket, or without one altogether, you will be required to pay a fine (currently 400Kč); if you refuse the police will be called. Remember to get a receipt from the inspector if you are unfortunate or careless enough to have to pay a fine.

44 GETTING AROUND

The Metro

Prague's metro, the city's underground rapid transit network, consists of three colour-coded lines forming a triangle of interchange stations in central Prague and extending out into the suburbs. Trains and stations are modern, clean and well-maintained, and the system is reliable and easy to use.

ON THE MOVE

Prague's modern metro is a planned network, conceived as the backbone of the city's fully integrated public transport system. It celebrated its 30th birthday in April 2005. The first section, part of Line C (colour-coded red), was opened between Florenc (then called Sokolovská) and Kačerov in 1975. The system now has 53 stations and a total length of nearly 54km (33 miles). Its steady extension over three decades has made it possible to remove trams and buses from central streets, enabling extensive pedestrianization to take place. New public transport hubs around metro stations like Anděl, Hradčany and Dejvická have been created on the edge of the city centre, where commuters and

other travellers can connect with tram and bus lines fanning out into outlying districts. The network continues to expand; Line C was extended under the Vltava to Kobylisy and Ládví in 2004 and by 2008 will reach out to the future trade fair grounds at Letňany. A fourth line is planned, and it is forecast that the metro will eventually largely replace trams.

TRAINS

The early planning of the metro envisaged the use of light rolling stock on the model of the Milan metro. After the Soviet invasion of 1968 this was no longer ideologically acceptable; heavier trains were ordered on the pattern of the Moscow metro, and much redesigning and

strengthening of structures like the Nusle bridge had to be carried out. More recent rolling stock is made locally by Siemens/ČKD.

● Earlier trains are being progressively modernized, with more attractive interiors and more varied seating.
● Trains travel at high speed with rapid acceleration and braking.

STATIONS

● Metro stations are indicated by a stylized M sign. In central Prague the metro was constructed very deep below street level, partly to provide shelter in case of nuclear attack.
● In the suburbs, stations may be at ground level or even above ground.

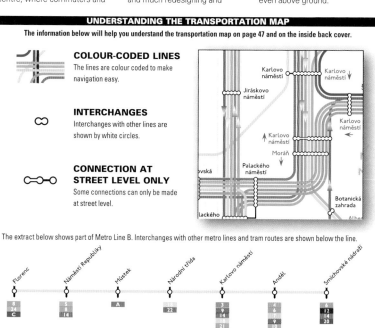

UNDERSTANDING THE TRANSPORTATION MAP

The information below will help you understand the transportation map on page 47 and on the inside back cover.

COLOUR-CODED LINES
The lines are colour coded to make navigation easy.

INTERCHANGES
Interchanges with other lines are shown by white circles.

CONNECTION AT STREET LEVEL ONLY
Some connections can only be made at street level.

The extract below shows part of Metro Line B. Interchanges with other metro lines and tram routes are shown below the line.

Muzeum

- Stations are generally approached via underground concourses, some of which may be very extensive, and by long stretches of escalator, on which most people remain standing rather than hurrying up or down.
- Platforms are normally laid out on either side of a broad central passageway to which they are connected by a series of arches.
- Electronic clocks at the end of the platform show the time as well as how many minutes have passed since the departure of the previous train.
- Stations are generally very clean and well ventilated.

FINDING YOUR WAY

- There are plans of the metro network—though not many of them—in stations.
- When you have decided which station you wish to travel to, note the colour of the line it is on and the name of the station at the end of that line.
- Remember to validate your ticket, then follow the coloured signs indicating your chosen line and look at the diagram in the central passageway to determine the correct platform.
- As the train is about to depart, a recorded announcement (in Czech) warns you to stand clear as the doors are closing. As the train gets under way, the next stop is announced (*Příští stanice, Hradčanská* for example).

SERVICES

- The metro runs between 5am and midnight. The interval between trains varies between 2.5 minutes or even less at peak times and up to 10 minutes at other times.

METRO LINES AND STATIONS

Line A (green)

Runs between Dejvická in the north and Skalka in the east.
- **Dejvická** station is named after the relatively affluent suburb of Dejvice and is at the city end of Evropská, the boulevard leading west towards the airport. It is an important interchange and is the terminus of the No. 119 and No. 254 airport buses.
- **Hradčanská** is the station for the Hradčany district, but is not convenient for the Castle area.
- **Malostranská** is the station for Malá Strana, though many parts of this historic quarter are some distance away. It is an important interchange with trams, including Nos. 22 and 23 serving the Castle and the upper part of the Hradčany district. It is possibly unique among the world's underground railway stations in having a garden.
- **Staroměstská** is not far from Karlův most (Charles Bridge), and is the station for Staré Město (Old Town), though again, many parts of the area are quite far away, some closer to Můstek or Náměstí Republiky station on Line B.
- **Můstek** is the interchange station with Line B at the lower end of Václavské náměstí (Wenceslas Square) and is convenient for many parts of Staré Město. it has an extensive underground concourse, with several exits, including one almost halfway up the square.
- **Muzeum** is the interchange station with Line C at the top of Václavské náměstí and named after the Národní Muzeum. It has a busy underground concourse with shops and a main DPP information office.
- **Náměstí Mírů** (Peace Square) serves part of the inner suburb of Vinohrady and several hotels.
- **Jiřího z Poděbrad** (George of Poděbrady Square) is the central station for Vinohrady.
- **Flora** is at the western end of Olšany cemeteries.

- **Želivského** is at the eastern end of Olšany cemeteries.

Line B (yellow)

Runs between Zličín in the far western suburbs to Černý most on the eastern edge of town.
- **Zličín** is the terminus for airport bus No. 100
- **Smíchovské nádraží** (Smíchov railway station) is the interchange with mainline trains and suburban buses (including the bus to Zbraslav).
- **Anděl** (Angel) is the station for Nový Smíchov mall and an important tram interchange.
- **Karlovo náměstí** (Charles Square) is centrally located in Nové Město (New Town) and is an important tram interchange.
- **Národní třída** is close to various attractions in both Staré Město and Nové Město and is an important tram interchange.
- **Můstek** (▷ Line A).
- **Náměstí Republiky** is at the eastern edge of Staré Město by the Prašná brána (Powder Tower) and the Obecni dům (Municipal House).
- **Florenc** is an interchange with Line C. It also serves Florenc long-distance bus station.

Line C (red)

Runs between the 2004 station of Ládví in the north to Háje in the southeastern suburbs.
- **Nádraží Holešovice** (Holešovice railway station) is an interchange with mainline trains and bus No. 112 to Troja.
- **Florenc** (▷ Line B).
- **Hlavní nádraží** (Main Station) is an interchange with mainline trains.
- **Muzeum** (▷ Line A).
- **I.P. Pavlova** is convenient for many Nové Město locations.
- **Vyšehrad** is the station for the Congress Center and Vyšehrad rock.

Don't be confused by older public transport maps which may show metro stations with their Communist-era names. Examples include Leninova (now Dejvická) and Moskevska (now Anděl).

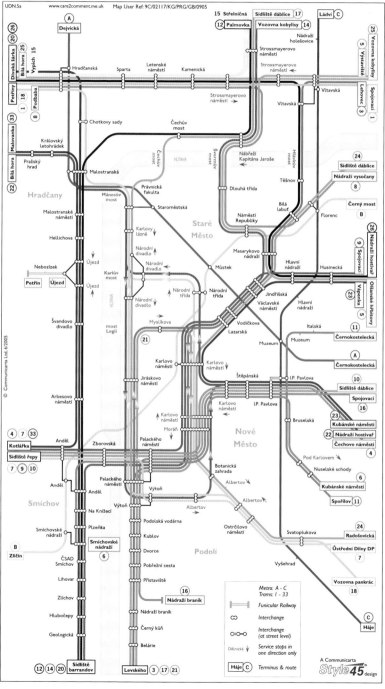

UDN.5a   www.care2comment.me.uk   Map User Ref: 9C/02117/KG/PRG/GB/0905

Hradčany

Staré Město

Nové Město

Smíchov

Podolí

Metro: A - C
Trams: I - 33

Funicular Railway

∞ Interchange

∞∞ Interchange (at street level)

Dělnická ─── Service stops in one direction only

Háje C Terminus & route

A Communicarta
Style 45 design

© Communicarta Ltd. 6/2005

Trams

Approximately 1,000 trams run through the streets of Prague, conveying more than a million passengers every day on 24 different routes. Supplanted by the metro as the backbone of the public transport system, they nevertheless remain an essential component of the network. For visitors, they offer a fascinating and unusual perspective on the city, as well as an efficient way of getting around.

Trams in Malá Strana (above). A typical tram stop (below)

While the metro offers the advantage of speed, there are few destinations of interest to visitors that cannot be reached by tram. If you are not pressed for time, you may find it more enjoyable to move around in a leisurely way by tram rather than use the metro.

TRAMS

While more modern trams are being steadily introduced, the bulk of the fleet consists of older vehicles, dating back to the 1960s and even the 1950s. They are still in good running order and many of them have modernized interiors with more comfortable padded seating in place of the traditional plastic bucket seats. They are designed, however, to carry more standing than sitting passengers. For most of the day the typical tram consists of two vehicles, a power car and trailer, though on some routes and outside busy times only a single vehicle may operate.

● Most trams are in a distinctive red-and-white livery, though some have been transformed into mobile advertising hoardings.

● The concertina-style doors—front, central and rear—are on the right side of the vehicle.

● Trams have powerful brakes

which can bring the vehicle to a halt almost instantly in an emergency, and you should consequently always be ready to use the grab handles.

● Stand at the back of the tram for the best views.

● Do not attempt to talk to the driver.

TIMES

● Normal tram services run between 4.30am and midnight, after which there is a skeleton night-time service which runs at half-hourly intervals.

● Daytime trams run at intervals ranging from 6 minutes at peak times to a maximum of 30 minutes at other times.

● Timetables for individual lines are obtainable from DPP information offices, while the timetables pasted up at every stop show the minutes past the

hour at which the service is due and the time taken to reach other stops on the line.

BOARDING AND ALIGHTING

● Trams halt at every stop.

● Most stops consist of a low platform separated from road traffic, sometimes with a rudimentary form of shelter.

● A number of old-fashioned stops still exist, where passengers wait on the pavement (sidewalk) and cross the road to board the tram when it arrives.

● Motorists are obliged to stop until boarding and alighting are completed.

● Entry to the tram is by the central or rear doors, with the front door used by passengers alighting (at least in principle).

● Once aboard the tram, remember to validate your ticket in one of the machines.

● Recorded announcements are made about stops.

● The tram's warning signal to other road users is a trilling bell, often sounded as it moves off.

ROUTES

● Numbered from 1 to 24, most of the daytime tram routes start and end at suburban terminuses, passing through central Prague on their way, while others remain in the outer districts.

● Lines through central Prague may be served by multiple routes, with trams arriving and departing at astonishingly frequent intervals.

● Trams display their route number and final destination. As well as noting the number of the route you wish to use, it's also a good idea to remember the final

destination in order to avoid heading off on the right tram but in the wrong direction.

NIGHT SERVICES
● Numbered from 51 to 59, these provide a basic service at 30-minute intervals at a time when the metro is closed down.
● All routes meet at the Lazarská stop near Národní třída in central Prague and, together with the buses connecting with

them at terminus and other stops, make it possible to reach most parts of the city, though not necessarily very speedily.

HISTORIC TRAMS
Trams have been part of the Prague street scene for more than a century. Many old-timers are on show in the Muzeum městské hromadné dopravy (▷ 92), and other splendidly preserved veterans from the

interwar period offer a seasonal 'nostalgia' service. Designated Line No. 91 operates at weekends and public holidays (April to November), between the museum at Střešovice and the Výstaviště Exhibition Grounds in Holešovice. The trip lasts about 40 minutes, and the tram leaves the terminus every hour on the hour between noon and 6pm. It's a fun way of seeing the city (adults 25Kč; children 10Kč).

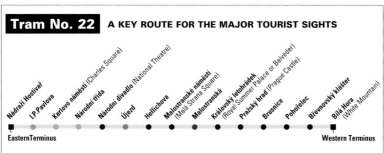

Tram No. 22 — A KEY ROUTE FOR THE MAJOR TOURIST SIGHTS

Nádraží Hostivař · I.P Pavlova · Karlovo náměstí (Charles Square) · Národní třída · Národní divadlo (National Theatre) · Újezd · Hellichova · Malostranské náměstí (Malá Strana Square) · Malostranská · Královský letohrádek (Royal Summer Palace or Belveder) · Pražský hrad (Prague Castle) · Brusnice · Pohořelec · Břevnovský klášter · Bílá Hora (White Mountain)

Eastern Terminus ─────────────────────── **Western Terminus**

Tram No. 22, Nádraží Hostivař-Bílá Hora (Hostivař railway station to White Mountain) runs from its terminus in the eastern suburbs, through Nové Město (New Town), across the most Legií (Bridge of the Legions), through the heart of Malá Strana, up to the Castle gates and on to the upper part of the Hradčany quarter and Strahovský klášter (Strahov Monastery) before continuing to its western terminus at Bílá Hora (White Mountain). For visitors it is probably the most useful and scenic of all routes, giving wonderful views of the Vltava and Malá Strana and sparing the climb up to the Castle. It can be joined conveniently at Malostranská metro station. Between Nové Město and Hradčany, tram No. 23 (between Kubánské náměstí and Malovanka) parallels the route of tram no. 22.

KEY
Interchange with metro:
● Line A
● Line B
● Line C
● Interchange with Petřín Hill funicular

MAIN STOPS:

Národní třída: interchange with metro Line B; close to lower end of Václavské náměstí (Wenceslas Square), Betlémské náměstí area of Staré Město (Old Town).

Národní divadlo (National Theatre): close to eastern end of Karlův most (Charles Bridge).

Újezd: interchange with Petřín Hill funicular; close to southern part of Malá Strana and Kampa Island.

Hellichova: southern part of Malá Strana and Kampa Island.

Malostranské náměstí (Malá Strana Square): middle of Malá Strana quarter; Svatého Mikuláš (Church of St. Nicholas); close to the western end of Karlův most (Charles Bridge).

Malostranská: interchange with metro Line A; close to foot of Staré zámecké schody (Old Castle Steps).

Královský letohrádek (Royal Summer Palace or Belvedér): entrance to Královská zahrada (Royal Garden).

Pražský hrad (Prague Castle): northern entrance to Castle.

Brusnice: close to Nový Svět.

Pohořelec: upper part of Hradčany quarter; Strahovský klášter (Strahov Monastery); Loreto; Petřín Hill.

Břevnovský klášter: Břevnov Monastery.

Bílá Hora (White Mountain): western terminus; alight at Vypích or Malý Břevnov for Letohrádek Hvězda (Star Castle).

Other Ways to Get Around the City

Although the metro and tram networks provide a comprehensive system for getting around Prague, there are many other ways that you can journey around the city ranging from buses and taxis to walking and bicycling, and even a funicular railway.

BUSES

A glance at the official public transport map of Prague will reveal the role city buses play in the integrated system. The map is dominated by the bright colours and thick lines of metro and tramway routes, while bus routes are shown in a thin, pale blue line. Few of these 196 routes penetrate central Prague, serving instead to fill in the gaps left by metro and tram in the suburbs and the countryside beyond. In these terms, the bus network is comprehensive; buses transport the same number of people every day as trams, and you will be hard put to find a Prague address more than a few hundred metres from a bus stop.

However, for most visitors to the city, buses are of limited use. Among the few places you are likely to want to visit that are accessible only by bus are the *zámek* at Zbraslav (▷ 150–151), and Troja (▷ 130–131), with its palace, zoo and botanical gardens. Zbraslav is reached by bus No. 243 and others from Smíchovské nádraží metro station and Troja by bus No. 112 from Nádraží Holešovice Metro.

Buses are red-and-white single-deckers with one-man crews, with doors at the front and the middle of the vehicle. Fares and ticketing are the same as for the metro and tram, though it is possible to buy a single ticket from the driver for 25Kč (with a 5Kč supplement). The frequency of service varies with the particular route, and ranges from peak-time intervals of 5 minutes to off-peak and weekend intervals of 30 minutes. Timetables are posted on the panels at stops in the same way as at tram stops.

Twelve night bus routes, Nos. 501–512, complement the night tramway service, and run at

intervals of 30 minutes to an hour. The main central stops are at Muzeum and I.P. Pavlova.

TRAINS

Prague's suburban railways do not form a coherent network like the metro. They are really only of interest to commuters and other local people and serve few, if any, places of visitor interest. Rail travel comes more into its own if you are visiting out-of-town destinations such as Karlštejn Castle (▷ 208–209). In the long term it is planned to develop the local rail network along the lines of the S-Bahn serving German cities, with new or modernized lines, for example, linking central Prague directly with the airport.

THE *LANOVKA*

The *lanovka* or funicular railway first creaked up Petřín Hill at the time of the Great Exhibition in

1891, easing the climb for the throngs visiting the newly built mini Eiffel Tower at the summit. It was originally powered by gravity; water was pumped into the car at the upper station, which then descended, drawing the other car up from the lower station. Today's funicular is electrically powered; it was reopened to passengers in 1985 after a 20-year break caused by landslides.

Just over 500m (1,640ft) long, the *lanovka* connects the lower station near Újezd tram stop to the summit station near the Štefánik Observatory, overcoming a difference in height of 130m (425ft). On the way the two cars pass each other, and stop at the intermediate station of Nebozízek, close to the panoramic restaurant of the same name. Just below the summit, the track passes through the medieval Hladová zed' (Hunger Wall), built in the 1360s. A ride aboard the funicular offers fabulous views over the whole of Prague and opens up all sorts of walking possibilities—to

The scenic funicular railway

Strahovský klášter (Strahov Monastery) and the upper part of Hradčany, or back down to town through orchards and parkland.

The funicular operates daily from 9am–11.30pm (11.20pm Nov–end Mar), at 10-minute intervals (15 minutes Nov–end Mar). You can use normal public transport tickets and passes (except the 14Kč single ticket).

50 GETTING AROUND

TAXIS

Over the years, Prague's taxi drivers have unfortunately built up a reputation for surliness and overcharging. Even the city's Lord Mayor was ripped off when, in 2004, he donned a disguise to check for himself whether they really were as awful as reported (▷ 21). Given the excellence of the public transportation and the city's walkability it is actually quite easy to avoid the use of taxis altogether. If you really do need to use one then follow these guidelines:

● Don't use the vehicles waiting at taxi ranks.

● Call a taxi from one of the firms listed below.

● Alternatively use a taxi firm recommended by a reputable hotel. This may be more reliable, and while expensive, is unlikely to be really outrageous.

● Agree to a fee before moving off, or check that the meter is switched on at the correct rate (this is Rate 1 in central Prague).

● Ask for and get a proper, printed receipt at the end of the journey.

Taxi prices

Registered taxis can be identified by a yellow roof lamp and by door panels giving tariffs and the firm's details.

Maximum official tariffs (liable to increase):
35Kč starting fee
25Kč per kilometre
5Kč per minute waiting time (including delays in traffic)

TAXI FIRMS	
COMPANY	TELEPHONE
AAA Taxi	140 14
Citytaxi	233 103 310
Credit taxi	235 300 000
Halotaxi	244 114 411
Prague Transport Service	732 328 510
Profitaxi	261 314 151
Radiotaxi	272 731 848
Sedop	271 726 666

WALKING

Prague is an eminently walkable place, and indeed many of its attractions can only be discovered on foot. Comprising the four originally separate towns of Hradčany, Malá Strana, Staré Město (Old Town) and Nové Město (New Town), the historic city is relatively compact, and can be crossed easily on foot in under an hour. The removal of traffic from many central streets and squares has increased safety for pedestrians and enhanced the pleasure of strolling. The Hradčany area is almost completely traffic-free. It is possible to walk the Royal Way from the Prašná brána (Powder Tower) at the eastern extremity of Staré Město via Karlův most (Charles Bridge) all the way to the Castle and only cross busy roads twice (though one of the crossing points is the perilous one at the eastern end of the bridge). This particular route, incidentally, is better followed in the reverse direction, in order to descend the hill from the Castle rather than climb it. Even during a short stay it's worth familiarizing yourself with public transport to ensure that exploration on foot remains enjoyable rather than exhausting.

A number of attractive walking routes are described on pages 192–201, but there are many other options, particularly those that make use of the promenades along both banks of the Vltava and of the paths threading through the various parks, especially those on Letná Plain, Kampa Island and Petřín Hill. The down side for pedestrians is the density of traffic on certain streets, particularly in Nové Město. The one-way streets feeding the Magistrála expressway are particularly noisy.

BICYCLING

Getting on a bike is certainly not the best way to explore Prague. There are simply too many people or vehicles competing for the space available; pedestrians will not thank you for intruding

WALKING TIPS

● Obey the rules at light-controlled crossings and avoid jay-walking.

● Watch out for trams, whose approach can often be fairly noiseless.

● Note that traffic drives on the right (though until the German occupation in 1939 it drove on the left).

Taking a break—touring Prague by bicycle can be hard work

into their domain and drivers may not even be aware of you. Tramlines and cobblestones can also cause difficulties. However, the city has designated a few numbered cycle routes, identified by pale brown signs. They make use of parks, quieter streets, the river embankments and cycleways along some major roads, but hardly add up to a comprehensive system. You can take your bicycle on the metro (10Kč ticket), but only outside peak hours, and it must travel in the last carriage. Cycling and Energy Futures (www.cyklopraha.cz) is a Prague-based organization promoting cycling.

Bicycle rental
City Bike
✉ Královdorská 5, Staré Město, Prague 1 ☎ 776 180 284
Ⓜ Náměstí Republiky

Praha-Bike
www.prahabike.cz
✉ Dlouhá 24, Staré Město, Prague 1 ☎ 732 388 880
🚋 Tram 5, 8, 14 to Dlouhá třída

ON THE MOVE

Driving

Most visitor attractions in Prague can be reached easily without the use of a car, but your own vehicle or a rental car comes into its own for excursions beyond the city limits.

Prague has a very high level of vehicle ownership, and traffic conditions are like those in any major western city, with hold-ups at traffic signals and congestion, while competition for road space with trams adds further stress. Through routes are reasonably well signposted, but finding your way around central Prague's labyrinth of narrow, one-way streets can be difficult, as can the search for a parking place.

RULES OF THE ROAD

Regulations are generally the same as in other European countries. Enforcement can be very strict, with no allowance made for minor mistakes or ignorance of the law.
● You must have a valid national driving licence (an International Driving Licence is not usually necessary).
● You must have the car's registration document and proof of insurance (Green Card if the car is your own).
● Drive on the right and overtake on the left.
● Seat belts must be worn.
● Headlights must be lit at all times between November and March.
● There is zero tolerance for drinking and driving. There must be no trace of alcohol in your bloodstream whatsoever. Never drink and drive.
● Children under 12 are not allowed in the front seat.
● Give way to people on foot at pedestrian crossings and when turning, even at a green light.
● Give way to trams, and at stops where there is no central refuge, halt and give way to passengers boarding and leaving the tram.
● A first-aid kit, warning triangle and spare light bulbs must be carried.

Road sign for a residential area

SPEED LIMITS
● 50kph (31mph) in built-up areas (start of the limit defined by the sign showing the name of the town or other settlement, end of the limit by a sign showing the name crossed out).
● 90kph (56mph) outside built-up areas.
● 130kph (80mph) on motorways (*vignette* necessary, ▷ 42).

PARKING
Parking is difficult in central Prague. Your hotel may have access to garages or parking spaces, usually at a high price. Many streets have no parking at all, or any spaces that exist are reserved for residents and season ticket holders. Other streets have parking meters allowing parking for a limited period at rates of up to 40Kč per hour. There are a number of multi-level or underground parking areas. Among those outside central Prague but close to metro stations are:
Nový Smíchov mall (2,000 spaces); Anděl metro station. Kongresové centrum (Congress Center; 1,100 spaces); Vyšehrad metro station.

Paying at a parking meter in central Prague

TIPS
● An essential aid if you are driving in Prague is the map Praha pro motoristy (available from the tourist information office, ▷ 271), which has information about through routes, one-way streets, parking and much more (the legend is in English, German and Czech).
● Car crime can be a problem in the Czech Republic. Always lock your vehicle, make sure that no possessions are visible inside and remove the radio if possible.

Parking facilities on the edge of Staré Město (Old Town) include: Kotva department store (300 spaces) on Náměstí Republiky close to the Obecni dům (Municipal House) and the Hotel InterContinental (200 spaces).

There are park-and-ride facilities at a number of suburban metro stations. If you are reduced to using these you should consider whether you need a car at all, though this may be a reasonable solution if, for example, you are passing through Prague en route to somewhere else and wish to spend a day in the city using public transport. The park-and-ride facilities at the following metro stations are well located in relation to major roads: Černý most: close to Motorway D11, main route No. 10 and eastern section of Pražský okruh (Outer Ring Road).
Ládví: close to Motorway D8.
Opatov: close to Exit 2 on Motorway D1.
Zličín: close to Exit 1 on western section of Pražský okruh.

VISITORS WITH A DISABILITY

Under Communism, few measures were taken to ease access to buildings and public transportation for people with disabilities. Today the situation is much improved but there is still a long way to go before Prague can be considered an easily accessible city.

GENERAL ADVICE

The city's newer buildings must be wheelchair accessible by law, but elsewhere ramps and aids are scarce, and the prevalence of cobblestones and massive kerbs is not helpful to navigation by wheelchair. But Prague has a very active local wheelchair association, the P.O.V, which promotes accessibility and the fullest possible integration of disabled people into the life of the city. It may be able to help with transfer from the airport and movement generally around the city if given sufficient notice. Its website lists (in Czech) accessible buildings (such as hotels, restaurants, museums, entertainment venues, post offices and banks) as well as parks and gardens. It also publishes the handbook *Přístupná Praha* (Accessible Prague) in Czech and English. Contact details: Pražská organizace vozíčkářů, Benediktská 688/6, Staré Město, Prague 1, tel 224 827 210, 224 826 078; www.pov.cz

USEFUL CONTACTS

AUSTRALIA
The Disability Information and Resource Centre Inc. 195 Gilles Street, Adelaide SA 5000; tel (08) 8223 7522; www.dircsa.org.au

CANADA
The Easter Seals Society 1185 Eglinton Avenue East, Suite 800, Toronto ON M3C6; tel 416/421-8377; www.easterseals.org

NEW ZEALAND
Disabled Persons Assembly (DPA) PO Box 27-524, Wellington 6035; tel 644 801 9100; www.dpa.org.nz

UK
RADAR 12 City Forum, 250 City Road, London EC1V 8AF; tel 020 7250 3222, 020 7250 0212; www.radar.org.uk
Tourism for All 7th Floor, Sunley House, 4 Bedford Park, Croydon, CR0 2AP; tel 0845 124 9971; www.holidaycare.org.uk

US
SATH 347 5th Avenue, Suite 610, New York City, NY 10016; tel 212/447-7274; www.sath.org

central Prague are operated by fully accessible buses (working days only).

● Route 1 runs between Chodov and Černý Most, stopping in central Prague at I.P. Pavlova, Náměstí Republiky and Florenc.

● Route 3 runs between Zličín and Sídliště Ďáblice, stopping in central Prague at Hradčanská, Malostranská, Náměstí Republiky and Nádraží Holešovice.

● These services are timed to connect with one another at Náměstí Republiky.

A sign at a bus stop shows that route 3 is wheelchair accessible

ARRIVING

By air
Ruzyně Airport (▷ 38) has been thoroughly modernized and is reasonably well equipped with facilities for people with disabilities. Most movement through the airport is on the same level and distances are relatively short.

● Let your airline know in good time if you need help on arrival. They should inform Ruzyně about any facilities you may require.

● Alternatively, contact ČSA (Czech Airlines), tel 020 7255 1898 (in UK); 00 420 220 113 393, 220 116 076 (in Czech Republic).

● The Ramada and Transit hotels located at the airport are both wheelchair friendly, and the Ramada has a fully equipped room for people with disabilities.

By train
● Praha hlavní nádraží (main station) and Praha Holešovice have self-operated elevators.

GETTING AROUND
Moving about the city by public transportation remains difficult, though the DPP (▷ 43) has made some progress.

By bus
Many bus routes use low-floor vehicles, and two routes between accessible housing and

By metro
Early metro stations were not built with wheelchair access in mind but more recent stations are fully accessible. Others have elevators which can only be operated by a member of staff. In total there are 22 stations with easy access, mostly in the suburbs. Only Line C has stations of this type in central Prague, including: Nádraží Holešovice, Florenc, Hlavní nádraží, Muzeum, I.P. Pavlova and Vyšehrad. All barrier-free stations are shown on an inset in the Plán Města Praha (Public Transport Map).

LEAVING PRAGUE

The Czech Republic is a small country, with a vast array of attractions, many of which can be easily visited on a day trip from Prague using a bus or train.

STATIONS

● Prague's main railway station (Praha hlavní nádraží) is on the edge of Nové Město (New Town), one metro stop from the top of Václavské náměstí (Wenceslas Square) and within walking distance of parts of central Prague. Though many trains start and terminate here, it

Waiting to greet passengers

is a through station and not a terminus as such. It consists of a mixture of century-old art nouveau buildings and a vast modern concourse and booking hall with many facilities. Both the station and the park outside are frequented by dubious-looking characters after dark, though the booking hall itself may be closed for a few hours at night. Hlavní is the most convenient starting point for most, but by no means all, rail trips out of town.

● Praha Masarykovo nádraží (Masaryk Station) was built in the 1840s as the city's first railway station. It is a true terminus, located within Nové Město, only a few hundred metres from the Obecní dům (Municipal House) and linked to Náměstí Republiky metro. It is the starting point for a number of local trains, eg to Nelahozeves (▷ 214–215).

● Praha Holešovice, with its own metro station (Nádraží Holešovice), is a modern

through station in Holešovice in the northern part of the city. A number of suburban and regional trains call here, as do certain international expresses, eg Berlin–Vienna.

● Praha Smíchov also has its own metro station (Smíchovské nádraží). This is also a modern station, in the southern suburb of Smíchov. Local trains call here on their way to destinations such as Karlštejn Castle (▷ 208–209) and Plzeň (▷ 205), as do all international expresses en route to destinations in southern and western Germany.

TRAINS

Most of the trains serving destinations within day-trip reach of Prague will be a *Rychlík* (express, designated by the letter R), a *Spěšný vlak* (fast train—Sp), or very likely, an *Osobní vlak* (passenger train—no identification). Long-distance national and international trains are variously identified as SuperCity (SC—first class only), EuroCity (EC), InterCity (IC) and Expres (Ex). If there is an alternative for a destination, avoid the *osobní*, which may be very slow. However, many local destinations are only served by such trains. Despite recent increases, fares remain below Western European levels.

INFORMATION

Timetable information is displayed on rollers at stations, while arrivals and departures are featured on overhead indicators and on white (arrivals) and yellow (departures) posters. A member of staff at the information offices in the stations listed on this page (but rarely elsewhere) should be able to answer enquiries in English. Rail enthusiasts might consider buying the current *Jízdní Řád*, the complete timetable of Czech Railways (in Czech, but decipherable with persistence).

The most straightforward access to train information in English is probably via the internet (www.cd.cz or www.jizdnirad.cz) or by phone (tel 221 111 122).

BUSES

The regional and national network of bus services in the Czech Republic is very well developed, and travel by bus can be faster as well as cheaper than rail. There are direct services from Prague to virtually every place of any size in the country, including many which are inaccessible by train. The once monolithic nationalized system has been broken down into numerous private firms, and information about routes and times can be difficult to obtain. Timetabling is not particularly convenient for visitors, and is based more on the needs of commuters, with few services at evenings or weekends.

● UAN (*Ústřední autobusové nádraží*—Central Bus Station), with its own metro station, Florenc, is Prague's main bus terminus. The different firms have their own ticket and information windows, usually manned by Czech-speakers. To find out about a particular service, you need to know the name of the destination, then find the route number and departure bay, and consult the timetables displayed in the middle of the hall. It's probably more straightforward to use the easy-to-follow internet service in English at www.jizdnirad.cz or take the easy option and enquire at a tourist information office.

● Fares are inexpensive; buy your ticket in advance if possible.

● Note that some services start from or call at suburban bus stations or stops, usually outside a metro station (eg Hradčanská and Zličín for Plzeň), and that using one of these instead of Florenc can reduce journey times.

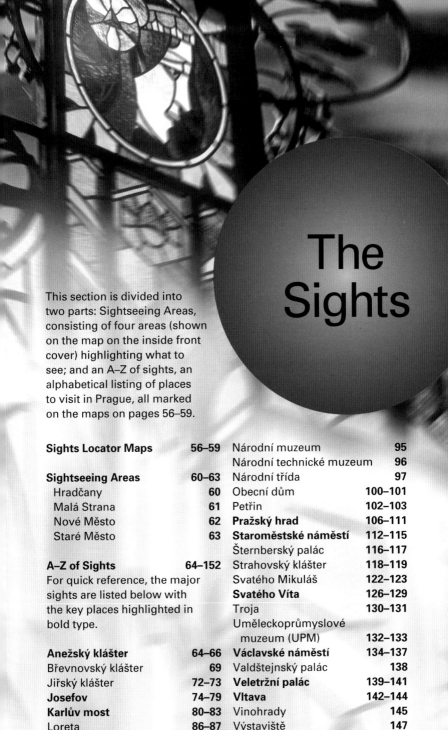

The Sights

This section is divided into two parts: Sightseeing Areas, consisting of four areas (shown on the map on the inside front cover) highlighting what to see; and an A–Z of sights, an alphabetical listing of places to visit in Prague, all marked on the maps on pages 56–59.

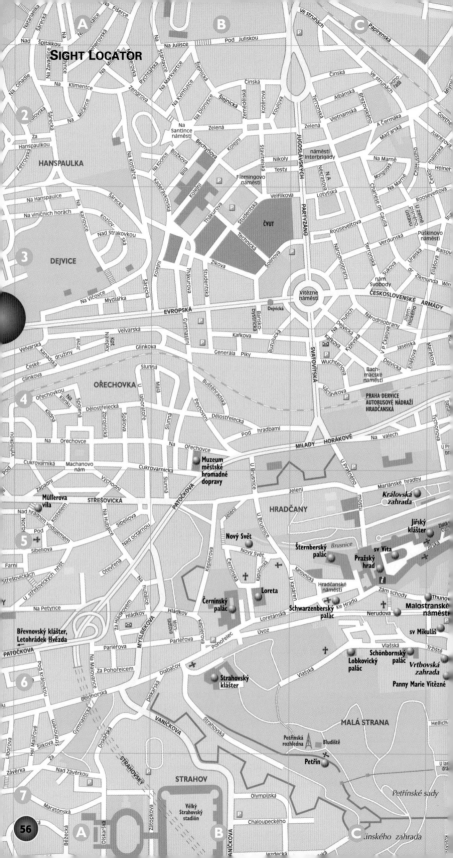

SIGHT LOCATOR

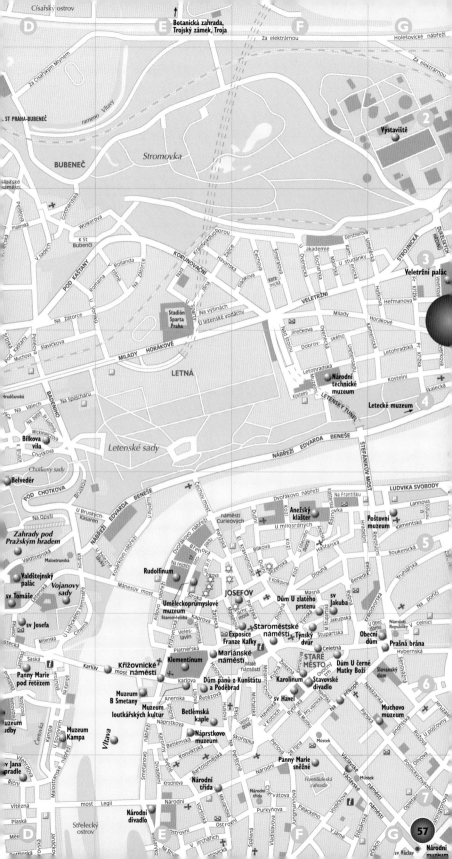

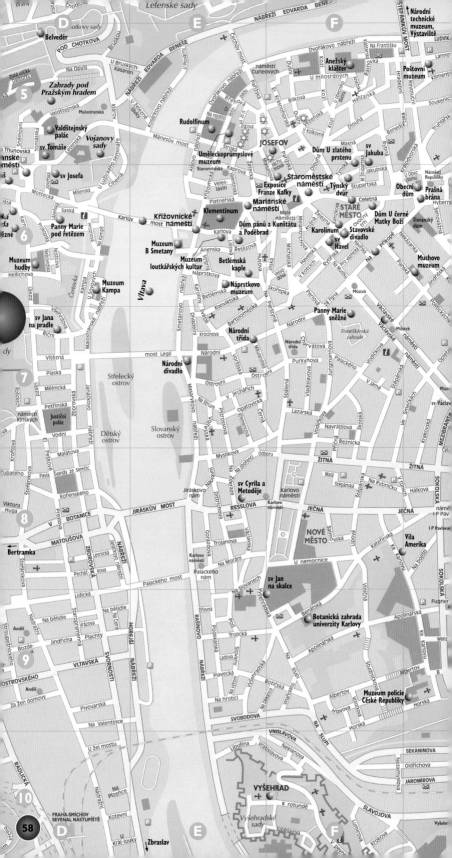

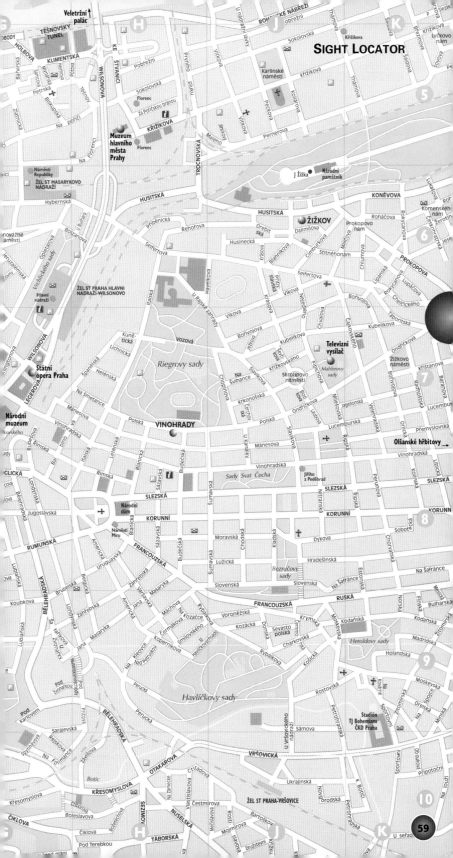

Hradčany

HOW TO GET THERE

🚆 Tram 22, 23 to Pražský hrad, Brusnice or Pohořelec

Prague's hilltop town not only includes Pražský hrad, the Castle, almost a little town in its own right, but also the built-up area running westwards along the rock spur which provided such a fine site for a citadel more than a thousand years ago.

Almost every visitor to Prague climbs (or more sensibly, takes the tram) up to the Castle quarter. Here, inside its gates and walls, are courtyards, churches, palaces, galleries and other attractions, as well as the great Gothic Cathedral of St. Vitus, the spiritual heart of the Czech nation. The Castle itself is the seat of the country's president; the blue-uniformed guardsmen protecting him put on a fine show at the hourly Changing of the Guard ceremony.

A uniformed guard standing outside his sentry box at Prague Castle

THE MAIN SIGHTS

Beyond the Castle's main gateway stretches one of the city's largest squares, Hradčanské náměstí, lined with the palaces and residences of noblemen and clergy. No through traffic disturbs the tranquillity of Hradčany, enhancing its character as a kind of time capsule in which little seems to have changed since the 18th century.

Further westward up the gentle slope are the district's other great attractions, the Loreto shrine and Strahovský klášter (Strahov Monastery), while hidden away is the secret little world of Nový Svět, its humble homes once the abode of Castle servants.

Bazilika svatého Jiří
St. George's Basilica, the country's finest Romanesque church (▷ 110).

Belvedér
The Royal Summer Palace, set in lovely gardens (▷ 67).

Jiřský klášter
St. George's Convent, full of Renaissance and baroque art (▷ 72–73).

Loreta
The baroque Loreto Shrine (▷ 86–87).

Starý královský palác
The Old Royal Palace, the heart of the Castle (▷ 109–110).

Šternberský palác
The Sternberg Palace, home to the National Gallery's collection of Old Masters (▷ 116–117).

Strahovský klášter
Strahov Monastery, famous for its baroque libraries (▷ 118–119).

Svatého Víta
The Cathedral of St. Vítus, with the jewel-like Wenceslas Chapel (▷ 126–129).

Zlatá ulička
Golden Lane, lined with little 'alchemists' cottages' (▷ 111).

OTHER PLACES TO VISIT
The Castle precincts shelter more museums and galleries, including the history museum in the Lobkovický palác (Lobkowicz Palace, ▷ 110–111),

the Obrazárna (Castle Picture Gallery, ▷ 106) and the Muzeum hraček (Toy Museum, ▷ 110–111). The huge Jízdárna (Riding School, ▷ 106) is often the setting for temporary exhibitions. Palaces to note include the

A floodlit view of Prague Castle and the Cathedral of St. Vítus

huge Schwarzenberský palác (Schwarzenberg Palace, ▷ 120–121), the future home of many of the treasures of the Národní Galerie (National Gallery), the sumptuous Arcibiskupský palác (Archbishop's Palace) opposite, and the huge Černínský palác (Černín Palace, ▷ 70). Outside the immediate confines of the Castle are lovely landscapes like the Královská zahrada (Royal Garden, ▷ 84).

WHERE TO EAT
Lobkowicz Palace Café
See page 237.

Lvi dvůr
See page 237.

THE SIGHTS

Malá Strana

HOW TO GET THERE

🚇 Malostranská

🚊 Tram 12, 20, 22, 23 to
Malostranské náměstí

Crouching at the foot of the
Castle, Malá Strana (Lesser
Town) is the most perfectly
preserved of Prague's
historic districts, a little
paradise of palaces and
gardens now colonized
by chic restaurants and
smart hotels.

With little space to expand
between the riverbank and the
slopes of Petřín Hill, Malá Strana
has kept something of the village-like character it must have
had a thousand years ago, when
merchants and other folk settled
near here, protected by the
Castle and close to the ford
across the as yet bridgeless
Vltava. Its present appearance
owes much to the 17th and 18th
centuries, when aristocratic

*Looking through an archway
into a square in Malá Strana*

families rebuilt their palaces and
laid out exquisite gardens in the
fashionable baroque style. The
city's finest baroque building,
Svatého Mikuláš (St. Nicholas'
Church), presides over
Malostranské náměstí (Malá
Strana Square), a stopping point
on the Royal Way between Karlův
most (Charles Bridge) and the
Castle. Malá Strana's lovely open
spaces include riverside Kampa
Park and the Petřín orchards.

THE MAIN SIGHTS

Prague's lovely pictorial house-
signs are much in evidence in
Malá Strana, and a stroll along
any of its charming streets and
lanes will reveal plenty of them,

above all in
Nerudova street
(▷ 98) leading up to the Castle.
You can get a stunning overview
of the area from the bell-tower of
St. Nicholas (▷ 122), though
some of the best views of Malá
Strana are from Hradčany high
above. Take the trouble to
explore hidden treasures like the
Vrtbovská zahrada (Vrtba
Garden, ▷ 146), and work out
your own way of getting up
and down from the Castle
instead of just following the
crowds along Nerudova.

Muzeum Kampa
The grand buildings of a former
mill are now a fascinating gallery
of modern art (▷ 92).

Panny Marie Vítězné
Pilgrims flock from all over the
Catholic world to admire The
Church of Our Lady of Victory's
wax figure known as the
Bambino di Praga (▷ 104).

Svatého Mikuláš
The baroque Church of St
Nicholas is a masterpiece of the
Dientzenhofer architectural
dynasty (▷ 122–123).

Valdštejnský palác
Now the home of the Senate, the
huge Wallenstein Palace has a
superb walled garden (▷ 138).

OTHER PLACES TO VISIT

Explore Petřín (▷ 102–103),
perhaps by using the *lanovka*
(funicular railway), which will lift
you effortlessly to the top,
where you will be within striking

distance of
the city's mini
Eiffel Tower, the Petřínská
rozhledna. Walk along the riverbank, from Kampa Island in the
south, beneath the arches of
Karlův most (Charles Bridge), to
the little park by Manesův most

*The Malá Strana and Judith
Bridge Towers, Charles Bridge*

(Mánes Bridge) in the north. Fans
will want to search out the John
Lennon Wall (▷ 194) near one
of the bridges over the Čertovká
(Devil's Brook), which separates
Kampa Island from the 'main-
land'. Cross the most Legií
(Bridge of the Legions) to
Střelecký ostrov (Shooters'
Island), for unusual views across
the river to Staré Město (Old
Town) and the Národní divadlo
(National Theatre, ▷ 94).

WHERE TO EAT

For wonderful views, climb up to
the U zlaté studně (Golden Well,
▷ 244), or for a riverside setting,
try the terrace of the Hergetova
cihelna (▷ 235).

THE SIGHTS

Nové Město

HOW TO GET THERE

Muzeum hlavního města Prahy
🚇 Florenc
🚋 Tram 8, 24 to Florenc
Národní divadlo
🚋 Tram 6, 9, 17, 18, 21, 22, 23 to Národní divadlo
Národní muzeum
🚇 Muzeum

Nové Město (New Town) is by far the largest of Prague's historic districts. 'New', because it was begun in the mid-14th century by Emperor Charles IV as a planned extension to the Old Town, it stretches in all directions from the ring of boulevards (Na příkopě, Národní třída) which follow the line of the long-demolished fortifications.

THE SIGHTS

Emperor Charles' plan for the New Town was so far-sighted that it was able to accommodate the growth of Prague right up to

Ornate ceiling decoration in the 19th-century National Theatre

the 19th century. Focused on three spacious squares—including Václavské náměstí (Wenceslas Square)—it now consists of mostly modern buildings, though among them plenty of treasures can still be seen.

The New Town is the commercial heart of the city, with offices, shops and department stores, and places of entertainment, the only part of the historic centre where locals easily outnumber tourists. Its visitor attractions tend to be widely scattered, and to see them all without wearing yourself out you will need to make use of public transport, or organize your sightseeing around certain areas.

THE MAIN SIGHTS

Wenceslas Square is an obvious focal point, as is Karlovo náměstí (Charles Square). The Národní divadlo (National Theatre) is a prominent landmark on the riverbank, and close by is Slovanský ostrov (Slavonic Island), one of the Vltava's many fascinating islands. Sometimes overlooked is the northeastern tip of the New Town, around Na Poříčí street.

Muchovo muzeum
The museum celebrates the work of the great art nouveau artist Alfons Mucha (▷ 89).

Muzeum hlavního města Prahy
Strictly speaking, the Prague City Museum is outside the New Town, but only just (▷ 90).

Národní divadlo
The sumptuous National Theatre is one of the great edifices of the 19th-century Czech National Revival (▷ 94).

Národní muzeum
The National Museum dominates Václavské náměstí (▷ 95).

OTHER PLACES TO VISIT

Historic monuments include the Novoměstská radnice (Town Hall of the New Town) and the city's second largest Gothic church Panny Marie sněžné (Church of Our Lady of the Snows, ▷ 104–105). Among the area's other churches is Svatého Cyrila a Metoděje (Church of St. Cyril and St. Methodius, ▷ 121),

where the assassins of Nazi Reichsprotektor Heydrich were cornered (▷ 33). Fascinating buildings in a variety of 20th-century styles line thoroughfares like Na příkopě (▷ 93) and Národní třída (▷ 97). The

Art nouveau Grand Hotel Evropa on Wenceslas Square

largest open space is the park occupying the middle of Karlovo náměstí (Charles Square), but for an unexpected refuge, you should make your way through the arcades off Václavské náměstí (Wenceslas Square) to the Františkánská zahrada (Franciscans' Garden, ▷ 136).

WHERE TO EAT

For a unique view while dining, try Zvonice, a restaurant high up in a bell-tower (▷ 244).

Globe
See page 234.

U Pinkasů
See page 243.

Staré Město

HOW TO GET THERE

Staroměstské náměstí
- 🚇 Staroměstská
- 🚊 Tram 17, 18 to Staroměstská

Karlův most
- 🚇 Staroměstská
- 🚊 Tram 17, 18 to Staroměstská or Karlovy lázně

Obecní dům
- 🚇 Náměstí Republiky
- 🚊 Tram 5, 8, 14 to Náměstí Republiky

Stavovské divadlo
- 🚇 Můstek

Staroměstské náměstí (Old Town Square), with its town hall and astronomical clock, is the heart of Staré Město (Old Town), and has the city's greatest concentration of historical monuments and other attractions. Lining its labyrinth of lanes and alleyways are plenty of intriguing shops, bars, restaurants and pubs.

The Týn Church and Jan Hus Memorial on Old Town Square

While Malá Strana was the aristocratic district, full of fine palaces, Staré Město was the merchants' quarter, its typical buildings not palaces (though there are several of these) but burghers' houses. Many of these still stand, some with 12th-century cellars testifying to their great antiquity and making fine settings for today's restaurants and bars. The rambling main artery of the district is the so-called Royal Way, the coronation route which leads from the Prašná brána (Powder Tower), via Celetná street, Staroměstské náměstí (Old Town Square) and Karlova street to Charles Bridge, and from there through Malá Strana to the Castle.

THE MAIN SIGHTS

Most people visit Staroměstské náměstí at some point during their stay. It's worth climbing the tower of the Staroměstská radnice (Town Hall) to orientate yourself. The Staroměstská mostecká věž (Old Town Bridge Tower) and the Prašná brána (Powder Tower) also offer great views. Don't confine your visit to the Royal Way—try to explore the courtyards and byways of this intriguing area.

Anežský klášter
St. Agnes' Convent has a superlative national collection of medieval art (▷ 64–66).

Obecní dům
The Municipal House is a glittering art nouveau complex (▷ 100–101).

Staroměstská radnice
Prague's biggest single draw is the hourly spectacle presented by the Orloj (Astronomical Clock) on the Old Town Hall (▷ 112).

Staronová synagóga
The Old-New Synagogue is the focal point of Josefov (▷ 75–76).

Stavovské divadlo
The 18th-century Estates Theatre was the scene of the première of Mozart's *Don Giovanni* (▷ 120).

Uměleckoprůmyslové muzeum
Beautifully presented works of art are on display at the Decorative Arts Museum (▷ 132–133).

OTHER PLACES TO VISIT

Galleries and museums include the Cubist Dům U černé Matky Boží (Black Madonna House, ▷ 70), and the **Muzeum loutkářských Kultur** (Puppet

The decorative calendar of the Astronomical clock

Museum, ▷ 92). Among the important churches are **Svatého Jakuba** (St. James, ▷ 124), the **Týn Church** (▷ 114), **Kostel svatého Mikuláš** (St. Nicholas in Old Town Square, ▷ 115) and the **Betlémská kaple** (Bethlehem Chapel, ▷ 67). Don't miss the **Týnský dvůr** (Týn Court or Ungelt), or a stroll through the courtyards of the **Klementinum**.

WHERE TO EAT

For sheer sumptuousness, dine in the Municipal House (▷ 100–101). Or for a view of the Orloj (Astronomical Clock), book a window seat in the first floor Grand Café (▷ 234–235).

THE SIGHTS

Anežský klášter

The national collection of medieval art, a superlative array of paintings and sculpture, is housed in the Convent of St. Agnes, lovingly rebuilt after a century of neglect.

Sunlight filters in through the windows lining the cloisters

A portrait of Emperor Charlemagne by Master Theodoric

Admiring the medieval works of art on display in the convent

SEEING ANEŽSKÝ KLÁŠTER

Close to the riverbank on the northern edge of Staré Město (Old Town) and Josefov, the 13th-century Convent of St. Agnes was rescued from near total decay and dereliction in the last decades of the 20th century. It makes a wonderfully appropriate home for the National Gallery's collection of medieval and early Renaissance art, one of the finest and most extensive to be found anywhere. Paintings, sculpture and other items are drawn not just from Bohemia, but from neighbouring regions of central Europe, enabling comparisons to be made and influences traced. The convent itself is a fascinating, rather rambling complex. It's the earliest example of Gothic architecture to be built in the Old Town, with halls and chambers of different size and character in which the works of art are displayed to great advantage. There are medieval cloisters and not one, but two churches; Kostel svatého Salvátor (Church of the Holy Saviour) and Kostel svatého Františka (Church of St. Francis), which was adapted during reconstruction for use as a concert hall. It is quite difficult to get an overall sense of the convent's layout by just wandering around, but there is a fine view of the complex as a whole from the heights of the Letná Plain on the far side of the Vltava (▷ walk, 192–193). From here you will be able to appreciate the convent's low-lying location by the river, which made it so vulnerable to the terrible flood of 2002. One of the worst affected victims of that natural disaster, the Convent of St. Agnes is still recovering, and for some time the arrangement and display of the collection is likely to be subject to change.

A carving of St. Agnes (left), who founded Anežský klášter in the 13th century

HIGHLIGHTS

MASTER THEODORIC

Master Theodoric (died c1381) was Emperor Charles IV's painter of choice. Working in the 1350s and 1360s, his robust, radiantly colourful, and sometimes earthy portraits of saints and dignitaries continue to exercise a strong appeal today, not least because they represent one of the earliest attempts to show individuals as they really are. Theodoric's main commission consisted of the dozens of portraits lining the walls of the Chapel of the Holy Cross at Karlštejn Castle (▷ 208–209). Here, a selection of his frame-filling portraits begins, appropriately enough, with St. Luke, the patron saint of painters, and continues with figures such as Emperor Charlemagne and St. Catherine, identified by the wheel she was put to death on.

ALTARPIECES

Among the gallery's greatest treasures are altarpieces and other works painted by 14th-century Bohemian masters, identified only by their place of origin. The Master of the Vyšší Brod Altarpiece is

TIPS

● It's worth walking around the convent to get an idea of what an impressive survival of medieval Prague it is. Even better, get a bird's-eye view of the whole complex from Letná Plain (▷ 192–193).
● Don't miss the lovely statue called the *Madonna of Český Krumlov*—it is an example of the 'Beautiful Style' that flourished around 1400.

The Resurrection *altarpiece (above) was painted by the Master of the Třeboň Altarpiece*

represented by an icon-like Madonna and by an altarpiece of nine panels painted in much the same glowing but rather static style. These works date from around 1350. Some 30 years later, the altarpiece painted by the Master of the Třeboň Altarpiece is of a different order altogether, its visionary intensity combined with dynamic detail. Christ is shown praying on the Mount of Olives with bloody drops of sweat on his forehead, while Judas and the soldiers lurk behind a wicker fence. Then, as the slim figure of the Saviour rises from the dead, his neglectful guardians recoil in disarray.

LATER WORKS

At the beginning of the 16th century, more than 100 years after the Třeboň Altarpiece was painted, the Master of the Litoměřice Altarpiece produced a superb triptych showing the Holy Trinity, a work whose greater realism marks the transition from the Middle Ages to the Renaissance. Somewhat earlier, from around 1482, and much more stiff in its representation of the human figure, is a picture showing St. Agnes herself engaged in nursing a bed-ridden patient. German artists are well represented, with a charming *Young Lady with Hat* by Lucas Cranach the Elder (c1472–1553), and a

Martyrdom of St. Florian by Albrecht Altdorfer (c1480–1538), showing the unfortunate saint at the mercy of a particularly repulsive band of thuggish tormentors.

Burial of St. Catherine *altarpiece (above), dating from around 1515*

BACKGROUND

St. Agnes was a princess of the Přemyslid line who escaped the possibility of an arranged marriage by becoming a nun. Inspired by the example of St. Francis, she founded a convent and hospital here on the banks of the Vltava, and in 1234 became its abbess. She seems to have obeyed the Franciscan vow of poverty to the letter, supposedly subsisting on a diet of raw onions and fruit. In her lifetime she became an object of popular veneration, which intensified after her death in 1282, and it seemed she was set to be declared a saint. In the event, this process took hundreds of years; Agnes was canonized only in November 1989, an event that took place just two days before the Velvet Revolution got under way. In the same year, she was declared the patron saint of all those working in the gas manufacture and supply industry.

The Madonna of Český Krumlov *carving (below) is an example of the 'Beautiful style'*

The institution founded by Agnes flourished, not least because of its easy access to the royal coffers, and coronations and kingly burials took place within its walls. But in 1420 the nuns were evicted by the Hussites (followers of Jan Hus, ▷ 27), who melted down its precious silver plate and used the buildings as an armoury. In the mid-16th century the convent passed into the hands of the Dominicans, who seem to have devoted themselves to business interests as much as to the contemplative life; they took in lodgers, brewed beer and set up a timber yard and glassworks. The convent and the surrounding area acquired a dubious reputation, which it kept until modern times, long after the convent had been closed by Emperor Joseph II in 1782. At the end of the 19th century, it might well have been redeveloped like nearby Josefov, but popular pressure saved it. Eventually the Communist regime restored it, using it initially as a home for the national collection of 19th-century art, since transferred to the Veletržní palác (Trade Fair Palace, ▷ 139–141).

The elegant Belvedér was built in the mid-16th century

BELVEDÉR

🞧 57 D5 • Letohradek královny Anny, Mariánské hradby, Hradčany, Prague 1
☎ 224 372 327/224 373 368
🕐 Tue–Sun 10–6 during showing of temporary exhibitions 🚻 Variable
🚃 Tram 22, 23 to Královský letohrádek
www.hrad.cz

Also known as the Královský letohrádek (Royal Summer Palace), the Belvedere closes off the eastern end of the Royal Garden (▷ 84) with an elegant flourish. It was one of the very first Renaissance buildings north of the Alps, built in the mid-16th century by Italian architects for Ferdinand I, who intended it as a place of retreat for his beloved spouse, Anna. Ringed by an exquisitely delicate arcade, it has a copper-clad roof in the form of an upturned boat. It is now used for temporary art exhibitions.

BETLÉMSKÁ KAPLE

🞧 57 E6 • Betlémské náměstí 4/256, Staré Město, Prague 1 ☎ 224 248 595 🕐 Apr–end Oct Tue–Sun 10–6.30; Nov–end Mar Tue–Sun 10–5.30 🚻 Adult 40Kč, child (6–16) 20Kč 🚃 Národní třída 🚃 Tram 6, 9, 18, 22, 23 to Národní třída
www.studenthostel.cz

The Bethlehem Chapel is where Jan Hus preached the Word of God to illiterate Czech townsfolk in their own language. Though Hus was burned at the stake as a heretic in 1415 (▷ 27), his chapel remained a stronghold of radical belief until it was handed over to the Jesuits in the Counter-Reformation. In the 19th century it virtually disappeared as bits of it were incorporated into the surrounding buildings. It was rebuilt in 1952 by the Communist regime. Big enough to hold a congregation of 3,000, the austere interior is very plain. The Chapel is now the ceremonial hall of the Technical University.

A tree shades the cobbled square in front of the Bertramka

BERTRAMKA

A must for Mozart lovers, this leafy villa is where the composer put the finishing touches to his opera *Don Giovanni*.

🞧 Off map 58 D8 • Mozartova 169, Smíchov, Prague 5 ☎ 257 316 753 🕐 Apr–end Oct daily 9–6; Nov–end Mar daily 9.30–4 🚻 Adult 110Kč, child (6–16) 50Kč 🚇 Anděl 🚃 Tram 4, 7,9 10 to Bertramka 🚻
www.bertramka.cz

RATINGS			
Cultural interest	●	●	● ●
Historic interest	●	●	● ●
Photo stops		●	● ●

TIP
● Make sure your visit to the Betramka coincides with one of the chamber concerts regularly staged here (in the open air in summer).

In the 18th century, the countryside just beyond Prague's walls was dotted with charming rural retreats, converted farmsteads and vintner's dwellings where the wealthy could escape the smells and summer heat of the city. Few are left today, but one of them, a green oasis in the industrial suburb of Smíchov, still exists as a shrine to the memory of Mozart.

THE VILLA
Named after one of its earlier owners, Franz von Bertram, the Bertramka was bought in 1784 for the glamorous singer Josefa Dušková and her much older husband, František Dušek, by one of her admirers, Count Clam. It was laid out on the lower slopes of Černý vrch (Black Hill), and consists of a delightful galleried dwelling facing other domestic buildings across a courtyard, together with an extensive garden shaded by trees. Prague's Mozart Museum could hardly have found a better home, nor could summer concerts be staged in a more appropriate setting. The Dušeks were old friends of Mozart, and played host to him at the Bertramka on more than one occasion. There were rumours of a romantic liaison between the composer and Josefa, who is also supposed to have forced him to finish the score of *Don Giovanni*, only hours before its first performance, by locking him in a room.

Mozart found the welcome in Prague he sadly lacked in Vienna; he revelled in the 'Figaromania' that swept the city following performances of his *Figaro* in 1787, joyfully declaring 'My Praguers understand me.' When Mozart died in 1791, the Viennese let his corpse be buried in a pauper's grave, but in Prague a capacity crowd more than filled Svatého Mikuláš (Church of St. Nicholas, ▷ 122–123) for his lavish funeral Mass. Tasteful restoration has overcome past neglect and fire damage, and the villa radiates the rococo atmosphere of Mozart's times, with memorabilia including the harpsichord on which he is supposed to have played. A 19th-century bust of the composer watches over the peaceful garden.

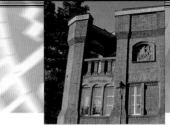

František Bílek designed the striking Bílkova Vila

Detail of a gargoyle on the exterior of the Carolinum

A group of statues above the portal of a house on Celetná

THE SIGHTS

BÍLKOVA VILA

✛ 57 D4 • Mickiewiczova 1, Hradčany, Prague 6 ☎ 224 322 021 ◉ Mid-May to mid-Oct Tue–Sun 10–6; mid-Oct to mid-May Sat–Sun 10–5pm 🏛 Adult 50Kč, child (6–16) 20Kč 🚊 Tram 18, 20 to Chotkovy sady 📷 Guided tour by prior arrangement (minimum 2 weeks notice) www.citygalleryprague.cz

Overlooking the last bend in the road on the way up to Prague Castle, the extraordinary villa designed by the Symbolist sculptor František Bílek (1872–1941) nevertheless escapes most visitors' attention. Bílek, an unfamiliar name to most foreigners, was famous in his day and much admired by Franz Kafka (1883–1924), among others, who spoke of his 'bare beseeching art full of visions, mystical longings and pangs of guilt.' The building he designed to live and work in is equally expressive, its Egyptian-style columns of the portico symbolizing stalks of corn, and its red-brick walls representing the good Earth. The sculpture in front shows the Czech educational reformer Comenius (1592–1670) bidding farewell to his native land, and there is more sculpture inside the house. Much of the furniture and fittings were designed by Bílek and reflect his intensely spiritual view of life.

BOTANICKÁ ZAHRADA

✛ Off map 57 E1 • Nádvorní 134, Troja, Praha 7 ☎ 234 148 111, 603 582 191 ◉ May–end Sep daily 9–7; Apr daily 9–6; Oct daily 9–5; Nov–end Mar daily 9–4 🏛 Gardens: adult 40Kč, child (6–16) 20Kč. Fata Morgana: adult 90Kč, child 45Kč. Combined ticket: adult 120Kč, child 60Kč. Free to external areas in winter 🚊 Bus 112 from metro Nádraží Holešovice to Zoologická zahrada www.botgarden.cz (in Czech)

These modern botanical gardens extend over the slopes just beyond Troja Palace, bringing a touch of exotic landscape to this already countrified part of the city. They are still being developed but there is plenty of interest, including a Japanese garden, Mediterranean plants and the 'Fata Morgana', a tropical paradise. Dating originally from the time of Emperor Charles IV (1346–78) or even earlier, the nearby vineyard around the delightful little Chapel of St. Clare features a vinotheque, with a selection of Moravian wines.

BOTANICKÁ ZAHRADA UNIVERZITY KARLOVY

✛ 58 F9 • Na Slupi 16, Nové Město, Prague 2 ◉ Daily 10–5 🏛 Free to gardens; glasshouses 20Kč 🚊 Karlovo náměstí 🚊 Tram 18, 24 to Botanická zahrada

The principal role of the Botanical Gardens of Charles University is academic, and you are likely to see students here making notes and sketching plants. But the 3.5ha (8-acre) gardens on their terraced site also function as a welcoming green oasis in this densely built-up part of the New Town. There's a wonderful array of plants of all kinds in a relatively small space, from tropical blooms in the steamy, refurbished hothouse to fine specimen trees, among them the oldest *metasequoia* in the country.

CAROLINUM

✛ 57 F6 • Ovocný trh 3–5, Staré Město, Prague 1 ◉ Gallery open to public 10–6 only during exhibitions 🏛 Price varies according to exhibition 🚊 Můstek

The university founded by Charles IV in 1348 and named after him is one of the oldest and most famous in Europe, with a current student body numbering nearly 40,000. Its history reflects the country's, with repeated disputes about its dual Czech/German character. Even after its division into completely separate Czech and German sections in 1882, squabbles continued about who should keep the university's original insignia. All this came to an end in 1945 with the expulsion of the German element altogether, and nowadays the Carolinum (or Karolinum) is a wholly Czech, or more correctly, cosmopolitan institution.

The university's departments are scattered all over the city, but its headquarters are still in this much rebuilt and altered Gothic edifice into which it moved in 1383. The most prominent original feature is the oriel window facing the Stavovské divadlo (Estates Theatre), while part of the interior is used as a gallery for temporary art exhibitions.

CELETNÁ

✛ 57 F6 • Celetná, Staré Město, Prague 1 🚊 Náměstí Republiky 🚊 Tram 5, 8, 14 to Náměstí Republiky

Forming the first stage of the Royal Way, pedestrianized Celetná is one of the principal thoroughfares of the Old Town, leading from the Prašná brána (Powder Tower) to Staroměstské náměstí (Old Town Square). A procession of mostly medieval buildings lines the route, nearly all of them later given charming baroque or rococo façades. Many now house trendy shops. There are a number of fascinating details to spot, among them the figures of Kutná Hora miners holding up the balcony of what was once the Mint at No. 36/587, opposite the Dům U černé Matky Boží (Black Madonna House, ▷ 70). Look into the *pavlač* of No. 11/598, a fine example of an old galleried courtyard.

BŘEVNOVSKÝ KLÁŠTER

One of Prague's great religious institutions, this baroque abbey complex was built by the Dientzenhofer family of architects.

The thousand-year-old Benedictine monastery of Břevnov, once deep in the countryside, still has a rustic atmosphere despite now being embedded in the city's western outskirts. Its baroque buildings are the work of the Dientzenhofers, and include not only one of their grandest churches, but an array of other edifices, such as the imposing granary dominating the approach to the complex.

LEGENDARY BEGINNINGS

All of these structures are only the latest in a series of buildings and rebuildings; one of the most fascinating aspects of a visit here is to descend into the crypt beneath the floor of the baroque church, where there are the squat columns and round arches of the original pre-Romanesque church, as well as fragments of Gothic masonry.

The monastery was founded by Prince Bořivoj and Bishop Vojtěch (or Adalbert) who, according to legend, dreamed identical dreams and met at the point where a spring gushed from the ground. Whatever the truth, Břevnov's origins can be traced to the year 993, when Vojtěch returned from Rome with a band of Benedictine monks and settled here. A nobleman and the first Slav Bishop of Prague, he set about the christianization of eastern Europe, eventually meeting a martyr's death in Poland. This earned him a place among the country's patron saints, and his bones were eventually returned to Prague.

LATER LUXURY

Vojtěch's later successors, the abbots of the 18th century, not only created one of Prague's most resplendent places of worship, but lived in some style themselves, as a tour of the sumptuous monastery buildings and their treasures reveals. The high point is the Theresian Hall, decorated for the visit of Empress Maria Theresa in 1753; the ceiling fresco, the biggest in Prague, depicts the miracle of the hermit Gunther (c955–1045), who avoided eating meat on a day of fast by causing a roast peacock to fly away from the table. For summer relaxation, the abbots retired to the charming garden pavilion, built over the site of the legendary spring. Břevnov was confiscated by the Communist regime in 1950, the monks were expelled and the buildings used to store books and police files. Restitution took place in 1990 and since then a steady schedule of repair and renewal has restored the institution to much of its former glory.

RATINGS	
Cultural interest	● ● ● ●
Historic interest	● ● ● ●
Photo stops	● ● ●

BASICS
✚ Off map 56 A6 • Markétská 1/28, Břevnov, Prague 6
☎ 220 406 111
🕐 Apr–end Oct Sat–Sun 10am, 2pm, 4pm; Nov–end Mar Sat–Sun 10am, 2pm
💰 Adult 50Kč, child (6–16) 30Kč
🚋 Tram 15, 22, 25 to Břevnovský klášter
📖 Guidebook 50Kč
🎧 Guided tours only
🚻

TIP
● If you've come this far into the western suburbs, continue a little further to Hvězda (Star Castle, ▷ 85), in its parkland setting, the site of the Battle of White Mountain in 1620 (▷ 29).

Intricate paintings adorn the interior vaults (top) of Břevnov Monastery (above)

The remarkable Cubist-style Black Madonna House

The huge Černín Palace has an impressive façade

DŮM U ČERNÉ MATKY BOŽÍ

The Black Madonna House, Prague's outstanding Cubist-style building, is an eminently suitable home for the museum of Czech Cubism.

🔢 57 F6 • Muzeum českého kubismu, Ovocný trh 19, Staré Město, Prague 1 ☎ 224 211 746 🕐 Tue–Sun 10–6 💰 Adult 100Kč, child (6–16) 50Kč. Free 1st Wed in month 3–8pm 🚇 Náměstí Republiky 🚊 Tram 5, 8, 14 to Náměstí Republiky 📖 Guidebook 135Kč 🎧 Guided tour by prior arrangement 🏛 Shop specializing in Cubist reproduction objects 🔌 www.ngprague.cz

RATINGS	
Cultural interest	●●●●
Photo stops	●●●●
Specialist shopping	●●●●

TIP

● Look out for the little Black Madonna who gave her name to the original baroque building on the site (she's in a gilded cage on the Celetná side of the building, ▷ below).

Built in 1911–12 by the progressive architect Josef Gočár, this extraordinary building occupies a landmark position on the Royal Way. It was originally a department store, with a famous first-floor café (▷ 21); its ground floor is now occupied by one of the city's best bookstores and by a shop selling superb—and expensive—reproductions of classic furniture and other objects designed by some of the artists and craftsmen whose original work is on show on the upper floors.

CUBISM

It was only in Bohemia that the Cubist movement in art extended into architecture, breaking down and recomposing building façades into complex, sometimes crystalline patterns, in the way that painters such as Braque and Picasso and their local counterparts had dramatically remodelled faces, landscapes and still lifes. Architectural Cubism was short-lived, at its peak in the two or three years immediately before World War I. After the war it evolved into the equally short-lived Rondo-Cubist style.

The near unique quality of the Black Madonna House will strike anyone who has started their walk along the Royal Way at the Obecní dům (Municipal House) just a few steps away. No contrast could be greater than that between the decorative opulence of the Municipal House and the disciplined crispness of this bold, glass and red sandstone façade. Yet only a few years separate the two buildings. Climb the splendid curving staircase to admire the collection of Cubist paintings, drawings, sculpture and furniture displayed on the first and second floor (labelling is in English).

ČERNÍNSKÝ PALÁC

🔢 56 B5 • Lorentánské náměstí 5, Hradčany, Prague 1 🚇 Not open to the public 🚊 Tram 22, 23 to Pohořelec

The Černín Palace, with its 150m (490ft) façade, lords it over the Loreto and the upper part of the Hradčany quarter. The biggest palace in Prague, it was begun by Jan Humprecht, Count Černín, in 1669, but remained unfinished on his death, and its construction and maintenance continued to eat up the family fortunes in the years to come. Eventually it was sold to the state; it served as an Austrian barracks, then in the 1920s became the Foreign Ministry of the new Czechoslovak state. During the Nazi Occupation it was the headquarters of the Reichsprotektor, and it was on his morning commute to the palace that 'Hangman' Heydrich was assassinated in 1942. Another death is also associated with the palace; in 1948, just after the Communist *coup d'etat*, the body of popular Foreign Minister Jan Masaryk (1886–1948) was found in the courtyard beneath his office window. The question of whether the last democratic member of the government fell or was pushed has never been resolved and remains a mystery.

DŮM PÁNŮ Z KUNŠTÁTU A PODĚBRAD

🔢 57 E6 • Řetězová 3, Staré Město, Prague 1 ☎ 608 273 849 🕐 Daily in summer 9am–10pm 💰 30Kč 🚇 Staroměstská 🚊 Tram 17, 18 to Karlovy lázně

Opening off narrow Řetězová street in the western part of the Old Town, the House of the Lords of Kunštat and Poděbrady has one of the city's oldest interiors accessible to the public.

A poster advertising the Franz Kafka exhibition in Staré Město

The House at the Golden Ring is home to modern Czech art

DŮM U ZLATÉHO PRSTENU

Discover little-known masterpieces of modern Czech art in the stimulating surroundings of one of the city's most venerable houses, the House at the Golden Ring.

🚏 57 F5 • Týnská 6, Staré Město, Prague 1 ☎ 224 827 022
🕐 Tue–Sun 10–6 🎫 Adult 80Kč, child (6–16) 40Kč 🚇 Náměstí Republiky 🚊 Tram 5, 8, 14 to Dlouhá třída or Náměstí Republiky
🎧 Guided tour by prior arrangement (minimum 2 weeks notice): 40Kč per person

RATINGS	
Cultural interest	● ● ● ●
Historic interest	● ● ●

An exhibition poster (below)

The narrow frontage of this medieval building stands at the meeting point of several lanes, archways and alleyways to the east of Staroměstské náměstí (Old Town Square). Penetrating deep into the surrounding urban fabric, the mysterious interior consists of a series of strangely shaped rooms connected by low doorways and spiral staircases. It's a disorientating environment, very much a part of 'magic Prague', and ideally suited to its present function, a gallery of the city's own collection of modern Czech art.

THE EXHIBITS

The building is basically a Gothic structure of the 13th century, though much rebuilt and modified in Renaissance times. Traces of wall-paintings from the building's early history are exposed at various spots, and there are occasional glimpses out to its huge neighbour, the Chrám Matky Boží pred Týnem (Týn Church), or down into the crooked course of rambling Týnská ulička. Though it's worth paying the entrance fee just to wander through the warren of rooms, the exhibits on display (on three floors) represent a good cross-section of 20th-century Czech art, and make an excellent alternative to the much more extensive array of works displayed in the Veletržní palác (Trade Fair Palace).

Nearly all the big names are represented by first-class works, though you should be aware that they are regularly rotated. They are also displayed thematically, not chronologically. You are certain to find pictures by the well-known figures of a century ago, like Max Švabinský (1873–1962) and Jan Zrzavý (1890–1977), as well as the often disturbing work of Surrealists like Jindřich Štyrský (1899–1942) and Marie Čermínová ('Toyen'; 1902–80), gloomy paintings by members of the wartime Group 42—a group of artists who came together in 1942 to work despite the pressure of the occupation—and other works by more recent artists.

Its vaulted 13th-century cellars are the building's original ground floor, converted into a basement when the ground level of most of the Old Town was raised in an attempt to combat regular flooding by the River Vltava. For a while in the 15th century it was the town residence of George of Poděbrady, the most illustrious of the 'Lords' (minor aristocrats from eastern Bohemia). In 1458, he was elected King of Bohemia, the only native Czech ever to have this honour, and is still a revered figure among democratically-minded Czechs.

EXPOSICE FRANZE KAFKY

🚏 57 F6 • Náměstí Franze Kafky 5, Staré Město, Prague 1 ☎ 222 321 675 🕐 Tue–Fri 10–6, Sat 10–5 🎫 40Kč 🚇 Staroměstská 🚊 Tram 17, 18 to Staroměstská

This small-scale exhibition on the life and work of Franz Kafka (1883–1924) is a focal point for anyone wishing to find out about Prague's most famous literary figure. Its displays are housed in the building on the corner of Maiselova and Kaprova streets, which replaced Kafka's birth-place, long since demolished. Though he changed his address many times, nearly all of the writer's life was spent within a short distance of this spot; 'a little mother with claws' is how he characterized the native city which never gave up her hold on him. As a Jew among Germans, a non-believer among his fellow-Jews, a German-speaker among Czechs, and a subject of the bureaucratically run Habsburg Empire, Kafka was well-qualified to become the 20th-century's spokesman on alienation; his novels and short stories evoke a darkly lit, sinister world, in which the powerless individual finds himself at the mercy of authority.

Jiřský klášter

The galleries of St. George's Convent, home to the national collection of Mannerist and baroque art, bring you into close contact with some of the most glorious paintings and sculpture ever produced in Bohemia.

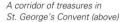

A corridor of treasures in St. George's Convent (above)

The exterior of the convent (above). Statue of St. John of Nepomuk (left)

RATINGS

Cultural interest	●●●●●
Good for kids	●●●
Historic interest	●●●

BASICS

✚ 56 C5 • Národní galerie, Jiřský klášter, Jiřské náměstí 33, Hradčany, Prague 1
☎ 257 531 644
🕐 Tue–Sun 10–6
💶 Adult 100Kč, child (6–16) 50Kč. Free 1st Wed in month 3–8pm
🚃 Tram 22, 23 to Pražský hrad
📖 Softback book *Mannerist and Baroque Art in Bohemia*, 190Kč
🎧 Guided tour by prior arrangement; price by agreement
🏪 Stall with limited selection of books and prints
🚻

www.ngprague.cz
The National Gallery's website with general information in English.

SEEING JIŘSKÝ KLÁŠTER

Next to, but separate from St. George's Basilica in the Castle precinct, are the convent's spacious galleries, laid out in chronological order on two floors. Beginning with the Mannerist art of Emperor Rudolf II's extravagant court, they continue with sublime examples of baroque painting and sculpture from Prague's golden age of the early 18th century, and end with the perhaps less substantial, but still delightful art of the rococo period. A final fascinating section examines in depth the whole business of art production in Prague, when there were no real barriers between art, craft and business, and masters and assistants turned out quality work in quantity for private and institutional patrons.

HIGHLIGHTS

RUDOLPHINE PRAGUE

Emperor Rudolf's appreciation of art of the highest quality, preferably with some sort of erotic undercurrent, is evident in the relatively small number of works from the age when his court attracted artists from all over Europe. Topless beauties are caught in the act of suicide by the Antwerp painter Bartholomeus Spranger (1546–1611), who also provided his master with coyly posed male figures. The Emperor sent Spranger's fellow countryman Roeland Savery (1576–1639) into the Bohemian forests and as far as the Alps in search of scenes which, in their atmosphere of romantic decay, would appeal to his restless and melancholic sensibility.

BAROQUE PAINTING

Large-scale paintings by Karel Škréta (1610–74) are a feature of many a Prague church interior. His creative genius is well displayed in the convent in ambitious works such as his *St. Charles Borromeo Visiting Plague Victims in Milan*, in which the artist himself appears as the Roman-nosed figure to the right of the saint. Almost like a scene from a slaughterhouse, the dramatic *Crucifixion of St. Andrew* by Michael Leopold Willman (1630–1706) reveals the influence he owes to Dutch painters such as Rembrandt and Rubens. Forced from his native Bohemia because of his Protestant faith, Johann Kupecký

Art students learning about the works on display; the large painting on the wall behind them is St. Charles Borromeo Visiting Plague Victims in Milan *by Karel Škréta (opposite top)*

An early 18th-century sculpture of Venus (below) by Matthias Bernhard Braun

(1667–1740) painted his masterly *Portrait of the Miniaturist Karl Bruni* in Vienna. However, the most fascinating figure of this period is Peter Brandl (1668–1735). A bon viveur and reckless spender, Brandl enjoyed the company both of aristocratic patrons and Prague's lowlife. His penetrating vision is especially evident in his merciless *Self-Portrait* of around 1725.

BAROQUE SCULPTURE

Outstanding among Prague's early 18th-century sculptors were Ferdinand Maximilian Brokoff (1688–1731) and the Tyrolean Matthias Bernhard Braun (1684–1738). Everyone notices Brokof's splendid pair of Moors holding up the balcony of the Morzin Palace in Nerudova street; the convent's gallery has their twins, taken from the Morzin family's country house. Braun was responsible for one of the most dynamic of the Karlův most (Charles Bridge) sculptures, the *Vision of St. Luitgard*. He is represented here by a number of fine works, among them a *Venus*, brought from its elevated perch on the parapet of the Clam-Gallas Palace in the Old Town. But the most astonishing sculpture of all is the extraordinarily dynamic *Virgin Mary and Archangel Gabriel*, the work of one of Braun's anonymous students, and a convincing demonstration of the master's skill as a teacher.

BACKGROUND

St. George's Convent was one of the earliest institutions of its kind, founded in 973 by Princess Milada, a niece of St. Wenceslas. Many of its later abbesses were of equally high rank, but this did not save the convent from the reforms of Emperor Joseph II; shut down in 1782, it then suffered an undignified fate as artillery barracks. Its unlikely saviour was the Communist regime, who rebuilt it between 1963 and 1976. Perhaps fortunately their original intention of turning it into the Museum of the Czechoslovak People came to nothing. A new home for the National Gallery's baroque collections in the Schwarzenberg and Salm palaces is likely to be ready by 2010.

Moor raising his shield (1718–19) by Ferdinand Maximilian Brokoff

TIPS

● Bear in mind that St. George's Convent is part of the National Gallery, and that entry to it requires a separate ticket from the one giving access to the interiors of the Cathedral and Castle.

● Much of the city's artistic heritage can seem rather out of reach; the intimate contact afforded here will give you a fresh appreciation of the glories of the Prague baroque.

Josefov

An atmospheric ancient cemetery and a cluster of synagogues are evocative testimony to a thousand years of Jewish life in Prague.

A busy street in Josefov (above). The Maisel Synagogue (right)

The entrance to the Old Jewish Cemetery (above)

SEEING JOSEFOV

Josefov—or Josephstadt—was the name given to Prague's famous ghetto after the emancipation of its inhabitants by enlightened Emperor Joseph II in 1781. The close-packed houses and the crooked streets of the ghetto were demolished in the late 19th century, but its synagogues remain. Some are museums, others are still used as places of worship by today's tiny community, successor to what was one of Europe's most flourishing Jewish communities. Almost every visitor to Prague is drawn towards the Gothic Staronová synagóga (Old-New Synagogue) and the unique Starý židovský hřbitov (Old Jewish Cemetery) with its 12,000 tombstones, but to experience Josefov fully and understand the past from which it has emerged, you need to take time and ponder the displays set out in the various synagogues. Bear in mind that the cemetery and five of the synagogues are administered by the Židovské muzeum (Jewish Museum), while the Old-New Synagogue belongs to the community; a collective ticket gives admission to the former, while a separate ticket has to be purchased for the latter. Men should cover their heads in both the cemetery and the Old-New Synagogue (paper *kippah* are available).

HIGHLIGHTS

STARONOVÁ SYNAGÓGA

Červená 2, Staré Město/Josefov, Prague 1 Sun–Thu 9.30–4, Fri 9–1; closed on Jewish holidays Adult 200Kč, child (6–16) 140Kč Staroměstská Tram 17, 18 to Staroměstská

Begun around 1270, the Old-New Synagogue is telling testimony to the ancient roots of Jewish life in Europe. Distinguished externally by its high brick gable, it may well have been built by the Christian masons working on the nearby Convent of St. Agnes. Its paradoxical name is the subject of legend and controversy; the most likely explanation, however, is that it was called the 'New' synagogue when it replaced an older building on the site, then had the 'Old' added when it was replaced in its turn in the 16th century by the synagogue in nearby Široká street.

RATINGS	
Cultural interest	●●●●
Historic interest	●●●●●
Photo stops	●●●●

BASICS

57 F5

Židovské museum (synagogues and Old Jewish Cemetery)

U Starého hřbitova 3a, Staré Město/Josefov, Prague 1

222 317 191

Apr–end Oct Sun–Fri 9–6; Nov–end Mar Sun–Fri 9–4.30

Adult 300Kč, child (6–16) 200Kč

Staroměstská

Tram 17, 18 to Staroměstská

Range of publications

Guided tours and group reservations: Reservační Centrum (tel 222 317 191)

www.jewishmuseum.cz
Description of the various establishments of the museum and their collections and events (in English).

A delightful art nouveau detail on Kaprova street in Josefov (opposite)

KEY TO THE MAP

1. Klausova synagóga
2. Starý židovský hřbitov
3. Pinkasova synagóga
4. Staronová synagóga
5. Vysoká synagóga
6. Maiselova synagóga
7. Španělská synagóga

THE SIGHTS

It is entered via a portal decorated with a vine, whose dozen roots represent the 12 tribes of Israel, its four stems the four rivers of the Creation. Inside, the nave is supported by vaults with five ribs instead of the usual four, which could be taken to symbolize the Christian cross. A central place, defined by a Gothic grille, is occupied by the *bimah* or pulpit. On display is the banner given by Emperor Ferdinand II to honour the Jewish community's part in the fight against the Swedes in the Thirty Years' War (1618–48); within its Star of David is a representation of a Swedish soldier's helmet. For many years, the synagogue's women worshippers sat separately, watching services from a side chamber through a number of window slits.

A local Jewish woman selling cardboard skull caps outside the Old-New Synagogue (above). The synagogue's bimah (pulpit) is surrounded by a Gothic iron grille (above right)

STARÝ ŽIDOVSKÝ HŘBITOV

Lit by whatever light filters down through the foliage of tall trees, the Old Jewish Cemetery is an eerie place, its toppling tombstones contained within the limited space defined by buildings and high walls. Despite the numerous visitors, the cemetery remains redolent of a Jewish Prague that has disappeared forever. In 1439, the Jews were forbidden to bury their dead outside the ghetto, and until Emperor Joseph's time every burial took place here, the grave sites being used again and again, until as many as a dozen dead were piled on top of each other. While the earliest tombstones were simple markers, later ones became more elaborate, with carved inscriptions and symbols evoking the names or achievements of the deceased.

Thus a fox would symbolize a member of the Fuchs family and a mouse the Meisels, while praying hands would evoke the priestly Cohens. The most visited tomb is that of Rabbi Loew (c1520–1609), legendary creator of the Golem (▷ 29). Remodelled in baroque style, the tomb is decorated with a lion and a bunch of grapes.

Just by the entrance to the cemetery, the little neo-Romanesque building of the Obřadní síň (Ceremonial Hall) is where bodies were once prepared for burial. It now houses displays on the rituals associated with death, burial and commemoration.

After the closure of the cemetery in the late 18th century, the community began to bury its dead elsewhere, eventually in the far more spacious surroundings of the Nový židovský hřbitov (New Jewish Cemetery, ▷ 99) in suburban Olšany; it is here that another much visited Jewish grave is located, that of Franz Kafka.

TIPS

● There are unusual views of the Old Jewish Cemetery from the upper floors of some of the surrounding buildings, notably the Pinkas Synagogue and the Uměleckoprůmyslové muzeum (▷ 132–133).

● The sheer numbers visiting Josefov can sometimes become oppressive; the best times to visit are early in the day or during the tourist lunch hour.

THE SIGHTS

ŽIDOVSKÁ RADNICE

The Jewish Town Hall is a reminder that the ghetto was once a self-governing town in its own right. The present pretty edifice is a mid-18th-century rebuilding of an earlier structure. Its charming belfry is topped by a Star of David and features a quartet of conventional clocks, but the Town Hall's most famous timepiece is mounted in a gable facing the Old-New Synagogue; much admired by devotees of the occult and a minor landmark of 'magic Prague', its hands move counterclockwise round a dial with Hebrew characters. The original Town Hall, like a number of the buildings in the ghetto, was the gift to the community from one of its most notable inhabitants, Mayor Mordecai Maisel, the richest man in Prague. Maisel also financed the building attached to the Town Hall, the Vysoká synagóga (High Synagogue), used by the community for worship and not accessible to the general public.

KLAUSOVA SYNAGÓGA

A baroque structure dating from 1689, but much modified in the late 19th century, the Klausen Synagogue was the successor to a group of buildings (klausen in German) erected in Mayor Maisel's time. It is now a museum, as are most of the Josefov synagogues, in this case devoted to everyday religious life. Among the most fascinating items is a series of paintings depicting in charming detail the activities of the burial association. Other exhibits recall Prague's importance as one of the foremost places in Europe of Jewish printing and bookbinding.

One of the Jewish Town Hall's clocks has Hebrew characters and hands that move counterclockwise (above). The tomb of Rabbi Loew in the Old Jewish Cemetery (above left)

The Pinkas Synagogue houses a poignant exhibition of children's drawings (below), dating from 1942–44, from the ghetto town of Terezín

THE SIGHTS

PINKASOVA SYNAGÓGA

The Pinkas Synagogue, now serving principally as a solemn memorial to the Jewish people of Bohemia and Moravia who were murdered by the Nazis, dates originally from the early 16th century, when it was built as a private place of worship for one of the ghetto's wealthiest families. Much altered and restored over the years, it combines late Gothic and Renaissance features and has retained a lovely rococo wrought-iron grille around its central *bimah* (pulpit). The names and dates of birth and death of the 77,297 who perished in the concentration camps are inscribed in simple black and red lettering on the walls. A more poignant means of commemoration could hardly have been devised. The meticulous work of lettering was carried out in the 1950s, taking a full five years, but in 1968 the synagogue was closed, ostensibly because of damp penetration, though it was widely believed that a more important factor was the Communist regime's anti-Zionist stance following the Israeli triumph in the Six-Day War. The building stayed closed until after the Velvet Revolution, since when the names have been painstakingly restored. An upstairs room houses an equally poignant exhibition of children's drawings from Terezín (Theresienstadt, ▷ 216–217), the ghetto town in northern Bohemia in which many Czech Jews perished.

MAISELOVA SYNAGÓGA

The Maisel Synagogue built by Mayor Maisel in 1592 as a private place of worship was the most lavish edifice ever to grace the ghetto. Unfortunately it was damaged more than once by fire, notably in a ghetto-wide blaze of 1689, and the present structure is an early

THE ASANACE

By the end of the 19th century, Josefov had been abandoned by those of its Jewish inhabitants who could afford more salubrious homes in the suburbs. The impoverished people who remained were joined by low-lifers of all kinds and it became an unsanitary slum. The response of the city fathers was to level its picturesquely tumbledown houses and straighten out its crooked alleyways, in a wholesale redevelopment of the area called the 'asanace' (sanitization).

A replica of a Jewish hat—an emblem of Prague's Jewish community—in the Maisel Synagogue (right)

A memorial to Jewish victims of the Holocaust from Bohemia and Moravia—the names of the 77,297 who perished in concentration camps are inscribed on the walls in the Pinkas Synagogue (left)

The Moorish-style Spanish Synagogue (below) was built in 1868

20th-century rebuilding in neo-Gothic style. Displays inside include a fine array of ritual objects in precious metals. The presence of these and other Jewish treasures in Prague is the result of a bizarre project undertaken by the Nazis; once the annihilation of European Jewry had been carried out, the Prague ghetto was to become the 'Museum of a Vanished Race', filled with objects looted from Bohemia and Moravia.

ŠPANĚLSKÁ SYNAGÓGA

In Vězeňská, to the east of the main group of ghetto buildings, the Spanish Synagogue of 1868 symbolizes the prestige and prosperity of Prague's Jewish community in the late 19th century. It is built in what was then the fashionable style for synagogues, an opulent version of the Moorish architecture of Spain's Alhambra. It contains displays on the modern history of Czech Jewry, including intriguing pictures of the ghetto before and after its late 19th-century redevelopment.

BACKGROUND

The Jewish presence in Prague goes back at least to the 10th century. Originally settled in Malá Strana, in the 13th century the Jews were made to move to what is now Josefov, which eventually became a walled town in its own right. The community's fortunes fluctuated; pogroms and expulsions alternated with periods of tolerance and prosperity, with rulers frequently aware of the economic benefits of protecting their Jewish subjects from Christian persecution. One 'Golden Age' occurred in the late 16th century, when men such as Mordecai Maisel and Rabbi Loew had the ear of Emperor Rudolf II. Another came in the late 19th and early 20th century, with Jewish people playing a prominent role in intellectual and commercial life. Many moved to the more spacious suburbs and the ghetto was redeveloped with handsome turn-of-the-20th-century buildings, like those lining Pařížká. The Nazis brought the long story of Jewish Prague to an end, though a small community has subsequently re-established itself.

Torah crown (1723) in the Maisel Synagogue (above)

MUSEUM OF A VANISHED RACE

In contrast to their wholesale desecration of Jewish property elsewhere, the Nazis set out to preserve the synagogues and other structures of the Prague ghetto. Not, however, with benevolent intentions. Plundered Jewish items from all over the country were accumulated here by the Nazis, and once the Jews of Europe had been exterminated, Josefov was to become the 'Museum of a Vanished Race', with costumed guides playing the roles of its former inhabitants.

Karlův most

The longest, and the loveliest, medieval bridge in Europe offers incomparable views of the river and city, as well as a superlative collection of open-air sculpture.

THE SIGHTS

SEEING KARLŮV MOST

At 516m (1,693ft) long, Charles Bridge has spanned the broad River Vltava between Staré Město (Old Town) and Malá Strana (Lesser Town) for more than 650 years. During that time it has served not only as a thoroughfare, but also as a processional way and a place of commerce, celebration and punishment. It carried one of Prague's first tramlines, but vehicular traffic of any kind has long since been banned, and the bridge's main function nowadays is as an incomparable viewing platform for the beauties of the city all around. Commerce, in the form of souvenir sellers, is still very much present, as is entertainment, in the shape of buskers and performers. The Royal Way (the coronation procession) passed this way en route between the Old Town's royal palace and the Cathedral, and the bridge remains a vital link along the tourist route between the city centre and the Castle district. It's worth remembering, however, that it is far from being the only crossing, and that there are plenty of alternative ways of moving from one bank of the river to the other. Charles Bridge can indeed become very crowded; the best times to enjoy its unique atmosphere are in the early morning and late evening.

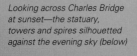

Looking across Charles Bridge at sunset—the statuary, towers and spires silhouetted against the evening sky (below)

HIGHLIGHTS

STAROMĚSTSKÁ MOSTECKÁ VĚŽ

✉ Karlův most, Staré Město, Prague 1 ☎ 224 220 569 🕐 Mar daily 10–6;
Apr–end May, Oct daily 10–7pm; Jun–end Sep daily 10–10pm; Nov–end Feb
daily 10–5 💰 Adult 50Kč, child (6–16) 40Kč 🚇 Staroměstská 🚊 Tram 17, 18
to Staroměstská

With its chisel-shaped roof and spiky corner turrets, the Old Town
Bridge Tower presents its unmistakable silhouette at the eastern end
of the bridge. The bridge's first arch is now concealed beneath the
paving of Křížovnické náměstí (Knights of the Cross Square), and the
tower's foundation is formed by the first of 16 massive piers. Both
the tower and the bridge itself are the work of Emperor Charles IV's
architect/engineer, Peter
Parler (1330–1399), who

HARD-BOILED HELP

When the great bridge was being
built, an appeal went throughout
the land for the wine and eggs
that needed to be mixed with
lime to make an immensely
strong mortar. The response was
magnificent, with towns and
villages delivering generous
quantities of the materials
required. But the builders were
nonplussed when the eggs
provided by one remote
community arrived hard-boiled!

designed them at the same
time as he worked on St.
Vitus Cathedral. The tower was given symbolic significance by means
of sculptural decoration; its eastern face is adorned with statues of
St. Vitus flanked by Charles and his son Wenceslas IV, as well as by
the patron saints of Bohemia and signs of the zodiac. Its defensive
function was a real one; in 1648, an improvised militia of students and
Jewish residents assembled here to beat back the Swedish soldiers
attempting to break into the Old Town, and barricades were thrown
up here on other occasions. There's a striking view of the bridge from
the tower's gallery, reached by 138 steps.

OUSTING THE SWEDES

Charles Bridge has been fought
over more than once. At the end
of the Thirty Years' War
(1618–48), the Swedish troops
who had occupied Malá Strana
stormed across the bridge but
were forced back by a motley
group of university students and
Jews from the ghetto, who
baricaded the Old Town Bridge
Tower. The dramatic scene is
re-created vividly in the diorama
in the Mirror Maze of Petřín
Hill (▷ 102).

*The splendid 14th-century
Charles Bridge (above middle)
is popular with tourists and is
thronged with an array of
street musicians (above left),
trinket sellers and portrait
artists (above right)*

As you walk across the bridge, try to stop and admire the following noteworthy statues and sculptures:

● St. Ivo, the patron saint of lawyers, by Matthias Bernard Braun. The saint is shown in the animated pose so characteristic of baroque sculpture.

● St. Cyril and St. Methodius, by Karel Dvořák. This group was added on the 20th anniversary of the founding of Czechoslovakia

MALOSTRANSKÁ MOSTECKÁ VĚŽ

✉ Mostecká, Malá Strana, Prague 1 ☎ 257 530 487 🕐 Apr–end Oct daily 10–6 💳 Adult 50Kč, child (6–16) 40Kč 🚇 Malostranská 🚊 Tram 12, 20, 22, 23 to Malostranské náměstí

Built in the mid-15th century, the Malá Strana Bridge Tower is modelled on the tower at the Old Town end of the bridge. It forms a much photographed pair with the smaller tower to its left. This early 12th-century defensive structure was part of the fortified approach to the Judith Bridge, the predecessor of the Charles Bridge. The Bridge Tower houses a small exhibition on the history of the bridge, and offers fine views from its gallery.

The 15th-century Malá Strana Bridge Tower and 12th-century Judith Bridge Tower form an archway into Malá Strana (below)

People strolling across medieval Charles Bridge (above)

and, however worthy, lacks the dynamism and emotional impact of its baroque counterparts.

● St. Francis Xavier, generally regarded as the finest work by Ferdinand Maximilian Brokoff. The Jesuit missionary is shown baptizing a pagan prince. One of the supporting figures may be a portrait of Brokoff.

● St. John of Nepomuk by M. Rauchmüller and Jan Brokoff, father of the talented Ferdinand Maximilian. It is placed at the spot from which the saint is supposed to have been thrown to a watery death by order of jealous King Wenceslas IV.

● The missionaries St. Vincent and St. Procopius, by F. M. Brokoff. Vincent is shown reviving a dead man, while Procopius stamps on a devil.

● St. Luitgard, by M. B. Braun. In a spasm of emotional intensity hardly equalled elsewhere, the blind nun Luitgard kisses one of the dying Christ's wounds.

● St. John of Matha, St. Felix of Valois and the Blessed Ivan, by F. M. Brokoff. These saints were responsible for rescuing Christians fallen into infidel hands, like those languishing in the cave here, guarded by a pot-bellied Turk and his dog.

STATUARY AND SCULPTURE

The statues grouped in opposite pairs all along the bridge's parapets (▷ 83) seem to have belonged to it forever, but for many years it remained unadorned, apart from a wooden Calvary. The statue of Bruncvík, a knightly figure in the same mould as Roland, the famous French hero, symbolizing civic rights and privileges, was added at the beginning of the 16th century, but he stands beneath the parapet on one of the piers, and does not form part of the glorious procession of baroque saints. Most of those you see now are copies, the originals having been removed to preserve them from the elements. All are worth a look, but some are real masterpieces by the foremost sculptors of the time and deserve closer attention (▷ side column).

BACKGROUND

Karlův most, known simply as 'The Bridge' or 'The Stone Bridge', was only given its present name in honour of Emperor Charles IV (1316–78) in 1870, when the building of other bridges meant it no longer formed the only crossing of the Vltava. A triumph of medieval engineering, its construction was ordered by Charles as part of his package of imperial improvements to the capital city. By 1378 it was sufficiently complete to carry his funeral procession. It had been preceded by a timber structure, then around 1160 by the first stone bridge, named after Queen Judith. The Juditín most (Judith Bridge) was destroyed by floods in 1342, but Charles Bridge, its mortar reinforced by a mixture of wine and eggs, has withstood most of whatever the Vltava has thrown at it, though three of its arches were destroyed in a terrible flood in 1890.

LESSER TOWN BRIDGE TOWERS

St. Wenceslas
by J. K. Böhm, 1858

SS. Cosmas and Damian
by J. O. Mayer, 1709

SS. John of Matha,
Felix of Valois and Ivan
and figure of a Turk
by F. M. Brokoff, 1714

St. Vitus
by F. M. Brokoff, 1714
(marble)

St. Adalbert
by F. M. Brokoff, 1709
(copy, 1973)

St. Philip Benizi
by M. B. Mandl, 1714

St. Luitgard
by M. B. Braun, 1710
(copy, 1995)

St. Cajetan
by F. M. Brokoff, 1709

St. Nicholas of Tolentino
by J. F. Kohl, 1706
(copy, 1969)

St. Augustine
by J. F. Kohl, 1708
(copy, 1974)

Roland Column
(originally
16th century;
copy, 1884)

SS. Vincent Ferrer
and Procopius
by F. M. Brokoff, 1712

St. Jude Thaddaeus
by J. O. Mayer, 1708

St. Francis Seraphicus
by E. Max, 1855

St. Anthony of Padua
by J. O. Mayer, 1707

SS. Ludmilla
and Wenceslas
workshop of
M. B. Braun, c1730
(copy, 1999)

St. John of Nepomuk
by M. Rauchmüller and J. Brokoff, 1683;
cast in bronze by W. H. Heroldt,
Nuremberg, 1683

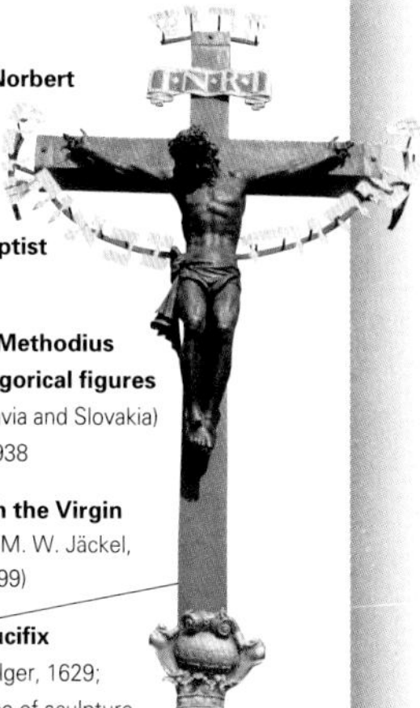

St. Francis Borgia
by J. and F. M. Brokoff,
1710 (restored by
R. Vlach, 1937)

SS. Wenceslas, Norbert
and Sigismund
by J. Max, 1853

St. Christopher
by E. Max, 1857

St. John the Baptist
by J. Max, 1857

St. Francis Xavier
by F. M. Brokoff, 1711
(copy, 1913)

SS. Cyril and Methodius
and three allegorical figures
(Bohemia, Moravia and Slovakia)
by K. Dvořák, 1938

St. Joseph
by J. Max, 1854

St. Anne with the Virgin
and Child by M. W. Jäckel,
1707 (copy, 1999)

Pietà
by E. Max, 1859
(originally 1695)

Bronze Crucifix
cast by J. Hilger, 1629;
the first piece of sculpture
on the bridge, set up 1657; Hebrew
inscription of 1696; figures by E. Max, 1861

SS. Barbara,
Margaret and
Elizabeth
by F. M. Brokoff,
1707 (copy)

Virgin with SS. Dominic and
Thomas Aquinas
by M. W. Jäckel, 1709 (copy, 1961)

St. Ivo
by M. B. Braun, 1711
(copy, 1908)

Virgin with St. Bernard
by M. W. Jäckel, 1709 (copy)

OLD TOWN BRIDGE TOWER

THE SIGHTS

The glorious baroque Library Hall

A statue outside the Ball Game Hall in the Royal Garden

KLEMENTINUM

The austere walls of the Klementinum conceal some of Prague's most lavish baroque interiors.

🔲 57 E6 ● Národní knihovna, Klementinum 190, Staré Město, Prague 1 ☎ 603 231 241 🕐 Tours of Library Hall and Astronomical Tower: Jul–end Aug Mon–Fri 10–7 (2–7pm according to staff holidays), Sat–Sun 10–7; May–end Jun, Sep–end Oct Mon–Fri 2–6pm, Sat–Sun 10–6; Mar–end Apr, Nov–end Dec Mon–Fri 2–6pm, Sat–Sun 11–6. Tours start on the hour 🎫 Adult 100Kč, child (6–16) 50Kč 🚇 Staroměstská 🚊 Tram 17, 18 to Staroměstská 🔲 45Kč 🌐 Guided tour in English

RATINGS	
Cultural interest	● ● ●
Historic interest	● ● ●

This great institution is Prague's second largest building complex after the Castle. Now a worthy home for the National Library, it was once the local headquarters of the Jesuit Order; its construction involved the demolition of dozens of houses and the realignment of several city streets.

The Jesuits were first invited to Prague in the mid-16th century by the Habsburg authorities to help stamp out the Czechs' tendency to Protestantism. Following Protestantism's brief triumph in 1618, they were thrown out of town, but returned after the 1620 Battle of the White Mountain, when they were put in charge of the Carolinum (Charles University). Their glory days finally came to an end when they were expelled and their splendid library confiscated by reform-minded Emperor Joseph II.

THE NATIONAL LIBRARY

The Klementinum consists of buildings of various dates arranged around a series of courtyards. Several churches, including the Kostel svatého Salvátora (Church of St. Saviour), cling to its rather forbidding exterior; the grandest façade, adorned with statues of Roman emperors, faces west. The Národní knihovna (National Library) is essentially a working institution, and if you are not the owner of a reader's card, access is limited. However, there is a guided tour of part of the complex, which takes in the Barokní knihovní (Library Hall) of 1727, one of the city's most splendid baroque interiors, with venerable tomes in oaken bookcases, a ceiling fresco in praise of Wisdom, and a display of geographical and astrological globes. To see the equally sumptuous Zrcadlová kaple (Mirror Chapel), all artificial marble, glass and gilded stucco, you will need a ticket for one of the public concerts held here. Rising over the middle of the Klementinum is the Hvězdárenská věž (Astronomical Tower), topped by a figure of Atlas and in use for astronomical and meteorological observations since 1722.

KRÁLOVSKÁ ZAHRADA

🔲 56 C5 ● Pražský hrad, Hradčany, Prague 1 ☎ 224 371 111, 224 373 368 🕐 Apr–end Oct daily 10–6 🎫 Free 🚊 Tram 22, 23 to Královský letohrádek or Pražský hrad www.hrad.cz

To the north of the Jelení příkop (Stag Moat), the Royal Garden offers unusual views of the Castle and Cathedral, as well as providing a restful green setting. Originally laid out in geometrical style in the mid-16th century, the gardens are now informal, with plenty of fine trees and floral displays. The only formal part of the area is the little *giardinetto* in front of the Belvedér (▷ 67), a 20th-century re-creation of a Renaissance garden. It makes a perfect setting for the bronze Zpívající fontána (Singing Fountain) of 1568. The gardens were particularly appreciated by Emperor Rudolf II, who had a lower level added to the bridge over the Stag Moat so that he could reach them without being observed. The name of the Lví dvůr (Lion Court) restaurant at the entrance nearest the Castle is a reminder of his menagerie, which included not only lions, but many other exotic beasts, housed in heated cages to protect them from the Prague winter. Another exotic import to the gardens was the tulip; it was here that the flower made its European debut, its seeds a gift from the Sultan to the Austrian ambassador in Constantinople. Opposite the Lion Court is the Jízdárna (Riding School), a large building now used for temporary exhibitions. Inside the gardens is the Renaissance pavilion known as the Míčovna (Ball-Game Hall); its sgraffito decoration was restored in Communist times, and if you look carefully you will find a hammer and sickle.

Star Castle was built in the shape of a six-sided star

Looking down over the lovely Knights of the Cross Square

LETECKÉ MUZEUM

🔲 Off map 57 G4 • Letiště Praha-Kbely, Mladoboleslavská 902, Kbely, Prague 9 ☎ 973 207 500 🕐 May–end Oct Tue–Sun 10–6 🎫 Free 🚇 Česko-moravská, then bus 259, 280, 302, 349, 354, 375, 376 to Letecké muzeum www.militarymuseum.cz

The collections of the Czech Republic's Aviation Museum are among the finest in Europe—a must for anyone interested in historic aircraft, despite its location in the far-off suburb of Kbely. Among the machines and memorabilia are several interwar products of Czechoslovakia's progressive Avia firm, but the stars of the show are the military aircraft of World War II—a Spitfire, a Russian Sturmovik and advanced jet fighters of the Luftwaffe. Erstwhile opponents of Cold War times include an American Phantom and Soviet MiGs and Suchois.

LETOHRÁDEK HVĚZDA

🔲 Off map 56 A6 • Liboc 25c, Liboc, Prague 6 ☎ 220 612 229 🕐 May–end Sep Tue–Sun 10–6; Oct–end Apr Tue–Sun 10–5 🎫 Adult 30Kč, child (6–16) 15Kč 🚊 Tram 15, 22, 25 to Vypich

This extraordinary hunting lodge deserves its name of Star Castle; it was built in the shape of a six-sided star in 1556 by Archduke Ferdinand of Tyrol to form the focal point of the game park laid out among the densely wooded Bílá hora (White Mountain) area to the west of Prague. Its elaborately stuccoed interior now houses occasional exhibits devoted to Czech writers. One of the final acts of the Battle of White Mountain (▷ 29) took place here, when the victorious Catholics butchered the defeated royal guardsmen of the Protestant Winter King, Frederick.

KŘIŽOVNICKÉ NÁMĚSTÍ

Sliced through by trams and traffic, this little open space at the Old Town end of Charles Bridge has still been called 'one of the most beautiful squares in Europe'.

🔲 57 E6
Kostel svatého Františka
✉ Křižovnické náměstí 3, Staré Město, Prague 1 ☎ 221 108 200 🕐 Visits by prior arrangement Apr–end Oct 🚇 Staroměstská 🚊 Tram 17, 18 to Staroměstská or Karlovy lázně
Galerie Křižovníků
✉ Křižovnické náměstí 3, Staré Město, Prague 1 ☎ 236 033 680/777 807 023 🕐 Daily 10–7 🎫 Adult 100Kč, child (6–16) 50Kč (varies according to exhibition) 🚇 Staroměstská 🚊 Tram 17, 18 to Staroměstská or Karlovy lázně 🚆

RATINGS			
Cultural interest	●	●	●
Historic interest	●	●	● ●
Photo stops	●	●	● ●

TIP
● It's easy to be swept along by the crowd crossing the road on the way to Charles Bridge, so do watch out carefully and only cross at the green light.

Knights of the Cross Square is defined by three of the loveliest buildings in Prague: the Staroměstská mostecká věž (Old Town Bridge Tower), Kostel svatého Františka (Church of St. Francis) and Kostel svatého Salvátor (Church of St. Saviour). Everyone passes this way as they approach Karlův most (Charles Bridge) on their way from Staré Město to Malá Strana and the Castle, but few linger and take in the square's exquisite character, probably because of its position on a main north–south traffic route. The pedestrians heading for the bridge from Karlova street do not mix well with traffic appearing unexpectedly from an archway and only stopped intermittently by a red light. Having braved the awkward crossing, most people are glad to get on to the bridge as soon as possible. Those who pause to look around are well rewarded.

THE SQUARE
A good place to start is the cast-iron statue of Charles IV. Beyond it is a wonderful view across the Vltava towards Malá Strana and the Castle. The north side of the square is lined by the buildings of the monastery of the Křižovnici, the Knights of the Cross of the Red Star, an ancient charitable order. As well as the Kostel svatého Františka, a domed early baroque masterpiece by French architect Jean-Baptiste Mathey (c1630–c1695), the Knights own the Galerie Křižovníků, a basement gallery used for temporary exhibitions. There's also a weird subterranean, grotto-like chapel with stalactite décor, and steps leading down to a surviving arch of the Judith Bridge, the Romanesque forerunner of Charles Bridge. To the east is Kostel svatého Salvátor, part of the Klementinum, with fine roof sculpture by Jan Bendl (1620–80).

Loreta

The Loreta is an irresistible example of baroque extravagance, inside and out, featuring a bearded lady, smartly dressed skeletons and the legend of a flying house.

SEEING THE LORETA

The Loreto Shrine and its famous carillon attracts crowds of tourists today, just as it once drew throngs of pilgrims, and is one of the Castle district's most popular sights. Its light-hearted baroque façade, alive with statuary, makes a striking contrast to the great mass of the Černínský palác (Černín Palace) on the high terrace opposite. Beyond the façade are cloisters whose focal point is the *santa casa*, a supposed replica of the house of the Virgin Mary in the Holy Land. On the far side of the courtyard is one of the city's most sumptuous baroque places of worship, the Kostel Narození Páně (Church of the Nativity). There's more evidence of the shrine's great wealth in the Treasury, with its extraordinary precious objects.

HIGHLIGHTS

EXTERIOR

The main façade of the Loreto was completed in 1724 by Kilián Ignác Dientzenhofer. In front of it is a splendid line-up of cherubs, cheerful counterparts to the figures higher up of saints, angels and the Virgin herself. The dominant feature is the elegant, tall tower. The 27 bells of its carillon were cast in Holland in 1694; every hour they ring out a much-loved Czech hymn of praise to Mary *A Thousand Times we hail Thee!*, in a version orchestrated by the composer Antonin Dvořák (1841–1904). The carillon can also be programmed to play other tunes.

SANTA CASA

The *santa casa* was originally quite a plain little building, until it was given its elaborate coating of stucco relief panels, which tell the story of its origins. It was built and paid for in the late 1620s by Kateřina Lobkowicz, a particularly pious noblewoman, and several members of her family are buried beneath it. Lacking windows, the simple brick interior is intended to evoke the humble surroundings in which the Holy Family lived. Apart from fragments of wall-paintings, the altar with its limewood figure of the Virgin Mary is the only decorative feature.

RATINGS	
Cultural interest	◑ ◑ ◑ ◑
Historic interest	◑ ◑ ◑ ◑
Photo stops	◑ ◑ ◑ ◑

BASICS
✚ 56 B5 • Loretánské náměstí 7/100, Hradčany, Prague 1
☎ 220 516 740
◷ Tue–Sun 9–12.15, 1–4.30
⬥ Adult 90Kč, child (6–16) 70Kč
▤ Tram 22, 23 to Pohořelec
▣ Guidebook in English 70Kč
⊞ Small shop with souvenirs and devotional items
⋔

www.loreta.cz
History, description of the buildings and interiors, opening hours and advice for pilgrims.

COURTYARD

The *santa casa* originally stood on its own, but in the 1660s it was surrounded by cloisters, to which a second floor was added a century later. The richly decorated chapels include one with an ecstatic painting of St. Francis receiving the stigmata, but it is the chapel dedicated to Our Lady of Sorrows which attracts most attention. The statue of a bearded lady here is that of St. Starosta (or Wilgefortis). Betrothed by her pagan father to an unwanted suitor, this unfortunate young woman prayed that she might be made so ugly that he would refuse her. Overnight she grew a beard, whereupon her father had her crucified.

KOSTEL NAROZENÍ PÁNĚ

Built by the Dientzenhofers in the first decades of the 18th century, the Loreto's baroque Church of the Nativity is one of the best

preserved of its kind in Prague, with particularly gorgeous decoration. The baroque idea of the Mass as a dramatic spectacle is confirmed here by the presence of first-floor oratories for the nobility, the equivalent of a box in the theatre. Amid the opulence, a macabre note is struck by the fully clothed and masked skeletons of St. Felicissimus and St. Marcia, and by the figure of St. Agatha bearing her severed breasts on a platter.

TREASURY

The Loreto's Treasury, on the first floor of the cloisters, was regularly raided by impoverished Habsburgs, but still possesses some of the most flamboyant liturgical objects in existence, among them the fabulous monstrance known as the 'Prague Sun', which incorporates some of the six and a half thousand diamonds bequeathed to the Loreto in 1695 by Countess Eva Franziska Kolowrat, whose portrait is on prominent display.

BACKGROUND

The Loreto legend has the Virgin Mary's humble home being spirited away by angels from the Holy Land when it was threatened by the advance of Islam. The little house was borne over sea and land, eventually coming to earth at Loreto in Italy. The shrine built there was imitated all over Europe, particularly in the Czech lands, and its cult was vigorously promoted in the course of the Counter-Reformation. The Prague Loreto was very popular with the nouveau-riche Catholic nobility, who had benefited from the share-out of Protestant spoils after the Battle of the White Mountain in 1620, and who were anxious to demonstrate both their wealth and piety.

TIP

● Try to time your arrival to coincide with the playing of the carillon, on the hour, every hour.

The opulent interior of the Church of the Nativity (top).
A grand bell tower rises above the façade of the baroque Loreto Shrine (above).
Detail of one of the statues adorning the exterior of the Loreto Shrine (opposite middle).
Beautiful ceiling frescoes decorate the vaulted cloisters (opposite bottom)

A view of Malá Strana Square from St. Nicholas's tower

The Lobkowicz Palace in Malá Strana dates from 1703

MALOSTRANSKÉ NÁMĚSTÍ

Overlooked by the city's greatest baroque church, Malá Strana Square is the hub of the Lesser Town and a focal point on the route between the Old Town and the Castle.

✚ 56 D6 • Malostranské náměstí, Malá Strana, Prague 1
🚊 Tram 12, 20, 22, 23 to Malostranské náměstí

RATINGS	
Cultural interest	●●●●
Historic interest	●●●●
Photo stops	●●●●●

The cliff-like bulk of the Svatého Mikuláš (Church of St. Nicholas, ▷ 122–123) may dominate, but there's plenty more to see and explore in and around the square and its adjoining streets and lanes. It's here in the heart of Malá Strana (Lesser Town) that most visitors pause before tackling the steep climb up to the Castle, not least because of the temptation offered by the numerous bars, cafés and restaurants.

TIP

● The square offers exciting possibilities for taking photographs at all times of day and night. Floodlighting transforms the great presence of the Church of St. Nicholas, especially when framed by the square's arcades.

THE BUILDINGS

St. Nicholas divides the sloping square into an upper and a lower half, each lined by the palaces and patrician houses so characteristic of this part of town. Some are very old, but most were rebuilt or given new façades in baroque style in the late 17th and 18th centuries. The grandest of the aristocratic edifices is the Lichtenštejnský palác (Lichtenstein Palace), which takes up the whole of the western side of the square. Built on the orders of Karl von Lichtenstein (1569–1627), the Catholic convert who presided with great zeal over the trial and execution of the Protestant rebels in Old Town Square in 1621, it now houses the music faculty of the University. The Palác Smiřických, Jan Albrecht Smiřický's pistachio-painted residence (No. 18/6), stands next to the Šternberský palác (Sternberg Palace) on the north side of the square. Smiřický (1594–1618) was briefly considered as an alternative to the Habsburgs as the monarch of Bohemia, and it was from his palace that the conspirators set off to the Castle on their mission of defenestration in 1618 (▷ 29). Take time to admire the broad arcades of the burgher's houses along the south of the square, and peer into the entrance of No. 1/272, a fine example of an old-fashioned Prague *pavlač* (galleried courtyard); it has the enchanting name of U petržílka (Parsley House).

LOBKOVICKÝ PALÁC

✚ 56 C6 • Vlašská 19/347, Malá Strana, Prague 1 🚊 Tram 12, 20, 22, 23 to Malostranské náměstí

This splendid baroque structure, one of several Prague palaces bearing the Lobkowicz name, stands on sloping Vlašská street at the point where the road opens out onto a small square. Begun in 1703, it was based on Bernini's ambitious design for the Louvre in Paris which was never carried out, a circular central vestibule with curving wings. The architect was one of Prague's master builders of Italian origin, Giovanni Battisa Alliprandi. An additional floor was added in the 1760s. The palace has had many owners, from its princely builders to the Ministry of Education and Public Enlightenment of interwar Czechoslovakia. In 1971 it became the seat of the West German Embassy, and it was in this role that it saw the most dramatic events in its history. In the summer of 1989, heralding the fall of Communist regimes all over Europe, East German tourists in their hundreds abandoned their rickety Trabant cars in the surrounding streets and lanes and clambered over the railings in search of sanctuary. Chaotic scenes reigned, as the fugitives milled around in the ever more muddy gardens and diplomats struggled to attend to their various needs. Eventually the East German government was forced to agree to a humiliating compromise; their citizens were allowed to proceed to West Germany, the only condition being that their trains pass through East Germany on the way. A giant golden Trabant on legs stands in the garden (not open to the public, but visible through the railings on the far side of the palace) in memory of those days.

The fine interior of the Mucha Museum (top).
A sculpture gracing the outside of the museum (above)

MUCHOVO MUZEUM

**The life and work of art nouveau artist Alfons Mucha
is expertly presented in this compact and
well laid out museum.**

Born in Moravia, Alfons Mucha (1860–1939), whose artistic
career took off in Paris, is still assumed by some of his many
admirers to have been a Frenchman. His fame was assured
when, in 1895, he designed a poster advertising Sarah Bernhardt's
Gismonda, and his subsequent sensuous depictions of maidens
with long tresses and flowing gowns promoting everything from
champagne to cigarettes became part of everyone's idea of what art
nouveau was all about. Mucha was an idealist from the start, and
hoped art nouveau would break down the barriers between high art
and everyday design. He was also a deeply patriotic Czech and
earnest Slavophile, and in 1910, when the allure of Paris began
to fade, he returned to his native land. Here he worked on an
extraordinary variety of projects, from decorating the interiors of the
Obecní dům (Municipal House, ▷ 100–101) to designing stamps
and banknotes for the new Czechoslovak Republic and stained glass
for St. Vitus Cathedral. After a long life, Mucha met an inglorious end;
this proud Czech patriot was interrogated by the Gestapo in the early
days of the Occupation, and died shortly after his release.

MUSEUM EXHIBITS

Housed in the 18th-century Kaunický palác, the museum exhibits
include drawings, pastels, sculpture and fascinating Mucha
memorabilia, as well as paintings. The atmosphere of his Paris studio,
which he shared with Rodin and Gauguin, is re-created convincingly,
with even a photograph of the latter playing the harmonium in
nothing but his underwear. The core of Mucha's later work was the
Slav Epic, a cycle of 20 immense canvases depicting key episodes in
Czech and Slav history. The paintings were intended to be put on
permanent show in Prague, but they still languish in far-off Moravský
Krumlov in southern Moravia; the museum however shows an
excellent English-language film about them.

*Princess Hyacinth lithograph
(1911) by Alfons Mucha*

RATINGS	
Cultural interest	●●●○
Specialist shopping	●●●

BASICS
✚ 57 G6 • Kaunický palác, Panská 7, Nové Město, Prague 1
☎ 224 216 415
🕐 Mar–end Dec daily 10–6; Jan–end Feb daily 10–5
💰 Adult 120Kč, child (6–16) 60Kč
Ⓜ Můstek or Náměstí Republiky
🚊 Tram 3, 9, 14, 24 to Jindřišská
📚 Range of guidebooks
☛ Guided tours by prior arrangement: 500Kč (tel 224 216 415)
🛍 Shop with stylish, specially designed souvenirs and other material
🚻

www.mucha.cz
Information about the exhibitions,
shop, and Mucha's life.

MUZEUM HLAVNÍHO MĚSTA PRAHY

This surprisingly little-visited municipal museum has much of interest, including a unique model of historic Prague.

➕ 59 H5 • Na poříčí 52, Karlín, Prague 8 ☎ 224 816 772/3
⏰ Tue–Sun 9–6 (8pm 1st Thu in month) 🎟 Adult 80Kč, child (6–16) 40Kč 🚇 Florenc 🚊 Tram 8, 24 to Florenc 📕 Guidebook 35Kč 🎧 Supplement for guided tour in English: 100Kč 🛍 Limited range of museum-related items 🏛 www.muzeumprahy.cz (in Czech)

RATINGS	
Cultural interest	●●●●
Good for kids	●●●
Historic interest	●●●●

Marian Square is home to the art nouveau New Town Hall

Prague's City Museum occupies one of those ponderous neo-Renaissance palaces built to boost the municipal image in the late 19th century, of which the prime example is the Národní Muzeum (National Museum). Its dignity took a hard blow when it acquired the urban motorway as a close neighbour, and the proximity of Florenc bus station has not enhanced its setting. It attracts few visitors from abroad, despite housing rich collections, possibly of greater potential interest than those of the National Museum.

Old Town Square in winter *(1862) by Ferdinand Lepie*

THE EXHIBITS

Prague's history up to the end of the 18th century is evoked through paintings, drawings, sculpture, models, plans and objects of all kinds, some of them extremely high quality. More recent history is dealt with by temporary exhibitions. One of the prize exhibits of the permanent collection is the original lower dial of the Orloj (Astronomical Clock) on the Old Town Hall; painted by Josef Mánes in 1865, it shows in delightful detail the signs of the zodiac and peasants performing their seasonal tasks. But the real star of the show is the famous Langweil model of Prague, in Room 7. This huge model, 20sq m (215sq ft) in area, was constructed with obsessive attention to detail between 1826 and 1834 by Anton Langweil, a lithographer by trade. Made from card and paper at a scale of 1:148, it covers the whole of Staré Město (Old Town) and much of Malá Strana and Hradčany. It is so accurate that it has proved an invaluable tool in urban conservation and city planning, showing the city exactly as it was some two centuries ago. The riverbanks are still a working environment, with timber yards and rubbish tips rather than elgant promenades; the Marian column still stands in Staroměstské náměstí (Old Town Square); the Josefov has not yet been redeveloped; and St. Vitus Cathedral remains far from finished. In the end, however, what is most extraordinary about Langweil's labour of love is that it shows just how little Prague has changed compared with most capital cities.

MARIÁNSKÉ NÁMĚSTÍ

➕ 57 E6 • Mariánské náměstí, Staré Město, Prague 1 🚇 Staroměstská 🚊 Tram 17, 18 to Staroměstská

Marian Square is a pleasant breathing space among the streets and lanes of the Old Town. It is defined by the Klementinum to the west, the City Library to the north, and the Nová radnice (New Town Hall) to the east. Built in 1911, this rather austere-looking art nouveau structure is not the town hall of New Town, but a replacement for the historic municipal headquarters on Staroměstské náměstí (Old Town Square), now used only for ceremonial purposes. Its façade is adorned with symbolic sculptures, and it is flanked by two quite remarkable statues by Ladislav Šaloun (1870–1946); to the left is the Iron Man, patron of armourers, to the right, Rabbi Loew (▷ 29). The fountain to the south is presided over by a female figure representing the Vltava, known to everyone as Terezka.

MUCHOVO MUSEUM

See page 89.

MÜLLEROVA VILA

➕ 56 A5 • Nad Hradním vodojemem 14, Střešovice, Prague 6 ☎ 224 312 012 ⏰ Apr–end Oct Tue–Thu guided tours at 9, 11, 1, 3, 5; Nov–end Mar Tue–Thu tours at 10, noon, 2, 4. Tours must be booked ahead 🎟 Adult 300Kč, child (6–16) 200Kč (tour in English 100Kč per person supplement) 🚇 Hradčanská, then tram 🚊 Tram 1, 2, 18 to Ořechovka www.mullerovavila.cz

The villa was built for the wealthy Müller family in 1930 in the middle-class suburb of Ořechovka (Walnut Grove) and is a key building in the evolution of the Functionalist architectural style.

The riverside façade of the Smetana Museum

The stunning, galleried interior of the Museum of Music

Its designer was the Viennese architect Adolf Loos (1870–1933), famous for his uncompromising statement 'Ornament is Crime' and for his concept of the *Raumplan*, in which the internal spaces of a building flowed into one another in a non-traditional way. The box-like Müller Villa is certainly unconventional. The exterior is severe in the extreme, but the spatial austerity of the interior is relieved by the use of precious materials. The Communists packed the Müller family off into a corner of their residence, subdividing the rest into offices. Since 1990, this icon of interwar architecture has been faithfully restored at great cost.

MUZEUM BEDŘICHA SMETANY

☐ 57 E6 • Novotného lávka 1, Staré Město, Prague 1 ☎ 222 220 082 ⚫ Wed–Mon 10–12, 12.30–5 💷 Adult 50Kč, child (6–16) 30Kč ☐ Staroměstská ☐ Tram 17, 18 to Karlovy lázně or Staroměstská

The museum devoted to the memory of the great Czech composer Bedřich Smetana (1824–1884) is housed in a handsome neo-Renaissance building at the end of the Novotného lavká, the jetty running out into the Vltava just upstream of Karlův most (Charles Bridge). Given that the orchestral suite *Vltava* is probably his most popular work, it seems a suitable location, though the building itself began life as part of the municipal waterworks. It is decorated with bold sgraffito work depicting the defence of the bridge against the marauding Swedish army in the Thirty Years' War (1618–48). Inside, there are mementoes of the man who was in effect the founder of modern Czech orchestral music, and you can listen to extracts from his works.

MUZEUM HUDBY

The National Museum of Music, in the stimulating setting of a Malá Strana church, exhibits instruments and memorabilia that more than do justice to this most musical of nations.

☐ 57 D6 • Karmelitská 2/4, Malá Strana, Prague 1 ☎ 257 327 285 ⚫ Wed–Mon 10–6 💷 Adult 100Kč, child (6–16) 50Kč ☐ Tram 12, 20, 22, 23 to Hellichová 📖 Guidebook 75Kč 🏠 www.nm.cz

RATINGS				
Cultural interest	●	●	●	●
Good for kids	●	●	●	
Historic interest	●	●	●	●

TIP
● The concerts staged in the Museum of Music often feature a more challenging repertoire than other venues and are well worth seeing.

No visitor to Prague can remain unaware for long of the Czechs' love of music and their eagerness to share their musical heritage with everyone. Bands and solo artists play in the streets and squares, the sound of students practicing pours from open windows, and concerts seem to be staged in every available interior. The country's great composers are national heroes, their memories honoured not only in performance, but in museums such as the Vila Amerika (▷ 146) devoted to Dvořák. For many years the national museum of music lacked a suitable home, but since 2004 its collections have been displayed in the old Church of St. Mary Magdalene (Sv. Maří Magdaleny) in Malá Strana.

THE MUSEUM
The building has had a varied history. It was deconsecrated at the end of the 18th century, and served as a warehouse, military hospital, customs building and riding school before becoming the home of the state archives. After costly conversion, the nave now functions as a fine concert hall, overlooked by several floors of side galleries in which the collections are expertly displayed. Every conceivable type of instrument is on show, from violins once owned by virtuosos to some extremely odd-looking bagpipes, a Czech speciality. Even odder are the bulbous brass instruments arranged in artful patterns in their showcases. There are also musical clocks on display. Some of the exhibits can be brought to life by using the clever interactive facilities. A visit to this unusual museum can be great fun as well as a serious introduction to the long and glorious history of music and musicians in the Czech lands.

The Muzeum Kampa (above). Apple *(1965)* by Jiří Kolář (below)

There is plenty to see at the Public Transport Museum

MUZEUM KAMPA

In an immaculately restored historic mill, this very personal collection presents works by two of the most important Czech artists of the 20th century.

➕ 57 D6 • Muzeum Kampa Nadace Jana a Medy Mládkových, U Sovových mlýnů 503/2, Malá Strana, Prague 1 ☎ 257 286 147 🕙 Daily 10–6 💰 Adult 120Kč, child (6–16) 60Kč 🚋 Tram 12, 20, 22, 23 to Hellichova 🍴

RATINGS	
Cultural interest	● ● ● ●
Historic interest	● ● ●
Photo stops	● ● ● ●

TIP
● There are intriguing views out from many of the galleries, but for a wonderful panorama over this part of town, climb up to the tilted glass 'cube' at the top of the building.

The Sova Mill was probably the first of its kind in Prague, grinding corn for nearly a millennium and for centuries providing the Castle with flour. The present building, a stately neo-Tudor edifice, has been adapted to its new purpose, and occupies a splendid position on Kampa Island, overlooking the great diagonal weir just upstream from Karlův most.

THE COLLECTIONS

The starting point for this unique collection was the belief of Jan (1912–89) and Meda Mládek that a nation's survival depended on freedom of artistic expression. During a long exile in the West, they overcame many obstacles to build up a collection of work by artists unrecognized or persecuted by the Communist regimes of Central and Eastern Europe. In Paris in the 1950s, Meda Mládek got to know František Kupka (1871–1957), the Czech pioneer of abstract art, who had lived in France since 1896. At the time, Kupka was little known in his homeland, and Meda, certain that his stature would eventually be recognized, acquired some of his work, from early studies in pencil and watercolour, to his later, dazzling oils.

Kupka is complemented in this collection by a very different figure, Otto Gutfreund (1889–1927), perhaps the outstanding Czech sculptor of the 20th century. In his 20s, Gutfreund created a number of astonishing Cubist sculptures in bronze, the first of their kind. Examples here include the tortured bust of *Viki* and a striking *Don Quixote*. But after World War I, Gutfreund moved away from this kind of expressiveness to more sober social concerns, represented here by endearing figures (*Trade, Industry*) engaged in everyday activities. Kupka's period of creativity is traced in the museum, one of the high points being his *Warm Chromatics* of 1911–12. Among the many works by more recent artists, look out for the dysfunctional *Family* (1967) by Karel Nepraš.

MUZEUM LOUTKÁŘSKÝCH KULTUR

➕ 57 E6 • Karlova 12, Staré Město, Prague 1 ☎ 222 220 913 🕙 Daily noon–8pm 💰 Adult 50Kč, child free 🚇 Staroměstská 🚋 Tram 17, 18 to Staroměstská www.puppetart.com

The Puppet Museum is one of the few authentic attractions among the souvenir shops lining Karlova street. It's associated with UNIMA, the International Institute of Marionette Art, which runs courses in the making and use of marionettes. The Czech tradition in puppetry goes back to the Middle Ages, though its real flowering has occurred in more recent times. The marionettes on display here include most of the familiar figures of puppet theatre, including the popular horned and cloven-hoofed devils. A real puppet theatre is on display and there are live performances too.

MUZEUM MĚSTSKÉ HROMADNÉ DOPRAVY

➕ 56 B4 • Vozovna Střešovice, Patočkova 4, Střešovice, Prague 6 ☎ 233 322 432 🕙 Late Mar to mid-Sep Sat–Sun and holidays 9–5; groups by arrangement at other times (tel 296 124 905) 💰 Adult 25Kč, child (6–16) 10Kč 🚇 Hradčanská, then tram 🚋 Tram 1, 2, 15, 18, 25 to Vozovna Střešovice

The city's Public Transport Museum is housed in a historic depot in the suburb of Střešovice. As well as paying tribute to the tram, it has a selection of other veteran vehicles such as trolley-buses and Škoda motor buses. The earliest vehicle is an open horse-drawn tram of 1886, and there are curiosities like the Lord Mayor's personal tram, as well as plenty of public transport memorabilia such as maps and posters.

NA PŘÍKOPĚ

A popular, pedestrianized shopping street, Na příkopě (On the Moat) is a lively central boulevard with a unique museum.

Running between the Municipal House and the lower end of Václavské náměstí (Wenceslas Square), traffic-free Na příkopě is one of central Prague's busiest streets, with banks, entertainment venues and prestigious shops. Together with its continuation to the west, Národní, it runs along the line of the medieval moat that for centuries separated the Old and New Towns, and which was only finally done away with in the 18th century.

CZECHS AND GERMANS

Until their expulsion, Prague's Germans regarded Na příkopě as 'their' street; the famous Café Continental was located here, and No. 22/859, the Vernierovský palác (Vernier Palace), functioned as a kind of community centre, the 'Deutsches Casino'. The regular Sunday promenade was an important social occasion which sometimes got out of hand when fights broke out between rival German and Czech students. Reflecting the changing times, after 1945 the Vernier Palace became the Slovanský dům (Slavonic House), and has now been redeveloped as a shopping mall. In the late 19th century, the rising tide of Czech nationalism reached the street with the construction, in 1896, of the Živnostenská banka (Investment Bank) at No. 20/858, intended to counter German dominance of trade and industry. With an overload of statuary, paintings and stained glass, the pomp and circumstance of the bank's interior rivals that of the Národní Muzeum (National Museum). In a further grandiose gesture, it is linked to its neighbour on the far side of Nekázanka street by a version of Venice's Bridge of Sighs. Other nearby banks fail to rival this sort of flamboyance as most of them were built in art nouveau or Functionalist style.

IDEALS AND ACTUALITY

Perhaps the most distinguished building on Na příkopě is No. 10/852, the Palác Sylva-Taroucca, a splendid rococo palace built in 1751 by the prestigious partnership of Anselmo Lurago and Kilián Ignác Dientzenhofer. It is now home to an incongruous range of tenants, including McDonald's, a casino and, well worth the climb to the first floor, the Muzeum komunismu (Museum of Communism, ▷ 16). A private venture which has attracted much controversy, the museum contrasts Communism's Utopian dreams with the grim reality of empty shops, meaningless slogans and pervasive policing. An upbeat note is struck at the end, however, with a short film about the Velvet Revolution, which brought an end to the oppressive regime.

RATINGS	
Chainstore shopping	●●●●
Cultural interest	●●●
Historic interest	●●●

BASICS
✚ 57 F6
🚇 Můstek

Muzeum komunismu
☎ 224 212 966
🕐 Daily 9–9
🎫 Adult 180Kč, child free
www.museumofcommunism.com

A poster advertising the Museum of Communism (above), housed in the 18th-century Sylva-Taroucca Palace (top) on Na příkopě

RATINGS

Cultural interest	●●●●●
Historic interest	●●●●○
Photo stops	●●●●○

BASICS

✚ 57 E7 • Národní třída 2, Nové
Město, Prague 1

☎ 224 901 448

🕐 Box office: daily 10–6 (second box
office at Ovocný trh 6, Staré Město)

🎫 Tickets for performances from
100Kč–1,000Kč

Ⓜ Národní třída

🚊 Tram 6, 9, 17, 18, 21, 22, 23 to
Národní divadlo

📕 Box office: books, recordings, etc.

www.narodni-divadlo.cz
Details of upcoming performances,
seating charts and ticket information.

*The elaborate ceiling and gilded
upper tiers of the auditorium
(above) at the National Theatre.
Superb ceiling paintings adorn
the theatre's grand foyer (top)*

NÁRODNÍ DIVADLO

**The opulent National Theatre, a citadel of Czech
culture overlooking the Vltava, is one of the
city's landmark buildings.**

The National Theatre is the country's flagship for the performing arts,
presenting the best of opera, ballet and theatre. It was begun in 1868,
with the laying of foundation stones taken from sites of national
significance around the country and even from abroad; the émigré
community in Chicago sent their own stone with the inscription 'What
blood unites, the sea will not sunder.' The building of the theatre was
a milestone in the Czechs' struggle to promote their own culture; with
the Stavovské divadlo (Estates Theatre) guarding its largely Germanic
character, they had for too long lacked an adequate building in which
to stage drama and music. The government refused all aid, but
the people—rich and poor—dug deep into their pockets, and the
great building was inaugurated in June 1881 with a performance of
Smetana's patriotic opera *Libuše*. Weeks later, a fire caused by
careless workmen reduced the building to a shell. Undaunted, Czechs
all over the country again contributed and sufficient funds were soon
gathered for reconstruction to start. Somewhat shamed by their
previous stinginess, the imperial family made a donation and sent
Prince Rudolf to attend this second inauguration.

THE 'NATIONAL THEATRE GENERATION'

No expense was spared to make the National Theatre worthy of its
vocation. Its first architect Josef Zítek (1832–1909) was succeeded by
Josef Schultz (1840–1917), who oversaw rebuilding following the
fire. In a dignified neo-Renaissance style, the theatre was lavishly decorated by the country's leading artistic talents, who ever after were
known as the 'National Theatre Generation'. They included Bohuslav
Schnirch (chariots atop the pavilions flanking the main entrance), Josef
Myslbek (balustrade sculptures), Mikoláš Aleš and František Ženíšek
(lobby scenes inspired by Smetana's *Má vlast*), and Voytěch Hynais
(safety curtain painting). The words *Národ sobě* ('The Nation to Itself')
written over the proscenium arch evoke the theatre's noble aspirations.

THE 'NEW SCENE'

Stretching along Národní třída, a new auditorium (the 'Nová scéna')
and other facilities were added to the National Theatre in 1983. While
providing much useful space and a home for the Laterna magika
(▷ 178), their architecture failed to win general approval, the glazed
exterior having been compared unflatteringly with bubble-wrap.

NÁRODNÍ MUZEUM

Of greater interest for its extravagant architecture than for its collections, the majestic National Museum is the crowing feature of Václavské náměstí (Wenceslas Square).

The long façade of the National Museum, topped by a gilded dome and corner towers, spans a greater width than the broad boulevard which rises gently towards it. It is self-evidently the most important building in town, and probably the reason why a Russian soldier raked it with machine-gun fire in the course of the Soviet invasion of 1968. Although it houses the headquarters of the National Museum, it contains only a fraction of the institution's vast collections, and they aren't necessarily the ones of greatest interest to visitors. However, it is well worth a visit for the sumptuousness and sheer scale of its interior.

THE MUSEUM
The museum stands on the site of the old Horse Gate (Koňská brána), which disappeared when the fortifications surrounding Nové Město (New Town) were demolished in the 1870s. It was completed in 1891 and, along with the National Theatre, immediately became one of the great symbols of Czech nationhood. The patriotic theme is heralded by the fulsome female figures adorning the entrance fountain; they represent the country's two main rivers, the Vltava and Elbe, along with *Czechia* herself. Inside, the huge staircase hall is surpassed by the even vaster first-floor Pantheon, with an exquisite tiled floor, statues of Bohemian worthies and ponderous history paintings. There is no way that the collections could match this splendour, though the exhibits of insects in showcases at least as old as the museum itself have the faded charm of a real period piece. Those with an interest in geology, prehistory, numismatics, botany and zoology will find much to intrigue them, while others may be tempted by one of the—often fascinating—temporary exhibitions.

RATINGS
Cultural interest	● ● ●
Good for kids	● ● ●
Historic interest	● ● ● ●
Photo stops	● ● ● ●

BASICS
🚇 59 G7 • Václavské náměstí 68, Nové Město, Prague 1
☎ 224 497 111
🕐 May–end Sep daily 10–6; Oct–end Apr daily 9–5. Closed 1st Tue in month
💳 Adult 100Kč, child (6–16) 50Kč. Free 1st Mon in month
Ⓜ Muzeum
📖 Guidebooks in English to some museum departments such as natural history. Audioguide 200Kč
📷
🏪 Bookshop, giftshop, mineral specimens shop
👪

www.nm.cz
Information on temporary exhibitions and branch museums throughout the Czech Republic.

TIPS
● It's worth remembering that the National Museum is one of Prague's few attractions to open on Mondays.
● Children seem to enjoy the museum's vast spaces and endless staircases.

Visitors pause on the grand staircase to admire the lavish interior of the National Museum (top).
A large sculpture outside the museum depicting a mother and child (left)

RATINGS

Cultural interest	●●●●
Good for kids	●●●
Historic interest	●●●

BASICS

➕ 57 F4 • Kostelní 2, Holešovice, Prague 7

☎ 220 399 111

🕐 Tue–Fri 9–5, Sat–Sun and holidays 10–6

🎫 Adult 70Kč, child (6–16) 40Kč

🚇 Vltavská or Hradčanská, then tram

🚊 Tram 1, 8, 15, 25, 26 to Letenské náměstí

🎧 Audioguide: adult 120Kč, child 80Kč. Free guided tours by arrangement

🏛 Museum shop

www.ntm.cz
Basic details in English, plus information in Czech on the country's other technical museums.

TIP

● Continuing modernization and reconstruction means that sections of the museum may be closed at any given time. Check before visiting if there are particular exhibits you wish to see.

A group of children on a guided tour learning about the Tatra motor cars displayed in the main hall of the National Technical Museum (top)

NÁRODNÍ TECHNICKÉ MUZEUM

Prague's major museum of science and technology has an outstanding collection of road and rail vehicles.

Its location high up on Letná Plain seems to deter many from visiting the National Technical Museum, but it's not difficult to reach by public transport, and its rich collections relating to almost every aspect of science and technology are well worth investigating.

THE TRANSPORT HALL

The core of the museum is the great glass-roofed hangar housing transport exhibits, with aircraft dangling from above and the floor occupied by a fascinating collection of vehicles of all kinds. Before the break-up of the Habsburg Empire, the Czech lands were the most industrialized and technically advanced part of the monarchy. Railways reflected this, and there are some fine old steam locomotives on display, including a superb express engine No. 375007, built in Prague in 1911 to haul the Emperor Franz Josef's personal train. His opulent Imperial Saloon Car is here, as is the luxurious carriage used by his appointed heir, the ill-fated Archduke Franz Ferdinand. After 1918, the new Republic of Czechoslovakia emerged as one of the leading manufacturers of automobiles in Europe, producing vehicles like the stately Tatra used by President Masaryk. In complete contrast to this conventional saloon is the streamlined, air-cooled Tatra 77a of 1937, capable of 160kph (100mph) and much sought after by German officers during the Occupation. Škoda is well represented, with sporty coupés from the 1970s and '80s as reminders that not all excellence was lost under Communism. As well as cars, there are bicycles and motorbikes, while the aircraft include veterans of the early days of flight, as well as more recent machines. More planes can be seen at the Letecké muzeum (Aviation Museum, ▷ 85) at Kbely airfield.

FROM THE UNDERWORLD TO THE HEAVENS

The museum's main individual attraction is probably the elaborate mock-up of a coal and ore mine in the basement, which can only be visited by guided tour. Elsewhere there are fabulous collections of timepieces, cameras and projectors, an exhibition on acoustics and an astronomy section. Given the country's lack of a sea coast, the skies have always exerted a special attraction in this part of the world, and it's fascinating to see on display here some of the instruments used to explore the mysteries of the heavens by pioneers like astronomers Tycho Brahe (1546–1601) and Johannes Kepler (1571–1630).

NÁRODNÍ TŘÍDA

The bustling thoroughfare running from Václavské náměstí (Wenceslas Square) to the Národní divadlo (National Theatre) and the Vltava has some of the city's most striking early 20th-century structures.

RATINGS	
Chainstore shopping	● ● ● ●
Cultural interest	● ● ●
Historic interest	● ● ●
Photo stops	● ● ●

BASICS

✚ 57 E7 • Národní třída, Nové Město, Prague 1

🔲 Můstek or Národní třída

🚊 Tram 6, 9, 18, 21, 22, 23 to Národní třída

The boulevard known as Národní třída (National Avenue), like Na příkopě to the east, marks the line of the medieval walls and moat that used to separate the Old and New Towns. Unlike Na příkopě, it has not been pedestrianized, and with its trams and traffic has a very different character. In the late 19th and early 20th century, with Na příkopě appropriated by Prague's German community, the city's Czechs took over Národní třída, and it was here that their Sunday *korzo* took place. People no longer promenade here in quite the same way, but Národní remains one of the streets in which the everyday life of the city is seen at its most vital.

ARCHITECTURAL ODDITIES

From the foot of Wenceslas Square, access to Národní is along 28 října (28 October), a short stretch of traffic-free street. Alternatively, and more interestingly, walk through the little arcade of the Baťa shoe store to the square beyond and discover a real curiosity, the Cubist street lamp. This unique object in chiselled concrete dates from around 1912, and is proof of the ability of Czech artists and designers to turn the insights of Cubism to practical use. To the south of the square rises the formidable mass of one of Charles IV's great projects, the Panny Marie Sněžně (Church of Our Lady of the Snows, ▷ 104–105), while beyond the statue of Josef Jungmann (1773–1847), one of the leaders of the Czech National Revival, stands another hulk of a building, the Palác Adrie (Adria Palace) of 1924. This craggy edifice, decorated with socially aware sculpture, is the city's largest example of the short-lived architectural style known as Rondo-Cubism.

VIOLENCE AND VELVET

It was from the basement auditorium of the Adria Palace that Václav Havel and his fellow plotters directed the course of the Velvet Revolution in late November 1989. The spark that set off the revolution was the brutal breaking-up of a student demonstration by riot police a few days earlier, on 17 November. Though no-one in fact died, this violent episode soon became known as the *masakyr* (massacre); it is commemorated by a sculpture of praying hands in the arcade on the south side of the street. Further along, on the far side, buildings Nos. 7/1011 and 9/1010 are ornate examples of art nouveau office buildings.

A statue of Josef Jungmann, one of the leaders of the Czech National Revival, on Národní třída (above).
The striking Rondo-Cubist façade of the Adria Palace (top)

Charming pictorial sign on the façade of The Three Little Fiddles

Detail above the courtyard entrance, Náprstkovo muzeum

NERUDOVA

With a wealth of house signs on exquisite baroque and rococo façades, steep Nerudova is one of the city's most perfectly preserved old streets.

🏛 56 C6 • Malá Strana, Prague 1 🚊 Tram 12, 20, 22, 23 to Malostranské náměstí

RATINGS	
Cultural interest	● ● ●
Historic interest	● ● ●
Photo stops	● ● ● ●

TIP
● Souvenir shops have colonized this most popular route to the Castle. If you have time, it's worth comparing their prices with shops elsewhere in the city.

Named after the 19th-century writer Jan Neruda (1834–91), the 'Dickens of Malá Strana', this steep street forms the final stretch of the Royal Way leading up to the Castle. It's part of an ancient route which once linked the Strahov Gate (Strahovská brána) to the west with the river crossing. Traces of the houses that lined it in medieval times remain in the vaulted cellars beneath the present, mostly 18th-century buildings, which give the street its lovely, harmonious character. More than anywhere else in the city, the buildings have kept the intriguing pictorial signs which once served to identify them. At the beginning of the street, beyond the famous old corner pub U kocoura (The Tomcat), look out for No. 6, U červeného orla (Red Eagle); No. 12/210, U tří housliček (The Three Little Fiddles), once the home of a family of violin-makers, and No. 16/212, U zlaté číše (The Golden Goblet). Striking a more pretentious note than these relatively modest burghers' houses is a pair of fine palaces. The sturdy Moors holding up the balcony of the Morzinský palác (Morzin Palace) are a pun on the Morzin family name—they are the work of F. M. Brokoff (1688–1731)—while the eagles performing the same task on the Thun-Hohenštejnský palác (Thun-Hohenstein Palace) opposite were sculpted by Matthias Bernard Braun (1684–1738). Like many of Malá Strana's palaces, both are now embassies (Romanian and Italian respectively). Number 33, the Bretfeldský palác (Bretfeld Palace), is where Mozart is supposed to have met Casanova, at a glittering ball held by Baron Bretfeld. Facing it, the Exposice historických lékáren—historic pharmacy—at No. 32/219 (tel 257 531 502; Apr–end Sep Tue–Fri 12–6, Sat–Sun 10–6; Oct–end Mar Tue–Fri 11–5, Sat–Sun 10–5) has been beautifully restored by the National Museum. Further up, No. 47/233 U dvou slunců (The Two Suns), now a restaurant, was Neruda's birthplace. The street now widens out, giving a choice of routes; straight ahead are steps leading up to Hradčanské náměstí (Hradčany Square), while slightly to the left, Úvoz continues towards Strahov. Most people turn sharp right at this point, and take the route to the Castle.

MUZEUM POLICIE ČESKÉ REPUBLIKY

🏛 58 F9 • Ke Karlovu 453/1, Nové Město, Prague 2 ☎ 224 923 619, 224 922 183 🕐 Tue–Sun 10am–5pm 💰 Adult 20Kč, child (6–16) 10Kč 🚇 I.P. Pavlova 🚊 Tram 6, 11 to Pod Karlovem

Housed in a former convent, the Czech Republic's police museum in Communist times celebrated such achievements as the capture of dissidents attempting to flee the country. Today the emphasis is more on solving such crimes as burglary and traffic offences, and it has a number of mildly horrifying reconstructions of crime scenes. The convent is on the outermost edge of Charles IV's New Town, and it was the Emperor himself who ordered its construction. The interior of its octagonal church is worth looking at for its star-studded vault, a magnificent technical achievement of its time.

NÁPRSTKOVO MUZEUM

🏛 57 E6 • Betlémské náměstí 1, Staré Město, Prague 1 ☎ 224 497 500 🕐 Tue–Sun 9–5.30 💰 Adult 60Kč, child (6–16) 30Kč. Free 1st Fri in month 🚇 Národní třída 🚊 Tram 6, 9, 18, 21, 22, 23 to Národní třída www.aconet.cz

The Náprstek Museum of Ethnography gets its name from its founder, Vojta Náprstek (1826–94). This energetic gentleman, embraced the spirit of the age, promoting technical inventions and female emancipation, while exhibiting limitless enthusiasm for 'primitive' cultures. Having taken part in the failed revolution of 1848, he had to flee the country, but profited from his period of exile in the US and Britain by catching up with technological developments and the idea of the museum as an

The grave of author Franz Kafka in the New Jewish Cemetery

educational tool. The museum he established in the family brewery makes up in charm and quality for what it lacks in comprehensiveness. There are a number of fascinating objects from the native cultures of North and South America, Australasia and Oceania. Temporary exhibitions are often of very high quality too.

OBECNÍ DŮM

See pages 100–101.

OLŠANSKÉ HŘBITOVY

✚ Off map 59 K7
Olšany cemeteries
✉ Vinohradská 153/1835, Žižkov, Prague 3 ☎ 267 310 652
⏰ May–end Sep daily 8–7; Mar–end Apr, Oct daily 8–6; Nov–end Feb daily 8–5 🚇 Flora or Želivského 🚊 Tram 5, 10, 11, 16 to Olšanské hřbitovy
New Jewish Cemetery
✉ Izraelská 1, Žižkov, Prague 3
☎ 272 741 893 ⏰ Apr–end Sep Sun–Thu 9–5, Fri 9–1; Oct–end Mar Sun–Thu 9–4, Fri 9–1. Closed Jewish holidays 🚇 Želivského 🚊 Tram 5, 10, 11, 16 to Želivského

The beautiful, leafy Olšany cemeteries cover a vast area and are a place of pilgrimage for many visitors. First laid out for the victims of a great plague in the late 17th century, they consist of several distinct sections. Among the thousands of graves in the main cemetery, entered from Vinohradská, is that of tragic student Jan Palach (▷ 35). To the east, the military cemetery has the graves of the Red Army men who fell liberating the city in May 1945, as well as those of renegade Russian soldiers, who fought alongside the Nazis. Surprisingly, there is also a small British war cemetery. Further east still, the Nový židovský hřbitov (New Jewish Cemetery) is a poignant place. The most visited grave here is that of Franz Kafka (1883–1924).

A view down pretty Černínská lane in the Nový Svět area

NOVÝ SVĚT

The Castle District's most tranquil and picturesque quarter, the 'New World' seems lost in a dream of long ago.

✚ 56 B5 • Hradčany, Prague 1
🚇 Hradčanská, then tram
🚊 Tram 22, 23 to Brusnice

RATINGS	
Cultural interest	●●●
Historic interest	●●●
Photo stops	●●●●

Nový Svět (New World) is the name given to both the secluded, village-like area north of the Loreto and to its main thoroughfare, a straggling lane which once led from the Castle to the countryside, but whose course is now blocked by the massive remains of baroque fortifications. Nowadays, the area's charming old houses are much sought after, but in the distant past Nový Svět was something of a slum, where the Castle servants were squeezed into squalid lodgings.

THE QUARTER

Two lanes lead gently downhill into the area from the Loreto: to the west, Černínská has a mascot atop a wall in the shape of a cheerful little figure of St. John Nepomuk, while its most prominent resident is the surrealist artist and film-maker Jan Švankmajer; to the east, Kapucínská gets its name from the Capuchin monastery facing Loreto Square, but its most famous, or notorious, building is at No. 10, once the headquarters of Communist Czechoslovakia's counter-intelligence service. The monastery is home to a real curiosity, a crib or Nativity scene with life-size figures, well worth seeing if you are here at Christmas time. In Nový Svět itself, most of the brightly painted houses are on the south side of the street, facing the high wall opposite. As well as numbers, many of them have names, frequently featuring the word 'gold'; there's a Golden Star, a Golden Sun and a Golden Lamb. The Golden Pear (U zlaté hrušky) is a famous restaurant, while the Golden Griffin (U zlatého noha) at No. 1/76 was for a while the residence of Emperor Rudolf II's court astronomers, Tycho Brahe and Johannes Kepler (▷ 28). The Capuchins' bell-ringing so annoyed Tycho that he persuaded the emperor that the monks were planning his assassination; ordered to leave the country, the Capuchins nevertheless managed to postpone their expulsion indefinitely by buying off the emperor with a painting of the Three Wise Men.

THE SIGHTS

Obecní dům

The name 'Municipal House' hardly does justice to this resplendent palace of the people, the city's foremost example of art nouveau architecture and interior design.

SEEING THE OBECNÍ DŮM

The Municipal House has something for everyone, and even the most hurried visitor should sit for a while in the sumptuous surroundings of its café and absorb the atmosphere of the classic coffee house of long ago. A meal in the refined Francouská restaurace (▷ 234) is a gastronomic experience, while the basement Plzeňská restaurace (▷ 239) has a cheerful beer-hall atmosphere. Music lovers will want to attend a concert in the Smetanova síň (Smetana Hall), the home of the Prague Symphony Orchestra; it is here that the Prague Spring music festival is launched, with a rousing performance of Smetana's *Má vlast* (My Home). The building's designers paid great attention to its functional spaces and fittings, and it's worth admiring such features as stairways, elevators and even the cloakroom. If you have responded to the spirit of the building and its lavish décor, you should join a guided tour of the opulent Ceremonial Rooms.

HIGHLIGHTS

EXTRAVAGANT EXTERIOR

The sumptuously decorated, pale ochre façade and glazed copper dome of the Obecní dům contrast with the sombre stonework of its venerable neighbour, the Prašná brána (Powder Tower). Architects Antonín Balšánek (1865–1921) and Osvald Polívka (1859–1931) were responsible for the building's design and, just as the 'National Theatre Generation' had worked on that great monument a quarter of a century earlier, so many of Prague's foremost art nouveau artists and sculptors collaborated on the embellishment of the Municipal House. The portal gives a foretaste of the delights to come, with filigree metalwork, jewel-like encrustations, allegorical figures, stucco medallions and a mosaic, the *Apotheosis of Prague*, by Karel Špillar (1871–1939). The gilt inscription around it reads '*Hail to Thee, Prague! Stand steadfast against Time and Malice as you have withstood the storms of ages*', and is from a poem by Svatopluk Čech (1846–1908).

SUMPTUOUS SUITES

The core of the Municipal House is formed by the spacious Smetanova síň (Smetana Hall), used for all kinds of events as well as a concert auditorium. The great composer is honoured, not only by

TIP

● It's possible to get a photograph of the whole of the Obecní dům if you stand far enough away, but it's much more rewarding to concentrate on close-ups if you want to record the jewel-like character of this opulent building and its extravagant details.

having the hall named after him, but by sculptures to either side of the stage representing his compositions *Vyšehrad* and *Slavonic Dances*. Splendid though the Smetana Hall is, it is in the sequence of ceremonial rooms on the first floor that the building's décor reaches its lavish climax. As well as a number of halls, an appetizing *patîsserie*, a folksy Moravian-Slovak Saloon and an Oriental Room, there is a Primatorský sál, or Lord Mayor's Parlour; the artist responsible here was Alfons Mucha (1860–1939), who excelled himself not only with patriotic paintings, but with stylish lettering and stained glass. Even the curtains were stitched under his supervision. Mucha would have liked to play an even greater role in the decoration of the building, but professional jealousy on the part of his fellow artists kept his ambition in check.

BACKGROUND

By the end of the 19th century it had become obvious that the growing city needed a multi-purpose building that would also express its now predominantly Czech character. With the demolition of the old Royal Palace next to the Powder Tower at the eastern end of Na příkopě, an ideal site offered itself; resonant with history, it would also serve to remind Prague's German community that they could no longer regard this part of the city as exclusively theirs. The architects were commissioned in 1903, and the Municipal House was completed in 1911. The building's role as a national, as well as municipal symbol was confirmed on 28 October 1918, when Czechoslovakia's independence from Austria-Hungary was proclaimed here.

By the 1980s, the building's beauty had become faded and its technical facilities outdated. In 1997 it emerged in lavishly restored glory from a reconstruction process that had lasted three years and which some commentators denounced as insensitive and overdone.

Many art nouveau details (above) feature in the Obecní dům including stunning stained glass in the café (above left)

Petřín

Petřín Hill is Prague's loveliest park, its woods, orchards and open spaces rising from Malá Strana to the twin towers of Strahovský klášter (Strahov Monastery).

SEEING PETŘÍN

Petřín Hill features as a gorgeous green background to many a view of Prague. Made up of several once distinct parks and gardens, it offers superb viewpoints over the city, stiff climbs and descents, or easy, graded walks. Over it rises Prague's miniature rival to the Eiffel Tower, the Rozhledna. Near the foot of the tower is a distinctly odd combination of mirror maze and historic diorama, while immaculate rose gardens form a floral framework to the Štefánikova hvězdárna (Štefánik Observatory). Tucked away among the trees of the Kinského zahrada (Kinsky Garden), which forms the southern part of the hill, are pools, grottoes, statues and a real surprise—a timber church, brought here all the way from the far-off Carpathian mountains. The easy way up the hill is to take the *lanovka*, the funicular which climbs up from Újezd in Malá Strana to the observatory. On its way it stops close to Nebozízek (▷ 238), a famous panoramic restaurant, which, like its rival establishment, Petřínské terasy, is an excellent spot to pause during your exploration of this wonderfully varied park.

HIGHLIGHTS

PETŘÍNSKÁ ROZHLEDNA

✉ Petřínské sady, Malá Strana, Prague 1 ☎ 257 320 112 ◷ May–end Aug daily 10–10 (last entry 9.30pm); Apr, Sep daily 10–7; Oct daily 10–6; Nov–end Mar Sat–Sun 10–5 🎟 Adult 50Kč, child (6–16) 40Kč 🚊 Tram 12, 20, 22, 23 to Újezd, then *lanovka* to Petřín; www.prague-info.cz

Petřín Hill's Rozhledna (viewing tower) was built for Prague's great Jubilee Exhibition in 1891; its inspiration, the Eiffel Tower, had been much admired by a Czech delegation to the Paris Expo of 1889. With a viewing gallery 53m (170ft) from the base, it makes no attempt to compete with its French counterpart, though having been sited on top of a hill, it hardly needs to. It is claimed that on a clear day the view from the top extends from the Giant Mountains in northern Bohemia to the distant Alps.

BLUDIŠTĚ

✉ Petřínské sady, Malá Strana, Prague 1 ☎ 257 315 212 ◷ May–end Aug daily 10–10 (last entry 9.30pm); Apr, Sep daily 10–7; Oct daily 10–5; Nov–end Mar Sat–Sun 10–5 🎟 Adult 50Kč, child (6–16) 40Kč 🚊 Tram 12, 20, 22, 23 to Újezd, then *lanovka* to Petřín; www.prague-info.cz

The Bludiště (Mirror Maze), next to the tower, is housed in a weird mock-Gothic structure which began life as one of the pavilions in the Jubilee Exhibition. After all those years, its distorting mirrors still defy you to keep a straight face. In the same building, the diorama entitled *The Fight of the Praguers with the Swedes on Charles Bridge in 1648* is exactly what it says, a 19th-century version of virtual reality which attempts to bring this historic episode to life.

KINSKÉHO ZAHRADA

The southern part of Petřín Hill was purchased by the aristocratic Kinský family in the early 19th century and turned into an English-style landscaped park. This romantic spot, part of it quite overgrown, is entered from the main part of the hill through the Hladová zed'

RATINGS	
Cultural interest	● ● ●
Good for kids	● ● ●
Photo stops	● ● ● ●

BASICS
✛ 56 C7 • Malá Strana, Prague 1
🚊 Tram 22, 23 to Pohořelec (for Strahov); tram 12, 20, 22, 23 to Újezd (for *lanovka*)

TIP
● If you are approaching Petřín Hill from Malá Strana, make sure you have a look at the Obětem komunismu (Memorial to the Victims of Communism). The controversial monument is up the hill close to the Újezd tram stop.

The baroque Church of St. Lawrence and the Calvary Chapel on Petřín Hill (above)

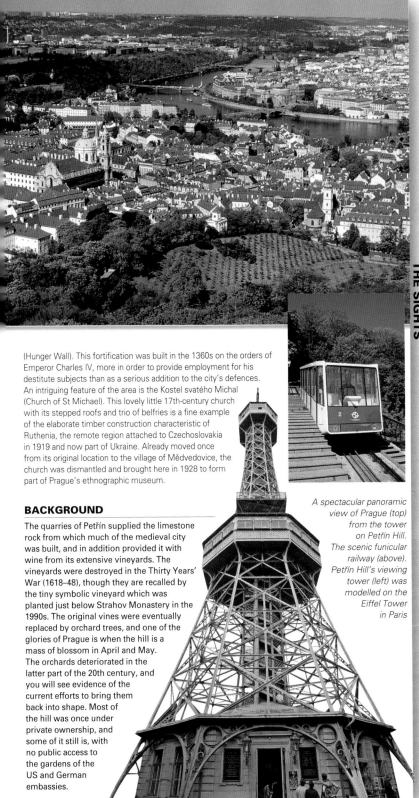

(Hunger Wall). This fortification was built in the 1360s on the orders of Emperor Charles IV, more in order to provide employment for his destitute subjects than as a serious addition to the city's defences. An intriguing feature of the area is the Kostel svatého Michal (Church of St Michael). This lovely little 17th-century church with its stepped roofs and trio of belfries is a fine example of the elaborate timber construction characteristic of Ruthenia, the remote region attached to Czechoslovakia in 1919 and now part of Ukraine. Already moved once from its original location to the village of Mĕdvedovice, the church was dismantled and brought here in 1928 to form part of Prague's ethnographic museum.

BACKGROUND

The quarries of Petřín supplied the limestone rock from which much of the medieval city was built, and in addition provided it with wine from its extensive vineyards. The vineyards were destroyed in the Thirty Years' War (1618–48), though they are recalled by the tiny symbolic vineyard which was planted just below Strahov Monastery in the 1990s. The original vines were eventually replaced by orchard trees, and one of the glories of Prague is when the hill is a mass of blossom in April and May. The orchards deteriorated in the latter part of the 20th century, and you will see evidence of the current efforts to bring them back into shape. Most of the hill was once under private ownership, and some of it still is, with no public access to the gardens of the US and German embassies.

A spectacular panoramic view of Prague (top) from the tower on Petřín Hill. The scenic funicular railway (above). Petřín Hill's viewing tower (left) was modelled on the Eiffel Tower in Paris

The twin towers of the Church of Our Lady beneath the Chain

Trees frame the tower of the Church of Our Lady of Victory

PANNY MARIE VÍTĚZNÉ

The Church of Our Lady of Victory welcomes pilgrims from all over the world, who come to venerate the wax figurine known as the *Bambino di Praga*.

✚ 56 D6 • Karmelitská 9, Malá Strana, Prague 1 ☎ 257 533 646 ◷ Church: Mon–Sat 8.30–6.30, Sun 9.30–8 (hours may vary). Museum: daily 10–5.30 🎟 Free 🚋 Tram 12, 20, 22, 23 to Hellichova or Malostranské náměstí 🏛 www.pragjesu.info

RATINGS	
Historic interest	● ● ●
Cultural interest	● ● ●

This church was completed in 1611 for a congregation of German Lutherans and was one of the first baroque places of worship to be built in Prague. Originally dedicated to the Holy Trinity, it was given its present name following the 1620 Battle of the White Mountain, when it was handed over to the Spanish Carmelite order. In 1628 the church was given the little figure of the infant Jesus, which subsequently became the focus of a widespread cult, particularly in Latin America. The *Bambino di Praga* (Little Child of Prague, ▷ above) presides over the church's dark interior, which, permeated with the atmosphere of intense Hispanic devotion, seems a world away from central Europe.

THE CHURCH

At Bílá hora (White Mountain) the Spanish troops, who made up a sizeable part of the Imperial army, were egged on against their Protestant opponents by a fiery sermon from a Carmelite fellow-countryman. Once Holy Trinity Church was in their hands, the Carmelites adapted it, constructing a cloister and removing the altar to the west end, thereby allowing a new façade to be built facing the street, which is still named after them (Karmelitská). The Carmelites enjoyed the patronage of Polyxena of Lobkowicz, an aristocratic lady with strong Catholic beliefs, who had given shelter to Vilém Slavata, one of the Imperial councillors ejected from the Castle windows in Prague's Second Defenestration (▷ 29). From her Spanish mother, Polyxena had inherited a little figure of the infant Jesus, a family heirloom made in Andalucia. In 1628 she presented it to the Carmelites, assuring them that it would protect them and their church. Miracles were soon reported, and the *Bambino di Praga* became known all over Catholic Europe and beyond. Set in a sumptuous silver casing in the north aisle of the church, and dressed in a variety of elaborate costumes, it has looked down on generations of admirers. A selection of the costumes can be seen in a little museum upstairs.

PANNY MARIE POD ŘETĚZEM

✚ 57 D6 • Velkopřevorské náměstí, Malá Strana, Prague 1 ☎ 257 530 876 ◷ Visits by advance arrangement. Mass: Sun 9am 🎟 Free 🚋 Tram 12, 20, 22, 23 to Malostranské náměstí or Hellichova

The Gothic Church of Our Lady beneath the Chain consists of two squat towers, a chancel and an open area where the nave should have been; it was never completed. The church belonged to the Knights of Malta, a Crusader Order. For centuries, the Knights ruled this part of town as a fully sovereign enclave; Maltézské náměstí (Maltese Square) is named after them, and the nearby Velkopřevorský palác is still the residence of their Grand Prior. It is one of several baroque palaces in the area. The finest is the Nostický palác (Nostic Palace), once the home of Count Franz Nostitz (1725–94), founder of the Estates Theatre, and now the Embassy of the Netherlands. Nearby is the graffiti-covered 'John Lennon Wall', where devotees of the former Beatle still pay their respects. In the 1980s, the wall was the scene of many a confrontation between the police and fans who renewed the bearded portrait of their hero each time it was erased.

PANNY MARIE SNĚŽNÉ

✚ 57 F7 • Jungmannovo náměstí 18, Nové Město, Prague 1 ☎ 224 490 350 ◷ Mon–Sat 9–5.15, Sun 12.30–5.15 (no visiting during Mass) 🎟 Free ◉ Můstek 🚋 Tram 6, 9, 18, 21, 22, 23 to Národní třída

The great Gothic Church of Our Lady of the Snows was intended by Emperor Charles IV to rival St. Vitus Cathedral and to dominate the skyline of the New Town. But

Mosaic of the Virgin with Child, Church of Our Lady of the Snows

An exhibit at the Postal Museum

The Powder Tower was once used as a gunpowder store

THE SIGHTS

the Hussite Troubles brought building to a stop, and only the chancel was completed. The best view of the exterior is from the Franciscans' Garden. The interior demonstrates both Gothic mastery of space and baroque determination not to be outdone; the huge black and gold high altar added in 1650 reaches up into the 30m-high (100ft) medieval vaults.

PETŘÍN

See pages 102–103.

POŠTOVNÍ MUZEUM

✚ 57 G5 • Nové mlýny 2, Nové Město, Prague 1 ☎ 222 312 006 🕒 Tue–Sun 9–12, 1–5 👜 Adult 25Kč, child (6–16) 10Kč 🚊 Tram 5, 8, 14 to Dlouhá třída
www.cpost.cz

In a little-visited corner of the New Town, the Postal Museum is housed in a 16th-century building that was once the home of a

rich miller. Its collections are vast and well organized. The emphasis is on stamps (▷ above) and other philatelic material from Czechoslovakia and its republics, but there are also stamps from many other countries. Even those without much interest in philately may be impressed by the stamps illustrating the often troubled course of Czech history and by the artistic talent which went into the design of many of them. During 1918 and 1919, the first Czechoslovak stamps were overprinted Austrian issues, giving the defunct Habsburg

Empire a short-lived afterlife; soon, artists like Alfons Mucha (1860–1939) were producing elaborate designs worthy of the new republic. These gave way during the Occupation to the German Führer. After 1948 the Communist regime celebrated its achievements with many a colourful stamp in Socialist Realist style. The upstairs rooms are used for changing exhibitions. In the mid-19th century, Václav Michalovic spent some of his fortune on having them decorated by the painter Josef Navrátil. There is a Green Room, an Alpine Room and a Theatre Room, with scenes from drama and opera and a self-portrait of the artist.

PRAŠNÁ BRÁNA

✚ 57 G6 • Náměstí Republiky/Na příkopě, Staré Město, Prague 1 ☎ 724 063 723 🕒 Apr–end Oct daily 10–6 👜 Adult 50Kč, child (6–16) 40Kč 🚇 Náměstí Republiky 🚊 Tram 5, 8, 14 to Náměstí Republiky
www.prague-info.cz

A distinctive Prague landmark, the famous Powder Tower stands guard over one of the eastern approaches to Staré Město (Old Town). It's well worth climbing to the gallery beneath the chisel-shaped roof for the view, with Celetná street guiding the eye over the rooftops towards Staroměstské náměstí (Old Town Square) and beyond to the Castle. The exhibition inside the tower, appropriately enough, is devoted to 'Prague Spires'.

The Powder Tower was built in 1475 as a ceremonial entrance to the Old Town. It occupied the site of one of the towers of the Old Town fortifications which, with the building of Nové Město (New Town) a century earlier, had become redundant. Its neighbour, where the Obecní

dům (Municipal House) now stands, was the royal palace, and the tower also served as a dignified starting point for the coronation procession along the Royal Way. It was unfinished when the court moved back to the Castle in the early 16th century, and for many years had only a temporary roof. For a while it was a gunpowder store—hence its name—and was badly damaged in the Prussian siege of 1757. In 1875 it was taken in hand by the conservation architect Josef Mocker (1835–99), who made it as good as, or even better than, new adding the chisel-shaped roof and a wealth of sculpture and other decoration.

PRAŽSKÝ HRAD

See pages 106–111.

RUDOLFINUM

✚ 57 E5 • Rudolfinum, Alšovo nábřeží 79/12, Staré Město, Prague 1 ☎ Gallery: 227 059 288 🕒 Gallery: Tue–Sun 10–6 👜 Gallery: adult 100Kč, under 15 free 🚇 Staroměstská 🚊 Tram 17, 18 to Staroměstská
www.galerierudolfinum.cz

The great neo-Renaissance Rudolfinum stands at the Old Town end of the Manesův most (Mánes Bridge). An art gallery as well as an outstanding concert venue—it's the home of the Czech Philharmonic—it was built in 1884, and given the full treatment in terms of ornamentation, with statues including lions, sphinxes and a procession of composers along the rooftop balustrade.

The Rudolfinum has two halls: the Dvořák Hall for orchestral music and the Suk Hall for chamber concerts. As a gallery, it has superlative top-lit exhibition rooms and is known for its promotion of contemporary international art.

Pražský hrad

Prague Castle, dominating the city from its rocky spur, has been the residence of princes, kings, emperors and presidents for more than 1,000 years.

BASICS

✚ 56 C5 • Informační středisko Pražského hradu, III nádvoří, Hradčany, Prague 1 (Castle Information Centre, Third Courtyard)

☎ 224 373 368, 224 372 434

⏰ Outside areas: Apr–end Oct daily 5am–midnight; Nov–end Mar daily 6am–11pm. Historical buildings: Apr–end Oct daily 9–5; Nov–end Mar daily 9–4. South Gardens: Apr–end Oct daily 10–6

💰 Outside areas: free. Tour A: Cathedral chancel, crypt and tower, Old Royal Palace, Story of the Castle exhibition, St. George's Basilica, Powder Tower, Golden Lane: adult 350Kč, child (6–16) 175Kč. Tour B: as for Tour A less Story of the Castle exhibition, Powder Tower, St. George's

continued on page 107

SEEING PRAŽSKÝ HRAD

Clustered within its walls are the great Gothic Cathedral of St. Vitus and the Romanesque Basilica of St. George, as well as museums, galleries, palaces, streets, squares and the tumble-down cottages of Zlatá ulička (Golden Lane). With so much to offer, the Castle presents a formidable challenge to visitors. Rather than joining the crowds toiling up the steep streets and steps leading from Malá Strana, you can take tram 22 or 23 to the Belvedér or Pražský hrad stops. Limit your first visit to a stroll through the courtyards and gardens, with perhaps a peep into the Cathedral and Golden Lane. Subsequent visits should include the lofty vaulted spaces of the Vladislavský sál (Vladislav Hall), while art enthusiasts will want to see the Renaissance and baroque treasures of Jiřský klášter (St. George's Convent), a separate institution which is part of the Národní Galerie (National Gallery, ▷ 72–73). There are some fine Old Master paintings in the Obrazárna (Castle Picture Gallery), and the temporary exhibitions staged in the Jízdárna (Riding School) are often well worth seeing. To get a sense of the deep roots of the Bohemian kingdom, spend time in the Cathedral with its crypt and its shrine to St. Wenceslas, then explore the labyrinthine substructure of the Starý královský palác (Old Royal Palace) with its enthralling displays on the Castle's long past. No visit is complete without enjoying the glorious prospect of Prague from the many viewpoints in and around the Castle; among the best are the Cathedral tower and the garland of gardens gracing the citadel's southern flank.

continued from page 106
Basilica: adult 220Kč, child (6–16) 110Kč. Tour C: Golden Lane and Daliborka tower only: 50Kč (free after 4pm in winter, 5pm in summer). Tour D: St. George's Basilica only: 50Kč

🚇 Malostranská, then steep walk via Staré zámecké schody (Old Castle Steps)

🚊 Tram 22, 23 to Pražský hrad

📖 Free leaflet with ticket; Prague Castle Hradčany guidebook, 350Kč

🎧 Guided tour in English (up to 5 people): 400Kč; 90Kč for each additional person. Audioguide: adult 250Kč, child (6–16) 200Kč

☕ Café in Lobkowicz Palace recommended

🍽 Lví dvůr restaurant opposite Riding School

🎁 Three well-stocked gift shops

👫

www.hrad.cz
Information on visiting the castle, its history, buildings and interiors.

www.story-castle.cz
Excellent summary in English of the Story of Prague Castle exhibition.

Looking across the River Vltava to the Castle District (top). Ornate iron railings line a curved staircase in St. George's Basilica (above left). A ceiling painting in the Chapel of the Holy Cross (opposite)

HIGHLIGHTS

CASTLE COURTYARDS

The western half of the Castle precinct is laid out around three court-yards, each with its distinct character. The První nádvoří (First Courtyard) serves as a grand entrance, its gates guarded by a pair of blue-uniformed soldiers and a brace of battling baroque giants above them. Crowds gather here at noon to watch the Ruritanian ceremony of Changing the Guard. The Druhé nádvoří (Second Courtyard) is reached through the Matyášova brána (Matthias Gate), a sandstone

structure of 1607 that serves to enliven the rather plain façades all around. The focal point here is a baroque fountain with the figure of Hercules. A passageway in the north wing (where the Castle Picture Gallery is) forms an alternative entrance to the Castle; beyond it, a bridge crosses the deep natural ravine known as the Jelení příkop (Stag Moat) towards the Riding School and Královská zahrada (Royal Garden; ▷ 84), while in the courtyard itself, the Kaple svatého Kříže (Chapel of the Holy Cross) houses a ticket office and one of the Castle's souvenir shops. The largest of the three, the Třetí nádvoří (Third Courtyard), serves mainly as a setting for the soaring architecture of the Cathedral, but it's worth paying attention to features like the granite obelisk, a memorial to the dead of World War I, and to the elegant statue of St. George and the Dragon. In the southeastern corner, close to the entrance to the Old Royal Palace, an unusual canopy covers the entrance to a spectacular stairway leading down to the Jižní zahrady (South Gardens). From the narrow lane to the north of the Cathedral, an opening leads to the fortifications and the massive Mihulka (Powder Tower), whose interior contains a variety of displays on military themes.

An equestrian statue in the largest of the Castle's three courtyards, the Třetí nádvoří

PRAGUE CASTLE OVERVIEW

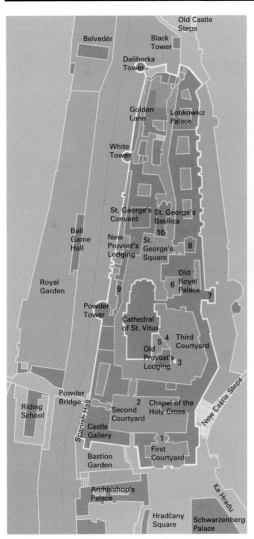

Attention! A guard standing outside his sentry box at Prague Castle (above). A bird's-eye view of the Castle complex (right)

KEY TO THE PLAN

1. Matthias Gate
2. Fountain
3. Obelisk
4. St. George
5. Romanesque remains
6. Palace Courtyard
7. Louis Wing
8. All Saints Chapel
9. Old Deanery (Mladota House)
10. Chapel of St. John of Nepomuk

The outstanding late-Gothic vaulted ceiling of the Vladislav Hall in the Old Royal Palace

STARÝ KRÁLOVSKÝ PALÁC

The Old Royal Palace contains a number of historic interiors, all of interest, but none with the impact of the Vladislavský sál (Vladislav Hall), perhaps the most extraordinary interior in Prague. At 62m (203ft) long and 16m (52ft) across, with delicate late-Gothic vaulting spiralling effortlessly upwards, it is the masterpiece of Castle architect Benedikt Ried (c1454–1534), who completed it in 1502. In the past the Hall was used on festive occasions, including tournaments; horsemen were able to spur their steeds up into the hall via the so-called Riders' Staircase, with its striking vault by Ried. Nowadays the hall really only comes into its own when the country's president is ceremonially sworn in. In one of the adjacent rooms is the window from which angry Protestant noblemen ejected the Emperor's Catholic councillors in Prague's most famous act of defenestration in 1618 (▷ 29).

Beneath the hall is a warren of chambers, corridors and other spaces from earlier phases of the Castle's construction. Long neglected, since 2002 they have housed an extensive and well-presented exhibition entitled 'The Story of Prague Castle'. Models, touch screens, arms and armour, artworks of all kinds and precious

The ceiling of the New Appeal Court in the Old Royal Palace is decorated with vibrant crests (right)

Detail of the decorative rib vaults on the ceiling of the Bohemian Chancellery in the Old Royal Palace (above)

A wall painting, surrounded by a stucco frame, in the Bohemian Chancellery of the Old Royal Palace (above)

objects such as the burial jewels of Bohemian rulers come together to give a lively account of the long evolution of the great citadel and of the fortunes of its inhabitants. There's a film in English and even a 'Castle Game' for children.

BAZILIKA SVATÉHO JIŘÍ
To the east of the Cathedral, Jiřské náměstí (St. George's Square) owes its name to St. George's Basilica and the adjoining Jiřský klášter (St. George's Convent), now the home of the National Gallery's superb collections of Renaissance and baroque art. Originally founded in the early 10th century, the basilica owes most of its present appearance to mid-12th-century rebuilding, though its main, red façade is a baroque addition, topped by landmark towers in pale limestone. The austere interior of the most important Romanesque edifice in the whole of Bohemia is a fine setting for concerts and a fascinating contrast to the Gothic complexity of the Cathedral.

LOBKOVICKÝ PALÁC AND MUZEUM HRAČEK
Lobkovický palác ✉ Jiřská 3, Hradčany, Prague 1 ☎ 257 535 121 🕐 Tue–Sun 9–5 💺 Adult 40Kč; child (6–16) 20Kč. Free 1st Wed of month; www.nm.cz
Muzeum hraček ✉ Jiřská 6, Hradčany, Prague 1 ☎ 224 372 294 🕐 Daily 9.30–5.30 💺 Adult 60Kč; child (6–16) 30Kč; www.muzeumhracek.cz
In the street descending towards the Černá věž (Black Tower) at the eastern end of the Castle are the Lobkovický palác (Lobkowicz Palace, ▷ 88) on the right, with the rather tired displays of the History

Museum, and the considerably more popular Muzeum hraček (Toy Museum) on the left. The Lobkowicz Palace has the Castle area's most inviting place of refreshment, a café serving tasty snacks.

ZLATÁ ULIČKA

Picturesque Golden Lane with its brightly painted 'alchemists' cottages' is the great attraction of the eastern part of the Castle precinct. Legend has it that the cobbled lane owes its name to the odd mixture of scientists and adventurers employed by Emperor Rudolf II to turn base metal into gold. But it's more likely that the name refers to goldsmiths who set up business here away from the rules and regulations of the city guilds. Franz Kafka found the lane's rather spooky atmosphere congenial, and spent many a night at No. 22 writing his short stories. Nowadays the little buildings house a range of superior souvenir shops.

Legendary Golden Lane with its brightly painted cottages

The baroque façade of St. George's Basilica

Strolling through the Castle Gardens on a sunny day

JIŽNÍ ZAHRADY

Running the whole length of the Castle's southern front and offering glorious views are the South Gardens, making a wonderful contrast to the sombre architecture and enclosed spaces of the rest of the complex. They were begun by Archduke Ferdinand in the mid-16th century, but their present appearance is largely the work of the early 20th-century Slovenian architect Josip Plečnik. He was President Masaryk's inspired choice as the right man to restore the run-down Castle and make it a suitable symbol for the new, democratic republic of Czechoslovakia, founded in 1918. Under the Communist regime the gardens were normally closed to the public, but one of the first acts of President Havel after 1989 was to order them to be opened. Entry is from either end, but the most dramatic approach is via the staircase leading down from the Third Courtyard. Features to note include the massive granite bowl placed as a (feminine) counterpart to the (masculine) monolith in the courtyard above, and the sandstone columns marking the spot where the defenestrated councillors of 1618 had their fall broken by a providential dungheap.

BACKGROUND

Not all the rulers of the Czech lands have lived in the Castle since the site was first fortified by Prince Bořivoj in the late 9th century. Some preferred the Vyšehrad rock and, while Emperor Charles IV built himself a sumptuous Gothic palace here, his son Václav IV preferred to reside downtown, where the present Obecní dům (Municipal House) now stands. Fear of the city mob drove subsequent rulers back to the easily defended hilltop, which Rudolf II converted from a fortress into a great centre of art and learning. Later Habsburgs abandoned Prague for Vienna, and the Castle was left to moulder away gently, its focal point the uncompleted Cathedral. The blank façades and countless identical windows added in the 18th century seemed an appropriate metaphor for the remote rule first of the Habsburgs, and later of the Communist regime. After the Velvet Revolution, President Havel strove to make the Castle a more welcoming place for citizens and visitors alike.

TIPS
- The best time to see the Changing of the Guard at the Castle gate is at midday, when there's a musical accompaniment, with buglers and trumpeters blowing a fanfare from the windows above. The guardsmen's bright uniforms are the work of Theodor Pištěk, the costume designer for the film *Amadeus* (1984).
- If you're not deterred by steep flights of steps, take the unusual way up to Hradčany from Malá Strana via the terraces of the Zahrady pod Pražským hradem (Gardens beneath Prague Castle, ▷ 146).
- The 'Castle Game' for children is fun as well as enlightening, and is highly recommended. It's also available on DVD. Adults will find it worthwhile to attend a screening of the English-language film about the Castle in an auditorium just off the Riders' Staircase.

Staroměstské náměstí

Merchants' houses, two great churches and the tall tower of the Old Town Hall, with its Astronomical clock, preside over this theatrical space, the stage for many a historic drama.

BASICS

➕ 57 F6 • Staré Město, Prague 1
🚇 Staroměstská, Můstek, Náměstí Republiky
🚋 Tram 17, 18 to Staroměstská

TIP

● The Old Town Square recaptures something of its medieval atmosphere as a trading place in the days before 25 December, when it is the site of a lively Christmas market (▷ 190).

Taking a break in a pavement café with a fantastic view of the Astronomical Clock on Old Town Square (above). A close-up of the upper face of the Astronomical Clock (opposite)

SEEING STAROMĚSTSKÉ NÁMĚSTÍ

Old Town Square is where Prague's ancient heart beats most strongly. It's the city's foremost meeting place, fed with streams of pedestrians from the converging streets and alleyways. The square attracts its largest crowd when the Orloj (Astronomical Clock) marks the passing hours. There's plenty of space for milling about and any number of places to eat and drink, inside and out. The Staroměstská radnice (Old Town Hall), made up of a picturesque conglomeration of buildings, now only has a ceremonial role, though it is also a fine home for the city's central tourist information office. From the Old Town Hall tower there is a dizzying view of the bustling activity in the square and an incomparable panorama over the Old Town's sea of red-tiled rooftops.

HIGHLIGHTS

STAROMĚSTSKÁ RADNICE

✉ Staroměstské náměstí 1 ☎ 224 482 751 🕐 Apr–end Oct Tue–Sun 9–6, Mon 11–6; Nov–end Mar Tue–Sun 9–5 💷 Adult 50Kč, child (6–16) 40Kč. Tower: adult 50Kč, child (6–16) 40Kč

The Town Hall of the Old Town consists of a rather random collection of buildings acquired at various dates from the early 13th century onwards. One of its most venerable features is the Gothic chapel on the first floor at the eastern end of the building; in the paving beneath its lovely oriel window are 27 crosses commemorating the rebel noblemen and burghers executed here in 1621. The Town Hall's main entrance is a richly carved, late Gothic doorway; the equally ornate Renaissance window to the west bears the inscription *Praga caput regni* (Prague, capital of the kingdom). Further west still, the beautifully sgraffitoed Dům U Minuty (Minute House) was lived in briefly by the Kafka family. Inside the Town Hall, the ceremonial rooms are worth inspection, but the real treat is the view from the tower.

ORLOJ

One of the most familiar symbols of 'magic Prague', the Astronomical Clock has three hands which tell not only the time in different ways, but also show the position of sun, moon and stars. It was first installed at the start of the 15th century, and the clock and its mechanism were steadily improved, most notably by Master Hanuš towards the end of the century. Legend has it that the city council had Hanuš's eyes put out to stop him ever passing on the secrets of his art; his revenge was to plunge his arm into the mechanism and immobilize it indefinitely. The lower dial, a 19th-century addition, shows the signs of the Zodiac and the labours of the seasons. As the hour strikes, the famous carved characters begin their shaky progress; the Apostles are accompanied by figures of a Turk, a Jew and Vanity, and by Death, waggling his hourglass. Finally a cockerel crows to bring the show to an end.

POMNÍK JANA HUSA (JAN HUS MEMORIAL)

The elaborate art nouveau Hus Memorial, a monument to the great reformist preacher and martyr Jan Hus, is the work of Ladislav Šaloun.

Crowds gathering in front of the Astronomical Clock on Old Town Square, with the twin towers of the Church of Our Lady before Týn dominating the skyline beyond (above). A local art student works on a water-colour painting of the Old Town Square (below)

It took 13 years to complete and was unveiled in 1915. The tall, spare figure of Hus gazes prophet-like into the distance, while beneath him are dynamically sculpted figures symbolizing the tribulations of his fellow countrymen and their eventual emancipation. The stylized inscription along the base of the memorial includes his terse pronouncement *Pravda vítězí* (Truth shall prevail), a comforting slogan much repeated by Czechs in difficult times.

CHRÁM MATKY BOŽÍ PŘED TÝNEM

✉ Staroměstské náměstí 14 ☎ 222 318 186 🕐 Doors open 30 min before services at 6pm (Wed, Thu, Fri), 8am (Sat), 9.30am, 9pm (Sun). Also Jul–end Aug 9–12, 1–2pm; other opening times possible 🎟 Free

The Gothic Church of Our Lady before Týn (Týn Church), with its formidable array of steeples and spiky belfries, is an inescapable presence in the square. It retains its lofty Gothic interior, though much of its furnishing dates from the baroque era. The most intriguing tomb is that of astronomer Tycho Brahe (1546–1601), clearly showing the artificial nose replacing the one sliced off in a duel (▷ 29).

HOUSES AND PALACES

Dům U kamenného zvonu ✉ Staroměstské náměstí 13 ☎ 224 827 526, 222 327 677 🕐 Tue–Sun 10–6 during temporary exhibitions 🎟 Adult 100Kč, child (6–16) 50Kč to temporary exhibitions; www.citygalleryprague.cz

Palác Kinských ✉ Staroměstské náměstí 12 ☎ 224 810 758 🕐 Tue–Sun 10–6 🎟 Adult 100Kč, child (6–16) 50Kč (long-term and temporary exhibitions). Free 1st Wed of month 3–8pm; www.ngprague.cz

Lining the south side of the square are the brightly painted façades of some of Prague's grandest town mansions, bearing names like U zlatého jednorožce (Golden Unicorn) and U kamenného beránka (Stone Lamb). The imposing Storchův dům (Štorch House) has a bold 19th-century fresco depicting St. Wenceslas, but the most fascinating buildings are perhaps those on the eastern side of the square. Beyond the rounded gables of the Týnská škola (Týn School), the chisel-roofed Dům

U kamenného zvonu (Stone Bell House) is a late 13th-century Gothic palace, whose true nature lay concealed until the 1970s beneath a baroque façade. It makes a fine home for temporary exhibitions staged by the City Gallery. Also used for long-term and temporary exhibitions (by the National Gallery), its neighbour, the Palác Kinských (Kinský Palace), is one of the city's loveliest rococo buildings. It has more than its fair share of Kafka associations; his father's haberdashery was on the ground floor, the family flat was on the first floor, and elsewhere in the building was the German grammar school attended by young Franz. On a freezing, fateful morning in February 1948, Communist leader Klement Gottwald stood on the palace balcony to proclaim the triumph of his *coup d'état* to thousands of supporters crammed into the snowbound square.

The baroque Church of St. Nicholas (below left) was built in 1735.
Beautiful sgraffito decoration on the façade of the Minute House (below middle).
The Jan Hus Memorial standing in front of the rococo Kinský Palace (below right)

KOSTEL SVATÉHO MIKULÁŠ

 Staroměstské náměstí 27a
☎ 224 190 991 ◷ Tue–Sat 10–4, Sun 12–3

Gleaming white, Prague's second great baroque church dedicated to St. Nicholas stands in a dominant position at the northwestern edge of the square. With twin towers and a dome, it's a masterpiece by Kilián Ignác Dientzenhofer (1689–1751), ingeniously designed to fit into what was then an awkwardly shaped space facing a narrow street. The demolition of part of the north side of the square to make Pařížská street around 1900, and the destruction of the north wing of the Town Hall in 1945, gave it a prominence Dientzenhofer never allowed for.

BACKGROUND

Originally a marketplace, the Old Town Square has also been the setting for many a symbolic moment in Bohemian history. In 1437, dozens of Hussite heretics were hanged here. Following their victory in the Battle of White Mountain in 1620, the Catholics took their revenge on their Protestant opponents, beheading the noblemen and hanging the commoners. In 1650, Catholic supremacy was commemorated with the erection of a column to the Virgin Mary Victorious. For three years, the Marian column stood in uneasy proximity to the Pomník Jana Husa (Jan Hus Memorial), before being torn down by a nationalist mob in 1918, who regarded it as a symbol of Austrian rule. In May 1945, the 19th-century north wing of the Town Hall fell victim to German gunfire, destroying the archi-tectural unity of the square and leaving a gap that has never been filled.

Stone Bell House (below) dates from the late 13th century

The elegant Ministry of Commerce building (below), on Old Town Square

Šternberský palác

The 18th-century baroque Sternberg Palace dazzles with the National Gallery's impressive collections of Old Masters and European art.

The entrance to the Sternberg Palace (above left).
Admiring the works of art on display (above right and below left)

SEEING THE ŠTERNBERSKÝ PALÁC

With a modest, easily missed entrance, the Sternberg Palace stands next to the far more flamboyant Arcibiskupský palác (Archbishop's Palace) on Hradčany Square. Beyond the archway, a cobbled passageway leads down to the 18th-century palace itself, an ambitious building worthy of a more prominent setting. Some of its rooms retain their original décor, but the point in coming here is not the architecture or the interior design, but the collection of Old Masters from European countries other than Bohemia ('Old Bohemian Art' is shown in St. George's Convent and St. Agnes' Convent). Although the scope of the gallery is wide-ranging, and there are some real treasures, it cannot be said to rank with Paris's Louvre or London's National Gallery. Many major names are represented with minor works, and the gallery has suffered a number of losses as paintings have been returned to the owners from whom they were confiscated in Communist times. Nevertheless, there is enough here to keep any art lover busy for the better part of a day, though it is probably best to concentrate on the relatively small number of outstanding works.

RATINGS
Cultural interest   ● ● ● ●
Historic interest   ● ● ●

BASICS
✚ 56 C5 • Hradčanské náměstí 15, Hradčany, Prague 1
☎ 233 090 570
🕐 Tue–Sun 10–6
💲 Adult 150Kč, child (6–16) 70Kč
🚋 Tram 22, 23 to Pražský hrad
📖 Art books and souvenirs
🎧 Guided tour by prior arrangement; price by agreement (tel 220 514 598)
☕ Attractive courtyard café
🏪 Gallery shop
🚻

www.ngprague.cz
The National gallery's website with general information in English.

HIGHLIGHTS
GERMAN PAINTING
The German and Austrian Renaissance painting displayed on the ground floor forms the heart of the collection. Among several pictures by Lucas Cranach the Elder (1452–1553) are parts of an altarpiece removed by Protestants from St. Vitus Cathedral in 1619, a superb *Adam and Eve*, and an exceptionally foolish *Old Man* blissfully unaware that his young female companion is less interested in his person than in her purse. The brutality of the age is conveyed by several paintings of martyrdoms, though the *Beheading of St. Dorothy* by Hans Baldung (called Grien; c1485–1545) shows the saint awaiting her horrible fate with equanimity. The gallery's most celebrated work by a German painter is the *Feast of the Rose Garlands* by Albrecht Dürer (1471–1528). Commissioned in 1506 for the German church in Venice, the crowded canvas shows the Virgin Mary crowning Emperor

Maximilian. The picture became a must-have item for passionate collector Rudolf II, who had it wrapped in carpets and borne over the Alps by four strong men. It is one of the very few paintings from Rudolf's famous collection to have remained in Prague.

FLEMISH AND DUTCH PAINTING

The quality of the paintings from the Netherlands shown on the first floor is a reminder that at one time the Habsburg Empire included not only Bohemia, but also the Low Countries, and that its rulers were well aware of their province's artistic riches. Among the earliest pictures on show here are a *Lamentation* by Dieric Bouts (c1415–1475) and *St. Luke Drawing the Virgin Mary* by Jan Gossaert (c1475–c1533), a wonderful exercise in complex architectural geometry. Later works include *St Bruno* by Van Dyck (1599–1641), a portrait of an arrogant-

looking *Jasper Schade van Westrum* by Frans Hals (c1581–1666), and several works by Rubens. Rembrandt (1606–69) is represented by his superb *Scholar in his Study*.

Studying Albrecht Dürer's *Feast of the Rose Garlands* (above), commissioned in 1506 for the German church in Venice

BACKGROUND

Begun in 1698, the palace bears the name of Count Wenzel Adalbert Sternberg (Václav Vojtěch Šternberk in Czech), supposedly the richest man in Prague. His great wealth had previously allowed him to build the huge palace at Troja (▷ 130–131). A relatively modest residence by comparison, the Šternberg Palace was completed in 1708 by Italian architect Giovanni Battista Alliprandi. Towards the end of the 18th century, a later Sternberg, Count Franz Josef, was instrumental in founding the Patriotic Association of the Friends of Art, whose collections were housed for a short while in the palace. They returned here only when the building was taken over by the National Gallery in 1946. In 1995, the Gallery's superlative collection of modern European art was moved from its cramped quarters here to the Veletržní palác (Trade Fair Palace, ▷ 139–141), then in 2003 a thorough restoration of the Sternberg Palace was completed, greatly improving the conditions in which the collection is shown.

TIP
● Make sure you see the 'Antique Cabinet' on the second floor; it has preserved its original décor of 1707 featuring a star—a play on the name Sternberg (*Stern* is German for star).

Strahovský klášter

Visible from all over the city, the twin towers of Strahov Monastery on top of Petřín Hill are an enticing landmark. The treasures within the monastery precincts include historic libraries of the utmost magnificence.

RATINGS

Cultural interest	●●●●
Historic interest	●●●
Photo stops	●●●●

BASICS

✚ 56 B6 • Strahovské nádvoří 1/132, Hradčany, Prague 1

☎ 233 107 718; picture gallery 233 107 722

🕐 Libraries: daily 9–12, 1–5. Picture gallery: Tue–Sun 9–12, 12.30–5

💷 Libraries: adult 80Kč, child (6–16) 50Kč. Picture gallery: adult 50Kč, child (6–16) 20Kč

🚋 Tram 22, 23 to Pohořelec

📖 Guidebook to libraries in English, 40Kč

🍴 Monastic restaurant and brewery; Oživlé dřevo restaurant on monastery terrace

♿

www.strahovskyklaster.cz
Extensive website with information on the history of the monastery, visiting conditions and details of libraries.

The grand entrance to Strahov Monastery (above).
A superb fresco decorating the ceiling of the former abbot's dining room at Strahov Monastery (above right)

SEEING STRAHOVSKÝ KLÁŠTER

The extensive monastery complex stretches westward from the clifflike slope at the top of Petřín Hill. Laid out around a rambling, cobbled courtyard, it has places to eat as well as museums, monastic quarters, churches, an art gallery and the two great libraries which constitute its greatest attraction. The main entrance is at the upper, western end of the courtyard, but there is also access from Petřín Hill and via steps leading up through a tunnel from Pohořelec Square. Of the museums, the Památník národního písemnictví (Museum of National Literature) is really only of interest to Czech speakers, though the Muzeum miniatur (Museum of Miniatures), with its collection of microscopic curiosities, may have wider appeal. The little Renaissance Kaple svatého Rocha (Chapel of St. Roch) at the main entrance is now an art gallery staging temporary exhibitions. The superb main church of the monastery is open only for services, but there is a view of the interior from the porch. The Strahovská obrazárna (Strahov Picture Gallery) has a number of masterpieces among its collection of paintings, prints, drawings and other artworks, but a visit here is probably only a priority for committed art-lovers.

HIGHLIGHTS

NANEBEVZETÍ PANNY MARIE
Although its stonework dates from Romanesque times, the monastery Basilica of the Assumption of the Virgin Mary was given very thorough baroque treatment in the mid-18th century by the architect Anselmo Lurago and the designer Ignaz Palliardi. The latter was responsible for the stucco work which sets off the dark furnishings and the wall and ceiling paintings. The church is the resting place of St. Norbert, founder of the Premonstratensian Order to which the monastery belongs.

FILOSOFICKÝ SÁL
The Philosophical Hall is the larger of Strahov's two libraries and was built by Palliardi at the end of the 18th century to accommodate the bookcases brought here from the monastery at Louka in Moravia. Carved in walnut, and with a single gallery, the bookcases are an

TIP

● Most of the bandmasters in the Austro-Hungarian army were Czechs. Drawing on this tradition, brass bands here are among the best in the world, but are less often heard in public than they were in Communist times. The courtyard restaurant at Strahov is one of the places you can often hear them oompahing away.

THE SIGHTS

astonishing 15m (50ft) high. They reach the ceiling painting, an ambitious work by the great Viennese artist Franz Anton Maulpertsch (1724–96); depicting the struggle of mankind to find true wisdom, it glorifies the great thinkers of all eras, with the exception of 18th-century heretics such as Voltaire and Diderot, who are shown being ushered into Hell. Intriguing items from the monastery's Kabinet kuriozit (Cabinet of Curiosities) are displayed at the library entrance.

TEOLOGICKÝ SÁL
The older of Strahov's two libraries, the Theological Hall, still has its original bookcases. It was begun in 1671 by Giovanni Domennico Orsi. With its richly stuccoed barrel vault, precious tomes displayed on lecterns and ancient globes scattered around, it is one of the most compelling interiors of 'magic Prague', with a mysterious atmosphere of arcane learning. The ceiling paintings by one of the monks proclaim the superiority of divine wisdom over mere rationality. Some of the bookcases have bars, behind which languish volumes once placed on the Church's index of forbidden reading.

STRAHOVSKÁ OBRAZÁRNA
Most of the works displayed in the Strahov Picture Gallery on the upper floor of the cloisters were collected in the 19th century, confiscated by the Communist regime in the 1950s and returned in the 1990s. Many are not of the highest quality, but worth seeking out are the icon-like 14th-century *Strahov Madonna*, a self-portrait by Peter Brandl (1668–1735), a revealing portrait of Rudolf II by Hans von Aachen (1552–1615) and a charming *Allegory of the Rule of Rudolf II* by Van Ravenstein (active in Prague 1589–1599 and 1606–1608).

BACKGROUND
Premonstratensian monks settled at Strahov in 1143. Having lived through repeated disasters over the centuries, their monastery managed to survive the Dissolution ordered by Joseph II in the late 18th century, when its eloquent abbot persuaded the emperor that Strahov was primarily a place of learning, fit to provide a home for the books confiscated from less fortunate institutions. In the 20th century, the Communists were less amenable; the Strahov monks were imprisoned or executed, and their libraries became part of the National Literature Museum.

Begun in 1671, the enchanting Theological Hall (above left) is the older of Strahov's two libraries.
The 18th-century Philosophical Hall (above) is lined with walnut bookcases that reach up to the ceiling painting

The bejewelled cover of the 9th-century Strahov Gospel (above), on display at Strahov Monastery

The pavilion in the garden of the Schönborn Palace (US Embassy)

Ice-skating in front of the neoclassical Estates Theatre

STAVOVSKÉ DIVADLO

The neoclassical Estates Theatre, one of Europe's finest historic opera houses, is indelibly associated with Mozart.

➕ 57 F6 • Ovocný trh 1, Staré Město, Prague 1 ☎ 224 902 322
🕐 Box office: daily 10–6
🎟 Tickets for performances from 100Kč–1,000Kč 🅜 Můstek
🚃 Tram 5, 8, 14 to Náměstí Republiky
www.narodni-divadlo.cz

RATINGS	
Cultural interest	●●●●○
Historic interest	●●●●○

TIP
● In the absence of a guided tour of the glittering interior of the Estates Theatre, buy a ticket for a performance; you won't be disappointed.

The stately green and cream neoclassical building of the Estates Theatre, one of the homes of the National Theatre company, closes off the western end of Ovocný trh with a spirited flourish. Its restored late 18th-century interior is a superb setting for drama, ballet and opera. For most of the 18th century, Prague theatre-goers had to make do with a variety of premises, including a market hall and a timber structure that could only be used in summer. The demand for a proper building was responded to by Count Nostitz, who provided funds for the construction of a theatre dedicated to 'The Fatherland and the Muses'; the gilt inscription *Patriae et Musis* still adorns the outside of the building. There was opposition to a theatre here; the Carmelites from the Church of St. Havel objected, as did the University. What was built by day was sometimes destroyed by hired gangs at night. It was originally named the Nostitz Theatre, after its founder, and was opened on 21 April 1783 with a performance of *Emilia Galotti* by the German playwright Gotthold Ephraim Lessing. In 1799, granted a subsidy by the governing body of Bohemia (composed of the 'estates' of nobility, clergy and burghers), it changed its name to the Estates Theatre. In 1920, what had become a largely German institution was forcibly taken over by a mob led by actors from the National Theatre and converted into a wholly Czech establishment. After 1948, it was renamed the Tyl Theatre, in honour of Josef Kajetán Tyl (1808–56), composer of the melody of *Kde domov můj (Where is my home?)*, the Czech national anthem.

Mozart had connections with the theatre; his *Figaro* was performed here, and there were triumphal premières of *La Clemenza di Tito* and *Don Giovanni*, as well as of the orchestral work later known as the *Prague Symphony*. The theatre made a splendid setting for scenes in Miloš Forman's 1984 film *Amadeus*.

SCHÖNBORNSKÝ PALÁC

➕ 56 C6 • Tržiště 15/365, Malá Strana, Prague 1 🚃 Tram 12, 20, 22, 23 to Malostranské náměstí

The baroque Schönborn Palace was built in the mid-17th century by Count Rudolf Colloredo. It shares its picturesque location in Malá Strana with the German Embassy in the Lobkowicz Palace, a short distance further uphill. In the 18th century it was extended and remodelled, but then in the 19th century it fell into disrepair and was divided up into apartments. In 1917, one of the flats was lived in briefly by Franz Kafka. In 1924 the palace was bought by the US as its legation, and became a full embassy in 1945. Its most attractive feature is the garden, laid out on the lower slopes of Petřín Hill and terminating in a delightful little pavilion, which was once a wine cellar and which is visible from many parts of town. The Stars and Stripes flown from the flagpole was a constant irritant to the Communist regime, whose secret police used the bell-tower of the Church of St. Nicholas to observe the embassy's activities.

SCHWARZENBERSKÝ PALÁC

➕ 56 C5 • Hradčanské náměstí 2/185, Hradčany, Prague 1 🚃 Tram 22, 23 to Pražský hrad

The Schwarzenberg Palace is Prague's outstanding Renaissance edifice, not least because of its prominent location on Hradčany Square and its spectacular sgraffito decoration. Built in the mid-16th century for the Lobkowicz family, it passed through tha hands of various aristocratic owners before becoming the property of the Schwarzenbergs. This Catholic family from Bavaria was

Prague's State Opera has a magnificent interior

Memorial plaque at the Church of St. Cyril and St. Methodius

rewarded for its loyalty to the emperor with land and property after the Battle of White Mountain in 1620. By the early 20th century, their estates extended over much of southern Bohemia, a miniature empire ruled from their great castle at Český Krumlov. Some of their property was nationalized in the 1920s, the rest of it confiscated under Communism. Their Hradčany palace first housed the Ministry of Forestry, then became a fine home for the historic collections of the Military Museum. After the Velvet Revolution, Prince Karel Schwarzenberg, who had never given up his Czechoslovak citizenship during exile in Austria, returned to serve as President Havel's Head of Chancellery. Together with the adjoining Salm Palace, the Schwarzenberg will be adapted in the long term as the home of the National Gallery's Renaissance and baroque collections.

STAROMĚSTSKÉ NÁMĚSTÍ

See pages 112–115.

STÁTNÍ OPERA PRAHA

➕ 59 G7 • Wilsonova 4, Nové Město, Prague 2 ☎ 296 117 111 🕐 Box office: Mon–Fri 10–5.30, Sat–Sun 10–12, 1–5.30 🎟 Tickets for performances from 150Kč–1,150Kč 🚇 Muzeum or Hlavní nádraží www.opera.cz

Prague's State Opera is housed in a neo-baroque building comparable in splendour, if not in size, with the National Theatre. Its location is less fortunate, cut off from the heart of the city by the Magistrála, the urban expressway, and approached via an

underpass. 'State Opera' is the most recent of the building's several names; it was originally the Neues Deutsches Theater (New German Theatre), built in 1888 by Prague's German community as a counterweight to the recently opened and entirely Czech-orientated Národní divadlo (National Theatre). The building's architects were the Viennese team of Helmer and Fellner and the opera chosen for the opening was Wagner's *Mastersingers of Nuremberg*. Over the years the theatre became a focus of excellence, hosting perform-ances by many of the great names in opera and introducing music by such figures as Mahler and Richard Strauss to the public. After the expulsion of Prague's Germans, in 1945 the theatre was renamed 'Theatre of the Fifth of May' and in 1948 the 'Smetana Theatre'. Following restoration over a six-year period starting in 1967, it was reopened as the State Opera in 1973.

ŠTERNBERSKÝ PALÁC

See pages 116–117.

STRAHOVSKÝ KLÁŠTER

See pages 118–119.

A scene from a performance of Cinderella at the State Opera

SVATÉHO CYRILA A METODĚJE

➕ 58 E8 • Resslova 9, Nové Město, Prague 2 ☎ 224 920 686 🕐 May–end Sep Tue–Sun 10–5; Oct–end Apr Tue–Sun 10–4 🎟 Adult 50Kč, child (6–16) 20Kč 🚇 Karlovo náměstí 🚊 Tram 3, 4, 6, 7, 10, 14, 16, 17, 18, 21, 22, 23, 24 to Karlovo náměstí

The baroque Church of St. Cyril and St. Methodius, built by Paul Ignaz Bayer and Kilián Ignác Dientzenhofer, was completed in 1736 and was originally a Catholic establishment dedicated to St. Charles Borromeo. It was closed during the reign of Emperor Joseph II, and used for various secular purposes until 1935, when it was reconsecrated as the cathedral of the Orthodox community of Czechoslovakia and dedicated to the Slav mis-sionaries Cyril and Methodius.

The church was the scene of the last stand of the resistance fighters who assassinated Reichsprotektor Heydrich. The wall plaque on the outside of the church recalls the high drama which was played out here on 18 June 1942. Having fulfilled their mission to kill Heydrich, the Czech and Slovak parachutists sent from England moved from one hiding place to another. Finally, they were given sanctuary in the crypt of the church but they were betrayed. The church was surrounded by SS troops who were driven back by a hail of bullets. The fire brigade was then ordered to flush out the defenders by pumping water into the crypt. Rather than fall into the hands of their enemy, they used their last bullets on themselves. The crypt is now the Národní památník hrdinů Heydrichiády (National Memorial to the Heroes of the Heydrich Terror).

Svatého Mikuláš

One of central Europe's most magnificent baroque churches, St. Nicholas's, with its great dome and tower, dominates Malá Strana. The church's ornate interior is a masterpiece of baroque theatricality.

St. Nicholas's green copper dome and bell-tower (above)

Detail of the church organ (above) once played by Mozart

SEEING SVATÉHO MIKULÁŠ

The monumental bulk of the great Church of St. Nicholas rises over Malostranské náměstí (Malá Strana Square). If the outside of the building is designed to impress, the interior is almost overwhelming in its dynamic interplay of space, light and colour, of painting and statuary. It is perhaps the supreme example in Bohemia of the way in which the Catholic Church of the Counter-Reformation sought to seduce the public by appealing directly to the senses rather than to the intellect. To experience something of what St. Nicholas's Jesuit builders intended, rather than just wandering around briefly, it's better by far to attend one of the evening concerts held here, when sound and artificial light enhance the sumptuous setting. Another kind of experience is offered by the tall belfry, which has a separate entrance on the southern side of the church; as well as a stunning bird's-eye view over this part of the city, there is also a small exhibition on 'The Music of Prague Organ Lofts'. Be warned: it's 215 stairs to the top!

RATINGS

Cultural interest	● ● ● ● ●
Historic interest	● ● ● ●
Photo stops	● ● ● ● ●

BASICS

✚ 56 D6 • Malostranské náměstí 25, Malá Strana, Prague 1
☎ Church: 257 534 215. Bell-tower: 251 512 516
◷ Church: Apr–end Oct daily 9–5; Nov–end Mar daily 9–4. Bell-tower: Apr–end Oct daily 10–5.30, Christmas 10–5
💰 Church: adult 50Kč, child (6–16) 25Kč. Bell-tower: adult 50Kč, child (6–16) 40Kč
🚊 Tram 12, 20, 22, 23 to Malostranské náměstí
📖 Guidebook 70Kč
🎫 Guided tour of church (2 weeks notice): no additional fee. Guided tour of bell-tower: no additional fee
www.psalterium.cz
Information in English about church tours and concerts.

A view up to the frescoes on the inside of the cupola (above)

HIGHLIGHTS

EXTERIOR

The dome and bell-tower of St. Nicholas's, both standing 74m (243ft) high, are inseparable elements in the Malá Strana townscape. The main body of the church terminates in a façade overlooking the western, sloping part of Malostranské náměstí (Malá Strana Square). It's a subtle composition of convex and concave surfaces, adorned with statuary proclaiming the triumph of the Jesuit Order under the patronage of the House of Habsburg. The founder of the Order, St. Ignatius of Loyola, and the great Jesuit missionary, St. Francis Xavier, feature prominently, as does the Habsburg eagle and St. Nicholas himself.

INTERIOR

Lined with statues of saints and with a huge ceiling painting celebrating the life and works of St. Nicholas, the nave leads towards the great central space beneath the dome. Here, four giant figures stand guard, representing the Fathers of the Church; one of them is brandishing a thunderbolt while another is making short work of a devil, using his

crozier as a lance. High above, the painting around the inside of the cupola commemorates the Holy Trinity. The great organ once played by Mozart is adorned with delightful figures of music-making cherubs, while the most ornate feature of the whole interior is the gorgeous pulpit, a rococo confection in gilt and rocaille (decorative shell work).

BACKGROUND

After the Catholic victory at the Battle of White Mountain in 1620, the Jesuits became firmly ensconced in the middle of Malá Strana. They propagated their message from the college which still abuts the Church of St. Nicholas to the north. They used the existing church in the square but regarded it as inadequate. Construction of a new building which would proclaim their prestige and power began in 1673. A succession of architects worked on the project, which eventually passed into the hands of the Dientzenhofer family. The nave was begun by Kryštof Dientzenhofer and completed after his death in 1722 by his son Kilián Ignác, who was also responsible for the dome. On Kilián's death in 1751 he was succeeded by his son-in-law, Anselmo Lurago, who added the bell-tower in 1755. The decoration of the interior was only finished in 1775. The Jesuits had just two years to enjoy the fruits of their century-long work, for in 1777 Emperor Joseph II had them expelled from the country. In 1791, the city that had taken Mozart to its heart marked his death with a requiem Mass in St. Nicholas's.

The ornate pulpit (above). Beautiful paintings decorate the ceiling of the Church of St. Nicholas (top)

Bustling Havel's street market in the Old Town with the church of St. Havel in the distance

The dynamic, baroque Church of St. John Nepomuk on the Rock at Vyšehrad

THE SIGHTS

SVATÉHO HAVEL

✛ 57 F6 • Havelská, Staré Město, Prague 1 ☎ 222 318 186 🅘 Visits possible half an hour before services (Mon–Fri 12.15pm, Sun 8am), or by arrangement 🅜 Můstek

The saint commemorated in the name of this church is St. Havel; also known as St. Gall, he was a 7th-century Irish monk who helped evangelize what is now Switzerland. His Prague church stands at the heart of the part of town also named after him— Havelské město. In the 13th century, an extension of the Old Town was laid out here, mainly in order to attract German merchants and tradesmen. With its straight streets and rectilinear marketplaces, it is quite distinct in character from the labyrinthine lanes and passageways of the rest of the Old Town, and its lively market stalls have something of its medieval atmosphere. St. Havel's Church has been rebuilt and extended more than once; its baroque façade is second only to Malá Strana's St. Nicholas in originality and liveliness. In the interior is the tomb of the great baroque painter Karel Škréta (1610–74).

SVATÉHO JAKUBA

✛ 57 F5 • Malá Štupartská 6, Staré Město, Prague 1 ☎ 224 828 816 🅘 Mon–Sat 9.30–12, 2–4; Sun 2–3.45 🅜 Náměstí Republiky 🚋 Tram 5, 8, 14 to Náměstí Republiky

St. James's is one of Prague's great churches, second in length only to St. Vitus Cathedral, its Gothic skeleton only partly disguised by the generous application of baroque ornament. Its acoustics are renowned, and this, together with its glittering interior, makes it a fine setting for concerts. The exuberant décor begins at the entrance, above which are animated stucco reliefs

depicting the lives of St. Francis and St. Anthony as well as St. James. Inside, a procession of gorgeous side altars leads towards the high altar with its monumental painting of the martyrdom of St. James by Václav Vavřinec Reiner (1689–1743). The most striking individual feature, however, is the tomb of Count Jan Václav Vratislav of Mitrovice. It was designed by the Viennese sculptor Johann Bernard Fischer von Erlach (1656–1723) and carried out by Ferdinand Maximilian Brokoff in 1716. The church has a gruesome reminder of a past crime. The thief who tried to pilfer the jewels from a figure of the Virgin Mary found that she held him fast by his arm, which had to be sliced off. The severed body part, somewhat decomposed after 400 years, hangs on the building's west wall.

SVATÉHO JANA NA PRADLE

✛ 57 D7 • Říční 1, Malá Strana, Prague 1 ☎ 776 366 650 🅘 Visits by prior arrangement 🚋 Tram 6, 9, 12, 20, 22, 23 to Újezd

Together with the adjoining hospice which it once served, the little Church of St. John at the Laundry brings a touch of rustic simplicity to this corner of Malá Strana. The originally Romanesque structure dates from the early 12th century, but was rebuilt in Gothic style a hundred years later. As with many religious institutions, the hospice closed down at the end of the 18th century; nearby Kampa Island, with its broad millstream, had always been a place where the city's washerwomen congregated, and it seemed only natural to turn the redundant church into a washhouse, hence its name.

SVATÉHO JAN NA SKALCE

✛ 58 F8 • Vyšehradská, Nové Město, Prague 2 ☎ 224 915 371 🅘 Not open to the public 🅜 Karlovo náměstí 🚋 Tram 3, 4, 6, 7, 10, 14, 16, 17, 18, 22, 23, 24 to Karlovo náměstí

The Church of St. John Nepomuk on the Rock is a minor masterpiece of baroque architecture by Kilián Ignác Dientzenhofer (1689–1751). The site on which it is built is high above the road and limited in extent. Dientzenhofer exploited these constraints to make a wonderfully dynamic composition, setting the church on top of a splendid double staircase, turning the towers inwards at an angle, and using the range of curvilinear, convex and concave forms so representative of the baroque. In the inaccessible interior there is a ceiling painting of the Apotheosis of St. John Nepomuk by Karel Kovář and Johann Brokoff's wooden figure of the saint, which served as the model for the bronze statue on Karlův most (Charles Bridge). Opposite the church is the Emauzy (Emmaus Monastery), endowed by Emperor Charles IV. It has cloisters with well-preserved wall paintings, a bare and lofty church, and an unusual pair of modern spires.

SVATÉHO JOSEFA

✛ 57 D6 • Josefská 4, Malá Strana, Prague 1 ☎ 257 532 100 🅘 Mon–Fri 10–4.15, Sun 2–4.15 🚋 Tram 12, 20, 22, 23 to Malostranské náměstí

St Joseph's Church stands in a Malá Strana side street. With a foundation stone laid by Emperor Leopold I in 1683, it was built for the Carmelite Order, whose monastery extended over what are now the Vojanový sady (Vojan Gardens) to the rear. Its richly sculpted façade with its

St. Joseph's Church has a richly sculpted façade

A silhouette of the statue of Winston Churchill on Thunovská

The cobbled Týn Court, or Ungelt, in the Old Town

banded columns and high gable are almost certainly the work of a member of the Order from Leuven in what is now Belgium and is more typical of the baroque style of the Low Countries than anything to be seen in Prague.

SVATÉHO MIKULÁŠ

See pages 122–123.

SVATÉHO TOMÁŠE

➕ 57 D5 • Letenská, Malá Strana, Prague 1 ☎ 257 530 556 🕐 Visits by prior arrangement. Regular services in English 🚋 Tram 12, 20, 22, 23 to Malostranské náměstí

St. Thomas's, tucked away just off Malostranské náměstí (Malá Strana Square), is one of the city's grandest churches and its single tower one of the area's most distinctive landmarks. The church was originally built in the 13th century for the Augustinians. Following its sacking by the Hussites in 1420, it later became one of the city's most fashionable places of worship. Its congregation of aristocrats and wealthy burghers could afford to employ Kilián Ignác Dientzenhofer to rebuild it, and from 1723 it was fitted out with fine paintings by the best artists of the age. The Augustinians were expert brewers, and beer first flowed from their brewery here in 1358. The dark brew dispensed in the adjoining beer hall is still famous, and very popular with tour groups.

SVATÉHO VÍTA

See pages 126–129.

TELEVIZNÍ VYSÍLAČ

➕ 59 J7 • Mahlerovy sady 1, Žižkov, Prague 3 ☎ 267 005 766 🕐 Daily 10am–11pm 🎟 Adult 60Kč, child under 10 free 🚇 Jiřího z Poděbrad 🚋 Tram 5, 9, 26 to Lipanská

The city's tallest structure, the Television Tower, rises more than 216m (708ft) over the plateau between the suburbs of Vinohrady and Žižkov. It was begun by the Communists in 1985, but only finished after the regime's fall. The tower's upper parts house all kinds of apparatus, some of it intended originally to jam West German television and protect the population from the temptations of consumerism. Just below the 100m (328ft) level are three levels of viewing galleries and a restaurant, reached by high-speed elevator. The view is said to extend for more than 100km (60 miles) in clear conditions. However, the historic parts of the city are some distance away and the immediate view comprises mostly the early 20th-century tenement blocks of Vinohrady and Žižkov. When the tower first began operating, people living nearby complained of headaches and of being able to pick up radio stations on their domestic appliances. The most recent innovation is the work of *enfant terrible* sculptor David Černý, whose giant babies can be seen climbing slug-like up the outside of the edifice (▷ right).

THUNOVSKÁ

➕ 56 D5 • Thunovská, Malá Strana, Prague 1 🚋 Tram 12, 20, 22, 23 to Malostranské náměstí

Narrow Thunovská street leads into Nové zámecké schody (New Castle Steps), an alternative to Nerudova street as a way up to the Castle. At the end of a short cul-de-sac is the Thunovský palác (Thun Palace); now the British Embassy, it was once the property of Walter Leslie, one of three mercenaries responsible for the assassination of General Wallenstein in 1634. Facing the palace, close to a bust of Sir Winston Churchill, is the cubby-hole from which Communist State Security kept an eye on comings and goings to and from the embassy.

TROJA

See pages 130–131.

TÝNSKÝ DVŮR

➕ 57 F6 • Staré Město, Prague 1 🚇 Náměstí Republiky 🚋 Tram 5, 8, 14 to Náměstí Republiky

Cobbled Týn Court, also called Ungelt, is a medieval courtyard, which can be entered only through its two gates. With its popular restaurants and shops, it has preserved something of the atmosphere of the Middle Ages, when it was a kind of free trade area for foreign, mostly German, merchants. On payment of tolls ('Ungelt' in old German), traders lived and operated here under the protection of the king and subject to their own laws. The Ungelt's finest feature is the Granovský palác (Granov Palace).

BANKA SLAVIE

Svatého Víta

Prague's greatest single landmark and a key national symbol, the Gothic Cathedral of St. Vitus is an essential destination for every visitor to the city. Six hundred years in the making, it is a treasure house of the art of every era.

SEEING SVATÉHO VÍTA

The Cathedral, its towers and pinnacles rising proudly above the enclosing walls of the Castle, is the spiritual heart of Czech Roman Catholicism. The building's atmosphere is best appreciated if you take part in one of the services; at other times the interior can seem overwhelmed by sheer numbers of visitors. Most people come to the Cathedral in the course of a visit to the Castle; the approach from the west is the most striking introduction to the great building, with the whole of the soaring west front revealed suddenly as you emerge from the passageway linking the Second and Third Courtyards. After this, it's a good idea to walk around the outside, admiring details like doors and screens as well as the delicacy, complexity and sheer scale of the architecture. Entry to the nave, from either the western or southern doorways, is free but if you have time it's worth investing in the ticket which, as well as allowing you into a number of Castle interiors, gives you access to the crypt, chancel and tower. The reward for climbing its 300 or so steps is a series of superb views of the city.

HIGHLIGHTS

WEST FRONT

Surprisingly, the face the Cathedral first presents to most of its visitors is a modern one. Along with the nave, the west front with its 82m (270ft) twin towers was built in faithful re-creation of the original Gothic style in the last years of the 19th century. Just as in the Middle Ages, it is rich in sculptural and other decoration. The bronze doors have fascinating relief panels showing the construction of the cathedral (middle) and scenes from the life of St. Vojtěch, the first Slav bishop of Prague (left). The right-hand door tells the story of St. Wenceslas; one panel depicts his assassination, with the saint clinging to a door-knocker in the shape of a lion's head, while his treacherous brother Boleslav stabs him in the back.

SOUTH FRONT

Dominating the Third Courtyard is the Cathedral's glorious southern tower, 95.5m (313ft) high. Its lower sections form part of the original medieval building, while the gallery dates from the mid-16th century and the elaborate cupola from the late 18th century. On the right, at

BASICS

✚ 56 C5 • Pražský hrad – III nádvoří, Hradčany, Prague 1

☎ 257 531 622

🕐 Apr–end Oct 9–5; Nov–end Mar 9–4

💶 Free admission to nave. Chancel, crypt, tower: adult 350Kč, child (6–16) 175Kč (ticket also gives admission to some Castle interiors). Adult 220Kč, child (6–16) 110Kč (ticket giving admission to fewer Castle interiors). Chancel, crypt and tower included in Prague Castle ticket; tower only: 20Kč (Apr–end Oct 9–5)

🚊 Tram 22, 23 to Pražský hrad

🎧 Audioguide from information office in Third Courtyard: adult 250Kč, child (6–16) 200Kč. 60-min guided tour in English (includes Castle interiors): 450Kč up to 5 people, 90Kč each additional person www.hrad.cz

Stained-glass window (1931), designed by Alfons Mucha, in the New Archbishop's Chapel (opposite). A Venetian mosaic (1371) above the Golden Gate (above left). Detail of the silver tomb of St. John of Nepomuk (above middle). The spires of the cathedral rise above the Castle complex (above right)

the foot of the tower, is the three-arched Zlatá brána (Golden Gate). Above is a wonderful Venetian mosaic of 1371 showing the Last Judgement, together with one of the Cathedral's many depictions of Charles IV; the Emperor is shown in supplication to the left of the arch, one of his wives to the right. The modern metal grille has fascinating depictions of the signs of the zodiac and the labours of the months.

NAVE

The lofty nave is lit by a remarkable series of stained-glass windows, the work of prominent Czech artists of the early 20th century. The rose window at the west end, made up of 27,000 pieces of glass, depicts the Creation of the World, and is the work of František Kysela (1881–1941), while the window in the first chapel on the right, showing the Descent of the Holy Ghost, was carried out by Max

ST. VITUS

The early Christian martyr Vitus is best known as the patron saint of sufferers from epilepsy and similar ailments once known as 'St. Vitus' Dance'. Why the greatest church in the Czech

lands should be dedicated to him remains unclear, though his name—Svatý Vít, in Czech—is suspiciously close to that of Svetovit, a pagan deity held in high esteem before the Czechs were Christianized.

A view of the south front of the Cathedral of St. Vitus (above right) showing the southern tower on the left and the three-arched Golden Gate on the right—the Venetian mosaic above the arches depicts The Last Judgement

Švabinský (1873–1962). Alfons Mucha (1860–1939) was responsible for the glass in the window of the third chapel on the left; it shows scenes from the lives of St. Cyril and St. Methodius in the art nouveau style for which the artist was famous.

CHANCEL AND CRYPT

Forming the medieval core of the Cathedral, the chancel is an example of the Gothic architect's ability to span space with seemingly weight-less stone. Very high up is a series of lifelike portrait heads, including not only Charles IV, but also his architect Peter Parler. Much more striking are the tombs at ground level, particularly that of St. John Nepomuk, a sumptuous creation. Below the chancel is the crypt, the resting place of many Bohemian rulers, among them emperors Rudolf II and Charles IV, the latter accompanied by all of his four wives.

ST. WENCESLAS CHAPEL

To commemorate his illustrious predecessor on the throne of Bohemia, Charles IV ordered this chapel built above the saint's original tomb. It is the Cathedral's most sacred space, decorated in the same

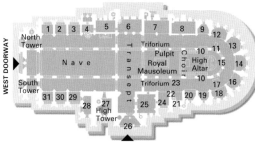

WEST DOORWAY

North Tower

1 2 3 4 5 6 7 8 9 12

Nave

Triforium

Pulpit

Royal Mausoleum

Choir

High Altar

10 11 13

10 15 14

South Tower

Triforium 23 10 17 16

31 30 29 22 20 19 18

28 27 High Tower 25 24 21

26

SOUTH DOORWAY

1. Bartoň of Dobenín Chapel
2. Schwarzenberg Chapel
3. New Archbishop's Chapel (Hora Chapel)
4. Old Treasury (Cathedral Treasury now in Chapel of Holy Rood in Second Courtyard)
5. New Sacristy
6. Wohlmut's Choir (Organ Gallery)
7. St. Sigismund's Chapel (Czernin Chapel)
8. Old Sacristy
9. St. Anne's Chapel (Nostitz Chapel)
10. Historical reliefs
11. Statue of Cardinal Friedrich von Schwarzenberg
12. Old Archbishop's Chapel
13. Chapel of St. John the Baptist (Pernstein Chapel)
14. Lady Chapel (Trinity Chapel, Imperial Chapel)
15. Tomb of St. Vitus
16. Reliquary Chapel (Saxon Chapel, Sternberg Chapel)
17. Tomb of St. John of Nepomuk
18. Chapel of St. John of Nepomuk (St. Adalbert's Chapel)
19. Wallenstein Chapel (Magdalene Chapel)
20. Royal Oratory (Vladislav Oratory)
21. Chapel of Holy Rood
22. Entrance to Royal Vault
23. Monument of Count Leopold Schlick
24. Martinitz Chapel (St. Andrew's Chapel)
25. St. Wenceslas's Chapel (above, Crown Chamber)
26. Golden Gate
27. Hasenburg Chapel
28. Chapter Library
29. Thun Chapel
30. Chapel of Holy Sepulchre
31. St. Ludmilla's Chapel (Baptistery)

THE SIGHTS

extravagant manner as the Chapel of the Holy Cross at Karlštejn Castle with paintings and semiprecious stones, and presided over by a limewood statue of the saint. The chapel's aura is increased by its inaccessibility; you are allowed to peer in from outside only. The upstairs chamber is where the crown jewels of Bohemia are hidden away and only shown to the public on very special occasions.

BACKGROUND

The cathedral reflects the spirit of its founder, Charles IV, who ordered it to be built in 1344 as part of his plan to make Prague a worthy capital of the Holy Roman Empire. Its first architect, Matthew of Arras (died 1352), was succeeded in 1353 by Peter Parler, but after Parler's death in 1399 work faltered, with just the chancel and lower part of the south tower completed. In the mid-19th century, with the founding of the 'Union for the Completion of the Cathedral', construction began again. Work proceeded steadily, and in 1929, on the millennial anniversary of the assassination of St. Wenceslas, the building was reconsecrated.

ORNATE DECORATION
The relief above decorates the metal grille of the Golden Gate and depicts the labours of the months.

An elaborate chandelier illuminates the Chapel of St. Wenceslas (above left) within the Cathedral of St. Vitus

Troja

The great baroque Troja palace, on the edge of the city, has
formal French-style gardens, stunning sculpture
and a sumptuously decorated interior.

*The late 17th-century Troja
Palace is set in formal gardens
on the edge of Prague
(above left).
A relief decoration on a large
urn crowning a wall in the
grounds of the palace
(above middle).
Chilling out—two polar bears
at Prague Zoo (above right)*

SEEING TROJSKÝ ZÁMEK

The Troja palace, built by ambitious aristocrat Count Sternberg in
the late 17th century, stands on the banks of the Vltava, a short
distance downstream from central Prague. It can be reached by a
combination of metro and bus or, more interestingly, by walking
through Stromovka Park and over the river by footbridge. Even
better is to take a boat and disembark at the Troja riverside as the
Count intended his guests to do, so that they would approach the
imposing main façade of his palace through its lavishly laid-out
gardens, then enter the building via the monumental staircase
with its fabulous array of sculpture. The entrance for today's
visitors is from the courtyard on the north side of the palace, but
you should certainly view the building from the garden front as
Sternberg's guests did; this is free of charge.

Inside, the sheer scale of what was intended to be a place for
summer use only is almost overwhelming, but the wall and
ceiling paintings are the main attraction, an epic glorification of
Sternberg's imperial superiors, the House of Habsburg. Within
easy reach of the city, but still with something of the country
about it, the Troja area has other 'green' attributes, which make
it a popular destination: to one side of the palace is the city zoo,
with the botanical gardens and a vineyard (▷ 68) covering
the slopes behind it.

HIGHLIGHTS

GARDENS AND STAIRCASE

Troja's gardens withered away under Communism, and have had to
be re-created from scratch rather than restored, at the cost of some
loss of atmosphere. They are laid out around a central axis running
from the river to the original main entrance to the palace. The lower
part, with clipped parterres and geometrical patterns, focuses on a
circular fountain, still with its original sculpture. The upper terrace is
bounded by a wall topped by huge terracotta vases, though these are
no match in size or scale to the horseshoe-shaped staircase and its
extraordinarily dynamic sculptures showing the struggle of gods and
giants (the giants are losing). The dark stonework of stairs and
statuary makes a striking contrast with the pale walls and red
highlights of the palace itself.

THE GREAT HALL

The core of the palace is formed by the Great Hall. Every inch of its walls and ceiling is covered in *trompe l'oeil* paintings, by the Godyn brothers from Flanders, who started work here in 1690. They are a shameless, utterly over-the-top tribute to Sternberg's imperial superior, the Habsburg Emperor, who had recently defeated the Turks at a great battle outside Vienna in 1683. Various episodes from Habsburg history are depicted, with an emphasis on the struggle of 'Western Christendom against the Sublime Porte'. One particularly vigorous scene shows a Turk with a turban being toppled from a balcony by valiant warriors in Roman costume. Elsewhere in the palace, the municipal collection of Czech 19th-century painting doesn't even begin to compete with all this baroque extravagance.

ZOO

✉ U Trojského zámku 3/120 ☎ 296 112 111 🕐 Jun–end Aug daily 9–7; Apr, May, Sep, Oct daily 9–6; Mar daily 9–5; Nov–end Feb daily 9–4 💰 Adult 90Kč, child (3–15) 60Kč. Oct–end Mar: adult 70Kč, child 40Kč. Free 1 June 🚌 Bus 112 from metro Holešovice to Zoologická zahrada 🚢 Steamer from New Town quayside; www.zoopraha.cz

Prague's extensive and well-stocked zoo is attractively laid out on the leafy slopes rising from the river bank. Years of under-investment and the grievous damage caused by the 2002 floods are being made good, and there is a continuing programme of improvement and expansion involving the addition of state-of-the-art buildings and enclosures. Most children will love the ride on the chairlift.

BACKGROUND

By building Troja, Count Sternberg hoped to embellish both his personal image and that of the native Bohemian aristocracy in general. He intended the palace to serve as a very superior hunting lodge, in which his sovereign could be entertained after hunting expeditions in the nearby Stromovka Park. As the richest man in Prague, Sternberg could afford to build on the most lavish scale. His architect was the Burgundian Jean-Baptiste Mathey (c1630–c1695), who brought the ideas of the French baroque to Prague. The site at Troja required much expensive earth-moving to place the palace exactly where Sternberg wanted it, on a direct line of sight with Prague Castle.

A baroque sculpture of a mermaid rises from an ornamental pond in front of the palace (above).
One of the superb ceiling frescoes at the extravagant Troja Palace (top)

Uměleckoprůmyslové muzeum (UPM)

The rich collections of the Decorative Arts Museum, among the finest of their kind in Europe, benefit from the original way in which they are displayed.

The exterior of the Decorative Arts Museum (above)

A 1920s poster on display (left); detailed stained glass decorating the stairway (middle); a craftsman in the museum's workshop (right)

Known familiarly as the UPM, the Decorative Arts Museum occupies a pompous neoclassical building of 1900, one of a group of stately public edifices around the Old Town end of the Manesův most (Mánes Bridge). It houses the country's largest collection of arts and crafts, comprising glassware, ceramics, porcelain, objects in silver, gold and other metals, graphic arts, posters, photography, fashion, furniture, and clocks and watches. Once shunned by visitors because of the static nature and tired look of the displays, the museum has been thoroughly revamped and now does justice to the superlative quality of its collections. Items range from late antiquity to the present and come from many European countries. The contribution of Bohemian artists and craftspeople is particularly striking, with wonderful examples of art nouveau and art deco work.

MATERIAL GOODS

The museum's treasures are arranged in a stimulating series of themed displays, based on the materials from which they are made, and accompanied by choice examples of furniture. 'Story of the Fibre' takes in textiles of all kinds, including lace and embroidery, though the most memorable items are the boldly designed interwar tapestries created by František Kysela (1881–1941) and Marie Teinitzerová (1879–1960). 'Born in Fire' contains the collection of glass and porcelain, and as well as masterpieces of 18th- and 19th-century Meissen porcelain there are beautiful examples of modern Czech ingenuity in the creation of highly original glass objects of various kinds. 'Print and Image' includes books, graphics and photography; perhaps the most fascinating objects here are posters from the period of the First Republic of Czechoslovakia (1918–38), with the optimistic and innovative atmosphere of the time reflected in an astonishingly varied use of forms, colours and typefaces. 'The Treasury' houses jewellery and metal items of all kinds, as well as articles which once graced the cabinets of curiosities of Renaissance rulers like Rudolf II; the emperor was responsible for commissioning the famous *pietra dura* picture of Hradčany from the Italian master craftsman Castrucci, which is on display here.

Václavské náměstí

Everyone is eventually drawn to Wenceslas Square, the city's most famous thoroughfare and meeting place.

RATINGS	
Cultural interest	● ● ● ●
Historic interest	● ● ● ●
Photo stops	● ● ● ●
Shopping	● ● ● ●

BASICS
✚ 57 F7 • Nové Město, Prague 1
Ⓜ Můstek (lower end of square); Muzeum (upper end)
🚊 Tram 3, 9, 14, 24 to Václavské náměstí

Sloping gently downhill from the Wenceslas Monument, busy Wenceslas Square buzzes with activity (top). Detail of the sgraffitoed façade of a building on the square (above, inset)

SEEING VÁCLAVSKÉ NÁMĚSTÍ

Despite its name, Wenceslas Square is more of a boulevard than a square. From its lower end, known as the Golden Cross, it runs gently uphill for just under 700m (765 yards) past the famous statue of St. Wenceslas to its crowning feature, the Národní muzeum (National Museum). Traffic has long since been minimized, the square is no longer the important through-route it used to be, and the once ubiquitous trams only make a brief appearance as they cross the square half-way along its length. The broad sidewalks are paved with the patterned (and slightly uneven and rather slippery) granite sets so characteristic of the city, and are lined with graceful lime trees. Crowds fill the square all day and for much of the night, swarming in and out of shops, arcades, hotels, restaurants and metro entrances. A stroll up and down is always a fascinating experience, both in terms of people-watching and appreciation of the townscape; Wenceslas Square has examples of every style of architecture from the last hundred years or so. The best overall view is from the terrace in front of the National Museum, but because of the presence of the traffic-choked *Magistrála*, the urban expressway, it can be reached only via an underpass.

TIPS

● To explore the square thoroughly, walk up one side and down the other, crossing to the middle for a good look at St. Wenceslas, and popping into at least some of the many arcades. If time is really short, get out at Muzeum metro station and walk downhill.

● For a break, stop off for a coffee or something stronger in one of the square's several cafés. The terrace establishments on the eastern side of the square catch the midday and afternoon sun.

● One of the best overall views of the busy life of Wenceslas Square is from the rooftop Duplex restaurant (No. 21), on the eastern side of the square.

THE SIGHTS

HIGHLIGHTS

THE WENCESLAS MONUMENT

A statue of St. Wenceslas stood in what was originally called the Horse Market as long ago as 1680, but the present, world-famous equestrian monument of the country's patron saint dates from 1913. The unmistakable icon of the Czech nation, it is the masterpiece of Josef Václav Myslbek (1848–1922), who worked on the project for decades, more than once changing his concept of Wenceslas. His final version shows the warrior-saint in relaxed yet alert pose astride his trotting steed, firmly holding his lance with its fluttering pennant. The massive granite plinth on which horse and rider stand is flanked by solemn statues of the country's other patron saints: Ludmila, Agnes, Prokopius and Vojtěch. On it are written words from a medieval Czech chorale: 'May we and our descendants not perish.'

Presiding over the square named after him, the equestrian statue of St. Wenceslas stands in front of the National Museum (above)

MŮSTEK

Muzeum is an understandable name for one of the square's metro stations, but the meaning of Můstek station is less obvious. *Most* in Czech means bridge, and *můstek* is a little bridge. Such a structure stood here in medieval times, spanning the moat between the Old and New Towns, though it was only discovered when the metro was built in the 1970s. Its remains can be seen near the top of the main escalator.

BUILDINGS

Mostly redeveloped in the first decades of the 20th century, the square is a kind of museum of modern architecture, with the Adria hotel (No.26, ▷ 250) as the sole survivor of the baroque edifices that once graced it. Looking much older, the many-gabled and exuberantly sgraffitoed Wiehlův dům (Wiehl Building; No. 34) on the corner with Vodičkova street dates in fact from 1895, and is a fine example of Czech neo-Renaissance style. Almost opposite stands one of Prague's outstanding art nouveau structures, the Evropa hotel (▷ 254) of 1905, the gable of its delicately worked façade topped by gilded figures holding a fairy lantern. Inside, the Evropa's famous café is even more sumptuous, its extravagant panelling, metalwork and mirrors all perfectly preserved. Just up the square, in complete contrast to all this lavishness, is the Jalta hotel (No. 45, ▷ 256).

The sumptuous café of the art nouveau Evropa hotel (above left). Notable statues on the façade of the Adam Pharmacy (above right)

Built in 1953–55, it is one of Prague's monuments of Communist architecture, and as such has often been derided, but its pale stone façade has a classic calm and repose. It can hardly be described as innovative, however, unlike a cluster of earlier structures at the lower end of the square; the most noticeable of these is the Functionalist Baťa building (No. 6), completed in 1929 for the boot and shoe magnate Tomáš Baťa, an enthusiast for modern architecture and design who had made his fortune supplying the Austro-Hungarian army with footwear in World War I. Its neighbours include a pair of art nouveau buildings, the Adamova lékárna (Adam Pharmacy, No. 8) of 1913 and the Peterkův dům (Peterka Building, No.12), completed in 1899 as one of the first of the city's buildings in this new and exciting style. At the foot of the square, art nouveau can be seen merging into art deco, in the shape of the monumental Palác Koruna, which turns the corner with Na příkopě. Closing off the foot of the square, and blocking the view into the Old Town, is the Communist-era glass and granite ČKD building. Built in 1983, it now houses offices and a nightclub.

Dating from 1895, the Wiehl Building (above and top) features splendid sgraffito decoration and is a fine example of Czech neo-Renaissance style

ARCADES

In the early 20th century, the Prague *pasáž*, or arcade, was given a new lease of life in and around Václavské náměstí (Wenceslas Square). New, multifunctional building complexes incorporated passageways giving access into an intriguing, labyrinthine world of shops, boutiques, bars, restaurants, cinemas, nightclubs and dancehalls. The most ambitious development of this kind is the Palác Lucerna (Lucerna Palace), masterminded by ex-President Havel's grandfather between 1907 and 1920. Look out for the satirical statue of Wenceslas on an upside-down horse. On a somewhat smaller scale, the arcades of the Palác Alfa (Alfa Palace) lead into the Františkánská zahrada (Franciscan Garden, tel 224 216 206/272 702 116; Mid-Apr to mid-Sep daily 7am–10pm; mid-Sep to mid-Oct daily 7am–8pm; mid-Oct to mid-Apr daily 8–7); this oasis in the heart of the city was once part of the Franciscan monastery attached to the Kostel Panny Marie Sněžné (Church of Our Lady of the Snows), and with its clipped hedges and secluded atmosphere still has something of the feel of monastic times.

Satirical statue of St. Wenceslas on an upside-down horse in the Lucerna Palace (left)

Three cloaked figures form part of the design crowning the art nouveau Koruna Palace (above) on the corner of Wenceslas Square

An array of different architectural styles, including sgraffito (below), can be seen on Wenceslas square

BACKGROUND

Wenceslas Square, one of the trio of public spaces laid out by Emperor Charles IV in the New Town, was originally called the Horse Market and functioned as such for centuries. Eventually it acquired a more dignified status, its size and position making it the city's central gathering place for meetings and demonstrations of all kinds. In 1848, the 'Year of Revolutions' began here with a ceremonial open-air Slavonic Mass. Returning from exile, President Masaryk passed this way in late 1918 on his way to the Castle, and the tanks and troops of the occupying Wehrmacht paraded here in 1939. In 1968, they were followed by their Warsaw Pact successors, and it was in protest against this suppression of the Prague Spring (▷ 35) that tragic student Jan Palach set himself on fire beneath the Wenceslas statue the following year (▷ 35). In 1989, half a million people roared their approval and rattled their key rings as Václav Havel proclaimed the end of the Communist regime from the balcony of the Melantrich building (No. 36).

VALDŠTEJNSKÝ PALÁC

Malá Strana's most ostentatious palace is a monument to the ambition of its builder, General Wallenstein. The palace's formal garden makes a magical setting for summer concerts.

Now the seat of the Czech Senate, the late-Renaissance Wallenstein Palace sprawls over a whole city block at the foot of the Castle. Built between 1624 and 1630, its construction involved the demolition of two dozen houses, a brickworks, and one of the city's gateways. Its main façade dominates the square of Valdštejnské náměstí, but its best-known feature is the superb, three-arched *Sala terrena* linking the palace to the parterres and statuary of its high-walled formal garden.

THE GREEDY GENERAL

Albrecht von Wallenstein (Valdštejn in Czech), a minor nobleman from northern Bohemia, rose to astonishing power and wealth before over-reaching himself and perishing at the hands of assassins. His fortune came first from his carefully calculated marriage to an elderly but immensely rich widow, then from the spoils of war; as the successful commander of the Catholic forces in the early stages of the Thirty Years' War (1618–48), Wallenstein not only led his men but enriched himself by taking charge of all their supplies. Initially much favoured by the emperor, he became the country's greatest landowner, purchasing the estates of exiled Protestant aristocrats at rock-bottom prices. Despite his success, he was a superstitious, fearful person, a believer in the occult, who regularly consulted astrologers and soothsayers. His ambition knew no bounds; from his little capital city of Jičín he ruled his vast ducal domain like a king, and he was rightly suspected of plotting with the emperor's enemies. On 25 February 1634, a mob of mercenary soldiers roused Wallenstein from his slumber in the town of Cheb (Eger) and ran him through with a halberd.

PALACE, GARDEN AND GROTTO

The spirit of Wallenstein seems to linger in the palace; the Great Hall has an extravagant ceiling painting depicting him as Mars, the God of War. From the wonderfully airy *Sala terrena*, an avenue of muscular bronze statues, masterpieces of sculptor Adrien de Vries (1545–1626), leads into the gardens. They are copies, the originals were taken to Stockholm by the Swedish army at the end of the Thirty Years' War. Against the garden wall are an aviary and a grotto, from whose dripping, globular stonework strange, half-distinguishable faces peer.

Don't miss A charming statue of Venus adorns the fountain in front of the *Sala terrena*.

RATINGS

Cultural interest	●●●○
Historic interest	●●●○
Photo stops	●●●○

BASICS

✚ 57 D5 • Valdštejnské náměstí 4, Malá Strana, Prague 1 (garden accesible from Letenská street or gateway from metro Malostranská)

☎ 257 071 111

◎ Palace: Sat–Sun 10–5; garden: Apr–end Oct daily 10–6

🎟 Free to palace and garden

Ⓜ Malostranská

🚋 Tram 12, 20, 22, 23 to Malostranské náměstí or Malostranská; tram 17 to Malostranská

www.senat.cz
Information about the Czech Senate.

An avenue of statues, created by sculptor Adrien de Vries, leads from the Sala terrena to the gardens (top).
Relief work decorating a heavy brass door on the exterior of the Wallenstein Palace (above)

Veletržní palác

The Trade Fair Palace, a glittering monument of early modern architecture, is a fine home for the national collections of 19th-, 20th- and 21st-century art. The palace is the best place to discover the excellence and originality of modern Czech art.

RATINGS

Cultural interest	● ● ● ● ●
Historic interest	● ● ●
Specialist shopping	● ● ● ●

BASICS

➕ 57 G3 • Dukelských hrdinů 47, Holešovice, Prague 7

☎ 224 301 111

🕐 Tue–Sun 10–6

💶 Varies according to floors visited. Floors 1–4: adult 250Kč, child (6–16) 120Kč (additional charge for temporary exhibits on the 5th floor). Free 1st Wed in month

🚃 Tram 5, 12, 17 to Veletržní

📖 Czech/English gallery plan with entrance ticket; *19th Century Art* paperback, 155Kč

🎧 Guided tour by arrangement. Audioguide

☕ Two ground-floor cafés

🏬 Gallery shop with above-average range of art books, postcards, etc.

🚹🚺

www.ngprague.cz
The National Gallery's website with general information in English on all its branches, including the collections in the Trade Fair Palace.

Early 20th-century Czech art on display in the Trade Fair Palace includes the Motorcyclist *(1924) by Otakar Sveč (right)*

SEEING THE VELETRŽNÍ PALÁC

Only part of the huge Trade Fair Palace is given over to the National Gallery's collection of art of the 19th, 20th and 21st centuries, but with more than 2,000 exhibits displayed on four floors there is more than enough to keep you busy for a whole day or longer. Paintings and sculpture predominate, but the cool white spaces of the galleries leading off the great building's central atrium are enlivened by furniture, applied arts, stage design, architectural models and drawings, and even a couple of motor cars. To avoid cultural indigestion, the best plan is to decide on priorities. The gallery is proud of its fine collection of modern art from other countries, and it's tempting to concentrate on works by French masters such as Cézanne, Dégas, Renoir, Gauguin, Matisse and Van Gogh, as well as by other European artists like Klimt, Kokoschka and Schiele, Miró, Munch and Chagall. However, if time is limited, it might be more rewarding to make the acquaintance of the work of 20th-century Czech artists, whose contribution is no less fascinating for being relatively

FUEL FOR THE FIRE

The great fire which devastated the Trade Fair Palace in 1974 is supposed to have raged all the more fiercely through being fuelled by the huge quantities of French cognac and Scotch whisky held here. Some firemen were said to have had more interest in liberating craved-for Western consumer goods than in quenching the blaze.

A 1960s Škoda convertible (above), one of the works representing Czech art from 1930 to 2000.
Wandering through a gallery displaying Czech art from 1930 to 2000 (opposite top): works include the painting Frutonium *by Milan Kunc (on the right-hand wall), a sculpture by Karel Pauzer (in the centre) and two paintings by Jiří Načeradský (on the far wall).*
A view of the impressive central atrium in the Trade Fair Palace (opposite bottom)

unfamiliar. The array of 19th-century work, both Czech and foreign, will also find its adherents, especially those impressed by large-scale history paintings and monumental sculpture. The palace's floors are linked by broad stairways, but time and energy can be conserved by using the elevators. There's a combined ticket for the whole building, or you can pay to visit individual floors.

HIGHLIGHTS

19TH-CENTURY ART

The most striking pictures in the 19th-century galleries on the fourth floor are those by artists like Mikoláš Aleš (1852–1913) and František Ženíšek (1849–1916) who set out to provide the reawakened Czech nation with a suitably epic version of its history. In his *Meeting of Jiří of Poděbrad with Matthias Corvinus* of 1878, Aleš has the 'Hussite king' standing in relaxed pose over his defeated Hungarian opponent, while Ženíšek's *Oldřich and Božena* of 1884 is based on the tale of the prince who preferred the charms of a native peasant girl to those of a haughty German princess. These somewhat overblown canvases should not distract you from more modest efforts like the delightful *Near the Cottage* (c1856) by Josef Mánes or the equally appealing *In an Alpine Valley* (1864) and *Ramble in the Mountains* (1870) by the sentimental Bavarian artist Karl Spitzweg. The most original Czech artist of this period is probably Jakub Schikaneder (1855–1924), whose atmospheric paintings evoke the appeal of misty twilights and the sun breaking through fog.

EARLY 20TH-CENTURY CZECH ART

The optimistic spirit of much Czech art of this period is symbolized by the sculpture at the entrance to the third-floor galleries, Otakar Sveč's *Motorcyclist* (1924), frozen in the act of scorching round a sharp bend. Everyday themes of the modern world are also taken up by Otto Gutfreund in charming little polychrome sculptures like *Trade* (1923) featuring a manager and his secretary engrossed in their work. Before concerning himself with such matters, Gutfreund was a pioneer of Cubism, and a number of his tormented heads from this period are on display, among them his *Don Quixote* (1912). The other leading figure of the short-lived Czech Cubist movement was the aptly named Bohumil Kubišta (1884–1918), represented here by several canvases

including his *Smoker* (1910), a wry self-portrait with a pipe. A wealth of pictures trace the evolution of the great painter František Kupka (1871–1957) from Symbolism to glorious, colourful Abstraction, but the most compelling painting on show here is Jan Zrzavý's gloriously pneumatic *Cleopatra II* (1942–57) showing the alluring temptress reclining in a magical setting of pyramids and palm trees.

CZECH ART (1930–2000)

As with Cubism, Czech artists developed their own distinctive take on Surrealism. Among the works shown on the second floor are paintings by Marie Čermínová, who used the name Toyen; her *Fright* (1937) is not, however, quite as terrifying as the truly horrific sculpture *Man With Machine* (1945) by Ladislav Zívr. The desolation of the Nazi occupation led to a unique and expressive movement in the Czech lands, known by the name of Group 42; examples of its work include *Railroad Station With a Windmill* (1941) by František Hudeček. Contrasting with such wartime gloom are ludicrously optimistic Socialist Realist paintings like *We Produce More, We Live Better* of the early 1950s by Alena Čermáková, one of the rare works of art to feature a sardine can. But artists of greater integrity continued to go their own way under Communism; look out for the menacing sculpture entitled *Chair—Usurper* by Aleš Veselý (born 1935) or the satirical shouting figures in *Big Dialog* by Karel Nepraš (1932–2002).

BACKGROUND

Occupying a whole city block, the Veletržní palác was completed in 1928 by the Czech architects Oldřich Tyl and Josef Fuchs as a home for industrial and trade fairs. This monument in glass, steel and concrete from the heroic period of modern architecture was an extraordinarily advanced structure for its time, not least because of its stunning atrium rising through many floors. Shown round shortly after it was opened, the great French/Swiss architect Le Corbusier (1887–1965) could only envy his Czech colleagues for having constructed the sort of building he had so far only dreamed of. Under Communism, the palace was used as a store, supplying hard-currency shops with Western consumer goods. It reopened in 1995 following restoration and conversion into a wonderfully appropriate home for modern art.

TIPS

● Even if you don't intend to wander through the 19th-century galleries on the fourth floor, it's worth starting your visit at this level in order to appreciate the scale and character of this extraordinary building.

● Temporary exhibitions, often of very high quality, are staged in the ground floor and other galleries.
● Of the two ground-floor cafés, the 'internet café' at the front of the building is larger, with outside views, and sometimes houses exhibitions.

Vltava

●

The broad River Vltava, rather than separating the different parts of the city, brings them together harmoniously. Bridges, islands and riverside walks and promenades invite you to enjoy it in all its varied moods.

SEEING THE VLTAVA

With its source in the rain-soaked forests along the borders with Austria and Bavaria, and fed by major tributaries such as the Sazava and Berounka, the Vltava joins the River Elbe (Labe in Czech) some 40km (25 miles) downstream from Prague, their combined waters eventually reaching the North Sea beyond Hamburg. The river passes through a series of gorges before reaching the city at the Vyšehrad cliff. Here it narrows and deepens, only to broaden out again as it approaches the rock spur on which the Castle of Vyšehrad stands, which forces it into a sharp turn eastward. The Vltava can be experienced in many ways. A trip by steamer is a popular way, or you can rent a rowing boat or pedalo. Strolling along the embankments and exploring the islands will reveal many unexpected vistas. Karlův most (Charles Bridge) reigns supreme among the various crossings, but some of the other bridges are fine examples of civic engineering, their detail and decoration well worth seeking out. Among fascinating remnants of the pre-industrial age are mill-wheels, weirs and the towers which once fed the city's water supply.

HIGHLIGHTS

BRIDGES

The monopoly of Karlův most (Charles Bridge) as the only river crossing came to an end in the 19th century with the construction of railway bridges and a chain bridge named after Emperor Ferdinand. In 1876 the granite Palackého most (Palacký Bridge) was built, named after the great 19th-century literary figure, whose elaborate monument stands just beyond the Nové Město (New Town) end of the bridge. Other monumental statues by Josef Václav Myslbek (1848–1922), the sculptor of the Wenceslas statue, once graced both ends of the bridge; damaged in the American air raid of 1945, they were moved to Vyšehrad, where they still stand. Bearing the name of Alois Jirásek (1851–1930), the popular author of historical romances, Jiráskův most (Jirásek Bridge) is a reinforced concrete structure of 1932. Far more elaborate, and built in a neo-baroque style with little pavilions at each end, the most Legií (Bridge of the Legions) gives access to Střelecký ostrov (Shooters' Island). Between here and Charles Bridge, a weir stretches diagonally across the river, providing a constant and splendid spectacle of roaring, foaming water. Although

BASICS

✚ 57 E6

TIPS

● Taking a steamer trip from Rašínovo nábřeží (Rašín Embankment) downstream to Troja is probably the best way of seeing Prague from the Vltava (▷ 218). The boat passes all the riverside attractions in the historic centre before terminating at Troja, with its palace, zoo and botanical gardens. The return trip can be made in the same way, or you can walk across Stromovka Park or take the bus or metro.
● Make sure you have your camera ready as you glide downstream. There are endless opportunities for capturing city sights at unusual angles.

The warm glow of the evening sky casts a golden hue over a couple in a rowing boat on the River Vltava (opposite). Bridges silhouetted against the sky at sunrise (opposite, inset). A weir on the Vltava (above left). River cruises are a popular way to experience the Vltava (above middle). A tranquil river scene (above right)

the somewhat severe appearance of Mánesův most (Mánes Bridge; 1914) is relieved by decoration by František Bílek (1872–1941) and Jan Štursa (1880–1925), it can in no way compete with the exuberant Čechův most (Čech Bridge). This memorial to the poet Svatopluk Čech (1846–1908), completed in the year of his death, is a full-blown essay in art nouveau, featuring fanciful ironwork and torch-bearing statues facing the waters. Otherwise undistinguished, Štefáníkův most (Štefáník Bridge) recalls the Slovak astronomer and aviator who was one of the founders of Czechoslovakia in 1918.

A picturesque view—looking across the river from the Bridge of the Legions to the towers and domes of the Old Town (below)

ISLANDS

The Vltava was—and still can be—a turbulent river, shifting restlessly in its bed and sometimes changing its course quite drastically. In medieval times it had a tendency to avoid the great bend beneath Pražský hrad (Prague Castle) by taking a short cut through the Old Town, much to the dismay of the citizens. In the end the problem could only be solved by raising the level of the whole area, a solution which turned the ground floor of many buildings, such as the Dům pánů z Kunštátu a Poděbrad (House of the Lords of Kunštát and Poděbrady) into basements. Material brought down by the river would form islands, which could change in shape or disappear altogether. The park-like islands that are such an attractive feature of today's river are more or less stabilized. Dětský ostrov (Children's Island) owes its name to its playgrounds and sporting facilities, while Slovanský ostrov (Slavonic Island) is so-called because it was the scene in the 19th century of many a patriotic event. Střelecký ostrov (Shooters' Island) was once the domain of the city's marksmen. Until recent times, Kampa Island was cut off from the rest of Malá Strana by the Čertovka (Devil's Brook), and remained largely undeveloped because of the constant risk of flooding. The largest island is Ostrov Štvanice (Štvanice Island), the site of the city's central tennis courts.

EMBANKMENTS

Broad thoroughfares run parallel to much of the river, lined by apartment buildings and great public edifices like the Národní divadlo (National Theatre) and the Rudolfinum. The most elegant riverside residences are those of Masarykovo nábřeží (Masaryk Embankment), an almost continuous wall of ornate dwellings in art nouveau style. The exception to such sophisticated treatment of the join between town and river is on the Malá Strana bank, where many much older buildings remain, and where, in places, the riverside has kept an almost rustic feel; just upstream from Mánesův most (Mánes Bridge), a little park has preserved the spot sweeping down to the waterside where carters and draymen once brought their horses for a drink.

This delicate wrought-iron statue (above) is an example of the splendid art nouveau ornamentation on Čech Bridge

BACKGROUND

The Vltava, with a major inland port just downstream from the heart of the city, is still a working river, though only a trickle of commercial traffic now ventures far upstream. Before the mid-20th century, the most important activity was timber rafting. Trees felled in the vast forests of central and southern Bohemia were lashed together in convoys up to 200m (650ft) long, then piloted skilfully downstream to the timber yards lining Prague's riverbank. This traditional traffic was brought to an end by the construction of dams for generating hydroelectric power, with the additional benefit of controlling the sudden floods which regularly wrought havoc along the river's course. The Romanesque Judith Bridge had been destroyed in 1342, and in 1890 three arches of the Charles Bridge were swept away. In 2002, the dams proved incapable of holding back the terrible flood, though all the city's bridges survived. Despite such disasters, the Vltava remains a much-loved river, the only major stream to run its entire course within the country's boundaries. Its changing moods were evoked in the second movement of Smetana's *Má vlast (My Country)*, given its première in the Žofín concert hall on Slavonic Island.

VINOHRADY

Opulent art nouveau apartment blocks surround a stunning church in this prestigious inner city suburb.

Before the Communists came to power, this highly desirable residential area was known as Královské Vinohrady (Royal Vineyards) in memory of the vines first planted here by Emperor Charles IV. The vines had long since disappeared when Prague's turn-of-the-20th-century building boom got under way, and seemingly endless ranks of middle-class apartment dwellings filled the newly laid-out grid of streets stretching eastward from central Prague. Developers vied with one another to give their buildings some distinction, and a stroll along almost any Vinohrady street will reveal a wealth of decorative detail in art nouveau style. Densely built-up though it is, the area has more than its fair share of squares and open spaces. Vinohrady's social hub is Náměstí Míru (Peace Square), dominated by the neo-Renaissance building of the Divadlo na Vinohradech (Vinohrady Theatre) and the twin towers of the 19th-century Kostel svatého Ludmily (Church of St. Ludmila), 60m (197ft) high; at an almost equal distance below the surface Náměstí Míru is the city's deepest metro station. Hardly known to visitors from abroad, Riegrovy sady (Rieger Gardens) is laid out on the slopes rising above the main railway station; it offers unusual views over the historic city. Vinohradská, the area's main artery, has a pair of smaller parks along its length: Sady Svatopluka Čecha (Svatopluk Čech gardens), and Náměstí Jiřího z Poděbrad (George of Poděbrady Square), at the heart of which stands Prague's most remarkable modern church.

MODERN MASTERWORK

The Chrám Nejsvětějšího Srdce Páně (Church of the Most Sacred Heart of Our Lord) is generally recognized as the masterpiece of the Slovenian architect Josip Plečnik (1872–1957). He was employed by President Masaryk to convert the Castle into a fitting symbol of the new democratic state of Czechoslovakia, yet found time to design this extraordinary church in a style utterly removed from the prevailing Functionalism of the period. A temple-like structure clad in dark brick-work and studded with stones of grey granite, it has a massive tower in which a huge clock is set in a glazed roundel. Inside, the simplicity of the vast nave is offset by ornate altarpieces and statuary designed by Plečnik himself. Underneath the church is a mysterious barrel-vaulted crypt. The church was completed in 1932, not long before Plečnik returned to work on the beautification of the Slovene capital.

RATINGS

Cultural interest	● ● ●
Historic interest	● ● ●
Walkability	● ● ●

BASICS

✚ 59 H7

Chrám Nejsvětějšího Srdce Páně
✉ Náměstí Jiřího z Poděbrad, Vinohrady, Prague 3
☎ 222 727 713
🕐 Open 30 min before morning services, 1 hour before other services, 1 hour after services. Mass: Mon–Sat 8am, 6pm, Sun 7am, 9am, 11am, 6pm
🎟 Free
Ⓜ Jiřího z Poděbrad
🚊 Tram 11 to Jiřího z Poděbrad; tram 10, 16 to Vinohradská vodárna

An art nouveau apartment block (top) and a decorative art nouveau detail (above) on Slavíkova street, Vinohrady. The huge tower of the Church of the Most Sacred Heart of Our Lord (above middle)

An ornate iron gateway frames the façade of the Vila Amerika

The Vojan Gardens offer a peaceful retreat in Malá Strana

A view across the terraced Gardens beneath Prague Castle

THE SIGHTS

VILA AMERIKA

✚ 58 G8 • Ke Karlovu 20, Nové Město, Prague 2 ☎ 224 918 013 🕓 Apr–end Sep Tue–Sun 10–1.30, 2–5.30; Oct–end Mar Tue–Sun 9.30–1.30, 2–5 🎫 Adult 40Kč, child (6–16) 20Kč 🚇 I.P. Pavlova 🚊 Tram 4, 6, 10, 16, 22, 23 to I.P. Pavlova **www.nm.cz**

This summer residence was built in 1720 by Kilián Ignác Dientzenhofer for Count Jan Václav Michna at a time when this part of the outer New Town was still an area of gardens and orchards. Set back from the street in a little formal garden, with sculptures by Matthias Bernard Braun (1684–1738) and flanked by a pair of identical pavilions, it is a delightful baroque palace in miniature. Since 1932 it has been the Muzeum Antonín Dvořáka (Dvořák Museum), a city counterpart to the composer's rustic birthplace in the village of Nelahozeves (▷ 214–215). Mementoes of the great man are relatively few, though one of the items on show is the gown he wore on being awarded an honorary doctorate by Cambridge University. The place is at its most enchanting when one of the frequent musical evenings is being staged.

VOJANOVY SADY

✚ 57 D5 • U Lužického semináře 17, Malá Strana, Prague 1 ☎ 257 531 839 🕓 Summer 8–7; winter 8–5 🎫 Free 🚇 Malostranská 🚊 Tram 12, 18, 20, 22, 23 to Malostranské náměstí

Far older than the other Malá Strana gardens described on this page, the Vojan Gardens originally formed part of the medieval Arcibiskupský palác (Archbishop's Palace), before becoming the property of the monastery attached to nearby Kostel svatého Josefa (St.

Joseph's Church). Hidden behind high walls, they form a peaceful retreat from the surrounding bustle, and although redesigned many times, still exude a faint air of medieval seclusion. Reminders of their great age exist in the form of a pair of chapels, one with a grotto-like interior. Lawns, shrubs and a scattering of exotic trees give them an informal character which contrasts with the baroque geometry of the area's other gardens.

VRTBOVSKÁ ZAHRADA

✚ 56 D6 • Karmelitská 25, Malá Strana, Prague 1 ☎ 257 531 480 🕓 Apr–end Oct daily 10–6 🎫 Adult 40Kč, child (6–16) 25Kč 🚊 Tram 12, 20, 22, 23 to Malostranské náměstí **www.vrtbovska.cz**

This baroque garden, laid out in terraces on the lower slopes of Petřín Hill, lies hidden behind a modest doorway on Karmelitská street, and is one of the loveliest secrets of Malá Strana. The courtyard through which it is approached has an archway topped by a gilded statue of Hercules by Matthias Bernard Braun, and one of the glories of the garden is its statuary from the workshop of this great sculptor. Stairways lead from the lower level with its aviary and *sala terrena* to a balustraded terrace, from where there is an unusual view of the rooftops of Malá Strana and the Svatého Mikuláš (Church of St. Nicholas, ▷ 122–123). Higher still, a little pavilion offers an even wider prospect. The garden was sadly neglected for many years and its recent restoration almost amounted to a complete reconstruction—as a result the garden has lost some of its period charm.

VYŠEHRAD

See pages 148–149.

ZAHRADY POD PRAŽSKÝM HRADEM

✚ 57 D5 • Valdštejnské náměstí 3, Malá Strana, Prague 1 ☎ 257 010 401/257 530 467 🕓 Apr–end Oct daily 10–6 (last entry 5.30pm) 🎫 Adult 69Kč, child (6–16) 39Kč 🚇 Malostranská 🚊 Tram 12, 20, 22, 23 to Malostranské náměstí **www.palacovezahrady.cz** (in Czech)

Also known as Palácové zahrady pod Pražským hradem (Gardens beneath Prague Castle), this glorious group of terraced gardens clings to the near-vertical slope dropping from the Prague Castle ramparts to the palaces lining Valdštejnská street far below. They were once the private preserve of such aristocratic families as the Pállfys, Ledebours, Kolowrats and Fürstenbergs, but now the palace gardens have been joined together and made accessible to the public. Apart from their intrinsic attractiveness, they form an intriguing alternative route to and from the Hradčany heights (though only in season). The area beneath the Castle was originally kept bare in order to provide a clear field of fire against anyone attempting to storm the complex, but from the mid-16th century palaces began to be built and provided with gardens, the only possible layout being in the form of terraces. Most of the gardens were remodelled in the 18th century, their designers exploiting to great effect the whole range of baroque features like steps and stairways, statuary and fountains, loggias, gazebos and other garden buildings. The Communist regime threw the gardens open to the public, but maintenance was a low priority, and restoration techniques crude. The gardens were closed for many years, but are once again open, some of their charm unfortunately erased by the need for almost total reconstruction.

VÝSTAVIŠTĚ

With a funfair, theatres, sculpture museum and weekend market, Prague's Exhibition Park has something for everyone.

The Výstaviště was originally laid out to celebrate Emperor Franz Josef's Jubilee in 1891. It attracted two million visitors then, and the crowds have been flocking here ever since. The 36ha (89-acre) site in the suburb of Holešovice at the eastern end of Stromovka Park is still dominated by the Průmyslový palác (Palace of Industry), built to house the principal exhibits. This splendid structure of steel and glass, with all sorts of fanciful details, including a spiral staircase wriggling up its central clock tower, is still used for trade fairs and events of all kinds. Among the other buildings and features scattered all over the park are theatres (including a reproduction of Shakespeare's Globe) and the rather run-down Luna Park funfair, and an exceptionally elaborate computer-operated fountain. There is also the wondrous Maroldovo panorama (Marold Panorama, open May–end Oct Tue–Fri 2–5pm; Sat–Sun 10–5; 20Kč), a late 19th-century attempt at virtual reality consisting of a huge circular painting depicting the 1434 Battle of Lipany in all its gruesome detail. Another important, albeit little-visited attraction is the National Museum's Lapidarium (Výstaviště 422, tel 233 375 636; open Tue–Fri noon–6, Sat–Sun and holidays 10–6; adult 40Kč, child 20Kč).

STONEWORK AND STATUARY

The word Lapidarium may conjure up visions of dusty chunks of badly labelled bits of stone, but some of the sculpture assembled here, in one of the spacious pavilions from the 1891 Exhibition, is of outstanding quality. Much of Prague's public statuary consists of reproductions; removed from their original locations to protect them from the elements, many superb examples of the real thing can be enjoyed here at close quarters. Among original works from Karlův most (Charles Bridge) are the statues of St. Ignatius of Loyala and St. Francis Xavier by Ferdinand Maximilian Brokoff (1688–1731) together with others rescued from the bed of the River Vltava after the great flood of 1890. From the Old Town Bridge Tower is a hierarchical group of sculptures with Emperor Charles IV at its centre.

Biding their time to return to the townscape are monuments to disgraced or forgotten figures. The most sensational of these is the memorial to one of Austria's most successful generals, Field marshal Radetzky, held aloft by several of his soldiers. The great man and his monument once enjoyed a prominent position in Malostranské náměstí (Malá Strana Square). However, Habsburg generals were not popular with the Czechs, and the statue was put into compulsory retirement soon after Czechoslovakia won independence in 1918.

RATINGS	
Cultural interest	●●●●
Good for kids	●●●●
Historic interest	●●●
Photo stops	●●●

BASICS

✚ 57 G2 • Výstaviště, Holešovice, Prague 7
☎ 220 103 111
🕐 Grounds: Daily 6am–midnight. Attractions: opening times vary
💰 Grounds: Free. Attractions: prices vary
🚊 Tram 5, 12, 14, 15, 17 to Výstaviště
🍴
📷
www.nm.cz
Information about the Lapidarium of the National Museum.

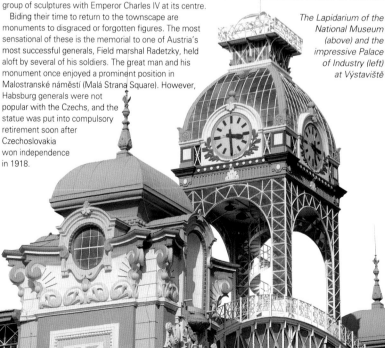

The Lapidarium of the National Museum (above) and the impressive Palace of Industry (left) at Výstaviště

Vyšehrad

A place of myth, legend and real history, this blackened crag dropping precipitously to the Vltava is an iconic site in the development of Czech national consciousness.

A view across the Vltava to Vyšehrad (left); The 17th-century Leopold Gate (middle left); Decorated door of the Church of St. Peter and St. Paul (middle right); Arched walkway, Vyšehrad Cemetery (right)

RATINGS

Cultural interest	● ● ●
Historic interest	● ● ● ●
Photo stops	● ● ● ●

BASICS

➕ 58 F10 ● Národní kulturní památka Vyšehrad, V Pevnosti 159/5b, Vyšehrad, Prague 2

☎ 241 410 352

Ⓜ Vyšehrad, then 10-min walk (▷ walk, 200–201)

🚊 Tram 3, 16, 17, 21 to Výtoň or 7, 18, 24 to Albertov, then 10-min walk uphill

ℹ Information point 'Špička' between Tábor and Leopold gates

📖 *Reflections on Vyšehrad* guidebook in English

🍴 Cafés and restaurants

🛗

www.praha-vysehrad.cz
History and general information in English.

A dramatic statue in Vyšehrad Park (opposite top).
The tomb of Antonín Dvořák at Vyšehrad Cemetery (opposite middle).
The façade of a Cubist apartment block (opposite bottom) designed by Josef Chochol (1880–1956)

SEEING VYŠEHRAD

A mixture of churches, chapels and other buildings, fortifications and landscaped areas on the castle rock at the southern edge of Nové Město make up a pleasant area in which to spend an hour or two away from the bustle of the city just downstream. The most important feature is the Vyšehradský hřbitov (National Cemetery), in which the nation's great and good are buried. Their close-packed tombs contain some excellent funerary sculpture, while other monumental figures by Josef Václav Myslbek (1848–1922), creator of the Wenceslas statue, adorn the nearby lawns. Visible from far away, the twin-towered Kostel svatého Petra a Pavla (Church of St. Peter and St. Paul), a 19th-century rebuilding of a much earlier structure, is one of Prague's most prominent landmarks. Vyšehrad's natural defences were strengthened at various periods; the formidable ramparts make a wonderful viewing platform, with a prospect northwards taking in much of the historic city and vistas southwards of other riverside cliffs and crags. Hollowed out beneath the ramparts are the mysterious spaces of the casemates, while amid the nondescript suburban development at the foot of the fortress is a cluster of buildings in the Cubist style, so peculiar to Prague.

HIGHLIGHTS

RAMPARTS

✉ Cihelná brána a kasematy 🕐 Apr–end Oct daily 9.30–6; Nov–end Mar daily 9.30–5 💰 Adult 30Kč, child (6–16) 20Kč

Most of the Vyšehrad rock is protected by the formidable natural defences of its cliffs. The fortress's most vulnerable side was to the southeast, the direction from which the ancient routeway from southern Bohemia approached Prague. This is also the route you are most likely to take when visiting the area, particularly if you have come from the Vyšehrad metro station. Fortified in medieval times, this flank is now protected by the Táborská brána (Tábor Gate), part of the extensive baroque defences added in the mid-17th century and which enclose most of the rock. The inner line of these defences includes another, much more elaborate gateway, the Leopoldova brána (Leopold Gate), designed by the architect Carlo Lurago (c1618–84). A walkway runs almost the whole way around the ramparts, though sections of it may be inaccessible because of repair work. The most dramatic views are from the southwestern corner, just above the small building housing the Vyšehrad art gallery; far below, toylike trams and cars pass in and out of the road tunnel driven through the rock in the late 19th century. On the northern side of the fortress, the massive Cihelná brána (Brick Gate) gives access to the Kasematy (Casemates). Extending beneath the ramparts for nearly 1km (0.5 miles), these fortifications include a vast hall once used—rather prosaically—as

a store for the city's supply of vegetables. The entrance chamber contains displays on the history of the fortress.

VYŠEHRADSKÝ HŘBITOV A SLAVÍN

🗺 K Rotundě 1 ☎ 224 919 815
🕑 May–end Sep daily 8–7;
Mar–end Apr, Oct daily 8–6; Nov–end Feb 8–5 💵 Free

The cemetery is a place of reverent pilgrimage for patriotic Czechs, and contains the tombs of some 600 worthies, many with internationally famous names. Bedřich Smetana (1824–84) is here, as is Antonín Dvořák (1841–1904), who is accommodated in the arcade which runs round three sides of the area. The cemetery's focal point is the Slavín, a monumental mausoleum built in 1887 as a kind of national pantheon; among the 50 or so great figures resting here are Alfons Mucha (1860–1939) and Josef Václav Myslbek (1848–1922).

CUBIST BUILDINGS

While the historically minded take photographs of the tombs of the famous, architectural students can often be found sketching the Cubist buildings below the Vyšehrad rock. Nowhere else in Prague is there quite such a concentration of these unique early 20th-century structures, though individually none is quite of the quality of the Dům U černé Matky boží (Black Madonna House, ▷ 70). Designed by Josef Chochol (1880–1956), they include two apartment blocks (Nos. 2/56 and 30/98 in Neklanova street), and a terrace of family houses on the Vltava embankment (Nos. 6–10/42 Rašínovo nábřeží), but the outstanding structure is the Vila Kovařovič (No. 3/49 Libušina street), immaculately restored and even boasting a Cubist-style garden.

BACKGROUND

It was on Vyšehrad that Princess Libuše supposedly fell into a swoon and foresaw the foundation of the city of Prague (▷ 24), and it was from here that warriors stormed out to battle their female opponents in the 'War of the Maidens' (▷ 25). Myth and legend aside, the rock was used by early Czech kings and princes as an alternative, easily defended, citadel to Hradčany. When fortresses of this kind became redundant in the 19th century, Vyšehrad's

romantic past was revived by nationalistically minded Czechs; the citadel's churches were restored or rebuilt, and what had been a humble parish graveyard became the National Cemetery. Solemn events of nationwide significance took place here, one of the most recent being the start of the student procession that precipitated the Velvet Revolution of 1989.

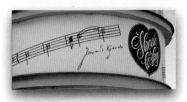

Zbraslav

●

The small town of Zbraslav is now part of Greater Prague and its splendid baroque palace has become a worthy home for the country's collections of Asian art.

RATINGS

Cultural interest	● ● ● ●
Historic interest	● ● ●
Photo stops	● ● ●

BASICS

✛ Off map 58 E10 • Zámek Zbraslav, Bartoňova 2, Zbraslav, Prague 5
☎ 257 921 638
🕙 Tue–Sun 10–6
💶 Adult 80Kč, child (6–16) 40Kč. Free 1st Wed in month 3–8pm
🚌 Bus 129, 241, 243, 255, 360 from Smíchovské nádraží metro station to Zbraslavské náměstí (14 min)
📷 Guided tour by prior arrangement; price by agreement
☕ Čajovna (tea room) with a range of exotic teas
🏪 Shop with museum-related souvenirs and books

www.ngprague.cz
The National Gallery's website with general information on all its branches, as well as descriptions of the collections at Zbraslav.

A painting from Hiroshige's 53 Stations of the Tokaido in the collection of Japanese art at Zbraslav (above left).
The baroque palace at Zbraslav (above middle) houses the National Gallery's collections of Asian and Islamic Art.
Chinese art—three soldiers (tomb guardians) dating from around 300BC (above right)

SEEING ZBRASLAV

In the first half of the 20th century, this little riverside town just south of Prague's built-up area was a popular destination with weekend trippers. Crowds would spend their days in the surrounding countryside or in the town's pubs and beer gardens. Nowadays visitors come here to see the Zbraslavský zámek, the baroque palace which is home to the National Gallery's collections of art and objects from China, Japan, India, Tibet, Southeast Asia and the Islamic world. The palace looks vast and imposing, but there's no need to feel intimidated; the collections are of the highest quality, and although quite wide-ranging, are not present in such quantity as to exhaust your interest. They are immaculately displayed, with labelling in English as well as Czech, and with explanatory panels in the form of scrolls. A couple of hours spent here, with a break on the cushions of the *čajovna* (tea room), is almost certain to be an enjoyable experience for even the least enthusiastic museum-goer.

HIGHLIGHTS

JAPANESE ART

Displayed in a series of rooms on the ground floor are exquisite Japanese enamels, ceramics, fans, screens, religious objects, lacquer-work, paintings and drawings. Many objects, such as boxes and walking-stick handles, are tiny, almost jewel-like, while others like the huge cloisonné dish hung on a wall are of an impressive scale, though none the less intricately worked. The gallery has a fine collection of paintings and graphic works by masters such as Hiroshige (1797–1858) and Hokusai (1760–1849); because of their fragility they are displayed in rotation, and you may not get to see Hokusai's famous *Breaking Wave off Kanagawa* with Mount Fuji in the far distance. However, other equally delectable pages from his album *36 Views of Mount Fuji* will almost certainly be on view, as will examples of Hiroshige's landscapes and scenes of everyday life in pre-industrial Japan.

CHINESE ART

Together with Japanese art, the Chinese art on the second floor forms the core of the National Gallery's collection, and is even more comprehensive, covering its evolution from the very earliest times.

TIP

● Good Czech cuisine can be enjoyed at the restaurant on the town square; it's called Škoda lásky, the Czech title of the musical hit, *What a shame about love,* by local-born composer Jaromír Vejvoda (1902–88) and has numerous mementoes belonging to him.

THE SIGHTS

Bronze Age items range from 4,000-year-old pots of great simplicity to the later funerary statuettes and other figures manufactured in quantity to provide companionship beyond the grave. As well as mythical animals, they include soldiers, officials, grooms and a pair of fiercely gesticulating guards with awesome teeth, no doubt intended to deter tomb raiders. By the 8th century AD the figures had become more ostentatious, with much use of glazed finishes; the horses in a variety of life-like poses are particularly fine. By the 11th century, true porcelain was being produced, and there are many superb examples of vessels of many kinds, among them a pair of monumental palace vases from the 17th century. A special section is devoted to the art of Buddhism, which culminates in a beautifully spotlit pantheon of deities.

BACKGROUND

Zbraslav's *zámek* was originally a monastery, founded by Cistercian monks as long ago as the 13th century. Its fortunes fluctuated; first destroyed by the Hussites in the early 15th century, it suffered the same fate in the Thirty Years' War (1618–1648). The present palatial baroque structure dates from the early 18th century and was the result of collaboration between the architects František Maximilian Kaňka (1674–1766) and Jan Blažej Santini-Aichl (1677–1723). Not long after its completion, the monks were expelled, and part of the complex was subsequently used as a sugar factory; a factory still dominates Zbraslav's main square. In the early 20th century the palace was restored by the civic-minded industrialist Cyril Dobenín, whose bust can be found at the end of the ground floor cloister. Under Communism, the palace became a somewhat incongruous home for the National Gallery's collection of modern Czech sculpture. Examples, such as a cast of Otto Gutfreund's charming *Family Group* , are still dotted around the attractive grounds, though the collection itself has moved to the Veletržní palác (Trade Fair Palace, ▷ 139–141).

Exhibits on display at Zbraslav include a beautiful early 19th-century Chinese tetrahedral vase (above), 19th-century (Qing Dynasty) silk embroidery (above left) and exquisite 17th-century Japanese porcelain (top)

ŽIŽKOV

This vibrant working-class district is famous for its authentic pubs, military museum, TV tower and an awesome, empty mausoleum.

RATINGS

Cultural interest	● ● ●
Historic interest	● ● ● ●
Photo stops	● ● ● ●

BASICS

✚ 59 J6 • Žižkov, Prague 3

Armádní muzeum

✉ U Památníku 2

☎ 973 204 924

🕐 Tue–Sun 10–6

🎟 Free

🚌 Bus 133, 207 from Florenc metro station to U Památníku, and a short steep walk

🏪 Limited range of souvenirs

🏛

www.militarymuseum.cz (in Czech)

Laid out a century ago at the foot of Žižkov Hill to the east of central Prague, the close-packed tenements of 'Red Žižkov' have always been a proletarian stronghold and have so far resisted gentrification. Feisty figures emerging from its dingy streets have included the Nobel Prize laureate Jaroslav Seifert (1901–86) and Olga Plíchalová (1933–96), better known as Olga Havlová, the former president's first wife. More recently it has become home to the city's largest Roma community. Its raucous drinking dens are treasured by regulars as unspoiled examples of what a Prague pub should be. The name of the area celebrates the Hussite general Jan Žižka (1360–1424), who won his most spectacular victory on the rock spur now crowned by the Národní památník (National Monument).

BIG AND BRASSY

Despite having only one eye, Žižka was the most successful general of the Hussite Wars. In 1420, on the hill now named after him, he led his peasant army to a decisive victory over the vastly superior professional force sent against him by pope and emperor (▷ 27). His fearsome equestrian statue in bronze, reputedly the biggest in the world, stands in front of the National Monument, which looks like a perfect example of Stalinist concrete architecture, but was built between 1925 and 1932 to commemorate the Czechoslovak Legions who had fought on the Allied side in World War I. The remains of the Unknown Soldier here were joined in Communist times by the corpses of Party dignitaries, mummified in the manner of Lenin in his Red Square tomb. They have long since been removed, and the empty National Monument awaits some new occupant. In the meantime, the reward for undertaking the stiff climb to the top of the hill is a fantastic view over central Prague. There's an even more stunning vista from the viewing gallery of the Televizní vysílač (TV tower, ▷ 125).

ARMÁDNÍ MUZEUM

Built at the same time as the National Monument, the Armádní muzeum (Army Museum), near the foot of the hill, tells the internationally little-known story of the Czechoslovak forces between 1914 and 1945. It's a stirring tale of difficult times and divided loyalties: of Czechs and Slovaks fighting on both sides in World War I; of the betrayal at Munich in 1938 of one of Europe's most modern and motivated armies, and of resistance at home and abroad in World War II.

A huge equestrian statue of the great Hussite general Jan Žižka (bottom) stands in front of the National Monument (below) on top of the hill named after him

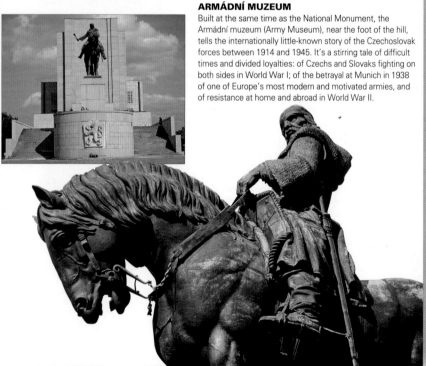

THE SIGHTS

This chapter gives information on things to do in Prague other than sightseeing. Shops are shown on the maps on pages 158–161 and entertainment venues on the maps on pages 170–173.

What to Do

SHOPPING

When it comes to shopping, Prague has plenty to offer: quirky and super-chic boutiques, antique shops, department stores, modern shopping malls, markets, bookstores and almost everything in-between. Among the local products on sale, don't miss the celebrated Czech crystal and glass or the beautiful Bohemian garnets.

FASHION

Unlike in other European cities, fashion in Prague hasn't had long to evolve. Communist department stores like Máj (now Tesco) didn't exactly follow international style trends. While developing their own sense of style, Praguers have been strongly influenced by other countries, especially Italy and Spain. The blonde in stilettos, faded jeans, and tank top (with a Dior bag) is the prototypical Slavic supermodel, and it is these women—their images all over the tabloids—who lead the trends.

Showing off a beautiful piece of porcelain in a shop in Prague

On Na příkopě, the main artery of the city's fashion district, you're never far from a branch of the Italian fashion chain Bloom, there are at least 15 shoe stores, and Spanish retailer Mango has expanded into the building next door. The exclusive designer boutiques, like Versace at the end of the avenue, are an enclave of exclusivity. H&M has opened two stores in central Prague, on Na příkopě and Jindřišská. There's nothing else like Pařížská street in Prague: from Hermès to Dior, the five-block-long boutique-studded avenue is the city's own Rodeo Drive.

Czech clothing designers have carved out their own niche and are gaining a following among the city's fashionistas. The small boutiques around Staroměstské náměstí are popular with stylists.

JEWELLERY

Bohemian garnets are among the most beautiful in the world. Whether set in gold or silver, the deep red stones always look elegant and timeless. Antique garnet jewellery, with its darker stones and delicate art deco designs, can be found at almost any antique shop. The prices and selection at the factory-direct Český Granát Turnov (branches on Dlouhá and Panská) are some of the best in town.

CRYSTAL, GLASS AND PORCELAIN

Prague is renowned for its fine crystal, glass and porcelain. The art of glass-blowing has been practiced in Bohemia since the 14th century and Czech crystal is a big source of national pride. Moser is the granddaddy of crystal houses, but prices reflect its status as 'the glass of kings'. The ancient thoroughfare of Celetná has several good shops, including Celetná Crystal (No. 15) and Celetná 7. Many stores will pack and send your purchases free of charge to local hotels so you don't have to carry breakables around with you.

FOOD

Culinary delights are easy to find, either fresh or packaged. There are some excellent Italian gourmet stores in central Prague, such as Sapori Italiana (Perlová 10, metro Národní třída). Czech delicacies such as tinned Prague ham, *oplátky* spa wafers and *Becherovka*, the herbal liqueur, can be found at any grocery store. Wine bars/ shops like Monarch and U Závoje have a huge selection of international, Moravian and regional wines, including Macedonian Vranac and Hungarian tokaj. Culinaria, on Skořepka, has goods from Fauchon and Maxim's de Paris.

ANTIQUES

For antiques, look for signs that say *starožitnosti*, and for antique books, *antikvariát*. Prices are marked, but you can make a

polite counteroffer if you feel justified. Lace items, small paintings and art deco tea sets are widely available and not very expensive. Art Décoratif, on Melantrichova, has lots of delightful old finds. The bazaar at the Palmovka metro stop is a treasure-hunter's paradise, with an array of old and antique furniture.

MARKETS

Signs saying *tržnice* point the way to the small markets usually run by Vietnamese vendors who sell cheaply made but useful goods,

A decorative, pictorial sign hanging ouside a wine shop on Celetná

from plastic suitcases for storing clothes to wallets, bags and shoes. These are normally down narrow passageways that open into interior courtyards. The largest outdoor market is Holešovická tržnice.

PRACTICALITIES

Most stores are open from 9 or 10am to 6pm Monday to Friday, with shorter hours on Saturday. In popular shopping areas most shops are also open on Sunday.

Check the door when you enter for a credit card sign; most clothing and shoe stores accept them, but many smaller boutiques do not (and some that do may not have a sign, so always ask).

Expect to hear *dobrý den* when you enter a shop and *na shledanou* as you leave; it's polite to return the greeting and farewell.

Malá Strana

🚇 Malostranská, then tram 22 or 23 to Pražský hrad

No visit to Prague is complete without a walk down charming Nerudova, the steep and ancient street that leads from the Castle to Malostranské náměstí (Malá Strana Square) and Karlův most (Charles Bridge). This was the last leg of the Royal Way in the time of kings, and up here it's easy to imagine the clatter of horse-drawn carriages on the cobblestones. It's a great place to find the artisan crafts that Czechs excel at—wooden toys, ceramics, marionettes and glass.

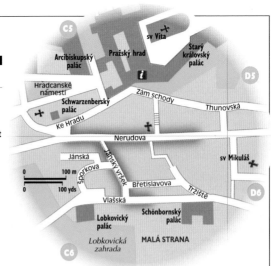

NERUDOVA

The easiest way to begin the walk is with a picturesque tram ride up to the castle. Take tram 22 or 23 to

Stamps on display in the window of Philately Antique Coins

Pražský hrad. If you've already seen the castle, simply walk through its courtyards and exit onto the square in front. The stunning panorama of Prague rooftops over the wall on your left is worth stopping for. Follow the sloping walkway along the wall to the bottom and turn left. You'll be at the top of Nerudova, in front of the splendid Zlatá Hvězda hotel.

Directly across the street is Turecká čajovna, a tiny tea room selling Turkish delight, nougat, halva, dried fruit and exotic teas (only open on weekends). Next door (No. 51) is Philately Antique Coins, which, as its name suggests, has a fascinating collection of old coins, as well as antique stamps, garnet rings, clocks and small paintings. Sharing the same number is Galerie Boema, with its pristine art deco jewellery, antique religious icons,

toy soldiers and military medals. As you pass the frescoed building at No. 47, look up to see the plaque commemorating this street's namesake: Czech writer and poet Jan Neruda lived here from 1834 to 1891.

The handmade wooden marionettes at Obchod s loutkami (No. 47) aren't just for children, but for keen collectors as well. Le Siants Galerie (No. 36) specializes in international contemporary paintings, graphics and sculpture and represents many artists from Central and Eastern Europe.

Another few steps and there's a stairway going off to your right. Walk down three flights of easy steps, past the wooden knight holding a *pivo* (beer) sign, to the Art Deco Gallery Shop (Jánský vršek 8) which has knick-knacks from the 1920s and 1930s and a quiet café in its courtyard. At the very bottom of the street is Signet (Vlašská 15), a respected dealer of old Czech, German and Russian books. Around the corner to the left is an important store in the city's fashion scene; the walls of Pavla & Olga (Vlašská 13, ▷ 164) are covered in snapshots of models wearing their clever, body-skimming designs.

Back up on Nerudova, the Czech natural crafts store Manufaktura (No. 31) has tiny quail-egg shaped vegetable soaps, beeswax candles, wooden wind chimes and hand-painted tin dishes.

Cross the street here and walk through the passageway at No. 32, to reach the Romen Little Shop, a gallery selling clothing, jewellery, bags, paintings and CDs by Roma (gypsy) artists from Central Europe. This unique non-profit store donates it proceeds to the communities where the artisans live.

There are some good crystal stores in this stretch, including Axel Crystal (No. 25), which has

beautiful crystal earrings, ornaments, vases and stemware. All manner of traditional nesting dolls (*matryoshka*) are for sale at Czech Traditional Handicrafts (No. 23).

For traditional Czech ceramics go into U Zeleného čaje (No. 17), a

Le Siants Galerie on Nerudova sells contemporary works of art

salon de thé that also sells more than 100 kinds of tea. Across from the Romanian Embassy, U Zlaté Číše (No. 16) is an atmospheric store filled with old postcards, posters, books, street signs and stamps. There are delightful oil paintings of the city's ancient landmarks—Prašná brána, Týn Church, Karlův most (Charles Bridge)—in all sizes at Galerie u Červeného beránka. And at Candele Artistche (No. 7) you can pick out your own colours for a custom-designed candle that looks like old-fashioned ribbon candy.

SQUARE
Malostranské náměstí 5/28, Prague 1
Tel 296 826 104
🚇 Daily 8am–1am
🚊 Tram 12, 20, 22, 23 to Malostranské náměstí

Nové Město

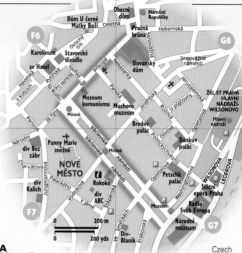

HOW TO GET THERE

🚇 Muzeum

The L-shaped area from Václavské náměstí (Wenceslas Square) to Na příkopě is the densest shopping area in the city, with European clothing chains dominating the scene. Václavské náměstí has an exhilarating mix of shops, hotels, casinos and restaurants competing for attention. Na příkopě, a pedestrian avenue that in ancient times was a moat, is full of people strolling, sitting at outdoor cafés and, of course, shopping.

VÁCLAVSKÉ NÁMĚSTÍ

At the square's midpoint two British retail giants face off: Marks & Spencer (No. 36) has smart clothes and sells popular English foods. Across the square, Debenhams (No. 21) has one of

Trendy shoes in the Baťa shop window on Wenceslas Square

the biggest shoe and cosmetics departments in the city. The British department store sits on the corner of Jindřišská, and on the opposite corner, at No. 19, is the city's newest Sephora branch.

There's an urban playground feel at the Nike store (No. 18), which has athletic shoes and soccer shirts. On the bottom left corner of the square is Pro Mod (No. 2), selling feminine clothes.

On the right corner of the square the Palác Koruna building (No. 1), dating from 1912, houses cafés and more than two dozen boutiques. Pinito Boutique has children's clothes with a Spanish flair and there are always glamorous dresses and jackets from the Italian designers at Anima Tua (▷ 164). Bontonland Megastore (▷ 167) on the lower level is the largest music store in Central Europe.

NA PŘÍKOPĚ

Leave Palác Koruna onto Na příkopě and to your right you'll see a splendid building edged in gold leaf that houses Benetton's Prague flagship store (No. 4). Next door, Mango's inexpensive and trendy clothes, bags and sunglasses have a carefree, Costa del Sol feel. Along this stretch are several more trendy clothing and shoe stores, including Clock House (No. 3) and Jackpot & Cottonfield (No. 13).

Still on the right, look for a narrow passage at No. 12 leading into the Černá růže (Black Rose) secessionist-era building. Here you'll find another gallery of sophisticated boutiques carrying designer labels, including Fashion Gate, which has elegant suits, ties and leather accessories from Valentino and Christian Dior. Roberto Cavalli has strappy heels and thigh-high boots in shiny metallic leather and snakeskin. The large Daniel Hechter/Pal Zileri store has hyper-stylish clothing for men and women who want to dress like rock stars.

Take the escalator to the second level to find Moser (▷ 163), the 'glass of kings', and its six plush rooms of exquisite, lead-free crystal. Up here you'll also find luxurious sleepwear at Madonna, and professional beauty products at Dermacol Studio (▷ 166). If Moser's prices are too steep, try Porcela Plus (outside at No. 17, ▷ 163).

After exiting Černá růže continue walking up Na příkopě, where the Zara flagship store (No. 15) is always crowded with fans of its sales and designer-inspired clothing. Further up on the left, the elegant Yanny boutique (No. 27, ▷ 165), with its collections from Alberta Ferretti's Philosophy, Jean Paul Gaultier, and Dolce & Gabbana, is a regular stop for women on Prague's best-dressed list.

A few more stores up is Taiza (No. 31, ▷ 165), where Paris-based Czech designers Katerina Baloun and Richard Rozbora create exclusive—and expensive—*prêt-a-porter* and couture dresses for a loyal clientele.

If you need an espresso to keep going, visit the *kavárna* in the Obecní dům (Municipal House), about 90m (100 yards) further on.

An exquisite vase on display in Moser in the Černá růže building

SLOVANSKÝ DŮM

Across the avenue, look for the yellow Slovánský dům (Slavonic House) at No. 22. Mexx, with its casual, sporty clothes for men, women and children, is the anchor retailer for the small boutiques within that sell exclusive brands. The Beltissimo store here is the only place in the city that carries coveted shoes and bags from Camper, but if you're curious about the patented Italian shoe technology that prevents sweating, have a look in GEOX (▷ 168), which has a devoted following.

WHERE TO EAT

KOGO

Na příkopě 22 (Slovanský dům), Prague 1
Tel 221 451 258-9
🕐 Daily 8am–11pm
🚇 Můstek, Náměstí Republiky
🚋 Tram 5, 8, 14 to Náměstí Republiky

Staré Město

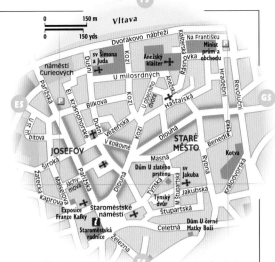

HOW TO GET THERE
🚇 Náměstí Republiky

The narrow, winding
streets around
Staroměstské náměstí (Old
Town Square) are popular
with young Czech
designers. You won't see
any chain stores in this
charming area, only small
ateliers and design studios
dotted among antique
stores and cafés. On the
other side of the square,
however, the mood shifts
from local to international.
Behind the leafy linden
trees on Pařížská (Paris
street) are some of the
most glamorous names in
fashion: Dior, Vuitton
and Hermès.

DLOUHÁ

Exit Náměstí Republiky metro
station and walk two blocks along
Revoluční to Dlouhá, which begins

*A charming poster in Philharmonia
music store on Pařížská*

on the left. On this winding street,
which ends at Staroměstské
náměstí, you can find everything
from Moravian wine to Bohemian
garnets. Antik v Dlouhé (No. 37) has
an eclectic mix of objects from the
19th century, including jewellery
and ceramics. Český Granát Turnov
(No. 28–30, ▷ 167) has the best
prices and selection of garnet
jewellery in the city. Sejto (No. 24,
▷ 167) has sumptuous pillows,
tablecloths and quilts made from
hand-screened silk.
    Follow Dlouhá to V Kolkovně, a
small street to the right, where
Alexandra Pavalová and Ivana
Satranková design tailored,
modern womenswear for Timoure
et Group (No. 6, ▷ 165). One
street over, on Dušní, a former
costume designer whips up slinky
evening dresses at Boutique Tatiana
(No. 1, ▷ 164). Back on Dlouhá,

the one-of-a-kind
sophisticated looks at Klára
Nademlýnská's *atelier* (No. 7,
▷ 164) suit women with a strong
sense of individual style.
    If you haven't visited
Staroměstské náměstí yet you'll
want to stop here and admire
the baroque, medieval and
Renaissance buildings that ring
this charming square. The huge
statue in the middle is of religious
reformer Jan Hus (▷ 27). The
next street leading off to the
right is Pařížská. Hold on to your
credit cards.

PAŘÍŽSKÁ

If Italian shoes or bags are your
weakness, you'll have a hard time
getting off this street without
emptying your wallet. Even if you
can resist the boots at Francesco
Biasia (No. 5) and sleek stilettos at
Ferragamo (No. 10), your willpower
will be seriously tested when you
see the chic designs in the
windows of Panucci (No. 10) and
Alberto Guardiani (No. 24, ▷ 168);
not to mention Louis Vuitton (No.
11, ▷ 168), where there's a huge
selection of totes, luggage and
shoes in the latest designs.
    On Pařížská not just diamonds,
but pearls, aquamarines, emeralds
and rubies are a girl's best friend.
Halada (No. 7) and Carollinum (No.
11, ▷ 167) both offer personalized
assistance to help you select from
their exclusive jewellery and
watches: pearls from Mikimoto,
chokers from Van Clef and Arpels,
watches by Chopard, Piaget,
Breitling and Rolex. For the
unmistakable glitter of Austrian
crystal, Swarovski (No. 16) has an
excellent selection of earrings
and necklaces.
    In summer there's always a
queue at Cremaria Milano (No. 20),
which sells Italian *gelato* (ice-cream).
A scoop and a seat at an umbrella-
covered table is a great way to relax.

Continuing
down the avenue,
you will find luxury accessories at
Hermès (No. 12) like carved
wood-handled umbrellas and
hand-folded ties. Hugo Boss (No. 6)
sells men's casual wear with a twist
of James Bond, and this shop
carries the designer's full line of

*Pařížská has a range of shops
selling stylish shoes*

clothes, shoes and accessories.
Hugo Boss Woman (No. 28) has
simple, elegant shifts, skirts and
jackets in neutrals like camel
and chocolate.
    If you've had your fill of fashion,
Antikvariát Grafika (No. 8) has
charming 19th-century postcards of
Prague and antique maps suitable
for framing. One-of-a-kind exotic
home furnishings from India and
South Asia are available at Le Patio
Lifestyle (No. 20, ▷ 167), where
you can buy anything from a candle
to a candelabra.

PRAVDA
Pařížská 17, Staré Město, Prague 1
Tel 222 326 203
www.pravda.bacchusgroup.cz
🕐 Daily 12–12
🚇 Staroměstská
🚋 Tram 17, 18 to Staroměstská

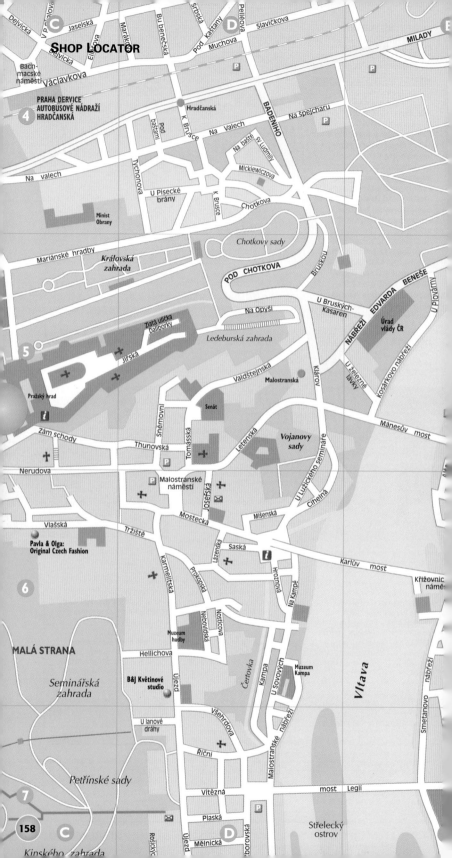

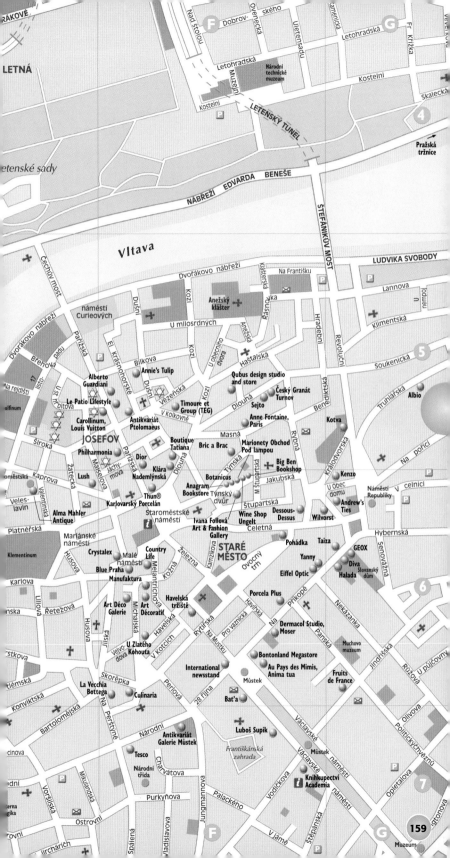

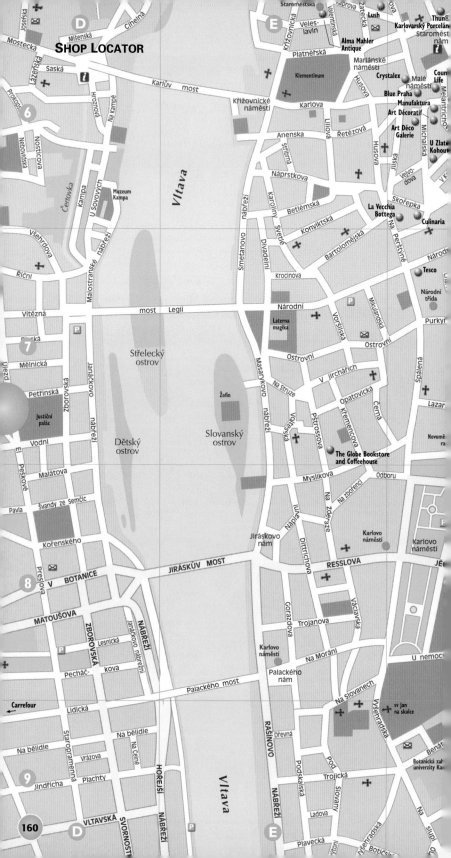

SHOP LOCATOR

Staroměstská
Kaprova
Žatecká
Valentinská
Lush
Thun®
Josefská
Mišenská
Karlovarský Porcelán
Staroměst
nám
Veles-
lavin
Mostecká
Cihelná
Platnéřská
D
E
Alma Mahler
Antique
Marlánské
náměstí
Lázeňská
Saská
Klementinum
Husova
Crystalex
Malé
náměstí
Coun
Life
Prokopská
Na Kampé
Karlův most
Blue Praha
Manufaktura
Nebovidská
Hrozňová
Křižovnické
náměstí
Karlova
Art Décoratif
Melantrichov
6
Nosticova
Karlova
Art Déco
Galerie
U Zlaté
Kohou
Anenska
Liliova
Řetězová
Husova
Jilská
Michalská
Stříbrná
Náprstkova
Vejvo-
dova
Čertovka
Kampa
U Sovových
Muzeum
Kampa
Karoliny
Betlémská
Skořepka
Malostranské
nábřeží
Smetanovo
Světlé
Konviktská
La Vecchia
Bottega
Všehrdova
Na Perštýně
Culinaria
Řiční
Divadelni
Bartolomějská
Národ
Vitézná
Krocinova
Tesco
Pinská
most
Legií
Národní
Národní
třída
7
Mélnická
Janáčkovo
Střelecký
ostrov
Laterna
magika
Voršilská
Mikulandská
Purkyř
Zborovská
Petřinská
Žofin
Ostrovní
Ostrovní
Spálená
Justiční
palác
Masarykovo
Na Struze
V jirchářích
Lazar
vodni
nábřeží
Dětský
ostrov
Slovanský
ostrov
Opatovická
Černá
Novomě
ra
Peškové
Pštrossova
Vojtéšská
Kremencova
The Globe Bookstore
and Coffeehouse
Pavla
Malátova
Myslíkova
Odboru
Švandy ze Semčic
Na Zderaze
Na zbořenci
Karlovo
náměstí
Karlovo
náměstí
F
Kořenského
Náplavní
Dittrichova
Jiráskovo
nám
Preslova
8
V BOTANICE
JIRÁSKŮV MOST
RESSLOVA
Je
MATOUŠOVA
Gorazdova
Václavská
ZBOROVSKA
Lesnická
Trojanova
Janáčkovo nábřeží
Pecháč-
kova
Karlovo
náměstí
Na Moráni
U nemoc
Palackého
nám
Palackého most
Carrefour
Lidická
Na slovanech
sv Jan
na skalce
Na bělidle
Dřevná
Vyšehradská
Na bělidle
Staropramenná
Vrázova
Na Celné
RAŠÍNOVO
9
Jindřicha
Plachty
HOŘEJŠÍ
Podskalská
Trojická
Botanická zah
univerzity Ka
Slovany
Benár
Ladova
160
D
VLTAVSKÁ
SVORNOST
NÁBŘEŽÍ
NÁBŘEŽÍ
E
Vltava
Piavecká
Botišc

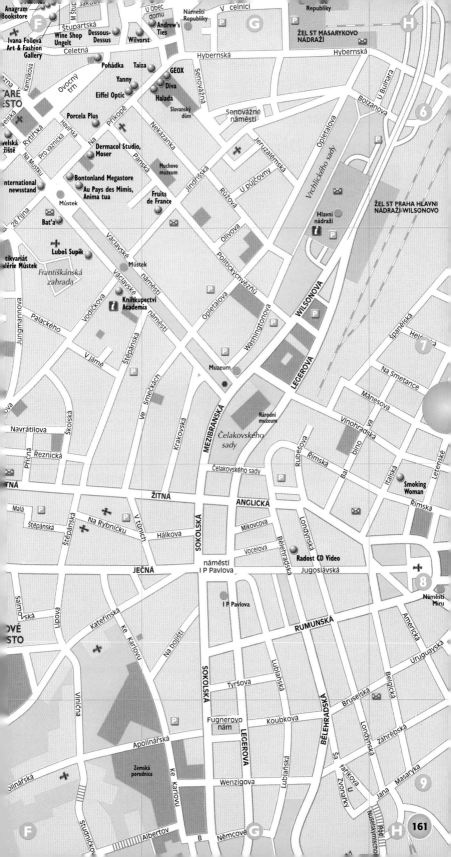

Shopping Directory

ANTIQUES & AUCTION HOUSES

ALMA MAHLER ANTIQUE
Map 159 E6
Valentinská 7, Josefov, Prague 1
Tel 223 258 65
www.almamahler.cz (online shopping at www.antiqueshop.cz)
The Czech family that owns this shop—there are two others at Radnické schody 9 and Týnská 7—is one of the largest antique dealers in the country. This one is in the cellar of an historic building in the Jewish quarter and sells a wide range of items, from lace tablecloths and delicate garnet jewellery to crystal chandeliers and cherry-wood wardrobes. Nearly every piece comes from a Bohemian home and dates from the 19th or early 20th century, and the prices are lower than at many other antique stores in central Prague.
◎ Daily 10–6 🚇 Staroměstská
🚊 Tram 17, 18 to Staroměstská

ANTIKVARIÁT GALERIE MŮSTEK
Map 159 F7
Národní 40 (Adria Palác), Nové Město, Prague 1
Tel 224 949 587
This shop sells fascinating old maps, sketches, antique books, graphics and posters, some dating as far back as the 16th century. Most items are Czech, German or Austrian in origin, but there are usually some interesting Asian prints as well. You'll find something here to suit every price range.
◎ Mon–Fri 10–7, Sat 12–4, Sun 2–6
🚇 Můstek

ANTIKVARIÁT PTOLOMAEUS
Map 159 F5
Široká 15, Josefov, Prague 1
Tel 222 329 985
Whether you're an armchair traveller or a globetrotter, you'll be entranced by the fascinating historical maps and old globes in this store. Some of the rare 16th-century maps can be quite pricey, but there are less expensive ones for sale. Don't forget to look around you: there are lovely old paintings and pencil sketches on the walls.
◎ Daily 10.30–6 🚇 Staroměstská
🚊 Tram 17, 18 to Staroměstská

ART DÉCO GALERIE
Map 159 F6
Michalská 21, Staré Město, Prague 1
Tel 224 223 076
A visit to this absorbing shop is like having free run of your eccentric grandmother's attic. Open for only a few hours a week, it specializes in mid-priced items from the 1920s to the 1950s. You'll probably lose all track of time rummaging through old Czech magazines, trying on hats and costume jewellery, and deciding if you should buy a martini set or a mantel clock.
◎ Mon–Fri 2–7 🚇 Národní třída
🚊 Tram 6, 9, 18, 22, 23 to Národní třída

Window shopping at Antikvariát Ptolomaeus in Josefov

ART DÉCORATIF
Map 159 F6
Melantrichova 5, Staré Město, Prague 1
Tel 224 222 283
Art Décoratif specializes in spot-on, high-quality reproductions of jewellery, glass and lamps from the secessionist and art nouveau period. Czech artists painstakingly re-create items like Tiffany lamps, chandelier earrings and swan-necked wine pitchers. The elegant shopfront is a perfect reproduction of the style popularized by the Czech painter from the same period, Alfons Mucha (1860–1939).
◎ Daily 10–8 🚇 Můstek

BRIC A BRAC
Map 159 F5
Týnská 7, Staré Město, Prague 1
Tel 222 326 484
There's something interesting everywhere you look in this cluttered but charming shop, down a passageway behind Týn Church: rows of battered Cyrillic typewriters, drawers stuffed with military medals, ladies' evening bags strung along a wire, old marionettes and stacks of 33-inch records. You could end up with a rare treasure or a curious trinket.
◎ Daily 11–7 🚇 Náměstí Republiky
🚊 Tram 5, 8 to Dlouhá třída

U ZLATÉHO KOHOUTA
Map 159 F6
Michalská 3, Staré Město, Prague 1
Tel 224 212 874
www.violin-hron.cz
The Hron family—Jiři, Pavlina and Roman—are expert dealers in what they call 'fine old and antique' violins, violas, cellos, double basses and bows.
◎ Variable hours, check the door
🚇 Můstek

BOOKS

ANAGRAM BOOKSTORE
Map 159 F6
Týnský dvůr (Ungelt courtyard), Staré Město, Prague 1
Tel 224 895 737
www.anagram.cz
In addition to a large section devoted entirely to Czech authors, this small English-language bookstore has an excellent selection of oversized art, architecture, photography and design books. A separate room has children's titles.
◎ Mon–Sat 10–8, Sun 10–7
🚇 Náměstí Republiky 🚊 Tram 5, 8 to Dlouhá třída

BIG BEN BOOKSHOP
Map 159 F5
Malá Štupartská 5, Staré Město, Prague 1
Tel 224 826 565
www.bigbenbookshop.com
You'll find the very latest American and British fiction and nonfiction titles at this well-stocked, English-language bookstore. Nominees and winners of major literary prizes get their own shelf, and the history section, in particular, is truly impressive.

WHAT TO DO

Mon–Fri 9–6.30, Sat 10–5, Sun noon–5 ⓂNáměstí Republiky 🚃Tram 5, 8 to Dlouhá třída

THE GLOBE BOOKSTORE AND COFFEE HOUSE
Map 160 E7
Pštrossova 6, Nové Město, Prague 1
Tel 224 934 203
www.globebookstore.cz
The Globe is part of Prague's expatriate lore—it was founded by five Americans in the early 1990s. In addition to the excellent café, there are English-language magazines, new and secondhand books and internet access.
Daily 10am–midnight ⓂNárodní třída 🚃Tram 6, 9, 18, 22, 23 to Národní třída

INTERNATIONAL NEWSSTAND
Map 159 F6
Bottom of Václavské náměstí, Nové Město, Prague 1
This is one of the best places in the city to find international magazines and major newspapers. Several racks display a wide selection of British, Italian, French, German, US and Russian publications.
Daily 8am–8pm ⓂMůstek

KNIHKUPECTVÍ ACADEMIA
Map 159 F7
Václavské náměstí 34, Nové Město, Prague 1
Tel 224 223 511
www.academia.cz
You could spend hours looking around this three-floor bookstore. There are several foreign-language sections, but you will also find the complete, untranslated works of authors like Klíma and Kafka. The travel section has great maps for hiking and cycling in the Czech countryside. When you've finished browsing, have a coffee or a glass of wine in the café on the second floor.
Store: Mon–Fri 9–8, Sat 9.30–7, Sun 9.30–6. Café: Mon–Fri 10–7, Sat 11–6, Sun 11–5 ⓂMůstek

CRYSTAL AND PORCELAIN
MOSER
Map 159 F6
Na příkopě 12 (Černá růže building), Nové Město, Prague 1
Tel 224 211 293
www.moser-glass.com
Founded in 1857, this celebrated Czech crystal company is known for making 'the glass of kings'. A stroll around the many rooms at their flagship store shows you

why: You will see photos of kings, queens and presidents toasting each other with Moser stemware. There is a dizzying number of crystal designs to choose from—delicate to substantial, silver-rimmed to gold-etched—and then the choice becomes traditional clear or brilliant tints like topaz, alexandrite, aquamarine and beryl. There is also another shop at Malé náměstí 11.
Mon–Fri 10–8, Sat–Sun 10–7 ⓂMůstek

The following three crystal and porcelain shops are part of the same company and stock a large selection of authentic Bohemia® lead crystal, porcelain tableware and decorative objects. The traditional pink porcelain might not be to everyone's taste, but the

An elaborate window display at Thun® Karlovarský Porcelán

whimsical designs—flamingos and elephants—will bring a smile.

CRYSTALEX
Map 159 F6
Malé náměstí 6, Staré Město, Prague 1
Tel 224 228 459
Daily 10–8 ⓂStaroměstská 🚃Tram 17, 18 to Staroměstská

PORCELA PLUS
Map 159 F6
Na příkopě 17, Nové Město, Prague 1
Tel 224 239 653
Daily 10–8 ⓂMůstek

THUN® KARLOVARSKÝ PORCELÁN
Map 159 F6
Pařížská 2, Josefov, Prague 1
Tel 224 811 023
Daily 10–8 ⓂStaroměstská 🚃Tram 17, 18 to Staroměstská

DEPARTMENT STORES
CARREFOUR
Off map 160 D9
Radlická 1 (Nový Smíchov shopping centre), Smíchov, Prague 5
Tel 257 284 111
www.carrefour.cz
This is the legendary French hypermarket where the staff has to use roller-skates to get around. It has a truly massive selection of foodstuffs, household goods, personal items, hardware and almost anything else you can think of.
Daily 7am–midnight ⓂAnděl 🚃Tram 4, 7, 9, 10, 12, 16 to Anděl

KOTVA
Map 159 G5
Náměstí Republiky 8, Nové Město, Prague 1
www.od-kotva.cz
Tel 224 801 438
The Swedish-designed Kotva store actually comprises dozens of independent shops, all with an open floor plan. The result is a fascinating, five-floor browsing experience through candle boutiques and jewellery counters, hat stores and furniture showrooms, kitchen stores and book shops. There's even a mushroom stand, a pharmacy and a natural cosmetics counter.
Mon–Fri 9–8, Sat 10–7, Sun 10–6 ⓂNáměstí Republiky 🚃Tram 5, 8, 14 to Náměstí Republiky

TESCO
Map 159 F7
Národní 26, Nové Město, Prague 1
Tel 222 003 111
www.tesco-shop.cz
Tesco offers six floors of everything from toiletries and stationery to toys and sporting goods. There's a big electronics department and a wide selection of clothes and footwear for men, women and children, but don't look for designer labels—this is strictly mid-range stuff. The large grocery store in the basement carries a number of imported foods from Germany and Britain.
Store: Mon–Fri 8am–9pm, Sat 9–8, Sun 10–8. Grocery: Mon–Fri 7am–10pm, Sat 8am–9pm, Sun 9–8. Small front food and essentials store: Mon–Fri 7am–10pm, Sat 8am–9pm, Sun 9–8
ⓂNárodní třída 🚃Tram 6, 9, 18, 22, 23 to Národní třída

FASHION

ANIMA TUA
Map 159 F6
Václavské náměstí 1 (Palác Koruna),
Nové Město, Prague 1
Tel 224 473 074
www.animatua.com
Anima Tua is a showcase for sexy
Italian fashion from designers like
Love Sex Money, Tenax and Pin
Up. Here you will find tiny bikinis
and *maillots* (bathing suits) with
plunging necklines, dramatic
dresses for making an entrance
and crystal-studded jeans.
There's also glamorous
costume jewellery.
🕐 Mon–Fri 10–8, Sat 10–7, Sun 12–6
🚇 Můstek

ANNE FONTAINE, PARIS
Map 159 F5
Masná 8, Staré Město, Prague 1
www.annefontaine.com
This romantic French designer
specializes in pristine white
blouses of every cut and design,
from ruffled tunics to modern
pleats. She also does beautiful
wool capes and shawls.
🕐 Tue–Fri 10.30–6.30, Sat 11–5
🚇 Náměstí Republiky 🚊 Tram 5, 8, to
Dlouhá třída

AU PAYS DES MIMIS
Map 159 F6
Na příkopě 12 (Černá růže), Nové Město,
Prague 1
Tel 221 014 344
The children's clothing in this
shop is delightful. Labels include
Lili Gaufrette, Petit Bateau, Jacadi
and Petit Boy.
🕐 Mon–Fri 10–8, Sat 10–7, Sun 11–7
🚇 Můstek

BOUTIQUE TATIANA
Map 159 F5
Dušní 1, Josefov, Prague 1
Tel 224 813 723
www.tatiana.cz
Taťána Kováříková was a theatre
costume designer before she
opened this shop, and her flair
for the dramatic shows in her
creations: an ankle-length white
winter coat with an off-centre
zipper and Nehru collar, a
hot-pink strapless dress covered
in black roses with stiff netting
underneath. Tatiana frequently
styles for the popular Czech
singer Helena Vondráčková.
🕐 Mon–Fri 10–7, Sat 11–4 (call Silvie if
you can't make the shop's hours: 224 934
850) 🚇 Náměstí Republiky 🚊 Tram 5, 8,
to Dlouhá třída

DESSOUS-DESSUS
Map 159 F6
Královdorská 7, Staré Město, Prague 1
Tel 222 316 915
Get your frothy French and
Italian lingerie, sleepwear and
undergarments from Lise
Charmel, Millesia and Au bade
here. The lace corsets, silk tap
pants and elegant dressing
gowns would suit a starlet.
🕐 Mon–Fri 10–7, Sat 10–6 🚇 Náměstí
Republiky 🚊 Tram 5, 8, to Náměstí
Republiky

DIOR
Map 159 F5
Pařížská 4, Josefov, Prague 1
Tel 222 310 134
www.dior.com
The biggest Christian Dior
boutique between Paris and
Moscow occupies prime real

*The Dior shop in Prague is in a
prime position on chic Pařížská*

estate on the most fashionable
street in Prague. The sight of all
the candy-coloured bags, heels
and dresses will make you want
to drape yourself from head to
toe in Dior. There's a private
room for viewing fine jewellery.
🕐 Mon–Fri 10–7, Sat 10–6, Sun 12–6
🚇 Staroměstská 🚊 Tram 17, 18, to
Staroměstská

IVANA FOLLOVÁ ART &
FASHION GALLERY
Map 159 F6
Týnský dvůr (Ungelt courtyard), Staré
Město, Prague 1
Tel 224 895 460
www.ifart.cz
Ivana Follová was an art dealer
and clothing designer before she
decided to combine her love of
both and open this store in 1998.
The serene, whitewashed space

displays her innovative
creations—cropped linen jackets,
wool wrap skirts and raw silk
shawls—and is also a showcase
for local jewellers, potters
and sculptors.
🕐 Daily 10.30–7 🚇 Náměstí Republiky
🚊 Tram 5, 8 to Dlouhá třída

KENZO
Map 159 G6
Obecní dům 2, Staré Město, Prague 1
Tel 222 002 302
www.kenzo.com
This Paris-based Japanese
designer continues to explore
ethnic influences in both his
men's and women's clothing
lines. His plush shop near the
Obecní dům (Municipal House)
carries a small sample of his
international collection, plus
perfumes, sunglasses, bags and
African-inspired jewellery.
🕐 Mon–Fri 10–7, Sat 10.30–6, Sun
11–5 🚇 Náměstí Republiky 🚊 Tram 5,
8, 14 to Náměstí Republiky

KLÁRA NADEMLÝNSKÁ
Map 159 F5
Dlouhá 7, Staré Město, Prague 1
Tel 224 818 769
www.klaranademlynska.com
Designer Klára Nademlýnská
makes a small selection of sexy
clothes for confident women.
You might walk out with a
pale-blue trench coat, satin
bustier or smart white jeans with
black stitching. The poured
concrete floor and rolling racks of
clothes give this shop the feel of
an *atelier* (artist's studio).
🕐 Mon–Fri 10–7, Sat 11–6 🚇 Náměstí
Republiky 🚊 Tram 5, 8 to Dlouhá třída

PAVLA & OLGA: ORIGINAL
CZECH FASHION
Map 158 C6
Vlašská 13, Malá Strana, Prague 1
Tel 728 939 872
Judging by the number of candid
snapshots on the walls, models
love this tiny shop in Malá
Strana. Pavla Michálková's body-
skimming dresses, skirts and
skinny long-sleeved T-shirts are
often featured in Czech *Elle* and
Harper's Bazaar.
🕐 Mon–Fri 2–7, Sat 3–6
🚇 Malostranská 🚊 Tram 12, 20, 22, 23
to Malostranské náměstí

SMOKING WOMAN
Map 161 H8
Italská 16, Vinohrady, Prague 2
Libuše Kultová combs the Czech
Republic for groovy old clothes to

stock her snug and cluttered secondhand store. Communist chic was actually pretty cool: some of her best finds are corduroy skirts, vintage jeans and belted princess coats. Kultová will be happy to help you sort through the racks and put together a look: how does a sheepskin coat, fuzzy white muffler, plaid flares and a leather messenger bag sound? © Mon–Fri 9–6 ⓜ Náměstí Míru 🚊 Tram 4, 10, 16, 22, 23 to Náměstí Míru

TAIZA
Map 159 G6
Na příkopě 31, Nové Město, Prague 1
Tel 225 113 308
www.taiza.com
Taiza offers sophisticated *prêt-a-porter* from this Paris-based Czech design house: think elegant long coats, perfectly cut wool trousers and tailored blouses. It excels at 'event dresses' made with ethereal fabrics and beaded in crystal and jet. The single couture wedding dress each spring is much-coveted by fashionable brides. © Mon–Sat 10–7, Sun 1–6 ⓜ Můstek

TIMOURE ET GROUP (TEG)
Map 159 F5
V Kolkovně 6, Josefov, Prague 1
Tel 222 327 358
www.timoure.cz
Alexandra Pavalová and Ivana Šafránková design clothes with an Armani-like sensibility: clean lines and modern shapes in grey, white, navy, black and red. A simple black shift is made subtly more exciting by a circle print, a black trench coat gets smart white piping, a beige and white herringbone skirt sports a tiny red buckle. © Mon–Fri 10–7, Sat 11–5 ⓜ Staroměstská 🚊 Tram 17, 18 to Staroměstská

WILVORST
Map 159 F6
U prašné brány 1-3, Staré Město, Prague 1
Tel 222 323 573
www.wilvorst.cz
Three separate branches of this venerable Austrian shop are clustered behind the Obecní dům (Municipal House). One carries conservative men's and women's separates from labels like Betty Barclay and Marco Polo, another carries trendier women's fashions and the third stocks casual separates for men.

Mon–Fri 10–7 (Men's store 9–7), Sat–Sun 10–6 ⓜ Náměstí Republiky 🚊 Tram 5, 8, 14 to Náměstí Republiky

YANNY
Map 159 F6
Na příkopě 27, Nové Město, Prague 1
Tel 224 228 117
Fashionistas love this sleek boutique with it's well-edited selection of women's shoes and clothing from some of the biggest international designers: Dolce & Gabbana, Versace and Gaultier. © Mon–Fri 10–8, Sat 10–7, Sun 10–6 ⓜ Můstek

FLORISTS

ANNIE'S TULIP
Map 159 F5
Bílkova 8, Josefov, Prague 1
Tel 222 311 013
www.anniestulip.cz

Taiza sells a range of elegant and sophisticated designs

Annie is the young daughter of Czech-Canadian Katherine Drbal, who owns this enchanting flower salon with her mother. Tulips and roses are the only traditional flowers in sight, however, since both women prefer modern blooms like hellborus and cosmos. The shop excels at creating unique bouquets for special events. © Mon–Fri 10–7, Sat 10–6 ⓜ Staroměstská 🚊 Tram 17, 18 to Staroměstská

B&J KVĚTINOVÉ STUDIO
Map 158 D6
Újezd 26, Malá Strana, Prague 1
Tel 257 320 455
This large, airy studio in Malá Strana specializes in perfect, traditional blooms—roses, lilies, gerber daisies, tulips,

peonies—but can also whip up more daring arrangements, like a towering stand of rustic pussy willows, exotic bamboo or a delicate bouquet of fresh lavender and rosemary sprigs. They also take telephone orders for delivery throughout the city. © Mon–Fri 7.30am–6pm, Sat 8.30am–6pm, Sun noon–6 ⓜ Malostranská 🚊 Tram 6, 9, 12, 20, 22, 23 to Újezd

FOOD & DRINK

COUNTRY LIFE
Map 159 F6
Melantrichova 15, Staré Město, Prague 1
Tel 604 203 265
www.countrylife.cz
Country Life is the city's best source of organic, vegetarian-friendly health food. It stocks several kinds of herbal tea, tofu and tempeh-based products, grains, gluten-free crackers and breads, tamari, tahini and much more. A vegan cafeteria next door serves hearty, hot food. © Mon–Thu 10–8, Fri 10–4, Sun 12–8 ⓜ Můstek

CULINARIA
Map 159 F6
Skořepka 9, Staré Město, Prague 1
Tel 224 247 237
www.culinaria.cz
In this gourmet imported food store, Pop Tarts and Doritos share space with English Branston pickle and Maldon sea salt. The American owners have stocked Culinaria with an eccentric collection of popular food from the US and Western Europe not readily available anywhere else. Look for the small section of items from Fauchon and Maxim's de Paris. The store also has tantalizing prepared foods and a fresh juice bar. © Mon–Fri 8.30–8, Sat 10–7, Sun 12–5 ⓜ Národní třída 🚊 Tram 6, 9, 18, 22, 23 to Národní třída

FRUITS DE FRANCE
Map 159 G6
Jindřišská 9, Nové Město, Prague 1
Tel 224 220 304
www.fdf.cz
This store is the city's primary source for hard-to-find vegetables and fruit, with two weekly deliveries from France. Even in the dead of winter, the shelves are overflowing with juicy melons and perfectly ripe tomatoes. It also offers French cheeses and pâtés, and condiments such as

walnut oil and Maille mustard. A second shop at Bělehradská 94, Vinohrady (metro I.P. Pavlova) sells a similar range of goods.
🕐 Mon–Fri 9.30–6.30, Sat 9.30–1 (both shops) Ⓜ Můstek

LA VECCHIA BOTTEGA
Map 159 E6
Na Perštýně 10, Staré Město, Prague 1
Tel 224 238 202
www.bottega.cz
The two rooms in this shop are filled to bursting with French, German and Italian cookware, kitchen gadgets and dishes. The Italian gourmet shop of the same name next door has spices, fresh pasta, Italian wines and liqueurs, hard-to-find cheeses like mascarpone and fontina, meats like prosciutto and mortadella, speciality oils and aged vinegars.
🕐 Mon–Fri 9–6, Sat 10–2 Ⓜ Můstek

WINE SHOP UNGELT
Map 159 F6
Týnský dvůr (Ungelt courtyard), Staré Město, Prague 1
Tel 224 827 501
www.flambee.cz/wine_shop/default.htm
Descend a flight of steep stone steps to reach this 14th-century wine cellar where owner Petr Pipek has personally selected the best varietals from around the world, including what he considers a few extraordinary Czech vintages. He even has bottles of the hard-to-find *eiswein*.
🕐 Daily 11–11 Ⓜ Náměstí Republiky
🚊 Tram 5, 8 to Dlouhá třída

BLUE PRAHA
Map 159 F6
Malé náměstí 14, Staré Město, Prague 1
Tel 224 216 717
www.bluepraha.cz
Blue Praha sells handmade modern glass, which is ideal for gifts or keeping as souvenirs of the city. There's a delightful selection of whimsical bowls, vases and stemware in bright-blue glass with accents of orange, yellow and red, as well as high-quality T-shirts with artists' renditions of landmarks like Karlův most (Charles Bridge) and Prague Castle. There are other shops at Pařížská 3, Josefov (metro and tram Staroměstská), Celetná 2 and Celetná 17 (metro Můstek).
🕐 Mon–Thu 9.30am–11.30pm, Fri–Sun 10.30am–11.30pm Ⓜ Můstek

BOTANICUS
Map 159 F6
Týnský dvůr (Ungelt courtyard), Staré Město, Prague 1
Tel 224 895 446
www.botanicus.cz
There's an intoxicating smell in this rustic shop selling organic natural products for the body, kitchen and bath. The wide range of herbal teas, essential oils, soaps, spices, herb-infused vinegars, oils and sea salts come with beautiful tags for giving as gifts. There's a second shop at Michalská 2 (metro Můstek).
🕐 Daily 10–8 Ⓜ Náměstí Republiky

LUBOŠ SUPÍK
Map 159 F7
Through the passageway next to Václavské náměstí 12, Nové Město, Prague 1

The exterior of the Wine Shop Ungelt—a 14th-century wine cellar

Popular with collectors, this shop has hundreds of hand-painted eggs decorated in different Moravian designs; prices are wholesale. After the Velvet Revolution, Supík was asked by the US Embassy to provide a selection of these traditional Czech eggs to sell in the American staff shop.
🕐 Daily 9–7.30 Ⓜ Můstek

MANUFAKTURA
Map 159 F6
Melantrichova 17, Staré Město, Prague 1
Tel 221 632 481
www.manufaktura.biz
Everything in this Czech craft store is handmade and uses natural or organic ingredients: soft wool blankets, painted ceramic mugs, olive-oil soaps and charming wooden ornaments.

There's also a branch at Nerudova 31, Malá Strana (metro Malostranská).
🕐 Mon–Sat 10–8, Sun 10–6 Ⓜ Můstek

ALBIO
Map 159 G5
Truhlářská 18, Nové Město, Prague 1
Tel 222 325 418
www.albiostyl.cz
At this organic, bio-grocery store there is a big selection of natural and cruelty-free cosmetics and skincare products, including the entire international German skincare line by Dr. Hauschka.
🕐 Mon–Fri 8–8, Sat 9–5 Ⓜ Náměstí Republiky 🚊 Tram 5, 8 to Dlouhá třída

DERMACOL STUDIO
Map 159 F6
Na příkopě 12 (Černá růže building), Nové Město, Prague 1
Tel 221 014 346
www.dermacol.cz
This company was begun in 1952 at Prague's Barrandov film studio, and claims to be the first manufacturer of 'cover makeup' for movies, the license for which it says it sold 'to Hollywood in 1969'. Go for its huge range of cosmetic and skincare products, professional makeup applications and spa services, including waxing, anti-cellulite treatments and facials.
🕐 Mon–Fri 9–8, Sat 9–7, Sun 11–7 Ⓜ Můstek

DIVA
Map 159 G6
Na příkopě 19, Nové Město, Prague 1
Tel 224 23 57 24
This well-stocked cosmetic and skincare boutique usually stocks the entire line of the major cosmetic brands it carries, making it easy to find just the right shade of pink lipstick.
🕐 Mon–Fri 9–8, Sat 10–6, Sun 11–6 Ⓜ Můstek

LUSH
Map 159 E6
Kaprova 13, Staré Město, Prague 1
Tel. 603 164 362
www.lush.com
This British soap shop is best known for its round 'bath ballistics' that fizz and release aromatherapy scents like jasmine, ginger and vanilla as they dissolve in your tub. All the quirkily named bath and body products are free of animal ingredients and scented with fruit and flower

WHAT TO DO

essential oils. Scoop up gooey honey, mud, avocado and seaweed facial masks or slice off a custom-size piece of soap from the various boulders piled on the counter.
🕐 Mon–Sat 10–7, Sun 12–6
Ⓜ Staroměstská

HOME DECOR
LE PATIO LIFESTYLE
Map 159 E5
Pařížská 20, Josefov, Prague 1
Tel 222 320 260
www.lepatio.cz
Le Patio's splendid store transports you to the British Colonial Empire. The owners travel extensively in India and South Asia to fill their shop with exclusive, one-of-a kind exotic furnishings and home décor, from serving trays to heavy chests. Czech blacksmiths create fantastical wrought-iron candelabras, and Indian carpenters make hand-carved armoires. There's something in every price range. You will find another shop and café at Národní 22, Nové Město (same opening times as Pařížská shop).
🕐 Mon–Sat 10–7, Sun 11–7
Ⓜ Staroměstská 🚊 Tram 17, 18 to Staroměstská

QUBUS DESIGN STUDIO AND STORE
Map 159 F5
Rámová 3, Staré Město, Prague 1
Tel 222 313 151
www.qubus.cz
A young group of Czech, British and German designers produce whimsical modern glass and ceramic items for the home at this studio and store. A pigeon-shaped wall sconce and ceramic Wellington boots are some of the more inventive offerings, but there are also sophisticated trays and glasses. This is the only place in Prague that carries the cult-status Austrian LOMO cameras.
🕐 Mon–Fri 10–6 Ⓜ Náměstí Republiky 🚊 Tram 5, 8 to Dlouhá třída

SEJTO
Map 159 F5
Dlouhá 24, Staré Město, Prague 1
Tel 233 373 908
www.sejto.cz
The name of this shop means screen in Czech, and that's what co-designers Alexandra Dýčková and Jarmila Dunderová do to their custom-designed natural

textiles. After hand-printing patterns, they create sumptuous pillows, quilts, tablecloths, placemats, scarves and bags.
🕐 Mon–Fri 10–7, Sat 11–4
Ⓜ Náměstí Republiky 🚊 Tram 5, 8 to Dlouhá třída

JEWELLERY
ČESKÝ GRANÁT TURNOV
Map 159 F5
Dlouhá 28-30, Staré Město, Prague 1
Tel 222 315 612
All the pieces at this well-stocked, factory-direct, garnet jewellery store are made at an artists' cooperative in Turnov, and all the stones are guaranteed to be real Bohemian garnets. There is a second shop at Panská 1 (metro Můstek).
🕐 Mon–Fri 10–6, Sat 10–1 Ⓜ Náměstí Republiky

Bright, funky bags on display in the window of Sejto on Dlouhá

HALADA
Map 159 G6
Na příkopě 16, Nové Město, Prague 1
Tel 224 221 304
www.halada.cz
Halada offers beautiful classic designs from legendary names: Nina Ricci diamond heart-shaped earrings and elegant Raymond Weil watches. There's a large selection of wedding rings cast in gold and silver, many featuring modern designs and interesting use of precious gems.
🕐 Mon–Sat 10–7, Sun 10–6 Ⓜ Můstek

CAROLLINUM
Map 159 E5
Pařížská 11, Josefov, Prague 1
Tel 224 810 890
www.carollinum.cz
Carollinum is a chic shop selling exclusive gems and watches.

When you're ready to splash out on an emerald necklace by Van Clef and Arpels, a 'Happy Diamonds' watch by Chopard, or a stunning Rolex, come here.
🕐 Mon–Fri 10–7, Sat 11–6, Sun 12–5
Ⓜ Staroměstská 🚊 Tram 17, 18 to Staroměstská

MARKETS
HAVELSKÁ TRŽIŠTĚ
Map 159 F6
Havelská at Melantrichova, Staré Město, Prague 1
The four-block long, central Havel's Market is an eclectic combination of fruit and vegetable stalls, cheap trinket hawkers and serious craftspeople. Much of the merchandise is forgettable (carved figurines, leather wallets with 'Prague' stamped on them), but every few stalls you'll find the works of a talented ceramacist or marionette artist for sale.
🕐 Apr–end Sep Mon–Fri 6am–6.30pm, Sat 7–6.30, Sun 8–6 Ⓜ Můstek

PRAŽSKÁ TRŽNICE
Off map 159 G4
Holešovice, Prague 7
This is the city's biggest outdoor market and resembles an outdoor shopping mall more than a street market. It can take hours to navigate the hundreds of stalls that sell every product imaginable—from jewellery to shoes, electronic equipment to housewares—but the prices are the lowest in the city and the quality of the goods is often the same as in shops. There are plenty of food and drink stands to fortify yourself midway through the adventure.
🕐 Mon–Fri 8–6, Sat 8–1 Ⓜ Vltavská 🚊 Tram 5 to Pražská tržnice

MUSIC
BONTONLAND MEGASTORE
Map 159 F6
Václavské náměstí 1 (Palác Koruna), Nové Město, Prague 1
Tel 224 473 080
www.bontonland.cz
A sprawling temple devoted to music worship in the lower level of Palác Koruna, Bontonland stocks a huge selection of artists in dozens of categories—classical to country, reggae to rock, dance to death metal. You may even find a group's entire catalogue of releases. Headphones allow you to hear tracks off the top-selling CDs.
🕐 Mon–Sat 9–8, Sun 10–7 Ⓜ Můstek

WHAT TO DO

PHILHARMONIA
Map 159 E5
Pařížská 13, Josefov, Prague 1
Tel 222 324 060
The range of classical CDs at this speciality music shop is truly staggering. Symphonies, operas, concertos, duets, quartets, orchestras and soloists are the only stars here. Along with such familiar names as Mozart and Chopin, there are obscure but fascinating CDs from Estonia, Bulgaria and Romania. There's also a section of historic recordings and a room devoted to Czech composers, such as Bedřich Smetana and Antonín Dvořák.
Ⓒ Mon–Fri 10–6.30, Sat–Sun 11–6 Ⓜ Staroměstská Ⓣ Tram 17, 18 to Staroměstská

RADOST CD VIDEO
Map 161 G8
Bělehradská 120, Vinohrady, Prague 2
Tel 224 252 741
www.radostfx.cz
Part of the Radost nightclub/lounge/café complex, this cutting-edge shop sells a selection of dance, pop, house, techno, drum & bass, jazz and world music. You can listen to any CD you want to by handing the case to the person behind the counter who'll put it on the stereo and give you head-phones and a remote control.
Ⓒ Mon–Fri 10–9, Sat 11–7, Sun 1–7 Ⓜ I.P. Pavlova Ⓣ Tram 4, 10, 11, 16, 22, 23 to I.P. Pavlova

WHAT TO DO

SHOES & ACCESSORIES

ALBERTO GUARDIANI
Map 159 F5
Pařížská 24, Josefov, Prague 1
Tel 222 422 821
www.albertoguardiani.it
The Japanese translation of the shop's name out front is your first clue that this Italian shoemaker has achieved cult status in some places. Women's shoes are high and pointy, men's are sleek and sporty.
Ⓒ Mon–Fri 10.30–7.30, Sat 11–7.30, Sun 12–7 Ⓜ Staroměstská Ⓣ Tram 17, 18 to Staroměstská

ANDREW'S TIES
Map 159 G6
U prašné brány 2, Staré Město, Prague 1
Tel 222 002 326
www.andrewsties.com
This little store packs hundreds of Italian silk ties and hand-tooled leather belts onto its racks. The store's location, tucked behind the Obecní dům concert hall, is

perfect for when you get those last-minute symphony tickets and want to spruce up your outfit.
Ⓒ Mon–Sat 10–7, Sun 11–5 Ⓜ Náměstí Republiky Ⓣ Tram 5, 8, 14 to Náměstí Republiky

BAŤA
Map 159 F6
Václavské námesti 6, Nové Město, Prague 1
Tel 224 218 133
www.bata.com
This is the flagship store of the world-famous Czech shoe company, with three floors of men's, women's and children's shoes and a large selection of purses and bags. Baťa sells mid-priced footwear in a huge range of styles, from trendy to classic.
Ⓒ Mon–Fri 9–9, Sat 9–7, Sun 10–7 Ⓜ Můstek

Wooden marionettes for sale at Marionety obchod pod lampou

EIFFEL OPTIC
Map 159 F6
Na příkopě 25, Nové Město, Prague 1
Tel 224 232 744
www.eiffeloptic.cz
You'll get the best selection of sunglasses in the city here, and frequent sales. Brands include Persol, Ray Ban, Armani, Cartier, Fendi, Hugo Boss, Chanel, Calvin Klein and Valentino. There are also excellent on-site eye doctors and an eyeglass repair service with no appointment necessary.
Ⓒ Mon–Fri 8–8, Sat 9–8, Sun 9.30–7 Ⓜ Můstek

GEOX
Map 159 G6
Na příkopě 22 (Slovanský dům), Nové Město, Prague 1
Tel 221 451 232
www.geox.cz

These Italian-made shoes have been patented for their secret technology that keeps feet from sweating or smelling anything other than sweet. They're not the trendiest around, but even rock stars have become devoted customers.
Ⓒ Daily 10–8 Ⓜ Náměstí Republiky Ⓣ Tram 5, 8, 14 to Náměstí Republiky

LOUIS VUITTON
Map 159 E5
Pařížská 11, Josefov, Prague 1
Tel 224 812 774
Label-conscious shoppers love this shop for its large selection of the latest shoes, bags and small leather accessories that carry the instantly recognizable LV logo. Multilingual assistants are on hand to help, and at the back of the store there's a good selection of current women's and men's shoes.
Ⓒ Mon–Fri 10–7, Sat 10–6, Sun 12–6 Ⓜ Staroměstská Ⓣ Tram 17, 18 to Staroměstská

TOYS

MARIONETY OBCHOD POD LAMPOU
Map 159 F5
Týnský dvůr (Ungelt courtyard), Staré Město, Prague 1
Tel 606 924 392
www.loutky.com
Wooden marionettes of all designs, shapes and sizes made by some of the country's best marionette artisans are for sale at the 'Shop Under the lamp'. Choose from brightly dressed kings and queens, princes and princesses, devils and gnomes.
Ⓒ Daily 10–9 Ⓜ Náměstí Republiky Ⓣ Tram 5, 8 to Dlouhá třída

POHÁDKA
Map 159 F6
Celetná 32, Staré Město, Prague 1
Tel 602 242 356
Wooden toys are a Czech specialty, and this shop claims to have the biggest selection in Prague. The shelves are packed full of wooden toys—painted and unpainted, large and small—with something to suit children of all ages. There are trains, dolls, puzzles and animals, fanciful wooden hot-air balloons dangling from the ceiling, and a delightful battery-operated carousel that features a parade of grinning bears, lions and monkeys.
Ⓒ Daily 9–8 Ⓜ Můstek

ENTERTAINMENT

Prague has a good selection of entertainment options, but not so many that you'll be overwhelmed by choice. Most venues are in the city centre, making them within easy reach of metro stations and tram stops. To find out what's on, pick up a copy of the *Prague Post*, published every Wednesday, and check the listings in the *Night & Day* insert. Alternatively, you can get information at www.prague.tv

CINEMA

Jan Sveřák's *Kolya*, which won the 1997 Academy Award for best foreign film, reinvigorated the Czech film industry. Barrandov Studios and Prague's excellent FAMU film school keep a steady stream of home-grown films on local screens. You can choose from Western-style multiplexes, independent art houses like Aero (▷ 174) and grand old theatres like Lucerna (▷ 175). Kino Světozor (▷ 175) offers a daily line-up of current

Prague hosts a wide range of pop concerts at a variety of venues

and classic Czech films with English subtitles. At other venues, look for the 'EN' symbol in listings, which denotes English-language films or English subtitles on foreign films.

CLASSICAL MUSIC

At the top end of Prague's classical music scene is an evening at the gilded Stavovské divadlo (Estates Theatre, ▷ 176), watching a production of *La Bohème* on one of Europe's most splendid stages. At the other is wandering into a baroque church in Malá Strana in the afternoon and hearing a string quartet bring Vivaldi's music to life. In between there are cellists on Karlův most (Charles Bridge) and stirring symphonies by the Czech Philharmonic at the Rudolfinum (▷ 176). For church concert

schedules, look for the people handing out flyers near popular tourist spots such as Staroměstské náměstí (Old Town Square). People in period clothing advertise concerts in the Obecní dům (Municipal House) around the hall, and the schedules for the Národní divadlo (National Theatre), Státní opera Praha (Prague State Opera) and Stavovské divadlo can be found at www.narodni-divadlo.cz

DANCE

Ballet is by far the most popular dance form on the city's stages, and at the Národní divadlo and Státní opera Praha, the Czech National Ballet company puts on regular performances of classics such as *Sleeping Beauty* and *Giselle*. For modern dance and touring companies the Divadlo Ponec (▷ 175) is the best venue.

JAZZ AND BLUES

The jazz and blues scene in Prague caters to both the serious aficionado and the casual fan. In 1994, when Bill Clinton grabbed a saxaphone and climbed onstage for a jam session at Reduta (▷ 176), popularity and audiences surged. A number of clubs now book both local and international groups. Some venues have a restaurant, such as Ungelt Jazz'N'Blues (▷ 177). Others, including AghaRTA (▷ 176), sell hard-to-find jazz CD recordings and U Malého Glena (▷ 177) has a popular amateur night. Clubs tend to be small and intimate, and an evening at one won't break your budget; cover charges are around 200Kč.

POPULAR MUSIC

Prague offers a wide selection of popular music. Palác Akropolis (▷ 184–185) books a regular schedule of African and ethnic music and Lucerna Music Club (▷ 177) is probably the most fun place to see a band—the semi-circular stage brings the music into the audience and there's always an enthusiastic crowd.

PLAYHOUSES

All professional plays in Prague are performed in the Czech language, though some theatres are beginning to introduce subtitles (▷ 15).

BOOKING TICKETS

In addition to the box offices of theatres and music clubs, there are several places in the city where you can find details of performances and buy tickets. There is usually a surcharge of around 50Kč per ticket. Ticketpro

A classical performance in the Mirror Chapel of the Klementinum

in the Prague Tourist Office (Rytířská 31) has a website in English (www.ticketpro.cz). Bohemia Ticket (www.ticketsbti.cz) is another central ticket company, with an office at No. 16 on Na příkopě and another on Malé náměstí. Church concerts don't require advance ticket purchases; just arrive a few minutes before and someone will be at the door.

DRESS CODES

The only real rule governing dress applies to performances of classical music, ballet and opera in formal auditoriums, where appropriate attire is expected.

SMOKING

Smoking is not permitted in the auditorium of cinemas and theatres, but there is often a smoking section in the lobby.

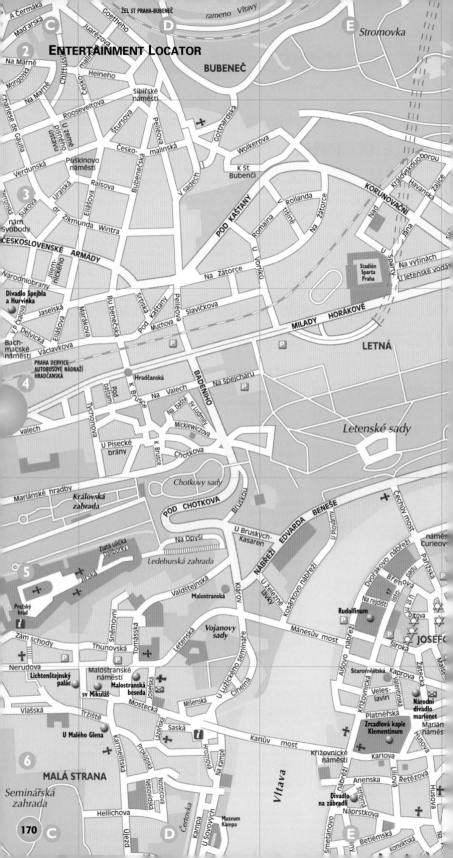

ŽEL ST PRAHA-BUBENEČ

rameno Vltavy

A Čermáka

Maďarská

Juarézova

Goetheho

Stromovka

Na Marně

Mongolská

Heineho

BUBENEČ

Na Marně

Chittussiho

Okseo

Rooseltova

Sibiřské
náměstí

Charlese de Gaulle

Verdunská

Štursova

Pelléova

Gotthardská

U země
pisného
ústavu

Česko-
malinská

Wolkerova

K St
Bubenči

Puškinovo
náměstí

Raisova

Bubenečská

Terronská

Uralská

V sadech

KORUNOVAČNÍ

dr Zikmunda Wintra

Rolanda

tišině

Na Zátorce

Havanská

Králova
dvorskou
porou

Sukova

Eliášova

Na
Zátorce

Romaina

U
sparty

Na
Stáří

Jana

nám
svobody

POD KAŠTANY

U vorníků

Na výšinách

ČESKOSLOVENSKÉ ARMÁDY

Na Zátorce

Stadión
Sparta
Praha

U letenské vodá

Národnlobrany

Jelenického

Bu benečská

Šrobárova

Muchova

Slavíčkova

Na špejcharu

MILADY HORÁKOVÉ

LETNÁ

Divadlo Špejbla
a Hurvínka

Jaselská

Eliášova

Maráková

Pod Kaštany

Pelléova

V Pražáku

Dejvická

Bachmacké
náměstí

Václavkova

PRAHA DERVICE
AUTOBUSOVÉ NÁDRAŽÍ
HRADČANSKÁ

Hradčanská

Pod
baštami

K Brusce

Na Valech

BADENIHO

Na špejcharu

valech

Tychonova

Na baště

sv Ludmily

Letenské sady

U Pisecké
brány

K Brusce

Mickiewiczova

Chotkova

Mariánské hradby

Královská
zahrada

Chotkovy sady

POD CHOTKOVA

Brusku

ČECHŮV most

náměs
Curieo

Ledeburská zahrada

NÁBŘEŽÍ EDVARDA BENEŠE

U Bruských
kasáren

U Plovárny

Dvořákovo nábřeží

Břehová

Pařížsk

Zlatá ulička
Daliborky

Na Opyši

Klárov

U železné
lávky

Kosárkovo nábřeží

Na rejdišti

15 n

bitova

Pražský
hrad

Jirská

Valdštejnská

Malostranská

Rudolfinum

Mánesův most

široká

JOSEFC

Zám schody

Sněmovní

Tomášská

Letenská

Aišovo nábřeží

Staroměstská

Kaprova

Nerudova

Thunovská

Vojanovy
sady

U Lužického semináře

Velesla-
vin

Jalentská

Lichtenštejnský
palác

Malostranské
náměstí

Cihelná

Platnéřská

Národní
divadlo
marionet

sv Mikuláš

Malostranská
beseda

Mišenská

Zrcadlová kaple
Klementinum

Marián
námès

Vlašská

Tržiště

Mostecká

Saská

Karlův most

Karlova

Liliová

Retězová

U Malého Glena

Lázeňská

Na kampě

Husova

Karmelitská

Prokopská

Hroznová

Křižovnické
náměstí

Anenská

Husova

MALÁ STRANA

Nosticova

Nebovidská

Divadlo
na zábradlí

Stříbrn

Seminářská
zahrada

Hellichova

Čertovka

Kampa

Újezd

U Sovových

Muzeum
Kampa

Vltava

Náprstkova

Betlémská

C   D   E

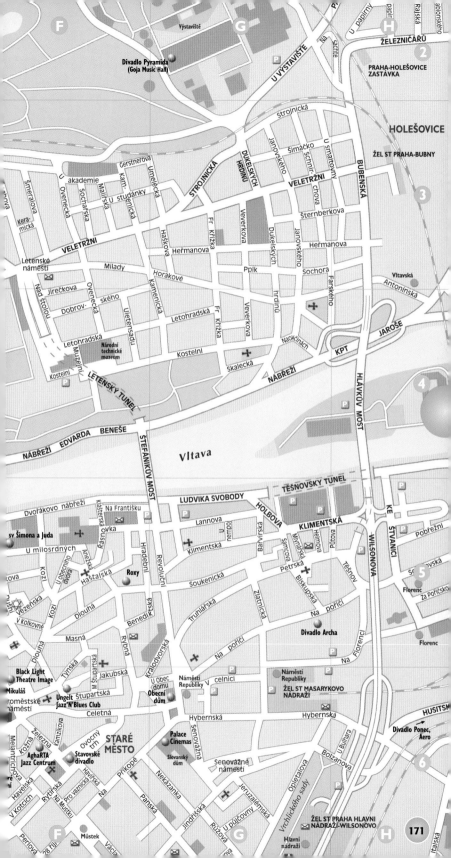

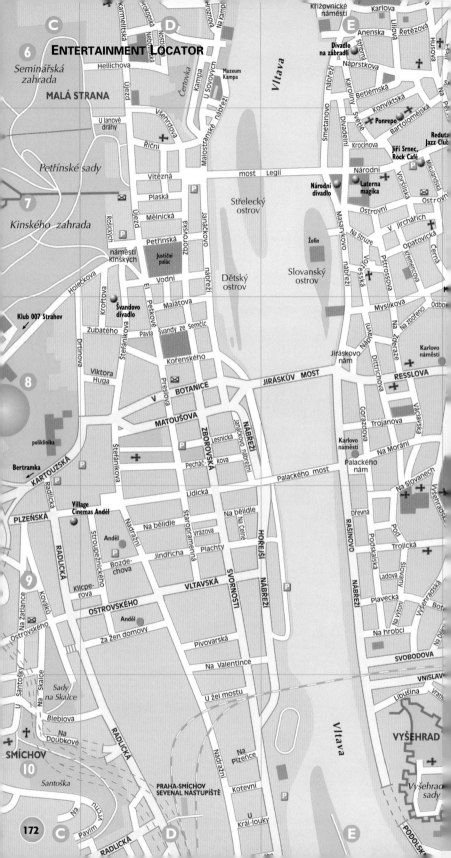

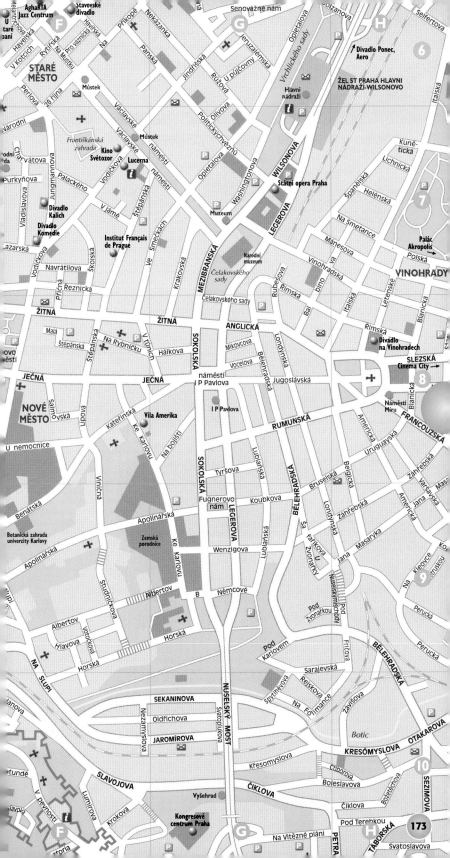

ARTS VENUES

DIVADLO ARCHA
Map 171 G5
Na Poříčí 26, Nové Město, Prague 1
Tel 221 716 333
www.archatheatre.cz
This is one of the city's premier venues for contemporary music, dance, drama and film screenings. There might be a concert by David Byrne, a modern production of Ibsen's *Nora*, an Irish author who reads and discusses his works accompanied by a harpist, or a performance by a conceptual dance company. Student film festivals and documentary premières also take place.
🕐 Varies according to performance. Café: Mon–Fri 9am–10.30pm, Sat 10–10, Sun 12–10 💷 Varies according to performance 🚇 Náměstí Republiky (exit at Na Poříčí) 🚋 Tram 3, 24, 26 to Bílá labuť

INSTITUT FRANÇAIS DE PRAGUE
Map 173 F7
Štěpánská 35, Nové Město, Prague 1
Tel 222 231 782 (cinema: 221 401 011)
www.ifp.cz
This cultural institute hosts readings by French authors, philosophy discussion evenings and exhibitions. The small theatre shows mainly French films with Czech and English subtitles, and Czech films with French subtitles. There is also a café on site.
🕐 Mon, Fri 8.30–7, Tue–Thu 8.30–7.30. Cinema: Screening days vary, most films start 8pm 💷 Varies according to performance. Cinema: 100Kč 🚇 Můstek 🚋 Tram 4, 6, 10, 16, 22, 23 to Štěpánská

ŠVANDOVO DIVADLO
Map 172 D8
Štefánikova 57, Smíchov, Prague 5
Tel 257 318 666
www.svandovodivadlo.cz
This is one of the five most important playhouses for classic and contemporary dramas, and is the country's first theatre to install subtitle technology for non-Czech speakers (▷ 15). The cool, 317-seat modern auditorium gives excellent views of the stage, which also hosts repertory companies, flamenco troupes, readings and concerts. There's usually an art or photography exhibition on the walls of the café.
🕐 Performances at 7pm. Box office: daily 2–7pm. Café: Mon–Sat 10am–midnight, Sun 2pm–midnight
💷 280Kč–365Kč 🚇 Anděl 🚋 Tram 9, 12, 20 to Švandovo divadlo

CHURCHES

SVATÉHO MIKULÁŠ, MALÁ STRANA
Map 170 D6
Malostranské náměstí, Malá Strana, Prague 1
Tel 257 534 215
www.psalterium.cz
The massive baroque Church of St. Nicholas (▷ 122–123) dominates Malá Strana Square. Although construction of the church was begun in 1673, the decoration of the interior was only finished in 1775. The 2,500-pipe organ was played by Mozart. There are daily classical music concerts here, but it can be chilly in winter.
🕐 Varies according to performance 💷 Varies according to performance 🚇 Malostranská 🚋 Tram 12, 20, 22, 23 to Malostranské náměstí

Prague's only IMAX screen is at the Palác Flora, Cinema City

SVATÉHO MIKULÁŠ, STARÉ MĚSTO
Map 171 F6
Staroměstské náměstí, Staré Město, Prague 1
Tel 224 190 994
www.husiti.cz/ccshpd/obce_seznam.htm
Classical music concerts are held daily inside the baroque Church of St. Nicholas, but tend to be pricey because of the location.
🕐 Varies according to performance 💷 Varies according to performance 🚇 Staroměstská 🚋 Tram 17, 18 to Staroměstská

SVATÉHO ŠIMONA A JUDA
Map 171 F5
Na Františku at Dušní, Josefov, Prague 1
Quartets, duos and choirs perform regular classical concerts in this church, which has a dramatic stained-glass semicircular wall.

🕐 Varies according to performance 💷 Varies according to performance 🚇 Náměstí Republiky

ZRCADLOVÁ KAPLE, KLEMENTINUM
Map 170 E6
Karlova 1, Staré Město, Prague 1
Tel 272 766 902
www.concerts-prague.cz
Classical performances by accomplished quartets, duets, trios and soloists take place in the Mirror Chapel of the Klementinum—it makes you feel like you're sitting inside someone's jewellery box.
🕐 Performances at 5pm 💷 Varies according to performance 🚇 Staroměstská 🚋 Tram 17, 18 to Staroměstská

CINEMAS

AERO
Off map 171 H6
Biskupcova 31, Žižkov, Prague 3
Tel 271 771 349
www.kinoaero.cz
If the city's film industry has an unofficial headquarters, it's this down-at-heel, independent art house. Revivals, foreign, classic, current and Czech films are shown in their original language with subtitles at this funky old complex. Buy a ticket in the courtyard and enjoy a beer at the bar inside before the show. The wooden seats are uncomfortable, and the sound system sometimes gives out for a minute, but everyone is good-natured about it.
🕐 Shows: 8.30pm. Bar: 4pm–1am
💷 90Kč 🚋 Tram 9, 10, 16 or 19 to Biskupcova

CINEMA CITY
Off map 173 H8
Palác Flora, Vinohradská 149, Žižkov, Prague 3
Tel 255 742 021
www.cinemacity.cz
The latest domestic and international films are shown in these modern multiplex theatres in two shopping centres. Many of the family-friendly US films (like *Shrek, The Incredibles* and *Harry Potter*) are dubbed into Czech. The Palác Flora venue features the city's only IMAX screen, and shows films in 3D.
🕐 Daily 11am–1am 💷 Adult 159Kč, child (under 12) 109Kč 🚇 Flora 🚋 Tram 5, 10, 11, 16 to Flora

INSTITUT FRANÇAIS DE PRAGUE
See this page.

WHAT TO DO

174 ENTERTAINMENT

KINO SVĚTOZOR
Map 173 F7
Vodičkova 41, Nové Město, Prague 1
Tel 224 947 566
www.kinosvetozor.cz
A self-proclaimed '100 percent popcorn-free zone', this popular art house has several daily screenings of Czech and foreign independent films in their original language with subtitles. It's also a co-host of the annual 'Days of European Film' festival and every week has Documentary Mondays. There are two lobby bars, rotating photo exhibits and Světozor T-shirts for sale.
⊙ Bar and box office: daily from 9.30am ⚡ 80Kč–100Kč ⊙ Můstek 🚋 Tram 3, 9, 14, 24 to Václavské náměstí

LUCERNA
Map 173 F7
Vodičkova 36 (pasáž Lucerna), Nové Město, Prague 1
Tel 224 216 972
www.lucerna.cz/kino.php
The show at Lucerna begins when you walk up the stairs to this art-deco gem. Bevelled mirrors and marble columns evoke the secessionist era and there's a great view of the famous upside-down horse sculpture in the passage below. The giant one-screen theatre has balconies and balustrades and alternates current Czech films in their original language with US hits. There's a lovely circular bar in the lobby.
⊙ Daily: first show 11am, last show 9.30pm. Café open until 1am ⚡ 110Kč ⊙ Můstek 🚋 Tram 3, 9, 14, 24 to Vaclavské náměstí

MAT
Map 172 F7
Karlovo náměstí 19, Nové Město, Prague 2
Tel 224 915 765
www.mat.cz
If you stop at this comfortable but tiny screening room, where a variety of subtitled Czech films and past Oscar winners are shown, leave time for the excellent American-style diner outside the cinema.
⊙ Shows: usually 6pm and 8.30pm. Box office: 9–5.30. Restaurant: Mon–Fri 9am–midnight, Sat–Sun 2pm–midnight ⚡ Adult 100Kč, child (under 12) 60Kč ⊙ Karlovo náměstí 🚋 Tram 3, 4, 6, 10, 14, 16, 18, 22, 23, 24 to Karlovo náměstí

PALACE CINEMAS
Map 171 G6
Na příkopě 22 (Slovanský dům), Nové Město, Prague 1
Tel 257 181 212
www.palacecinemas.cz
This central multiplex cinema offers comfy chairs, huge screens and all the usual refreshments. Come here to see Hollywood blockbusters, usually just days after their UK première. Films are in their original language, many with English subtitles.
⊙ Daily 11am–1am ⚡ Adult 179Kč, child (under 12) 129Kč ⊙ Náměstí Republiky

PONREPO
Map 172 E7
Bartolomějská 11, Staré Město, Prague 1
Tel 224 233 281
www.nfa.cz

An open-air Mozart performance at the lovely Bertramka villa

Ponrepo is an old jewel box of a theatre with red velvet chairs and ornate white woodwork, and screens noncommercial and classic foreign and Czech movies in their original language. It also holds the national film archives for the Czech Republic. There's a tiny bar in the lobby.
⊙ Box office: Mon–Fri 3.30–8.15. Shows at 5.30 and 8 ⚡ Adult 150Kč, child (under 12) 100Kč; yearly pass required: adult 40Kč, child 30Kč ⊙ Národní třída

VILLAGE CINEMAS ANDĚL
Map 172 C9
Plzeňská, between Radlická and Stroupežnického, Smíchov, Prague 5
Tel 251 115 111
www.villagecinemas.cz
This modern, 14-screen cineplex has all the usual bells and

whistles, but it's the only one in the city that offers 'gold class' service. For around 350Kč you can watch films in a comfortable screening room and sit in a jumbo recliner. Waiters serve snacks and drinks throughout the screening. Check listings to see which film is in 'gold class' each week.
⊙ Daily 10am–1am ⚡ Adult 159Kč, child (under 12) 119Kč ⊙ Anděl

CLASSICAL MUSIC, DANCE AND OPERA

BERTRAMKA
Off map 172 C8
Mozartova 169, Smíchov, Prague 5
Tel 257 317 465
www.bertramka.cz
Wolfgang Amadeus Mozart lived here when he spent time in Prague in the late 18th century. Now it's a museum that holds classical concerts in an elegant salon and summer garden.
⊙ Concerts: Apr–end Oct Wed and Sat at 5pm ⚡ Adult 390Kč, child (under 12) 250Kč; prices may vary ⊙ Anděl, then tram 4, 7, 9, 10, 14 to Bertramka

DIVADLO PONEC
Off map 171 H6
Husitská 24A, Žižkov, Prague 3
Tel 224 817 886
www.divadloponec.cz
Divadlo Ponec is a respected centre for contemporary dance and movement where the house company stages avant-garde performances and hosts visiting international groups. Don't be dissuaded by the location outside central Prague, there's nothing else like it in the city. The Theatre Club opens one hour before shows and stays open afterwards.
⊙ Varies according to performance. Box office: 6pm–8pm on performance days ⚡ Adult 140Kč, child (under 12) 80Kč; prices may vary ⊙ Florenc

LICHTENŠTEJNSKÝ PALÁC
Map 170 C6
Malostranské náměstí 13, Malá Strana, Prague 1
Tel 257 534 206
Opera soloists and classical music groups give intimate concerts in an elegant salon in the Lichtenstein Palace.
⊙ Shows at 7.30pm ⚡ Adult 200Kč, child (under 12) 50Kč; prices may vary ⊙ Malostranská 🚋 Tram 10, 20, 22, 23 to Malostranské náměstí

NÁRODNÍ DIVADLO
Map 172 E7
Národní 2, Nové Město, Prague 1
Tel 224 901 448
www.narodni-divadlo.cz
The grand Renaissance National Theatre on the River Vltava is a Prague landmark. Opera and ballet performances take place in the stunning triple-balconied auditorium. Before you pass under the front portico look up to see Bohuslav Schnirch's magnificent gold sculpture of Apollo and the nine muses.
◉ Performances from 7pm. Box office: Mon–Fri 10–6 and 45 min before curtain 🎭 Opera: adult 930Kč, child (under 12) 430Kč. Ballet: adult 850Kč, child 300Kč. Prices may vary 🚇 Národní třída 🚊 Tram 6, 9, 17, 18, 21, 22, 23 to Národní divadlo

OBECNÍ DŮM
Map 171 G6
Náměstí Republiky 5, Staré Město, Prague 1
Tel 222 002 111
www.obecni-dum.cz
Classical music concerts take place in the 1,500-seat Smetana Hall of the Municipal House and regularly feature the works of well-loved composers like Smetana, Dvořák, Vivaldi and Mozart. Leave time to soak up the legendary art nouveau architecture and interior of this famous building dating from 1912. The dress code is somewhat relaxed and there is an excellent café, restaurant and bar on-site.
◉ Daily performances from 7pm. Box office: Mon–Fri 10–6 and 1 hour before concerts 🎭 Adult 1,200Kč, child (under 12) 700Kč; prices may vary 🚇 Náměstí Republiky 🚊 Tram 5, 8, 14 to Náměstí Republiky

RUDOLFINUM
Map 170 E5
Alšovo nábřeží 12, Josefov, Prague 1
Tel 227 059 359
The world-renowned Czech Philharmonic Orchestra calls the Rudolfinum's Dvořák Hall home when it's not on tour. The auditorium's wooden seats don't offer much legroom, but during the intermission you can stretch your legs along the river, and there's a bar for refreshments. The Sůk Hall hosts chamber orchestras.
◉ Performances from 7pm. Box office: Mon–Fri 10–6 and one hour before curtain 🎭 Adult 900Kč, child (under 12) 150Kč; prices may vary 🚇 Staroměstská 🚊 Tram 17, 18 to Staroměstská

STÁTNÍ OPERA PRAHA
Map 173 G7
Wilsonova 4, Nové Město, Prague 1
Tel 224 227 266
www.opera.cz
Opera and ballet are performed in the majestic red and gold U-shaped auditorium of the Prague State Opera house—a neo-baroque building—and people certainly dress up for the occasion. The box seats are worth splashing out on if you want to feel like royalty for a night.
◉ Evening performances 7pm; Sunday matinee 2pm. Box office: Mon–Fri 10–5.30, Sat–Sun 10–12, 1–5.30 🎭 Opera: adult 1,200Kč, child (under 12) 400Kč. Ballet: adult 850Kč, child 300Kč. Prices may vary 🚇 Muzeum

A dramatic scene from Cinderella *at the Státní opera Praha*

STAVOVSKÉ DIVADLO
Map 171 F6
Ovocný trh 1, Staré Město, Prague 1
Tel 224 901 448
www.narodni-divadlo.cz
This neoclassical wedding cake of a theatre is famous for the fact that Mozart conducted the world première of Don Giovanni here in 1787, and had a warmer reception than he got in Vienna. The breathtaking auditorium of the Estates Theatre, with its five golden tiers of box seats, gives opera one of its most beautiful stages in Europe. Smartly dressed patrons reflect the formal surroundings. A bar opens during the intermission.
◉ Performances at 7.30pm and week-end matinees. Box office at Ovocný trh 6: Mon–Fri 10–6 and 30 min before curtain 🎭 Opera: adult 1,030Kč, child (under 12)

780Kč. Ballet: adult 680Kč, child 310Kč. Prices may vary 🚇 Můstek 🚊 Tram 5, 8, 14 to Náměstí Republicky

VILA AMERIKA
Map 173 G8
Ke Karlovu 20, Vinohrady, Prague 2
Tel 224 918 013
www.nm.cz/mad
Villa Amerika dates from 1717 and houses a museum dedicated to Czech composer Antonín Dvořák. In its elegant salon, the Original Music Theatre of Prague puts on a vocal and music show in period costumes, called 'Wonderful Dvořák'.
◉ Performances: Apr–end Oct Tue and Fri 8pm. Museum: Tue–Sun 10–5 🎭 Concerts: 545Kč. Museum: 40Kč. Prices may vary 🚇 I.P. Pavlova 🚊 Tram 4, 6, 10, 11, 16, 22, 23 to I.P. Pavlova

CONTEMPORARY LIVE MUSIC

JAZZ

AGHARTA JAZZ CENTRUM
Map 171 F6
Železná 16, Staré Město, Prague 1
Tel 222 211 275
www.agharta.cz
This club, now occupying the space where the former Železná Jazz Club used to be, is an established showcase for modern instrumental, vocal jazz and jazz fusion. Some impressive names in the European jazz community stop by, and there's an impressive CD counter.
◉ Shows nightly at 9pm. Club: daily 9pm–midnight. Bar: daily 6pm–1am. CD shop: 6pm–midnight 🎭 100Kč 🚇 Můstek

REDUTA JAZZ CLUB
Map 172 E7
Národní 20, Nové Město, Prague 1
Tel 224 933 487
www.redutajazzclub.cz
Prague's oldest and most important jazz club was also the first place Czechs could hear rock 'n' roll in the 1950s; it was famous for playing smuggled Elvis albums. Now it's known for the time President Bill Clinton played a jam session during a visit in 1994. It offers snug banquettes, clear sightlines and a mix of modern, fusion, Latin, Dixieland and trumpet jazz with the occasional big band and swing group. A good selection of CDs is on sale, including a cult-classic recording of Clinton's performance.

⊙ Shows nightly at 9.30pm. Box office: Mon–Fri at 3pm, Sat–Sun at 7pm 🖐 220Kč 🚇 Národní třída 🚃 Tram 6, 9, 18, 22, 23 to Národní třída

U MALÉHO GLENA
Map 170 D6
Karmelitská 23, Malá Strana, Prague 1
Tel 257 531 717
www.malyglen.cz
The musical offerings at the informal and popular American-owned Little Glen's might feature jazz, blues, modern or Latin. Thursdays, Fridays and Saturdays are devoted to Czech jazz groups. There are frequent jam sessions that welcome amateurs, a kitchen serving hot food, and lots of people who come here for the lively atmosphere.
⊙ Daily 10am–2am (kitchen open until midnight). Shows: Sun–Thu 9.30pm, Fri–Sat 10pm 🖐 150Kč
🚇 Malostranská 🚃 Tram 12, 20, 22, 23 to Malostranské náměstí

U STARÉ PANÍ
Map 171 F6
Michalská 9, Staré Město, Prague 1
Tel 603 551 680
www.jazzinprague.com
This sophisticated club is in the cellar of a hotel of the same name, and offers evenings of modern and contemporary jazz. With an elevated stage and grand piano, 'At the Old Woman' attracts serious names and serious fans. Sightlines can be interrupted by pillars, so arrive early and grab a good spot. There's a restaurant and bar.
⊙ Daily 7pm–2am, music at 9pm 🖐 150Kč–200Kč 🚇 Můstek

UNGELT JAZZ'N'BLUES CLUB
Map 171 F6
Týn 2, Staré Město, Prague 1
Tel 224 895 748
www.jazzblues.cz
This popular but small club behind the Týn Church occupies the 15th-century cellar of a Renaissance building. The line-up is a mix of jazz, blues, funk and fusion performed by a reliable rotation of local groups who always put on a solidly entertaining show. A pub serves hot food until midnight.
⊙ Pub opens daily at noon; club opens daily at 8pm. Music: daily at 9pm 🖐 120Kč 🚇 Náměstí Republiky 🚃 Tram 5, 8, 14 to Náměstí Republiky

ROCK AND OTHER

KLUB 007 STRAHOV
Off map 172 C8
Strahov dormitory complex (Koleje ČVUT), Block 7, Vaníčkova 7, Strahov, Prague 6
Tel 257 211 439
www.klub007strahov.cz
Hardcore rap, hip hop, reggae and punk acts take the stage here most nights before the DJ comes on. It's a bit out of the way, but it's the only club of its kind in Prague.
⊙ Sun–Thu 7.30pm–1am, Fri–Sat 7.30pm–2am. Shows at 7.30pm 🖐 120Kč 🚇 Dejvická, then bus 143, 149 or 217 to Chaloupeckého

KONGRESOVÉ CENTRUM PRAHA
Map 173 G10
5 května 65, Nusle, Prague 4
Tel 261 172 222
www.kcp.cz

Live acts perform at the Ungelt Jazz'n'Blues Club in the Old Town

Major international music acts and local extravaganzas appear at this modern indoor arena. It was built in 1980 and for many years was one of the largest, most modern cultural centres in Europe. When the big Czech names play here the house is packed with locals.
⊙ Varies according to performance 🖐 500Kč–1,300Kč 🚇 Vyšehrad

LUCERNA MUSIC CLUB
Map 173 F7
Vodičkova 36 (pasáž Lucerna), Nové Město, Prague 1
Tel 224 217 108
www.musicbar.cz
A popular and beloved old theatre with tons of character, the Lucerna was built by former President Václav Havel's grandfather. Catch a Beatles'

cover band, a Cure revival, or an appearance by Bo Diddley, Eva Cesoria or Petr Kolář. There's a very popular 1980s and '90s video party on Saturdays and Sundays.
⊙ Daily 8pm–3am 🖐 Varies according to performance 🚇 Můstek 🚃 Tram 3, 9, 14, 24 to Václavské náměstí

MALOSTRANSKÁ BESEDA
Map 170 D6
Malostranské náměstí 21, Malá Strana, Prague 1
Tel 257 532 092
www.mb.muzikus.cz
The former Malá Strana town hall building now hosts folk, oldies, rock and country music bands for appreciative local audiences of all ages. The auditorium fills up early, especially on weekends, and there's a lively bar scene.
⊙ Bar: 5pm–1am. Shows at 8.30pm 🖐 80Kč–100Kč 🚇 Malostranská 🚃 Tram 12, 20, 22 23 to Malostranské náměstí

PALÁC AKROPOLIS
See page 184–185.

ROCK CAFÉ
Map 172 E7
Národní 20, Nové Město, Prague 1
Tel 224 933 947
www.rockcafe.cz
In the front room of this semi-gritty but friendly café-by-day and club-by-night, one wall is painted to resemble the inside of a cave, there's local art on the walls and internet access. In the evenings the crowd is a mix of 20- and 30-somethings who come for the featured band, be it speed metal, ska-reggae-rap or local pop star Fatty Lumpkin. There are no chairs or tables in the raw, 400-capacity, low-ceilinged room where the bands play.
⊙ Mon–Fri 10am–3am, Sat 7pm–3am, most shows at 8.30pm 🖐 89Kč 🚇 Národní třída 🚃 Tram 6, 9, 18, 22, 23 to Národní třída

ROXY
See page 185.

MARIONETTE, BLACK LIGHT AND MUSICAL THEATRE

BLACK LIGHT THEATRE IMAGE
Map 171 F6
Pařížská 4, Josefov, Prague 1
Tel 222 314 448
www.imagetheatre.cz
The small troupe at this, the second-oldest black light theatre in Prague, stages elaborate and inventive shows incorporating

dance, pantomime and projection. It's perfect family entertainment. The Image Bar has live music on Friday evenings and there's a café (open 4.30pm–2am).
🎭 Performances: daily at 8pm. Box office: daily 9–8 💰 400Kč
🚇 Staroměstská 🚊 Tram 17, 18 to Staroměstská

DIVADLO PYRAMIDA (GOJA MUSIC HALL)
Map 171 G2
Výstaviště, Holešovice, Prague 7
Tel 227 658 955
www.goja.cz
This pyramid-shaped glass theatre on Prague's Fairgrounds stages Czech versions of international musical hits like *Les Misérables*, *Cats* and *Miss Saigon*.
🎭 Varies according to performance
💰 600Kč–700Kč 🚇 Nádraží Holešovice, then tram 5,12, or 17 to Výstaviště

DIVADLO SPEJBLA A HURVÍNKA
Map 170 C4
Dejvická 38, Dejvice, Prague 6
Tel 224 316 784
www.spejbl-hurvinek.cz
Created in 1945 by Josef Skupa, the tales of Spejbl and Hurvínek, the father and son characters, are a much-loved tradition. The lobby has a display on the history of the theatre and the marionettes that have been used over the years.
🎭 Children's shows: Wed–Fri 10am, Sat–Sun 2 and 4.30pm. Shows for older children and adults: 7pm, days vary. Box office: Tue–Fri 10–2, 3–6, Sat–Sun 1–5
💰 Adult 80Kč, child (under 12) 70Kč
🚇 Dejvická

JIŘÍ SRNEC: THE BLACK LIGHT THEATRE OF PRAGUE
Map 172 E7
Národní 20, Nové Město, Prague 1
Tel 257 921 835/721 589 244
www.blacktheatresrnec.cz
This theatre is the birthplace of the black light. Its founder, Jiří Srnec, introduced this form of wordless illusion theatre to the world at the Edinburgh Fringe Festival in 1958, and its standards are among the highest in the city. Recent shows have included *Alice in Wonderland*, *Peter Pan* and the *Flying Velocipede*.
🎭 Performances: Wed, Thu, Sat, Sun at 7.30pm. Box office: daily 10–6 💰 400Kč
🚇 Národní třída 🚊 Tram 6, 9, 18, 22, 23 to Národní třída

LATERNA MAGIKA
Map 172 E7
Národní 4, Nové Město, Prague 1
Tel 224 931 482
www.laterna.cz
The Laterna Magika's modern building—a giant cube of glass—is a startling contrast to the majestic neoclassical Národní divadlo next door, but both are part of the country's National Theatre group. The performances here are in a wordless medium that uses a combination of projection, dance, music, light and pantomime to create fantastical 'narrations' of dramatic tales. The 400-seat theatre has a bar in the lobby (open during performances).
🎭 Performances: Mon–Sat at 8pm. Box office: Mon–Sat 10–8 💰 Adult 680Kč, child (under 12) 300Kč 🚇 Národní třída 🚊 Tram 6, 9, 18, 22, 23 to Národní třída

A wordless performance at the modern Laterna Magika theatre

NÁRODNÍ DIVADLO MARIONET
Map 170 E6
Žatecká 1, Staré Město, Prague 1
Tel 224 819 322
www.mozart.cz
The National Marionette Theatre has been staging Mozart's *Don Giovanni* with life-size, opera-singing marionettes for more than 10 years and it remains popular.
🎭 Performances: daily 8pm. Box office: 10–8 💰 490Kč 🚇 Staroměstská 🚊 Tram 17, 18 to Staroměstská

PLAYHOUSES
DIVADLO KALICH
Map 173 F7
Jungmannova 9, Nové Město, Prague 1
Tel 296 245 311
www.kalich.cz
Contemporary comedies and dramas are performed by the

high-energy repertory company in this intimate 400-seat auditorium. Occasionally there's a concert by a popular Czech singer. Plays are in Czech.
🎭 Performances: Wed–Sat at 8pm. Box office: daily 10–6 💰 90Kč–190Kč 🚇 Můstek

DIVADLO KOMEDIE
Map 173 F7
Lazarská 7, Nové Město, Prague 1
Tel 224 222 734
www.prakomdiv.cz
This popular repertory company stages both dramas and comedies. Tickets can be hard to come by because many of the regular performers are also well-known film and television actors. All plays are performed in Czech.
🎭 Box office: Mon–Fri 12–7.30, Sat–Sun 2 hours before curtain
💰 100Kč–180Kč 🚇 Národní třída 🚊 Tram 3, 9, 14, 24 to Vodičkova

DIVADLO NA VINOHRADECH
Map 173 H8
Náměstí Míru 7, Vinohrady, Prague 2
Tel 224 257 601
www.dnv-praha.cz/
One of the grandest playhouses in Prague, Divadlo na Vinohradech opened in 1907 and stages classic dramas in Czech. The 45-strong ensemble includes some of the country's best actors. Recent seasons included works by Thomas Becket, Shakespeare and Edward Albee. The art nouveau lobby has an ornate carved wooden bar, and the 665-seat auditorium has two balconies. Theatre director Martin Stropnický once served as Culture Minister.
🎭 Performances: 7.30pm. Box office: Mon–Fri 11–7, Sat 1–4, 4.30–7 💰 Adult 60Kč–280Kč 🚇 Náměstí Míru 🚊 Tram 4, 10, 16, 22, 23 to Náměstí Míru

DIVADLO NA ZÁBRADLÍ
Map 170 E6
Anenské náměstí 5, Staré Město, Prague 1
Tel 222 868 868
www.nazabradli.cz
The legendary Theatre on the Balustrade was the first place former President Václav Havel worked as a playwright. It now stages new interpretations of contemporary plays in Czech. A café serves drinks and light meals.
🎭 Performances: 7.30pm. Box office: Mon–Fri 2–8 (closed 4–4.30), Sat–Sun and holidays 2 hours before curtain. Café: Mon–Fri 10am–1am, Sat–Sun 4pm–1am 💰 Adult 100Kč–325Kč 🚇 Staroměstská 🚊 Tram 17, 18 to Karlovy Lázně

WHAT TO DO

Nightlife

Nightlife in Prague comes in many forms, from casinos to beer halls, sleek cocktail bars to arty cafés. The drink of choice almost everywhere is beer. With so many excellent Czech beers to choose from, it's the easiest and cheapest choice, but there are now scores of trendy cocktail bars that pride themselves on book-length menus of drinks.

PUBS AND BARS

With beer occupying a sacred place in Czech life, it's no surprise that Prague is full to bursting with bars (look for signs that say *hospoda* or *pivnice*) and pubs. Czech pubs are friendly places, but the service can seem a little abrupt at times. When ordering a beer (*pivo*) you might be asked *normalni* or *male*. This means normal or small. The former is half a litre, the latter a third. Generally, each drink order is marked on a piece of paper that stays on the table—don't pick it

A neon sign advertises one of the city's many nightclubs

up or fiddle with it or the staff might think you're altering it. When you ask for the bill you'll have the choice of paying separately or all together. In the many Irish and English pubs dotted throughout central Prague, the rules of etiquette are much the same. There's usually a larger menu of food available at these pubs, with generous breakfasts, and in many places, multiple televisions for soccer matches. These pubs are a haven for large groups of visiting stag (bachelor) parties from the UK and can sometimes get a little bit rowdy.

CAFÉS

The city's café scene isn't as bustling as it was during the secessionist era, but fortunately most of the cafés from that time are still open and have been

expertly restored to their former glory. The grand dames are Café Imperial, Café Louvre, the *Kavárna* at the Obecní dům (Municipal House) and Café Slavia, where Václav Havel used to meet his fellow dissidents in the 1970s. All are delightful places to linger over a cup of tea, a glass of wine or a traditional Czech meal. They retain their original glorious interiors, massive windows and efficient service. Most are open by 8am and close around 11pm or midnight. Only Café Louvre has a non-smoking area, but all have high ceilings and the smoke generally wafts upwards, not around other diners. Look for a rack with a selection of newspapers; most major Czech dailies are available everywhere, and some cafés also stock *The Guardian* and the *International Herald Tribune*.

CLUBS

As you club hop around the city, you don't have to fear withering looks from doormen unless your destination is one of the glitzier places, like Mecca or Duplex. Dress codes are practically non-existent, but that doesn't mean you can show up in a ripped shirt. At the handful of truly glamorous clubs, standards are basically that you resemble the fashionable crowd inside; there are no rules like 'no trainers (sneakers) or jeans'. Generally, clubs open around 7pm for drinks and the DJ starts up around 10pm. If there's a live act on the bill, expect it start start around 8.30pm or 9pm.

GAY AND LESBIAN SCENE

Prague's gay and lesbian scene is not overly obvious to the casual observer, but the city does have some excellent gay-friendly venues: high-energy nightclubs such as Gejzeer on Vinohradská and Termis on Trebizského are super stylish, then there are sleek cocktail bars such as Escape on V jámě and a gay-friendly beer hall, U Rudolfa, on Mezibranská. Look for a copy of *Amigo* at larger

newsstands and *tabaks* in the city for complete listings (in Czech). You could also try the following websites for more information on accommodation and entertainment (www.praguegaycity.com and www.feminismus.cz).

CASINOS

Prague has a number of casinos, so if you're feeling lucky you can try your hand at a number of venues. In addition to the major hotels—including the Marriott, the Hilton and the President—Václavské náměstí and Na

Feeling lucky? There are several casinos in Prague

příkopě both have casinos with professional staff and plush surroundings in which to lose your shirt or win big. You can use euros or Czech crowns, and you must be over 18 and dressed reasonably well to gain entrance. Banco Casino (Na příkopě 27) is a luxurious 24-hour gaming palace with every game you can think of; Casino Ambassador (Václavské náměstí 5) is a sophisticated hall with the traditional vices—poker, roulette, blackjack, slots; Casino Palais Savarin (Na příkopě 10) has elegant, almost royal surroundings. The city's only English-style casino is in a regal building right on the River Vltava and offers free transport to the casino if you call in advance (check their website for more information: www.spearmintcasino.cz).

BARS

ALCOHOL BAR
Dušní 6, Josefov, Prague 1
Tel 224 811 744
www.alcoholbar.cz
You descend a spiral stairway to get to this polished bar that prides itself on its huge selection of cocktails. A constantly refilled bowl of roasted peanuts on the table keeps you thirsty, and an attentive serving staff keeps you sated. A DJ spins tunes from the '70s, '80s and '90s most nights, and on Thursdays and Fridays there's live music, usually a guitar and a drum set, doing respectable covers of popular songs from the Beatles to REM. A high-tech air filter keeps the smoke-level down.
🕓 Daily 7am–2am 🚇 Staroměstská
🚊 Tram 17, 18 to Staroměstská

BAR AND BOOKS
Týnská 19, Staré Město, Prague 1
Tel 224 808 250
www.barandbooks.net
The Prague branch of the very classy New York bar has the same red walls, leather booths and floor-to-ceiling bookcases as its sister establishment. The mood is sophisticated and smart, from the Brazilian jazz on the sound system to the champagne to the complimentary cigars for women on Mondays.
🕓 Mon–Fri 2pm–4am, Sat 6pm–4am, Sun 6pm–3am 🚇 Náměstí Republiky
🚊 Tram 5, 8, 14 to Dlouhá třída

BAR BAR
Všehrdová 17, Malá Strana, Prague 1
Tel 257 312 246
www.bar-bar.cz
Hidden on a small street near the river in Malá Strana, this tiny cellar bar has a loyal following of cool locals and expatriates who crowd around the semicircular wooden bar every night. The décor is eclectic: plaster masks and abstract photography, and whimsical sculptures that convey the bar's friendly vibe.
🕓 Noon–late 🚇 Malostranská
🚊 Tram 9, 12, 22, 23 to Újezd

LA BODEGA FLAMENCA
Šmeralova 1, Bubeneč, Prague 7
Tel 233 374 075
This great local spot borrows heavily from Spanish bar culture, with its high tables, tiled floor and bar serving a variety of small tapas such as garlicky olives and spicy cheese spreads. Occasionally a flamenco dancer

or singer makes an appearance. The sangria-soaked vibe is happy and congenial.
🕓 Mon–Thu 5pm–1am, Fri–Sat 5pm–3am 🚇 Hradčanská, then tram to Letenské náměstí 🚊 Tram 1, 25, 26 to Letenské náměstí

LA BODEGUITA DEL MEDIO
Kaprova 5, Staré Město, Prague 1
Tel 224 813 922
www.bodeguita.cz
Rumored to be owned by the Castro family, the other two branches of this Cuban cocktail bar and restaurant are in Old Havana and Oman, UAE. The atmosphere here is thick with references to Ernest Hemingway's Cuban period; there are photos of the bearded author, a massive oak bar, ceiling fans and humidors full of Cuban cigars.

Dancing the night away—Prague has a lively nightlife scene

The staff can't do enough for the customers, and when you add in pitchers of *mojitos*, it's no wonder everyone always seems excited to be here. The Latin dancers that take to the floor spontaneously ramp up the energy level.
🕓 Daily 10am–2am 🚇 Staroměstská
🚊 Tram 17, 18 to Staroměstská

BOMBAY COCKTAIL BAR
Dlouhá 13, Staré Město, Prague 1
Tel 721 882 557
www.rasoi.cz
Inside this pretty cocktail bar, dark wood, brick pillars and saffron walls lend a strong Indian feel, as do the jugs and urns dangling from the ceiling. A wall-size painted mural of the Taj Mahal leads the way to an excellent Indian restaurant downstairs, but the real action is upstairs, where

the Indian-influenced pop and swirling lights tempt people to the dance floor.
🕓 Daily noon–4am 🚇 Staroměstská
🚊 Tram 5, 8, 14 to Dlouhá třída

BOND'S COCKTAIL BAR
Polská 2, Vinohrady, Prague 2
Tel 222 733 871
www.jamesbondcafe.cz
Intimate low leather seating clustered around even lower tables in this narrow cocktail bar create a mellow but hip vibe. Deep red lighting and cool music on the stereo attracts a well-heeled local crowd at night.
🕓 Mon–Sat 5pm–2am, Sun 5pm–midnight 🚇 Jiřího z Poděbrad 🚊 Tram 11 to Vinohradská tržnice

BUGSY'S
Pařížská 10, Josefov, Prague 1
Tel 224 810 287
www.bugsybar.cz
Bugsy's is a very stylish, below-ground bar that draws a fashionable crowd of suits and starlets; the doorman who greets you at the entrance will probably subtly size you up for appropriate dress. Bartenders in starched white shirts put on a performance as they mix cocktails and this place is legendary for its martinis. The complimentary cheese sticks on every table are a tasty bonus.
🕓 Daily 7pm–2am 🚇 Staroměstská
🚊 Tram 17, 18 to Staroměstská

CHATEAU BAR
Jakubská 2, Staré Město, Prague 1
Tel 222 316 328
www.chateau-bar.cz
This self-proclaimed local legend of a bar has had several incarnations (and reputations) over the years, but has always kept the same blood-red interior and clientele of 20-and-30-something decadent partiers. It has added a cellar club, and DJs keep the dancers happy on the second level. The mood starts out mellow in the afternoon and early evening, but gets increasingly raucous as the night goes on.
🕓 Daily noon–5am 🚇 Náměstí Republiky 🚊 Tram 5, 8, 14 to Dlouhá třída

CHEERS
Belgická 116, Vinohrady, Prague 2
Tel 222 513 108
Cheers is one of the new generation of Czech *hospodas*, which means a beer-centric but modern atmosphere in which to

drink, and eat if you choose. Beers on offer include Stella Artois, Budvar, Radegast, Leffe Blonde and Belle-Vue Kreik. The long bar features an interesting light fixture that brings to mind a giant metal cheese grater, and the picture windows that look onto St. Ludmila Church make this a comfortable place to relax in.

🕐 Daily 11am–1am 🚇 Náměstí Míru 🚊 Tram 4, 10, 16, 22, 23 to Náměstí Míru

CONFESSIONS
U Milosrdných 4, Staré Město, Prague 1
The Lebanese owners of the Karma Lounge café next door opened this chill-out space to give people a place to go after dining. It's decorated in an ethereal blue Moroccan theme and the music is usually Arab-influenced pop.

🕐 Sun–Fri 1pm–2am, Sat 5pm–2am 🚇 Staroměstská 🚊 Tram 17, 18 to Staroměstská

DEBRUG
Masná 5, Staré Město, Prague 1
Tel 224 819 283
This dark but appealing pub is just a few blocks off Staroměstské náměstí (Old Town Square) and bills itself as 'an Amsterdam pub in the heart of Prague'. Delightful black-and-white photos of 1950s Amsterdam and models of old sailing ships line the walls. The friendly bar staff offer Dutch and Belgian beers on tap and a menu of 'Dutch finger food.'

🕐 Daily noon–2am 🚇 Náměstí Republiky 🚊 Tram 5, 8, 14 to Dlouhá třída

DÉFILE FASHION BAR & LOUNGE
Vodičkova 17, Nové Město, Prague 1
Tel 296 239 020
www.defile.cz
The city's fashion contingent—models, designers, photgraphers, editors—congregate here, perhaps because the all-white space is as pretty as they are. This is a sleek café by day that turns into a stylish cocktail lounge at night. A giant plasma screen runs videos of fashion shows and life-size photos of models stare down from the walls. The downstairs club feels exclusive, but is open to the public, and features couches, a good-sized dance floor and an 18m-long (60ft) glass 'catwalk.'

🕐 Daily 8am–1am 🚇 Můstek 🚊 Tram 9, 14 to Vodičkova

DUPLEX
Václavské náměstí 21, Nové Město, Prague 1
Tel 224 232 319
www.duplexduplex.cz
Occupying what is easily one of the city's best locations, this ultra-chic club is on the top floor of a building overlooking Wenceslas Square. After a wardrobe check by the bouncers at street level, an elevator whisks you up five floors and opens onto a vast white, red and pink interior that looks like it was designed by Gucci. Film and rock stars love this place, so it was no surprise that Mick Jagger chose to dance away his birthday here in 2004.

🕐 Daily 10pm–5am 💶 300Kč–500Kč 🚇 Můstek 🚊 Tram 3, 9, 14 to Václavské náměstí

Chilling out at the stylish Défile Fashion Bar & Lounge

ESCAPE
V jámě 8, Nové Město, Prague 1
Tel 602 403 744
www.volny.cz/cz/escapeclub/
Less than two blocks off Václavské náměstí is Escape, a sleek, medium-size cocktail bar with a chic gay-friendly vibe. There's a glamorous central bar, a fabulous dance floor for when the DJ starts up around 10pm and lots of seating for those who just want to relax and watch the scene, which might include a strip show, go-go dancers or something equally entertaining. A full menu of international dishes is available if you need to fortify yourself for what lies ahead.

🕐 Daily 7pm–5am 🚇 Můstek 🚊 Tram 4, 10, 22, 23 to Štepanská

FRAKTAL
Šmeralova 1, Bubeneč, Prague 7
Fraktal is not just a bar, it's a lifestyle. The Canadian owner has installed a mismatched collection of couches, battered tables and some threadbare chairs in a cramped, but very relaxed, carpeted underground space. The crowd is young, international and laid-back to an extreme; dogs are welcome. Sandwiches and snacks are available if you get hungry.

🕐 Daily 11am–3am 🚇 Hradčanská, then tram 25, 26, 8, or 1 to Letenské náměstí

JET SET
Radlická 1C, Smíchov, Prague 5
Tel 257 327 251
With sleek black-and-white modular sofas and eye-catching modern art, this is a trendy playground for a hard-partying clientele that fancies itself part of the international jet set. Relax, dance or try the Mediterranean-inspired menu offered by the Greek owners.

🕐 Mon–Thu 12pm–2am, Fri–Sat 12pm–3am, Sun 12pm–1am 🚇 Anděl 🚊 Tram 4, 9, 10, 16 to Anděl

JO'S BAR
Malostranské náměstí 7, Malá Strana, Prague 1
Tel 602 971 478
This faded expatriate institution is tucked in the shadow of the Svatého Mikuláš (Church of St. Nicholas) in Malá Strana, and for years was a popular meeting place where homesick Americans could commiserate and get the only authentic *burritos* in Prague. American and British students still make up a healthy proportion of the crowd in this multilevel bar, with a dance club downstairs and a dining room in the back.

🕐 Daily 11am–2am 🚇 Malostranská 🚊 Tram 12, 20, 22, 23 to Malostranské náměstí

KOZIČKA
Kozí 1, Staré Město, Prague 1
Tel 224 81 83 08
www.kozicka.cz
It can be hard to get a table at 'The Goat', a frenetic, slightly cramped underground bar and late-night pub. This is a nice place to camp out if you're in the Old Town for a long night of drinking and snacking.

🕐 Mon–Fri 12–4am, Sat 6–4, Sun 6–3 🚇 Náměstí Republiky 🚊 Tram 5, 8, 14 to Dlouhá třída

MONARCH WINE BAR
Na Perštýně 15, Nové Město, Prague 1
Tel 224 239 062
Monarch is a serious wine bar that doesn't take itself seriously. The handsome, high-ceilinged room is full of warm colours, with sturdy tables and old wine barrels scattered around. Several international wines by the glass, including some excellent Czech varietals, are listed on the giant chalkboard and change daily, and an impressive range of French cheeses and crusty French bread is available to soak it all up. A wine store in the back stocks hard-to-find labels.
🕐 Daily 9am–8pm 🚇 Můstek
🚊 Tram 9, 18, 22, 23 to Národní třída

PIANO BAR
Milešovská 10, Vinohrady, Prague 2
Tel 226 275 467
www.sweb.cz/pianobar/
Piano Bar is a warm, semi-rustic retreat from the city's clubs and boisterous bars. Its brick walls, 100-yaer-old piano and scruffy but still-operational billiards table attracts a cabaret-loving, gay-friendly clientele. Come for the camaraderie and the sing-alongs.
🕐 Daily 5pm–5am 🚇 Jiřího z Poděbrad
🚊 Tram 11 to Jiřího z Poděbrad

RED HOT AND BLUES
Jakubská 12, Staré Město, Prague 1
Tel 222 323 364
This authentic American jazz restaurant features live jazz, Creole music or blues every night from 7.30pm until 10.30pm in a pretty winter garden. It serves excellent Bloody Mary's and the menu offers jambalaya, gumbo, giant burritos and nachos.
🕐 Daily 9am–11pm 🚇 Náměstí Republiky 🚊 Tram 5, 8, 14 to Dlouhá třída

RETRO
Francouská 4, Vinohrady, Prague 2
Tel 603 17 61 11
www.kavarnaretro.cz
Retro has a gorgeous 1960s-inspired décor of pale blues, light yellows and browns, a long leather banquette running along one wall and small tables that create the perfect atmosphere for a romantic tête-à-tête. It's a café during the day, a hip restaurant by night and, after the kitchen closes, a music bar until 5am. A great location and large front windows allow passersby to get a peek at the cool scene inside.

🕐 Sun–Thu 8am–1am, Fri–Sat 8am–5am 🚇 Náměstí Míru 🚊 Tram 4, 10, 16, 22, 23 to Náměstí Míru

RIEGROVY SADY
Vinohrady, Prague 2
On a warm summer evening it seems like all of Prague is at the beer garden in this lovely, hilly park sipping a beer or a *béton* (Becherovka and tonic). Couples, skateboarders, families and dogs gather at the picnic tables under the stars and pass the hours pleasantly. In one corner a screen is sometimes set up to show football matches, and there's a makeshift stage for the occasional musical performance, but there are plenty of quiet places too.
🕐 May–end Sep daily 5pm–midnight 🚇 Jiřího z Poděbrad 🚊 Tram 11 to Vinohradská tržnice

There is live music every night at the Red Hot and Blues restaurant

RINCON
Na zábradlí 1, Nové Město, Prague 1
Tel 222 222 173
www.rincon.cz
Rincon's Spanish influence only extends to the red and yellow paint on the walls, but this is a pleasant enough two-level café, restaurant and bar right near Karlův most (Charles Bridge). The windows look across to the Castle, there are drink specials on many nights, and the large tables make it good for groups.
🕐 Daily 1pm–1am 🚇 Staroměstská 🚊 Tram 17, 18 to Karlovy lázně

ST. NICHOLAS
Tržiště 10, Malá Strana, Prague 1
St. Nicholas is one of the most comfortable cellar bars in the city. On the same street as several embassies, this pub wraps you in

warmth when you descend from the street, with a low stone ceiling and tiny table lights. Don't miss the plaque identifying the 'political table' in the far right corner, so named for the embassy staff who like to gather here at the end of the day.
🕐 Mon–Fri 12pm–1am, Sat–Sun 2pm–1am 🚇 Malostranská 🚊 Tram 12, 20, 22, 23 to Malostranské náměstí

TRETTERS
V Kolkovně 3, Staré Město, Prague 1
Tel 224 811 165
www.tretters.cz
Tretters is the cocktail bar of choice for Hollywood actors in town for a film shoot. The crowd at this narrow, elegant bar tends toward the sophisticated. Inside, the mood is 1930s Paris and New York, with red leather booths and oak-panelled walls hung with old photos of stars of stage and screen. There's great service and the cocktails are perfectly mixed.
🕐 Daily 7pm–3am 🚇 Staroměstská 🚊 Tram 17, 18 to Staroměstská

U ZÁVOJE
Havelská 25, Nové Město, Prague 1
Tel 226 006 120
www.uzavoje.cz
U Závoje is set inside an historic building known as The House of the Veil after the textile merchants who once did business here. This wine bar is as elegant and smooth as the varietals it offers—at least 40 corked bottles are clustered on the long farmhouse table that serves as a bar, and a wine 'bookcase' of at least 100 more vintages flanks the wall. The back room feels like someone's porch, with sturdy wicker furniture and giant arty photos.
🕐 Daily 11am–midnight 🚇 Můstek

BRITISH AND IRISH PUBS
CAFFREY'S IRISH BAR
Staroměstské náměstí 10, Staré Město, Prague 1
Tel 224 828 031
www.caffreys.cz
A counterpoint to the George and the Dragon English soccer bar next door (▷ 183), this Irish pub has snug booths with stained-glass panels. It's a quiet place during the day but at night, when the soccer comes on the TV, the inevitable stag parties drop in, the Guinness starts flowing, and it becomes a loud Irish party. From spring to autumn, the outside tables are much coveted.

Sun–Fri 9am–1am, Sat 9am–2am
Staroměstská 🚊 Tram 17, 18 to Staroměstská

GEORGE AND THE DRAGON
Staroměstské náměstí 11, Staré Město, Prague 1
Tel 222 326 137
www.georgedragon.cz
For some people it doesn't get any better than this handsome English soccer bar in Old Town Square. This long, vaulted-ceiling pub in the Palác Kinských has deep-red walls and white woodwork which lend it a dignified air. Every table has a view of one of many hanging televisions. There's Fosters on tap and, near the bar, a large photo of Queen Elizabeth and the English National Football team.
Daily 9am–2am Staroměstská 🚊 Tram 17, 18 to Staroměstská

MOLLY MALONE'S
U Obecního dvora 4, Staré Město, Prague 1
Tel 224 818 851
www.mollymalones.cz
The giant, crackling fireplace is reason enough to seek out this inviting Irish pub, with weathered wooden floors and a snug attic table for those lucky enough to snag it. Excellent Irish cooking and Guinness on tap are two more reasons. Laid-back expatriates and locals come here for long nights of conversation by the fire.
Daily 9am–1am Náměstí Republiky 🚊 Tram 5, 8, 14 to Dlouhá třída

O'CHE'S
Liliova 14, Staré Město, Prague 1
Tel 222 221 178
www.oches.cz
A casual crowd congregates at this Irish pub for darts, televised soccer games and serious drinking. Pictures of the pub's namesake adorn the walls.
Daily 10am–1am Staroměstská 🚊 Tram 17, 18 to Staroměstská

CAFÉS AND COFFEHOUSES
BLATOUCH
Věženská 4, Staré Město, Prague 1
Tel 222 328 643
www.blatouch.cz
This narrow, intimate café with old bookcases, small wooden tables and interesting artwork is on a quiet street in the Old Town. It offers a pleasant refuge from the tourist crowds, but can get quite smoky at night.

Mon–Thu 11am–midnight, Fri 11am–2am, Sat 1pm–2am, Sun 1pm–midnight Náměstí Republiky 🚊 Tram 5, 8, 14 to Dlouhá třída

CAFÉ IMPERIAL
Na Poříčí 15, Nové Město, Prague 1
Tel 222 316 012
www.hotelimperial.cz
The atmospheric Café Imperial, dating from 1914, has an interior unlike any in Europe: cream, blue and orange ceramic tiles in floral patterns cover the walls, ceiling and pillars. A swing or Dixieland jazz band plays on Friday and Saturday nights. Don't miss the photos near the door of the famed 'doughnut-throwing' (▷ 13).
Mon–Fri 8am–midnight, Sat 9am–1am, Sun 9am–11pm No cover charge Náměstí Republiky 🚊 Tram 5, 8, 14 to Dlouhá třída

Dating from 1914, the Café Imperial has a majestic interior

CAFÉ LOUVRE
Národní 20, Nové Město, Prague 1
Tel 224 930 949
www.cafelouvre.cz
One of the few surviving coffee-houses from the First Republic, the Louvre has retained its original features, including the wacky turtle tank in the front room. The elegant, second-floor café a few blocks from the river in Nové Město has 6m-high (20ft) ceilings and large windows over-looking the street. It's a perfect spot for cake and coffee or for sipping wine late into the night and summoning the ghosts of Kafka and Einstein, both of whom were regulars. There's a lovely billiard parlor in the back room and also a non-smoking area.
Daily 8am–11pm Národní třída 🚊 Tram 9, 18, 22, 23 to Národní divadlo

CAFÉ SLAVIA
Smetanovo nábřeží 2, Nové Město, Prague 1
Tel 224 239 604
www.cafeslavia.cz
Café Slavia, a landmark art nouveau café, once renowned as a dissident meeting spot under Communism, is now popular with dance and film students from the schools next door, tourists who come for the stunning view of Prague Castle across the river, and local people who come to read the paper. The location can't be improved on: one wall of windows faces the Národní divadlo (National Theatre) and the other, the River Vltava. When the trams rumble by, the floor shakes.
Daily 8am–midnight Národní třída 🚊 Tram 9, 18, 22, 23 to Národní třída

LITERÁRNÍ KAVÁRNA
Týnská 6, Staré Město, Prague 1
Tel 224 827 807
A heavy wooden door leads into this serene café, the haunt of writers and artists. It's far removed from the crowds, but just a few steps from the Old Town Square.
Daily 10am–10pm Staroměstská 🚊 Tram 17, 18 to Staroměstská

SHAKESPEARE AND SONS
Krymská 12, Vršovice, Prague 10
Tel 271 740 839
www.shakes.cz
Shakespeare and Sons, an elegant old bookstore and café, is tucked away in a quaint district just outside central Prague. Poetry and prose readings are regular features, chess and backgammon sets are scattered about, works by local artists are on the walls, and a small bar serves beer and wine. You will also find current US magazines like *The New Yorker*, *Harpers* and *The New York Review of Books*.
Daily noon–midnight Náměstí Míru, then tram 22, 23, or 4 to Krymská

CLUBS
LA FABRIQUE
Uhelný trh 2, Staré Město, Prague 1
Tel 224 233 137
www.lafabrique.cz
Down a steep stairway off a pretty square, this rather plain dance club somehow manages to feel glitzy despite the worn wooden floors and hard-to-negotiate hallways. It can be impossibly crowded after 1am, so get there before 11pm to grab a seat at one

of the many tables in the rooms off the main dance area. Enthusiastic DJs spin their own mix and take requests, so everyone's usually happy.

🕐 Daily 11pm–4am 💰 150Kč
Ⓜ Národní třída 🚊 Tram 9, 18, 22, 23 to Národní třída

FRIENDS
Bartolomějská 11, Staré Město, Prague 1
Tel 224 236 772
www.friends-prague.cz/site/en
Billing itself as 'gay Prague's premier venue', this large, super-modern, central gay-orientated club has much to offer whether you're gay or straight. With a different theme every night—disco fever, mambo latin and video party are just a few—a massive dance floor and bar, private lounge rooms and cutting-edge sound system, the vibe here is super cool and happy. Sunday's 'chillout night' features movies and beer for only 20Kč. Rumour has it that the 'cutest waiters in Prague' work here.

🕐 Daily 6pm–5am 💰 100Kč
Ⓜ Národní třída 🚊 Tram 9, 18, 22, 23 to Národní divadlo

FUTURUM MUSIC BAR
Zborovská 7, Smíchov, Prague 5
Tel 257 328 571
www.musicbar.cz
This dance club, in an historic building, has excellent DJs and live acts, and the innovative metal and brick interior creates an appealing industrial atmosphere. Every Friday and Saturday at 9pm there's a popular '80s and '90s party.

🕐 Daily 8pm–3am 💰 100Kč Ⓜ Anděl
🚊 Tram 4, 9, 10 to Anděl

GURU
Rokycanova 29, Žižkov, Prague 3
Tel 222 783 463
www.guruclub.cz/cz
There are oriental rugs on the brick walls and velvet couches surrounding the large dance and stage floor in this slightly avant-garde, cave-like dance and music club. Upstairs is a coffee-house with balcony booths that provide a great view of the action downstairs, but come early if you want one. Live music is followed by a DJ most nights.

🕐 Daily 7pm–5am 💰 30Kč–50Kč for live acts Ⓜ Flora 🚊 Tram 5, 9, 26 to Olšanské náměstí

IRON DOOR
Křemencova 10, Nové Město, Prague 1
Tel 224 930 343
The appealing Iron Door, down a flight of stairs in a wide brick cellar, has oriental rugs on the floor, lumpy sofas, ottomans and comfy chairs. It caters to a younger crowd who alternate lounging around with jumping up to dance in front of the bar when the DJ spins a song they like. In the back a door leads to the smaller 'Club Nebe', which has a more sophisticated vibe.

🕐 Daily 7pm–5am Ⓜ Národní třída
🚊 Tram 9, 18, 22, 23 to Národní třída

KARLOVY LÁZNĚ
Novotného lávka 1, Staré Město, Prague 1
Tel 222 220 502
www.karlovylazne.cz

Radost FX lounge-club features a different party theme every night

This superclub proclaims itself the biggest music club in middle Europe, for good reason. It occupies an entire building on the banks of the River Vltava and provides several ways to entertain you—a band room with live music, a chill-out room, three DJ dance areas and a café with free internet access in the base-ment. Women should be aware of the famous transparent dance floor. Queues start forming around midnight.

🕐 Café: daily 10am–5am. Club: daily 9pm–5pm 💰 150Kč Ⓜ Staroměstská
🚊 Tram 17, 18 to Karlovy Lázně

KLUB LÁVKA
Novotného lávka 1, Staré Město, Prague 1
Tel 222 222 156
www.lavka.cz

In a spectacular setting, on the end of a jetty on the river, is Lavka—a multi-level disco that gets going late and draws a mixed crowd of tourists and locals looking to let loose and make a match. It has several dance areas and a balcony with a stunning view of Karlův most (Charles Bridge) for when you need some fresh air.

🕐 Daily 9.30pm–5am 💰 150Kč
Ⓜ Staroměstská 🚊 Tram 17, 18 to Karlovy Lázně

MECCA
U průhonu 3, Holešovice, Prague 7
Tel 283 870 522
www.mecca.cz
This ultra-cool disco outside central Prague has won the vote for coolest club and best dance music in town several years running. This is the club for you if your scene is beautiful people: it's a notorious model hangout so don't be surprised to find a bevy of the long-limbed beauties lounging on the white leather couches. The multilevel club has several theme rooms and serves what some say are the smallest beers in town, so the drink of the night is definitely cocktails.

🕐 Daily 10pm–6am 💰 150Kč–250Kč
Ⓜ Vltavská, then tram 15 to Dělnická

N11
Narodni 11, Nové Město, Prague 1
Tel 222 075 705
www.n11.cz
N11 is a labyrinthine cellar club made up of several rooms for eating, drinking and dancing. Arched ceilings, metal tables and chairs, and a concrete floor give the place a somewhat sterile feel but it warms up when the younger crowd starts to pour in around midnight. There's 40 wines by the glass and a different musical theme every night—soul, R&B, Latin, hip hop or dance.

🕐 Daily 4pm–4am Ⓜ Národní třída
🚊 Tram 9, 28, 22, 23 to Národní třída

PALÁC AKROPOLIS
Kubelíkova 27, Žižkov, Prague 3
Tel 296 330 913
www.palacakropolis.cz
This converted theatre is now the hub of Prague's alternative music scene. Ethnic, regional and international acts take the stage in the main room most nights, and a DJ keep things lively in the dance bar. Wandering from room to room

WHAT TO DO

to experience the different vibes is half the fun. The *malé sal*, or little room, has music but is also good for conversations.

🕐 Bar: daily 7pm–3am. Restaurant: daily 11.30–1am. Café: Mon–Fri 10–midnight, Sat–Sun 4–midnight
💰 50Kč–400Kč 🚇 Jiřího z Poděbrad
🚊 Tram 11 to Jiřího z Poděbrad

RADOST FX

Tel 224 254 776
Bělehradská 120, Vinohrady, Prague 2
www.radostfx.cz
Originally based on an East Village club in New York, this world-famous lounge-club complex looks nothing special from the outside, but inside are some of the best DJs this side of London. Every night there's a different party theme, such as 'Ibiza', 'Soulrider' and 'Bikini'. Scantily-dressed professional dancers keep things exciting. Upstairs, there's a cool vegetarian café serving some of the city's best food until the small hours, and a swinging Moroccan lounge complete with mosaic tiles, mirrors and acres of tapestry-covered seating areas. Downstairs in the club the action starts up around midnight.

🕐 Café: daily 10–1am. Lounge: daily 11–4am. Club: daily 10pm–6am
💰 Club entry: around 200Kč
🚇 I.P. Pavlova 🚊 Tram 4, 10, 16, 22, 23 to I.P. Pavlova

ROXY

Dlouhá 33, Staré Město, Prague 1
Tel 224 82 62 96
www.roxy.cz
Roxy is one of Prague's most popular clubs, on a winding street that leads from Staroměstské náměstí (Old Town Square). Kids come here for cutting-edge international acts specializing in trance, Asian dub and techno. A former theatre, this sprawling club is a bit grungy, but always fun, and is popular with British acts like Trance Global Underground and guest DJs from across Europe. The crowd is a mix of young locals and backpacking students who spill over from the hostel next door.

🕐 Daily 1pm–1am. Shows start around 8pm 💰 100Kč–400Kč (depending on the show) 🚇 Náměstí Republiky
🚊 Tram 5, 8, 14 to Dlouhá třída

U ZLATÉHO STROMU

Karlova 6, Staré Město, Prague 1
Tel 222 22 04 41
www.zlatystrom.cz
'At the Golden Tree' is on the main tourist street leading from Karlův most (Charles Bridge) to Staroměstské náměstí (Old Town Square). A predominantly tourist crowd populates this disco, where anything goes, including topless pole dancing. There are two dance floors—one is straight out of *Saturday Night Fever*—and three bars. Especially popular are the party nights with drink specials like *mojitos* and Red Bull. The kitchen serves salads, pizza, pasta and the usual Czech dishes.

🕐 Daily 8pm–6am 💰 Sun–Tue free, Wed–Thu 60Kč, Fri–Sat 80Kč
🚇 Staroměstská 🚊 Tram 17, 18 to Staroměstská

A stained-glass window in a Švejk restaurant in Josefov

TRADITIONAL CZECH PUBS

PIVOVARSKÝ DŮM

Ječná 15, Nové Město, Prague 1
Tel 296 216 666
www.gastroinfo.cz/pivodum
Banana is just one of the unusual tasting beers made on-site at this popular brewpub in the New Town. Beer samplers that let you taste a variety of brews, from sour cherry to champagne, are a fun way to work your way through the list. Make sure you check out the fascinating photos of turn-of-the-20th-century Prague on the walls. A full menu of traditional Czech food is available.

🕐 Daily 11am–11.30pm 🚇 Karlovo náměstí 🚊 Tram 4, 10, 16, 22, 23 to Štěpánská

ŠVEJK RESTAURANT HOSTINEC 'U KALICHA'

Na Bojišti 12, Vinohrady, Prague 2
Tel 296 189 600
www.ukalicha.cz
This pub bills itself as the 'original Švejk' pub for the reference to it in Jaroslav Hašek's famous novel—*The Good Soldier Švejk*—as the place where the two characters plan to meet but never do ('at 6 in the evening after the war'). It's very popular, so reservations are necessary.

🕐 Daily 11am–11pm 🚇 I.P. Pavlova
🚊 Tram 4, 10, 16, 22, 23 to I.P. Pavlova

U ČERNÉHO VOLA (AT THE BLACK OX)

Tel 220 513 481
Loretánské náměstí 1, Hradčany, Prague 1
This grand and beautiful spot is justly praised by locals and tourists alike for offering a true beer hall experience in the quaint Castle district, but for much lower prices than you'd expect in this part of town. As a bonus, the hard-to-find, excellent Kozel beer is on tap.

🕐 Daily 11–11 🚊 Tram 22, 23 to Pohořelec

U FLEKŮ

Křemencova 11, Nové Město, Prague 1
Tel 224 934 019
www.ufleku.cz
The world-famous U Fleků brewery and beer garden is on most tourists' itineraries for its famous dark Flek beer and jovial oom-pah-pah band atmosphere. The historic building dates from the 14th century and there's indoor or outdoor seating in a charming courtyard (even in winter) at long wooden tables. Take note: the offered shots of schnapps and brandy are not complimentary.

🕐 Daily 9am–11pm 🚇 Národní třída
🚊 Tram 9, 18, 22, 23 to Národní třída

U VEJVODU

Jilská 4, Staré Město, Prague 1
Tel 224 219 999
www.uvejvodu.cz
U Vejvodu is an authentic Czech beer hall on three levels, where locals and tourists mix happily and eat heartily in a cavernous and fun atmosphere. It's worth noting that it's open later than almost anywhere else.

🕐 Mon–Thu 10am–3am, Fri–Sat 10am–4am, Sun 11am–2am 🚇 Národní třída 🚊 Tram 9, 18, 22, 23 to Národní třída

SPORTS AND ACTIVITIES

Czechs are avid sports enthusiasts and fans. Their biggest passions are ice hockey and tennis, and both sports have produced a long history of Czech champions. Major events on the annual Prague sporting calendar include the World Cup ice hockey playoffs in February and March, the Prague Open Tennis Championship in August, and the Prague Marathon (www.pim.cz), which crosses Karlův most (Charles Bridge), every May.

There's major rivalry between the two Prague soccer teams, Sparta and Slavia, and each has its own devoted fans. As soon as the snow melts, the impromptu softball games start up at Letna Park. Tickets for spectator sports such as ice hockey and soccer are available through TicketPro (www.ticketpro.cz), Ticketcentrum (Rytířská 31, Prague 1) and other outlets.

There are plenty of tennis courts in the city and Stromovka Park has acres of paths for joggers and rollerbladers (skate rental is available on the path to the Planetarium). The closest 18-hole golf course has a bucolic setting under the castle at Karlštejn, but truly world-class courses are in the spa towns of Karlovy Vary and Mariánské Láznê.

If your taste runs to extreme sports then your options include bungee jumping and parachuting (Aviate Centrum Praha; www.clever.cz/~alarez/acp.htm).

Water sports are plentiful, whether you want to paddle around the River Vltava in the heart of the city (there's a boat rental business on Žofin Island) or head out to the country for some canoeing or sailing.

WHAT TO DO

BICYCLING

CENTRAL EUROPEAN ADVENTURES PRAGUE
Jáchymova 4, Josefov, Prague 1
Tel 222 328 879
http://cea51.tripod.com/Eng1d.htm
This company runs one-day cycling tours in the countryside near Prague. Participants meet at 8.30am in front of the Orloj (Astronomical Clock) in Prague, then take a 30-minute train ride to Karlštejn. A day of cycling through Český Kras natural reserve follows. The route goes along the Berounka River, stops at Koniprusy Cave and ends in the charming Karlštejn Village.
🕐 Apr–end Sep Tue–Sun 💰 680Kč
🚇 Staroměstská

BILLIARDS

HARLEQUIN
Vinohradská 25, Vinohrady, Prague 2
Tel 224 217 240
There are 15 tables in this well-ventilated pool hall (go past the *herna*—slot-machines in front), and what some say is the best cue selection in the city. There's a bar area with tables for non-players. Thursday is league night.
🕐 Daily 2pm–4am 💰 80Kč per hour
🚇 Jiřího z Poděbrad

BOWLING

BOWLING CENTRUM RAN
V Celnici 10, Nové Město, Prague 1
Tel 221 033 020
www.bowlingran.cz
With seven modern lanes, a café and bar, and billiard tables, there's something for everyone at this central bowling alley. Many

An ice-hockey fan—the sport is very popular in the Czech Republic

leagues play here, so you should make a reservation on the website or call beforehand.
🕐 Daily noon–midnight 💰 200Kč per hour 🚇 Náměstí Republiky

BUNGEE JUMPING

K. I. BUNGEE JUMP AND GAMMA STUDIO
Hvězdova 2, Vyšehrad, Prague 4
Tel 777 250 126
www.bungee.cz
If adrenalin is your thing, there's no shortage of it here, where you can jump off a bridge (in a harness). Most of the activities take place in beautiful nature settings. There's a range of bungee-related thrills, including 'bungee running' and 'bungee trampoline'.
🕐 Opening hours vary. Call for locations 💰 700Kč per jump 🚇 Vyšehrad

FITNESS CLUBS

CYBEX HEALTH CLUB AND SPA
Hilton Hotel, Pobřežní 1, Karlín, Prague 8
Tel 224 842 375
www.cybexprg.cz
The swankiest fitness club in the city has a blonde Scandinavian wood interior and a luxurious full-service spa. The 500sq m (5,400sq ft) airy gym is built on two open levels, with 40 cardio machines, 30 strength stations and 15 free weight stations. Private training, spinning and aerobics classes are offered, and there's also a squash court, pool, Jacuzzi and sauna.
🕐 Daily 5.30am–11pm 💰 Day pass for all facilities: 900Kč 🚇 Florenc

WORLD CLASS HEALTH ACADEMY
V Celnici 10 (Millennium Plaza), Nové Město, Prague 1
Tel 221 033 033
Also Václavské náměstí 22, Nové Město, Prague 1
Tel 234 699 100
www.worldclassfitness.net
With two locations in central Prague, each boasting 1,800sq m (19,400sq ft) of space, equipment from Life Fitness and Hammer Strength, 40 cardio stations and a long list of group classes, it's no wonder this gym is so popular. Day passes are available.
🕐 Daily 6am–11pm 💰 Day pass: 300Kč 🚇 Náměstí Republiky or Můstek

GOLF

GOLF CLUB PRAHA
Plzeňzká 401/2, Motol, Prague 5
Tel 257 216 584
www.gcp.cz

This nine-hole course near the city has a putting green, driving range, pro-shop and restaurant. It was built in 1926 and is popular for its tranquil setting and challenging drives.

🕐 Apr–end Nov daily 8–7. Restaurant: Apr–end Oct daily 9–8
💰 500Kč–1,100Kč 🚇 Anděl

ICE HOCKEY

HC SLAVIA
Sazka Arena, Vysočany, Prague 8
Tel 266 121 122
www.hc-slavia.cz
Slavia play in the city's largest indoor arena, built for the 2004 World Ice Hockey Championship.
🕐 Check website for details 💰 Prices vary 🚇 Českomoravská

HC SPARTA
T-Mobile Arena, Výstaviště Exhibition Grounds, Holešovice, Prague 7
Tel 266 727 475
www.hcsparta.cz
In both ice hockey and soccer, Sparta and cross-town Slavia are fierce rivals.
🕐 Check website for details 💰 Prices vary 🚇 Nádraží Holešovice

ICE SKATING

ZIMNÍ STADION NIKOLAJKA
U Nikolajky 28, Smíchov, Prague 5
Tel 251 560 269
This is a good-sized skating rink with skate rental available.
🕐 Mon–Fri 8am–noon (Fri also 8–10pm), Sat–Sun 1–3.30pm; hours may vary, call ahead 💰 35Kč 🚇 Anděl, then 10-min walk

ROCK WALL CLIMBING

LOKALBLOK
Nám. 14. října 10, Smíchov, Prague 5
Tel 251 511 490
www.lokalblok.cz
Lokalblok claims to be the third-largest climbing bar in Europe. It has several climbing areas of varying levels of difficulty, shoe rental and trained staff to help novices. The popular pub and restaurant upstairs provide a place to relax after a workout.
🕐 Mon–Fri 9am–10pm, Sat–Sun noon–10pm 💰 60Kč, plus 25Kč shoe rental 🚇 Anděl

SOCCER

AC SLAVIA
Střešovice, Prague 6
Tel 233 081 753
www.slavia.cz
AC Slavia is building a new stadium, but remains the under-dog in the cross-town rivalry.

🕐 Stadium ticket office: Mon–Fri 9–12, 1–4 💰 Prices vary 🚇 Anděl, then bus 217 to Stadion Strahov

AC SPARTA
Milady Horákové 98, Bubeneč, Prague 7
Tel 220 570 323
www.sparta.cz
Sparta are usually the defending Czech champions and the club has the largest following. At certain games violence has broken out amongst some of the fans.
💰 Prices vary 🚇 Hradčanská, then tram 1, 8, 15 to Sparta

SPORTS COMPLEX

HAMR SPORTS COMPLEX
Záběhlická, Spořilov, Prague 4
Tel 272 772 762
www.hamrsport.cz
This vast sports complex features 24 excellent clay tennis courts,

The Prague Marathon takes place in May each year

squash courts, table tennis and indoor cycling. A pro-shop sells clothing, equipment and restrings racquets, and private lessons are available. There's also a restaurant with a deck overlooking the tennis courts.
🕐 Daily 8am–midnight 💰 Tennis: one hour in summer 150Kč; in winter 300Kč 🚇 I.P. Pavlova, then tram 11 to Spořilov, then 10-min walk

SQUASH

SQUASH CENTRUM HAŠTAL
Haštalská 20, Staré Město, Prague 1
Tel 224 828 561
Reservations are required 24 hours in advance for one of the multiple modern courts at this smart squash centre. There are instructors for novices, and show courts with glass walls and seating areas for matches.

🕐 Mon–Fri 6am–9pm, Sat–Sun 8–8
💰 160Kč–360Kč depending on time of day. Racquet and ball rental available 🚇 Náměstí Republiky

SWIMMING

HOTEL OLŠANKA
Táboritská 23, Žižkov, Prague 3
Tel 267 092 202
The pool at this central hotel may not be Olympic-size, but its perfect for doing a few lengths, and there's no problem if you are not a hotel guest. There's also a massage service and a sauna for an additional charge.
🕐 Mon–Fri 6am–9pm, Sat–Sun 8–8
💰 60Kč per hour 🚇 Flora 🚊 Tram 5, 9, 26 to Olšanské náměstí

PODOLI POOLS
Podolská 74, Podolí, Prague 4
Tel 241 433 952
www.pspodoli.cz
Set in a wooded valley, there's an outdoor Olympic-size pool here and plenty of space for sunbathing. You will also find a fitness centre on-site.
🕐 Mon–Fri 6am–9.45pm (no entry after 8pm), Sat–Sun 8–8 (no entry after 7pm)
💰 80Kč–150Kč 🚇 Karlovo náměstí, then tram 3, 16, 17, 21 to Kublov

TAI CHI

TAIJI AKADEMIE
Polska 1, Vinohrady, Prague 2
Tel 777 053 225
www.taiji.cz
You can join a group class or sign up for individual lessons at this academy—for the ancient, calming martial art of tai chi—run by Radek Kolar.
🕐 Daily 8am–midnight; you must call ahead 💰 Prices vary 🚇 Jiřího z Poděbrad

TENNIS

BENDVIK
Diskařská 1, Hradčany, Prague 1
Tel 251 611 129
www.tenis-kurty.cz
At these Hradčany clay courts a stray lob might accidentally hit the Castle. Everyone just calls this club 'tennis by the castle' because of its proximity to Pražský hrad—literally just around the corner. Play is open to the public but it can be hard to get court time on one of the three courts because of the club's popularity.
🕐 Opening times vary; call ahead 💰 110Kč–250Kč per hour, depending on day and time 🚇 Malostranská
🚊 Tram 22, 23 to Pohořelec

HEALTH AND BEAUTY

The Czech spa towns of Karlovy Vary and Mariánské Lázně are justly famous for their extensive medical spa facilities and tranquil surroundings. A few days spent in either of these is completely rejuvenating but if you can't make the trip from Prague, you can achieve the same feeling in the city with a few visits to places that specialize in well-being and health. Most gyms offer drop-in sessions with personal trainers and saunas and steam rooms for post-workout relaxation. Massage studios are common around the city—look for salons with signs that says *masáž*. An array of skin care products and cosmetics are available at the beauty emporium Sephora, which has several branches in the city. Dermacol Studio (▷ 166) offers a wide range of spa and beauty treatments. For inner health you will find a great selection of herbal teas, organic breads and grains at Country Life (▷ 165) and at Albio (▷ 230), an organic food store and restaurant.

WHAT TO DO

BEAUTY TREATMENTS

CYBEX HEALTH CLUB AND SPA
Hilton Hotel, Pobřežní 1, Karlín, Prague 8
Tel 224 842 375
www.cybexprg.cz
It may sound like an odd combination, but the coffee peeling and chocolate wrap treatment makes perfect sense if you're after baby-smooth skin. A masseuse applies finely ground coffee mixed with sesame oil to remove dead skin and open your pores, followed by a satiny, thick layer of chocolate, with plenty of cocoa butter to make your skin incredibly soft. When you rinse off, you smell intoxicatingly sweet.
🕒 Daily 5.30am–11pm 💆 75-minute treatment 2,000Kč 🚇 Florenc

HOTEL LE PALAIS
U Zvonařky 1, Vinohrady, Prague 2
Tel 234 634 111
There are a number of massage and spa treatments at the spa in this 5-star hotel (▷ 258), but the most popular is the stress-relieving stone massage. As the attendant places the flat, heated and oiled stones along the pressure points on your back and neck, the entire world slips away.
🕒 Spa: daily 8–8 🚋 Tram 6, 11 to Bruselská

SABAI STUDIO
Na příkopě 22 (Slovanský dům), Nové Město, Prague 1
Tel 221 451 180
www.sabai.cz
Muscle aches and stress disappear under the hands of the licensed massage physiotherapists at this studio specializing in Thai techniques, a thousand-year-old form based on the healing theory of intrinsic energy flows and balance. Nine kinds of treatment are offered, including 'foot nirvana' (an acupressure massage of the reflex muscles of the feet), 'relax' (massage of the head, shoulders, neck and ears), 'twiggy' (an anti-cellulite treatment that uses a ginger rub to improve circulation) and 'ritual' (herbal oils to open pores, then peppermint oil to restore vitality).

Enjoying a relaxing facial can be a great way to unwind

🕒 Daily 10–10 💆 Massages 550Kč–1,500Kč 🚇 Náměstí Republiky

SALONS

JAMES HAIR
Malá Štupartská 9, Staré Město, Prague 1
Tel 224 827 373
www.jameshair.cz
This chic but unpretentious hair salon is run by James, a former New York-based celebrity hairdresser. Models come here for the painstaking attention to detail and knowledge of the latest cutting techniques and colours. Everyone on the staff has experience cutting hair in London, New York or Amsterdam.
🕒 Tue–Fri 8–8, Sat 9–6 💆 Cuts: prices start from 500Kč 🚇 Náměstí Republiky

MARK PHILLIPS SALON
Mánesova 47, Vinohrady, Prague 2
Tel 222 254 096
One pedicure by Elizabeth Phillips and you'll compare all others to her. The cheery British expatriate rubs, files, grinds and buffs with a variety of instruments until your feet are lovely and smooth, then she gives your toenails a perfect paint job (appointments available on Mondays and Wednesdays).
🕒 Opening hours vary 💆 Pedicure: 850Kč. Cuts with Mark 750Kč; foil highlights 2,200Kč; blow dry and set 750Kč 🚇 Jiřího z Poděbrad

SPAS

SALON PELUX
Štěpánská 61 (pasáž Lucerna), Nové Město, Prague 1
Tel 224 215 959
Email: salon@pelux.cz
A pampering team of Czech, Russian and Japanese beauty technicians is on hand to see to your every need at this full-service spa. In their expert hands you can choose from a variety of luxurious facials, massages, manicures, pedicures or waxing treatments. There's also a hair salon for cuts, colour and styling.
🕒 Daily 9–8 💆 450Kč–1,500Kč depending on treatment 🚇 Můstek

YVES ROCHER
Václavské náměstí 47, Nové Město, Prague 1
Tel 221 625 570
www.yvesrocher.cz
At this no-nonsense French spa they'll tweeze, wax and pluck you, give you a rejuvenating facial, and send you out the door with polished fingers and toes in no time at all. You also have the opportunity to buy the products used in your treatment.
🕒 Mon–Fri 7am–9pm, Sat 8–6, Sun 10–6 💆 300Kč–2,000Kč depending on treatment 🚇 Muzeum

FOR CHILDREN

A city where there are puppets at every turn, and red and yellow trams that ring their bells when pulling into a stop, Prague fascinates most children without even trying. Special experiences include the mirror maze on Petřín Hill and the butterfly garden near the zoo, while an afternoon on Dětský ostrov can turn into a delightful opportunity to feed the ducks. At Jungleland kids can play around in an enclosure full of plastic balls, while older children may enjoy the antique planes and trains at the Národní technické muzeum. Many of the city's marionette theatres have matinees, and the mix of dance, pantomime, music and illusion at the black light shows will hold even young children's interest. Or hop on a tram, like the charming antique No. 91, which makes a stop at the fairgrounds.

DĚTSKÝ OSTROV
Vltava River, Malá Strana, Prague 1
Entrance on Janáčkovo nábřeží (closest bridge Jiráskův most)
There's a safe, enclosed playground on the delightful, wooded Children's Island that is easily accessible from the Malá Strana side of the river. Plenty of benches allow watchful adults to sit and take in the sweeping views.
🚊 Karlovo náměstí, then tram to Zborovská

JUNGLELAND
Výmolova 2, Radlice, Prague 5
Tel 251 091 437
www.fitness-station.cz
This enclosed, modern playground has lots of safe, fun diversions for energetic kids, and is divided into two sections: one for children aged 1–6, the other for those aged 7–13. The main attraction is a massive pen filled with bright, plastic balls which kids can jump around in safely.
🕐 Daily 9–7 💰 70Kč 🚊 Radlická

MUZEUM HRAČEK
Prague Castle, Jiřská 6, Hradčany, Prague 1
Tel 224 372 294
www.muzeumhracek.cz
The Toy Museum has a display of antique and modern toys from the 18th, 19th and 20th centuries. There is also an impressive collection of historic Barbie dolls.
🕐 Daily 9.30–5.30 💰 Adult 60Kč; child (6–16) 30Kč 🚊 Malostranská

NÁRODNÍ DIVADLO MARIONET
See page 178.

NÁRODNÍ TECHNICKÉ MUZEUM
Kostelní 42, Holešovice, Prague 7
Tel 220 399 111
www.ntm.cz
At the National Technical Museum old planes and hot-air balloons hang from the ceiling, antique bicycles ring the balcony and a giant locomotive looks ready to

start steaming down the track at any minute. This glass-roofed museum displays everything in one spacious main hall, so there's no endless trudging through room after room.
🕐 For opening hours and prices, ▷ 96
🚊 Tram 1, 8, 15, 25, 26 to Letenské náměstí

Delightful wooden puppets can be seen throughout the city

PETŘÍNSKÁ ROZHLEDNA AND BLUDIŠTĚ
Petřínské sady, Malá Strana, Prague 1
Most children will enjoy the 360°, bird's-eye view from the top of Petřín Hill's Rozhledna (viewing tower), modelled on the Eiffel Tower. In the small Gothic castle nearby, there's the delightful Bludiště, a maze filled with convex and concave mirrors. Enjoy a ride in the *lanovka* (funicular) to reach the top of this wooded hill.
🕐 For opening hours and prices, ▷ 102
🚊 Tram 12, 20, 22, 23 to Újezd, then *lanovka* to Petřín

SEA WORLD
Výstaviště, Holešovice, Prague 7
Tel 220 103 305
www.morsky-svet.cz
Tanks of exotic, rainbow-coloured fish will keep children facsinated,

but this is an excursion for the younger set; there are plenty of small fish, but no 'exciting' forms of sealife like sharks or dolphins at this aquarium.
🕐 Daily 10–7 💰 220Kč 🚊 Holešovice, then tram 5, 12, or 17 to Výstaviště

TETA TRAMTARIE
Jungmannova 28, Nové Město, Prague 1
Tel 296 165 174
Adults enjoy this indoor, urban playground as much as kids. There is an extensive, modern jungle gym, a children's bookstore and a small theatre where puppet shows and plays are performed. Parents can keep an eye on their kids from the café which serves sandwiches and light snacks.
🕐 Daily 10–8 🚊 Můstek 🚊 Tram 3, 14 to Vodičkova

VÝSTAVIŠTĚ
Holešovice, Prague 7
www.krizikovafontana.cz
The fairgrounds at Výstaviště have sprawling pavilions, a marine park, theatres and amusement rides, and in the evenings, the brilliantly lit Křižík Fountain 'dances' to music. You can take the antique tram No. 91 there (▷ 49), which stops throughout the city.
🕐 Opening hours vary 💰 Prices vary
🚊 Tram 5, 12, 14, 15 or 17 to Výstaviště

ZOOLOGICKÁ ZAHRADA
U Trojského zámku 3/120, Troja, Prague 7
Tel 296 112 111
www.zoopraha.cz
The addition of a new tropical hall has helped Prague Zoo recover from the devastation of the 2002 floods, and there are delights around every corner, from gorillas to giraffes. You can walk to the zoo from Stromovka Park or the fairgrounds via a footbridge.
🕐 For opening hours and prices, ▷ 131
🚊 Bus 112 from metro Holešovice to Zoologická zahrada

WHAT TO DO

FESTIVALS AND EVENTS

Throughout the year, Prague plays host to several cultural, traditional, artistic and sporting events. Whenever there's a major holiday, Staroměstské náměstí (Old Town Square) will set something up—a craft market, a tree or a stage for local singers and dancers to perform on. The major music festivals include Prague Spring, in May and June, and Prague Autumn in October. Verdi takes over the State Opera House in August. Every May the marathon is run and the route crosses the scenic 14th-century Karlův most (Charles Bridge). In February Praguers celebrate the pre-Lenten festival, *Masopust*, complete with papier-mâché puppets. Other highlights of the city's calendar include the summer Prague Fringe Festival and the autumn wine harvest festivals. Check the *Night & Day* section of the English-language weekly, the *Prague Post*, for details of what's on.

FEBRUARY

MASOPUST
Žižkov, Prague 3
www.praha3.cz
This pre-Lenten festival runs for five days, beginning the Friday before Ash Wednesday. Though not as wild as Mardi Gras, it includes giant puppets and a parade. At night, there's music and events at Palác Akropolis and Kino Aero.
⊙ Jiřího z Poděbrad

APRIL

FEBIOFEST
www.febiofest.cz
Despite the name, this international film and documentary festival is usually held the first week in April. The schedule of screenings includes film student debuts, alternative films and a few big-studio releases.
⊙ Early April ❓ See website for details

PÁLENI ČARODĚJNIC
The traditional spring festival called 'Witches' Night' is marked by bonfires in the countryside and broom burning supposedly to ward off evil. In Prague, the best places to see bonfires are on Kampa Island and Petřín Hill. Check that week's *Prague Post* for details of where the bonfires will be in the city.
⊙ 30 April 🚊 Kampa Park: Tram 9, 22 or 23 to Újezd. Petřín Hill: Tram 9, 22 or 23 to Újezd, then funicular to the top

MAY

MAJÁLES
In this commemorative May Day parade, students traditionally lead a procession from náměstí Jana Palacha to Staroměstské náměstí.
⊙ 1 May ⊙ Staroměstská

PRAGUE MARATHON
www.pim.cz
The annual marathon has one of the most picturesque running paths in the world—it crosses the

14th-century Karlův most (Charles Bridge) and ends in Staroměstské náměstí (Old Town Square).
⊙ May ⊙ Staroměstská 🚊 Tram 17, 18 ❓ See website for details

WORLD ROMA MUSIC FESTIVAL KHAMORO
This annual festival of Roma music and culture began in 1999.

Concerts are often held at many of Prague's splendid churches

The six-day event features music from several countries, films, seminars and exhibits.
🎫 260Kč–360Kč (for individual concerts through Ticketpro and at venues)
⊙ Reduta Jazz Club (▷ 176): Národní třída. Roxy (▷ 185): Náměstí Republiky. Lucerna Music Club (▷ 177): Můstek

MAY/JUNE

PRAGUE SPRING
Tel 257 312 547
www.festival.cz
Every year this world-famous music festival begins on 12 May, the anniversary of the death of Czech composer Bedřich Smetana (1824–84). Since 1952 it has opened its three-week concert series with his *Má vlast (My Country)* and closed with Beethoven's *Ninth Symphony*. It attracts conductors and musicians from all over the world. A smaller,

sister festival called Prague Autumn is held in October.
⊙ 12 May–3 June ❓ See website for details of venues and performances

JUNE

FRINGE FESTIVAL PRAHA
www.praguefringe.com
Modelled on the Edinburgh Fringe Festival, this week-long celebration of alternative music, theatre and dance takes place on various indoor and outdoor stages across the city.
⊙ First week in June 🎫 Tickets start from 50Kč ❓ See website for details

AUGUST

VERDI FESTIVAL
www.opera.cz
An entire month of Verdi operas at the Státní opera Praha (Prague State Opera, ▷ 176).
⊙ August 🎫 Tickets: 300Kč–1,100Kč
⊙ Muzeum or Hlavní nádraží

SEPTEMBER

VINOHRADY GRAPE HARVEST
www.praha2.cz; www.praha3.cz
In late September the district of Vinohrady (which means royal vineyards) celebrates the grape harvest. There are traditional crafts, performers in period costume and the first bottles of *burčak*—a young Czech wine that tastes like apple cider.
⊙ 3rd or 4th weekend in September
⊙ Náměstí Míru 🚊 Tram 4, 10, 16, 22, 23

DECEMBER

CHRISTMAS MARKET
Every year on the first Sunday of Advent a craft market and a huge Christmas tree are set up in the Old Town Square. Dozens of wooden huts sell handmade Czech Christmas ornaments and other festive gifts and decorations. To ward off the chill, grab a cup of *svařené víno* (hot mulled wine).
⊙ Craft huts: daily 10–10 from first Sun in Dec to first Sun in Jan (approximately)
🎫 Free ⊙ Staroměstská

Prague is compact enough to explore on foot, and this section describes five walks and a trip along the River Vltava that take in some of the most interesting parts of the city. The start points of the walks are marked on the map on the inside front cover of the book. This chapter also gives suggestions for excursions outside the city. These are marked on the map on page 204.

Out and About

ALONG THE HEIGHTS

This 'green' approach to the Castle is almost entirely on one level. It takes you through a chain of parks and gardens with wonderful views over the River Vltava and the city.

THE WALK

Distance: 3km (2 miles)
Allow: 1.5 hours
Start at: Letenské náměstí tram stop
End at: Pražský hrad (Prague Castle) or Pražský hrad tram stop

HOW TO GET THERE

🚊 Tram 1, 8, 15, 25, 26 to Letenské náměstí

Cross to the far side of Milady Horákové street and go down it for a short distance, turning first right on to Ovenecká street. At the end turn right, then left and cross the esplanade in front of the sober-looking buildings housing the Národní technické muzeum (National Museum of Technology, ▷ 96) to the east.

You are now at the eastern end of Letenské sady (Letná Gardens), the attractively landscaped parkland running high above the Vltava along the edge of Letná Plain.

❶ Letná Plain is the eastward extension of the rock spur on which the Castle stands. Its shrub-clad cliffs drop down to the river and form a backdrop to many vistas from the Old Town, while the edge of the plateau offers ever-changing views of the great bend in the river and the Old Town on the far bank. The clifftop section of Letná is lavishly planted with fine trees and is a popular promenading area; to the north

is a much more open section, used in the past by the Communists for their May Day parades. One of the key events in the 1989 Velvet Revolution took place here when, on 26 November, a crowd of almost a million called for a general strike against the regime.

Walk past the Letenský zámeček (▷ 237), a restaurant with a huge beer garden and bandstand, and enjoy the views of river and city from the lip of the plateau. Continue west among the trees along the cliff-top path, eventually descending a ramp which brings you to the massive, granite-faced plinth which once supported the Stalin statue.

Flowers in the Royal Garden (above left). Looking towards the Old Town from Letná park (above)

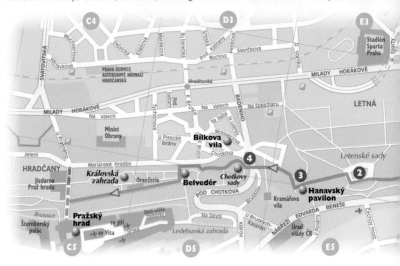

OUT AND ABOUT

❷ Communist Czechoslovakia was ahead of the other Soviet satellites in its official adoration of Stalin, and the monument to the dictator was intended to join the Castle, Vyšehrad and the National Monument on Žižkov Hill in their domination of the city skyline. At 30m (100ft) high, the monster figure of Stalin was backed by two lines of workers, Soviet on one side, Czechoslovak on the other. Local wits instantly dubbed the monument 'the meat queue'. It was completed in 1955, just in time for the cult of Stalin to be denounced in his homeland. His statue in Prague lingered on embarrassingly, but in 1962 it was demolished in an operation that lasted two weeks and involved a series of explosions. In Stalin's place, a mysterious giant metronome now beats out the passing of time.

Go up the steps to the left of the plinth and turn left, then half left up the steep path leading to the Hanavský pavilon (▷ 235).

❸ Now a restaurant, this little neo-baroque pavilion was one of the stars of the show at the Jubilee Expo of 1891. It was commissioned by the Duke of Hanau as a showcase for the products of his ironworks, and is itself assembled from cast-iron sections. You don't have to patronize the restaurant to enjoy the prospect—an enticing vista of the Vltava and its series of bridges. To the west are substantial remains of the brick-built baroque fortifications, on top of which perches the Kramářova vila (Kramář Villa). Karel Kramář (1860–1937) was one of the architects of Czechoslovak independence and the country's first prime minister. His villa is now the Czech prime minister's residence.

Go round the Hanavský pavilon and continue downhill to rejoin the main path, turning half left almost immediately to cross the modern footbridge over the main road. From the bridge there is a view of Bílkova vila (▷ 68), built by the artist František Bílek. At the far end of the bridge you enter Chotkovy sady (Chotek Gardens).

Golden art nouveau statue (above right), Hanavský pavilon

❹ The leafy little park bears the name of Count Chotek, Governor of Prague between 1826 and 1843. The energetic and public-spirited count was responsible for a whole array of 'civic improvements', including the Vltava embankments and the serpentine road between city and Castle that you have just crossed. The park named after him has an extraordinary central feature, a grotto with statues of a youth and a bevy of wistful maidens. It is a memorial to the neo-Romantic, 19th-century author Julius Zeyer, and the statues represent characters from his writings. At the far end of the park there is an unusual view of the Kralovský letohrádek or Belvedér (▷ 67).

Leave Chotek Gardens by the exit to the right of the Belvedér, turn left and left again into the Královská zahrada (Royal Garden, ▷ 84). There are many attractive features to detain you here, among them a view of the Castle and Cathedral on the far side of the Jelení příkop (Stag Moat). Walk along the southern edge of the garden and look down on to the glittering Oranžerie (Orangery), a modern replacement for the one built in Emperor Rudolf's time. At the far end of the Royal Garden turn left towards the Castle or right towards the Pražský hrad tram stop if you wish to return downtown.

WHEN TO GO
This is essentially a summer walk, not least because the Royal Garden is closed between November and March.

WHERE TO EAT
Sitting at one of the many outside tables of the Letenský zámeček (▷ 237) can be very enjoyable. The view from the Hanavský pavilion (▷ 235) will certainly complement your meal.

...he Chotek Gardens

The huge metronome (above)

OUT AND ABOUT

AROUND MALÁ STRANA

This rewarding route twists and turns through the streets, squares and alleyways of the most picturesque and best preserved quarter of town, with unusual glimpses of the riverside along the way.

THE WALK

Distance: 3.5km (2 miles)
Allow: 2 hours
Start/end at: Malostranská metro and tram stop

HOW TO GET THERE

🚇 Malostranská
🚊 Tram to Malostranská

From Malostranská metro station or tram stop walk down Klárov street towards Manesův most (Mánes Bridge). From the bridge's southern approach, go down into the little riverside park.

❶ The unkempt area running down to the water's edge is where working horses used to be brought to cool down and enjoy a drink. From the park there is an unusual view upstream to Karlův most (Charles Bridge) and Staré Město (Old Town).

Leave the park and turn left along Cihelná street and the pretty little square, which is really just a widening of the street called U lužického semináře. As you approach Charles Bridge, bear left, crossing over the Čertovka ('Devils Brook') millstream and passing beneath one of the bridge's broad arches into the oval-shaped square known as Na Kampě. You are now on Kampa Island.

❷ Kampa Island lies between the Čertovka and the main channel of the Vltava. For much of its existence it remained free of building because of the risk of flooding. Most of the island was turned into a public park in 1940; from the balustrade there are fine views across the river, this time looking downstream to Charles Bridge. The Čertovka has kept the big old water-wheel of one of its mills, while another, the Sova Mill, is now the home of the Muzeum Kampa (▷ 92), a private galley of modern Czech art.

Prague's coat of arms

Go back towards Na Kampě, but turn left before entering the square and follow the street round until you come to a bridge over the Čertovka, which brings you into Velkopřevorské náměstí (Grand Priors Square).

❸ Dominating Velkopřevorské náměstí are two splendid palaces—the rococo Buquoyský palác (Buquoy Palace), now the French Embassy, and the Velkopřevorský palác (Grand Priors Palace), the residence of the Grand Prior of the Knights of Malta. Here you will see the famous John Lennon Wall, with its graffitied tributes to the assassinated Beatle.

Continue in the same direction out of the square and, leaving Kostel Panny Marie pod řetězem (Church of Our Lady of the Chain, ▷ 104) to the right, go across the upper end of Maltézské náměstí (Maltese Square) into narrow Prokopská street, turning right into Karmelitská street and Malostranské náměstí (Malá Strana Square, ▷ 88), with the awesome bulk of Svatého Mikuláš (Church of St Nicholas, ▷ 122–123). For a bird's-eye view, climb the church's tall bell-tower to the viewing gallery. After, go through the gap in the southwestern corner of the square into Tržiště street.

❹ Tržiště runs gently uphill, becoming Vlašská street higher up. The US and German embassies occupy the two finest palaces in this part of town, the Schönbornský in Tržiště (▷ 120) and the Lobkovický in Vlašská (▷ 88) respectively. The area was once the home of the Italian builders and craftsmen whose skills went into the building of much of Renaissance and baroque Prague (Vlašská means 'Italian').

Just beyond the German Embassy, bear right uphill and follow little Šporkova street right round to the foot of a flight of steps on the left. Go up the steps and turn right into Nerudova (Neruda street, ▷ 98). You could spend a good part of the day spotting house signs among the street's baroque and rococo town houses, but for now go down the street into Malostranské náměstí (Malá Strana Square) and turn left along Sněmovní street which leads past the Czech Chamber of Deputies (No. 176) into Pětikostelní náměstí (Fünfkirchen Square).

❺ This charming little square is one of the few places in town to have kept its bilingual German/Czech street sign. Centuries ago, the main approach to the Castle passed this way, but the narrow lane winding up steeply from the square is now a cul-de-sac. Called U zlaté studně (The Golden Well), it leads up to an exclusive hotel and terrace restaurant of the same name.

Go downhill into Valdštejnské náměstí, where the dominant feature is the main façade of the great Valdštejnský palác (Wallenstein Palace, ▷ 138). To the left, along curving Valdštejnská street, is a row of aristocratic palaces built at the foot of the Castle, with access to their wonderful terraced gardens through the courtyard of the Ledeburský palác (Ledebour Palace). Turn right and walk along the arcade on the near side of Tomášská street.

OUT AND ABOUT

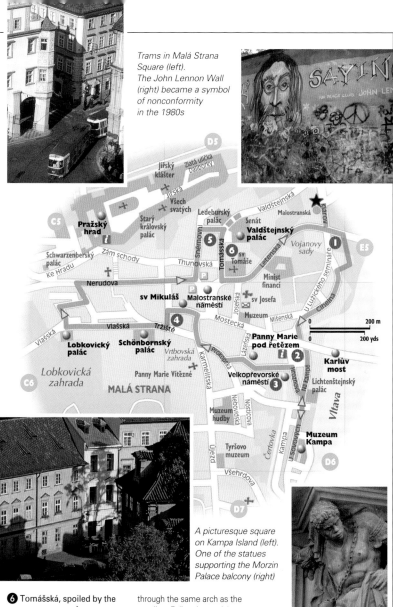

Trams in Malá Strana Square (left).
The John Lennon Wall (right) became a symbol of nonconformity in the 1980s

A picturesque square on Kampa Island (left). One of the statues supporting the Morzin Palace balcony (right)

OUT AND ABOUT

6 Tomášská, spoiled by the constant stream of one-way traffic, is nevertheless worth taking in for its baroque houses. None is finer than No. 26/4, U zlatého jelena (The Golden Stag), built by the great baroque architect Kilián Ignác Dientzenhofer in 1726. Gracing the portal is a life-size sculpture of a stag in the company of St. Hubert, the patron saint of hunting, by Ferdinand Maximilian Brokoff (1688–1731).

At the end of Tomášská, cross to the far side of the road, turn left and go through the pedestrian archway; on no account walk through the same arch as the tramline. Follow Letenská street as it curves along the high wall of the Valdštejnská zahrada (Wallenstein Garden). Turn left at the end of the street to return to Malostranská metro station or tram stop.

WHEN TO GO

You can do this walk at any time, though note that the bell-tower of the Church of St. Nicholas is open only from April to the end of October.

WHERE TO EAT

Malá Strana could almost be described as Prague's restaurant quarter, and there is no shortage of places to eat and drink. Hergetova cihelna (▷ 235), close to the start (and end) of the walk, is a stylish riverside restaurant, while David (▷ 234), near the German Embassy, has a reputation as one of the most welcoming gastronomic establishments in town.

HRADČANY AND MALÁ STRANA

This walk avoids the usual stiff trek up to the Castle by using the tram to whisk you up to Hradčany, with its breathtaking views, charming lanes and baroque palaces. After strolling through the courtyards and gardens of the Castle, you can take the easy, downhill route to the perfectly preserved district of Malá Strana.

THE WALK

Distance: 4km (2.5 miles)
Allow: 2 hours
Start at: Pohořelec tram stop
End at: Malostranské náměstí
(Malá Strana Square)

HOW TO GET THERE

🚇 Malostranská, then tram 22, 23 to Pohořelec

From the Pohořelec tram stop, cross Keplerova street and head for the far side of Pohořelec square. Turn right, walk up the ramp and enter the precincts of Strahovský klášter (Strahov Monastery, ▷ 118–119) through its baroque gateway. Continue across the courtyard of the monastery, passing the entrance to its libraries and the Church of the Assumption of Our Lady (Kostel Nanebevzetí Panny Marie), both on your right. Go through the opening at the far end of the precinct and turn almost immediately right into the vineyard viewpoint.

❶ In front of you, the slopes of Petřín Hill drop away almost precipitously. Petřín was once covered in vineyards, which have long since been replaced by orchard trees. The little vineyard here, laid out in the 1990s, is a kind of memorial to them. The view takes in almost all of historic Prague.

Retrace your steps into the monastery courtyard. Turn right and go down steps, which lead beneath the house called U zlatého stromu (The Golden Tree), one of several ancient buildings lining Pohořelec square.

❷ A statue of St. John Nepomuk stands in the upper section of the partly arcaded square, whose name 'place of fires' recalls its devastation in a series of fires and sieges.

Walk down Loretánská street, turning left on to the terrace on which the gigantic Černínský

palác (Černín Palace, ▷ 70) stands. From here you can look down on the Loreta (Loreto Shrine, ▷ 86–87). Go down the steps, head diagonally left across the square and down narrow, cobbled Černínská lane, past the little Nepomuk statue on top of a garden wall. You are entering the secluded little area known as Nový Svět (New World, ▷ 99).

sgraffitoed Schwarzenberský palác (Schwarzenberg Palace, ▷ 120–121) and to the left, the sumptuous Arcibiskupský palác. Tucked away at the side of the Archbishop's Palace, and reached by a sloping lane, is the Šternberský palác (Sternberg palace, ▷ 116–117), home of the National Gallery's Old Master paintings.

A group of visitors outside the grand Archbishop's Palace, Hradčany

Turn right and walk along Nový Svět itself, admiring its picturesque old houses. Continue down Kanovnická street into Hradčanské náměstí (Hradčany Square).

❸ The vast, traffic-free Hradčanské náměstí is surrounded by the palaces of the nobility and the residences of the cathedral clergy. The first palace on your left, the Renaissance Martinický palác (Martinic Palace), was the home of one of the Imperial councillors famously defenestrated from a Castle window in 1618 (▷ 29). To your right at the top end of the square is the monumental Toskánský palác (Tuscan Palace), but the square's two great landmarks face each other at its lower end; to the right the boldly

Go through the gateway, with its blue-uniformed guardsmen, into the Castle precincts. Return another day to visit the interiors of Pražský hrad (Prague Castle, ▷ 106–111); for now walk through the First and Second Courtyards to the Third Courtyard, dominated by Svatého Víta (St. Vitus Cathedral, ▷ 126–129). Entry to the nave is free, and it is worth looking in for a moment to admire its stained-glass windows. Cross Jiřské náměstí (St. George's Square) at the east end of St. Vitus's and go down the lane to the right of the baroque west front of Bazilika svatého Jiří (St. George's Basilica). Leave the Castle through the Černá věž (Black Tower) at the end of the lane and turn almost 180 degrees right into the Jižní zahrady (South Gardens, ▷ 111). The gardens

WHEN TO GO

The Castle's South Gardens are closed in winter so this walk is best done in summertime (Apr–end Oct).

WHERE TO EAT

The most attractive place in the Castle precincts for a drink and snack is the café in the Lobkovický palác (Lobkowitz Palace, ▷ 237). There are also numerous cafés, restaurants and pubs in and around Malá Strana Square.

St. John of Nepomuk statue (left), Nový Svět. New Castle Steps (right)

are open between April and October; at other times you can rejoin the walk by retracing your steps to the western entrance to the Castle.

4 A stroll through the South Gardens reveals lovely vistas over the rooftops of Malá Strana, as well as striking views of the sheer walls of the Castle. One of the best viewpoints, marked by a slim column topped by a golden sphere and lightning flashes, is the Moravská bašta (Moravian Bastion); another, close to the strange stone pyramid towards the far end of the gardens, is formed by a little colonnaded belvedere.

An intriguing way of descending to Malá Strana is to go down the stairway by the Moravian Bastion and buy a ticket for the Zahrady pod Pražským hradem (Gardens

A sculpture in the New World Garden

beneath Prague Castle, ▷ 111), the series of baroque terraced gardens belonging to various palaces. For now, continue along the South Gardens, climb the broad steps at their western end and emerge at the top of Zámecké schody (Castle Steps).

5 Known as the New Castle Steps to distinguish them from Staré zámecké schody (Old Castle Steps), this picturesque link between Malá Strana and the citadel is in fact an older

The impressive gateway to Prague Castle (above)

approach to the citadel, already in use in the 13th century.

Go down the ramped steps, with the high wall of the Castle gardens to your left. Admire the Renaissance Palác pánů z Hradce (Palace of the Lords of Hradec) to your right. The steps lead into narrow Thunovská street (▷ 125), with the British Embassy just up a little lane to the left. Turn first right into Sněmovní street and into Malostranské náměstí (Malá Strana Square, ▷ 88), dominated by Svatého Mikuláš (Church of St. Nicholas, ▷ 122–123).

STREETS AND SQUARES OF STARÉ MĚSTO

The Royal Way leads directly along Celetná and Karlova streets to Charles Bridge but this longer route offers an insight into some of the most fascinating places in the Old Town.

THE WALK

Distance: 1.8km (1.2 miles)
Allow: 1 hour
Start at: Náměstí Republiky
End at: Smetana statue on Novotného lávka

HOW TO GET THERE

🚇 Náměstí Republiky
🚋 Tram 5, 8, 14 to Náměstí Republiky

From Náměstí Republiky metro station or tram stop, cross the square and walk along the front of the Obecní dům (Municipal House, ▷ 100–101).

❶ The Obecní dům is the outstanding example of Prague art nouveau architecture. Its café is a great place to soak up atmosphere and prepare yourself for the walk ahead.

Come out of the Municipal House, turn right beneath the bridge linking it to the landmark Prašná brána (Powder Tower, ▷ 105) and bear slightly left into Celetná street (▷ 68). The Powder Tower marks the start of what came to be known as the Royal Way, the route followed by the coronation procession. This would make its way from the old royal palace (on the site of the Municipal House), through the Old Town, across the river and up to the Cathedral where the crowning ceremony would take place. Continue along Celetná past the wonderful Cubist building known as the Dům U černé Matky Boží (Black Madonna House, ▷ 70), and turn right into the courtyard of No. 17/595. This leads into Malá Štupartská street, the site of Svatého Jakuba (Church of St. James, ▷ 124), one of Prague's great medieval churches. It was given a baroque interior in the 17th and 18th centuries. Even if you don't go inside, you can admire the virtuoso plaster relief sculptures above the doorway. Go back a few steps and turn right into the courtyard of Týnský dvůr (Týn Court, ▷ 125) or Ungelt.

A statue of Terezka adorns a fountain on Marian Square

❷ In the Middle Ages, and almost into modern times, the Týnský dvůr was like a little world on its own, an enclave where foreign merchants could live and trade under the protection of the king, obeying their own laws and exempt from ordinary taxes. It has now been restored and has attracted specialist shops and sophisticated places to eat and drink.

Leave the Týn Court by the far entrance and walk along the side of Chrám Matky Boží před Týnem (Church of our Lady before Týn) into Staroměstské náměstí (Old Town Square).

❸ The broad cobbled esplanade of the Staroměstské náměstí (▷ 112–115), with its wealth of fine buildings, is a popular gathering place. There is far too much to take in at one go, so just have a leisurely stroll through and enjoy the general atmosphere.

Walk out of the square past the Staroměstská radnice (Old Town Hall) with the Orloj (Astronomical Clock) and into the next, far smaller square, Malé náměstí (Little Square).

❹ The mansions lining Malé náměstí are just as fascinating as those in Staroměstské náměstí. The most striking is No. 3/142; its façade was painted by the distinguished 19th-century artist Mikuláš Aleš (1852–1913) for its owner, the hardware merchant V. J. Rott. In the middle of the square, the old well is covered by a 16th-century wrought-iron canopy, topped by a gilt Bohemian lion.

Go right, leaving behind the crowds heading along the Royal Way towards Karlova street, and out of Malé náměstí to the north, turning immediately left on Linhartská along the side of the Nová Radnice (New Town Hall) and entering Mariánské náměstí (Marian Square, ▷ 90).

❺ Mariánské náměstí is dominated by the New Town Hall, whose façade features a pair of formidable statues of the Iron Man (to the left), and the famous Rabbi Loew (▷ 29), creator of the Golem (to the right). A more graceful figure, part of the fountain on the far left-hand side of the square, is that of the female spirit of the Vltava, also known as Terezka.

Turn left along Husova street, named after martyr Jan Hus, who was burned at the stake in 1415. Just beyond the giants holding up the portal of the massive Clam-Gallasovský palác (Clam-Gallas Palace), walk across Karlova street into the continuation of Husova, then turn right into Řetězová street. Number 3, the Dům pánů z Kunštátu a Poděbrad (House of the Lords of Kunštát and Poděbrady, ▷ 70), was once the residence of George of Poděbrady, known as the 'Hussite King'. Opposite, at No. 8, is one of the city's oddest house signs, 'The Black (and very battered) Boot'. Continue along Řetězová and Anenská, turning left into Anenské náměstí (Agnes Square), home of the Divadlo na zábradlí (Theatre at the Balustrade, ▷ 178).

The charming Týnský dvůr (above). Iron Man statue on the New Town Hall (right). Gazing across the River Vltava (below)

The magnificent art nouveau Obecní dům (left). Bustling Old Town Square (right)

6 The theatre won fame as an island of dissent in Communist times; it was here that playwright and later president Václav Havel began his career, as a stagehand.

Go across the square into Stříbná and turn right at the end of this narrow alleyway into Náprstkova street. Cross Karoliny Světlé street, go up the steps at the side of the Bellevue restaurant, turn left and cross busy Smetanovo nábřeží (Smetana Embankment) by the pedestrian crossing. Turn right towards Karlův most (Charles Bridge) and left along the pier called Novotného lávka, which terminates in the old waterworks building housing the Muzeum Bedřicha Smetany (Smetana Museum, ▷ 91).

7 The Muzeum Bedřicha Smetany is worth seeing in its own right, but for the moment, lean on the railing by the seated statue of the great composer and enjoy the spectacle of the river crashing over the weir and the classic view of Charles Bridge, Malá Strana and the Castle.

WHEN TO GO
The walk can be done at any time.

WHERE TO EAT
Here in the heart of Prague you will find a number of places to eat. Apart from the Obecní dům (Municipal House), a good place to stop is the Grand Café Praha (▷ 234–235), with views of the Orloj (Astronomical Clock).

VYŠEHRAD AND NOVÉ MĚSTO

This walk takes you from one of the key buildings of Communist Prague, around the attractions of the Vyšehrad rock, then back through Charles IV's New Town, via one of the city's lost villages.

THE WALK

Distance: 5 km (3 miles)
Allow: half a day
Start at: Vyšehrad metro station
End at: Václavské náměstí

HOW TO GET THERE

🚇 Metro Line C, direction Háje to Vyšehrad

The metro emerges from below ground to cross the deep valley of the Botič brook on the lower level of the spectacular Nusle expressway bridge, though you will only be aware of this once you have reached the glass-walled Vyšehrad station. From the station, go up steps to the breezy esplanade in front of the huge building of the Kongresové centrum Praha (Congress Centre).

❶ The Kongresové centrum Praha, formerly called the Palác kultury (Palace of Culture), was one of the great construction projects of the Communist regime, intended as the Party's own citadel on a par with historic Hradčany. Completed in 1980, it hosted a run of Communist congresses until the Velvet Revolution put a stop to such events. It is now used, among other things, for pop concerts and NATO summits. From the esplanade there are fine views across the valley to the remaining ramparts of the New Town and beyond to the Castle.

Walk west along the esplanade to the Business Centrum Vyšehrad, turn left down a broad stairway, then left again along a pathway. Follow the path as it turns sharply to the right, cross the road at the pedestrian crossing and follow the line of fortifications to the Táborská brána (Tábor Gate).

❷ The mid-17th-century Táborská brána guards the southeastern approach to the Vyšehrad fortress (▷ 148–149). It is part of the baroque defences built all around

Doorway of the Church of St. Peter and St. Paul, Vyšehrad

Prague after the Thirty Years' War. Beyond it, on the right, are remains of the far older Gothic gate, called Špička, now used as an information point.

Continue through the next gate, the baroque Leopoldova brána (Leopold Gate), named after the emperor of the time. Ahead of you, on the right, is a remarkable survival, the 11th-century Romanesque Rotunda svatého Martina (St. Martin's Rotunda). Before reaching the rotunda, turn left along the footpath which runs along the top of the ramparts, and continue to the far southwestern corner of the fortress where there is a viewpoint.

❸ The steep and blackened cliff drops sharply to the river far below, though the scene is somewhat diminished by the road and tram tunnel which was driven through the rock in the early 20th century. There are panoramic views of the upstream course of the Vltava to the south.

Come down from the ramparts, cross the meadow with its giant statues of figures from Czech

mythology, pass in front of the west front of Kostel svatého Petra a Pavla (Church of St. Peter and St. Paul), and enter Vyšehradský hřbitov (Vyšehrad Cemetery). Famous figures are buried in this national cemetery and in its Pantheon, the Slavín. Leave the cemetery via the eastern entrance close to the Slavín, turn left and go down steps to the Cihelná brána (Brick Gate), the northern gateway to the fortress. Follow the curving road downwards and turn first right into Přemyslová street. The building on the left-hand corner at the bottom of the street (No. 2/56) is one of the cluster of Cubist structures in Vyšehrad. Turn left along Neklanova street to find another of these unusual buildings (No. 30/98) and continue to Rašínovo nábřeží (Rašín Embankment) where, on the left, there is the best example of all, the Vila Kovařovic (No. 3/49 Libušina street). Walk north beneath the railway bridge, going over the busy roads by the light-controlled crossings. You are now at the spot once occupied by one of Prague's 'lost' villages, Podskalí.

❹ For centuries, Podskalí ('Beneath the Rocks') was the domain of a rough-and-ready riverside community of sand merchants, ice-cutters and, above all, the raftsmen responsible for floating vast quantities of lumber downstream from the forests to the south. This traditional way of life was brought to an end in the early 20th century, when hydroelectric dams upstream blocked navigation and the riverbank was tidied up with the construction of the embankment roadway. Nothing is left of Podskalí now except the fine 16th-century Výtoň Customs House, which has become an attractive little museum.

From the customs house, walk 'inland' along Na hrobci street and turn left along Vyšehradská street. The road rises between

OUT AND ABOUT

the little baroque Svatého Jan na skalce (Church of St. John Nepomuk on the Rock, ▷ 124) on the right, and the Emauzy (Emmaus Monastery) on the left, and brings you into Karlovo náměstí (Charles Square).

5 Karlovo náměstí, with its central park, is the largest of the squares laid out in Emperor

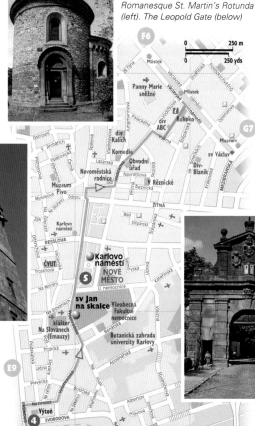

Romanesque St. Martin's Rotunda (left). The Leopold Gate (below)

The tower of the New Town Hall (above). Monumental statuary, Vyšehrad (below)

Charles IV's New Town, and originally served as the cattle market. A number of fascinating buildings here include Faustův dům (Faust House) at No. 41 to the south (lived in by a succession of characters suspected of alchemy and pacts with the Devil, rather than by Dr. Faustus himself); the Kostel svatého Ignace (Church of St. Ignatius) to the east; and the Novoměstská radnice (Town Hall of the New Town) to the north, whose tower can be climbed for a view of the area.

From the Town Hall walk along Vodičkova street, turning right into V Jámě street and left into the early 20th-century U Nováku arcade. A stroll through here brings you to Václavské náměstí (Wenceslas Square, ▷ 134–137).

WHERE TO EAT

You will find places to eat at Vyšehrad, but more attractive alternatives in the New Town include the Literarní kavárna (Vyšehradská 53; daily 9–6) and the Příčný řez restaurant (▷ 240).

WHEN TO GO

This walk is best during the day, when the various attractions are open (the Výtoň museum is closed Mon).

PLACE TO VISIT

Výtoň Customs House
Podskalská celnice na Výtoni, Rašínovo nábřeží 412, Nové Město, Prague 2
Tel 224 919 833
🕐 Tue–Sun 10–6
🎫 Adult 30Kč, child 20Kč
🚊 Tram 3, 7, 16, 17, 21 to Výtoň

OUT AND ABOUT

VYŠEHRAD AND NOVÉ MĚSTO 201

ALONG THE VLTAVA

A cruise along the Vlatva is a wonderful way to see Prague from a different angle. Some of the bridges are works of art in their own right, and there are many other fascinating sights associated with the river immortalized by Bedřich Smetana.

THE RIVER TRIP

Distance: 4.5km (3 miles)

Allow: 1.5 hours

Start at: Rašínovo nábřeží (Rašín Embankment) upstream from Jiráskův most (Jirásek Bridge)

End at: Čechův most (Čech Bridge) near the InterContinental hotel

HOW TO GET THERE

🚇 Karlovo náměstí metro (Palackého náměstí exit); tram 3, 4, 7, 10, 14, 16, 17, 21 to Palackého náměstí

The steamer begins its journey at the landing stage on the embankment named after Alois Rašín, the First Republic's Minister of Finance who was assassinated by an anarchist in 1923. The most prominent landmark on the embankment, just before Jiráskův most (Jirásek Bridge), is the Tančící dům (Dancing Building).

❶ Also named 'Fred & Ginger', the idiosyncratic 'Dancing Building' was the first self-consciously postmodern structure in Prague, built in 1996 to a design by Vlado Milunič and Frank Gehry. It houses offices and a stylish rooftop restaurant.

The boat passes beneath the reinforced concrete Jirásek Bridge, built in 1932 and named after the popular author of historical romances Alois Jirásek (1851–1930). On the right bank, beyond the weir, Slovanský ostrov (Slavonic Island) is one of the largest islands in the Vltava. The steamer heads left into the navigation channel and a series of locks, separated from the main channel by the long, thin Dětský ostrov (Children's Island), with its playgrounds and recreational facilities. The dark stone tower at the entrance to the channel is the Malostranská vodáren věž (Malá Strana Water Tower).

❷ Built in 1483, the tower is one of several surviving examples of the structures which formed a vital part of the city's ingenious medieval water

supply system. Water was pumped up into towers like this one, from where it was led via conduits throughout the city, supplying buildings and public fountains. Another water tower can be glimpsed near the tip of Slovanský ostrov on the far bank, where it has been cleverly incorporated into the Mánes cultural complex.

Before leaving the navigation channel, the boat passes beneath the most Legií (Bridge of the Legions). The bridge, dating from

1901, was built as a replacement for an earlier chain bridge. Its name commemorates the legionnaries who fought alongside the Allies in World War I, their efforts proving decisive in the creation of an independent Czechoslovakia in 1918. The bridge gives access to Střelecký ostrov (Shooters' Island).

❸ The 'Shooters' after whom Střelecký ostrov is named were the marksmen who used to practice their art here right up to the Communist period. The island is now one of the city's most attractive parks, with great views.

To the left, as the boat emerges from beneath the most Legií, is the entrance to the Čertovka or Devil's Brook, which separates Kampa Island from the 'mainland' of Malá Strana. It is really a millrace, dug out in the Middle Ages to drive a series of mills. Three of

the mills survive; the only one visible from the boat is the largest, the Sova Mill, now home to the Muzeum Kampa (▷ 92). Beyond the Sova Mill, the boat finally emerges from the navigation channel. To the right, the waters of the Vltava thunder over the Old Town Weir.

❹ The weir is a splendid sight, especially when the river is in spate. It's one of many such works carried out long ago to make the Vltava more navigable. The gap in the middle

A scenic river view, with the Čech Bridge in the distance

allowed raftsmen to pilot their great chains of timber rafts downriver. On the right bank, the weir is linked to Novotného lávka (Novotný Jetty), above which rises another ancient but much restored water tower, the city's tallest and oldest.

One of the high points of the trip is seeing Karlův most (Charles Bridge) from water level, with its massive timber cutwaters protecting its piers from debris brought down by the river. To the left, the outlet of the Devil's Brook forms a kind of Little Venice, while a short distance further on, beyond the Hergetova cihelna restaurant (▷ 235), is a little park where carters and draymen would water their horses in the shallows of the river. The boat now passes beneath Mánesův most (Mánes Bridge).

OUT AND ABOUT

The impressive
Tančící dům
(Dancing
Building)

A tranquil scene: Charles Bridge spanning
the River Vltava

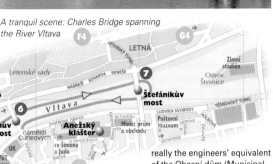

A boat sailing past Shooters'
Island on the Vltava

To avoid the heights of Letná Plain, the Vltava now begins its great bend to the east. The palatial building on the left bank is the seat of the Czech government. High above it is the opulent villa built by Czechoslovakia's first prime minister, Karel Kramář; it's now the prime ministerial residence. Further along, on the same level is jaunty little Hanavský pavilon (▷ 235), a panoramic restaurant, and further along still, the plinth on which the monstrous Stalin statue once stood. The boat now approaches the Čechův most (Čech Bridge).

6 The Čechův most, named in honour of the lyric poet Svatopluk Čech, was completed in 1908, just a few years before the Mánesův most, but a greater contrast in styles can hardly be imagined; Čechův is

really the engineers' equivalent of the Obecní dům (Municipal House), with splendid ironwork and elaborate statuary.

Beyond the bridge, there are pleasant views of Anežský klášter (St. Agnes Convent) on the Old Town bank. The final bridge on this trip is the Štefánikův most (Štefánik Bridge).

7 Completed in 1951, the modern Štefánikův most recalls Milan Rastislav Štefánik (1880–1919), the Slovak astronomer, aviator and general who was the third member of the triumvirate responsible for the foundation of independent Czechoslovakia in 1918.

Steamers heading downstream to Troja and Prague Zoo pass through the locks of Ostrov Štvanice (Štvanice Island) straight ahead, but this boat now turns round, and returns upstream to moor at the landing stage by the Čech Bridge.

OUT AND ABOUT

0   250 m

0   250 yds

5 Originally named after the tragic Habsburg Crown Prince Rudolf, who commited suicide, then after the assassinated Archduke Franz Ferdinand, the bridge now commemorates the 19th-century artist Josef Mánes (1820–71). Built in 1914; it is a relatively plain structure, with late art nouveau detailing.

BASICS

Prague Steam Navigation Co.

✉ Rašínovo nábřeží

☎ 224 931 013, 224 930 017

🕐 Mid-Mar to early Nov daily 3.30pm

💷 Adult 250Kč, child 125Kč

❓ Until the completion of road improvements, cruises may start from a temporary landing stage upstream www.paraplavba.cz

WHEN TO GO

It's worth choosing a fine day and sitting on the open deck but you will be exposed to the sun—so don't forget to wear sunscreen.

EXCURSIONS

The Czech Republic is a small country with an extraordinary wealth and variety of attractions. Prague lies almost at the geographical heart of Bohemia, and few places in the province are beyond the range of a day trip from the capital, though many of them are tempting destinations for a longer stay.

The Renaissance castle at Nelahozeves is home to a superb art collecion

Looking up from the battlements to medieval Karlštejn Castle

Konopiště Castle is set among extensive forests and parkland

No capital city is entirely representative of the country as a whole, and Prague is no exception. The trips described in this section take in a small selection of provincial towns which will give some idea of the richness of the republic's urban scene: they include Plzeň, the bustling industrial centre which gave its name to what is probably the world's most famous beer; Kutná Hora, a classic 'gold rush' little city which has preserved many mementoes of its history and, in the tranquil countryside of southern Bohemia, exquisite medieval Český Krumlov, contained within a bend of the River Vltava and overlooked by the country's biggest castle.

You could spend a lifetime exploring the Czech Republic's castles. The most visited of all of them is Karlštejn; built by Emperor Charles IV as a repository for the crown jewels, it rises dramatically from the forests along the winding River Berounka, a short distance from Prague. Just as fascinating is Konopiště, the sumptuously furnished country residence of Habsburg Archduke Franz Ferdinand, whose murder at Sarajevo in June 1914 unleashed World War I. A very different kind of castle, also on Prague's doorstep, but seemingly a world away in its village setting, is Renaissance Nelahozeves; restored to its princely owners after Communist confiscation, it now houses the country's finest private art collection. In the village at its foot is the humble birthplace of the much-loved Czech composer, Antonín Dvořák (1841–1904).

The Czech lands have seen more than their fair share of tragedies, few more chilling than the conversion by the Nazis of the fortress town of Terezín into a ghetto-prison. Under its German name of Theresienstadt, it became a sinister clearing house for the Jews of Czechoslovakia and elsewhere en route to the Final Solution. The town is now a sombre memorial to this inhuman episode in the country's history.

PLZEŇ

The historic capital of western Bohemia, and now a busy industrial city, Plzeň is proud of its most famous product, Pilsner beer.

Tourist information office
Náměstí Republiky 41, 301 16 Plzeň
☎ 378 035 330
🕒 Apr–end Sep daily 9–6; Oct–end
Mar Mon–Fri 10–5, Sat–Sun 10–3.30
http://info.plzen-city.cz;
www.zcu.cz/plzen

HOW TO GET THERE

Plzeň is 88km (55 miles) southwest of Prague

By car: Plzeň is an easy drive from Prague on the D5 motorway. Leave at the interchange with Route No. 20

By train: Semi-fast trains from Prague Hlavní nádraží (main station) and Smíchov to Plzeň Hlavní nádraží (main station) more or less hourly. Journey time: 1 hour 40 minutes

By bus: Frequent buses from Prague Florenc bus station (most also call at Hradčanská and Zličín metro stations) to Plzeň central bus station. Journey time: around 1 hour 30 minutes (less from Hradčanská and Zličín)

OVERVIEW

Straddling the old highway between Prague and the great cities of Bavaria, and known to the world by its German name of Pilsen, Plzeň has prospered throughout most of its history. In the 19th century it became the home of great industrial concerns like the Škoda engineering and

A lively display of historical fencing in Plzeň (below)

Gambrinus, a character linked to the history of beer brewing

armament works, but its most renowned product was, and is, Pilsner, the hoppy, bottom-fermented beer repeatedly imitated but never equalled.

Plzeň was one of the few places in Czechoslovakia to have been liberated by the US army in the last days of World War II. General Patton's troops entered the city on 6 May 1945, and could have gone on to free Prague had this prize not been conceded to the Soviet Union by Allied agreement.

THE TOWN

Plzeň has retained its medieval checkerboard layout, focused on Náměstí Republiky—one of the biggest squares in Bohemia—lined with buildings from most periods of the city's history. There is a spectacularly decorated Renaissance Town Hall, but the dominant building is the Gothic Kostel svatého Bartoloměje (St. Bartholomew's Church). Its tower is the country's tallest, and there is a fine view of the city from its gallery. Other Plzeň superlatives include the Velká synagóga (Great Synagogue), the second largest in Europe, now used as a concert and exhibition hall.

THE BREWERY

Just outside central Plzeň, the city's great visitor attraction is Plzeňský Prazdroj, the Pilsen Brewery, though there is also an excellent Pivovarské muzeum (Brewing Museum) in town. Plzenský Prazdroj, better known abroad by its German name of Pilsner Urquell, offers excellent guided tours around its vast establishment, ending with a tasting of the product.

WHERE TO EAT

Na Spilce
Plzeňský Prazdroj
Tel 337 062 755
The Pilsen Brewery's huge restaurant serves hearty Bohemian dishes.
🕒 Mon–Sat 11–10, Sun 11–9

PLACE TO VISIT

Plzeňský Prazdroj
U Prazdroje, Plzeň
Tel 377 062 888
www.pilsner-urquell.com
🕒 Apr–end Sep daily tours at 10.30, 12.30, 2, 3.30; Oct–end Mar Mon–Fri tours at 12.30, 2
🎟 120Kč

ČESKÝ KRUMLOV

A rival to Prague's Hradčany in sheer size, Český Krumlov's huge castle looks down over Southern Bohemia's most enchanting medieval town.

BASICS

Tourist information office
Infocentrum, Náměstí Svornost, 381 01 Český Krumlov
🕐 Jul–end Aug daily 9–8; Jun, Sep daily 9–7; Apr–end May, Oct daily 9–6; Nov–end Mar daily 9–5
www.ckrumlov.cz

HOW TO GET THERE

Český Krumlov is 161km (100 miles) south of Prague

By car: Drive southeast from Prague on motorway D1 and at Exit 21 take Route No. 3 towards Tábor then České Budějovice. About 4km (2.5 miles) beyond České Budějovice turn right on to Route No. 159 towards Český Krumlov. An alternative, only slightly longer route is by highway No. 4 and Route No. 20 via Příbram and Písek to České Budějovice

By train: Through summer-only express 'Šumava' direct from Prague Hlavní nádraží (main station) to Český Krumlov (about 3 hours 30 minutes each way). Otherwise change at České Budějovice (not recommended)

By bus: Fairly frequent direct services from Prague Florenc or Na knízeci bus stations to Český Krumlov (about 3 hours)

OVERVIEW

The crag-top castle (hrad) and the tiny town crammed into a loop of the fast-flowing Vltava together make a near-perfect ensemble. The castle was here before the town. Probably dating from the early 13th century, the first fortification was the sturdy round tower which forms the base of the brightly painted Renaissance tower (věž) that is such a landmark today. The earliest urban settlement was the little Latrán quarter, which straggles up from the riverbank to the castle gate. Only later was the area within the river bend developed, though the constricted site foiled the medieval planners' attempts to lay out a regular street plan. Town and castle were handed on to a succession of aristocratic owners—the Víteks, the Rožmberk dynasty, the Austrian Eggenbergs and finally the Schwarzenbergs, great magnates who ruled their vast domains like

a little kingdom, complete with its private army, until they were expropriated in 1947. By then they had long since abandoned Krumlov as their main residence, and castle and town mouldered away in obscurity, seemingly lost amid the forests stretching along the border between Bohemia and Austria. Few visitors made their way here, one exception being the Viennese artist Egon Schiele (1890–1918), whose mother was a native of Krumlov. His stay here in the summer of 1911 came to an abrupt end when he was thrown out of town by the local people who objected to him using under-age girls as nude models. Expulsion on a far greater scale occurred between 1945 and 1946, with the removal of Krumlov's German-speaking inhabitants, some three-quarters of the town's population.

THE CASTLE COURTYARDS

The castle's countless rooms and buildings are arranged around a series of courtyards. The first, reached through a gateway with the Schwarzenberg coat of arms, is lined with a pharmacy, a salt-house and stables. Approached across a moat inhabited by bears,

Looking out over the rooftops of medieval Český Krumlov

the second courtyard is the core of the castle, with the former mint and the medieval-cum-Renaissance palace. The long climb up to the viewing gallery of the tower is rewarded by a superlative panorama over the town and river, and beyond to the wooded hills of the Šumava (Bohemian Forest). Tours of the interior begin from the third courtyard, while beyond the fourth courtyard is an extraordinary multi-tiered bridge leading across a ravine to the baroque theatre and the gardens on the plateau beyond.

THE CASTLE INTERIORS

The interiors are so varied and extensive that it takes two tours to see even a sample of them. One tour focuses on the earlier periods in the development of the castle, with a visit to the medieval chapel and a series of rooms furnished in Renaissance and baroque style. A highlight is the gilded carriage built in Rome for a member of the Eggenberg family who was the Habsburg ambassador to the Vatican in the mid-17th century, but the real climax of this tour is the mid-18th-century Maškarní sál (Masquerade Hall). Dances, celebrations and other festivities would have been held in this opulent ballroom, with its brightly painted background of illusionistic masked revellers, flirting, parading behind balustrades, leaning from balconies or playing musical instruments. A second tour concentrates on life in the castle during the 19th century and on the long history of the Schwarzenberg family.

THE BAROQUE THEATRE
Of the very few private baroque theatres that survive, this one, built by the last of the Eggenbergs in 1680 and remodelled in the mid-18th century, is the most ornate (May–end Oct Tue–Sun 10–3; adult 180Kč, child 90Kč; guided tours only). It has preserved intact not only its auditorium, but also its complete stage equipment and lighting, its Italian-inspired scenery and its archives, making it possible to recreate authentic baroque operas and other spectacles. Previously closed, it has been restored and brought back into occasional use.

THE GARDENS
The formal baroque gardens, laid out on the plateau beyond the ravine, are some of the biggest to have largely escaped being relandscaped in the English, romantic style in the 19th century (May–end Sep daily 9–7; Apr, Oct daily 8–5; free). They include most of the typical features of the era, including a balustraded terrace with an elaborate fountain and a prospect of geometrical parterres. But there is more, including a more informal area, a riding school and the delightful Bellaria—a rococo summer

Detail of a painting in the castle's Masquerade Hall (left)

palace painted in lovely, subtle tones. Nearby is a modern outdoor revolving theatre.

THE TOWN
Once remote and, in Communist times, seriously neglected, Krumlov is now on UNESCO's World Heritage list and attracts many visitors. Some of its charm is now submerged beneath souvenir shops and over-restored façades, but a stroll in any direction from the central square will reveal a number of fine old buildings of medieval or later date. The sloping square itself has a plague column and an arcaded town hall decorated with the coats of arms of the town's successive rulers. The Gothic Kostel svatého Víta (St. Vitus's Church), with its tall and slender tower, is a magnificent landmark. Egon Schiele's connection with Krumlov has inspired the Egon Schiele Art Centre; occupying the building which once housed the municipal brewery, it has a small permanent collection of the artist's works but devotes itself mainly to changing exhibitions of modern art.

WHERE TO EAT
Zlatý Anděl
Hotel Zlatý Anděl, náměstí Svornosti, 381 01 Český Krumlov
Tel 380 712 310-15
The historic Golden Angel Hotel on Český Krumlov's main square has two restaurants, a pub and a cocktail bar.
⏱ Daily 11–10

TIP
● Český Krumlov is in the heart of Southern Bohemia, the region regarded by Czechs as quintessentially Bohemian. If you have come this far, it's worthwhile stopping overnight and exploring the villages, historic towns and lovely landscapes in the area.

The landmark Renaissance tower at Český Krumlov castle (above). Visitors strolling beneath the dramatic arches of the castle (above left)

WHERE TO STAY
The Zlatý Anděl (▷ below left) has a range of tastefully furnished rooms.
🛏 Double rooms: 2300Kč–3400Kč

PLACES TO VISIT
Hrad
Státní hrad a zámek Český Krumlov, Zámek 59, 38 101 Český Krumlov
Tel 380 704 710
⏱ Tours 1 and 2: Jun–end Aug Tue–Sun 9–5; Apr–end May, Sep–end Oct Tue–Sun 9–4
💰 Tour 1: adult 160Kč, child 80Kč. Tour 2: adult 140Kč, child 70Kč
🎫 Guided tours only

Věž
⏱ Jun–end Aug Tue–Sun 9–5.30; Apr–end May, Sep–end Oct Tue–Sun 9–4.30
💰 Adult 35Kč, child 20Kč

Egon Schiele Art Centrum
Široká 71, 381 01 Český Krumlov
Tel 380 704 011
⏱ Daily 10–6; may be closed in winter
💰 Adult 180Kč, child 105Kč

KARLŠTEJN

The medieval outline of Karlštejn Castle, one of the iconic images of medieval Bohemia, rises over a romantic framework of deep forests and winding river gorge.

BASICS

Hrad Karlštejn

✉ 267 18 Karlštejn

☎ 311 681 617

🕒 Jul–end Aug Tue–Sun 9–12, 12.30–6; May–end Jun, Sep Tue–Sun 9–12, 12.30–5; Apr, Oct Tue–Sun 9–12, 1–4; Mar Tue–Sun 9–12, 1–3; 1–20 Nov, 26–31 Dec, 1–8 Jan Tue–Sun 9–12, 1–3 (hours may vary)

🎫 Tour 1: adult 200Kč, child 100Kč. Tour 2: adult 300Kč, child 100Kč

📷 Guided tours only. Tour 2 must be booked in advance: Národní památkový ústav, P.O. Box 45, 130 11 Praha 3, tel 274 008 154/156; e-mail: reservace@stc.npu.cz. Reservation fee: 30Kč

🏨 🍴 📷

www.hradkarlstejn.cz

HOW TO GET THERE

Karlštejn is 28km (17 miles) southwest of Prague

By car: 10km (6 miles) via Route No. 4, then via Route No. 116 and then park in Karlštejn village

By train: Frequent suburban trains from Prague's main station Hlavní nádraží (around 35 minutes) or Smíchov (around 30 minutes) to Karlštejn station

Note: There is no public access by motor vehicle to the castle, which is 1.5km (1 mile) uphill from the village on foot or by horse-drawn carriage

OVERVIEW

The countryside starts right on Prague's doorstep, but the beautifully wooded valley of the River Berounka, a 30-minute trip by suburban train, seems a world away from the capital. In 1348 it was in this seemingly remote and inviolate setting that Emperor Charles IV ordered work to begin on a great stronghold. Karlštejn was not built for any strategic reason, but as a kind of sacred strongbox in stone, a repository for religious relics and crown jewels. The deeply devout Charles had an obsession with acquiring the body parts of assorted saints (▶ 26) and resonant relics such as the thorns from Christ's Cross. Securely held in close proximity to the crown jewels of the Holy Roman Empire and of the Kingdom of Bohemia, they would affirm the

Detail of a painting decorating the Imperial Palace, Karlštejn

spiritual foundation of Charles' rule and that of his successors from the House of Luxembourg.

The Emperor's ambitious project, intended to endure for all eternity, was carried out in the short space of seven years, but his hopes for the future were not to be fulfilled. At the start of the Hussite troubles in the early 15th century (▶ 27), the imperial jewels were taken to Nuremberg and then to Vienna, never to be returned, while the Bohemian jewels were removed in 1619 at the start of the Thirty Years' War and placed in a strongroom above the Wenceslas Chapel in St. Vitus Cathedral for safe keeping, where they remain to this day. Having lost its principal purpose, Karlštejn remained in relative obscurity until the beginning of the 19th century, when its picturesque potential was realized. A start was made on restoration, a process taken over late in the century by the over-zealous conservation architect, Josef Mocker (1835–99). What you see today is largely the result of his attempts to return the castle to its original appearance; this involved demolition and rebuilding on a scale unthinkable today, and says less about the reality of Karlštejn than

what people in the 19th century thought a medieval castle should look like. But the spiritual core of the castle—the jewel-bedecked chapels where the Emperor would lose himself in religious rapture—remains intact.

EXTERIOR

The castle presents an unforgettable silhouette of battlements and chisel-roofed towers rising from the treetops high above the river. It looks utterly impregnable, and this was confirmed when the Hussites tried to take it, failed, and settled down to a siege which lasted seven months. Despite their best efforts, Karlštejn held out and was never attacked again. The castle's unusual layout is best understood as a kind of pilgrimage route, which leads upwards from the state rooms of the Císařský palác (Imperial Palace), first to the Mariánská věž (St. Mary's Tower) with the Kaple svatého Kateřiny (St. Catherine's Chapel), and from there via a timber bridge to the Velká věž (Great Tower) with the holy of holies, the Kaple svatého Kříže (Chapel of the Holy Cross).

After the long trek up from Karlštejn village, you enter the castle through the outer ward. While waiting for the guided tour to begin you can go along the battlemented spur to the tower housing the 80m-deep (263ft) well hewed into the rock by miners brought from Kutná Hora; the views over the valley and surrounding countryside are vast.

TOUR ONE

The castle interiors can only be visited on a guided tour. The first tour focuses on the Imperial Palace and the lower floors of St. Mary's Tower, including the castle prison. Most of the interiors of the palace were thoroughly reconstructed by Mocker and his colleagues and are rather bare, enlivened only by a number of artworks and displays on the history of Karlštejn. The Audience Hall is an exception. With its original panelling and coffered ceiling,

OUT AND ABOUT

Karlštejn Castle, set on a forest-clad hilltop (above). The Chapel of St. Catherine at Karlštejn Castle (left)

this is where the Emperor, his back to the light, would receive his subjects.

TOUR TWO

The second tour, by far the more interesting, takes in Karlštejn's most precious interiors (reservations needed in advance). On the upper floor of St. Mary's Tower is the Church of Our Lady (Kostel Nanebezvetí Panny Marie), which has kept much of its original Gothic decoration. Beneath a ceiling painted with countless angels, somewhat faded wall-paintings show scenes of the Apocalypse and of Charles IV taking possession of various holy relics. An annual Mass is still held here on 29 November, the anniversary of the Emperor's death. From the church, a narrow passageway leads to the tiny Chapel of St. Catherine, decorated in the same opulent fashion as the Wenceslas Chapel in St. Vitus Cathedral, with walls of gilded plaster studded with semi-precious stones. A painting over the door shows Charles with one of his four wives, Anna of Schwednitz. The Emperor would spend days in contemplation here, preparing himself for the final ascent to the holy of holies in the Great Tower. Now reached via the timber bridge built by Josef Mocker, the tower contains the vaulted Chapel of the Holy Cross (Kaple svatého Kříže), the climax of the imperial pilgrimage. Its décor is truly extraordinary, featuring not only the now familiar jewel-encrusted walls, but a heavenly host of more than 100 saints, an array of portraits from the brush of Charles's favourite painter, Master Theodoric (died c1381).

Karlštejn is a tourist village and there is no shortage of places to eat and drink. One pleasant spot is the restaurant of the Hotel Mlýn (tel 311 744 411; Wed–Sun 11–10), overlooking the waters of the River Berounka.

A delicate statue in the Chapel of the Holy Cross (right)

KONOPIŠTĚ

The medieval castle of Konopiště has sumptuously furnished interiors which reflect the complex personality of tragic Archduke Franz Ferdinand.

OUT AND ABOUT

BASICS

Státní zámek Konopiště

✉ 256 01 Benešov

☎ 317 721 366

🕐 May–end Aug Tue–Sun 9–12, 1–5;
Sep Tue–Fri 9–12, 1–4, Sat–Sun 9–5;
Oct Tue–Fri 9–12, 1–3, Sat–Sun 9–4;
Nov Tue–Fri groups by arrangement,
Sat–Sun 9–12, 1–3; Apr Tue–Fri 9–12,
1–3, Sat–Sun 9–12, 1–4. Possibly
open some days in late Mar

🎫 Tours I and II: adult 150Kč, child
80Kč. Tour III: 250Kč

🎧 Guided tours only 🏢 👫

www.zamek-konopiste.cz

HOW TO GET THERE

Konopiště is 40km (25 miles)
southeast of Prague

By car: Drive southeast from Prague on
motorway D1, taking Exit 21 towards
Benešov/Tábor. At Benešov, turn right
on main road 106 and continue for 1km
(0.5 miles) to Konopiště

By train: Fast (around 50 minutes) and
stopping (around 1 hour 10 minutes)
trains from Prague Hlavní nádraží (main
station) to Benešov u Prahy, then 2.5km
(1.5-mile) walk on signposted path

By bus: From Roztyly metro station
(around 40 minutes) or Florenc bus
station (around 1 hour) to Benešov bus
station or Benešov-odbočka (turning),
then 2.5km (1.5-mile) walk on
signposted path

OVERVIEW

Set among extensive forests and
parkland, the castle at Konopiště
dates originally from the 13th
century, but its present
appearance and character is due
to its transformation into a
prestigious country residence in
the late 19th century by
Archduke Franz Ferdinand, the
heir to the Habsburg throne. Few
places are as evocative of the
atmosphere of the last years of
the doomed Austro-Hungarian
Empire as Konopiště.

The middle-aged Archduke, the
nephew of Franz Josef, had
become heir to the throne after
the suicide of the emperor's son,
Prince Rudolf. An instinctive
conservative, Franz Ferdinand
nevertheless hoped to reform the
moribund realm he was to
inherit, not least by giving more
say in its running to underrepre-
sented Slav peoples like the
Czechs. Although of royal blood,
he was ostracized by the
snobbish Viennese court for
marrying a mere aristocrat,
Sophie Chotek, a member of an
old Bohemian family. This
devoted family man and faithful
husband was uncomfortable and
formal in company, lacking in

charm and subject to terrible
rages. He is remembered mostly
for his assassination in Sarajevo
in June 1914, the event which
precipitated the outbreak of
World War I. His murderer, the
young Bosnian Serb Gavrilo
Princip, was arrested, brought
to Bohemia and imprisoned
at Terezín, where he died
of tuberculosis.

Konopiště, the Archduke's
favourite residence, has been
state property since 1921, apart
from a brief interlude in World
War II, when it became an SS
headquarters and was earmarked
as a potential future residence for
Heinrich Himmler.

THE EXTERIOR

With its tall round tower rising
above the tree tops, Konopiště
has a romantic appearance when
first glimpsed. The tower, part of
the original stronghold built by
Tobiáš of Benešov in the 1290s,
along with the rest of the castle,
was extensively remodelled by
Franz Ferdinand, and its present
look, with its conical cap, owes
more to the architecture of the
Austrian Tyrol than to Bohemia.
The Archduke's architect was
Josef Mocker (1835–99), who

TIP
● If you have acquired a taste for Bohemian castles, a trip to Konopiště can easily be extended to take in one of the most romantically situated piles in the country. Český Šternberk is perched on a crag overlooking the River Sázava, 25km (15 miles) to the east, reached by minor roads.

A magical winter view of Konopiště Castle (opposite)

Hunting trophies on display inside the castle (right)

Detail of an ornate gateway in the castle grounds (below left)

'Dogleader' statue outside the castle (below)

was also responsible for the virtual reconstruction of Karlštejn Castle. Mocker swept away everything built at Konopiště since the end of the Middle Ages, except for the baroque gateway and its statues.

THE INTERIORS
The castle interiors are extensive, and you would need to take no fewer than three guided tours to visit all of them. The paintings, portraits, furniture and decorative objects of all kinds reflect Franz Ferdinand's taste, and create a rather heavy atmosphere. The Archduke was a keen fan of modern coveniences of the day: among the up-to-date facilities at Konopiště were hot and cold running water, central heating and even a lavishly furnished elevator. The first tour takes in the suite of rooms in the castle's south wing, including the almost nightmarish 'corridor of hunting trophies'. With its horns, antlers and stuffed and snarling bears, it gives a good idea of the Archduke's passion for the chase—he enjoyed slaughtering wild animals on an almost industrial scale. Some of the rooms are arranged to evoke the visit to Konopiště of German Kaiser Wilhelm II and Grand Admiral Tirpitz, which took place only two weeks before Franz Ferdinand met his end in Sarajevo. The second tour includes other guest rooms, a study and the castle chapel with its Gothic paintings and sculpture. The highlight of this tour, however, is the armoury. The Archduke's collection of arms and armour is one of the finest of its kind; its most spectacular item is its 16th-century Italian tournament armour. The third tour concentrates on the family's private apartments and includes the master bedroom, the study used by the Archduchess, and the children's quarters. Other parts of the castle you can visit (admission 25Kč) include the original shooting gallery and the St. George museum; one of Franz Ferdinand's obsessions was his collection of items associated with the saint.

THE GROUNDS
The park and gardens, like the castle's interior, bear the imprint of Franz Ferdinand. He was particularly proud of the vast rose garden he created, and the grounds were adapted to show off his extensive sculpture collection. Exotic trees and shrubs were planted, while the more remote parts of the estate were managed as game preserves.

WHERE TO EAT
The castle offers snacks, a bistro and a café, but the tastiest option is the Stará Myslivna game restaurant in the grounds (tel 317 721 148; daily 10.30am–11pm).

OUT AND ABOUT

KUTNÁ HORA

One of Bohemia's best-preserved old towns has abundant relics from the glory days when it was a great silver mining centre. The ossuary at nearby Sedlec is one of the country's oddest attractions.

BASICS

Tourist information office

Sankturinovský dům, Palackého náměstí, 284 01 Kutná Hora

☎ 327 512 378

www.kutnohorsko.cz

HOW TO GET THERE

Kutná Hora is 70km (43 miles) east of Prague

By car: Motorway D11 to Exit 39, then Route 38 via Kolín; alternatively, Route 12 via Kolín, or Route 333 via Říčany (slower but more attractive)

By train: Limited number of direct trains from Prague Hlavní nádraží (main station) to Kutná Hora Hlavní nádraží (main station), around 1 hour, then by local train to Kutná Hora město (town station) or by local bus No. 1 or 4 to town centre

By bus: From Florenc bus station, frequent direct buses (around 1 hour 15 minutes)

TIP

● Kutná Hora has several railway stations. If you come by train, bear in mind that the Kutná Hora Hlavní nádraží (main station) is about 2km from the town itself. The branch line from here to the town station (Kutná Hora město) passes first through Kutná Hora Sedlec, the station for the ossuary.

OVERVIEW

This fascinating little city once rivalled the capital in size and was the source of much of its wealth. Immensely productive silver deposits were responsible for the rise of medieval Kutná Hora, while their exhaustion led to its decline as early as the 16th century. Drained of most of its population, the town lingered on, but centuries of obscurity have been its salvation in the end. Much of its medieval and later heritage is intact, and in recent years Kutná Hora has undergone something of a renaissance; its accessibility from Prague makes it one of the most popular tourist destinations in the country. A stroll around the charming streets leads past many minor treasures, such as the Gothic Kamenný dům (Stone House) and the venerable 12-sided public fountain. However, the town's finest monument is the great Chrám svaté Barbory (St. Barbara's Church), a cathedral-size structure which is one of the most extraordinary achievements of late Gothic architecture in Europe. In the suburb of Sedlec is a rather macabre attraction, the bones from some 40,000 burials arranged in a vaulted ossuary.

CHRÁM SVATÉ BARBORY

A monastery was founded at Sedlec early in the 13th century. Its church was one of the largest and finest Gothic buildings in the

kingdom, but by the end of the 14th century the miners of Kutná Hora were rich enough to try and beat it. Nothing but the best would do; Jan Parler, the son of the architect of Prague's St. Vitus Cathedral, was summoned from the capital in 1388 to begin work. He was followed, in due course, by such masters as Matyáš Rejsek (c1445–c1506) and Benedikt Ried (died 1534). Ried was responsible for the church's unmissable roof, an extraordinary skyline of exotic tented forms visible from far away. He also designed the equally unusual vaulting of the nave, taking as his

An elaborate stone fountain in Kutná Hora (below)

OUT AND ABOUT

model his own ideas for the vault of the Old Royal Palace in Prague Castle, and pushing stonework to its limits in fanciful patterns of extreme delicacy. Ried's vault was completed, after his death, in 1547 but building then stopped, only to be resumed in modern times. St. Barbara is the patron saint of miners, and her church has plenty of reminders of where the town's wealth came from, particularly in the side chapels with their wall paintings of mining scenes.

The church stands at one end of the curving plateau on which Kutná Hora is built. There are fine views of the town and its sur-roundings from Barborská street, which runs along the lip of the plateau, its balustrade graced by baroque statues of saints. Behind is the enormously long façade of the town's Jesuit college.

HRADEK

Meaning 'little fort', this building has a history going back to the 13th century. It is now the home of the České muzeum stříbra (Czech Museum of Silver), which tells you about the precious metal and the role it played in the rise of Kutná Hora. There are two sections: 'Silver Town' deals with the town, and 'Silver Route' traces the whole process of turn-ing ore into coin. You can also don miner's gear and go down a nearby medieval mineshaft.

VLAŠSKÝ DVŮR

While St. Barbara's Church pro-claimed the faith as well as the wealth of Kutná Hora's miners, it was here, in the Vlasský dvůr (Italian Court), that the silver they extracted was turned into the currency of the realm. Conceived as a stronghold at the end of the 13th century, by 1330 the build-ing had been converted into a mint to process the precious metal, which was mined in ever greater quantities. Italian experts were brought from Florence to instruct local people in the art and craft of creating such coins as the famous Prague *groschen* or groat. The *groschen* became legal tender over much of Europe, only being displaced in the 16th century by the even more famous *Joachimsthaler* from Bohemia, the coin which gave the world the word 'dollar'.

The importance of Kutná Hora was confirmed around 1400, when King Wenceslas IV made the Italian Court into an official royal residence.

SEDLEC

Once an independent settlement, focused on its great monastery, Sedlec is now part of Kutná Hora. The monastery's fortunes varied dramatically over the centuries; its golden age of wealth and influence came in the 13th century, but in 1420 it was sacked by the Hussites. A revival took place at the beginning of the 18th century, when the 'Great Santini', the Prague architect of Italian descent, rebuilt the abbey church in his highly individual style, an inspired combination of baroque and Gothic. Sedlec was closed down at the end of the 18th century, and its buildings were put to use as a tobacco factory. Santini's church has been undergoing restoration for many years and is still closed to the public, but Sedlec draws plenty of visitors to its other attraction, the Kostnice (Ossuary). The origins of this extraordinary charnel house go back to the Middle Ages, when war and plague filled the adjoining cemetery to bursting point and extra space had to be found to house the surplus skeletons. A blind monk is said to have arranged the bones in simple patterns early in the 16th century, but the present fascinating displays date from the late 19th century, when František Rint and his family used the bones at their disposal to create fantastical chandeliers, chalices, bells and even the coat of arms of the Schwarzenberg family, who had become the owners of the chapel. It is not a sight for the squeamish.

WHERE TO EAT

There is a reasonable choice of places to eat in Kutná Hora including Restaurant Kometa (Barborská 29, tel 327 515 515; open daily 9am–midnight).

The Church of St. John of Nepomuk in Kutná Hora (opposite left).
Detail of a stained-glass window (opposite right) in St.Barbara's Church (below)

PLACES TO VISIT

Chrám svaté Barbory
Barborska, 284 01 Kutná Hora
☼ May–end Sep Tue–Sun 9–5.30; Apr, Oct Tue–Sun 9–11.30, 1–4; Nov–end Mar Tue–Sun 9–11.30, 2–3.30
🎫 Adult 30Kč, child 15Kč

Hradek
České muzeum stříbra, Barborska 28, 284 01 Kutná Hora
Tel 327 512 159
☼ Jul–end Aug Tue–Sun 10–6; May, Jun, Sep Tue–Sun 9–6; Apr, Oct Tue–Sun 9–5
🎫 Museum only: adult 60Kč, child 30Kč. Museum and silver mine: adult 130Kč, child 80Kč
🔲 Guided tour in English: 400Kč

Vlašský dvůr
Havlíčkovo náměstí 552, 284 24 Kutná Hora
Tel 327 512 873
☼ Apr–end Sep Tue–Sun 9–6; Mar, Oct Tue–Sun 10–5; Nov–end Feb Tue–Sun 10–4
🎫 Adult 40Kč, child 20Kč
🔲 Tour: adult 70Kč, child 50Kč

Sedlec Ossuary
Kostnice, Zámecká 127, 284 03 Kutná Hora
Tel 728 125 488; www.kostnice.cz
☼ Apr–end Sep daily 8–6; Oct daily 9–12, 1–5; Nov–end Mar daily 9–12, 1–4
🎫 Adult 35Kč, child 20Kč

OUT AND ABOUT

NELAHOZEVES

This tiny village on the Vltava to the north of Prague has two noteworthy treasures. One is the humble birthplace of the composer Antonín Dvořák, the other a unique Renaissance castle, the home of the country's finest private art collection.

HOW TO GET THERE

Nelahozeves is 27km (17 miles) north of Prague on the River Vltava

By car: From Prague take motorway D8, leaving at Exit 18, and driving south on main road No.16. Turn left after 2km (1.2 miles) towards Veltrusy, then right after less than 1km (0.5 miles) on to a minor road parallel to the Vltava, which leads to Nelahozeves in 4km (2.5 miles)

By train: Local train approximately every 2 hours from Prague Masarykovo nádraží (Masaryk station) and Holešovice station to Nelahozeves zastávka (halt). Journey time around 50 minutes

OVERVIEW

Long before Antonín Dvořák was born here in 1841, this village was chosen as a suitable spot for his castle by Florian Griespeck von Griesbach. Originally from the Tyrol, Griespeck was the high official responsible for all royal building in Bohemia, able to commission work from the very best designers and craftsmen. The architect of Nelahozeves may well have been the great Bonifaz Wohlmut, for the castle, begun in 1553, was a state-of-the-art structure, incorporating all sorts of new-fangled ideas from Renaissance Italy. It soon passed into the hands of the Lobkowicz family who, apart from periods of dispossession at the hands of the Nazis and Communists, have owned it ever since. The family were among the highest in the land, supplying Habsburg rulers with faithful chancellors and military men, though perhaps the outstanding member among them was the half-Spanish Polyxenia, renowned for her rescue of one of the defenestrated Catholic councillors in 1618 and for her gift of the *Bambino di Praga* to the Church of Our Lady of Victories (▷ 104). In the early 20th century, despite democratic Czechoslovakia's abolition of aristocratic titles, Prince Maximilian Lobkowicz was Ambassador to London and then a member of the wartime government in exile. Following the fall of Communism, the Lobkowicz properties were

restituted to the family, along with much of what they contained, including priceless paintings that had been among the most prized possessions of the Národní galerie (National Gallery) in Prague.

THE CASTLE

Nelahozeves remains much as it was when built in the mid-16th century. Despite its formidable appearance standing on top of a rise in the ground, it is a *zámek* rather than a *hrad*. *Hrad* translates as castle or fortress, whereas a *zámek* is more along the lines of a French château or a German Schloss. Nelahozeves was conceived more as a prestigious residence than as a stronghold able to withstand a determined siege, though the corner bastions in the style of an Italian *castello* look serious enough. Griespeck seems to have run out of money before his castle was completed, and only three of its four wings were built.

The north wing is the most flamboyant, with splendid sgraffito decoration depicting biblical and mythological scenes. Approached via a bridge across a dry moat, the three completed

wings of the partly arcaded courtyard are in different styles. The east wing has a doorway featuring the Griespeck coat of arms. The castle interiors are now visited mostly for their collections, but many are fascinating in their own right, particularly the Arkádové haly (Arcade Hall) and the vaulted Rytířský sál (Knights Hall).

THE COLLECTIONS

The collections reassembled here include superb examples of the decorative arts, as well as a wealth of paintings. Great care has been taken to place items in their context, with individual rooms arranged in such a way as to reflect the personality and

Memorial to the composer Antonín Dvořák in Nelahozeves (above)

A winter view of the Renaissance castle, Nelahozeves (left)

The splendid castle dining room (below left)

Antonín Dvořák's birthplace, Nelahozeves (right)

period of a particular Lobkowicz member. Among the outstanding family portraits is one of Polyxenia's husband, the first Prince Lobkowicz, a fine work by Emperor Rudolf II's court painter, Bartolomaeus Spranger (1546–1611). Rudolf himself makes an appearance, as does Polyxenia, shown attending to the wounded victims of the defenestration. Other portraits evoke the family's Spanish connections, among them one of the Infanta Margarita attributed to Velázquez (1599–1660). In the mid-18th century, a Lobkowicz returned from a trip to London without the horses he had intended to buy; instead he had bought two magnificent Canalettos of the River Thames. Perhaps the greatest treasure though is *Haymaking*, one of Pieter Brueghel the Elder's (c1520–69) wonderful depictions of the seasons of the year, the only one of the series to be in private possession, and a loss to Prague's Národní galerie (National Gallery). Other masterpieces include pictures by Lucas Cranach the Elder, Rubens and Veronese. Many members of the Lobkowicz family were musical;

they had their own orchestra, and supported needy composers. One of these was Beethoven, a firm friend of Prince Josef Franz Maximilian, to whom he dedicated a number of works, including the Eroica Symphony, originally intended to honour Napoleon. The Music Room evokes this and other fascinating connections, with all kinds of musical memorabilia.

DVOŘÁK BIRTHPLACE

Antonín Dvořák's father was the village butcher in Nelahozeves. He also kept a pub, part of a two-floor house overlooking the village green, and this was where the family lived, along with several other residents. Music influenced the young Dvořák from an early age; his father played the zither and led the local band, his teacher was a talented musician, and the Italian workmen building the nearby railway spent their evenings singing in the pub. This may have given young Antonín not just a taste for song, but also for railways; he became a lifelong trainspotter. After launching himself on what eventually became a glittering musical career, he rarely returned

to Nelahozeves, but always kept his love of the countryside. His birthplace (Památník Antonína Dvořáka) is now a small museum.

OUT AND ABOUT

TEREZÍN

Nazi propaganda claimed this 18th-century fortress town was a 'model ghetto' for the Jews forced to live in it, but the reality was quite different. Terezín is now a poignant memorial to the suffering endured there.

BASICS

General information

Terezín–Památník (Terezín–Memorial), Principova alej 304, 411 55 Terezín

☎ 416 782 225/416 782 442

www.pamatnik-terezin.cz

HOW TO GET THERE

Terezín is 65km (40 miles) northwest of Prague

By car: Drive north from Prague on Motorway D8, leaving at Exit 35 and following signs to Terezín

By train: Terezín has no station of its own. The nearest is at Bohušovice nad Ohří, 2km (1.2 miles) to the south, which is only served by stopping trains. From Prague Hlavní nádraží (main station) and Holešovice or Masarykovo nádraží (Masaryk station) take a fast train to Roudnice nad Labem and change to a local train with destination Ústí nad Labem (around 1 hour 15 minutes)

By bus: Frequent direct buses from Prague Florenc bus station (around 1 hour)

A bleak, forbidding interior (below) at the former Terezín ghetto

OVERVIEW

As a perfectly preserved baroque fortress town, Terezín rates more than a mention in the history of town planning, but its great fame, or rather notoriety, is due to its role in World War II, when the Nazis emptied it of its inhabitants and turned it into a Jewish ghetto, a staging post on the way to the Final Solution.

The fortress was originally built on the orders of Austrian Emperor Joseph II, who was disturbed by the growing power of the Prussian kingdom to the north, and originally named Theresienstadt in honour of his mother, Empress Maria Theresa. Blocking the direct route to Prague, it embodied the latest in military technology of the period, with a double line of star-shaped ramparts linked by a network of subterranean passageways and protected by a broad moat, part of which was formed by diverting the River Ohře. Within the walls, a classic grid layout of intersecting streets was lined with dour barrack buildings and a cheerless neoclassical church. Beyond the moat, the outlying Malá pevnost (Small Fortress) was used as a military prison. Although up to 50,000 soldiers were garrisoned here, Theresienstadt was never called upon to prove its effectiveness; when the Prussians eventually invaded in 1866, they simply bypassed it.

In 1941, the first consignment of Czech Jews arrived at the fortress, and a year later the place was cleared of all its original inhabitants in order to make way, not just for Jews from the Protectorate of Bohemia-Moravia, but for privileged Jews from Germany, such as decorated war veterans and those married to 'Aryans'. Theresienstadt was never an extermination camp as such. A semblance of normal life was maintained, not least for propaganda purposes; a misleading film entitled *The Führer Gives the Jews a Town* was made, portraying Terezín as a kind of health spa. But some 30,000 people died here, quite apart from the other tens of thousands who perished after being

OUT AND ABOUT

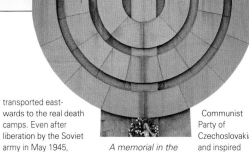

transported eastwards to the real death camps. Even after liberation by the Soviet army in May 1945, many more victims were claimed by typhus.

A memorial in the cemetery at Terezín

Communist Party of Czechoslovakia and inspired by the Soviet Union.

MUZEUM GHETTA

The Ghetto Museum tells the story of Terezín between 1941 and 1945 with informative displays incorporating much original material. Some of the more chilling moments of a visit come with the showing of a film, which includes sequences from the Nazis' cynical but successful attempt to present the place in a good light.

The museum was only established in the 1990s. Under Communism, the particular sufferings of Jewish people tended to be glossed over, with far more attention paid to the heroics of the 'Anti-Fascist Struggle' led, of course, by the

MAGDEBURSKÁ KASÁRNA

The former Magdeburg Barracks complement the Muzeum Ghetta by giving a full account of the extraordinary cultural life that flourished in Terezín, some of it officially approved, some of it clandestine. Many members of the pre-war Czech cultural élite were of Jewish origin, and the ghetto had a disproportionate number of artists, musicians, writers, journalists and academics. The children's opera *Brundibar* was composed here and performed dozens of times, and there was even a jazz band called the Ghetto Swingers. But Viktor Ullman's opera The

Emperor of Atlantis was banned when the Germans realised that it could be interpreted as a satire on Hitler and the Third Reich.

MALÁ PEVNOST

In front of the Small Fortress is a vast symbolic cemetery, dominated by a Christian Cross and a Star of David. Entered through a gateway bearing the infamous Nazi slogan *Arbeit Macht Frei* (Work Makes Free), the fortress was used for many years by the Austrians as a military prison. Incarcerated here were hundreds of World War I Czech mutineers, while the most famous prisoner was Gavrilo Princip, the Serb responsible for the assassination of Archduke Franz Ferdinand and his wife in Sarajevo in 1914. Horrible though conditions were in Austrian times, under the Nazis they became unspeakable. The fortress now served mostly as a prison for Czechs in the anti-German resistance, but also incarcerated here were representatives of more than a dozen Allied nations. Many were executed, others worked to death, and in all some 2,500 perished here. Between 1945 and 1948 the Small Fortress served as a detention centre for Germans, many of them arrested quite arbitrarily. Of the 4,000 or so interned here, some 600 did not survive. It is now an excellent museum on the role it played and a memorial to those who suffered here, though a tour of its grim cells and execution grounds is not a pleasant experience.

The Nazi slogan 'Work Makes Free' above the gateway to the courtyard at Terezín (above). Specially designed banknotes, valid only in the Terezín ghetto (left)

QUITTUNG ÜBER HUNDERT KRONEN
100
100

023586
Quittung über 50
FÜNFZIG KRONEN
50

WHERE TO EAT

A range of cafés and restaurants can be found in the town of Litoměřice, just 2km (1.2 miles) north of Terezín.

PLACES TO VISIT

Muzeum Ghetta and Magdeburská kasárna
Komenského, 411 55 Terezín
🕐 Apr–end Oct daily 9–6; Nov–end Mar daily 9–5.30
🎫 Adult 160Kč, child 130Kč. Combined ticket with Small Fortress: adult 180Kč, child 140Kč
📷 Guided tour: no additional charge

Malá pevnost
Principova alej 304, 411 55 Terezín
🕐 Apr–end Oct daily 8–6; Nov–end Feb daily 8–4.30

OUT AND ABOUT

The best—and in some parts of Prague the only—way to get to know the city is on foot, and to help you achieve this there are plenty of guided walking tours, often with a special theme. A river cruise is a delight in itself, and offers unexpected perspectives, while a bus tour can give you an instant appreciation of the city's overall layout.

BUS TOURS

MARTIN TOUR
Štěpánská 61, Nové Město, Prague 1
Tel 224 212 473
A variety of trips, including an introductory tour of Prague aboard an open panoramic bus.
🕐 2-hour historical city tour: daily 9.15, 10.30, 11.30, 1.45, 2.45, 4 from Staroměstské náměstí (Old Town Square). Also picks up at several other stops 🚌 Adult 350Kč, child 200Kč

PRAGUE SIGHTSEEING TOURS
Klimentská 52, Nové Město, Prague 1 (office). Start point: Náměstí Republiky
Tel 222 314 661; mobile 602 375 552
www.pstours.cz
A range of bus tours, some of which involve leaving the bus and walking. Out-of-town excursions are also available.
🕐 2-hour bus-only tour of city: daily 11, 1.30 🚌 Adult 390Kč, child 300Kč

PREMIANT CITY TOUR
Na příkopě 23, Staroměstské náměstí, Prague 1
Tel 606 600 123
www.premiant.cz
A range of city tours, by bus or bus and foot, plus numerous excursions outside Prague.
🕐 1-hour 'Prague in Brief' tour: up to 5 times daily 🚌 Adult 240Kč, child 180Kč

RIVER TOURS

EVROPSKÁ VODNÍ DOPRAVA (EVD)
Čechův most (Čech Bridge), Staré Město, Prague 1 (Na Františku quayside near InterContinental hotel)
Tel 224 810 030
www.evd.cz
One- and two-hour daytime cruises, and a three-hour evening cruise.
🕐 One-hour cruise: 10, 11, noon, 1, 2, 3, 4, 5, 6. Two-hour cruise: noon, 3. Evening cruise: 7pm 🚢 One-hour cruise: adult 220Kč, child 110Kč. Noon two-hour cruise: adult 640Kč (includes lunch), child 320Kč

PRAŽSKÁ PAROPLAVEBNÍ SPOLEČNOST A.S.
Rašínovo nábřeží (Rašín Embankment), Nové Město, Prague 2
Tel 224 931 013
www.paroplavba.cz

Cruising along the River Vltava

There is a range of cruises and one-way trips available, as well as excursions to destinations beyond Prague, including the historic town of Mělník, the Slapy reservoir recreational area and a single trip to Troja for the zoo, palace and gardens.
🕐 55-min round tour to Vyšehrad rock: mid-Mar to early Nov daily 11, noon, 1, 2, 3, 4, 5, 6. 90-min tour past city centre to Štvanice Island and return to Čechův most (Čech Bridge): mid-Mar to early Nov daily 3.30pm (▷ 202–203); lunch, evening, and disco cruises to order. All-day trip to Mělník: occasionally only 7am. Slapy: May–end Aug Fri–Sun 9am. One-way trip to Troja (75-min): 1 May–30 Jun Mon–Fri 8.30am; 26 Mar–30 Apr, 19 Sep–31 Oct daily 9.30, 12.30, 3.30; 1 May–31 Aug daily 9.30, 12.30, 3.30. Round trips possible 🚢 Vyšehrad tour: adult 170Kč, child 85Kč. City centre tour: adult 250Kč, child 125Kč. Mělník: adult 420Kč, child 210Kč. Slapy: adult 300Kč, child 150Kč. Troja (one-way): adult 90Kč, child 60Kč

PRVNÍ VŠEOBECNÁ ČLUNOVACÍ SPOLEČNOST S.R.O.
Platnerská 4, Staré Město, Prague 1 (office); landing stage nearby, others near Malá Strana end of Mánesův most (Mánes Bridge) and Čertovká
Tel 603 819 947
www.prague-venice.cz
This small-scale operation has cruises taking in the Čertovká (Devil's Brook) millstream, close-ups of a hidden arch of Karlův most (Charles Bridge) and remains of the Romanesque Judith Bridge.

🕐 Hourly departures. Winter 10.30–6; mid-season 10.30–8; Summer 10.30am–11pm. Trips last 45 minutes 🚢 Adult 270Kč, child (90–140cm tall) 135Kč, child under 90cm tall free

WALKING TOURS

A reliable source of qualified guides is the Pragotur Guides Centre in the tourist information office in the Old Town Hall.

CITY WALKS
Tel 222 244 531; mobile 0608 200 912
www.praguewalkingtours.com
City Walks offers a wide choice of themed walks, plus an Insider Tour as an introduction to the city. Walks start from the Orloj (Astronomical Clock) in Old Town Square, except the Insider Tour which begins 'beneath the horse' at the top of Wenceslas Square.
🕐 Various times and duration 🚶 Adult from 300Kč, child from 150Kč

PRAGUE WALKS
Jakubská 4, Staré Město, Prague 1
Tel 603 271 911
www.praguewalks.com
Expert guides lead tours through the city on themes such as the Velvet Revolution, Literary Prague and Spooky Prague, as well as taking you to pubs you might not discover on your own. There's an introductory tour of the highlights of Prague, with an optional steamer trip. All walks start from the Orloj (Astronomical Clock) in Old Town Square.
🕐 Various times and duration 🚶 Adult from 300Kč, child from 150Kč

WITTMANN TOURS
Mánesova 8, Nove Město, Prague 2
Tel 222 252 472
www.wittmann-tours.com
Wittman specializes in tours with a Jewish theme, including excursions to Terezín and Lidice, as well as walks around the Josefov. Walks start from the square in front of the InterContinental Hotel.
🕐 Usually Sun–Fri 10.30am (also 2pm in summer). Times may vary.
🚶 Adult 650Kč, child 500Kč

OUT AND ABOUT

This chapter focuses on places to eat and stay, listed alphabetically. Restaurants are also listed by area on page 224 and by cuisine on page 225.

Eating and Staying

EATING OUT IN PRAGUE

Restaurant standards in Prague have improved immeasurably since the Velvet Revolution. Today the city has a wealth of places to eat, providing everything from revamped versions of the traditional, rather heavy Czech cuisine to fine food from around the world.

There are plenty of options for eating out in Prague, whether indoors or out

TRADITIONAL CUISINE

Conventional Bohemian cooking draws heavily on the country's abundant natural resources. The landscape is threaded with rivers and studded with ponds, the home of freshwater fish like pike-perch, trout and, above all carp. Deep forests and broad fields provide a habitat for all kinds of game—deer, hare, rabbit, pheasant, partridge, even wild boar—yet the most popular meat with Czechs is pork, served, like most main courses, with the traditional accompaniments of pickled cabbage and dumplings. The latter are made from a surprising variety of ingredients, including bread, potatoes and semolina, as well as flour, and serve to soak up lashings of sauce. A starter, usually in the form of soup, may precede the main course, while desserts are often omitted, leaving room for cakes—generally light and delicious.

RESTAURANT TYPES

The *restaurace* varies enormously in character and price. At one end of the scale are unpretentious establishments serving lunch to office workers at unbelievably low prices; at the other end are glittering palaces of fine cuisine catering to local nouveaux-riches and visitors from abroad. Some of the best places in the latter category are the restaurants attached to the grand hotels (Zlatá Praha in the InterContinental, Sarah Bernhardt in the Paříž), as well as purpose-built establishments that rely on design and atmosphere as much as the food served, such as restaurants in the Bacchus, Ambiente and Zátiší groups. In between is a new kind of pub, carefully styled by breweries like Plzeňský Prazdroj and Staropramen to attract the drinkers and diners of today, while even the unreformed type of pub (*hospoda* or *pivnice*) will normally provide food of some kind.

Strictly speaking, a *vinárna* is a wine bar, but the term has come to mean a restaurant in which wine rather than beer accompanies the meal.

CAFÉS

Early and mid-20th-century Prague was one of the strongholds of central European café culture. A few historic establishments survive—Slavia, the cafés of the Obecní dům (Municipal House) and the Hotel Evropa—but more typical of today's city are the refuges of Anglo-Saxon expatriates (Globe, Bohemia Bagel) or chic places such as Cukr Káva Limonáda. Contemporary tea rooms have made an appearance too (Dobrá čajovná).

PRICES

It's easy to economize when eating out in Prague; the golden rule is to follow the habits of the local people. The best deals tend to be off the tourist trail and in the suburbs, but the listings that follow include several inexpensive establishments in central Prague. Look out for dishes of the day, which may be fresher and tastier anyway. Sophisticated eating comes at a higher cost, though less so than in most Western cities. You will often pay for the atmosphere as much as for the food. The price of a meal can rise quite steeply if you unwittingly take items from the tray of hors d'oeuvres offered at the start of the meal, which are unlikely to be complimentary. Prices normally include VAT, so beware of waiters adding it to the bill again. Service is also usually included, though it is standard practice to round up the final amount. One way of keeping costs down is to patronise fast-food outlets. But rather than entering a familiar establishment, with a predictable range of offerings, try a sausage from a street stall, accompanied by a liberal splodge of

EATING

mild mustard. Alternatively, look out for a buffet serving the same sort of thing, plus, if you are lucky, a range of small open sandwiches. Called *obložený chlebíčky*, these can be delicious combinations of ingredients such as cheese, salmon, fish roe, hard-boiled egg, and mayonnaise, with salad trimmings and a sprinkling of paprika powder.

OPENING TIMES

A lot of Czechs set off to work early, and with this in mind, many restaurants close well before midnight, but plenty of others, especially those with a substantial tourist clientele, stay open much later.

ETIQUETTE

Dress codes are generally informal, and smart casual attire is suitable for virtually any occasion. The more fashionable restaurants still try to get diners to leave their coats with the lady at the cloakroom. At humbler establishments it is normal to share a table if there are no free seats elsewhere; simply ask the permission of those already seated. Wish everyone *dobrou chut'!* (bon appétit!) before starting to eat, or *na zdraví!* (cheers!) before downing your drink. In a pub, your glass of beer may be replaced automatically by a wandering waiter unless you say otherwise.

Try some local cuisine while you are in the city, washed down with a coffee or a cocktail

CHAIN RESTAURANTS

Most of the global fast-food chains have a presence in the city, so those in search of a burger or pizza in familiar surroundings need never go hungry. There's a particularly large concentration of such establishments on the top floor of the huge Nový Smíchov mall in the suburbs.

More interesting perhaps, and certainly more in tune with the character of the city, are the chains of pub-restaurants run by two of the big Czech breweries. Plzeňský Prazdroj (Pilsner Urquell) has had great success with its range of renovated pubs, while Staropramen of Prague has targeted a trendier clientele with its cooler version of the same thing, Potrefená husa (The Shot Goose). Both offer a cheerful atmosphere, beer on tap and good, affordable food: traditional Bohemian at Plzeňský Prazdroj; contemporary international at Potrefená husa.

At the upper end of the scale are the gourmet restaurant groups founded mostly by enterprising foreigners. The Zátiší Group was the first to move into this field in the early 1990s, and has been joined by others, such as Kampa and Bacchus, providing sophisticated settings for the enjoyment of fine food with a cosmopolitan touch.

RESTAURANT CHAIN	RESTAURANT	PRICE OF A MEAL FOR ONE (Kč)	PAGE REFERENCE/ ADDRESS
BACCHUS	Barock	700–900	Page 231
www.bacchusgroup.cz	Hot	800–1,200	Hotel Jalta, Václavské náměstí
	Pravda	900–1,250	Page 239
KAMPA	Hergetova Cihelna	600–900	Page 235
www.kampagroup.com	Kampa Park	1,000–1,500	Page 235
	Square	700–900	Page 241
PLZEŇSKÝ PRAZDROJ	Celnice	200–300	Page 233
(Kolkovna Group)	Kolkovna	200–300	Page 236
www.kolkovna.cz	Lary Fary	200–650	Page 236
	Olympia	200–300	Page 238
POTREFENÁ HUSA	Potrefená husa	300–400	Page 239
www.potrefenahusa.com	Potrefená husa	300–400	Kolínská 19, Vinohrady
	Potrefená husa	300–400	Resslová 1, Nové Město
	Potrefená husa	300–400	Verdunská/Terronská 11, Dejvice
ZÁTIŠÍ	Bellevue	1,300–1,600	Page 231
www.zatisigroup.cz	Mlýnec	600–1,000	Page 238
	V Zátiší	1,000–1,300	Page 244

EATING

BASICS
brynza sheep's cheese
česnek garlic
chléb bread
cukr sugar
domácí home-made, local
džem jam
hořčice mustard
klobása sausage
křen horseradish
kysaná smetana sour cream

čočková polévka lentil soup
dršťková polévka tripe soup
drůbeží krém cream of
chicken soup
francouzská cibulačka French
onion soup
gulášová polévka goulash
soup
hovězí polévka beef broth
hrachová polévka pea soup
kapustnicá cabbage soup

moravský vrabec
'Moravian sparrow' (pork with
caraway seeds)
svíčková na smetaně beef in
cream sauce with cranberries
telecí ledvinky veal kidneys
telecí řízek Wiener
schnitzel (veal)
vepřová pečeně roast pork
vepřové řízek Wiener
schnitzel (pork)

majonéza mayonnaise
maso meat
máslo butter
mléko milk
oběd lunch
ocet vinegar
olej oil
omáčka sauce
ovoce fruit
párek frankfurter
pepř pepper
rohlík roll
ryba fish
rýže rice
šlehačka whipped cream
smetana cream
snídaně breakfast
sůl salt
sýr cheese
tartarská omáčka tartare
sauce
večeře dinner
vejce egg
    míchaná vejce scrambled
    egg
    vařená vejce boiled egg
    vejce na měkko soft-boiled
    egg
    vejce na tvrdo hard-boiled
    egg
    vejce se slaninou egg and
    bacon
voda water

POLÉVKY (SOUPS)
boršč beetroot soup
bramborová polévka potato
soup

slepičí vývar chicken soup
zelná polévka cabbage soup

PŘEDKRMY
(HORS D'OEUVRES)
husí játra goose liver
kozí sýr goat's cheese
krabí koktejl crab cocktail
krevety scampi
losos salmon
omeleta s cibulí onion
omelette
ruské vejce Russian eggs
studené předkrmy cold
hors d'oeuvres
teplé předkrmy warm
hors d'oeuvres

SALÁTY (SALADS)
hlávkový lettuce
listový green leaf
mrkvový carrot
rajčatový tomato

HLAVNÍ JÍDLA
(MAIN COURSES)

SPECIALITIES
biftek beefsteak
čevapčiči spicy meatballs
Balkan style
hovězí guláš beef goulash
játra liver
jehněčí karé rack of
lamb
koleno knuckle
kotleta cutlet
krkovice roast neck of pork

DRŮBEŽ (POULTRY)
husa pečená roast goose
kachna duck
krůtí medailonky medallions
of turkey
kuře chicken
smažená kuřecí prsa fried
breast of chicken

ZVĚŘINA (GAME)
bažant pheasant
daňčí hřbet saddle of
venison
holub pigeon
jelení venison
kančí boar
koroptev partridge
králík rabbit
perlička guinea-fowl
srnčí venison (roebuck)
zajíc hare

RYBY (FISH)
filé fillet (of white fish)
humr lobster
kapr carp
    kapr na černou carp in
    dark sauce
krevety prawns
losos salmon
pstruh trout
sardelka anchovy
sardinka sardine
sled' herring
štika pike
treska cod
úhoř eel
zavináč pickled herring

EATING

**BEZMASÁ JÍDLA
(MEAT-FREE DISHES)**
pečená špenátová roláda
roast spinach roulade
smažený sýr fried cheese
smažené žampionové
klboučky fried mushrooms
zapečený chřest se sýrem
baked asparagus with cheese
zeleninová omeleta
vegetable omelette

jablko apple
jahoda strawberry
kompot stewed fruit/
compote
malina raspberry
meruňka apricot
pomeranč orange
rozinky raisins
rybíz currants
švestka plum
třešeň cherry

EATING OUT
V kolik hodin otevírá ta
restaurace?
What time does the restaurant
open?

Stůl pro ..., prosím
A table for ..., please

číšník/číšnice
waiter/waitress

**PŘÍLOHY/ZELENINA
(SIDE ORDERS/VEGETABLES)**
bramborák potato pancake
brambory potatoes
bramborový knedlík potato
dumpling
brokolice broccoli
celer celery root
chřest asparagus
cibule onion
fazole beans
houby mushrooms
houskový knedlík bread
dumpling
hranolky potato chips
hrášek peas
kapusta curly kale
knedlíky dumplings
květák cauliflower
lečo ratatouille
okurka gherkin
pórek leek
rajče tomato
rýže rice
špenát spinach
vařený brambor boiled
potatoes
žampiony mushrooms
zelí cabbage

OVOCE (FRUIT)
ananas pineapple
borůvky blueberries
banán banana
broskev peach
citrón lemon
hrozny grapes
hruška pear

**DESERTY/MOUČNÍKY
A PEČIVO
(DESSERTS/PÂTISSERIE)**
buchty yeast buns with fruit or
jam filling
dort tart/cream cake
jablečný závin apple strudel
koláč cake
ovocné knedlíky fruit
dumplings
palačinky filled crêpes
tvaroh curd cheese
zmrzlina ice-cream

NÁPOJE (DRINKS)
Becherovka Carlsbad aperitif
borovička gin-like spirit
čaj tea
   čaj s mlékem tea with milk
   čaj se citrónem tea with
lemon
džus juice
horká čokoláda hot chocolate
káva coffee
minerální voda/minerálka
mineral water
   perlivá voda sparkling water
   neperlivá voda still water
pivo beer
   světlé pivo lager
   černé pivo dark beer
sekt sparkling wine
slivovice plum brandy
stará myslivecká 'Old
Huntsman' digestif
víno wine
   červené víno red wine
   bílé víno white wine

Prosím jídelní/nápojový
lístek
Please could we see the
menu/drinks list?

Máte ten jídelní lístek
anglicky?
Do you have the menu in
English?

Máte denní nabídku?
Is there a dish of the day?

Co je specialita podniku?
What is the house special?

Kolik stojí to jídlo?
How much is this dish?

Jsem vegetarián(ka)
I am a vegetarian

Dám si...
I'd like...

Sůl a pepř, prosím
Could we have some salt and
pepper please?

Jídlo bylo výborné
The food was excellent

Zaplatím!
Can I have the bill, please?

For more words and phrases
relating to restaurants and
eating out, ▷ 282.

EATING

The restaurants below and on page 225 are listed alphabetically on pages 230–244.

CENTRAL PRAGUE

HRADČANY

Lobkowicz Palace Café
Lví dvůr
Peklo
U Císařů
U Labutí
U Ševce Matouše
U Zlaté Hrušky

The stylish Alcron Restaurant

MALÁ STRANA

Around Malostranské náměstí (Malá Strana Square) and Nerudova
Bazaar
David
Gitanes
Square
U Mecenáše
U Sedmi Švábů

Northern Malá Strana
Hergetova Cihelna
Hungarian Grotto
Kampa Park
Pálffy Palác
U Zlaté Studně

Southern Malá Strana and Kampa Island
Alchymist
Bakeshop Diner
Bohemia Bagel
Café Savoy
C'est La Vie
Cukr Káva Limonáda
Olympia
Rybářský Klub
U Malířů
U Maltézských Rytířů
U Modré Kachničky

NOVÉ MĚSTO

Around Václavské náměstí (Wenceslas Square)
Alcron
Casa Mia
Dobrá čajovna

Kogo
U Pinkasů
Zahrada v Opeře
Zen Zen
Zvonice

South of Národní třída
Café Louvre
Globe
Tulip Café
U Fleků
Universal
Velryba

Southern Nové Město
Cicala
Lemon Leaf
Mánes
La Perle de Prague
Příčný Řez
U Kalicha

Northern Nové Město
Albio
Café Imperial
Celnice
Řecká Taverna
U Sádlů

PETŘÍNSKÉ SADY

Nebozízek
Oživlé Dřevo

STARÉ MĚSTO

Around Staroměstské náměstí (Old Town Square)
Ambiente Brasileiro
Country Life
Grand Café
Havelská Koruna
Metamorphis
Palác Kinských
Rybí Trh
U Modré Růže

Around the Obecní dům (Municipal House)
Francouzská Restaurace
Kavárna Obecní dům
Plzeňská Restaurace
Le Saint Jacques
Sarah Bernhardt

Josefov and northern Staré Město
Amici Miei
Barock
Le Café Colonial
Cartouche
Chez Marcel
King Solomon Restaurant
Kolkovna
Lary Fary

Potrefená Husa
Pravda
Rasoi Restaurant/Bombay Café
Zlatá Praha

Southern Staré Město and Karlův most (Charles Bridge)
Allegro
Bellevue

Lavish décor in the Café Savoy

Clementinum
Don Giovanni
Káva Káva Káva
Klub Architektů
Konvikt
Mlýnec
Parnas
Reykjavik
Slavia
U Medvídků
V Zátiší

SUBURBS

Bubeneč
Le Bistrot de Marlène

Holešovice
Hanavský Pavilón
Letenský zámeček

Nusle
U Pastýřky

Smíchov
La Cambusa

Vinohrady
Ambiente The Living Restauants
Modrá Řeka
Myslivna
Radost FX

Vršovice
Včelín

Žižkov
Kuře v Hodinkách
Mailsi

American
Ambiente The Living
Restaurants
Bakeshop Diner
Bohemia Bagel
Globe

Asian
Lemon Leaf
Mailsi
Rasoi Restaurant/Bombay Café

Top cuisine at Restaurant David

Balkan
Modrá Řeka

Czech
Café Imperial
Café Louvre
Celnice
David
Havelská Koruna
Klub Architektů
Kolkovna
Konvikt
Olympia
Peklo
Plzeňská Restaurace
U Císařů
U Fleků
U Kalicha
U Labutí
U Maltézských Rytířů
U Mecenáše
U Medvídků
U Modré Růže
U Pastýřky
U Pinkasů

French
Le Bistrot de Marlène
Chez Marcel
Francouzská restaurace
Letenský zámeček
La Perle de Prague
Le Saint Jacques
Sarah Bernhardt
U Malířů
Universal

Game
Myslivna
U Modré Kachničky

Hungarian
Hungarian Grotto

International
Alchymist
Allegro
Barock
Bellevue
Le Café Colonial
Café Savoy
C'est La Vie
Clementinum
Hanavský pavilion
Hergetova Cihelna
Kampa Park
Kuře v Hodinkách
Lary Fary
Lví dvůr
Mánes
Metamorphis
Mlýnec
Nebozízek
Oživlé Dřevo
Palác Kinských
Pálffy Palác
Parnas
Potrefená Husa
Pravda
Příčný Řez
Square
U Ševce Matouše
U Zlaté Hrušky
U Zlaté Studně
V Zátiší
Včelín
Zahrada v Opeře
Zlatá Praha
Zvonice

Italian
Amici Miei
Casa Mia
Cicala
Don Giovanni

Kosher
King Solomon Restaurant

Latin American
Ambiente Brasileiro

Medieval
Cartouche
U Sádlů
U Sedmi Švábů

Mediterranean
Bazaar
La Cambusa
Gitanes
Kogo
Řecká Taverna

Seafood
Alcron
Casa Mia
Reykjavik

A bubbling pot of mussels

Rybářský Klub
Rybí trh

Snacks
Cukr Káva Limonáda
Dobrá Čajovna
Grand Café
Káva Káva Káva
Kavárna Obecní dům
Lobkowicz Palace Café
Slavia
Tulip Café
Velryba

Vegetarian/Organic
Albio
Country Life
Radost FX
Zen Zen

EATING

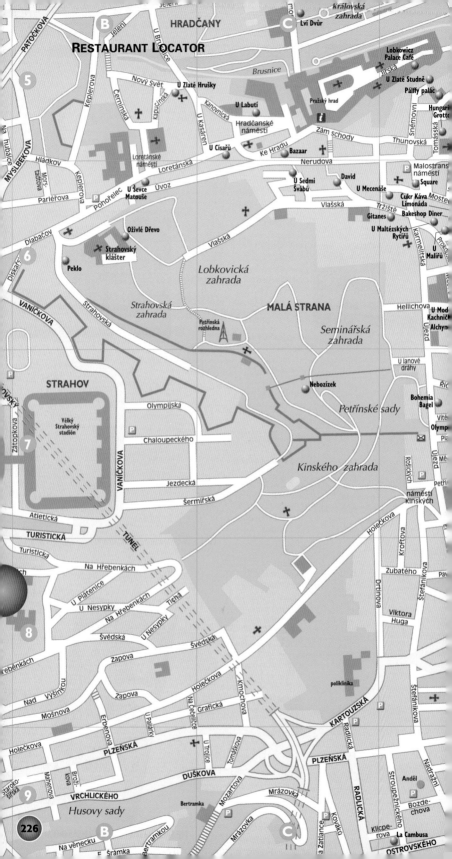

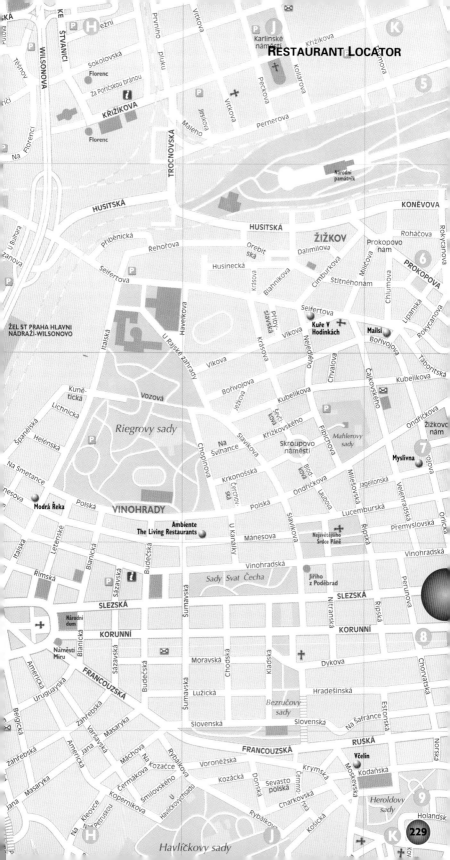

RESTAURANTS

PRICES AND SYMBOLS

The restaurants are listed alphabetically (excluding Le and La). The prices given are for a two-course lunch (L) for one person and a three-course dinner (D) for one person, without drinks. The wine price is for the least expensive bottle.
For a key to the symbols, ▷ 2.

ALBIO
Map 228 G5
Truhlářská 18–20, Nové Město, Prague 1
Tel 222 325 414
www.albiostyl.cz

Just a few steps from the sumptuous Obecní dům (Municipal House), whose restaurants serve the richest food imaginable, the Albio represents a very different approach to nutrition. It claims to be the country's only organic café and restaurant, and is also a food store and information centre promoting sensible eating. The menu is extensive and far from wholly vegetarian, the air is smoke-free, children are made especially welcome, and you are sure to leave with a warm glow of satisfaction after dining on such delicacies as pike-perch twists washed down with organic wine or unpasteurized beer.
🕐 Daily 11–10
🍴 L 128Kč, D 128Kč, Wine 195Kč
🚇 Náměstí Republiky
🚊 Tram 5, 8, 14 to Náměstí Republiky

SPECIAL
ALCRON
Map 228 G7
Štěpánská 40, Nové Město, Prague 1
Tel 222 820 000
www.prague.radissonsas.com
This exclusive restaurant, with only a couple of dozen seats, opens off the lobby of the prestigious Radisson SAS hotel (▷ 259). It specializes in exquisite fish dishes, using ingredients flown in freshly from the world's oceans or drawn from Bohemia's lakes and rivers. It is quite distinct from the hotel's much larger French-style establishment. The glory days of the old Alcron (the hotel's former name) are evoked with a superb sweeping mural in art deco style.
🕐 Mon–Sat 5.30–10.30pm; Sunday brunch
🍴 L, D 1,500Kč (gourmet menu), Wine 890Kč
🚇 Můstek
🚊 Tram 3, 9, 14, 24 to Václavské náměstí

ALCHYMIST
Map 226 D6
Hellichova 4, Malá Strana, Prague 1
Tel 257 312 518
www.alchymist.cz
Nothing will quite prepare you for the extraordinary interior of this fascinating restaurant, down a side street in Malá Strana. Delicately painted vaults, plush sofas, chairs upholstered in zebra-skin and objects of all kinds combine to create a total decorative overload. In the end its exuberance is convincing, as is the attentive service and well-considered international cuisine. Opened in 2004, the Alchymist seems certain to take its place among the most talked-about restaurants in town.
🕐 Apr–end Oct daily 8–3, 7–midnight; Nov–end Mar Tue–Sun 8–3, 7–midnight
🍴 L 450Kč, D 1,000Kč, Wine 560Kč
🚊 Tram 12, 20, 22, 23 to Hellichova

ALLEGRO
Map 227 E6
Veleslavínova 2a, Staré Město, Prague 1
Tel 221 426 880
www.fourseasons.com
The opulent, wood-panelled restaurant of the luxurious Four Seasons Hotel Prague (▷ 254) not only offers some of the most refined and delicious food in Prague, but also has a superlative riverside location by Karlův most (Charles Bridge). The timeless view across the Vltava to Malá Strana and the Castle is best enjoyed from the terrace. Dishes like roasted milk-fed mountain lamb or braised veal cheek are highly recommended. Bohemian and Mediterranean cuisine of this quality does not come cheap, but you may well consider it worth the money.
🕐 Daily 6.30am–11pm
🍴 L 1,200Kč, D 2,100Kč, Wine 750Kč
🚇 Staroměstská
🚊 Tram 17, 18 to Staroměstská

AMBIENTE BRASILEIRO
Map 228 F6
U Radnice 8, Staré Město, Prague 1
Tel 224 234 474
www.ambi.cz

This 'eat as much as you like' establishment is devoted to the South American love of meat. From chicken hearts to fillet steak, all is prepared on skewers in a special grill, then served by the cheerful chefs. Here in Prague it's a bit of a gimmick, but a good one. Choose between the atmospheric and rather noisy cellar or the quieter ground floor.
🕐 Daily 11am–midnight
🍴 L 450Kč, D 550Kč, Wine 329Kč
🚇 Staroměstská
🚊 Tram 17, 18 to Staroměstská

AMBIENTE THE LIVING RESTAURANTS

Map 229 J7
Mánesova 59, Vinohrady, Prague 2
Tel 222 727 851
www.ambi.cz

A big photo of James Dean looks down over the gingham tablecloths and wicker chairs of this American-style cellar diner. The menu is extensive and fun, ranging from burritos to buffalo wings, and from tacos to T-bone steaks. It's only a short walk from Náměstí Mírů metro station, in the pleasant inner borough of Vinohrady.

🕐 Mon–Fri 11am–midnight, Sat–Sun 12–12 (5–12 in Jul, Aug)
🍽 L 200Kč, D 400Kč, Wine 200Kč
Ⓜ Náměstí Míru
🚋 Tram 4, 10, 16, 22, 23 to Náměstí Míru

AMICI MIEI

Map 228 F5
Vězeňská 5, Staré Město, Prague 1
Tel 224 816 688
www.amicimiei.cz

In a quiet little side-street, this smart Italian restaurant is one of the best places to eat during a visit to the Jewish Quarter. A chic atmosphere and the friendly service enhance the pleasure of choosing dishes from the tempting menu. There is an excellent wine list, and in summer you can eat outside.

🕐 Daily 11.30–4, 6.30–11
🍽 L 700Kč, D 850Kč, Wine 450Kč
Ⓜ Staroměstská
🚋 Tram 17, 18 to Staroměstská, 17 to Právnická fakulta

BAKESHOP DINER

Map 226 D6
Lázeňská 19, Malá Strana
Tel 257 534 244
www.bakeshop.cz

Opened in 2002, following the success of a similar establishment in Staré Město, this American-style diner stands in a Malá Strana side-street just away from the main stream of tourists on their way to and from Karlův most (Charles Bridge). As well as a choice of international newspapers, it offers burgers, salads and substantial snacks in a relaxed and uncrowded atmosphere.

🕐 Daily 7am–10pm
🍽 L 350Kč, D 450Kč, Wine 180Kč
🚋 Tram 12, 20, 22, 23 to Malostranské náměstí

BAROCK

Map 228 F5
Pařížská 24, Staré Město, Prague 1
Tel 222 329 221
www.barock.bacchusgroup.cz

This glitzy establishment attempts to match the trendy offerings of the city's most expensive shopping street with its floor-to-ceiling windows, long bar and life-size photographs of celebrities and film stars. The fashionable clientele does its best to live up to the image, choosing items from the mainly Asian-style menu; the best bargain is undoubtedly the sampler plate, changed daily.

🕐 Daily 10am–midnight
🍽 L 700Kč, D 900Kč, Wine 800Kč
Ⓜ Staroměstská
🚋 Tram 17, 18 to Staroměstská, 17 to Právnická fakulta

BAZAAR

Map 226 C5
Nerudova 40, Malá Strana, Prague 1
Tel 296 826 106
www.restaurantbazaar.cz

Bizarre might be a better word for the experience offered in this cavernous interior just beneath the Castle, where run-of-the-mill Mediterranean food takes second place to exotic atmosphere and exuberant evening entertainment. The reward for climbing the 68 steps of the winding stairway leading up from the main restaurant is a spectacular terrace and two-floor winter garden, with wonderful views over Malá Strana and Petřín Hill—an unbeatable location for lingering on long summer evenings.

🕐 Daily 12–11 (bar to 2am)
🍽 L 650Kč, D 850Kč, Wine 475Kč
🚋 Tram 12, 20, 22, 23 to Malostranské náměstí

BELLEVUE

Map 227 E6
Smetanovo nábřeží 18, Staré Město, Prague 1
Tel 222 221 443
www.pfd.cz

This first-floor riverside restaurant deserves its name—the view of the Vltava, Karlův most (Charles Bridge) and the castle is beautiful and is best appreciated on the summer terrace. The international cuisine lives up to the setting and the service is impeccable. Nowhere else are you likely to be offered juniper-scented deer consommé, followed by cod with puréed sweet potato. Jazz accompanies the Sunday brunch.

🕐 Mon–Sat 12–3, 5.30–11, Sun 11–3.30, 7–11
🍽 L 1,300Kč, D 1,600Kč, Wine 690Kč
Ⓜ Národní třída
🚋 Tram 17, 18 to Karlovy lázně, 6, 9, 22, 23 to Národní divadlo

LE BISTROT DE MARLÈNE

Off map 227 D5
Schwaigerova 59/3, Bubeneč, Prague 6
Tel 224 921 853
www.bistrotdemarlene.cz

The attractively refurbished French Bistrot de Marlène, close to Stromovka park, prides itself on producing superlative food from fresh ingredients (mostly imported). The choice of dishes is deliberately limited, but you will not be disappointed.

🕐 Mon–Fri 12–2.30, 7–10.30, Sat 7–10.30pm
🍽 L 1,500Kč, D 2,000Kč, Wine 660Kč
Ⓜ Hradčanská

BOHEMIA BAGEL

Map 226 D7
Újezd 16, Malá Strana, Prague 1
Tel 257 310 694
www.bohemiabagel.cz

Opened in the 1990s by expatriate entrepreneur and jazz-man Glenn Spicker as a little bit of America in Malá Strana, Bohemia Bagel offers a variety of stone-baked bagels, as well as soups, desserts, newspapers and a cheerful atmosphere. There's another branch, with internet access, at Masná 2 in Staré Město. Credit cards are not accepted.

🕐 Mon–Fri 7am–midnight, Sat–Sun 8am–midnight
🍽 Bagels up to 75Kč, Wine 35Kč (small glass)
🚋 Tram 6, 9, 12, 20, 22, 23 to Újezd

LE CAFÉ COLONIAL

Map 227 E5
Široká 6, Staré Město,
Prague 1
Tel 224 818 322
www.lecafecolonial.cz

Le Café Colonial is in the heart of the Jewish Quarter. It has brightly painted walls, darkwood furnishings, heavy chandeliers and a slightly decadent atmosphere. The delicious food is mainly French, and the wines are international, with a good selection of reds and whites from Moravia. The restaurant merges with an equally stylish café.

🕐 Daily 10am–midnight
🍽 L 600Kč, D 750Kč, Wine 315Kč
Ⓜ Staroměstská
🚋 Tram 17, 18 to Staroměstská

CAFÉ IMPERIAL

Map 228 G5
Na poříčí 15, Nové Město,
Prague 1
Tel 222 316 012
www.hotelimperial.cz

The Imperial of 1914, like the Slavia (▷ 241) and the Café Louvre (▷ right), is one of the few monuments remaining from the Prague café society of a century ago, but unlike them it seems to have escaped the attention of visitors from abroad. This is surprising, given its flamboyant décor—Oriental-style wall-to-ceiling ceramic tiles—and its general air of a bustling central establishment. It's on the

ground floor of the equally stylish Imperial hotel (▷ 255). Credit cards are not accepted.

🕐 Daily 9am–midnight (Sun to 11pm)
🍽 L 125Kč, D 250Kč, Wine 150Kč
Ⓜ Náměstí Republiky
🚋 Tram 5, 8, 14 to Náměstí Republiky; tram 3, 24, 26 to Bílá Labuť or Masarykovo nádraží

CAFÉ LOUVRE

Map 228 E7
Národní třída 20, Nové Město,
Prague 1
Tel 224 930 949
www.cafelouvre.cz

This spacious first-floor café has a grandstand view from its big windows of the activity in the busy boulevard of Národní třída. A city institution, so far it has resisted the temptation to revamp its rather garish décor, and remains resolutely untrendy. This guarantees a mixed rather than tourist/expatriate clientele, with locals enjoying unpretentious food and drink while perusing the daily newspapers. There's a popular pool room at the back.

🕐 Mon–Fri 8am–11.30pm, Sat–Sun 9am–11.30pm
🍽 L 200Kč, D 250Kč, Wine 160Kč
Ⓜ Národní třída
🚋 Tram 6, 9, 18, 21, 22, 23 to Národní třída

CAFÉ SAVOY

Map 227 D7
Vítězná 5/Zborovská 68, Malá Strana,
Prague 5
Tel 257 311 562
www.ambi.cz
A useful landmark close to the Malá Strana end of the Most Legií (Bridge of the Legions), the stylish Savoy occupies an airy corner room with an upper gallery floor and a most elaborate ceiling. Breakfast, snacks and full meals are available at reasonable prices, and the service is good.

🕐 Mon–Fri 8am–10.30pm, Sat–Sun 9am–10.30pm
🍽 L 300Kč, D 375Kč, Wine 189Kč
🚋 Tram 6, 9, 12, 20, 22, 23 to Újezd

LA CAMBUSA

Map 226 D9
Klicperova 2, Smíchov,
Prague 5
Tel 257 317 949
www.lacambusa.cz
This excellent fish restaurant is easily accessible, right by Anděl metro station in suburban Smíchov. The

seafood is guaranteed fresh, and its preparation is inspired by the distinctive cuisines of Livorno and Provence; there's probably no better bouillabaisse in Prague.

🕐 Mon–Sat 7pm–midnight (lunch by arrangement)
🍽 D 1,000Kč, Wine 380Kč
Ⓜ Anděl
🚋 Tram 4, 6, 7, 9, 10, 12, 14, 20 to Anděl

CARTOUCHE

Map 228 F5
Bílkova 14, Staré Město,
Prague 1
Tel 224 819 597/222 317 103
www.cartouche.cz
The rough-hewn wooden furnishings, bare brick walls and wrought-iron fixtures of this cellar establishment, lit by flickering candles and the glow of the fire beneath a slowly turning spit, conjure up all the atmosphere of medieval France. You almost expect some musketeer to rip away the sword which functions as a door handle and come leaping down the timber stairway. Wash down generous portions of spit-roasted meat with tankards of foaming ale and (on Friday evenings) be entertained by the music of medieval songstresses.

🕐 Mon–Fri 11–11, Sat–Sun 1–11pm
🍽 L 600Kč, D 800Kč, Wine 390Kč
Ⓜ Staroměstská
🚋 Tram 17 to Právnická fakulta

CASA MIA

Map 228 F7
Vodičkova 17/Jungmannova 14,
Nové Město, Prague 1
Tel 296 238 204
www.casamia.cz
It's worth penetrating the *pasáž* (arcade) connecting Vodičkova and Jungmannova streets in the New Town to find this attractive establishment. There's a classy restaurant and a cellar pizzeria, and both have extensive menus. The restaurant features a choice of ocean and freshwater fish, according to availability. The pizzeria offers a wide range of pastas as well as pizzas. You can dine outside in the pleasant courtyard in summer.

🕐 Daily 11am–midnight
🍽 Restaurant: L 650Kč, D 1,000Kč, Wine 240Kč. Pizzeria: L 150Kč, D 250Kč, Wine 150Kč
🚋 Tram 3, 9, 14, 24 to Vodičkova

EATING

CELNICE

Map 228 G6
V Celnici 4, Nové Město,
Prague 1
Tel 224 212 240
www.celnice.com

Right by Náměstí Republiky (Republic Square) and the Obecní dům (Municipal House), the 'Custom House' is a highly successful attempt by the Pilsner Urquell brewery to bring the Prague pub up to date. As well as a cheerful atmosphere, beer on tap and traditional food such as *koleno* (pork knuckle), there are steaks and salads and, in the cellar, a sensational sushi bar. On weekends the cellar is a popular (and noisy music) venue.

🕐 Sun–Wed 11am–2am, Thu–Sat 11am–4am
🍴 L 200Kč, D 300Kč, Wine 354Kč
Ⓜ Náměstí Republiky
🚊 Tram 5, 8, 14 to Náměstí Republiky

C'EST LA VIE

Map 227 D7
Říční 1, Malá Strana,
Prague 1
Tel 721 158 403
www.cestlavie.cz

This chic riverside restaurant at the southern end of Kampa Island was badly affected by the great flood of 2002, and has undergone complete restoration, including the revival of its previous enviable reputation for fine food. The extensive (and expensive) menu features dishes from a number of world cuisines, occasionally in rather confusing combinations, but the overall quality is outstanding. Try the pesto baked salmon, or veal entrecôte with asparagus risotto.

🕐 Daily 11.30am–1am
🍴 L 600Kč, D 1,200Kč, Wine 495Kč
🚊 Tram 6, 9, 12, 20, 22, 23 to Újezd

CHEZ MARCEL

Map 228 F5
Haštalská 12, Staré Město,
Prague 1
Tel 222 315 676

Chez Marcel is as authentic as it gets—a French-run brasserie with all the usual characteristics such as newspaper racks, old posters, a blackboard with *plats du jour* and a main menu featuring classic dishes at more-than-acceptable prices. The location overlooking a little square close to Anežský klášter (St. Agnes Convent) in the northern end of Staré Město is an added attraction. And there's another plus: a non-smoking section. Marcel also has a branch at Americká 20 in Vinohrady. Credit cards are not accepted.

🕐 Mon–Fri 8am–1am, Sat–Sun 9am–1am
🍴 L 400Kč, D 500Kč, Wine 420Kč
Ⓜ Náměstí Republiky
🚊 Tram 5, 8, 14 to Dlouhá třída

CICALA

Map 228 F8
Žitná 43, Nové Město, Prague 1
Tel 222 210 375
www.trattoria.cicala.cz

One-way Žitná is an unattractive, heavily trafficked, inner city bypass, but you'll forget all this as soon as you enter this basement restaurant, where the Italian proprietor dispenses both charm and choice Italian food. The fresh pasta is considered to be the best in town by expatriates, and there's much more to choose from, all served in generous portions at pared-down prices. Signed photographs testify to visits by many a satisfied celebrity. Credit cards are not accepted.

🕐 Mon–Sat 11.30–10.30
🍴 L 250Kč, D 325Kč, Wine 290Kč
Ⓜ I.P. Pavlova or Karlovo Náměstí
🚊 Tram 4, 6, 10, 16, 22, 23 to Štěpánská

CLEMENTINUM

Map 227 E6
Platnéřská 9, Staré Město,
Prague 1
Tel 224 813 892
www.clementinum.cz

There's a fascinating view of that great citadel of the Jesuit Order, the Klementinum, from the large windows of the restaurant that shares its name. Devastated by the 2002 flood, it has been reopened and restyled in an inviting, contemporary manner. The menu is mainly French-inspired, with a fairly limited range of reasonably priced dishes, which are suitable for a light lunch or a more substantial dinner. The former basement dining room is now a beer hall.

🕐 Daily 11–midnight
🍴 L 325Kč, D 400Kč, Wine 135Kč
Ⓜ Staroměstská
🚊 Tram 17, 18 to Staroměstská

COUNTRY LIFE

Map 228 F6
Melantrichova 15,
Staré Město, Prague 1
Tel 224 213 366

Tucked away in the heart of the Old Town, Country Life was in the front line of the vegetarian fight in this meat-addicted country, first with its wholefood shop, then with this very popular, cafeteria-style eatery. Pick up a tray and choose a healthy lunch from the wide selection of soups, casseroles, salads and fruit, all at very acceptable prices. Credit cards are not accepted.

🕐 Mon–Thu 8–7, Fri 8–6, Sun 11–6
🍴 Main courses around 50Kč
Ⓜ Můstek

CUKR KÁVA LIMONÁDA

Map 226 D6
Lázeňská 7, Malá Strana,
Prague 1
Tel 257 530 628

This newly opened, very chic café is just a step away from the Malá Strana end of Karlův most (Charles Bridge). Choose from a good selection of teas, coffees, soft and alcoholic drinks, and from an inventive menu featuring delicious cakes, crêpes and other inviting snacks.

🕐 Mon–Sat 8.30–7.30, Sun 8.30–7
🍴 L, D 200Kč, Wine 210Kč
🚊 Tram 12, 20, 22, 23 to Malostranské náměstí

EATING

DAVID

Map 226 C6
Tržiště 21/611, Malá Strana,
Prague 1
Tel 257 533 109
www.restaurant-david.cz

Ring the doorbell of what appears to be a private house tucked away up a quiet little lane in the further reaches of Malá Strana and you will be shown, with exemplary courtesy, into an attractive dining room, hung with vivid paintings by the well-known contemporary artist Michal Halva. After 1989, this was one of the first restaurants to cater to foreign visitors. You won't be disappointed by any of the reinvented traditional Bohemian dishes featured on the menu. International dishes include an excellent chateaubriand and a variety of ocean fish, including 'sea wolf' or catfish. The 'Old Prague' dish (boar, crispy duck and pork) is particularly satisfying.

🕐 Daily 11.30–11
🍴 L 650Kč, D 800Kč, Wine 390Kč
🚋 Tram 12, 20, 22, 23 to Malostranské náměstí

DOBRÁ ČAJOVNA

Map 228 F7
Václavské náměstí 14, Nové Město,
Prague 1
Tel 224 231 480
www.tea.cz

Just off Václavské náměstí (Wenceslas Square), this quiet courtyard retreat ('The Good Tea-House') offers an extraordinary range of teas, properly presented in a pot, quite a departure in a country where lukewarm water and a tasteless teabag are all too often the norm. There's a ban on mobile phones, and the tea can be enjoyed without breathing in other people's cigarette fumes—an ideal place to escape from city stress. There's a limited range of snacks. Credit cards are not accepted.

🕐 Mon–Fri 10–9.30, Sat–Sun 2–9.30pm
🍴 Tea around 65Kč
Ⓜ Můstek
🚋 Tram 3, 9, 14, 24 to Václavské náměstí

DON GIOVANNI

Map 227 E6
Karoliny Světlé 34,
Staré Město,
Prague 1
Tel 222 222 060
www.dongiovanni.cz

Reckoned to be the first authentic Italian restaurant to open in Prague, the Don Giovanni is popular with expatriates from south of the Alps. People come not only for the genuinely Italian dishes, made from the freshest of proper ingredients, but also for the formal though unpretentious atmosphere. The wine list represents the best from Italy's wine regions.

🕐 Daily 11am–midnight
🍴 L 550Kč, D 1,000Kč, Wine 420Kč
🚋 Tram 17, 18 to Karlovy lázně

FRANCOUZSKÁ RESTAURACE

Map 228 F6
Obecní dům, Náměstí Republiky 5,
Staré Město,
Prague 1
Tel 222 002 770
www.obecnidum.cz

The French Restaurant in the art nouveau Obecní dům (Municipal House) was *the* place to dine a century ago. Sitting amid all its gloriously restored magnificence, you might feel as if you're taking part in a period performance of some kind; the tablecloths are blindingly white, the chandeliers are glittering, the service is attentive and the mostly French cuisine is excellent. It's a Prague experience not to be missed, and the package combining dinner with a concert in the Municipal House's Smetana Hall is well worth investigating (www.oliverius.cz for details).

🕐 Daily noon–4, 6–11
🍴 L 1,000Kč, D 2,000Kč, Wine 790Kč
Ⓜ Náměstí Republiky
🚋 Tram 5, 8, 14 to Náměstí Republiky

GITANES

Map 226 C6
Tržiště 7, Malá Strana,
Prague 1
Tel 257 530 163
www.gitanes.cz

This individual little restaurant, just off Malostranské náměstí, consists of two small, very comfortable and brightly decorated rooms. The food, wine and atmosphere are that of

former Yugoslavia and its Mediterranean neighbours. There's a good selection of pasta and fish dishes, as well as Balkan specials like *čevapčiči* (spicy lamb sausages) and veal roasted over an open fire. Highly recommended.

🕐 Daily 12–12
🍴 L, D 600Kč, Wine 260Kč
🚋 Tram 12, 20, 22, 23 to Malostranské náměstí

GLOBE

Map 227 E7
Pštrossova 6, Nové Město,
Prague 1
Tel 224 934 203
www.globebookstore.cz

The Globe Bookstore and Coffeehouse has been a Prague institution since 1993, when it began life on the far bank of the Vltava in the then unfashionable inner suburb of Holešovice. It has now relocated to a more central site in the New Town, not far from the Národní divadlo (National Theatre) and, with its stock of thousands of books, internet facilities, changing exhibitions, congenial atmosphere, good coffee and snacks, it remains a hang-out for the more cultured patron.

🕐 Daily 10am–midnight
🍴 L 95Kč, D 195Kč, Wine 160Kč
🚋 Tram 6, 9, 17, 18, 22, 23 to Národní divadlo; Tram 21 to Myslikova

GRAND CAFÉ

Map 228 F6
Staroměstské náměstí 22,
Staré Město,
Prague 1
Tel 221 632 520
www.grandcafe.cz

With a grandstand view of the Old Town Hall's Orloj (Astronomical Clock), this newly reopened and extended first-floor café has built on the popularity of its predecessor, the Café Milena, named after

EATING

Franz Kafka's most famous lover. When the clock's procession of puppets has stopped performing you will be able to give your attention to the delicious cakes on offer—not cheap, but definitely worth the money. Try the Schwarzwaldský dort (Black Forest cake), one of many delights on the menu.

🕐 Daily 7am–midnight
🍴 L 650Kč, D 800Kč
Ⓜ Staroměstská
🚊 Tram 17, 18 to Staroměstská

HANAVSKÝ PAVILON

Off map 227 E5
Letenské sady 173,
Holešovice,
Prague 7
Tel 233 323 641
www.hanavskypavilon.cz

The view is the main attraction at the Hanava Pavilion, a light-hearted little structure in glass and cast iron, built for the Jubilee Expo of 1891, and subsequently moved to this prominent location at the western end of Letná Plain. Window tables and the spacious terrace command a wonderful vista of the Vltava and its bridges, Staré Město to the left, Malá Strana to the right. The cuisine, served to the accompaniment of a piano, is a mixture of modernized Old Bohemian and international.

🕐 Daily 10am–11pm
🍴 L 500Kč, D 1,000Kč, Wine 590Kč
🚊 Tram 18, 20 to Chotkovy sady

HAVELSKÁ KORUNA

Map 228 F6
Havelská 21–23,
Staré Město,
Prague 1
Tel 224 239 331
Just along from the Havelská market is this well-run, self-service establishment, which is extremely popular with locals and visitors, and not just because of the excellent value

offered. There's a good selection of conventional Czech food, from hearty soups and meat and dumplings to filling desserts. The well-stocked salad bar is more than just a nod to healthy eating. Drinks include beer on tap. The ticket collected on entry is filled out as you move around with your tray from counter to counter, and you pay your modest bill at the desk on the way out.

🕐 Daily 9–8
🍴 L, D 150Kč
Ⓜ Můstek

HERGETOVA CIHELNA

Map 227 E6
Cihelná 2b, Malá Strana,
Prague 1
Tel 257 535 534
www.cihelna.com

This ambitious conversion of a historic brickworks enjoys a prime location on the banks of the Vltava, just downstream from Karlův most (Charles Bridge). Beneath the stylish, spacious bar on the upper floor is a fascinating barrel-vaulted dining room opening out onto a 75m (245ft) riverside terrace with an unforgettable view of the bridge and the Old Town. The food and drink matches the quality of the setting.

🕐 Daily 11.30am–1am (kitchen closes 11pm)
🍴 L 600Kč, D 900Kč, Wine 500Kč
Ⓜ Malostranská
🚊 Tram 12, 18, 20, 22, 23 to Malostranská

HUNGARIAN GROTTO

Map 226 D5
Tomášská 12, Malá Strana,
Prague 1
Tel 257 532 344
www.hungarian-grotto.cz
You will find this cellar establishment a stone's throw from Malostranské náměstí. It has several comfortable and plushly furnished rooms, and serves a wide range of dishes

from the land of the Magyars, such as goose liver, pörkölt (a type of beef stew) and, of course, gulyas. Good Hungarian wines accompany the carefully prepared dishes, while piped music evokes the landscape of the far-off puszta.

🕐 Daily 11.30–11.30
🍴 L 300Kč, D 700Kč, Wine 290Kč
🚊 Tram 12, 20, 22, 23 to Malostranské náměstí

KÁVA KÁVA KÁVA

Map 228 F7
Pasáž Platýz, Národní 37,
Staré Město,
Prague 1
Tel 224 228 862
www.kava-coffee.cz
Káva Káva Káva looks out onto an attractively paved courtyard, which is part of a pasáž (arcade) linking Národní to Uhelný trh (Coal Market) and Staré Město. It claims to serve the best coffee in town, as well as cakes and bagels. There are newspapers on a rack and internet facilities. When the weather permits, you can sit outside.

🕐 Mon–Fri 7am–9pm, Sat–Sun 9–9
🍴 Snacks from 30Kč, Wine 180Kč
Ⓜ Národní třída
🚊 Tram 6, 9, 18, 21, 22, 23 to Národní třída

KAMPA PARK

Map 227 D6
Na Kampě 8b,
Malá Strana,
Prague 1
Tel 296 826 102
www.kampagroup.cz
This doyenne of fine food served in stylish surroundings continues to attract A-list diners and a host of ordinary folk as well, despite being inundated in the great flood of 2002. It has a wonderful location at the tip of Kampa Island, almost beneath the arches of Karlův most (Charles Bridge). Choose from a selection of superb, mainly seafood dishes, such as seared scallops, and an excellent wine list. The service is impeccable.

🕐 Daily 11.30am–1am
🍴 L 1,000Kč, D 1,500Kč, 495Kč
🚊 Tram 12, 20 , 22, 23 to Malostranské náměstí

EATING

SPECIAL
KAVÁRNA OBECNÍ DŮM
Map 228 G6
Náměstí Republiky 5, Staré Město,
Prague 1
Tel 222 002 763-4
www.vysehrad2000.cz/obecnidum

There's no grander place to sip coffee and enjoy delicious cake than the splendid café of the art nouveau Obecní dům (Municipal House). The refreshments may seem expensive, but not when you reflect on what it must have cost to build, decorate and restore this spacious interior, an architectural gem of a century ago. There's a terrace in summer, but even the sun finds it difficult to compete with the brilliance within.
🕐 Daily 7.30am–11pm
🍴 L, D 300Kč, Wine 250Kč
Ⓜ Náměstí Republiky
🚊 Tram 5, 8, 14 to Náměstí Republiky

KING SOLOMON RESTAURANT
Map 227 E5
Široká 8, Staré Město, Prague 1
Tel 224 818 752
www.kosher.cz
The acclaimed kosher King Solomon Restaurant stands in the heart of Josefov, Prague's old Jewish Quarter. The interior is full of atmosphere, but it's the fine food that tempts people here. Based on the freshest ingredients, it offers the very best of traditional Middle Eastern and Eastern European dishes, not least its superlative *gefilte* fish. There are kosher wines too, from France, Israel, Hungary and the Czech Republic.
🕐 Sun–Thu 12–11; Fri dinner and Sat lunch only by reservation
🍴 L 550Kč, D 1,000Kč, Wine 450Kč
Ⓜ Staroměstská
🚊 Tram 17, 18 to Staroměstská

KLUB ARCHITEKTŮ
Map 227 E6
Betlémské náměstí 5a, Staré Město,
Prague 1
Tel 224 401 214
www.klubarchitektu.com
This vaulted cellar restaurant, attached to the headquarters of the professional association of Czech architects, with its fascinating art and design bookshop, has plenty of atmosphere and attracts a varied clientele. The food is not outstanding—a selection of Czech staples and international dishes—but is good value.
🕐 Daily 11.30am–midnight (kitchen closes at 11pm)
🍴 L 125Kč, D 300Kč, Wine 120Kč
Ⓜ Národní třída
🚊 Tram 6, 9, 18, 21, 22, 23 to Národní třída

KOGO
Map 228 G6
Na příkopě 22, Nové Město, Prague 1
Tel 221 451 258-9
www.kogo.cz
Deep within the state-of-the-art Slovanský dům shopping mall is this glittering Italian-style restaurant, one of the city's prime places to see and be seen. It's always buzzing with life and offers a huge range of Mediterranean food—steaks, salads, seafood, pastas, pizzas and risottos—which can be eaten in the winter garden-like interior or outside in summer.
🕐 Daily 8am–11pm
🍴 L, D 450Kč, Wine 490Kč
Ⓜ Můstek, Náměstí Republiky
🚊 Tram 5, 8, 14 to Náměstí Republiky

KOLKOVNA
Map 228 F5
V Kolkovně 8, Staré Město, Prague 1
Tel 224 819 702
www.kolkovna.cz
Kolkovna is one of the highly successful attempts by the Pilsner Urquell brewery group to bring the traditional Czech pub up to date. It's cleaner, less smoky and the food is certainly better. Choose between the ground floor with its gleaming brewery vat or the more intimate cellar to indulge in traditional dishes such as pork knuckle, washed down with the incomparable hoppy brew.
🕐 Daily 11am–midnight
🍴 L 200Kč, D 300Kč, Wine 380Kč
Ⓜ Staroměstská
🚊 Tram 17, 18 to Staroměstská; Tram 17 to Právnická fakulta

KONVIKT
Map 227 E6
Bartolomějská 11, Staré Město,
Prague 1
Tel 224 231 971/602 355 806
The name of this pub-restaurant has nothing to do with prisoners, but refers to the building's past as a residence of the Jesuit Order (*konvikt* means students' residence). It's a cheerful place, popular with office workers at lunch time. The standard Czech food is competitively priced, and there's a good selection of beers. Credit cards are not accepted.
🕐 Daily 11am–midnight
🍴 L 100Kč, D 250Kč, Wine 135Kč
Ⓜ Národní třída
🚊 Tram 6, 9, 18, 21 22, 23 to Národní třída

KUŘE V HODINKÁCH
Map 229 J6
Seifertova 26, Žižkov, Prague 3
Tel 222 734 212
www.kurevhodinkach.com
The curiously named 'Chicken in the Watch' is a celebration of a 1960s hit by Czech rock legend Vladimír Mišík. Posters of the great man and other rock 'n' roll memorabilia give this pub-restaurant in inner suburban Žižkov its distinct identity, but there's much more to the place than mere image-making; nothing could be more substantial than the succulent pork knuckle (*koleno*) served here. This and other hearty dishes are best accompanied by a glass of one of the several beers on tap.
🕐 Mon–Sat 11am–1am, Sun noon–1am
🍴 L 150Kč, D 250Kč, Wine 140Kč
🚊 Tram 5, 9, 26 to Lipanská

LARY FARY
Map 228 F5
Dlouhá 30, Staré Město, Prague 1
Tel 222 320 154
www.laryfary.cz
This restaurant, just a few steps from Staroměstské náměstí (Old Town Square), has gone to great lengths to impress with its originality. An eclectic mix of vaguely Oriental objects fills the vaulted interior, while the menu offers a range of Czech dishes.
🕐 Daily 11am–midnight
🍴 L 200Kč, D 650Kč, Wine 149Kč
Ⓜ Náměstí Republiky
🚊 Tram 5, 8, 14 to Dlouhá třída

EATING

LEMON LEAF

Map 227 E8
Na Zderaze 14, Nové Město, Prague 2
Tel 224 919 056
www.lemon.cz
The Lemon Leaf serves mostly Thai cuisine, though there are plenty of international choices, as well as pastas and salads. The restaurant, a block away from Karlovo náměstí (Charles Square), is inviting and spacious, with high ceilings, yellow walls and plenty of natural light from the large windows. The food is sensibly priced, and the inclusive lunch menus (89Kč–139Kč) offer amazing value and inevitably attract crowds of diners. There's also a good choice of beers on tap.

Mon–Thu 11–11, Fri 11am–12.30am (kitchen closes at 10.30), Sat 12.30–12.30, Sun 12.30pm–11pm
L 140Kč, D 500Kč, Wine 150Kč
Karlovo náměstí
Tram 3, 4, 6, 10, 14, 16, 18, 22, 23, 24 to Karlovo náměstí

LETENSKÝ ZÁMEČEK

Off map 227 E5
Letenské sady 341, Holešovice, Prague 7
Tel 233 378 200
www.letenskyzamecek.cz
The 'Letna Mansion' is adjacent to what is probably the largest beer garden in Prague, with an enviable location on Letná Plain, overlooking the Vltava and Staré Město (Old Town). Nicely shaded by trees, it attracts a large and sometimes raucous crowd in summer, and is certainly a place to absorb some local atmosphere. For more refined refreshment, try the upper floor of the mansion itself, where the Belcredi restaurant offers the freshest of French food. There is also the Ullmann restaurant on the ground floor and the garden restaurant.

Daily 11–11
Restaurant: L 750Kč, D 1,000Kč, Wine 240Kč
Tram 1, 8, 15, 25, 26 to Letenské náměstí

LOBKOWICZ PALACE CAFÉ

Map 226 D5
Jiřská 3, Hradčany, Prague 1
Tel 233 356 978
www.lobkowiczevents.cz
Far and away the most pleasant place to take a break from seeing the Castle sights, this aristocratic establishment occupies a pair of elegant rooms in one of the town palaces of the Lobkowicz dynasty. The spacious balcony, heated in winter, gives a privileged view of the Castle gardens and Malá Strana. The snacks, soups and salads are out of the ordinary too.

Daily 10–6
L 375Kč, Wine 440Kč
Malostranská
Tram 12, 18, 20, 22, 23 to Malostranská

LVÍ DVŮR

Map 226 C5
U Prašného mostu 6/51, Hradčany, Prague 1
Tel 224 372 361
www.lvidvur.cz
Upholding the memory of the wild beasts once kept here for the pleasure of the emperor, the busy 'Lion Court' enjoys a strategic position on the northern approach to the Castle. It has attractive interiors and a terrace with castle and cathedral views. The cuisine is Bohemian and international. The real speciality is the tasty suckling pig; you can get a whole one for 5,500Kč or a more manageable portion for around 500Kč.

Daily 11–11
L 650Kč, D 800Kč, Wine 450Kč
Tram 22, 23 to Pražský hrad

MAILSI

Map 229 K6
Lipanská 1, Žižkov, Prague 3
Tel 222 717 783
The Mailsi is the first Pakistani restaurant in Prague, and is still quite a rarity. It's worth seeking out in the inner, multi-ethnic borough of Žižkov, should you find yourself in need of a curry to combat dumpling fatigue. The setting is unpretentious, the service amiable, the minced beef and tiger shrimp are just as they should be, and the prices are more than reasonable. Credit cards are not accepted.

Daily 12–3, 6–11
L, D 250Kč, Wine 165Kč
Tram 5, 9, 26 to Lipanská

MÁNES

Map 227 E8
Masarykovo nábřeží 250, Nové Město, Prague 1
Tel 224 931 112
www.restaurace-manes.cz

The white Mánes building was constructed in 1930 as the headquarters of the prestigious art association of the same name. Picasso, Dalí and Frank Lloyd Wright were members. The building is a riverside landmark. Linking the 'mainland' to Slovanský ostrov (Slavonic Island), it's a key structure in the history of Modernist Czech architecture, but also incorporates the onion-domed water tower which had stood here since the Middle Ages. Enjoy standard Czech and international fare inside or on the summer terrace.

Daily 11–11
L 250Kč, D 450Kč, Wine 170Kč
Tram 17, 21 to Jiráskovo náměstí

METAMORPHIS

Map 228 F5
Malá Štupartská 5/636, Staré Město, Prague 1
Tel 221 771 068
www.metamorphis.cz
Reached by a winding staircase, the Romanesque cellar of this ancient building at the eastern entrance to the Týn Court (or Ungelt) is now a romantic restaurant serving a range of Czech and international dishes, as well as providing breakfast for the hotel guests. The ground-floor café specializes in fairly standard pizzas and pastas, but the great attraction here is to sit outside and enjoy the atmosphere of the medieval courtyard with the view of the spiky spires of the Týn Church poking up above the rooftops.

Daily 9am–1am
L 350Kč, D 600Kč, Wine 435Kč
Náměstí Republiky
Tram 5, 8, 14 to Náměstí Republiky

MLÝNEC

Map 227 E6
Novotného lávka 9, Staré Město,
Prague 1
Tel 221 082 208
www.zatisigroup.cz

This establishment has an
unusual location on Novotného
lávka, the pier-like structure
protruding into the Vltava just
by Karlův most (Charles
Bridge). The plush interior
leads to a glazed wall and
an outdoor terrace with an
incomparable close-up view of
the bridge itself and of the Old
Town bridge tower. The
cosmopolitan cuisine is first
class—let yourself be tempted
by the baked sea bass
with baby bokchoy and
coconut condiment.
🕐 Daily 12–3, 5.30–11
🍽 L 600Kč, D 1,000Kč, Wine 690Kč
🚊 Tram 17, 18 to Karlovy lázně

MODRÁ ŘEKA

Map 229 H7
Mánesova 13, Vinohrady,
Prague 2
Tel 222 251 601
Tucked away in a side-street
on the slope above the main
railway station is the little 'Blue
River', a Balkan hideaway run
by a husband and wife. They
serve their regular customers
with hearty, well-spiced fare
typical of the former
Yugoslavia, and you are
unlikely to find more authentic
čevapčiči (spicy meatballs)
anywhere else in town.
🕐 Mon–Fri 12–11, Sat–Sun 5–11pm
🍽 L 200Kč, D 250Kč, Wine 200Kč
🚊 Tram 11 to Italská

MYSLIVNA

Map 229 K7
Jagellonská 21, Vinohrady,
Prague 3
Tel 222 723 252
www.myslivna-restaurant.com
Somewhat off the beaten track,
but only two metro stops and a
short walk from Václavské

náměstí (Wenceslas Square),
the long-established
'Gamekeeper's Lodge' claims
to be Prague's best game
restaurant, and it's certainly
worth coming to Vinohrady to
check it out (reservations are
recommended). The suppliers
and chefs are all specialists,
and your hearty plateful of
venison, boar, pheasant or
roebuck will be succulent,
tender and very satisfying—as
well as excellent value. You
may or may not be put off by
the animal parts and hunting
memorabilia with which the
place is decorated.
🕐 Daily 11am–midnight
🍽 L 300Kč, D 500Kč, Wine 230Kč
🚇 Jiřího z Poděbrad
🚊 Tram 11 to Jiřího z Poděbrad

NEBOZÍZEK

Map 226 C7
Petřínské sady 411, Malá Strana,
Prague 1
Tel 257 315 329
www.nebozizek.cz
The 'Little Auger' occupies a
wonderful panoramic position
on Petřín Hill, where it was
once an aristocrat's summer
retreat set among the
vineyards. Its name comes
from the corkscrew course of
the paths which thread the
hillside. The international
dishes served inside or on the
terrace are perfectly adequate,
but the view is what people
come for, so reserve your table
early. You can also stay here,
in one of the restaurant's
two apartments.
🕐 Daily 11–11
🍽 L 450Kč, D 550Kč, Wine 160Kč
🚊 Tram 6, 9, 12, 20, 22, 23 to Újezd,
then to middle station of the *lanovka*
(funicular)

OLYMPIA

Map 226 D7
Vítězná 7, Smíchov,
Prague 5
Tel 251 511 079
www.olympia-restaurant.cz
The Olympia, like the Celnice
(▷ 233) and the Kolkovna
(▷ 236), is one of the
super-pubs established by the
Plzeňský Prazdroj brewery. It's
just on the Malá Strana side of
the Most legií (Bridge of the
Legions), and has proved to be
a hit with people looking for
something superior to the
ordinary pub, yet with all the
traditional atmosphere. Solid

Czech food is served with what
many consider to be the
world's best beer.
🕐 Daily 11am–midnight
🍽 L 200Kč, D 300Kč, Wine 350Kč
🚊 Tram 6, 9, 12, 20, 22, 23 to Újezd

OŽIVLÉ DŘEVO

Map 226 B6
Strahovské nádvoří 1, Hradčany
Tel 220 517 274
www.ozivledrevo.cz
The strangely named 'Revived
Wood' enjoys a breathtaking
view of the Castle and the red
rooftops of Malá Strana,
perched over the orchards
dropping away from the
Strahov monastery complex
(of which it forms part). Dining
on the terrace is consequently
quite an experience, but the
vaulted interior has attractions
too. The cuisine is international
and refined Bohemian, of
a quality that tempted
ex-President Havel to bring
the Rolling Stones this way.
🕐 Daily 11–11
🍽 L 800Kč, D 1,000Kč, Wine 650Kč
🚊 Tram 22, 23 to Pohořelec

PALÁC KINSKÝCH

Map 228 F6
Týnská ulička 606/3,
Staré Město, Prague 1
Tel 224 810 750
www.palac-kinskych.cz
The Kinský Palace is
considered to be the city's
loveliest rococo edifice.
Originally divided up into
shops and apartments (Franz
Kafka once lived there), it now
houses some of the treasures
of the Národní galerie (National
Gallery), as well as this sophisticated restaurant, reached
from the lane to the rear. The
Czech and international dishes
are prepared by an acclaimed
chef, and have been appreciated by a galaxy of stars and
celebrities. The wine list is
exceptionally interesting.
🕐 Mon–Fri 12–3, 6–11, Sat–Sun
6–11pm
🍽 L 450Kč, D 900Kč, Wine 490Kč
🚇 Staroměstská
🚊 Tram 17, 18 to Staroměstská

PARNAS

Map 227 E7
Smetanovo nábřeží 2, Staré Město,
Prague 1
Tel 224 218 521
www.restaurantparnas.cz
The Parnas is a sister
establishment to the famous

PÁLFFY PALÁC

Map 226 D5
Valdštejnská 14, Malá Strana,
Prague 1
Tel 257 530 522
www.palffy.cz

You could ride a horse up the splendid staircase of this building, one of several Malá Strana palaces lining Valdštejnská, just below the Castle. The high-ceilinged, second-floor dining room, with its crystal chandeliers, offers a rare chance to dine in baroque splendour. There's a small terrace too. The refined international cuisine more than matches the setting and represents exceptional value, especially if you book the lunchtime *table d'hôte* meal in advance. There's an extensive and well-considered wine cellar.
🕐 Daily 11–11
🍴 L 750Kč, D 1,000Kč, Wine 490Kč
Ⓜ Malostranská
🚋 Tram 12, 18, 20, 22, 23 to Malostranská

Slavia café next door (▷ 241), and looks out on to the same fabulous view of river and Castle. Even without the view, it would still be worth coming here for the superb art deco interior, with its marble floor and panelled walls, and the excellent cuisine. The sophisticated versions of traditional Czech stomach-fillers like goulash, beef sirloin and breast of pheasant, complemented by an equally refined and extensive wine list, are unlikely to disappoint.
🕐 Daily 12–11
🍴 L 450Kč, D 600Kč, Wine 220Kč
🚋 Tram 6, 9, 17, 18, 21, 22, 23 to Národní divadlo

PEKLO

Map 226 B6
Strahovské nádvoří 1/132, Hradčany, Prague 1
Tel 220 516 652
www.peklo.com
The monks of the Strahov monastery were great horticulturalists and they called the garden they created at the very top of Petřín Hill 'Paradise'; the wine cellar dug beneath was named 'Hell' (*Peklo*). The restaurant now installed here has kept the name, though the vines that once grew all around have long since disappeared and the wine list features Moravian rather than Czech wines. It's quite an experience to sit here deep underground and dine on such dishes as 'Mephisto pork'.
🕐 Daily 12–12
🍴 L 500Kč, D 650Kč, Wine 225Kč
🚋 Tram 22, 23 to Pohořelec

LA PERLE DE PRAGUE

Map 227 E8
Rašínovo nábřeží 80, Nové Město, Prague 2
Tel 221 984 160
www.laperle.cz
The two-floor 'Pearl of Prague' is one of the most spectacularly sited of the city's eating places. It sits atop the controversial Frank Gehry-designed 'Dancing Building' on its prominent riverside site. With a panorama stretching up and down the Vltava, and an immaculate interior, the scene is set for some of the best French cuisine, accompanied by a selection of fine wines. The restaurant's signature dish is rack of lamb.
🕐 Tue–Sat 12–2, 7–10.30, Mon 7–10.30pm
🍴 L 600Kč, D 1,200Kč, Wine 550Kč
Ⓜ Karlovo náměstí
🚋 Tram 17, 21 to Jiráskovo náměstí; tram 3, 4, 6, 10, 14, 16, 18, 22, 23, 24 to Karlovo náměstí

PLZEŇSKÁ RESTAURACE

Map 228 G6
Náměstí Republiky 5, Staré Město, Prague 1
Tel 222 002 770
www.obecnidum.cz
The 'Pilsner Restaurant' is the basement beer hall of the sumptuous art nouveau Obecní dům (Municipal House). The decoration is fabulous, featuring lively ceramic murals of rustic scenes. You sit at long central tables or side alcoves, and dine on well-prepared traditional Bohemian dishes, washed down with *Plzeňský prazdroj*—Pilsner Urquell—all the while being serenaded by a wandering accordionist.
🕐 Daily 12–11
🍴 L 250Kč, D 500Kč, Wine 280Kč
Ⓜ Náměstí Republiky
🚋 Tram 5, 8, 14 to Náměstí Republiky

POTREFENÁ HUSA

Map 228 F5
Bílkova 5, Staré Město, Prague 1
Tel 222 326 626
www.potrefenahusa.com
www.pivovarystaropramen.cz
The 'Shot Goose' is one of a chain of new-style bars and restaurants designed to appeal to the new generation of prosperous young Czechs tired of supping half-litres of *pivo* in smoky, old-fashioned pubs. It's bright, sleek and cheerful, and offers good, standard food, such as roast goose or duck breast with dumplings, as well as a wide range of drinks (including several types of beer). This particular branch occupies the lower ground floor of the 'House of Teachers', one of Prague's rare Cubist buildings. Other branches are at Resslova 1 in Nové Město and at Vinohradská 104 in Vinohrady.
🕐 Daily 11am–midnight
🍴 L 300Kč, D 400Kč, Wine 155Kč
Ⓜ Staroměstská
🚋 Tram 17 to Právnická fakulta

PRAVDA

Map 228 F5
Pařížská 17, Staré Město, Prague 1
Tel 222 326 203
www.pravda.bacchusgroup.cz
This trendy establishment is very much at home among the chic fashion stores and boutiques on Prague's most fashionable shopping street. The interior is designed in a beautifully calculated minimalist style, and the cuisine is as cosmopolitan as the crowd it attracts, featuring stylishly prepared dishes from places as diverse as Scandinavia and Thailand, Iceland and Italy.
🕐 Daily 12–12
🍴 L 900Kč, D 1,250Kč, Wine 800Kč
Ⓜ Staroměstská
🚋 Tram 17, 18 to Staroměstská

EATING

PŘÍČNÝ ŘEZ

Map 228 F7

Příčná 3, Nové Město, Prague 1

Tel 222 233 283

www.pricnyrez.cz

Opened in 2002, the stylish Příčný Řez has proved to be sensationally popular, offering friendly service, an attractive ethnic-themed atmosphere on three levels, and sizeable portions of inventive, tasty food at extremely reasonable prices. The 100Kč lunch deal is a real bargain and there is a special menu for Sunday brunch. You are unlikely to find a table if you haven't booked in advance. Credit cards are not accepted.

🕑 Mon–Fri 10.30am–11pm, Sat–Sun 11.30–11

🍴 L 250Kč, D 300Kč, Wine 175Kč

🚇 Karlovo náměstí

🚊 Tram 3, 4, 6, 10, 14, 16, 18, 22, 23, 24 to Karlovo náměstí

RADOST FX

Map 228 G8

Bělehradská 120, Vinohrady, Prague 2

Tel 224 254 776

www.radostfx.cz

This bar, café and nightclub, a short walk from Václavské náměstí (Wenceslas Square) is also reckoned by many to be the city's best vegetarian restaurant. There's an exceptionally wide range of healthy eating options to tempt the trendy customers, who can admire the funky surroundings while sitting on one of the old sofas. The serving staff are as hip as the food and atmosphere, and clubbers will appreciate the liberal opening hours. Credit cards are not accepted.

🕑 Restaurant: Mon–Fri 9am–3am, Sat–Sun 10.30am–5am

🍴 L, D 300Kč, Wine 150Kč

🚇 I.P. Pavlova

🚊 Tram 4, 6, 10, 11, 16, 22, 23 to I.P. Pavlova

RASOI RESTAURANT/ BOMBAY CAFÉ

Map 228 F5

Dlouhá 13, Staré Město, Prague 1

Tel 222 328 400/721 882 557

www.rasoi.cz

While the Bombay Café specializes in lip-smacking cocktails, the Rasoi restaurant in the cellar serves tasty dishes from its north Indian repertoire, cooked to perfection in a Tandoor oven. Indian restaurants are a rarity in central Prague, and Rasoi is well placed, just a short stroll along curving Dlouhá street from Staroměstské náměstí (Old Town Square).

🕑 Restaurant: daily 12–11. Café: daily 5pm–4am

🍴 L, D 650Kč, Wine 500Kč

🚊 Tram 5, 8, 14 to Dlouhá třída

ŘECKÁ TAVERNA

Map 228 G5

Revoluční 16, Nové Město, Prague 1

Tel 222 317 762

www.gyros-gr.com

The 'Greek Tavern' is on Revolution Street, the road that divides the Old Town from the northern section of the New Town. It offers standard, but very acceptable, Grecian fare in a characteristic setting of fake columns and Mediterranean murals. There's another branch—'Old Athens'—at the Nový Smíchov shopping mall.

🕑 Daily 11am–midnight

🍴 L 300Kč, D 375Kč, Wine 140Kč

🚇 Náměstí Republiky

🚊 Tram 5, 8, 14 to Dlouhá třída

REYKJAVIK

Map 227 E6

Karlova 20, Staré Město, Prague 1

Tel 222 221 218

www.reykjavik.cz

Right in the middle of the tourist trail between Old Town Square and Karlův most (Charles Bridge), this Icelandic establishment was one of the first private restaurants founded after the Velvet Revolution. It serves succulent dishes made from fresh seafood flown in from Iceland, and attracts a faithful clientele to its comfortable interior and summer garden. Fish is the obvious choice, but there are meat-based dishes as well.

🕑 Daily 11am–midnight

🍴 L 600Kč, D 750Kč, Wine 150Kč

🚇 Staroměstská

🚊 Tram 17, 18 to Staroměstská

RYBÁŘSKÝ KLUB

Map 227 D6

U Sovových mlýnů 1, Malá Strana, Prague 1

Tel 257 534 200

www.rybklub.cz

This modest establishment lies on the banks of the Vltava at the southern tip of Kampa Island, and is the restaurant arm of the 'Fishermen's Club'. It serves inexpensive dishes based on the fish that fill the country's rivers and countless ponds. Rybářský Klub is definitely the place to try such Czech dishes as smoked eel, roasted pike-perch or carp with garlic. Moravian white wine makes a good accompaniment.

🕑 Daily 12–11

🍴 L 350Kč, D 450Kč, Wine 379Kč

🚊 Tram 6, 9, 12, 20, 22, 23 to Újezd

RYBÍ TRH

Map 228 F6

Týnský dvůr 5, Staré Město, Prague 1

Tel 224 895 447

www.rybitrh.cz

At the other end of the spectrum from the 'Fishermen's Club' on Kampa Island is the sophisticated 'Fish Market' in the Týnský dvůr (Ungelt courtyard). Seafood from oceans all over the world is flown here daily. The restaurant prides itself on the freshness of its ingredients, the expert preparation and its stylish setting, which includes aquaria filled with tropical fish.

🕑 Daily 11am–midnight

🍴 L 750Kč, D 850Kč, Wine 600Kč

🚇 Staroměstská

🚊 Tram 17, 18 to Staroměstská

LE SAINT JACQUES

Map 228 F6

Jakubská 4, Staré Město, Prague 1

Tel 222 322 685

www.saint-jacques.cz

This family-run restaurant serves regional French cuisine. The menu uses fresh, imported ingredients. The atmosphere is calm, elegant and welcoming without being over-pretentious. Musical accompaniment is provided by a pianist and violinist whose repertoire seems inexhaustible.

🕑 Mon–Fri 12–3, 6–12, Sat–Sun 6pm–midnight

🍴 L, D 650Kč, Wine 500Kč

🚇 Náměstí Republiky

🚊 Tram 5, 8, 14 to Náměstí Republiky

SARAH BERNHARDT

Map 228 G5
U Obecního domu 1, Staré Město,
Prague 1
Tel 222 195 900
www.hotel-pariz.cz

The splendid restaurant of the Hotel Paříž (▷ 258) is the equal in over-the-top art nouveau sumptuousness to the adjacent Obecní dům (Municipal House). It still has something of the atmosphere of its early days, immortalized in Bohumil Hrabal's novel *I Served the King of England*, and if you are looking for a formal dining experience, this is the place to come. The menu combines the best of French and traditional Bohemian cuisine.

🕐 Daily 6.30–10, 12–4, 6–midnight
🍴 L 600Kč, D 1,000Kč, Wine 360Kč
Ⓜ Náměstí Republiky
🚋 Tram 5, 8, 14 to Náměstí Republiky

SLAVIA

Map 227 E7
Smetanovo nábřeží 2, Staré Město,
Prague 1
Tel 224 218 493/224 239 604
www.cafeslavia.cz

With its unsurpassable location opposite the Národní divadlo (National Theatre) and its superb view over the Vltava to the Castle, the Slavia still trades on its reputation as Prague's foremost literary café, the century-old haunt of artists, poets and, in Communist times, dissidents. Nowadays you are more likely to be sitting in its restored art deco splendour in the company of fellow tourists, but the Slavia remains an essential stop-off in your exploration of Prague.

🕐 Daily 8am–11pm
🍴 L 200Kč, D 300Kč, Wine 220Kč
🚋 Tram 6, 9, 17, 18, 21, 22, 23 to Národní divadlo

SQUARE

Map 226 D6
Malostranské náměstí 5/28,
Malá Strana, Prague 1
Tel 296 826 104
www.kampagroup.com

In the shadow of the great baroque Kostel svatého Mikuláš (Church of St. Nicholas), the Malostranská *kavárna* was one of the city's most popular cafés and meeting places. It still is, though the name has changed and the café has transformed into an extremely chic restaurant. Subtle designer interiors, outside seating and a Mediterranean-style menu draw a fashionable crowd of expatriates and prosperous young Czechs who come to dine in some style. You may find the atmosphere more appealing than what is actually put on your plate.

🕐 Daily 8am–1am
🍴 L 700Kč, D 900Kč, Wine 475Kč
🚋 Tram 12, 20, 22, 23 to Malostranské náměstí

TULIP CAFÉ

Map 227 E7
Opatovická 3, Nové Město,
Prague 1
Tel 224 930 019
www.tulipcafe.cz
Tucked away in the tightly packed streets to the south of the Národní divadlo (National Theatre), this cool and stylish café has been described as a cross between a Viennese coffee-house and a Californian cocktail bar (with an emphasis on California rather than Vienna). It's one of the strongholds of American expatriate life in Prague, with an inventive schedule of events, including cabaret, comedy, music and readings, as well as drinks, snacks and Sunday brunch.

🕐 Mon–Wed 11am–midnight, Thu–Sat 11am–1am, Sun 11–11
🍴 L 100Kč, D 300Kč, Wine 145Kč
Ⓜ Národní třída
🚋 Tram 6, 9, 18, 21, 22, 23 to Narodní třída

U CÍSAŘŮ

Map 226 C5
Loretánská 5/175, Hradčany,
Prague 1
Tel 220 518 484
www.ucisaru.cz
The atmospheric 'Emperor' evokes a distinguished past, with royal portraits and its generally over-the-top décor of arms and armour and the occasional bearskin. Imperial visitors may be rare nowadays, but the roll-call of recent visitors includes presidents and prime ministers. You dine beneath vaulted ceilings from a menu of Bohemian and international dishes, including game such as boar and elk. The 13th-century cellars are particularly well-stocked and feature wines from around the world.

🕐 Daily 9am–1am
🍴 L 600Kč, D 700Kč, Wine 690Kč
🚋 Tram 22, 23 to Pohořelec

U FLEKŮ

Map 227 E7
Křemencova 11, Nové Město,
Prague 1
Tel 224 934 019-20
www.ufleku.cz
Regulars and visitors have been crowding into this famous pub for more than 500 years. Its picturesque interiors and beer garden have room for an astounding 1,200 guests, all efficiently served with Old Bohemian cuisine and the excellent dark beer brewed on the premises. Brass bands and a cabaret provide background noise and entertainment, and there's even a museum.

🕐 Daily 9am–11pm
🍴 L 300Kč, D 450Kč, Wine 183Kč
Ⓜ Národní třída
🚋 Tram 6, 9, 18, 21, 22, 23 to Národní třída

U KALICHA

Map 228 G8
Na Bojišti 12–14, Nové Město,
Prague 2
Tel 296 189 600
www.ukalicha.cz

'The Chalice' is perhaps the most famous pub in Prague, and a visit here is a high priority for fans of Jaroslav Hašek's immortal comic creation, the *Good Soldier*

Švejk (1921–23). This was Švejk's regular watering hole, the place where he was arrested for inadvertently mocking Emperor Franz Josef at the outbreak of World War I. You might see his reincarnation here as one of the members of the brass band that entertains visitors from all over the world as they down their half-litres of Pilsner and tuck into their duck and dumplings. Reserve ahead.

🕓 Daily 11–11
🍽 L, D 450Kč
Ⓜ I.P. Pavlova
🚋 Tram 4, 6, 10, 16, 22, 23 to I.P. Pavlova

U LABUTÍ

Map 226 C5
Hradčanské náměstí 11, Hradčany,
Prague 1
Tel 220 511 190
www.ulabuti.cz

On the square in front of the Castle, in a building dating back to the 14th century, U Labutí is a useful though quite expensive port of call in the Hradčany district. In the mid-20th century it was briefly the residence of the family of former US Secretary of State Madeleine Albright. The menu offers a mixture of traditional Czech and international cuisine, along with an extensive wine list, and you can eat outside in the pleasant courtyard in summer. There is also

U MALÍŘŮ

Map 226 D6
Maltézské náměstí 11,
Malá Strana, Prague 1
Tel 257 530 318
www.umaliru.cz

This lovely old building 'At the Painter', on a quiet square in the southern part of Malá Strana, was a restaurant as long ago as the 16th century. Its present owners offer the best of French cuisine. Dishes of impeccable quality are prepared and served with the utmost care and attention to detail, in an intimate setting enhanced by murals and ceiling paintings. An exceptional wine list complements one of Prague's most refined dining experiences. The *chateaubriand flambé à la sauce aux champignons Shii-také* is only one of many temptations. Reserve ahead.

🕓 Daily 11.30–11.30
🍽 L 1,000Kč, D 1,800Kč, Wine 950Kč
🚋 Tram 12, 20, 22, 23 to Malostranské náměstí

a pub serving simpler, less expensive meals and Pilsner on tap.

🕓 Restaurant: daily 12–11.30. Pub: daily 10–10
🍽 L 550Kč, D 800Kč, Wine 420Kč (less in pub)
🚋 Tram 22, 23 to Pražský hrad

U MALTÉZSKÝCH RYTÍŘŮ

Map 226 D6
Prokopská 10/297, Malá Strana,
Prague 1
Tel 257 530 075
www.umaltezskychrytiru.cz

This intimate, family-run restaurant, in a quiet corner of Malá Strana, occupies a building which was once part of the domain of the Knights of

Malta. The friendly welcome, the candlelit charm and the good Czech cooking have made it a popular venue, and you are unlikely to find a table unless you have booked well in advance.

🕓 Daily 1pm–11pm
🍽 L 500Kč, D 700Kč, Wine 140Kč
🚋 Tram 12, 20, 22, 23 to Malostranské náměstí

U MECENÁŠE

Map 226 C6
Malostranské náměstí 10,
Malá Strana, Prague 1
Tel 257 531 631

Housed in 'The Golden Lion', one of the arcaded Renaissance houses lining the south side of Malá Strana Square, this is one of Prague's most atmospheric restaurants, the haunt of the famous 17th-century executioner Jan Mydlář. The hangman's signature forms part of the décor of the two-roomed interior, along with firearms, swords, fragments of the gallows and darkwood furnishings. The food is a mixture of refined traditional Bohemian and international dishes.

🕓 Daily 11am–11.30pm
🍽 L 450Kč, D 650Kč, Wine 290Kč
🚋 Tram 12, 20, 22, 23 to Malostranské náměstí

U MEDVÍDKŮ

Map 228 E7
Na Perštýně 7, Staré Město,
Prague 1
Tel 224 211 916
www.umedvidku.cz

'At the Little Bears' is one of the most famous pubs in town, and fairly unusual in that it serves not the beers of Prague or Plzeň (Pilsen), but the distinctive products of the České Budějovice (Budweis) brewery in southern Bohemia. You can choose from a range of hearty meat-based traditional dishes.

🕓 Daily 11.30–11
🍽 L 250Kč, D 300Kč, Wine 195Kč
Ⓜ Národní třída
🚋 Tram 6, 9, 18, 21, 22, 23 to Národní třída

U MODRÉ KACHNIČKY

Map 226 D6
Nebovidská 6, Malá Strana, Prague 1
Tel 257 320 308/257 316 745
www.umodrekachnicky.cz

In an obscure little lane in Malá Strana, the 'Blue Duckling' has been an institution since it first opened in the early 1990s, so much so that it has spawned another branch, U Modré Kachničky II, in Staré Město (Michalská 16, tel 224 213 418; open daily 11.30–11). Its success is partly due to its refined Bohemian cuisine, with the emphasis on game (including half-a-dozen varieties of duck), and the intimate atmosphere of its comfortable little dining rooms, each decorated individually and furnished with antique pieces.

🕐 Daily 12–4, 6.30–midnight
🍴 L 600Kč, D 1,000Kč, Wine 420Kč
🚊 Tram 12, 20, 22, 23 to Hellichova

U MODRÉ RŮŽE
Map 228 F6
Rytířská 16, Staré Město, Prague 1
Tel 224 225 873
www.umodreruze.cz
Many of the historic houses in the Old Town have vaulted cellars, which once formed the ground floor of the building, and only disappeared below surface when the whole ground level of the area was raised to combat frequent flooding. The 'Blue Rose' occupies one of these atmospheric interiors, and serves a good selection of traditional Bohemian dishes. People with a small appetite might think twice before ordering the set meal, which consists of trout, goose liver, duck and neck of pork and finishes off with a hearty strudel.

🕐 Daily 11.30–11.30
🍴 L 1,000Kč, D 1,150Kč, Wine 870Kč
🚇 Můstek

U PASTÝŘKY
Off map 228 G9
Bělehradská 15, Nusle, Prague 4
Tel 222 564 335
www.pastyrka.cz
'At the Shepherdess' is a koliba, or log cabin, first built as part of the Czechoslovak contribution to the 1967 World Expo in Montreal, and re-erected in the Prague suburb of Nusle. It's rather large for a log cabin, with room for 350 diners, who enjoy hearty mountain fare while being serenaded by a gypsy band. Very much a tour group attraction, it's great fun, and only a short tram trip from central Prague.

🕐 Daily 6pm–1am
🍴 D 350Kč
🚊 Tram 6, 11 to Náměstí bratří Synků

U PINKASŮ
Map 228 F6
Jungmannovo náměstí 16, Nové Město, Prague 1
Tel 221 111 150
www.upinkasu.cz
This historic pub/restaurant in the heart of the city has been thoroughly refurbished without losing any of its traditional atmosphere. The ground floor is for drinking the excellent draught Prazdroj (Urquell) beer; it was here in 1843 that Prague was first introduced to this tasty brew. The more elegant upstairs dining rooms are the place to tuck into refined versions of typical Bohemian cuisine. You can eat outside in summer.

🕐 Daily 10am–1am
🍴 L 100Kč, D 200Kč, Wine 170Kč
🚇 Můstek

U SÁDLŮ
Map 228 G5
Klimentská 2, Staré Město, Prague 1
Tel 224 813 874
www.usadlu.cz
The world of medieval chivalry is thoroughly re-created in the Knight Hall and Armament Room, hung with weaponry and lit by iron lamps. The menu is equally formidable, featuring challenges like 'Master Wenceslas's Gradual' (beefsteak in wild pepper) and 'Meat of the Apocalyptic Piglet' (variations of pork), to say nothing of the dessert named 'Cold Fairy'. It's all quite tasty and surprisingly good value.

🕐 Daily 11–11
🍴 L 150Kč, D 400Kč, Wine 200Kč
🚊 Tram 5, 8, 14 to Dlouhá třída

U SEDMI ŠVÁBŮ
Map 226 C6
Jánský vršek 14, Malá Strana, Prague 1
Tel 257 531 455
www.svabove.cz
On a little lane in the upper part of Malá Strana, the 'Seven Swabians' pub is one of the city's several 'medieval' establishments, and one of the most ambitious. Here you can roister the evening away drinking mead, eating food prepared according to time-honoured recipes and being entertained by fire-eaters, jugglers, swordsmen and gypsy dancers.

🕐 Daily 11–11
🍴 L, D 350Kč, Wine 90Kč
🚊 Tram 12, 20, 22, 23 Malostranská

U ŠEVCE MATOUŠE
Map 226 B6
Loretánské náměstí 4, Hradčany, Prague 1
Tel 220 514 536
'Matouš the Shoesmith's', which still shows signs of its former incarnation as a cobbler's workshop, specializes in steaks served with a variety of sauces. Footwear features in the décor and diners sit at former workbenches. The food is unpretentious and good value for this very touristy location in the Castle quarter.

🕐 Daily 11–4, 6–11
🍴 L 400Kč, D 500Kč, Wine 160Kč
🚊 Tram 22, 23 to Pohořelec

U ZLATÉ HRUŠKY
Map 226 B5
Nový svět 3, Hradčany, Prague 1
Tel 220 514 778
www.uzlatehrusky.cz
Next door to where court astronomer Tycho Brahe (▷ 28) once lived, the 'Golden Pear' is one of the city's most famous historic restaurants, enjoying an enviable reputation even in Communist times. In a lovely baroque building, on the delightful winding lane of Nový svět in the Castle quarter, it has a garden section on the far side of the lane. Czech and international dishes feature on the menu.

🕐 Daily 11.30am–1am
🍴 L 800Kč, D 1,500Kč, Wine 590Kč
🚊 Tram 22, 23 to Brusnice

UNIVERSAL
Map 227 E7
V Jirchářích 6, Nové Město, Prague 1
Tel 224 934 416
www.universalrestaurant.cz
This inexpensive, French-style restaurant not far from the Národní divadlo (National Theatre) is popular with the young crowd. It serves excellent salads and a range of special dishes, including rarities (in Prague) like choucroute from Alsace and magret of duck. The daily menu is especially good value.

🕐 Mon–Sat 11.30am–midnight, Sun 11–11
🍴 L 150Kč, D 375Kč, Wine 160Kč
🚇 Národní třída
🚊 Tram 6, 9, 18, 21, 22, 23 to Národní třída

U ZLATÉ STUDNĚ

Map 226 D5

U Zlaté studně 4/166, Malá Strana, Prague 1

Tel 257 533 322

www.zlatastudna.cz

Hidden away at the top of a steep lane is the 'Golden Well', both a luxury hotel and an elegant restaurant. The restaurant reopened early in the 21st century after a long period of renovation. Its international menu featuring sophisticated versions of Bohemian specials, including game, makes it worth the climb, but an added reward is the glorious view over the city from the terrace.

🕐 Daily 7am–11pm

🍴 L 1,100Kč, D 1,300Kč, Wine 1,000Kč

Ⓜ Malostranská

🚋 Tram 12, 20, 22, 23 to Malostranská or Malostranské náměstí or 18 to Malostranská

VČELÍN

Map 229 J9

Kodaňská 5, Vršovice, Prague 10

Tel 271 742 541

The 'Beehive' is a cool pub-type eatery in the rapidly gentrifying inner suburb of Vršovice, just a few tram stops from central Prague. It attracts a young and trendy crowd with its cosmopolitan menu, which represents excellent value for money. There are also several kinds of beer on tap.

🕐 Mon–Fri 11am–midnight, Sat 11.30am–midnight, Sun 11.30–11

🍴 L 125Kč, D 175Kč, Wine 130Kč

🚋 Tram 4, 22, 23 to Ruská

VELRYBA

Map 228 F7

Opatovická 24, Nové Město, Prague 1

Tel 224 931 444

This cellar café-bar, founded soon after the Velvet Revolution, is popular with youngish intellectual types. Part of the attraction is the exhibitions put on in the room to the rear. It serves a good selection of vegetarian and other light dishes, as well as an extensive choice of drinks.

🕐 Daily 11am–midnight

🍴 L, D 125Kč, Wine 144Kč

Ⓜ Národní třída

🚋 Tram 6, 9, 18, 21, 22, 23 to Národní třída

V ZÁTIŠÍ

Map 227 E6

Liliová 1, Staré Město, Prague 1

Tel 222 221 155/222 220 627

www.zatisigroup.cz

Just off Betlémské náměstí (Bethlehem Square), the 'Retreat' or 'Still Life' was one of the first gourmet restaurants to open after the Velvet Revolution, and it has often been acclaimed as the best restaurant in Prague. It is still among the leading restaurants of its kind, with elegant interiors, sophisticated Czech and international cuisine, and an exceptional wine list—at a price.

🕐 Daily 12–3, 5.30–11

🍴 L 1,000Kč, D 1,300Kč, Wine 290Kč

Ⓜ Národní třída

🚋 Tram 6, 9, 18, 21, 22, 23 to Národní třída

ZAHRADA V OPEŘE

Map 228 G7

Legerova 75, Nové Město, Prague 1

Tel 224 239 685/724 138 020

www.zahradavopere.cz

The 'Garden in the Opera' has the Státní opera Praha (Prague State Opera) as a neighbour, and is popular with opera-goers before and after the show. The restaurant's décor is the highly individual and contemporary creation of the design team responsible for remodelling the Castle's presidential suite. The high-quality Czech and international dishes are more conventional, but offer excellent value, given the unique surroundings.

🕐 Daily 11.30am–midnight

🍴 L 350Kč, D 600Kč, Wine 215Kč

Ⓜ Muzeum

ZEN ZEN

Map 228 F7

Ve Smečkách 21, Nové Město, Prague 1

Escape from city stress into this attractive restaurant, with its restful atmosphere

permeated with delicious aromas. The café and tea room serve connoisseur brews and homemade cakes, while the restaurant offers tasty and inexpensive vegetarian, vegan and gluten-free dishes. Credit cards are not accepted.

🕐 Restaurant: Mon–Fri 11–10, Sat–Sun 12–10. Café: Mon–Sat 2–10

🍴 L 90Kč, D 150Kč, Wine 150Kč

Ⓜ Muzeum

ZLATÁ PRAHA

Map 227 E5

Náměstí Curieových 43/5, Staré Město, Prague 1

Tel 296 639 914

www.zlatapraharestaurant.cz

The 'Golden Prague' rooftop restaurant of the InterContinental hotel (▷ 256) was perhaps the most prestigious restaurant of the Communist period. It has continued to maintain the highest standards of comfort and cuisine, as well as providing a romantic view over many of the city's spires. The changing menu features tempting interpretations of traditional Czech cooking—the leg of rabbit and saddle of venison are some of the best you'll find—plus sophisticated international dishes, with wines to match. Its Sunday brunches are popular.

🕐 Daily 12–3, 6–11.30

🍴 L 1,000Kč, D 1,350Kč, Wine 690Kč

Ⓜ Staroměstská

🚋 Tram 17 to Právnická fakulta

ZVONICE

Map 228 G6

Jindřišská věž, Jindřišská ulice, Nové Město, Prague 1

Tel 224 220 009

www.restaurantzvonice.cz

This is one of the most unusual places to eat in Prague. The bell-tower of Kostel svatého Jindřicha (St. Henry's Church) has been restored and opened to the public. There are fabulous views over Prague from the top floor and from the restaurant on two of the lower—but still high—floors. It's a romantic setting, with the old beams of the belfry all around, as well as the 'Maria' bell of 1518. The fine Czech and international cuisine has prices that reflect the uniqueness of the surroundings.

🕐 Daily 11.30am–midnight

🍴 L 600Kč, D 1,000Kč, Wine 690Kč

🚋 Tram 3, 9, 14, 24 to Jindřišská

EATING

STAYING IN PRAGUE

Prague excels in historic properties, which have been carefully restored and made into comfortable, characterful places to stay. After several years when the demand for hotel beds outstripped supply, the accommodation situation in the city is now much more balanced. Occupancy rates are nevertheless high and it is best to make reservations well in advance. A range of options is available and the number of good, mid-range hotels is increasing.

A suite in the Radisson SAS Alcron Hotel

The reception desk at Le Palais, Vinohrady

Views from the roof garden of the Hotel Aria

The elegant lobby of the Hotel Evropa

LUXURY
International hotels tend to provide the comforts, services and facilities implied in their rates. Many are in converted historic buildings: The Four Seasons is an outstanding example, and also has a key location by the river, just downstream from Karlův most (Charles Bridge). Modern, purpose-built hotels include the Hilton and InterContinental.

MID-RANGE
The city is full of four-star hotels, often rather small, occupying buildings of character in the central districts. Rates are likely to be at international four-star level, but facilities may not be. A previous deficiency in three-star hotels is well on the way to being remedied, often in areas outside the centre, but linked by public transportation.

BUDGET
The number of one- and two-star hotels is limited, but there are plenty of hostels. Remember that many hotels will put an extra bed in a room for a nominal charge. For longer stays, it may make sense to rent an apartment. Some have a central location, but there are plenty more in the suburbs. Pensions are small, privately run hotels or guest houses.

WHERE TO STAY
The city's excellent public transportation system means that most places in the metropolitan area are accessible by metro, tram or bus. However, Prague is a delight to explore on foot, and your stay will be much enhanced if your lodgings are within walking distance of at least some of the major attractions. This is not difficult, as most hotels are either in one of the historic districts or very near. The Castle quarter, Hradčany, is quiet

and full of atmosphere, but with a more limited choice of places to stay, and it is, of course, at the top of the hill. Lovely left-bank Malá Strana is a popular choice, tranquil except for a very few streets, and with many hotels in converted palaces and historic houses. On the other side of Karlův most (Charles Bridge), Staré Město (Old Town) is in the middle of things, with plenty of historic places to stay and lots of restaurants and entertainment venues. Much more extensive, Nové Město (New Town) has a great variety of accommodation. Of the suburbs, the inner boroughs of Vinohrady (middle-class) and Smíchov (working-class, but well on the way to gentrification) are the most interesting, with places to stay ranging from modest pensions to the luxurious Mövenpick, whose two sections are linked by a spectacular funicular. Elsewhere outside central Prague, the key factor is the quality of public transportation—aim to be near a metro station.

High season runs from April to the end of October, plus Christmas and New Year, but special deals are often available, especially for weekend stays.

ACCOMMODATION AGENCIES
The most reliable is probably the city's official information agency, PIS (▷ 271). Staff at its offices will help with immediate accommodation. For advance bookings contact Pragotour, Prague 5, Arbesovo náměstí 4, tel 221 714 133, e-mail: pragotour@pis.cz. You can also try AVE, Hlavní nádraží (main station), Nové Město, Prague 2, tel 224 223 226, or at the airport, tel 220 114 650; www.avetravel.cz

For apartment rentals booked in advance from the UK try Escape to Prague, tel 07971 581675; www.escapetoprague.com

STAYING

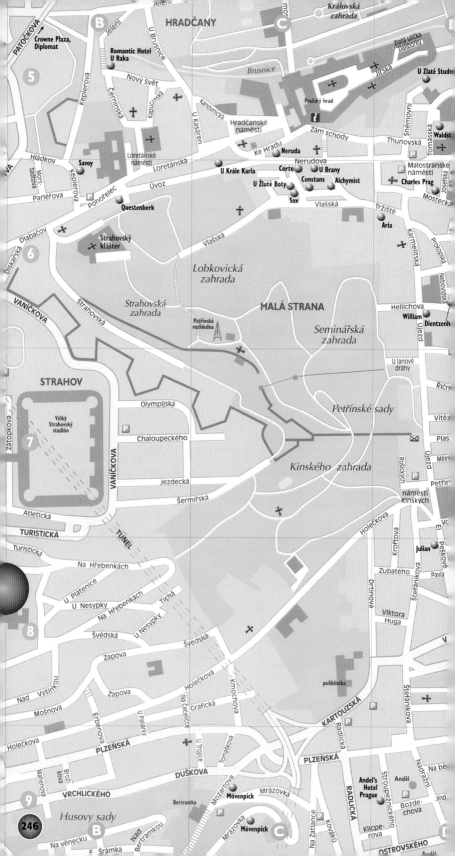

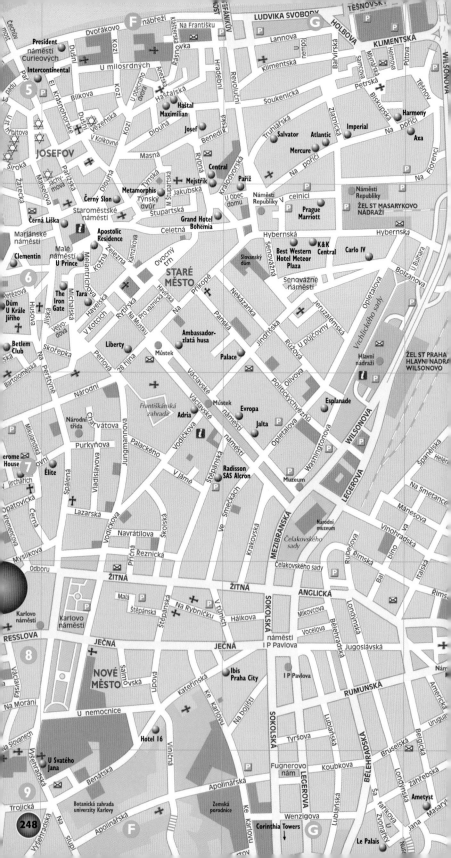

Hilton Prague

H

Pobřežní

P

Sokolovská

Florenc

Za Poříčskou bránou

i

KŘIŽÍKOVA

Florenc

Prunílu

Malého

TROCNOVSKÁ

Vítkova

Jirsíkova

Sokolovská

J

Karlínské
náměstí

P

Peckova

Kollárova

Křižíkova

Vítkova

Pernerova

Pernerova

Křižíkova

Sokolovská

Křižíkova

K

Thámova

5

Národní
památník

Lyčkovo
nám

Řeřinova

Sovova

Pernerova

Lukášova

Roháčova

Komeňského
nám

České

Žerotínova

HUSITSKÁ

HUSITSKÁ

Řehořova

KONĚVOVA

Roháčova

Rokycanova

Lukášova

Roháčova

ŽIŽKOV

Orebit
ská

Dalimilova

Prokopovo
nám

PROKOPOVA

6

Příběnická

Seifertova

Husinecká

Biskupcova

krásova

Biskupcova

Cimburkova

Štítnéhonám

Milíčova

Chlumova

Lipanská

Rokycanova

Lupáčova

Jeseniova

ská

Dům
odborových
svazů

Havelkova

Seifertova

Chlumova

Bořivojova

Chelčického

Italská

U Rajské zahrady

Přibý-
slavská

Vlkova

Nejedlého

Chvalova

Bořivojova

Lipanská

Táboritská

Ondříčkova

Sudoměřská

Vozová

Bořivojova

Ježkova

Kubelíkova

Čajkovského

Kubelíkova

Žižkovo
nám

Křišťanova

anova

Riegrovy sady

P

Na
Švihance

Slavíkova

Křížkovského

Šeříc-
kova

Skroupovo
náměstí

Fibichova

Mahlerovy
sady

Bořivojova

Radhošťská

7

Lucemburská

Choceradská

Krkonošská

Čerchov-
ská

Ondříčkova

Bloc
kova

Laubova

Milešovská

Jagellonská

Velehradská

Orlická

Přemyslovská

Polská

VINOHRADY

Polská

Slavíkova

Lucemburská

Ripská

U kanálky

Mánesova

Nejsvětějšího
Srdce Páně

Vinohradská

Blanická

Budečská

Sázavská

i

Vinohradská

Sady Svat Čecha

Jiřího
z Poděbrad

Perunova

Kolínská

SLEZSKÁ

8

SLEZSKÁ

SLEZSKÁ

Nitranská

Ripská

árodní
úm

KORUNNÍ

KORUNNÍ

KORUNNÍ

Blanická

Sázavská

Budečská

Šumavská

Tosca

Moravská

Chodská

Kladská

Dykova

Soběcká

Chorvatská

FRANCOUZSKÁ

Záhřebská

Masaryka

Máchova

Na Kozačce

Lužická

Šumavská

Hradešínská

Na Šafránce

Varšavská

Jana

Bezručovy
sady

Slovenská

Slovenská

Na Šafránce

Estonská

RUSKÁ

Norská

Finská

Bulharská

9

Abri

Čermákova

Smilovského

U
Havlíčkových

Voroněžská

Kozácká

Donská

Sevasto
polská

Krymská

Moskevská

Kodaňská

Heroldovy sady

Madrid

ŽIž

Slovinská

249

H

Rybalkova

Charkovská

košická

J

K

Holandská

HOTELS

ABRI

Map 249 H9
Jana Masaryka 36,
Vinohrady,
Prague 2
Tel 222 515 124/222 511 568
www.abri.cz

In a quiet side-street in the up-and-coming residential district of Vinohrady, this is an unpretentious, modest-sized hotel. The staff are courteous and the rooms are larger than you might expect. Half-board (including breakfast and dinner) rates are very reasonable, and the food served in the hotel restaurant, while not exciting, is perfectly adequate. It's useful in this densely built-up area to be able to park your car in the hotel courtyard. You can walk to Václavské náměstí (Wenceslas Square) in less than 15 minutes, or you can take the No. 22 tram to Malá Strana and the Castle from the end of the street.
🛏 2,800Kč–3,600Kč
🛏 27
💺 In some rooms
🚇 Náměstí Míru
🚊 Tram 4, 22, 23 to Jana Masaryka

ADMIRAL BOTEL

Map 247 E9
Hořejší nábřeží, Smíchov, Prague 5
Tel 257 321 302
www.admiral-botel-cz
A number of botels, converted from river barges, were launched in the 1960s and 1970s as an ingenious way of solving the problem of the city's acute lack of hotel rooms. The rooms, or rather cabins, are not spacious, but this is more than made up for by the thrill of staying on the water. Moored on the left bank of the Vltava in suburban Smíchov, the *Admiral* is the most shipshape of the fleet. Some cabins have views across the river of Vyšehrad and Nové Město. There is an onboard restaurant and Captain's Club.
🛏 2,160Kč–3,380Kč
🛏 87
🚇 Anděl
🚊 Tram 4, 7, 10, 14 to Zborovská

SPECIAL
ALCHYMIST

Map 246 C6
Tržiště 19, Malá Strana, Prague 1
Tel 257 286 011-6
www.alchymistresidence.com
A prominent corner building opposite the American Embassy in Malá Strana has been converted into an exclusive residence for well-heeled visitors with a taste for over-the-top, Italian interior design and attentive service. The décor features 16th- to 19th-century paintings and sculpture, as well as flamboyant furnishings. The small number of suites range from the merely luxurious to the utterly sumptuous. There's a café, a restaurant looking out over an internal courtyard, a sushi bar, massage rooms and a pool set in an original Gothic cellar. The Residence Nosticova, also in Malá Strana, offers a similar experience.
🛏 5,550Kč–20,700Kč (excluding breakfast)
🛏 10
💺 🌊
🚊 Tram 12, 20, 22, 23 to Malostranské náměstí

ADRIA

Map 248 F7
Václavské náměstí 26,
Nové Město, Prague 1
Tel 221 081 111
www.adria.cz
In a privileged position at the lower end of Václavské náměstí (Wenceslas Square), this family-owned and impeccably run hotel offers every comfort in a location that could hardly be better. The rococo building was first turned into a hotel nearly a century ago, and has undergone several thorough renovations since then. The rooms at the rear of the building have fascinating views over the charming central oasis of the Franciscan Gardens. The Triton restaurant in the basement offers outstanding cuisine.
🛏 4,500Kč–5,400Kč
🛏 87
💺
🚇 Můstek
🚊 Tram 3, 9, 14, 24 to Václavské náměstí

AMBASSADOR—ZLATÁ HUSA

Map 248 F6
Václavské náměstí 5–7,
Nové Město, Prague 1
Tel 224 193 111, 224 193 876
www.ambassador.cz

Originally two separate hotels, the art deco Ambassador and the 'Golden Goose' are a city institution, once the haunt of the rich and famous. The location, at the lower end of Wenceslas Square, is unbeatable, and the lobby always seems to be buzzing with life, not least because of the adjoining casino and night club. Complete renovation has restored some of the traditional glitter, and the rooms are comfortable, with good facilities. The hotel also has a large deluxe restaurant and Pilsner beer restaurant.

🏨 4,000Kč–9,300Kč
🛏 162
♿
Ⓜ Můstek

AMETYST
Map 248 H9
Jana Masaryka 11,
Vinohrady, Prague 2
Tel 222 921 921/222 921 946-7
www.hotelametyst.cz

The spotless Ametyst, in the same quiet street of inner suburban Vinohrady as the Abri (▷ 250), is less than a quarter of an hour on foot to Václavské náměstí (Wenceslas Square) and is well placed for tram connections to all parts of Prague. Virtually rebuilt in 1994, this attractive boutique hotel has been refurbished regularly since then. The best of the attractive and spotlessly maintained rooms are those with balconies on the top floor. The hotel restaurant specializes in traditional Czech and Austrian dishes and prides itself on its wine list. Parking is available.

🏨 3,050Kč–6,560Kč
🛏 84
♿ In some rooms
Ⓜ Náměstí Míru
🚋 Tram 4, 22, 23 to Jana Masaryka

ANDEL'S HOTEL PRAGUE
Map 246 D9
Stroupežnického 21, Smíchov,
Prague 5
Tel 296 889 688, 296 882 201
www.andelshotel.com
Rooms in this ultra-contemporary establishment are extremely comfortable and lavishly equipped. The hotel is the keystone in the glittering business and retail complex that has brought bustling new life to the formerly rather run-down inner suburb of

Smíchov. All parts of the historic central area are within a few minutes reach by public transportation. Sumptuous facilities include the Delight Restaurant and a spacious fitness and relaxation centre. The luxurious and convenient Andel's Suites, which are ideal for longer-term visitors, were added to the hotel in 2004.

🏨 7,650Kč–9,750Kč
🛏 239, 51 suites
📺 ♿
Ⓜ Anděl
🚋 Tram 4, 6, 7, 9, 10, 12, 14, 20 to Anděl

APOSTOLIC RESIDENCE
Map 247 F6
Staroměstské náměstí 25,
Staré Město, Prague 1
Tel 221 632 206/221 632 222
www.prague-residence.cz
'The House at the Blue Star' on Old Town Square is directly opposite the Old Town Hall, with privileged views of the Orloj (Astronomical Clock). It has only seven 'residences'. The top-floor apartment, with its Jacuzzi, is ideal for

| SPECIAL |
ARIA
Map 246 D6
Tržiště 9, Malá Strana, Prague 1
Tel 225 334 111
www.aria.cz
This immaculate establishment, on the same street as the American Embassy, has created a unique identity through clever and original use of a musical theme. The comfortable rooms are named after musicians and the floors are labelled 'classical', 'contemporary', 'jazz' and 'opera'. There is also a music salon and a musical director is on hand to advise on appropriate entertainment during your stay. Some of the rooms have views over the Vrtbovská zahrada, one of Prague's finest baroque gardens. The international restaurant has a winter garden and a panoramic summer terrace.

🏨 10,500Kč–12,750Kč
🛏 52
📺 ♿
Ⓜ Malostranská
🚋 Tram 12, 20, 22, 23 to Malostranské náměstí

honeymooners and there's a stylish restaurant with an open-air section on the ground floor.

🏨 3,530Kč–4,590Kč
🛏 7
♿
Ⓜ Staroměstská
🚋 Tram 17, 18 to Staroměstská

ATLANTIC
Map 248 G5
Na poříčí 9, Nové Město, Prague 1
Tel 224 812 084
www.hotel-atlantic.cz
Just a few steps from the Obecní dům (Municipal House), the Atlantic occupies a former 16th-century inn upgraded to a hotel when the railway arrived at nearby Masaryk Station in 1845. Thoroughly refurbished in 2004, it offers no-frills accommodation at very reasonable rates. The hotel's Fiesta Restaurant has a winter garden.

🏨 2,300Kč–4,100Kč
🛏 62
Ⓜ Náměstí Republiky
🚋 Tram 5, 8, 14 to Náměstí Republiky; tram 3, 24, 26 to Masarykovo nádraží

AXA
Map 248 H5
Na poříčí 40,
Nové Město, Prague 1
Tel 227 072 489
www.hotelaxa.com
The early 1930s Axa was a pioneering building in the Functionalist style, and with its cool lines and wide range of modern facilities, it soon became a Prague landmark. It stands on characterful Na poříčí, a shopping and business artery running eastwards from the Obecní dům (Municipal House), not far from Florenc metro station and Masaryk railway station, and directly by a tram stop. The plain but perfectly adequate rooms vary in amenities, outlook and noise levels. The hotel has a restaurant serving Czech and international dishes, as well as a fitness centre and 25m (82ft) pool.

🏨 2,850Kč–4,400Kč
🛏 138
🏊 📺
Ⓜ Florenc
🚋 Tram 3, 8, 24, 26 to Bílá labuť

BEST WESTERN HOTEL KAMPA

Map 247 D7

Všehrdova 16, Malá Strana, Prague 1

Tel 257 404 444

www.euroagentur.cz

Despite its name, this hotel is not quite on Kampa Island, but stands on the far side of the Čertovká (Devil's Brook), which divides it from the mainland. The bedrooms at the rear of the 17th-century building enjoy views over the brook and the leafy park beyond, and all offer good standard comforts at a reasonable price. You may find that the hotel's Knight Hall is used by noisy private gatherings.

🛏 3,200Kč–4200Kč

🛈 84

🚊 Tram 6, 9, 12, 20, 22, 23 to Újezd

BEST WESTERN HOTEL METEOR PLAZA

Map 248 G6

Hybernská 6, Nové Město, Prague 1

Tel 224 192 111/224 192 559

www.hotel-meteor.cz

Once known as The White Lion, this establishment was first recorded as long ago as 1307, and in the 18th century received a visit from future Emperor Joseph II. Rebuilt in baroque style, it has been comprehensively modernized, and offers all amenities and very acceptable accommodation a stone's throw from the Prašná brána (Powder Tower) and Obecní dům (Municipal House), and within easy walking distance of all central attractions. There's also an atmospheric barrel-vaulted wine cellar restaurant.

🛏 4,470Kč–5,700Kč

🛈 88

🛇 🔄

🚇 Náměstí Republiky

🚊 Tram 5, 8, 14 to Náměstí Republiky

BETLEM CLUB

Map 247 E6

Betlémské náměstí 9, Staré Město, Prague 1

Tel 222 221 574-5

www.betlemclub.cz

Once the property of one of the Protestant nobles executed on Staroměstské náměstí (Old Town Square) for their part in the rebellion of 1618 (▷ 29), this historic building stands opposite the Betlemské kaple (Bethlehem Chapel). The hotel, furnished in 1970s style, offers

affordable accommodation in an unbeatable location. The bedrooms are on the small side, but very comfortable. The atmospheric restaurant is in the medieval cellars.

🛏 3,300Kč–4,500Kč

🛈 21

🚇 Národní třída

🚊 Tram 6, 9, 18, 22, 23 to Národní třída

CENTRAL

Map 248 F5

Rybná 8, Staré Město, Prague 1

Tel 224 812 041

www.orfea.cz

Dating from the 1930s, the Central, tucked away in the labyrinth of Old Town streets behind the Obecní dům (Municipal House), certainly lives up to its name. Once out of the door, it is literally a few minutes to Staroměstské náměstí (Old Town Square) and the Orloj (Astronomical Clock). The hotel offers unpretentious accommodation at attractive prices, and an art deco restaurant to dine in.

🛏 3,200Kč–4,650Kč

🛈 68

🚇 Náměstí Republiky

🚊 Tram 5, 8, 14 to Náměstí Republiky

ČERNÁ LIŠKA

Map 247 F6

Mikulášská 2, Staré Město, Prague 1

Tel 224 232 250

www.hotelcernaliska.cz

It's impossible to find a more central place to stay than the 'Black Fox', some of whose rooms look straight at Svatého Mikuláš (Church of St. Nicholas) in Staroměstské náměstí (Old Town Square). The small and friendly hotel has comfortable rooms, some with exposed beams and painted ceilings, in a charming Renaissance building. The only potential downside is noise: The square never sleeps.

🛏 3,540Kč–5,980Kč

🛈 12

🔄

🚇 Staroměstská

🚊 Tram 17, 18 to Staroměstská

ČERNÝ SLON

Map 247 F6

Týnská 629/1, Staré Město, Prague 1

Tel 222 321 521, 222 329 353

www.hotelcernyslon.cz

The 'Black Elephant' is tucked away in the very core of the Old Town, with views from its

CARLO IV

Map 248 G6

Senovážné náměstí 13, Nové Město, Prague 1

Tel 224 593 111/224 593 033

www.boscolohotels.com

The ornate former central post office and savings bank has been converted into what is claimed to be the city's most opulent hotel. Beyond the stunning reception area, once the main banking hall, are rooms that are the last word in style and comfort. In addition, you will find inviting bars, a restaurant, a health club and a fabulous swimming pool with a mosaic floor.

🛏 8,970Kč–19500Kč

🛈 152

🛇 🔄 🔄

🚇 Hlavní nádraží

🚊 Tram 3, 9, 14, 24 to Jindřišská; tram 5, 9, 26 to Hlavní nádraží

windows of the Týn Church and the Ungelt. It's one of the oldest buildings in the area, with foundations dating back to the 13th century, and offers tastefully furnished rooms and an atmospheric restaurant with ribbed vaulting. Extra beds can be provided on request.

🛏 3,500Kč–5,700Kč

🛈 16

🔄 In some rooms

🚇 Staroměstská or Náměstí Republiky

🚊 Tram 17, 18 to Staroměstská; tram 5, 8, 14 to Náměstí Republiky

CHARLES PRAG

Map 246 D6

Josefská 1, Malá Strana, Prague 1

Tel 257 532 913

www.selectmarketinghotels.com

This small, elegant hotel is in a side street near Karlův most (Charles Bridge), named after Malá Strana's Svatého Josefa (Church of St. Joseph). The building is in baroque style and the comfortable, spacious rooms have traditional solid wood furnishings. The hotel has a loyal clientele: Rooms are often reserved well in advance.

🛏 4,500Kč–12,500Kč (excluding breakfast)

🛈 31

🚊 Tram 12, 20 ,22, 23 to Malostranské náměstí

STAYING

CLEMENTIN

Map 247 E6
Seminářská 4,
Staré Město, Prague 1
Tel 222 221 798/605 283 054
www.clementin.cz

In a side-street in the heart of the Old Town, this tiny hotel claims to be the narrowest surviving house in Prague. The building dates originally from the 14th century, but has Renaissance, baroque and neo-classical features. The rooms are of a good standard and there is a friendly welcome.

🛏 3,500Kč–6,300Kč
🛉 9
💺
🚇 Staroměstská
🚊 Tram 17, 18 to Staroměstská

CLOISTER INN

Map 247 E7
Konviktská 14,
Staré Město, Prague 1
Tel 224 211 020
www.cloister-inn.com

This highly recommended hotel, in a former convent whose history goes back to the Middle Ages, was part of the notorious StB (Secret Police) HQ in nearby Bartolomějská street. It now offers well-kept, standard rooms and is ideally placed just off the main tourist beat in the Old Town, a few minutes away from Karlův most (Charles Bridge).

🛏 3,300Kč–4,500Kč
🛉 75
🚇 Národní třída
🚊 Tram 6, 9, 22, 23 to Národní divadlo; tram 17, 18 to Karlovy lázně

CONSTANS

Map 246 C6
Břetislavova 309,
Malá Strana, Prague 1
Tel 234 091 818
www.hotelconstans.cz

Charming Constans is tucked away in one of Malá Strana's narrow lanes, and occupies three 17th-century houses. It has a historic atmosphere and comfortable rooms with solid furnishings; some with balconies. Extra beds can be provided on request. There is a breakfast room/restaurant, and full-board rates (breakfast, lunch and dinner) are available.

🛏 4,980Kč–7,170Kč
🛉 32
💺 Some rooms only
🚊 Tram 12, 20, 22, 23 to Malostranské náměstí

CORINTHIA TOWERS

Off map 248 G9
Kongresová 1, Nusle, Prague 4
Tel 261 191 111/261 191 239
www.corinthia.cz

This skyscraper rises up over the motorway bridge connecting the southern suburbs with central Prague. Vyšehrad metro station is practically part of the hotel, and it's only a couple of stops to Václavské náměstí (Wenceslas Square). The hotel offers every comfort, including fitness centre and a swimming pool with a spectacular view over Prague. There's a choice of bars, and the two restaurants serve Czech, international and Mediterranean cuisine.

🛏 7,800Kč–9,000Kč
🛉 544
🅿 📺 💺
🚇 Vyšehrad

CORTO

Map 246 C6
Nerudova 27, Malá Strana, Prague 1
Tel 257 534 281/224 215 313
www.corto.cz

The modest Corto pension provides affordable accommodation in one of the fine old houses in Malá Strana, just a stone's throw from the Castle. The rooms are basic, but some have extraordinary views over the rooftops. There's another Corto pension in Staré Město.

🛏 2,050Kč–3,500Kč
🛉 13
🚊 Tram 12, 20, 22, 23 to Malostranské náměstí

CROWNE PLAZA

Off map 246 B5
Koulova 15, Dejvice, Prague 6
Tel 296 537 111/296 537 858
www.crowneplaza.cz

Still referred to as the Hotel International by many, luxury Crowne Plaza is one of the few Stalinist skyscrapers in 'wedding-cake' style to have been built outside the former Soviet Union. Now a protected national monument, it's a visitor attraction in its own right, with a richly decorated interior featuring tapestries, mosaics, stained glass and chandeliers by the best artists and craftsmen of the time. Rooms on the upper floor have extensive views over the city. It's a little off the beaten track, in the fashionable western suburb of Dejvice, but this is no disadvantage as the tram terminus is just outside the door. There is a wine cellar and restaurant serving Czech and international dishes.

🛏 3,000Kč–9,000Kč
🛉 254
📺 💺
🚊 Tram 8 to Podbaba

DIENTZENHOFER

Map 246 D6
Nosticova 2, Malá Strana, Prague 1
Tel 257 320 888
www.dientzenhofer.cz

This friendly, welcoming little pension is in a pleasant part of Malá Strana south of Karlův most (Charles Bridge) and near the Čertovká millstream and Kampa Island. The building was home to the Dientzenhofer dynasty of architects, who did so much to give this quarter its glorious baroque character. It offers straightforward accommodation with private facilities, and there is a delightful courtyard and garden.

🛏 3,700Kč–4,200Kč
🛉 9
🚊 Tram 12, 20, 22, 23 to Hellichova

DIPLOMAT

Off map 246 B5
Evropská 15, Dejvice, Prague 6
Tel 296 559 111/296 559 213
www.diplomatpraha.cz

Large, purpose-built Diplomat is popular with business people as it is only 20 minutes from the airport by city bus (less by hotel limousine). It has a spacious, spotless interior, comfortable, contemporary rooms and excellent facilities. From here you can walk (uphill) to the Castle, and the historic central area is only a couple of stops on the metro. There is a choice of three restaurants.

🛏 7,200Kč–7,900Kč
🛉 398
📺 💺
🚇 Dejvická
🚊 Tram 2, 8, 20, 26 to Dejvická; bus 119 to airport

DŮM U KRÁLE JIŘÍHO
Map 247 E6
Liliova 10, Staré Město, Prague 1
Tel 221 466 100
www.kinggeorge.cz
Dating originally from the late 14th century, the 'House at the Sign of King George' stands on Liliova, one of the oldest and most central streets in Prague. The building once formed part of Anenský klášter (St. Anne's Convent), one of the many such establishments abolished in the 18th century by the reforming Emperor Joseph II; its present state as a charming small pension dates from a conversion in the early 1990s. It has pleasant rooms, some with sloping ceilings, and there is a pub and music club on site.
🛏 2,700Kč–3,100Kč
🛈 17
🚇 Staroměstská
🚋 Tram 17, 18 to Staroměstská

ÉLITE
Map 247 F7
Ostrovní 32, Nové Město, Prague 1
Tel 224 932 250-1/224 501 172
www.hotelelite.cz
A member of the small 'Hotels of Charm' group, the Élite on 'Island Street' is a stone's throw from Národní třída metro station and tram stop. The building goes back to the 14th century, and has some fascinating features, including one room with a Renaissance painted ceiling. There is a cellar bar, nightclub and grill-restaurant serving French, Spanish and Argentinian dishes. Enjoy breakfast in the courtyard in summer.
🛏 3,990Kč–6,450Kč
🛈 79
🔒
🚇 Národní třída
🚋 Tram 6, 9, 18, 21, 22, 23 to Národní třída

ESPLANADE
Map 248 G7
Washingtonova 1600/19, Nové Město, Prague 1
Tel 224 501 111/224 501 172
www.esplanade.cz
The Esplanade was one of the élite hotels of interwar Czechoslovakia, built to the highest specifications in 1927 in late art nouveau style. Somewhat faded by the end of the 20th century, it now has refurbished rooms of widely varying character, so it's worth

inspecting a few before making your choice. The hotel over-looks the main rail station and State Opera. There is a terrace café and the restaurant serves international and Czech dishes.

🛏 4,500Kč–9,800Kč
🛈 74
🔒 In some rooms
🚇 Hlavní nádraží or Muzeum

EVROPA
Map 248 G7
Václavské náměstí 25, Nové Město, Prague 1
Tel 224 215 387
www.hotelevropa.cz
The Evropa is a glittering creation of art nouveau architecture. The rooms may be shabby and run-down, and there's a definite lack of facilities, but for some it is reward enough to stay in such an iconic building, in the heart of things on Wenceslas Square.

Alternatively, just sit for a while over a coffee in the fabulous ground-floor café.
🛏 2,200Kč–4,000Kč
🛈 92
🚇 Můstek
🚋 Tram 3, 9, 14, 24 to Václavské náměstí

GRAND HOTEL BOHEMIA
Map 248 F6
Králodvorská 4, Staré Město, Prague 1
Tel 234 608 111/234 608 152
www.grandhotelbohemia.cz
Originally called the Hotel Steiner, after its first owner, this art deco city institution

FOUR SEASONS HOTEL PRAGUE
Map 247 E6
Veleslavínova 2a, Staré Město, Prague 1
Tel 221 427 000, 221 427 777
www.fourseasons.com/prague
The Four Seasons is a supremely tasteful conversion of three historic buildings—one baroque, one neoclassical and one neo-Renaissance. It offers the ultimate in comfort, elegance and facilities, as well as a riverside location by Karlův most (Charles Bridge). Rooms range from standard (an understatement) to the supremely luxurious presidential suite, and some have river and Castle views. The Allegro Restaurant (▷ 230) is one of the most sophisticated in Prague.
🛏 8,850Kč–17,850Kč
🛈 161
🍴 🔒
🚇 Staroměstská
🚋 Tram 17, 18 to Staroměstská

welcomed its first guests in 1927. It was refurbished as a luxury hotel in the 1990s. The comfort offered is difficult to beat, as is the location, in the heart of the Old Town just behind the Obecní dům (Municipal House). There's a ballroom and restaurant.
🛏 5,850Kč–9,600Kč
🛈 78
🔒
🚇 Náměstí Republiky
🚋 Tram 5, 8, 14 to Náměstí Republiky

HARMONY
Map 248 H5
Na poříčí 31, Nové Město, Prague 1
Tel 222 319 807/222 321 187
www.hotelharmony.cz
This no-nonsense hotel is on a busy commercial street

running eastward from the Obecní dům (Municipal House). A Functionalist building from the 1930s, its rooms are plainly furnished but comfortable. The two restaurants serve Czech and international cuisine.

💶 2,640Kč–3,900Kč
🛏 60
Ⓜ Florenc or Náměstí Republiky
🚊 Tram 3, 8, 24, 26 to Bílá Labuť

HAŠTAL
Map 248 F5
Haštalská 16/1007,
Staré Město, Prague 1
Tel 222 314 335
www.hastal.com
In the northern part of the Old Town, close to Anežsky klášter (St. Agnes' Convent) and the Vltava embankment, this dignified building has been a brewery and, after the 1968 invasion, the Soviet Army Kommandatura. Today it is a welcoming small hotel, ideally placed for visiting the central sights and attractions. Some of the pleasantly modernized rooms face the market place, others look out over the interior courtyard. It has a pleasant summer garden.

💶 3,060Kč–4,410Kč
🛏 24
📺 🔌
🚊 Tram 5, 8, 14 to Dlouhá třída

HILTON PRAGUE
Map 249 H5
Pobřežní 1, Karlín, Prague 8
Tel 224 841 111/224 842 737
www.prague.hilton.com
The Prague Hilton is a huge glass cube overlooking the urban expressway, just outside the city's historic area. It makes up for its location by being a self-contained world of its own, with an extravagant range of amenities, among them one of the city's best restaurants. The rooms are spacious and comfortable and the hotel is a natural choice for visiting celebrities.

💶 4,480Kč–8,480Kč
🛏 788
📺 📶 🔌
Ⓜ Florenc
🚊 Tram 8, 24 Florenc

HOFFMEISTER
Map 247 D5
Pod Bruskou 7, Malá Strana, Prague 1
Tel 251 017 111
www.hoffmeister.cz
At the foot of the hairpin bend leading up to the Castle district and just a few steps from Malostranská metro station, the luxury Hoffmeister enjoys a privileged position. The interiors are spacious and pleasingly contemporary in style, and the décor features original works by the owner's father, artist Adolf Hoffmeister. The comfortable rooms are individually designed, with traffic noise kept to a minimum by effective double glazing. A wellness centre with 'aromatherapy stone bath treatment' occupies a 15th-century grotto, and there is a gourmet restaurant.

💶 6,000Kč–9,000Kč
🛏 37 rooms
📶 🔌
Ⓜ Malostranská
🚊 Tram 12, 18, 20, 22, 23 to Malostranská

HOTEL 16
Map 247 F8
Kateřinská 16, Nové Město, Prague 2
Tel 224 920 636
www.hotel16.cz
This small family-run hotel extends a friendly welcome to its guests in what might seem a somewhat out-of-the-way location in the New Town. However, it's only a 10-minute walk to the top end of Václavské náměstí (Wenceslas Square), and the Botanická zahrada (Botanical Gardens) are nearby. Rooms are unpretentious, but comfortable, and are furnished in an attractive contemporary Italian style.

💶 3,100Kč–4,000Kč
🛏 14
🔌
Ⓜ I.P. Pavlova
🚊 Tram 4, 6, 10, 16, 22, 23 to Štěpánská

IBIS PRAHA CITY
Map 248 G8
Kateřinská 36,
Nové Město, Prague 2
Tel 222 865 777/221 104 926
www.hotelibis.cz

The Ibis is not the place to stay if you want to soak up the local atmosphere 24 hours a day, but it offers reliable accommodation with a few frills in a modern building. The location is not particularly atmospheric either, but it's right by a metro station and tram stop and only a short walk from the Národní muzeum (National Museum) at the top of Václavské náměstí (Wenceslas Square). Facilities include a swimming pool and the Estaminet restaurant, which serves Czech and international cuisine.

💶 2,670Kč–3,210Kč (without breakfast)
🛏 181
📶 🔌
Ⓜ I.P. Pavlova
🚊 Tram 4, 6, 10, 16, 22, 23 to I.P. Pavlova

IMPERIAL
Map 248 G5
Na poříčí 15, Nové Město, Prague 1
Tel 222 316 012
www.hotelimperial.cz
The art nouveau Imperial is on a corner site by Masaryk

station and just a short walk along busy Na poříčí to the Obecní dům (Municipal House) and Staré Město (Old Town). It was one of the grandest hotels of its day, and though the grandeur has faded, it offers a budget experience in characterful surroundings. The Café Imperial (▷ 232) on the ground floor remains one of Prague's great institutions.

💶 1,180Kč–2,500Kč
🛏 286
Ⓜ Náměstí Republiky
🚊 Tram 5, 8, 14 to Náměstí Republiky; tram 3, 5, 14, 24, 26 to Masarykovo nádraží; tram 3, 8, 24, 26 to Bílá Labuť

INTERCONTINENTAL

Map 247 E5
Náměstí Curieových 43/5,
Staré Město, Prague 1
Tel 296 631 111/296 631 118-9
www.prague.intercontinental.com

Dating from the 1970s, the InterContinental was the Communist era's flagship hotel. It still exudes the luxurious atmosphere of a grand hotel of those times and provides its guests with every amenity, one being its fine location overlooking the art nouveau Čechův most (Čech Bridge) on the northern edge of the Old Town. Its foyer, café and bar are popular meeting places, and the rooftop Zlata Praha (Golden Prague restaurant, ▷ 244) is one of the best in town. It also has a state-of-the-art fitness centre.

6,180Kč–10,800Kč (excluding breakfast)
372
Tram 17 to Právnická fakulta

JALTA

Map 248 G7
Václavské náměstí 45,
Nové Město, Prague 1
Tel 222 822 111
www.jalta.cz

The Jalta is one of the Communist era's most distinguished buildings, in a restrained and elegant architectural style. The interiors have been carefully refurbished and are warm and welcoming.

THE IRON GATE

Map 247 F6
Michalská 19, Staré Město,
Prague 1
Tel 225 777 777/225 999 902-4
www.irongate.cz

Hidden in the warren of streets just south of Staroměstské náměstí (Old Town Square), this wonderful historic building, with its internal courtyard, has been carefully converted into superior accommodation consisting of a range of well-equipped suites and studios. One privileged suite is in a tower, with a wonderful view over the rooftops. Tasteful furnishings complement original features from the building's long history, which dates back to the 14th century. The restaurant serves dishes from the different cuisines of the Habsburg Empire.

4,800Kč–29,700Kč
43
Staroměstská or Můstek
Tram 17, 18 to Staroměstská

The hotel is popular with business people and conference delegates. The 'Hot' restaurant offers global fare, and there is also a casino.

4,200Kč–5,100Kč
94
Muzeum

JEROME HOUSE

Map 247 E7
V Jirchářích 13/153,
Nové Město, Prague 1
Tel 224 933 207/224 933 140
www.jerome.cz

You will find straightforward accommodation at the Jerome House, which has a very central but quiet location just around the corner from the lively Národní třída metro station and tram stop. The building dates back to the Middle Ages, but the rooms are unpretentiously contemporary in style. Some have multiple beds and shared facilities.

3,000Kč–4,500Kč
52
Národní třída
Tram 6, 9, 18, 21, 22, 23 to Národní třída

JULIAN

Map 246 D8
Elišky Peškové 11,
Smíchov, Prague 5
Tel 257 311 144/257 311 150
www.julian.cz

This small, family-run hotel in Smíchov, the up-and-coming inner-city borough on the left bank of the Vltava, has been cleverly converted from a century-old apartment block and offers superior three-star value. The southern end of Malá Strana is within easy walking distance, and it's just minutes by tram from central Prague. The attractively furnished rooms have tea- and coffee-making facilities, and the restaurant serves light meals. The hotel is a stone's throw from the Kinsky Gardens, which merge with the parkland of Petřín Hill and make possible a 'green' walk all the way to Hradčany.

2,980Kč–3,980Kč
32
In attic rooms
Tram 6, 9, 12, 20 to Švandovo divadlo

K&K CENTRAL

Map 248 G6
Hybernská 10,
Nové Město, Prague 1
Tel 225 022 000/225 022 606
www.kkhotels.com/central

The Central was one of Prague's very first distinctive art nouveau buildings, and served for many years as a theatre. Just as beautiful as the Evropa (▷ 254), the work of the same architects, it far outclasses it in terms of comfort. The rooms are well equipped and attractive, but don't expect art nouveau opulence—the style is strictly international contemporary. The location is excellent too, just a few steps from the Obecní dům (Municipal House). It also has an attractive restaurant.

7,920Kč–8,520Kč
127
Náměstí Republiky
Tram 5, 8, 14 to Náměstí Republiky; tram 3, 5, 14, 26, 24 to Masarykovo nádraží; tram 3, 9, 14, 24 to Jindřišská

JOSEF

Map 248 F5
Rybná 20, Staré Město, Prague 1
Tel 221 700 111/221 700 901
www.hoteljosef.com
The Josef is a designer hotel par excellence, the work of the architect Eva Jiřičná, who has left her distinctive mark elsewhere in Prague. The ultimate in minimalism is combined with elegance and comfort, and the rooms offer every amenity. There is also an attractive, private garden and a rooftop fitness centre.

🛏 4,092Kč–6,417Kč
🛈 108
🔧 🔸
Ⓜ Náměstí Republiky
🚋 Tram 5, 8, 14 to Dlouhá třída

LIBERTY

Map 248 F6
28 října 11/376,
Staré Město, Prague 1
Tel 224 239 598
www.hotelliberty.cz
This small luxury art nouveau hotel has an enviable central location on the traffic-free street linking Národní třída with the lower end of Václavské náměstí (Wenceslas Square). There are lavish antique-style furnishings and a summer terrace. The top-floor suites enjoy a fine view over the rooftops of the Old Town to the Castle.

🛏 4,950Kč–10,200Kč
🛈 32
🔧 🔸
Ⓜ Můstek

MAXIMILIAN

Map 248 F5
Haštalská 14, Staré Město, Prague 1
Tel 225 303 111/225 303 118
www.maximilianhotel.com
The Maximilian was built in the early 20th century as an upper middle-class city residence,

and its refurbishment has been at pains to re-create and enhance the atmosphere of the time. The hotel prides itself on its warm welcome and on the services offered. Rooms have exquisitely tasteful furnishings, and guests are served complimentary refreshments in the tea and coffee lounge.

🛏 4,650Kč–6,240Kč
🛈 71
🔧 🔸
🚋 Tram 5, 8, 14 to Dlouhá třída

MEJSTŘÍK

Map 248 F5
Jakubská 5, Staré Město, Prague 1
Tel 224 800 055
www.hotelmejstrik.cz
This privately run hotel dates from the 1920s, and the refurbished décor of its public spaces pay tribute to the art deco era, while the well-equipped and attractive rooms are more contemporary in style. It has an excellent position just behind the Obecní dům (Municipal House) and is within walking distance of all central attractions. The restaurant and bistro serve Czech and international dishes, and you can dine and drink outside in summer.

🛏 2,600Kč–6,200Kč
🛈 29
🔸 In upper-floor rooms
Ⓜ Náměstí Republiky
🚋 Tram 5, 8, 14 to Náměstí Republiky

MERCURE

Map 248 G5
Na poříčí 7, Nové Město, Prague 1
Tel 221 800 800
www.accorhotels.com
The Mercure is probably the best of the clutch of hotels on and around Na poříčí, the busy commercial street leading east from the Obecní dům (Municipal House). It makes the most of its Franz Kafka connection; the writer once worked in the building as an insurance

executive. Rooms are attractive and contemporary, and the hotel has a good range of facilities, a brasserie, bar and even a library with works by Kafka and other authors.

🛏 4,160Kč–6,220Kč
🛈 174
Ⓜ Náměstí Republiky
🚋 Tram 5, 8, 14 to Náměstí Republiky; tram 3, 5, 14, 24, 26 to Masarykovo nádraží

METAMORPHIS

Map 248 F6
Malá Štupartská 5/636,
Staré Město, Prague 1
Tel 221 771 011/221 771 020
www.metamorphis.cz
This hotel enjoys a privileged location in the medieval courtyard known as the Ungelt (Týnský dvůr), just to the rear of the Týn Church and a few steps from Staroměstské náměstí (Old Town Square). Its origins go back to the 9th century, and the sensitively converted, comfortable rooms have some historic features such as beams and vaulting. You can even sleep in the former chapel. The hotel restaurant serves Czech and international dishes, and light meals can be taken in the café with its summer terrace.

🛏 4,980Kč–7,170Kč
🛈 24
🔸 In most rooms
Ⓜ Náměstí Republiky
🚋 Tram 5, 8, 14 to Náměstí Republiky

STAYING

MÖVENPICK

Map 246 C9
Mozartova 261/1,
Smíchov, Prague 5
Tel 257 151 111/257 153 108
www.moevenpick-prague.com
The Mövenpick's high standard
of comfort and lavish facilities
more than compensate for its
out-of-the-way location. The
two parts of the hotel are
connected by a spectacular
funicular, which offers breathtaking views during its short,
steep trip. It is built on the
slopes rising above the
Smíchov district, and some
rooms overlook the Mozart
Museum in the Vila Bertramka.
There is a choice of
restaurants and bars.
🍴 4,350Kč–5,100Kč
🛏 436
📺 💲
🚇 Anděl
🚋 Trams 6, 12, 14, 20 to Anděl; trams
4, 7, 9, 10 to Bertramka

NERUDA

Map 246 C5
Nerudova 44,
Malá Strana, Prague 1
Tel 257 535 557-61
www.hotelneruda.cz
Almost at the top of steep
Nerudova street, the exclusive
small hotel named after the
19th-century Prague writer,
sometimes called the 'Charles
Dickens' of Malá Strana, is just
a stone's throw from the
Castle. The historic building it
occupies has been carefully
converted to provide attractive
and comfortable rooms. The
glass-roofed restaurant and
Café Carolina provide snacks,
meals and drinks in a pleasant
atmosphere.
🍴 7,650Kč–9,900Kč
🛏 34
💲
🚋 Tram 12, 20, 22, 23 to
Malostranské náměstí

PALACE

Map 248 G6
Panská 12,
Nové Město, Prague 1
Tel 224 093 111/224 093 120
www.palacehotel.cz
Dating from 1909, this purpose-
built luxury hotel more than
lives up to its prestigious
address at the corner of
'Gentleman's Street', where the
Muchovo Muzeum is also
located. Successive restora-
tions and refurbishments have

removed some of the early
20th-century patina, but the
rooms and public spaces are
attractive and comfortable, and
the service is exemplary. There
is a gourmet restaurant, as well
as a pleasant lounge for light
refreshments, and Václavské
náměstí (Wenceslas Square) is
just one block away.

🍴 10,080Kč–34,200Kč
🛏 124
💲
🚇 Můstek
🚋 Tram 3, 9, 14, 24 to Václavské
náměstí or Jindřišská

LE PALAIS

Map 248 G9
U Zvonařky 1,
Vinohrady, Prague 2
Tel 234 634 111/234 634 634
www.palaishotel.cz
Le Palais is a fine example of
exuberant late 19th-century
neo-Renaissance architecture,
with a wealth of decorative
details by the renowned
Prague artist Luděk Marold.
The building has been restored
with great sensitivity and offers
luxurious rooms and suites
with every contemporary
amenity, including marble
bathrooms. Le Papillon
restaurant serves international
and refined Czech cuisine, and
the summer terrace offers a
view over the Nusle valley.

🍴 7,200Kč–11,100Kč
🛏 72
📺 💲
🚋 Tram 6, 11 to Bruselská

PAŘÍŽ

Map 248 G5
U Obecního domu,
Staré Město, Prague 1
Tel 222 195 195/222 195 666
www.hotel-pariz.cz

The luxurious and very grand
'Paris' almost matches its
neighbour, the sumptuous
art nouveau Obecní dům
(Municipal House), in architectural and design extravagance,
though the public spaces
have retained more original
character than the rooms. It
offers top-class amenities and
facilities in what many consider
to be among the very best
hotels in Prague, and certainly
one which captures the atmosphere of the turn of the 20th
century, not least in the Sarah
Bernhardt restaurant (▷ 241).
🍴 9,600Kč
🛏 86
📺 💲
🚇 Náměstí Republiky
🚋 Tram 5, 8, 14 to Náměstí Republiky

POD VĚŽÍ

Map 247 D6
Mostecká 2,
Malá Strana, Prague 1
Tel 257 532 041
www.podvezi.cz
The tiny Pod Věží has a
charming location in a historic
building on the corner of the
Malá Strana approach to
Karlův most (Charles Bridge).
It's not the most tranquil spot
in town, but the hotel combats
this with double glazing and a
pleasant atrium restaurant
serving Czech and international
dishes. The comfortable rooms
are pleasantly furnished.
🍴 5,200Kč–8900Kč
🛏 11
💲
🚋 Tram 12, 20, 22, 23 to
Malostranské náměstí

RADISSON SAS ALCRON
Map 248 G7
Štěpánská 40,
Nové Město, Prague 1
Tel 222 820 000/222 820 047
www.prague.radissonsas.com

Just off Václavské náměstí (Wenceslas Square), the sumptuous Alcron was completed in 1930, and for much of the following decade was the haunt of politicians and of journalists covering the successive crises afflicting pre-World War II Czechoslovakia. The hotel's restoration has retained its traditional feel while bringing it into the contemporary world, and it remains one of the best of the city's luxury hotels. The beautifully furnished rooms have marble bathrooms and lavish facilities, including in-room entertainment systems. Choose from two gourmet restaurants (▷ 259).

⚏ 4,770Kč–6,870Kč
🛈 211
🖾 📺 🌀
🚇 Můstek, Muzeum
🚊 Tram 3, 9, 14, 24 to Václavské náměstí

PRAGUE MARRIOTT
Map 248 G6
V Celnici 8, Nové Město, Prague1
Tel 222 888 888/222 888 822
www.marriott.com

This big hotel is well equipped for its business clients, but caters just as comfortably to other guests. It offers high-quality rooms, as well as a variety of suites, generous public spaces and an exceptional fitness centre, the large 'Fitness Academy'. The Brasserie Praha serves a wide range of cuisines, from Czech to Californian.

⚏ 5,070Kč–13,500Kč
🛈 293
🖾 📺 🌀
🚇 Náměstí Republiky
🚊 Tram 5, 8, 14 to Náměstí Republiky; tram 3, 5, 14, 24, 26 to Masarykovo nádraží

PRESIDENT
Map 247 F5
Náměstí Curieových 100,
Staré Město, Prague 1
Tel 234 614 110/234 614 169
www.hotelpresident.cz

The monolithic-looking President was reopened in 2004 following extensive reconstruction after suffering damage during the great flood of 2002. The hotel's riverside location is one of its great assets, with views of the Vltava enjoyed by many of its spacious and luxurious rooms, but other rooms have equally fine panoramas over Staré Město. The hotel also has a casino, a riverside restaurant serving international dishes, and a piano bar.

⚏ 4,800Kč–7,440Kč
🛈 99
📺
🚊 Tram 17 to Právnická fakulta

QUESTENBERK
Map 246 B6
Úvoz 15/155,
Hradčany, Prague 1
Tel 220 407 600
www.questenberk.cz

The 17th-century Questenberk has a rather church-like appearance with a calvary crowning its stepped approach. Its original function was as the Hospital of St. Elisabeth and St. Norbert and, following its conversion in 2003, guests are now served breakfast in the chapel dedicated to St.

ROMANTIC HOTEL U RAKA
Map 246 B5
Černínská 10/93,
Hradčany, Prague 1
Tel 220 511 100
www.romantikhotel-uraka.cz

This log-built farmhouse, with its shingle roof, would seem to belong deep in the Bohemian forests rather than in the city. It offers a unique lodging experience to those lucky enough to succeed in reserving one of its half-dozen rooms. It is furnished with exquisite taste and presided over by a sophisticated host. Don't be put off by the seemingly remote location at the back end of the Nový Svět area of Hradčany; the Castle is a delightful 10-minute walk away, and the tram stop is even nearer.

⚏ 6,200Kč–7,400Kč
🛈 6
🌀
🚊 Tram 22, 23 to Brusnice

Elisabeth. The rooms are comfortable and the atmosphere is intimate, but the real attraction of this historic building is its location just below Strahovsky klášter (Strahov Monastery), a short stroll from the Castle.

⚏ 5,100Kč–8,400Kč
🛈 30
🚊 Tram 22, 23 to Pohořelec

SALVATOR
Map 248 G5
Truhlářská 10,
Nové Město, Prague 1
Tel 222 312 234
www.salvator.cz

Built around an internal courtyard, the Salvator provides basic accommodation in a side street just a two-minute walk from the Obecní dům (Municipal House). The cheaper rooms have shared facilities. Breakfast is served in the cellars, pleasingly decorated with old film posters and the like. The hotel is linked to the adjoining La Boca restaurant.

⚏ 2,200Kč–3,100Kč
🛈 32
🚇 Náměstí Republiky
🚊 Tram 5, 8, 14 to Náměstí Republiky

STAYING

SAVOY

Map 246 B6
Keplerova 6,
Hradčany, Prague 1
Tel 224 302 430
www.hotel-savoy.cz

The art nouveau Savoy, dating from 1911, was rescued from near-oblivion in the 1990s and lovingly restored. It combines turn-of-the-20th-century elegance with every modern amenity and prides itself on its mastery of the art of pampering its guests. From the open fireplace in the library to the tasteful décor of the rooms and suites, every detail is calculated to induce a mood of relaxation and well-being. The restaurant has a retractable cupola and serves sumptuous international cuisine. A short, gentle downhill walk brings you to the gates of the Castle.
💷 9,900Kč–10,500Kč
🛏 61
📺 🔄
🚃 Tram 22, 23 to Pohořelec

SAX

Map 246 C6
Jánský vršek 3,
Malá Strana, Prague 1
Tel 257 531 268
www.sax.cz

This dignified, early 19th-century building is now a well-run boutique hotel. It stands in what was once the Italian quarter of Malá Strana, just a short uphill walk from the Castle. Inside, it is furnished and decorated in a restful, contemporary style, with comfortable rooms opening off an attractive atrium.
💷 3,500Kč–4,400Kč
🛏 22
🚃 Tram 12, 20, 22, 23 to Malostranské náměstí

TARA

Map 247 F6
Havelská 15,
Staré Město, Prague 1
Tel 224 228 083

This pension overlooks the Havelská market in the very heart of the Old Town. Accommodation is on the third and fourth floors and is easily reached without the aid of an elevator. The rooms are simply but attractively furnished, though only the 'de luxe' rooms with sloping ceilings have private bathrooms. Credit cards are not accepted.
💷 1,500Kč–2,500Kč (excluding breakfast)
🛏 30
🚇 Můstek

TOSCA

Map 249 H8
Blanická 10,
Vinohrady, Prague 2
Tel 221 506 111

The thoroughly reconstructed Tosca offers affordable accommodation in the increasingly fashionable inner borough of Vinohrady. The rooms are modestly furnished and comfortable. Náměstí Mírů—the heart of Vinohrady, with church, theatre, tram stop and metro station—is at the end of the street, and Václavské náměstí (Wenceslas Square) is within easy walking distance or there is a tram direct to the Castle.
💷 2,660Kč–4,600Kč
🛏 38
🚇 Náměstí Mírů
🚃 Tram 4, 10, 16, 22, 23 to Náměstí Mírů

U BRANY

Map 246 C6
Nerudova 21,
Malá Strana, Prague 1
Tel 257 531 227-8
www.ubrany.cz

This small hotel, on steep and picturesque Nerudova street, is in a great location halfway between Karlův most (Charles Bridge) and the Castle. The rooms are quiet and comfortable, and the staff are discreet and friendly. There's a good choice of bars, pubs and restaurants just a few minutes walk away.
💷 5,200Kč–6,500Kč
🛏 10
🚃 Tram 12, 20, 22, 23 to Malostranské náměstí

U KRÁLE KARLA

Map 246 C6
Úvoz 4,
Hradčany, Prague 1
Tel 257 531 211
www.romantichotels.cz

Nestling at the foot of steps leading up to Hradčanské náměstí—the square in front of the Castle—the 'King Charles' occupies a building whose history goes back to the Middle Ages, though its present appearance is baroque. Furnishings and fittings contribute to the historic atmosphere, and include painted ceilings and stained glass in the comfortable bedrooms, as well as in the hotel's two charming dining rooms. It's quite a distance to the tram stop though.
💷 4,200Kč–5,800Kč
🛏 19
🔄
🚃 Tram 12, 20, 22, 23 to Malostranské náměstí

U PAVA

Map 247 D5
U lužického semináře 32,
Malá Strana, Prague 1
Tel 257 533 360
www.romantichotels.cz

The 'Peacock' belongs to the same group as the U Krále Karla (▷ above) further up the hill, and offers an equivalent experience near the riverside, in one of the most picturesque parts of Malá Strana. Originally Gothic, the house was rebuilt by the great baroque architect Kilián Ignác Dientzenhofer, and its restoration has respected and enhanced this fine example of Prague's heritage. The interiors feature darkwood furnishings, crystal chandeliers and artworks, and there's an atmospheric wine restaurant in the cellar.
💷 4,800Kč–7,200Kč
🛏 27
🔄
🚇 Malostranská
🚃 Tram 12, 18, 20, 22, 23 to Malostranská

U PRINCE
Map 247 F6
Staroměstské náměstí 29,
Staré Město, Prague 1
Tel 224 213 404
www.hoteluprince.cz

The location of this hotel
opposite the Orloj
(Astronomical Clock) on
the Old Town Hall is
unsurpassable, as is its
rooftop terrace with fabulous
views across a good part of
the city's 'hundred towers'.
The building originally dates
from the 12th century
and refurbishment in 2001
has given the very comfortable
bedrooms a cosy, antique
feeling. There's a busy café
and restaurant on the ground
floor, but noise is kept at bay
by double glazing.
🛏 6,000Kč–10,000Kč
🚪 24
Ⓜ Staroměstská
🚊 Tram 17, 18 to Staroměstská

U SVATÉHO JANA
Map 247 F9
Vyšehradská 28,
Nové Město, Prague 2
Tel 224 911 789
www.accomprague.com/usvjana
The rectory attached to Kilián
Ignác Dientzenhofer's glorious
little baroque Svatého Jan na
Skalce (Church of St. John
Nepomuk on the Rock) has
been converted into a
comfortable small guest
house. The rooms are soberly
decorated and comfortable,
and represent excellent value,
while the surroundings are
delightful. It's just a short walk
from Karlovo náměstí (Charles
Square), and there's a tram
stop just outside the door.
🛏 1,690Kč–2,090Kč
🚪 14
Ⓜ Karlovo náměstí
🚊 Tram 18, 24 to Botanická zahrada

SPECIAL

U ZLATÉ STUDNĚ
Map 246 D5
U Zlaté studně 166/4,
Malá Strana, Prague 1
Tel 257 011 213
www.zlatastudna.cz

Without an invitation from
the President, you can't stay
closer to the Castle than in
this utterly charming small
hotel, at the top of the steep
lane which once led up to
Hradčany from Malá Strana.
The lane is now blocked,
so peace and quiet is
guaranteed, as are some of
the best views in Prague,
which range from the
terraced gardens of baroque
palaces to the far side of the
city. The luxurious bedrooms
have whirlpool baths and
exquisitely tasteful antique-
style furnishings, and the
gourmet restaurant makes
the most of the view.
🛏 4,350Kč–7,100Kč
🚪 20
Ⓢ
🚊 Tram 12, 20, 22, 23 to
Malostranské náměstí

U ŽLUTÉ BOTY
Map 246 C6
Jánský vršek 11,
Malá Strana, Prague 1
Tel 257 532 269
www.zlutabota.cz
'At the Sign of the Yellow Boot'
is an attractive and characterful
small hotel in a Malá Strana
alleyway just a few (steep)
steps below the Castle. Rooms
are individually decorated,
some with rustic panelling and
tiled stoves. They connect with
one another, which is useful for
larger families, and offer good
value for the location.
🛏 3,400Kč–4,300Kč
🚪 8
🚊 Tram 12, 20, 22, 23 to
Malostranské náměstí

WALDSTEIN
Map 246 D5
Valdštejnské náměstí 6/19,
Malá Strana, Prague 1
Tel 257 533 938/251 051 111
www.avehotels.cz

Fitting snugly into a corner of a
tiny square at the side of the
massive Valdštejnský palác
(Wallenstein Palace), the
Waldstein hotel does not
announce its presence to the
outside world, but is well worth
searching out. Its location
guarantees peace and quiet,
and the comfortable rooms all
have an individual character
and furnishings. The 'Master
Jan Hus' suite in the courtyard
extension is full of character.
A spectacular view up to the
Castle greets you as you step
outside the hotel.
🛏 4,656Kč–8,673Kč
🚪 15
Ⓜ Malostranská
🚊 Tram 12, 20, 22, 23 to
Malostranské náměstí

WILLIAM
Map 246 D6
Hellichova 5,
Malá Strana, Prague 1
Tel 257 320 242
www.euroagentur.cz
This rather unprepossessing
corner building at the junction
of busy Újezd and Hellichova
conceals a thoroughly
refurbished interior
offering reasonably priced
accommodation. The blue
and white décor of the
public spaces may not be to
everyone's taste, but the
rooms are more neutral in
design. Street noise aside,
the Malá Strana location is
excellent, and what better way
to get your bearings than by
letting yourself be whisked
up Petřín Hill aboard the
nearby funicular?
🛏 3,000Kč–5,500Kč
🚪 40
🚊 Tram 12, 20, 22, 23 to Hellichova

STAYING

HOTEL CHAINS

Name of Hotel Chain	Description	Number of Hotels in Prague	Telephone Numbers and Websites
Ave	A local chain with properties in Prague ranging from the first-class, central Hotel Mucha to three-star establishments in the suburbs.	8	00 420 251 091 111 (Prague) www.avehotels.cz
Best Western	The world's largest hotel group has several hotels close to the historic city centre and in convenient suburban locations.	8	0800 393 130 (UK) 1 800 780 7234 (US) www.bestwestern.com
Hilton	The Prague Hilton is a landmark building on the edge of central Prague.	1	800 888 44 888 (UK) 1-800-HILTONS (US) www.hilton.com
Holiday Inn	Holiday Inn's hotels in Prague include the city's only Stalinist-style skyscraper, the Crowne Plaza.	3	0800 40 50 60 (UK) 1-877-HOLIDAY (US) www.ichotelsgroup.com
Ibis	This reliable French group of modern hotels has three establishments in slightly out-of-the-way but easily accessible locations.	3	0892 686 686 (France) www.ibishotel.com
K & K Hotels	This private, Austrian-based chain of superior boutique hotels has two central properties.	2	00 43 662 842 157 (Austria) www.kkhotels.com
Marriott	This international brand has two large, luxury hotels and an exclusive executive apartment in Prague.	2	0800 221 222 (UK) 800 932 2198 (US) www.marriott.com
Mövenpick	This reliable Swiss group of luxury and business hotels has one large establishment in Prague, its two sections linked by spectacular funicular.	1	00 33 1 42 81 19 00 (France) www.moevenpick-hotels.com
Novotel	Prague has two hotels belonging to this well-known international group.	2	020 8283 4500 (UK) www.novotel.com
Radisson	This US-based global chain has acquired and completely renovated the famous five-star Alcron just off Václavské náměstí (Wenceslas Square).	1	0800 37 44 11 (UK) 888 201 1718 (US and Canada) www.radisson.com
Ramada	The global Ramada group is represented with one central hotel in Wenceslas Square and another purpose-built establishment at the airport.	2	0808 1000 783 (UK) 1 800 854 7854 (US) www.ramadainternational.com
Small Luxury Hotels	Small- to medium-size establishments of distinction offering superior comfort and service.	2	00800 525 48000 (UK) www.slh.com
Vienna International	An Austrian-based chain with several hotels (and one apartment) of exceptional quality in Prague.	5	00 43 1 333 73 73-72 (Austria) www.vi-hotels.com

STAYING

Planning

BEFORE YOU GO

CLIMATE AND WHEN TO GO

Prague lies in the middle of the Bohemian basin, enclosed by ranges of border uplands, and the historic heart of the city is in a small basin of its own, bounded by Hradčany and the other heights. This means that temperature inversions are not uncommon, and air pollution can be severe. In the past, the main atmospheric poison was the discharge from the countless boilers used to heat buildings; these were fired by brown coal or lignite, an inefficient and smoky fuel. Most boilers now use natural gas, and the main contributor to pollution is vehicle exhaust; Prague has a very high ratio of car ownership and use.

At the heart of Central Europe, Prague has a continental climate, to some extent modified by Atlantic influences. This means warm, sometimes very humid summers, and cold, occasionally very cold, winters. Summer is also characterized by sudden thundery downpours, especially in August.

The city is often said to be at its best in spring, when the trees in the streets and parks are fresh and green and the orchards of Petřín Hill a sea of blossom. This is when the city's premier music festival, the Prague Spring, takes place. September and even early October are also good times to come, when the days are still quite long and the sun can still be warm. But detailed weather patterns are unpredictable, and you can have good or bad luck at any time of the year. Temperatures can fluctuate quite quickly. Winter snowfall makes the city even more magical than usual, and the pre-Christmas period is very jolly; destined to be the focal point of dinner on the 24th, live carp are on sale in the streets (▷ 12) and there's a lively Christmas market in Staroměstské náměstí (Old Town Square, ▷ 190).

(▷ 12)

(Old Town Square, ▷ 190)

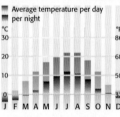

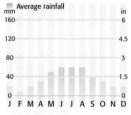

TEMPERATURE

- Average temperature per day
- per night

RAINFALL

- Average rainfall

WEATHER WEBSITES

SERVICE	WEBSITE
12-day forecast	www.prague.ic.cz/prague-weather.htm
24-hour forecast	www.myczechrepublic.com/weather/prague-weather.html

TIME ZONES

Prague is on Central European Time, one hour ahead of GMT (Greenwich Mean Time). Czech Summer Time operates (variably) between March and October, when clocks go forward one hour.

CITY	TIME DIFFERENCE	TIME AT 12 NOON IN PRAGUE
Amsterdam	0	12 noon
Berlin	0	12 noon
Brussels	0	12 noon
Chicago	-7	5am
Dublin	-1	11am
Johannesburg*	+1	1pm
London	-1	11am
Madrid	0	12 noon
Montreal	-6	6am
New York	-6	6am
Paris	0	12 noon
Perth, Australia*	+7	7pm
Rome	0	12 noon
San Francisco	-9	3am
Sydney*	+9	9pm
Tokyo*	+8	8pm

* One hour less during Czech Summer Time

WHAT TO TAKE

- Essentials include travel documents, currency or the means to obtain it (cash and credit cards, traveller's cheques), and any medication you may need. You will also need your driving licence if you intend to rent a car, and car registration and insurance documents if bringing your own car (▷ 52).
- Bearing in mind the

(▷ 52)

A magical winter scene (above). Be prepared for sudden summer showers (below right)

PLANNING

COUNTRY		ADDRESS	CONTACT DETAILS
Australia	E	8 Culgoa Circuit O'Malley, Canberra ACT 2606	Tel 02 6290 1386; www.mfa.cz/canberra
	C	169 Military Road, Dover Heights, Sydney, NSW 2030	Tel 02 9371 8878; www.mfa.cz/sydney
Canada	E	251 Cooper St. Ottawa, Ontario K2P 0G2	Tel 613 562 3875; www.mfa.cz/ottawa
	C	1305 Avenue des Pins Ouest, Montreal, Quebec H3G 1B2	Tel 514 849 4495; www.mfa.cz/montreal
Germany	E	Wilhelmstrasse 44, 10117 Berlin-Mitte	Tel 030 226 38; www.mfa.cz/berlin
Ireland	E	57 Northumberland Road, Ballsbridge, Dublin 4	Tel 01 668 1135; www.mfa.cz/dublin
New Zealand	C	Level 3, BMW Mini Centre, 11–15 Great South Road, corner of Margot Street, Auckland	Tel 09 522 8736
South Africa	E	936 Pretorius St., Arcadia, Pretoria	Tel 27 12 431 2380; www.mfa.cz/pretoria
UK	E	28 Kensington Palace Gardens, London W8 4QY	Tel 020 7243 1115; www.mfa.cz/london
USA	E	3900 Spring of Freedom Street NW, Washington DC 20008	Tel 202 274 9100; www.mfa.cz/washington
	C	1109 Madison Avenue, New York, NY 10028	Tel 212 717 5643; www.mfa.cz/newyork

Key: E = Embassy C = Consulate

unpredictability of the weather, you need to be prepared for sudden changes. An umbrella or light waterproofs are likely to come in useful at any time of the year, while summer wear may be needed from late April onwards. It's worth repeating that winter days and evenings can be really cold, and a mere fleece or thin anorak may well prove inadequate; think warm coat, gloves and headgear. However, should you be caught out, virtually anything you might need can be bought in Prague.

● One priority is comfortable footwear; Prague's cobblestones are definitely not foot-friendly.

● Czechs dress quite casually, and formal wear is unnecessary in most situations, though you might like to put on something smart for an evening out at the opera or a fine restaurant.

● Take addresses and phone numbers of emergency contacts, including the number to call if you lose your credit cards. Note the serial numbers of any traveller's cheques and the registration numbers of expensive items like laptops in case you need to report a loss or theft to the police.

● Electricity sockets in the Czech Republic require the standard, two-pin plugs (▷ 266).

● It's a good idea to make photocopies of all important documents (passport, driver's licence, etc) and to keep these separate from the originals.

PASSPORTS AND VISAS

● All visitors to the Czech Republic must carry a valid passport or, in the case of those EU citizens whose countries provide them, a national identity card. A visa is not required for visitors from most Western countries, however you should

CUSTOMS

The following are guidelines for the quantity of goods visitors from abroad (aged 18 years and over) can take into the Czech Republic providing they travel with the goods and they are for their own personal use.

● 200 cigarettes or
100 cigarillos or
50 cigars or
250g of smoking tobacco

● 2 litres of wine or
1 litre of spirits

● 50ml of perfume or
250ml of eau de toilette

Allowances can change so always check before you travel.

always check before you travel. It is worth noting that Canadian citizens may require a visa.

● Passport and visa rules can change at short notice, and it's worth verifying the current situation with the Czech Embassy or consulate in your home country before you travel. Alternatively, visit the Czech Ministry of Foreign Affairs website: www.mzv.cz

● Citizens of countries requiring a visa to visit the Czech Republic must obtain it in advance from the Czech Embassy or consulate in their home country; visas are not issued at the border.

● It's a good idea to leave your passport in the hotel safe and carry a photocopy with you.

CUSTOMS

● Most items imported into the Czech Republic for personal use are not subject to customs duty. However, it is advisable to check before you travel.

● Items which may not be imported include plants, tea and coffee.

● When exporting items from the Czech Republic there are restrictions on items of historic or cultural value. Valuable antiques may come into this category and

may require an official certificate.

● Before exporting any goods from the Czech Republic, always check the relevant customs allowances and regulations.

● There are customs offices at Sokolovská 22, Prague 8, tel 224 816 256, and at Ruzyně Airport, Aviatická 12/1048, tel 220 113 529 or 220 114 447.

● Visitors from non-EU countries can claim back value-added tax on items purchased in the Czech Republic for more than 2,000Kč. Present the receipt for such goods to the customs officer on leaving the country.

TRAVEL INSURANCE

● In addition to covering the loss or theft of money or belongings, make sure your travel insurance covers repatriation in the event of an emergency.

● If you are a frequent traveller, consider taking out an annual insurance policy. Whatever insurance you are offered, always compare the cost and conditions with those offered by other companies.

● Ensure you have the helpline number of your insurer.

● Full health insurance is advisable (▷ 272–273).

PRACTICALITIES

ELECTRICITY

The power supply in the Czech Republic is 220 volts AC and sockets take plugs with two round pins. If you are planning to bring appliances with you from the UK or USA such as laptops or hairdryers, you will need an adaptor (usually on sale at international airports). US appliances will also require a transformer.

LAUNDRY

There are many dry-cleaners and some self-service laundrettes in Prague. They include:
● **Laundryland** Londýnská 71, Nové Město, Prague 2, Tel 777 333 466, 222 516 692; open daily 8am–10pm. There is also another branch at: Černá růže, Na příkopě 12, Staré Město, Prague 1; open daily 9am–8pm.
● **Laundry Kings** Dejvická 16, Dejvice, Prague 6, Tel 233 343 743; open Mon–Fri 7am–10pm, Sat–Sun 8am–10pm.

LAVATORIES

● Public toilets are generally few and far between, though every metro station has one.
● Department stores and fast-food establishments such as McDonald's usually have toilets that you can use.
● It's perhaps a good idea to time your sightseeing with café and restaurant stops in mind so you can use their facilities. There is usually a small charge for use, and if there is an attendant and the facilities are in reasonably good condition you should leave a crown or two as a tip, especially if you have been given a sheet or two of toilet paper.
● *WC* or *záchod* means lavatory, while *muži* or *páni* means gents and *dámy* or *ženy* means ladies.

SMOKING

● Many Czechs are still enthusiastic smokers. Bars and pubs can be oppressive for non-smokers, though some restaurants now have non-smoking sections. About the only place where smoking is definitely not permitted is on public transport (metro, trams, buses), while mainline trains have non-smoking carriages.

CLOTHING SIZES

Use the clothing sizes chart below to convert the size you use at home.

UK	Metric	US	
36	46	36	SUITS
38	48	38	
40	50	40	
42	52	42	
44	54	44	
46	56	46	
48	58	48	
7	41	8	SHOES
7.5	42	8.5	
8.5	43	9.5	
9.5	44	10.5	
10.5	45	11.5	
11	46	12	
14.5	37	14.5	SHIRTS
15	38	15	
15.5	39/40	15.5	
16	41	16	
16.5	42	16.5	
17	43	17	
8	36	6	DRESSES
10	38	8	
12	40	10	
14	42	12	
16	44	14	
18	46	16	
20	46	18	
4.5	37.5	6	SHOES
5	38	6.5	
5.5	38.5	7	
6	39	7.5	
6.5	40	8	
7	41	8.5	

MEASUREMENTS

The metric system is in use throughout the Czech Republic.

Distances	measured in kilometres
Speed	measured in kilometres per hour
Food	sold in grams and kilograms
Liquids	sold in litres
Fuel	sold in litres

VISITING WITH CHILDREN

Many of Prague's tourist attractions will appeal to children as much as to adults. The city has enough of a fairy-tale character to entrance most children, at least for a while. The buskers and street performers

CONVERSION CHART

FROM	TO	MULTIPLY BY
Inches	Centimetres	2.54
Centimetres	Inches	0.3937
Feet	Metres	0.3048
Metres	Feet	3.2810
Yards	Metres	0.9144
Metres	Yards	1.0940
Miles	Kilometres	1.6090
Kilometres	Miles	0.6214
Acres	Hectares	0.4047
Hectares	Acres	2.4710
Gallons	Litres	4.5460
Litres	Gallons	0.2200
Ounces	Grams	28.35
Grams	Ounces	0.0353
Pounds	Grams	453.6
Grams	Pounds	0.0022
Pounds	Kilograms	0.4536
Kilograms	Pounds	2.205
Tons	Tonnes	1.0160
Tonnes	Tons	0.9842

A collection of puppets for sale on a stall on Charles Bridge

along the tourist trail are a great source of entertainment, as is the midday Changing of the Guard at the Castle. Not many children will have seen anything like the Orloj (Astronomical Clock) on the Staroměstská radnice (Old Town Hall), and getting around by tram will be a novel experience for many, especially aboard the vintage model. Some will enjoy a ride in one of the horse-drawn carriages based in the Staroměstské náměstí (Old Town Square), others a river trip or a go on a rowboat or pedalo. And there are plenty more specific attractions:
● Prague Zoo, including a ride aboard its chairlift (▷ 131).

PLANNING

CAR RENTAL COMPANIES IN PRAGUE

COMPANY	ADDRESS	TELEPHONE	WEBSITE
A Rent Car	Washingtonova 9, Nové Město, Prague 1	224 233 265	www.a-rentcar.cz
AT Car-Budget	Reservation Centre, Hotel InterContinental		
	Náměstí Curieových 5, Staré Město, Prague 1	235 325 713	www.budget.cz
Czechocar	5. května 65, Nusle, Prague 4	261 222 079	www.czechocar.cz
Dvořák – Rent a Car	Revoluční 25, Staré Město, Prague 1	224 826 260	www.dvorak-rentacar.cz
Europcar	Pařížská 28, Staré Město, Prague 1	224 811 290	www.europcar.cz
Have Car	Vodičkova 26, Nové Město, Prague 2	296 329 602	www.have-car.cz
Hertz	Karlovo náměstí 28, Nové Město, Prague 2	222 231 010	www.hertz.cz
Sixt Speed Rent	Hotel Hilton, Pobřežní 1, Prague 8	296 622 407	www.e-sixt.cz

● The Muzeum loutkářských kultur (Puppet Museum, ▷ 92) and Puppet Theatre (▷ 178).
● The fairground-type facilities at the Výstaviště exhibition grounds (▷ 189).
● Technically-minded kids will appreciate the Technical Museum (▷ 96) and the Public Transport Museum (▷ 92), while junior fans of costume and dance will enjoy folklore

shows such as those staged regularly by the Czech Song and Dance Ensemble at the Pyramida Hotel.
● The Bludiště, or Mirror Maze, (▷ 102) near the top of Petřín Hill will entertain, especially if combined with a trip aboard the funicular railway.
● The Communist-era House of Sport is now Teta tramtarie (▷ 189) a kind of mall for the young, with toys, games and all kinds of children's gear for sale, plus a milk bar, pizzeria, puppet theatre and cinema.

CAR RENTAL
The major international car rental firms are represented in Prague, and arranging a car in advance through one of them may entitle you to a discount. It

will normally be less expensive, however, to rent a vehicle from one of the many local firms (▷ 39). The rental firms in the chart above all have downtown offices.

LOCAL WAYS
● Manners are mildly formal. Titles such as Dr. and Ing. (Engineer) are respected and should be acknowledged. Hands are shaken on meeting, on being introduced, and sometimes on leaving.
● If you are invited into someone's home, be prepared to leave your shoes at the door and don borrowed slippers. A small gift, such as chocolates or flowers, will be appreciated, but should not be too ostentatious.
● Tables can be shared with strangers in restaurants, with permission (*je tu valno?*). Always wish your fellow-diners *dobrou chuť* (bon appétit) before eating and *na zdraví* (good health) before drinking (anything alcoholic).
● When riding the escalators down to and up from the metro, you should stand on the right-hand side; Czechs in a hurry use the left to pass.
● On trams and metros, be aware of fellow passengers and offer your seat to the elderly, pregnant women and people with a disability.

PLACES OF WORSHIP
Anglican
Svatého Klimenta, Klimentská 5, Nové Město, Prague 1, tel 284 688 575, tram 5, 8, 14 to Dlouhá třída (Sunday service 11am).

Baptist
International Baptist Church, Vinohradská 68, Vinohrady, Prague 3, tel 731 778 735, metro Jiřího z Poděbrad (Sunday service 11am).

Catholic
Svatého Tomáše, Josefská 8, Malá Strana, Prague 1, tel 257 532 675, tram 12, 20, 22, 23 to Malostranské náměstí (Mass Saturday 6pm, Sunday 11am).

Panny Marie Vítězné (▷ 104), Karmelitská 9, Malá Strana, Prague 1, tel 257 313 646, tram 12, 20, 22, 23 to Malostranské náměstí (Mass Sunday at noon).

The baroque Church of St. Nicholas on Old Town Square

Jewish
Bejt Simcha Reform Synagogue, Mánesova 8, Vinohrady, Prague 2, tel 222 52 472, metro Muzeum. Services are also held in the Old-New, Spanish and Jerusalem synagogues.

Muslim
Islamic Center & Mosque, 14 Politických vězňů, Nové město, Prague 1, tel 732 111 611, metro Muzeum or Můstek.

Orthodox
Orthodox Cathedral of Saints Cyril and Methodius, Resslova 9, Nové město, Prague 2, tel 249 206 686, metro Karlovo náměstí.

MONEY

One Czech crown is made up of 100 hellers. Banknotes come in denominations of **50, 100, 200, 500, 1,000, 2,000** and **5,000** crowns.

The currency is the Czech crown (*koruna česká*, abbreviated to Kč or CZK). The crown is divided into a hundred virtually worthless hellers (*halíř* abbreviated to h). Coins come in denominations of 1, 2, 5, 10, 20 and 50 Kč; notes in denominations of 50, 100, 200, 500, 1,000, 2,000 and very rarely 5,000 Kč.

EXCHANGE RATES

There are approximately 42Kč to £1, 30Kč to 1 euro or 24Kč to $1 (US). The Czech government plans to enter the euro zone in the future, and some hotels and businesses already post their prices in euros.

BEFORE YOU GO

● It is advisable to take a combination of cash, traveller's cheques and credit and debit cards, so you don't have to rely on any one means of payment in the event of an emergency.

● Change a small amount of cash before you go (or at the airport), enough to cover you for your first expenses on arriving.

CREDIT AND DEBIT CARDS

● Check that your credit or debit card can be used to withdraw money from cash machines in the Czech Republic.

● Interest is normally payable on cash withdrawals on credit cards, and most banks charge a fee when you use a debit card. It's worth comparing the rates from a range of banks.

EVERYDAY ITEMS AND HOW MUCH THEY COST

ITEM	PRICE (Kč)
Cup of coffee	40–60
Bottle of mineral water	40–50
Beer (half litre)	25–35
Glass of house wine	45–70
The Prague Post newspaper	50
International newspaper	80–150
Camera film	220
Litre of fuel	35
Public transport ticket	20
Small open sandwich	30

● There are plenty of cash machines in Prague (including the airport) and elsewhere in the country, and instructions are usually in English and German as well as Czech.

● Most establishments used to dealing with visitors from abroad accept payment by credit card, but a significant number do not, and others may enforce a minimum spending limit.

TRAVELLER'S CHEQUES

● Traveller's cheques offer security, as long as you keep a separate record of their serial numbers, but commission can be high when you change them. For a short stay they may be more of a hindrance than a help.

BANKS AND BUREAUX DE CHANGE

● Banks and savings banks are plentiful in Prague and around the country generally, and most have a *směnárna* (currency exchange).

● Commission varies between

one bank and another, but is invariably less than in on-street bureaux de change, and is rarely more than 3 per cent.

● The Komerční banka has traditionally offered some of the lowest rates (central branch at Na příkopě 33, Staré Město, Prague 1, tel 222 432 111).

● Bureaux de change solicit your business along the tourist trails throughout the city but, despite the competition, tend to charge high rates of commission, even though the exchange rate quoted may appear generous.

● Banks are normally open between 8am and 5pm.

● Many bureaux de change seem to stay open as long as there is any prospect of business.

● Hotel reception desks will often change money, but don't expect a particularly generous rate.

WIRING AND TRANSFERRING MONEY

● Wiring money from home should only be undertaken as a last resort, as the commission charged can be expensive and it may take some time.

● Conventional banks such as the central branch of the Komerční banka (▷ above) can undertake this service. Alternatively use American Express (Václavské náměstí 56, Nové Město, Prague 1, tel 224 219 992, open daily 9–7).

● The Czech Post Office (*Česká pošta*) has an arrangement with Western Union whereby money

PLANNING

can be transferred to and from abroad relatively quickly. The necessary documents are in English, as well as Czech, and the service is available at selected post offices (www.cpost.cz).

DISCOUNTS

Children, students and senior citizens are eligible for substantial discounts for many services and attractions in Prague, from public transport to museum admissions. With this in mind, it's always a good idea to carry some proof of age or status, such as a passport, International Student Identity Card (ISIC) or International Youth Travel Card (IYTC). You can get

Bright signs outside a bureau de change in Prague

an ISIC from your student union or from CTS. Contact www.ctstravelusa.com in the US or www.ctstravel.co.uk in Britain. Children under 6 travel free on

public transport within Prague, as do permanent residents over the age of 70.

TIPPING

● At restaurants and cafés a service charge is sometimes included in the bill, in which case tipping is not compulsory. However, it is common practice to round up the total paid.

● Foreign visitors are expected to be more generous than locals.

● Only round up the amount paid for a taxi ride if service has been reasonable.

● It is customary to give lavatory attendants a few crowns.

FINDING HELP

EMERGENCY TELEPHONE NUMBERS

GENERAL
112
AMBULANCE
155
FIRE
150
POLICE
156 (municipal)
158 (national)

POLICE STATIONS

THE CENTRAL POLICE STATION IS AT:
✉ Bartolomějská 14, Staré Město, Prague 1 ☎ 974 851 700 🚇 Národní třída 🚊 Tram 6, 9, 18, 21, 22, 23 to Národní třída or 6, 9, 17, 18, 21, 22, 23 to Národní divadlo

OTHER POLICE STATIONS IN CENTRAL PRAGUE INCLUDE:
✉ Vlašská 3, Malá Strana, Prague 1 ☎ 974 851 730 🚊 Tram 12, 20, 22, 23 to Malostranské náměstí

✉ Benediktská 1, Staré Město (rear of Kotva department store), Prague 1 ☎ 974 851 710 🚇 Náměstí Republiky

✉ Jungmannovo náměstí 9, Nové Město (near lower end of Václavské náměstí), Prague 1 ☎ 974 851 750 🚇 Můstek

✉ Hybernská 2, Nové Město (near Obecní dům/Municipal House), Prague 1 ☎ 974 851 500 🚇 Náměstí Republiky

✉ Krakovská 11, Nové Město (near upper end of Václavské náměstí), Prague 1 ☎ 974 851 720 🚇 Muzeum

Prague and the Czech Republic generally do not present serious hazards, crime or safety problems to visitors, and crime rates, while rising, are still much lower than in most comparable Western cities. However, sensible precautions should be taken. This includes taking out adequate travel insurance to cover any health emergencies, thefts or legal

Remember to keep your belongings close by at all times

costs that may arise. Violent crimes against the person are most unlikely. The most common problem is petty theft such as pickpocketing and stealing passports.

PERSONAL SECURITY

● Carry only as much cash on your person as you are likely to need during the course of the day, and leave valuable items in the hotel safe or in the care of the hotel reception.

● Carry bags and cameras slung diagonally across your chest rather than over the shoulder, and position them under one arm in busy places. Backpacks are a tempting prospect to thieves, some of whom are expert at slicing them open unobtrusively and

removing the contents.

● Keep belongings close by. Don't leave items like wallets, mobile phones and cameras on café and restaurant tables. If you place a handbag on the floor,

PLANNING

make sure the strap is wound round the leg of the table or chair.

● Crowded places present great opportunities for pickpockets and bag-snatchers. Be especially vigilant on Karlův most (Charles Bridge) and in other busy areas frequented by tourists.

● Beware of anyone offering to change money on the street. It is illegal and not worth doing anyway; the money-changer may be in league with a 'false policeman' who will demand to inspect your passport and then make off with it.

● Some parts of the city are frequented at night by less-than-savoury characters, including street-walkers. Areas you might wish to avoid after nightfall include the park outside Hlavní nádraží (Main Railway Station) and the interior of the station itself, while Václavské náměstí (Wenceslas Square), Uhelný trh in Staré Město, and Florenc bus station can get pretty sleazy, though not actually dangerous.

● Cars are a popular target for thieves. After parking your vehicle—preferably in a supervised parking area—don't leave anything visible in the interior and take

LOST/STOLEN CREDIT CARDS

● Before you set off, make a note of the telephone number to ring if your credit card is lost or stolen. Remember to keep the number separate from the card itself.

LOST PROPERTY

CENTRAL LOST PROPERTY OFFICE
✉ Karoliny Světlé 5, Staré Město, Prague 1
☎ 224 235 085
🕐 Mon, Wed 8–5.30, Tue, Thu 8–4, Fri 8–2
Ⓜ Národní třída
🚋 Tram 6, 9, 17, 18, 21, 22, 23 to Národní divadlo

valuables, including the radio if possible, with you.

● If you become the victim of a robbery, report it to the police. Although you are unlikely to see the criminals apprehended and your possessions recovered, you will need a police document in order to file a claim with your insurance company.

Your insurer or broker should also be informed as soon as possible.

● Loss or theft of your passport should be reported to the police and then to your embassy. Making a photocopy of the page giving your personal details before you leave home will save a great deal of time.

POLICE

Two kinds of police (*policie*) operate in the Czech Republic. The national police are identified by their navy-blue jackets, grey trousers and green and white patrol cars, while the municipal police (*městská policie*) are dressed in black and are invariably on foot. Policemen are generally helpful to visitors from abroad.

Be patient when dealing with the sometimes ponderous police bureaucracy. If you wish to report a theft, look for a police officer on the street or contact the nearest local police station rather than using the emergency telephone number. Police stations are shown on most city maps, usually by a green star on a yellow background.

The friendly face of the police in Prague

EMBASSIES AND CONSULATES IN PRAGUE			
COUNTRY	CONTACT DETAILS	TELEPHONE	METRO/TRAM STOP
Australia	6th floor, Solitaire Building, Klimentská 10, Nové Město, Prague 1; open Mon–Fri 9–1, 2–5	296 578 530	Tram 5, 8, 14 to Dlouhá třída
Canada	Muchova 6, Hradčany, Prague 6 (www.canada.cz); open daily 8.30–12.30, 1.30–4.30	272 101 800	Metro: Hradčanská
Ireland	Tržiště 13, Malá Strana, Prague 1; open Mon–Fri 9.30–12.30, 2.30–4.30	257 530 061-4	Tram 12, 20, 22, 23 to Malostranské náměstí
New Zealand	Dykova 19, Vinohrady, Prague 3; open Mon–Fri 9–noon	222 514 672	Tram 10, 16 to Vinohradská vodárna
UK	Thunovská 14, Malá Strana, Prague 1 (www.britain.cz); open Mon–Fri 9–noon	257 402 111	Tram 12, 20, 22, 23 to Malostranské náměstí
US	Tržiště 15, Malá Strana, Prague 1 (www.usembassy.cz); open Mon–Fri 9–noon	257 530 663	Tram 12, 20, 22, 23 to Malostranské náměstí

OPENING TIMES AND TICKETS

OPENING TIMES

Banks
Mon–Fri 8am–5pm (possibly earlier on Friday). Smaller branches may close at midday.

Churches
Some churches are open the same hours as museums and galleries, but many are only opened shortly before services.

Museums and galleries
Tue–Sun 10am–6pm. Nearly all museums and galleries are closed on Monday. There may be an evening opening on Thursdays.

Pharmacies
Mon–Sat 8am–6pm. 24-hour pharmacies are available (▷ 273). Details are usually posted on the doors of all pharmacies.

Post offices
Mon–Fri 8am–6pm. Central post office 2am–midnight (▷ 274).

Restaurants
Some restaurants open for lunch, then take a break before opening again in the early evening. Some local restaurants may close at 10pm or 11pm. Establishments with a foreign clientele normally stay open until midnight or later.

Shops
In general shops open Mon–Fri 8am/9am–5pm, Sat 9am–noon. Supermarkets and Department Stores: Mon–Fri 8am/9am–8pm, Sat 10am–7pm (guidelines only). Malls: Sun 10am–7pm. Nový Smíchov mall: daily 7am–midnight.

TICKETS
The cost of travel, entry fees and entertainment in Prague is generally low by Western European and US standards. However, there are ways to reduce costs further still.
● Buy concert and similar tickets direct from the venue rather than through a ticket agency.
● Check whether museums and galleries have free, or reduced-rate, admission on certain days of the month.
● Holders of an International Student Identity Card (ISIC) are entitled to discounts for public transport, museums, galleries and theatres. Senior citizens aged over 70 (60 in some cases) with appropriate ID may be entitled to similar discounts.
● Consider buying a Prague Card (▷ 44) or public transport pass, as it may save you money.

NATIONAL HOLIDAYS
1 January
New Year's Day; Establishment of the Czech Republic (1993)
March/April
Easter Monday
1 May
Labour Day
8 May
Liberation Day (Prague freed from German occupation 1945)
5 July
Cyril and Methodius Day
6 July
Master Jan Hus Day
28 September
State Day of the Czech Republic (Saint's Day of St. Wenceslas)
28 October
Foundation of the Republic of Czechoslovakia (1918)
17 November
Day of the Struggle for Liberty and Democracy (Velvet Revolution 1989)
24 December
Christmas Eve
25 December
Christmas Day
26 December
Christmas festival continues

TOURIST OFFICES

Prague is served by a highly professional tourism organization, the P.I.S. (*Pražská informační služba*—Prague Information Service; www.prague-info.cz). It publishes maps and visitor information on a variety of subjects and in several languages, including English, and also manages a number of visitor attractions. Manned by helpful, multilingual staff, its information offices can provide advice on what to do and where to go, as well as selling tickets for events and finding accommodation. Most towns in the Czech Republic frequented by visitors from abroad have tourist offices, though the quality of information provided can vary.

● The main P.I.S. office in Prague is in the Lucerna passage, Vodičkova 36, Prague 1; open Apr–end Oct Mon–Fri 9–7, Sat–Sun 9–6; Nov–end Mar Mon–Fri 9–6, Sat–Sun 9–5.
● There is another office in the Staroměstská radnice (Old Town Hall) at Staroměstské náměstí 1, Staré Město, Prague 1; opening times as above.
● Other offices are in the hall of the Hlavní nádraží (main railway station) and, from April to the end of October, in the Malá Strana bridge tower at the western end of Karlův most.

Czech Tourism is the overall organization promoting tourism in the Czech Republic. Its head office in Prague is at Vinohradská 46, Vinohrady, Prague 2, tel 221 580 111; www.czechtourism.com

It is also represented abroad:
Canada Czech Tourism
401 Bay Street, Suite 1510, Toronto, Ontario M5H 2Y4, tel 416 363 9928
UK Czech Tourism
13 Harley Street, London W1G 9QG, tel 020 7631 0427
US Czech Tourism
Czech Center, 1109 Madison Avenue, New York, NY 10028, tel 212 288 0830

Czech Republic

Look out for the logo above to direct you to Czech Tourism

PLANNING

HEALTH

The Czech Republic generally has a good reputation for health care, despite shortage of funds and the emigration of skilled personnel tempted by higher salaries elsewhere.

There are reciprocal health care arrangements with EU member countries, including the UK. Care will normally be provided free of charge at the hospital or clinic, but otherwise a refund may be claimed (▷ 273). Medicines may have to be paid for and a refund claimed in the same way. Citizens of the UK and other EU countries should ensure that they are in possession of a European Health Insurance Card (EHIC).

Taking out comprehensive medical insurance before you travel is advisable (this will give you more control of any treatment you require) and is essential if you live in a non-EU country. Always check the cover provided, particularly regarding repatriation.

BEFORE YOU GO
● No inoculations are required for visiting the Czech Republic, though you might want to make sure that your tetanus protection is up to date (boosters are required every 10 years).
● If you are taking any medication and may need a repeat prescription while away, ask for it well before you travel. Also ask your doctor to give you a note of the pharmaceutical name of any medication you are taking—trade names for various medicines may differ in the Czech Republic.
● If you are planning to be away for a month or more, it may also be a good idea to have a full medical and dental check-up before you go.

FINDING A CLINIC OR HOSPITAL
Many people in the medical profession speak English, and are used to treating visitors from abroad. If you need medical treatment you could ask at your hotel for a local doctor, but Nemocnice Na Homolce (Na Homolce Hospital) is particularly recommended. It offers full services including emergency treatment and has a special section for foreigners with

---

HEALTHY FLYING
● Visitors to Prague from as far as the US, Australia or New Zealand may be concerned about the effect of long-haul flights on their health. The most widely publicized concern is deep vein thrombosis, or DVT. Misleadingly called 'economy class syndrome', DVT is the forming of a blood clot in the body's deep veins, particularly in the legs. The clot can move around the bloodstream and could be fatal.
● Those most at risk include the elderly, pregnant women and those using the contraceptive pill, smokers and the overweight. If you are at increased risk of DVT see your doctor before departing. Flying increases the likelihood of DVT because passengers are often seated in a cramped position for long periods of time and may become dehydrated.

To minimize risk:
Drink water (not alcohol)
Don't stay immobile for hours at a time
Stretch and exercise your legs periodically
Do wear elastic flight socks, which support veins and reduce the chances of a clot forming

EXERCISES
1 ANKLE ROTATIONS   2 CALF STRETCHES   3 KNEE LIFTS

Lift feet off the floor. Draw a circle with the toes, moving one foot clockwise and the other counterclockwise

Start with heel on the floor and point foot upward as high as you can. Then lift heels high, keeping balls of feet on the floor

Lift leg with knee bent while contracting your thigh muscle. Then straighten leg, pressing foot flat to the floor

Other health hazards for flyers are airborne diseases and bugs spread by the plane's air-conditioning system. These are largely unavoidable, but if you have a serious medical condition seek advice from a doctor before flying.

English-speaking doctors in attendance.

Contact details
✉ Roentgenova 2, Smíchov, Prague 5
☎ 257 272 146/257 271 111
🕐 24 hours for emergencies
🚌 Bus 167 from Anděl metro to Nemocnice Na Homolce
www.homolka.cz

The downtown first-aid clinic of the medical faculty of Charles University is in Charles Square:

✉ Karlovo náměstí 32, Nové Město, Prague 2
🕐 Mon–Fri 7–4
🚊 Tram 4, 6, 10, 14, 16, 18, 22, 23, 24 to Karlovo náměstí

Emergency care is also provided nearby at the First Medical Clinic of Prague Ltd:
✉ Vyšehradská 35, Nové Město, Prague 2
☎ 224 918 201
🕐 Daily 24 hours
🚇 Karlovo náměstí

North American visitors should be aware of the following establishments:

Canadian Medical Care
☒ Veleslavínská 1, Dejvice, Prague 6
☎ 235 360 133
◉ Weekdays 8–6 (24-hour on–call, tel 724 300 302)
▣ Tram 20, 26 to Nádraží Veleslavín
www.cmc.praha.cz

Health Center Prague
☒ Vodičkova 28, 2nd floor, Nové Město, Prague 1
☎ 224 220 040, 296 236 000 (appointments); 603 433 833, 603 481 361 (emergency)
◉ 24 hours for emergencies; appointments Mon–Fri 8–5
▣ Můstek
▣ Tram 3, 9, 14, 24 to Václavské náměstí

WATER

Tap water may not be particularly palatable, but it is safe to drink, though most people drink mineral water (*minerální voda* or *minerálka*) at home and when eating out. In a country famous for its spas, several brands are available, of which the most widespread is the mildly fizzy *Mattoni* from Karlovy Vary.

DENTAL TREATMENT

Dental treatment is subject to the same conditions as other medical care. Even if you are from an EU country, make sure your

insurance covers the cost of dental treatment.

Free, or reduced cost, emergency treatment should be available at:
☒ Palackého 5, Nové Město, Prague 1
☎ 224 946 981
◉ 24 hours
▣ Můstek
▣ Tram 3, 9, 14, 24 to Václavské náměstí

Private dental clinics with experience in treating visitors from abroad include:

European Dental Center
☒ Václavské náměstí 33, Nové Město, Prague 1
☎ 224 228 984
◉ Mon–Fri 8am–11pm, Sat 9–6; 24 hours for emergencies
▣ Můstek
▣ Tram 3, 9, 14, 24 to Václavské náměstí
www.edcdental.cz

American Dental Associates
☒ Stará Celnice Building, 2nd floor atrium, V Celnici 4/1031, Nové Město, Prague 1
☎ 221 181 121
◉ Mon–Thu 8.30–8, Fri 8.30–5, Sat 10.30–9
▣ Náměstí Republiky
▣ Tram 5, 8, 14 to Náměstí Republiky
www.americandental.cz

PHARMACIES

Pharmacies are identified by the international green cross sign and the word *Lékárna*. They are generally well-stocked, though not necessarily with all the brands familiar at home, and staff are usually knowledgeable and helpful.
24-hour pharmacies:
☒ Palackého 5, Nové Město, Prague 1
☎ 224 946 982
▣ Můstek
▣ Tram 3, 9, 14, 24 to Václavské náměstí

☒ Belgická 37, Vinohrady, Prague 2
☎ 222 513 396
▣ Náměstí Míru

▣ Tram 4, 10, 16, 22, 23 to Náměstí Míru

OPTICIANS

If you wear glasses or contact lenses, take spares with you, and have a copy of your prescription handy in case you break or lose them. If you are going to be away for a long time and don't want to carry lots of contact lens solution with you, supplies are available at pharmacies and opticians. Major optician chains with several branches in Prague include Eiffel Optic and GrandOptical.

Contact details
Eiffel Optic
☒ Na příkopě 25, Staré Město, Prague 1
☎ 224 234 966
◉ Mon–Sat 8–8, Sun 9.30–7
▣ Můstek

GrandOptical
☒ Myslbek, Na příkopě 19–21, Staré Město, Prague 1
☎ 224 238 371
◉ Mon–Fri 9.30–8, Sat 10–7, Sun 10–6
▣ Můstek

ALTERNATIVE MEDICINE

Czechs are great believers in herbal remedies, and pharmacies stock 'cures' not normally available in such establishments. Prague has its share of practicioners of complementary therapies, who can be found by consulting the *Zlaté stránky* (Yellow—or rather 'golden'—Pages) telephone directory, which has an English index (www.zlatestranky.cz).

A traditional pharmacy in Malá Strana with wooden shelves and decorative plasterwork

COMMUNICATION

It is easy to keep in touch with home while you are in Prague with internet cafés, dataports and mobile phones.

TELEPHONES

The telephone system has improved beyond recognition in the last few years, though it may be the memory of its unreliability that has impelled so many Czechs to invest in mobile phones.

● Most pay phones accept only telephone cards, which can be obtained from post offices, newsagents and any establishment displaying the blue and yellow *Český Telecom* logo. They come in denominations of 50 units upwards.

● Many phones have instructions in English; if not, insert the card, pause for the LCD display to appear, listen for the dial tone, then dial the number. The ringing tone is a series of long beeps; the engaged tone is short and fast.

● Charges per unit are at their maximum between 7am and 7pm, less outside those hours and on weekends and public holidays.

● International calls from a pay phone are expensive. The LCD display will reveal how fast your units are disappearing.

● Phoning from your hotel may be convenient, but it will also be expensive, possibly up to four times as much as the normal rate.

● It is slightly cheaper to make an international call from the annexe of the main post office at Politických vězňů 4, by booking it at the counter and waiting to be sent to a phone. You can also make reverse-charge (collect) calls from here.

USEFUL TELEPHONE NUMBERS	
Emergency	112
Directory enquiries (national)	1180
Directory enquiries (International; operators should speak English)	1181
Prague Information Service (P.I.S; Mon–Fri 8–7)	12 444

● Phoning home with your mobile is usually possible, but will be expensive. If you are staying for any length of time, it's worth buying a pay-as-you-go SIM card.

POST OFFICES

● Česká Pošta has local post offices with variable opening hours all over Prague, including one in the Castle. The central post office (www.cpost.cz) offering the whole range of facilities, including poste restante, is just off Václavské náměstí (Wenceslas Square):

✉ Hlavní pošta, Jindřišská 14, Nové Město, Prague 1
☎ 221 131 111
🕐 Daily 2am–midnight
Ⓜ Můstek
🚋 Tram 3, 9, 14, 24 to Václavské náměstí

● The postal service's corporate colour is orange. Don't mistake the letter boxes attached to walls for litter bins.

● Stamps (*známky*) can be bought from news kiosks, tobacconists, some hotels and shops, as well as at post offices.

● The postal service is rather unpredictable, but letters and postcards to the UK should take no more than a week, and up to two weeks to the US.

● Make sure your letters and cards sent abroad have a *Par Avion* sticker.

● Parcels weighing up to 2kg (4.4 pounds) can be sent from

CALLING THE CZECH REPUBLIC FROM ABROAD

The Czech Republic's country code from abroad is 420. To phone Prague from the UK, dial 00 420 followed by the local nine-digit number (which includes the Prague code of 2). To phone Prague from the US, dial 011 420, then as above.

CALLING ABROAD FROM THE CZECH REPUBLIC

To call home from the Czech Republic, dial the international access code (00), followed by the country code, the area code (for UK area codes omit the first zero), then the number.

COUNTRY CODES

Dial 00 followed by:

Australia	61
Canada	1
New Zealand	64
Republic of Ireland	353
UK	44
US	1

any post office. Large packages must be sent from the customs post office (Celní pošta), Plzeňská 139, Smíchov, Prague 5, tel 257 019 111, tram 4, 7, 9, 10 to Klamovka.

● Alternatively, and much quicker, use a courier service such as DHL, at Václavské náměstí 53, tel 800 103 000, metro Muzeum.

INTERNET ACCESS

You can get online at many hotels, and there are plenty of cybercafés scattered around Prague, among them:

Bohemia Bagel Masná 2, Staré Město, Prague 1, open Mon–Fri 7am–midnight, Sat–Sun 8am–midnight, tram 5, 8, 14 to Dlouhá třída.

Globe Bookstore & Coffeehouse Pštrossova 6, Nové Město, Prague 1, tel 224 934 203, open daily 10am–midnight, tram 6, 9, 17, 18, 21, 22, 23 to Národní divadlo.

Jáma V jámě 7, Nové Město, Prague 1, tel 224 222 383, open daily 11am–midnight, tram 3, 9, 14, 24 to Vodičkova.

MAILING RATES			
		to non-European countries	to Europe
Postcards and letters			
(surface mail)	up to 10g	12Kč	9Kč
	up to 20g	9Kč	9Kč
	up to 50g	17Kč	17Kč
(airmail)	up to 20g	14Kč	14Kč
	up to 50g	26Kč	26Kč

		to non-European countries	to Europe
Parcels			
(surface mail)	up to 500g	95Kč	95Kč
(airmail)	up to 500g	181Kč	181Kč

Note: International postal charges are liable to increase

MEDIA

NEWSPAPERS

Many of the leading European newspapers can be bought in Prague, though they normally arrive on the day after publication. One exception is the *Guardian*, which is printed in Frankfurt and is usually on sale by mid-morning. The *International Herald Tribune* and *USA Today* are also on the newsstands on the day of publication. With the exception of the *Guardian*, newspapers from abroad are sold at several times their price at home. News magazines such as *Time* and *Newsweek* are widely available. The best-stocked newsstand is probably the one at the lower end of Václavské náměstí (Wenceslas Square). The leading Czech papers include the liberal *Lidové noviny*; *Právo*, the completely reformed and respected former organ of the Communist Party; and *Mladá fronta Dnes*, aimed in its previous incarnation at Communist youth. The most successful sensationalist tabloid is *Blesk*.

Local English-language newspapers and journals
The Prague Post
This weekly paper is quite an institution, having been founded in 1991 with American author and journalist Alan Levy as its editor-in-chief (he died in 2004).

Its weekly *Night & Day* supplement gives an excellent run-down on events and its restaurant and other listings are a great help to visitors.
www.praguepost.com

Prague Tribune
A bi-monthly aimed at the expatriate business community.
www.prague-tribune.cz

The New Presence/ Přítomnost
The successor to the leading liberal intellectual journal of prewar Czechoslovakia.
www.new-presence.cz

Listings periodicals include:
Culture in Prague
Published monthly in English as well as Czech.

Kulturní přehled (Cultural overview)
A very thorough monthly; in Czech only, but just about decipherable.

TELEVISION

Most hotel rooms have a TV set receiving a variety of international channels, many of them German and Italian, though CNN and Sky News usually feature and you may also be able to get BBC News 24.

Czech state television consists of two channels, ČT 1 and ČT 2. The latter is more 'serious'; it broadcasts a daily early news programme in English and shows some English-language films with Czech subtitles. The most successful private channel is TV Nova, whose output is largely of US origin.

RADIO

The excellent range of programmes includes news provided by the BBC World Service which can be listened to on 101.1 FM. Of the four Czech state radio stations, ČR1 concentrates on news and current affairs, while ČR3 plays mostly classical music. There is news in English on 92.6 FM. Local commercial stations are dominated by fast-talking DJs playing the usual mixture of pop.

BOOKS, MAPS AND FILMS

BOOKS
History and culture
● Among the many books published in English on the history of Prague and the Czech lands, the most appealing and erudite is probably *Prague in Black and Gold* (1997) by Peter Demetz, who grew up in Prague before emigrating to the USA.
● Richard Burton's softback *Prague – A Cultural and Literary History* (2003) in the series 'Cities of the Imagination' is a good introduction to its subject.
● In *The Coasts of Bohemia* (1998), the Canadian academic Derek Sayer has written an exhaustive, often witty, account of how modern Czechs developed a sense of themselves as a nation by the selective rewriting of their history.

● Illustrated with black-and-white photographs, *Prague in the Shadow of the Swastika* (1995) by Callum MacDonald and Jan Kaplan evokes the dire days of the Nazi occupation.
● *Prague: the Turbulent Century* (1997) by Jan Kaplan and Krystyna Nosarzewska is a great compendium of photos, magazine illustrations, postcards and ephemera of all kinds.
● British journalist and writer Timothy Garton Ash stood on the Wenceslas Square balcony with Václav Havel as the future president greeted the crowds during the Velvet Revolution of 1989, and *We the People* (1990) is his eyewitness account of the fall of Communism.
● British-based Czech journalist and wit Benjamin Kuras has

produced the Czech equivalent of *1066 and All That* in a sardonic history book entitled *Czechs and Balances—a Nation's Survival Kit* (1996).
● There are plenty of beautifully illustrated books about the glories of Prague's architecture, but to understand the why as well as the what, look at *Prague—Eleven Centuries of Architecture: Historical Guide* (1992) by various authors. Supplement it for the modern age with the handy guide *Prague—Twentieth Century Architecture* (2002).

Literature
● The Czech classic everyone has heard of is *The Good Soldier Švejk and His Fortunes in the World War* (1973) by the

PLANNING

prankster Jaroslav Hašek. It is a hilarious account of a wise fool drafted into the shambolic Austro-Hungarian army in World War I.

● Prague's most-loved novelist was Bohumil Hrabal, best known abroad for the film adaptation of his tragic-comic *Closely Observed Trains* (1990, ▷ Films). Even more readable is *I Served the King of England* (1989) the breathless life story of an all-too-clever Prague waiter.

● In permanent exile in Paris, Milan Kundera now writes in French and is more widely admired abroad than at home. But his *The Unbearable Lightness of Being* (1984) remains a classic, as does his less well-known *The Joke* (1984), written much earlier as a satire on Communism.

● Another author who chose to remain in exile (in Canada) after 1989 is Josef Škvorecký. *The Cowards* (1972) is his equivalent of *The Catcher in the Rye*, a debunking account of Czech behaviour in the last days of World War II.

● The novelist, short-story writer and essayist Ivan Klíma survived incarceration in Terezín as a child. *The Spirit of Prague* (1994) reviews the many influences on his development as a writer.

● A painless way of sampling the literary riches of Prague is to purchase Paul Wilson's *Prague: A Traveller's Literary Companion* (1995), which contains extracts from works by most of the city's great writers.

● The Norwegian journalist Terje Englund has lived in Prague long enough to take the lid off the Czech character in his 'User's Manual for Foreigners' *The Czechs in a Nutshell* (2004).

MAPS

The larger bookshops in Prague all have a selection of maps and plans. The widest range is probably in the bookshop in the Black Madonna House (▷ 70, open Mon–Fri 9.30–7, Sat 9.30–6).

The maps in this book are ideal for your stay in Prague but you could also try the following:

● Marco Polo městský plan Praha-Prag-Prague 1:12,000. A beautifully printed and very detailed town plan. Legend in English and street index.

● Marco Polo městský plan Praha-Prag-Prague 1:6,000. Even more detailed plan of central Prague.

● EuroCity velký městský atlas. A 126-page A–Z atlas at a scale of 1:20,000. Includes plan of central Prague and public transport map.

● Plán města Prahy: městská hromadná doprava—public transit plan 1:23,000. Detailed and ultra-clear city plan of public transport services, including every metro station, tram and bus stop and inset plan of night services.

● Praha pro motoristy (Prague for motorists). Includes 1:10,000 plan of central Prague with details of one-way streets and parking garages; inset plan of parking zones; 1:30,000 plan of Greater Prague showing through routes, park-and-ride facilities; 1:150,000 road map of region. Available from P.I.S. information offices (▷ 271).

Relaxing with a good book

For trips outside Prague, and for walking in the countryside, the individual sheets of the official topographical map at 1:100,000, 1:50,000 and 1:25,000 are excellent. They are supplemented for popular tourist areas by maps with additional visitor information published by the Austrian firm Freytag & Berndt and the German firm Kompass. If you plan to explore the Czech Republic, the indispensable companion is the 288-page Autoatlas Česká Republika.

● If your trip involves driving across Germany to Prague, the 3 miles to 1 inch Big Road Atlas Germany published in Britain by the AA includes the western part of the Czech Republic.

● Alternatively, for a detailed plan of the city try www.mapy.cz (in Czech, but easy to follow).

FILMS

Prague has played a starring role in several films, and has been a background presence in many others. The Czech film industry has had more than its fair share of ups and downs; its heyday came in the mid- to late 1960s, when the Communist censor's grip was relaxed, and films like *A Blonde in Love* (Miloš Forman, 1965), *Intimate Lighting* (Ivan Passer, 1966) and *Closely Observed Trains* (Jiří Menzel, 1966) won international fame as the heralds of the Czech 'New Wave'. Émigré Forman used his native Prague to stand in for Mozart's Vienna in his acclaimed 1984 *Amadeus*. The intensely claustrophobic atmosphere of the Communist era is eerily evoked in Karel Kachyňa's *The Ear* (1970), set in the bugged apartment of a paranoid Party official and his wife. The invasion itself forms the background of Milan Kundera's *The Unbearable Lightness of Being* (1988), whose protagonists agonize about their convoluted lives as the Prague Spring is crushed by the Soviet tanks. The happier events of the 1989 Velvet Revolution form the setting for the popular Czech film *Kolya* (1996), made by the father-and-son team of Zdeněk and Jan Svěrák. It tells the bittersweet story of a grumpy, middle-aged Praguer redeemed by having to care for a little boy. The same team were subsequently responsible for a wartime mini-epic, *Dark Blue World* (2001), which paid tribute to the Czech pilots whose heroic exploits in the RAF were rewarded by imprisonment under Communism. Another recent evocation of wartime is *Divided We Fall* (2000) by Jan Hřebejk; with a wry and typically Czech view of human frailty.

Animated films are a Czech speciality, raised to the level of fine art in the work of Jiří Trnka, though the work of the Surrealist Jan Švankmajer is better known abroad. The latest of Švankmajer's witty but disturbing films is *Little Otik* (2000), the story of a monster child growing from an uprooted tree.

Nowadays, the considerable but relatively inexpensive resources of the Czech film industry are much in demand by foreign film-makers.

PLANNING

USEFUL WEBSITES

BACKGROUND INFORMATION
www.prague.tv
Everything you need to know about Prague, including an accommodation finder, expatriate gossip and tips on using taxis.

www.radio.cz
Draws on the very considerable resources of state radio to give a wealth of information on current affairs, culture and business.

www.myczechrepublic.com
A well-written and researched compendium of useful facts and advice about the Czech Republic generally, as well as Prague.

www.czech.cz
The official Foreign Ministry site of the Czech Republic, with basic information on the country, plus entry requirements, etc.

CULTURE
www.ngprague.cz
An introduction to Prague's Národní galerie (National Gallery) and its various outposts.

www.nm.cz
Details of all of the many branches of the Národní muzeum (National Museum), including several outside Prague.

DRIVING
www.uamk.cz
If you click on 'UK' and then 'Tourist Information' you will find some useful driving information.

EATING OUT
www.squaremeal.cz
Online and updated version of a booklet which reviews and classifies hundreds of restaurants.

EVENTS
www.praguepost.com
The online version of the city's leading English- or rather American-language journal, with current listings plus some visitor information.

www.sdmusic.cz
What's on in the world of Czech music of every kind.

www.ticketsbti.cz
Information on venues and ensembles, with online booking for classical concerts and opera.

GENERAL VISITOR INFORMATION
www.pis.cz or
www.prague-info.cz
The website of Prague's official tourism information service, *Pražská informační služba* (P.I.S.), with comprehensive information on all aspects of the city.

www.czechtourism.com
Updated general travel information on the Czech Republic and on places to visit.

www.xe.com
Currency converter.

GETTING AROUND
www.jizdnirad.cz
Timetable information for rail and long-distance bus travel.

www.vlak-bus.cz
An alternative to the above.

www.cdrail.cz
The official site of *České drahy* (Czech Railways) with timetable and other information, including reduced-fare deals.

www.dpp.cz
Comprehensive public transport information from *Dopravní podnik hl.m.Prahy*, the city's transit authority.

WEATHER
www.prague.ic.cz/prague-weather.htm
General Prague website with 12-day weather forecast.

www.myczechrepublic.com/weather/prague-weather.html
General information on climate and detailed daily forecast for the Prague area.

KEY SIGHTS QUICK WEBSITE FINDER		
SIGHT	**WEBSITE**	**PAGE**
Anežský klášter	www.ngprague.cz	64–66
Jiřský klášter	www.ngprague.cz	72–73
Josefov	www.jewishmuseum.cz	74–79
Loreta	www.loreta.cz	86–87
Muchovo muzeum	www.mucha.cz	89
Národní divadlo	www.narodni-divadlo.cz	94
Národní muzeum	www.nm.cz	95
Národní technické muzeum	www.ntm.cz	96
Obecní dům	www.obecnidum.cz	100–101
Pražský hrad	www.hrad.cz	106–111
Šternbeský palác	www.ngprague.cz	116–117
Strahovský klášter	www.strahovskyklaster.cz	118–119
Svatého Mikuláš	www.psalterium.cz	122–123
Svatého Víta	www.hrad.cz	126–129
Troja	www.citygalleryprague.cz	130–131
UPM muzeum	www.upm.cz	132–133
Valdštejnský palác	www.senat.cz	138
Veletržní palác	www.ngprague.cz	139–141
Výstaviště	www.nm.cz	147
Zbraslav	www.ngprague.cz	150–151

PLANNING

WORDS AND PHRASES

Czech is one of the most phonetic of all European languages and, unlike English, particular combinations of letters are nearly always pronounced the same way. If you master a few basic rules, particularly concerning the accents, you will find Czech easier to read and pronounce.

Vowels are pronouned as follows:

a	as **a** in	m**a**t
e	as **e** in	v**e**t
i/y	as **i** in	b**i**t
o	as **o** in	n**o**t
u	as **oo** in	b**oo**k
ě	as **ye** in	**ye**ll
ů	as **oo** in	s**oo**n

Adding an accent (´) over the vowel will lengthen the sound. For example:

á	as **a** in	f**a**r
í	as **ee** in	s**ee**

Note also these combinations:

au	as **ow** in	c**ow**
ou	as **oe** in	t**oe**

Consonants as in English except:

c	as **ts** in ma**ts**
j	as **y** in **y**es
ch	in the back of the throat like the Scottish lo**ch**
č	as **ch** in **ch**at
š	as **sh** in **sh**are
ž	like a French '**j**' (the sound in the middle of the word plea**s**ure)
ň	as **ny** in ca**ny**on
ř	combines rolled **r** and **zh** sound in mea**s**ure
ý	as **ie** in bel**ie**f
ď	as in **d**uration
ť	as **t** in over**t**ure
w	pronounced as **v**

All Czech nouns can be masculine, feminine or neuter. They also have case endings that change according to how the noun is used in a sentence. An adjective's ending also changes to match the ending of the noun. Expect to see multiple variations of the same word. For this reason, it is easier to treat basic phrases as a whole.

CONVERSATION

I don't speak Czech
Nemluvím česky

I only speak a little Czech
Mluvím česky jenom trochu

Do you speak English?
Mluvíte anglicky?

I don't understand
Nerozumím

Please repeat that
Můžete to zopakovat

Please speak more slowly
Mluvte pomalu, prosím

Please spell that
Jak se to píše?

Please could you write that down for me
Napište mi to, prosím

My name is...
Jmenuji se...

What's your name?
Jak se jmenujete?

Hello, pleased to meet you
Těší mě

This is my friend
To je můj přítel/moje přítelkyně

This is my wife/husband/ daughter/son
To je moje žena/můj muž/moje dcera/můj syn

Where do you live?
Kde bydlíte?

I live in...
Bydlím v...

I'm here on holiday
Jsem tady na dovolené

Good morning
Dobrý den

Good afternoon/evening
Dobrý den/dobrý večer

Goodbye
Na shledanou

Bye-bye/hello
Ahoj (a common greeting used for both)

See you tomorrow
Na shledanou zítra

See you soon
Uvidíme se brzy

What is the time?
Kolik je hodin?

How are you?
Jak se máte?

Fine, thank you
Díky, dobře

I'm sorry
Promiňte

USEFUL WORDS

yes	thank you	where	when	why
ano	**děkují**	**kde**	**kdy**	**proč**
no	you're welcome	here	now	who
ne	**prosím/nemáte zač**	**tady**	**ted'?**	**kdo**
please	excuse me!	there	later	may I/can I
prosím	**Promiňte!**	**tam**	**později**	**můžu**

Could you help me, please?
Pomůžete mi, prosím?

How much is this?
Kolik to stojí?

I'm looking for...
Hledám...

Where can I buy...?
Kde dostanu...?

How much is this/that?
Kolik stojí tohle/tamto?

When does the shop open/close?
Kdy tady otevíráte/zavíráte?

I'm just looking, thank you
Děkují, jenom si prohlížím

This isn't what I want
Není to ono

I'll take this
Vezmu si to

Do you have anything less expensive/smaller/larger?
Máte něco levnějšího/menšího/většího?

Are the instructions included?
Jsou u toho pokyny pro uživatele?

Do you have a bag for this?
Máte na to tašku?

I'm looking for a present
Hledám dárek

Can you gift wrap this please?
Zabalte to jako dárek, prosím

Do you accept credit cards?
Můžu platit kreditní kartou?

I'd like a kilo of...
Prosím kilo...

Do you have shoes to match this?
Máte boty, které by s tím ladily?

This is the right size
To je správná velikost

Can you measure me please?
Můžete mě prosím změřit?

This doesn't suit me
To není pro mě

Do you have this in...?
Máte to v...?

Should this be dry cleaned?
Musí se to nechat čistit?

Is there a market?
Je tady někde trh/tržnice?

0 **nula**	6 **šest**	12 **dvanáct**	18 **osmnáct**	40 **čtyřicet**	100 **sto**
1 **jedna**	7 **sedm**	13 **třináct**	19 **devatenáct**	50 **padesát**	1,000 **tisíc**
2 **dvě**	8 **osm**	14 **čtrnáct**	20 **dvacet**	60 **šedesát**	million **milión**
3 **tři**	9 **devět**	15 **patnáct**	21 **dvacet jedna**	70 **sedmdesát**	quarter **čtvrt**
4 **čtyři**	10 **deset**	16 **šestnáct**	22 **dvacet dva**	80 **osmdesát**	half **půl**
5 **pět**	11 **jedenáct**	17 **sedmnáct**	30 **třicet**	90 **devadesát**	three quarters **tři čtvrtě**

Where is the nearest post office/mail box?
Kde je tady nejblíž pošta/poštovní schránka?

What is the postage to...?
Kolik stojí poštovné do...?

One stamp, please
Jednu známku prosím

I'd like to send this by air mail/registered mail
Leteckou poštou/rekomando prosím

Can you direct me to a public phone?
Kde je tady telefonní budka?

What is the charge per minute?
Kolik stojí hovor za minutu?

Can I dial direct to...?
Můžu točit přímo...?

Do I need to dial 0 first?
Musím nejprve točit nulu?

Where can I find a phone directory?
Kde najdu telefonní seznam?

Where can I buy a phone card?
Kde koupím telefonní kartu?

What is the number for directory enquiries?
Číslo telefonních informací, prosím?

Please put me through to...
Spojte mě prosím s...

Have there been any calls for me?
Nevolal mi někdo?

Hello, this is...
Haló, tady je...

Who is this speaking please?
Kdo je u telefonu?

I'd like to speak to...
Chtěl(a) bych mluvit s...

Extension ... please
Klapka ... prosím

Please ask him/her to call me back
Vyřiďte mu/jí prosím, ať mi zavolá

Is there a bank/currency exchange office nearby?
Je tady někde blízko banka/směnárna?

I'd like to change sterling/dollars into crowns (Kč, Czech currency)
Anglické libry/americké dolary za české koruny (Kč) prosím...

Can I use my credit card to withdraw cash?
Mohu vybírat hotovost na svoji kreditní kartu?

WORDS AND PHRASES 279

I'd like to cash this traveller's cheque
Mám tady cestovní šek k proplacení

Can I cash this here?
Můžu si tady nechat proplatit šek?

What is the exchange rate today?
Jaký je dnešní kurz?

GETTING AROUND

Where is the train/bus station?
Kde je tady vlakové/autobusové nádraží?

Does this train/bus go to...?
Jede ten vlak/autobus do...?

Does this train/bus stop at...?
Staví ten vlak/autobus v...?

Please stop at the next stop
Zastavte mi na další zastávce, prosím

Where are we?
Kde jsme?

Do I have to get off here?
Musím tady vystoupit?

Where can I buy a ticket?
Kde si mohu koupit lístek?

Is this seat taken?
Je tady obsazeno?

Where can I reserve a seat?
Kde si mohu rezervovat místo?

Please can I have a single/return ticket to...
Prosím jízdenku/zpáteční jízdenku do...

Where is the timetable?
Kde je jízdní řád?

COLOURS

black **černá**	blue **modrá**
brown **hnědá**	purple **fialová**
pink **růžová**	white **bílá**
red **červená**	gold **zlatá**
orange **oranžová**	silver **stříbrná**
yellow **žlutá**	grey **šedá**
green **zelená**	turquoise **tyrkysová**

SHOPS

baker's **pekařství**	fishmonger's **ryby**	lingerie shop **prádlo**
bookshop **knihkupectví**	florist **květinářství**	newsagent's **trafika**
butcher's **maso uzeniny**	gift shop **suvenýry/dárky**	perfume shop **drogerie**
cake shop **cukrárna**	grocer's **potraviny**	photographic shop **fotopotřeby**
clothes shop **oděvy**	hairdresser's **kadeřnictví**	shoe shop **obuv**
delicatessan **lahůdky**	jeweller's **klenoty**	sports shop **sportovní zboží**
dry-cleaner's **čistírna**	launderette **prádelna**	tobacconist's **tabák**

When is the first/last bus to...?
Kdy jede první/poslední autobus do...?

I would like a standard/first-class ticket to...
Prosím lístek druhé třídy/první třídy do...

Where is the information desk?
Kde jsou informace?

Do you have a metro/bus map?
Máte mapu metra/autobusů?

Where can I find a taxi (rank)?
Kde najdu (stanoviště) taxi?

Please take me to...
...(address), prosím

How much is the journey?
Kolik platím?

Please turn on the meter
Zapněte prosím taxametr

I'd like to get out here please
Dovolíte, vystoupím tady

Could you wait for me, please?
Můžete na mě počkat, prosím?

Is this the way to...?
Je to správný směr k/do...?

TOURIST INFORMATION

Where is the tourist information office/tourist information desk, please?
Kde je informační středisko pro turisty, prosím?

What can we visit in the area?
Co stojí za vidění tady v okolí?

Do you have a city map?
Máte mapu města?

Can you give me some information about...?
Prosím informace o...?

What sights/hotels/restaurants can you recommend?
Co doporučíte k vidění/které hotely/restaurace doporučujete?

Please could you point them out on the map?
Můžete mi je ukázat na mapě, prosím?

What is the admission price?
Kolik stojí vstupné?

Is there a discount for senior citizens/students?
Máte slevu pro důchodce/studenty?

Are there guided tours?
Máte obhlídku s průvodcem?

Are there boat trips?
Dá se jet na výlet lodí?

Where do they go?
Kam to jezdí?

Is there an English-speaking guide?
Máte anglické průvodce?

Are there organized excursions?
Organizujete výlety?

Can we make reservations here?
Můžeme si tady rezervovat místo?

What time does it open/close?
V kolik hodin otevíráte/zavíráte?

Is photography allowed?
Je možné tady fotografovat

DAYS/ TIMES/ MONTHS/ SEASONS/ HOLIDAYS

Monday	night	month	March	October	Easter
pondělí	**noc**	**měsíc**	**březen**	**říjen**	**Velikonoce**
Tuesday	day	year	April	November	National Holiday
úterý	**den**	**rok**	**duben**	**listopad**	**Státní svátek**
Wednesday	morning:	today	May	December	All Saints' Day
středa	(until about	**dnes**	**květen**	**prosinec**	**Všech svatých**
	9 am)				
Thursday	**ráno**	yesterday	June	spring	Christmas
čtvrtek		**včera**	**červen**	**jaro**	**Vánoce**
	(the rest of the				
Friday	morning)	tomorrow	July	summer	26 December
pátek	**dopoledne**	**zítra**	**červenec**	**léto**	**Štěpána**
Saturday	afternoon	January	August	autumn	New Year's Eve
sobota	**odpoledne**	**leden**	**srpen**	**podzim**	**Silvestr**
Sunday	evening	February	September	winter	New Year's Day
neděle	**večer**	**únor**	**září**	**zima**	**Nový rok**

Do you have a brochure in English?
Máte brožuru v angličtině?

What's on at the cinema(s)?
Máte program kina/kin, prosím?

Where can I find a good nightclub?
Kde najdu dobrý klub/disko?

What time does the show start?
V kolik hodin začíná představení?

Could you reserve tickets for me?
Chci si rezervovat lístky, prosím

How much is a ticket?
Kolik stojí lístek?

Should we dress smartly?
Je nutný večerní oděv?

IN TROUBLE
Help!
Pomoc!

Stop, thief!
Pozor, zloděj!

Can you help me, please?
Pomozte mi prosím

Call the fire brigade/police/an ambulance
Zavolejte hasiče/policii/ sanitku

I have lost my passport/ wallet/purse/handbag
Ztratil(a) jsem pas/náprsní tašku/peněžnku/kabelku

Is there a lost property office?
Jsou tady ztráty a nálezy?

Where is the police station?
Kde je policejní stanice?

I have been robbed
Okradli mě

I have had an accident
Měl(a) jsem nehodu

Here is my name and address
Tady je moje jméno a adresa

Did you see the accident?
Viděli jste tu nehodu?

Are you insured?
Máte pojištění?

Please can I have your name and address?
Mohu si vzít vaše jméno a adresu?

I need information for my insurance company
Potřebuji informace pro svoji pojišťovnu

Excuse me, I think I am lost
Promiňte prosím, asi jsem se ztratil(a)

ILLNESS
I don't feel well
Není mi dobře

Could you call a doctor please
Zavolejte prosím doktora

Is there a doctor/pharmacist on duty?
Má tady službu lékař/lékárník?

I need to see a doctor/dentist
Potřebuji doktora/zubaře

Where is the hospital?
Kde je nemocnice?

When is the surgery open?
Kdy má tato ordinace otevřeno?

I need to make an emergency appointment
Potřebuji nutně vidět lékaře

Do I need to make an appointment?
Musím se objednat?

I feel sick
Je mi zle

I am allergic to...
Mám alergii na...

I have a heart condition
Mám nemocné srdce

I am diabetic
Mám cukrovku

I'm asthmatic
Mám astma

I've been stung by a wasp/bee
Štípla mě vosa/včela

Can I have a painkiller?
Prosím prášek proti bolesti

How many tablets a day should I take?
Kolik tabletek mám denně brát?

How long will I have to stay in bed/hospital?
Jak dlouho budu muset zůstat v posteli/v nemocnici?

I have a bad toothache
Moc mě bolí zub

I have broken my tooth/crown
Ulomil se mi zub/korunka

A filling has come out
Vypadla mi plomba

Can you repair my dentures?
Opravíte mi zubní protézu?

IN THE TOWN

on/to the right	**vpravo/doprava**	north	**sever**	open	**otevřeno**	palace	**palác**	river	**řeka**
on/to the left	**vlevo/doleva**	south	**jih**	closed	**zavřeno**	gallery	**galerie**	bridge	**most**
around the corner	**za rohem**	east	**východ**	daily	**denně**	town	**město**	theatre	**divadlo**
opposite	**naproti...**	west	**západ**	cathedral	**katedrála**	town hall	**radnice**	garden	**zahrada**
straight on	**rovně**	free	**zdarma**	church	**kostel**	square	**náměstí**	chateau	**zámek**
near	**blízko**	donation	**dobrovolné vstupné**	castle	**hrad**	street	**ulice**	no entry	**zákaz vstupu**
in front of	**před**	lavatories (WC)	**záchod/toalety**	museum	**muzeum**	avenue	**alej/třída**	entrance	**vchod**
behind	**za**	men **muži** women **ženy**		monument	**pomník/památník**	island	**ostrov**	exit	**východ**

RESTAURANTS

For more words and phrases relating to restaurants, ▷ 223.

I'd like to reserve a table for ... people at ...
Rezervujte mi stůl pro ... osob na ... hodin

We have/haven't booked
Máme/nemáme rezervaci

Could we sit there?
Můžeme si sednout tady?

Is this table taken?
Je ten stůl obsazen?

Are there tables outside?
Je možné sedět venku?

Where are the lavatories?
Kde jsou toalety?

We would like to wait for a table
Počkáme, až se uvolní místo

Could you warm this up for me?
Ohřejete mi to prosím?

We'd like something to drink
Dáme si něco k pití

What do you recommend?
Co doporučujete?

I can't eat wheat/sugar/salt/ pork/beef/dairy
Mám dietu a nejím lepek/cukr/sůl/vepřové/hovězí/ mléčné výrobky

Could I have bottled still/sparkling water?
Prosím láhev minerálky bez bublinek/perlivé minerálky

The food is cold
Jídlo je studené

The meat is overcooked/too rare
To maso je příliš propečené/syrové

I ordered...
Objednal(a) jsem si...

This is not what I ordered
To jsem si neobjednal(a)

Is service included?
Je v tom spropitné?

The bill is not right
Účet nesouhlasí

I'd like to speak to the manager, please
Chci mluvit s vedoucím, prosím

HOTELS

I have made a reservation for ... nights
Mám rezervaci na ... nocí

Do you have a room?
Máte volný pokoj?

How much per night?
Kolik stojí pokoj na jednu noc?

Double/single room
Pokoj pro dva/pro jednu osobu

Twin room
Pokoj se dvěma postelemi

With bath/shower
S koupelnou/se sprchou

May I see the room?
Mohu ten pokoj vidět?

Could I have another room?
Je možné dostat jiný pokoj?

Is there a lift in the hotel?
Je v tom hotelu výtah?

Are the rooms air-conditioned/ heated?
Mají pokoje klimatizaci/topí se na pokojích?

Is breakfast included in the price?
Je snídaně v ceně?

Do you have room service?
Máte room service?

When is breakfast served?
Kdy se podává snídaně?

I need an alarm call at...
Potřebuji budíček v ... hodin

The room is too hot/too cold/ dirty
Na pokoji je moc horko/zima/pokoj je špinavý

I am leaving this morning
Dnes ráno/dopoledne odjíždím

Please can I pay my bill?
Mohu zaplatit?

Please order a taxi for me
Objednejte mi prosím taxík

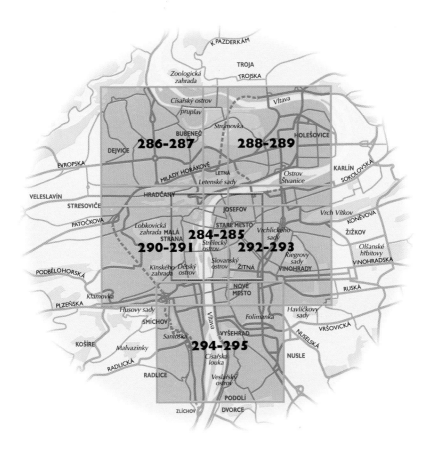

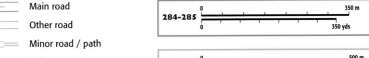

Main road

Other road

Minor road / path

Railway

City wall

Park

Railway station

Important building

Featured place of interest

Monument / statue

Tourist information office

Church

Synagogue

Post office

Metro station

Parking

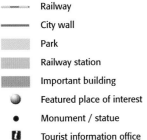

284-285

0 — 350 m

0 — 350 yds

286-295

0 — 500 m

0 — 500 yds

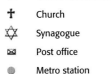

Maps

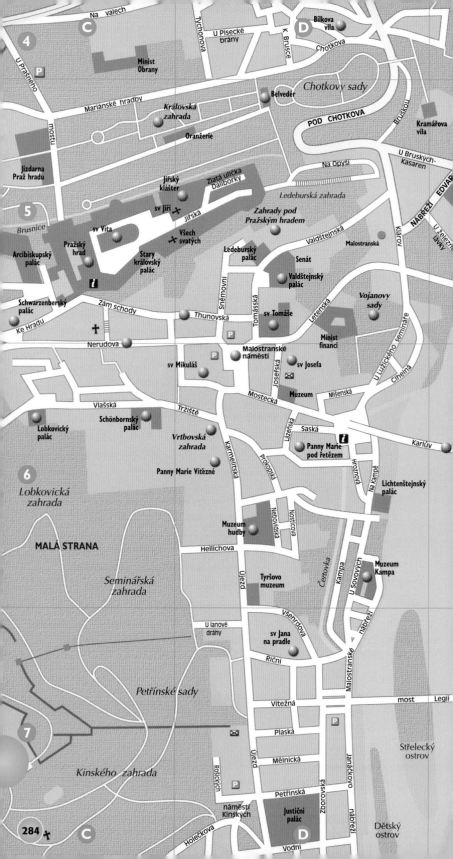

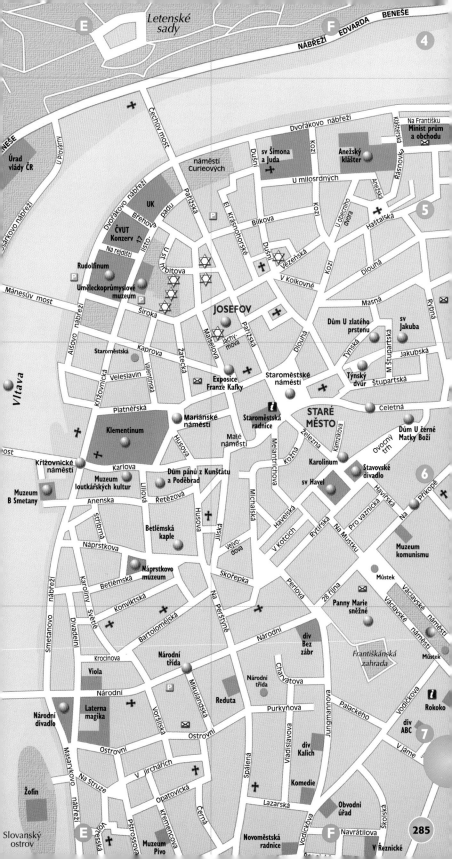

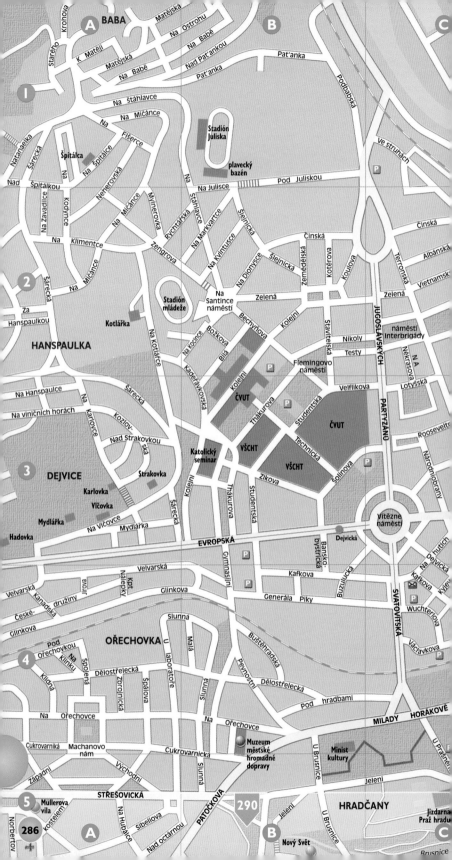

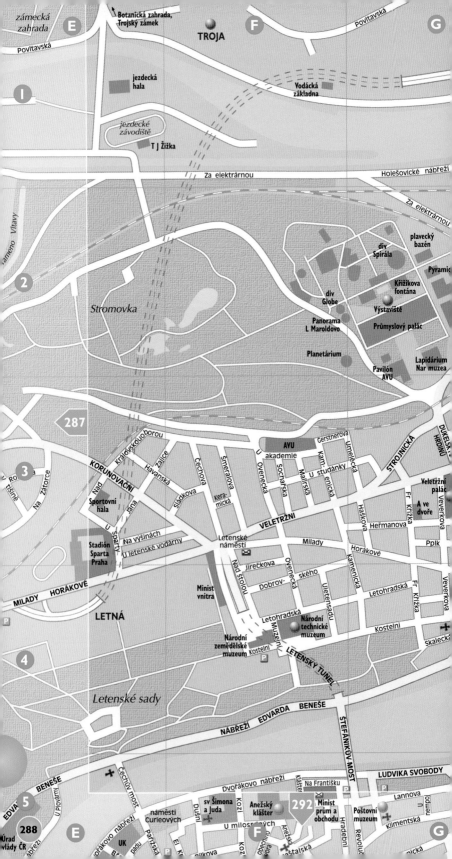

zámecká zahrada

E

Botanická zahrada, Trojský zámek

F

Povltavská

G

Povltavská

TROJA

I

jezdecká hala

Vodácká základna

jezdecké závodiště

T J Žižka

Holešovické nábřeží

Za elektrárnou

za elektrárnou

plavecký bazén

div Spirála

Pyramic

2

Křižíkova fontána

Stromovka

div Globe

Výstaviště

Panorama L Maroldovo

Průmyslový palác

Planetárium

Lapidárium Nar muzea

Pavilón AVU

287

AVU akademie

Gerstnerová

Umělecká

STROJNICKÁ

DUKELSKÝ HRDINŮ

KORUNOVAČNÍ

Královskouborou

Zálice

Havanská

Čechova

Šmeralova

U akademie

Kamenická

Sochařská

U studánky

Umělecká

Veletržní palác

3

Na Zátorce

Sportovní hala

Jana

Sládkova

Keramická

Malířská

Haškova

Fr Křižíka

A ve dvoře

Veverkova

U Sparty

Nad

Na výšinách

VELETRŽNÍ

Heřmanova

Pplk

Stadión Sparta Praha

U letenské vodárny

Letenské náměstí

Milady

Horákové

Kamenická

Letohradská

Fr Křižíka

Veverkova

MILADY HORÁKOVÉ

Nad štolou

Jirečkova

Ovenecké ského

Uletensadu

LETNÁ

Minist vnitra

Dobrov- ského

Kostelní

Skalecká

4

Letenské sady

Letohradská

Muzejní

Národní technické muzeum

LETENSKÝ TUNEL

Národní zemědělské muzeum

Kostelní

NÁBŘEŽÍ EDVARDA BENEŠE

ŠTEFÁNIKŮV MOST

LUDVÍKA SVOBODY

Lannova

5

BENEŠE

EDVA

U Plovárny

Čechův most

Dvořákovo nábřeží

Na Františku

Klášter

sv Šimona a Juda

Dušní

Kozí

Anežský klášter

292

Minist prům a obchodu

Poštovní muzeum

Klimentská

288

Úřad vlády ČR

náměstí Curieových

UK

U milosrdných

Anežská

Hradební

Revoluční

E

F

G

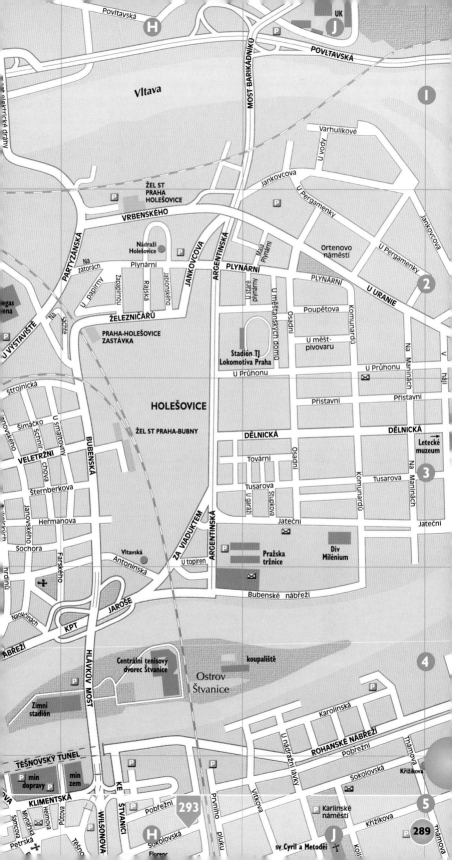

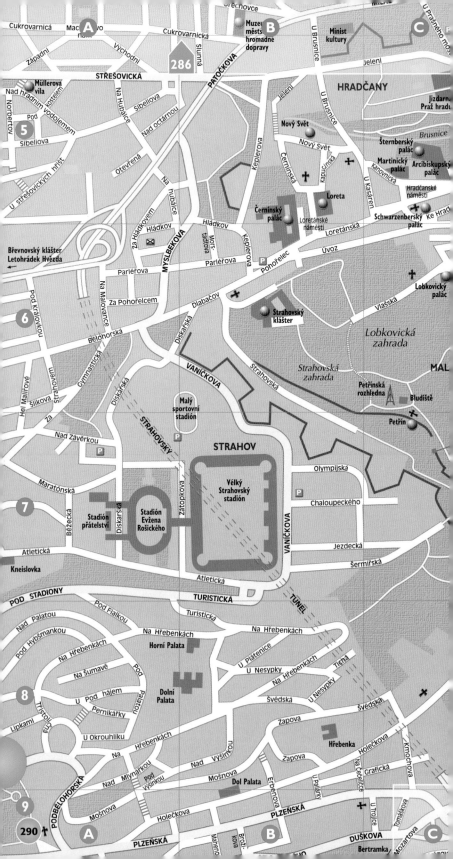

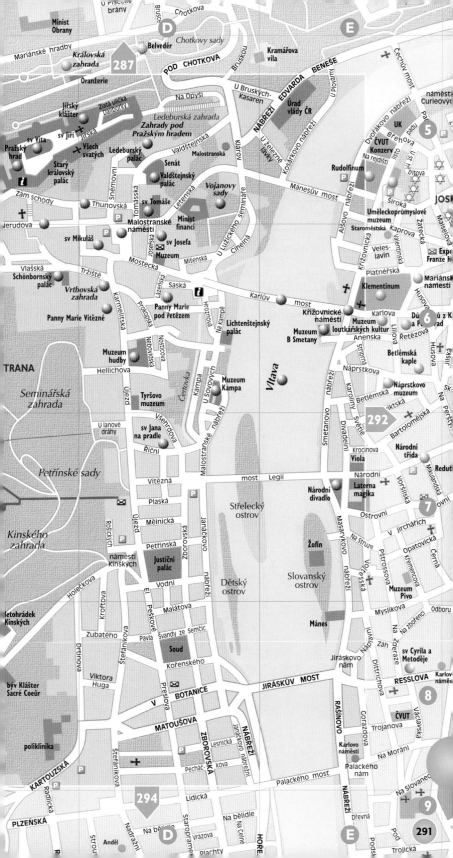

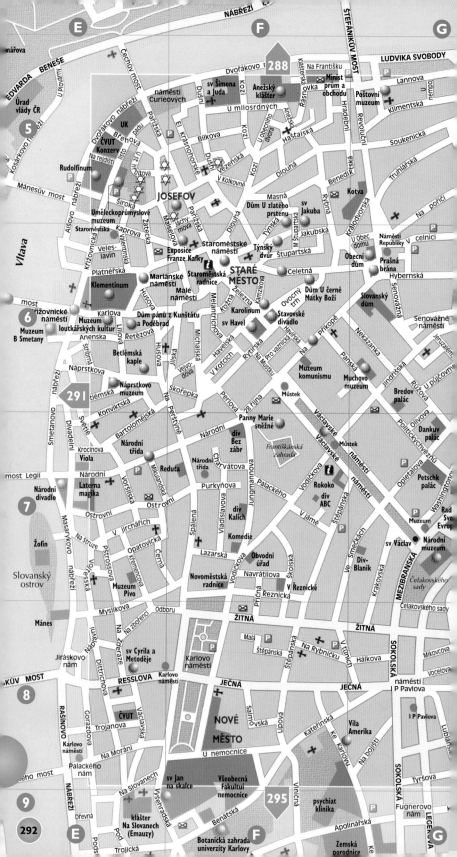

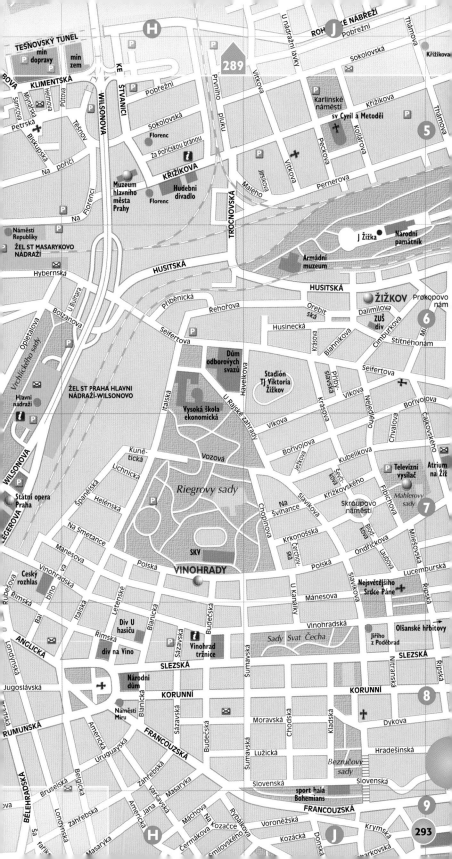

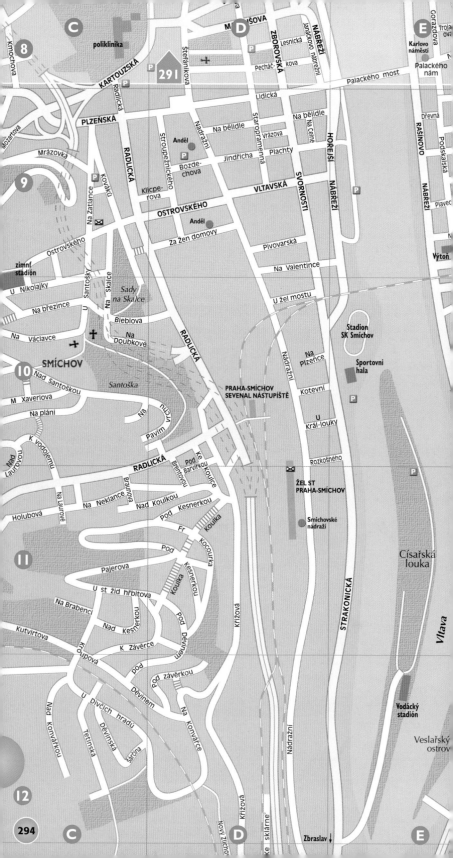

ACKNOWLEDGMENTS

Abbreviations for the credits are as follows:
AA = AA World Travel Library, **t** (top), **b** (bottom), **c** (centre), **l** (left), **r** (right), **bg** (background)

Every effort has been made to trace the copyright holders, and we apologise in advance for any unintentional errors or omissions. We would be pleased to apply any corrections in any future edition of this publication.

UNDERSTANDING PRAGUE

5cl AA/Clive Sawyer; 5cc AA/Jon Wyand; 5cr AA/Simon McBride; 8tr AA/Simon McBride; 8cl AA/Tony Souter; 8cr AA/Clive Sawyer; 8/9c AA/Jon Wyand; 8br AA/Jonathan Smith; 9tr AA/Jonathan Smith; 9tl AA/Jonathan Smith; 9cr AA/Tony Souter; 9br Moser; 10tr AA/Jonathan Smith; 10cl AA/Jon Wyand; 10cr Hotel Aria; 10bl AA/Simon McBride/Alphonse Mucha/Mucha Trust, 2005/Bridgeman Art Library; 10cr Statni opera Praha/Peter Bremkus; 10br AA/Jonathan Smith

LIVING PRAGUE

11 AA/Jonathan Smith; 12/13bg David Wasserman/brandxpic-tures; 12tl Czech Tourism; 12tr Czech Tourism; 12cl AA/Jon Wyand; 12cr Czech Tourism; 12c AA/Jonathan Smith; 12b AA/Jon Wyand; 13tl AA/Jonathan Smith; 13tc AA/Jonathan Smith; 13tc AA/Jonathan Smith; 13tr AA/Jonathan Smith; 13cl AA/Jonathan Smith; 13cc AA/Jonathan Smith; 13c AA/Jonathan Smith; 14/15bg AA/Jon Wyand; 14tl Czech Tourism; 14tr Czech Tourism; 14cc Statni opera Praha/Peter Bremkus; 14cr Monica Hatley; 14b AA/Jonathan Smith; 15tl Statni opera Praha/Peter Bremkus; 15tc Radim Beznoska/Spectrum Pictures; 15tr AA/Jonathan Smith; 15cl AA/Jonathan Smith; 15cr Moser; 16/17bg AA/Jonathan Smith; 16tl Nguyen Phuong Thao/AFP/Getty Images; 16tr AA/Jonathan Smith; 16cl AA/Jonathan Smith; 16cc Czech Tourism; 16cr AA/Jonathan Smith; 16cl AA/Jonathan Smith; 17t Czech News Agency; 17cl AA/Jon Wyand; 17cc Czech News Agency; 17cr Pension Unitas; 18/19bg Czech Tourism; 18tl/c Michal Cizek/AFP/Getty Images; 18tr Czech Tourism; 18cr SK Slavia Praha/Martin Maly; 18b AA/Jonathan Smith; 19tl Czech Tourism; 19tr Czech Tourism; 19cl Michal Cizek/AFP/Getty Images; 19cc Menahem Kahana/AFP/Getty Images; 19cr Frantisek Ortmann; 20/21bg AA/Jonathan Smith; 20tc AA/Jonathan Smith; 20tr Czech Tourism; 20cc AA/Jonathan Smith; 20cr AA/Jonathan Smith; 20cl Czech Tourism; 21tc AA/Jonathan Smith; 21tr Stepan Lutansky/Rex; 21cl Czech News Agency; 21cc AA/Jonathan Smith; 22bg AA/Simon McBride; 22tl AA/Jonathan Smith; 22tr Czech News Agency; 22cl Sean Gallup/Getty Images

THE STORY OF PRAGUE

23 AA/Jon Wyand; 24/25bg AA/Clive Sawyer; 24tl AA/Jonathan Smith/Jewish Museum, Prague; 24cr AA/Jon Wyand; 24bl AA/Simon McBride; 24bc/r Jan Kaplan; 25cl AA/Jonathan Smith; 25cc AA/Clive Sawyer; 25bc Werner Forman Archive/ Narodni Museum, Prague; 25br Jan Kaplan; 26/27bg AA/Clive Sawyer; 26cl AA/Simon McBride; 26cr AA/Clive Sawyer; 26bl Jan Kaplan; 26br Czech Tourism; 27cl AA/Simon McBride; 27cc AA; 27bc akg-images; 27br AA/Simon McBride; 28/29bg AA/Jon Wyand; 28tl AA/Simon McBride; 28cc Jean-Loup Charmet/Science Photo Library; 28cr Sheila Terry/Science Photo Library; 28bl AA/Simon McBride; 28br Bibliotheque Nationale, Paris, France/Bridgeman Art Library; 29cl AA/Simon McBride; 29cc AA/Jon Wyand; 29cr AA/Clive Sawyer; 29bc/r Jan Kaplan; 30/31bg Czech Tourism; 30tl AA/Clive Sawyer; 30cr AA/Clive Sawyer; 30bl AA/Clive Sawyer; 30br AA/Jonathan Smith; 31cc Jan Kaplan; 31cr AA/Jonathan Smith; 31bc Bibliotheque Nationale, Paris, France, Archives Charmet/Bridgeman Art Library; 31br Jan Kaplan; 32/33bg Jon Wyand; 32cl Bettmann/Corbis; 32bl AA/Jonathan Smith; 32bc/r Bettmann/Corbis; 33cl Bettmann/Corbis; 33cc AA/Clive Sawyer; 33cr AA/Jon Wyand; 33bc AA; 34/35bg AA/Clive Sawyer; 34cc

AA/Jonathan Smith; 34bl akg-images; 34br Peter Turnley/Corbis; 35cc AA/Jon Wyand; 35bc Rex; 35br AA/Tony Souter; 36bg Czech Tourism; 36cr EPA Photo CTK/Michal Krumphanzl/hf mda; 36bl AA/Jon Wyand; 36br Nguyen Phuong Thao/AFP/Getty Images

ON THE MOVE

37 AA/Jon Wyand; 38–39t Digital Vision; 39c CSA Czech Airlines; 40t AA/Alex Kouprianoff; 41t AA/Clive Sawyer; 41c Eurolines; 42t Digital Vision; 42 Marek Bubnik/UAMK; 43–47t Czech Tourism; 43c Czech Tourism; 43c Czech Tourism; 44t AA/Jonathan Smith; 44c AA/Jonathan Smith; 46 AA/Clive Sawyer; 48–49t AA/Jonathan Smith; 48c AA/Jonathan Smith; 48b Czech Tourism; 50–51t AA/Jonathan Smith; 50cr AA/Jonathan Smith; 50cr AA/Clive Sawyer; 51c AA/Tony Souter; 52t Digital Vision; 52c AA/Jonathan Smith; 52c AA/Jonathan Smith; 53t AA/Nicholas Summer; 53 AA/Jonathan Smith; 54t AA/Jonathan Smith; 54 Czech Tourism

THE SIGHTS

55 AA/Clive Sawyer; 60cl AA/Jonathan Smith; 60cr AA; 61cl AA/Clive Sawyer; 61cr AA/Jon Wyand; 62cl AA/Tony Souter; 62cr AA/Jonathan Smith; 63cl AA/Simon McBride; 63cr AA/Simon McBride; 64t AA/Jonathan Smith; 64cl AA/Clive Sawyer; 64cc AA/Jonathan Smith; 64cr AA/Jonathan Smith; 64b AA/Jonathan Smith; 65 AA/Jonathan Smith; 66t AA/Jonathan Smith; 66b AA/Jonathan Smith; 67bg Clive Sawyer; 67tl AA/Simon McBride; 67tr AA/Tony Souter; 68tl AA/Jonathan Smith; 68tc AA/Clive Sawyer; 68tr AA/Jon Wyand; 69t AA/Jon Wyand; 69c Czech Tourism; 70tl AA/Jonathan Smith; 70tr AA/Clive Sawyer; 70c AA/Clive Sawyer; 71tl AA/Jonathan Smith; 71tr AA/Jonathan Smith; 71cr AA/Jonathan Smith; 72t AA/Jonathan Smith; 72cl AA/Jonathan Smith; 72cc AA/Jonathan Smith; 72cr AA/Jonathan Smith; 73tl AA/Jonathan Smith; 73tr AA/Jonathan Smith; 73cr AA/Jonathan Smith; 74 AA/Jonathan Smith; 75t AA/Jon Wyand; 75cl AA/Simon McBride; 75cc AA/Jonathan Smith; 75cr AA/Tony Souter; 76c AA/Jon Wyand; 76b AA/Jon Wyand; 77c AA/Jon Wyand; 77b AA/Jon Wyand; 78t AA/Jonathan Smith/Jewish Museum, Prague; 78b AA/Jonathan Smith/Jewish Museum, Prague; 79tl JMP/M. Dunayevsky; 79tr AA/Jonathan Smith; 79cr AA/Jonathan Smith/Jewish Museum, Prague; 80t AA/Clive Sawyer; 80/81b AA/Clive Sawyer; 81cl AA/Simon McBride; 81cc AA/Jon Wyand; 81cr AA/Tony Souter; 82cl AA/Clive Sawyer; 82cr AA/Clive Sawyer; 83tl AA/Simon McBride; 83tr AA/Simon McBride; 83cl AA/Jon Wyand; 83cr AA/Jon Wyand; 83bl AA/Simon McBride; 84tl AA/Jonathan Smith; 84tr AA/Simon McBride; 85tl Czech Tourism; 85tr AA/Simon McBride; 86t AA/Simon McBride; 86cl AA/Simon McBride; 86cl AA/Jon Wyand; 87t AA/Jon Wyand; 87cr AA/Clive Sawyer; 88tl AA/Simon McBride; 88tr AA/Jonathan Smith; 89t Mucha Trust, 2005; 89cl AA/Simon McBride; 89cr Alphonse Mucha/Mucha Trust, 2005/Bridgeman Art Library; 90tr AA/Jonathan Smith; 90c AA/Jonathan Smith; 91tl AA/Clive Sawyer; 91tr Czech Tourism; 92tl Muzeum Kampa; 92tr AA/Jonathan Smith; 92bl Museum Kampa-Jan and Meda Mladek Foundation; 93t AA/Jonathan Smith; 93b AA/Jonathan Smith; 94t AA/Tony Souter; 94c AA/Jon Wyand; 95t AA/Jon Wyand; 95b AA/Jon Wyand; 96t AA/Jon Wyand; 97t AA/Jonathan Smith; 97b AA/Jonathan Smith; 98tl AA/Clive Sawyer; 98tr AA/Jonathan Smith; 99tl AA/Jon Wyand; 99tr AA/Jonathan Smith; 100t AA/Tony Souter; 100cl AA/Clive Sawyer; 100cc AA/Clive Sawyer; 100cr Czech Tourism; 101tl AA/Clive Sawyer; 101cr AA/Simon McBride/Alphonse Mucha/Mucha Trust, 2005/Bridgeman Art Library; 102t AA/Jim Holmes; 102cl Roger Hatley; 103t AA/Jonathan Smith; 103cr AA/Jonathan Smith; 103b AA/Jon Wyand; 104tl AA/Clive Sawyer; 104tr AA/Clive Sawyer; 104c

AA/Tony Souter; **105tl** AA/Jon Wyand; **105tc** AA/Jon Wyand; **105tr** AA/Tony Souter; **105c** AA/Clive Sawyer; **106/107t** AA/Clive Sawyer; **106c** AA/Clive Sawyer; **107c** AA/Jon Wyand; **108t** AA/Clive Sawyer; **108c** AA/Jonathan Smith; **108c bg** Jon Wyand; **109t** AA/Simon McBride; **109b** Czech Tourism; **110cl** AA/Clive Sawyer; **110cr** AA/Simon McBride; **110bl** AA/Clive Sawyer; **111cl** AA/Simon McBride; **111cc** AA/Jon Wyand; **111cr** AA/Clive Sawyer; **112tc** AA/Simon McBride; **112c** AA/Simon McBride; **113** AA/Clive Sawyer; **114t** Czech Tourism; **114b** AA/Tony Souter; **115cl** AA/Clive Sawyer; **115cc** AA/Tony Souter; **115cr** AA/Clive Sawyer; **115r** AA/Clive Sawyer; **115b** AA/Simon McBride; **116t** AA/Clive Sawyer; **116cl** AA/Jonathan Smith; **116cr** AA/Jonathan Smith; **116c** AA/Jonathan Smith; **117** AA/Jonathan Smith; **118t** AA/Simon McBride; **118cl** AA/Simon McBride; **118cr** AA/Jon Wyand; **119cl** AA/Simon McBride; **119cr** AA/Simon McBride; **119b** AA/Simon McBride; **120tl** Czech Tourism; **120tr** AA/Clive Sawyer; **121tl** Statni Opera Praha; **121tr** AA/Clive Sawyer; **121b** Peter Bremkus/Statni Opera Praha; **122t** AA/Simon McBride; **122cl** AA/Jon Wyand; **122cc** AA/Jon Wyand; **122cr** AA/Simon McBride; **123t** AA/Simon McBride; **123b** AA/Tony Souter; **124tl** AA/Simon McBride; **124tr** AA/Jonathan Smith; **125tl** AA/Jonathan Smith; **125tc** AA/Jon Wyand; **125tr** AA/Jonathan Smith; **125b** AA/Jonathan Smith; **126** AA/Simon McBride; **127t** AA/Jon Wyand; **127cl** AA/Simon McBride; **127cc** AA/Jon Wyand; **127cr** AA/Tony Souter; **128cl** AA/Jonathan Smith; **128cr** AA/Simon McBride; **129cl** AA/Jon Wyand; **129br** AA/Tony Souter; **130t** AA/Jon Wyand; **130cl** AA/Clive Sawyer; **130cc** AA/Jon Wyand; **130cr** AA/Jon Wyand; **131t** AA/Clive Sawyer; **131cr** AA/Clive Sawyer; **132t** AA/Jon Wyand; **132cl** AA/Jonathan Smith; **132cc** AA/Jonathan Smith; **132cc** AA/Jonathan Smith; **132cr** AA/Jon Wyand; **132b** AA/Jonathan Smith; **133** AA/Jonathan Smith; **134/135t** AA/Simon McBride; **134c** AA/Jonathan Smith; **135c** AA/Clive Sawyer; **136cl** AA/Clive Sawyer; **136cc** AA/Jon Wyand; **136cr** AA/Simon McBride; **136b** AA/Jonathan Smith; **137tl** AA/Jonathan Smith; **137cr** AA/Jonathan Smith; **137br** AA/Jonathan Smith; **138t** AA/Clive Sawyer; **138c** AA/Jon Wyand; **139t** AA/Jonathan Smith; **139b** AA/Jonathan Smith; **140** AA/Jonathan Smith; **141t** AA/Jonathan Smith/copyright DACS 2005; **141b** AA/Jonathan Smith; **142** AA/Jon Wyand; **142c** AA/Jon Wyand; **143t** Czech Tourism; **143cl** Czech Tourism; **143cc** AA/Clive Sawyer; **143cr** AA/Simon McBride; **144c** AA/Simon McBride; **144c** AA/Clive Sawyer; **145t** AA/Jonathan Smith; **145cr** AA/Jonathan Smith; **145cr** AA/Jonathan Smith; **146tl** AA/Jon Wyand; **146tc** AA/Jonathan Smith; **146tr** AA/Simon McBride; **147cr** AA/Clive Sawyer; **147b** AA/Clive Sawyer; **148t** AA/Simon McBride; **148cl** AA/Jonathan Smith; **148cc** AA/Clive Sawyer; **148cc** AA/Jon Wyand; **148cr** AA/Simon McBride; **149t** AA/Simon McBride; **149c** AA/Simon McBride; **149b** AA/Clive Sawyer; **150t** AA/Jonathan Smith; **150cl** AA/Jonathan Smith; **150cc** AA/Jonathan Smith; **150cr** AA/Jonathan Smith; **151tl** AA/Jonathan Smith; **151cr** AA/Jonathan Smith; **151br** AA/Jonathan Smith; **152c** AA/Clive Sawyer; **152b** AA/Clive Sawyer

WHAT TO DO

153 AA/Jonathan Smith; **154t** AA/Jon Wyand; **154cl** AA/Jon Wyand; **154cr** AA/Jonathan Smith; **155cl** AA/Jonathan Smith; **155cr** AA/Jonathan Smith; **156cl** AA/Jonathan Smith; **156cr** AA/Jonathan Smith; **157cl** AA/Jonathan Smith; **157cr** AA/Jonathan Smith; **162-168t** AA/Jon Wyand; **162c** AA/Jonathan Smith; **163c** AA/Jonathan Smith; **164c** Czech Tourism; **165c** AA/Jonathan Smith; **166c** AA/Jonathan Smith; **167c** AA/Jonathan Smith; **168c** AA/Jonathan Smith; **169t** AA/Simon McBride; **169cl** Czech Tourism; **169cr** Czech Tourism; **174-178t** AA/Simon McBride; **174c** Czech Tourism; **175c** Czech Tourism; **176c** Statni opera Praha/Peter Bremkus; **177c** AA/Jonathan Smith; **178c** Laterna magika; **179-185t** AA/Clive Sawyer; **179cl** AA/Jon Wyand; **179cr** AA/Jon Wyand; **180c** Brand X Pics; **181c** AA/Jonathan Smith; **182c** AA/Simon McBride; **183c** AA/Jonathan Smith; **184c** AA/Jonathan Smith; **185c** AA/Jonathan Smith; **186-187t**

Photodisc; **186c** AA/Jonathan Smith; **187c** AA/Jonathan Smith; **188t** Image 100; **188c** Image 100; **189t** AA/Jon Wyand; **189c** AA/Jonathan Smith; **190t** AA/Steve Day; **190c** Czech Tourism

OUT AND ABOUT

191 AA/Jonathan Smith; **192cl** AA/Jonathan Smith; **192c** AA/Clive Sawyer; **193cl** AA/Jonathan Smith; **193r** AA/Clive Sawyer; **193b** AA/Clive Sawyer; **194** AA/Clive Sawyer; **195tl** AA/Simon McBride; **195tr** AA/Jon Wyand; **195cl** AA/Clive Sawyer; **195cr** AA/Tony Souter; **196** AA/Clive Sawyer; **197tl** AA/Jonathan Smith; **197tr** AA/Clive Sawyer; **197cl** AA/Tony Souter; **197cr** AA/Jon Wyand; **198** AA/Jon Wyand; **199tc** AA/Jonathan Smith; **199tr** AA/Jonathan Smith; **199cl** AA/Simon McBride; **199bl** AA/Simon McBride; **199br** AA/Jonathan Smith; **200** AA/Jon Wyand; **201t** AA/Tony Souter; **201cl** AA/Jon Wyand; **201cr** AA/Clive Sawyer; **201b** AA/Clive Sawyer; **202** AA/Jonathan Smith; **203tl** AA/Jonathan Smith; **203tr** AA/Simon McBride; **203c** AA/Jonathan Smith; **204cl** AA/Clive Sawyer; **204cc** The Lobkowicz Collections, Nelahozeves Castle, Czech Republic; **204cr** Czech Tourism; **205t** Czech Tourism; **205b** Czech Tourism; **206** Czech Tourism; **207tc** AA/Jon Wyand; **207cl** AA/Jon Wyand; **207cr** Czech Tourism; **208** AA/Clive Sawyer; **209t** AA/Clive Sawyer; **209c** AA/Clive Sawyer; **209b** AA/Jon Wyand; **210** Czech Tourism; **211cl** AA/Jon Wyand; **211tr** Czech Tourism; **211cc** AA/Jon Wyand; **212tl** Czech Tourism; **212tr** AA/Jon Wyand; **212b** Czech Tourism; **213** Czech Tourism; **214t** Czech Tourism; **214c** The Lobkowicz Collections, Nelahozeves Castle, Czech Republic; **215t** Czech Tourism; **215c** Czech Tourism; **216** AA/Jon Wyand; **217t** AA/Jon Wyand; **217c** AA/Jon Wyand; **217b** Jan Kaplan; **218** AA/Jonathan Smith

EATING AND STAYING

219 Hotel Aria; **220cl** AA/Tony Souter; **220cc** AA/Clive Sawyer; **220cc** AA/Jonathan Smith; **220cr** AA/Jon Wyand; **221cl** ImageState; **221cc** Czech Tourism; **221cc** AA/Jon Wyand; **221cr** AA/Jon Wyand; **222cl** AA/Philip Enticknap; **222cc** Photodisc; **222cr** AA/J Edmanson; **223cl** David Wasserman/brandxpictures; **223cc** Photodisc; **223cr** AA/Clive Sawyer; **224cl** Radisson SAS Alcron Hotel; **224cr** Ambiente Group; **225cl** Restaurant David; **225cr** AA/Tony Souter; **225br** AA/Jonathan Smith; **230cl** AA/Jonathan Smith; **230cr** Ambiente Group; **231t** AA/Jonathan Smith; **232tl** AA/Jonathan Smith; **232bl** AA/Jonathan Smith; **233tl** AA/Jonathan Smith; **233c** AA/Jonathan Smith; **234** AA/Jonathan Smith; **235cl** AA/Tony Souter; **235cc** AA/Jonathan Smith; **236** AA/Simon McBride; **237** AA/Jonathan Smith; **238** AA/Jonathan Smith; **239** AA/Jonathan Smith; **240** AA/Jonathan Smith; **241tl** AA/Jonathan Smith; **241bl** AA/Simon McBride; **241c** AA/Jonathan Smith; **242tl** AA/Jon Wyand; **242c** AA/Jon Wyand; **244** AA/Jonathan Smith; **245cl** Radisson SAS Alcron Hotel; **245cc** AA/Jonathan Smith; **245cc** Aria Hotel; **245cr** AA/Simon McBride; **250cl** AA/Jonathan Smith; **250br** AA; **251** Hotel Ametyst; **253** AA/Jonathan Smith; **254t** AA/Jonathan Smith; **254c** AA/Jonathan Smith; **254br** AA/Jonathan Smith; **255bl** AA/Jonathan Smith; **255cr** AA/Jonathan Smith; **256tl** AA/Jonathan Smith; **256bl** AA/Jonathan Smith; **257bl** AA/Jonathan Smith; **257tc** AA/Jonathan Smith; **257tr** AA/Jonathan Smith; **257br** AA/Jonathan Smith; **258c** AA/Jonathan Smith; **259bc** AA/Jonathan Smith; **258tr** AA/Jonathan Smith; **259c** AA/Jonathan Smith; **259b** AA/Jonathan Smith; **260** AA/Jonathan Smith; **261tl** AA/Jonathan Smith; **261tc** www.zlatastudna.cz; **261tr** AA/Jonathan Smith

PLANNING

263 AA/Jonathan Smith; **264c** Czech Tourism; **264b** AA/Jonathan Smith; **266** AA/Jon Wyand; **267r** AA/Clive Sawyer; **268** Currency information courtesy of MRI Bankers Guide to Foreign Currency, Houston, USA; **269t** AA/Jonathan Smith; **269c** AA/Clive Sawyer; **269b** AA/Jonathan Smith; **270** AA/Simon McBride; **271t** AA/Jonathan Smith; **271c** Czech Tourism; **273c** AA/James A Tims; **273b** AA/Clive Sawyer; **275** AA/Jonathan Smith; **276** AA/Jonathan Smith; **277** Digital Vision

Project editor
Cathy Hatley

Design work
David Austin

Picture research
Alice Earle

Internal repro work
Susan Crowhurst, Ian Little, Michael Moody

Production
Lyn Kirby, Helen Sweeney

Mapping
Maps produced by the Cartography Department of AA Publishing

Main contributors
Michael Ivory (Understanding Prague, The Story of Prague, On the Move, The Sights,
Out and About, Eating and Staying, Planning); Heather Maher (Living Prague, What to Do);
Ky Krauthamer, Maureen Fronczak-Rogers (verifiers); Marie Lorimer (indexer);
Sheila Hawkins (proofreader)

Copy editor
Karen Kemp

Published by AA Publishing, a trading name of Automobile Association Developments Limited,
whose registered office is Fanum House, Basing View, Basingstoke, Hampshire, RG21 4EA, UK.
Registered number 1878835.

A CIP catalogue record for this book is available from the British Library.

ISBN-10: 0-7495-4821-5
ISBN-13: 978-0-7495-4821-6

Binding style with plastic section dividers by permission of AA Publishing.
Key Guide is a registered trademark in Australia and is used under license.

Colour separation by Keenes, UK
Printed and bound by Leo, China

Find out more about AA Publishing and the wide range of travel publications and services
the AA provides by visiting our website at www.theAA.com/bookshop

A02405
Maps in this title produced from mapping © MAIRDUMONT / Falk Verlag 2005
Relief map images supplied by Mountain High Maps ® Copyright © 1993 Digital Wisdom, Inc
Weather chart statistics supplied by Weatherbase © Copyright (2005) Canty and
Associates, LLC
Transport map © Communicarta Ltd, UK

We believe the contents of this book are correct at the time of printing. However, some
details, particularly prices, opening times and telephone numbers do change. We do not
accept responsibility for any consequences arising from the use of this book. This does
not affect your statutory rights. We would be grateful if readers would advise us of any
inaccuracies they may encounter, or any suggestions they might like to make to improve
the book. There is a form provided at the back of the book for this purpose, or you can
email us at Keyguides@theaa.com

COVER PICTURE CREDITS

Front cover, top to bottom: AA/Jon Wyand; AA/Clive Sawyer; AA/Clive Sawyer; AA/Jon Wyand
Back cover, top to bottom: AA/Clive Sawyer; AA/Jonathan Smith; AA/Jonathan Smith; AA/Jonathan Smith
Spine: AA/Jon Wyand

Dear Key Guide Reader

●

Thank you for buying this Key Guide. Your comments and opinions are very important to us, so please help us to improve our travel guides by taking a few minutes to complete this questionnaire.

You do not need a stamp (unless posted outside the UK). If you do not want to cut this page from your guide, then photocopy it or write your answers on a plain sheet of paper.

Send to: Key Guide Editor, AA World Travel Guides
FREEPOST SCE 4598, Basingstoke RG21 4GY

Find out more about AA Publishing and the wide range of travel publications the AA provides by visiting our website at
www.theAA.com/bookshop

ABOUT THIS GUIDE
Which Key Guide did you buy? _____

Where did you buy it? _____

When? _ _ month/ _ _ year

Why did you choose this AA Key Guide?
- ❏ Price ❏ AA Publication
- ❏ Used this series before; title _____
- ❏ Cover ❏ Other (please state) _____

Please let us know how helpful the following features of the guide were to you by circling the appropriate category: very helpful (**VH**), helpful (**H**) or little help (**LH**)

Size	**VH**	**H**	**LH**
Layout	**VH**	**H**	**LH**
Photos	**VH**	**H**	**LH**
Excursions	**VH**	**H**	**LH**
Entertainment	**VH**	**H**	**LH**
Hotels	**VH**	**H**	**LH**
Maps	**VH**	**H**	**LH**
Practical info	**VH**	**H**	**LH**
Restaurants	**VH**	**H**	**LH**
Shopping	**VH**	**H**	**LH**
Walks	**VH**	**H**	**LH**
Sights	**VH**	**H**	**LH**
Transport info	**VH**	**H**	**LH**

What was your favourite sight, attraction or feature listed in the guide?

Page _____ Please give your reason _____

_____

Which features in the guide could be changed or improved? Or are there any other comments you would like to make?

_____

_____

ABOUT YOU

Name (*Mr/Mrs/Ms*) _____

Address _____

_____

_____

Postcode _____ Daytime tel nos_____
Please *only* give us your mobile phone number if you wish to hear from
us about other products and services from the AA and partners by text or mms.

Which age group are you in?
Under 25 ❑ 25–34 ❑ 35–44 ❑ 45–54 ❑ 55+ ❑

How many trips do you make a year?
Less than1 ❑ 1 ❑ 2 ❑ 3 or more ❑

ABOUT YOUR TRIP

Are you an AA member?   Yes ❑ No ❑

When did you book?   _ _ month/ _ _ year

When did you travel?   _ _ month/ _ _ year

Reason for your trip?   Business ❑ Leisure ❑

How many nights did you stay? _____

How did you travel?   Individual ❑ Couple ❑ Family ❑ Group ❑

Did you buy any other travel guides for your trip? _____

If yes, which ones? _____

_____

Thank you for taking the time to complete this questionnaire. Please send it to us as
soon as possible, and remember, you do not need a stamp (*unless posted outside
the UK*).

Titles in the Key Guide series:
Australia, Barcelona, Britain, Brittany, Canada, Costa Rica, Florence and Tuscany,
France, Germany, Ireland, Italy, London, Mallorca, Mexico, New York, New Zealand,
Normandy, Paris, Portugal, Prague, Provence and the Côte d'Azur, Rome,
Scotland, South Africa, Spain, Venice, Vietnam.

To be published in November 2006:
Thailand
